Social Finance

Social Finance

Edited by

Alex Nicholls, Rob Paton, and Jed Emerson

OXFORD
UNIVERSITY PRESS

Great Clarendon Street, Oxford, OX2 6DP,
United Kingdom

Oxford University Press is a department of the University of Oxford.
It furthers the University's objective of excellence in research, scholarship,
and education by publishing worldwide. Oxford is a registered trade mark of
Oxford University Press in the UK and in certain other countries

© Oxford University Press 2015

The moral rights of the authors have been asserted

First Edition published in 2015

Impression: 1

Published in the United States of America by Oxford University Press
198 Madison Avenue, New York, NY 10016, United States of America

British Library Cataloguing in Publication Data
Data available

Library of Congress Control Number: 2015933905

ISBN 978-0-19-870376-1

Printed and bound by
CPI Group (UK) Ltd, Croydon, CR0 4YY

ACKNOWLEDGEMENTS

Alex Nicholls

My thanks go, first, to all the contributors to this volume. Many have been very patient and all have provided high quality chapters across various iterations of this, at times, epic project. I would also like to acknowledge the support of the editorial and publishing team at Oxford University Press, particularly Clare Kennedy. Clare has remained steadfastly supportive of this book—despite the delivery date repeatedly slipping out of view. My personal thanks go to my various co-authors: Rosemary Addis, Jed Emerson, Jeremy Nicholls (thanks, brother), Anna Oleksiak, Rob Paton, Aunnie Patton, Roger Spear, and Emma Tomkinson. All (in different ways!) have been a pleasure to work with. Finally, this collection is dedicated to my amazing children, Samuel, Harriet, and Juliette: each one is different and each one is wonderful. This book is also dedicated to my extraordinary mother, Catherine Nicholls: in memoriam.

Jed Emerson

My deep thanks go to Alex Nicholls for his steadfast leadership on this writing project and his significant work to see that its potential was attained. I would also thank my collaborator Rob Paton for his vision and ideas regarding how to make the most of this opportunity. Thanks go to my co-authors of the chapter on impact investing, Anna Oleksiak and Alex Nicholls, for their good work and ideas—even those that differed from my own experience in practicing impact investing over many years. I would also acknowledge the good editors at Oxford University Press for their patience and support throughout our lengthy writing process. And finally, I would think my wife, Mia Haugen, for her continuing support and affirmation of my work and efforts to advance innovative approaches to finance and living.

Rob Paton

It has been a privilege to work with Alex and Jed, who have been long-time indefatigable leaders of this field in theory, policy development, and practice. Thanks are also due to the UK Economic and Social Research Council whose award of funding for a seminar series on social investment gave me and others the chance to learn from innovative practitioners, extended our networks internationally, and laid a foundation for this collection. I salute my ARNOVA colleagues Rich Steinberg and Dennis Young for being model contributors to work with (and patient as well). I also enjoyed the support of Open University colleagues, especially Roger Spear on our co-authored chapter, but also recently Dr Michael Ngoasong whose work on impact investing in Africa is ensuring our continued presence in developing this academic area. As always, my wife Josephine provided the requisite mix of generous support and well-targeted scepticism.

CONTENTS

LIST OF FIGURES   ix
LIST OF TABLES   xi
ABOUT THE AUTHORS   xiii

Social finance: Capitalizing social impact   1
Alex Nicholls and Jed Emerson

PART I CONTEXTS AND DEBATES

1 **Social finance: Does 'investment' add value?**   45
Geoff Mulgan

2 **What should social finance invest in and with whom?**   64
Richard Steinberg

3 **Financing social innovation**   96
Dennis R. Young

4 **Philanthrocapitalism comes of age**   113
Matthew Bishop and Michael Green

PART II THE LANDSCAPE

5 **Co-operative and mutual finance**   133
Jonathan Michie

6 **Microfinance: A field in flux**   156
Nicholas Sabin

7 **Venture philanthropy: Development, evolution, and scaling
   around the world**   185
Rob John and Jed Emerson

8 **Impact investing: A market in evolution**   207
Anna Oleksiak, Alex Nicholls, and Jed Emerson

PART III MODELS AND METRICS

9 **Measuring social impact**   253
Alex Nicholls, Jeremy Nicholls, and Rob Paton

10 **Risk and return in social finance: 'I am the market'**   282
Alex Nicholls and Emma Tomkinson

11 **Projection, valuation, and pricing in social finance**   311
Alex Nicholls and Aunnie Patton

12 **The Peterborough Pilot Social Impact Bond** 335
Alex Nicholls and Emma Tomkinson

PART IV **INFRASTRUCTURE**

13 **The roles of government and policy in social finance** 383
Rosemary Addis

14 **Public policy for social finance in context** 460
Roger Spear, Rob Paton, and Alex Nicholls

15 **Building the social finance infrastructure** 488
Rodney Schwartz, Clare Jones, and Alex Nicholls

PART V **FUTURE DIRECTIONS**

16 **Crowdfunding in social finance** 521
Othmar M. Lehner

17 **Investing for social impact: Direct foreign investment and private
equity in Africa and South Asia** 543
Peter Hinton and Sweta Penemetsa

18 **Islamic finance as social finance** 572
Natalie Schoon

19 **Environmental impact investing: Co-managing the ecological
and economic household** 589
Jacob Harold, Joshua Spitzer, Jed Emerson, and Marieke Spence

Postscript: Is there a co-operative alternative to capitalism? 616
Dan Gregory

INDEX 629

LIST OF FIGURES

0.1	Spectrum of social finance	5
0.2	Spectrum of social finance instruments	5
1.1	The lifecycle of social finance	53
3.1	A benefits theory of social enterprise capital finance	107
6.1	Growth of microfinance programmes and clients	163
6.2	Geographic coverage of microfinance	164
6.3	Microfinance market structure by institution type	166
6.4	Need for broader range of microfinance products and services	170
8.1	Stages of new market development	214
8.2	Geographic focus of impact investing	217
8.3	Sector focus	218
8.4	A layered investment structure	230
8.5	The Rikers Island Social Impact Bond	231
8.6	A GIIRS rating	232
8.7	Individual deal size, $m	238
9.1	A contingency model for social impact measurement	276
10.1	Financial returns in social finance	287
10.2	Risk and return across a portfolio in conventional finance	289
10.3	Financial risk and return in social enterprise investment	290
10.4	Probability risk	294
10.5	Data availability and risk	295
10.6	Variance risk	295
10.7	Uncertainty risk	296
10.8	Population risk	299
10.9	Population risk/social outcome	300
11.1	The projection-valuation-pricing model	313
11.2	Gatekeepers of capital	317
12.1	The structure of a Social Impact Bond	339
12.2	Innovations in modelling the role of government	340
12.3	Structure of the Peterborough SIB	346
12.4	The measurement and payment system	348
13.1	The dynamics of the market for social finance	398

13.2 A framework for policy design and analysis   401

13.3 Framework for government action   405

13.4 The policy toolbox   407

13.5 An overview of the systemic development required for the social
       finance market   414

13.6 The elements of the enabling market infrastructure for social finance   415

13.7 Layered capital structures for investment in social finance   432

13.8 Structure of Social Impact Bond contract   448

15.1 Social impact investment infrastructure   489

16.1 Major forms of pledging capital ranked by complexity   526

16.2 A matchmaking model   531

17.1 Comparative financial instruments analysis   551

17.2 Comparative sector analysis   552

17.3 Comparative geographical analysis   554

17.4 Acumen Fund's sector focus   560

17.5 The Abraaj Group's portfolio distribution   561

19.1 Temporal issues in environmental investment valuations   600

▨ LIST OF TABLES

0.1 Social finance instruments and purposes   14

6.1 Microfinance market structure by institution size   165

6.2 Historical private equity transactions in microfinance   172

7.1 Venture philanthropy matrix   187

7.2 European venture philanthropy funds originated by private equity, hedge fund, or family offices (family or individually owned private investment houses)   195

8.1 Examples of impact investments   211

8.2 Impact investing instruments   222

8.3 Social and environmental impacts   225

8.4 Market actors   225

8.5 Examples of impact investors   226

8.6 Demand-side actors in developing countries   229

9.1 Who is the customer for social impact?   262

9.2 Different approaches to social impact measurement   266

10.1 Social risk in social finance investment   297

10.2 Social risk–social return correlations   302

11.1 Projection calculations in mainstream finance   314

11.2 Discount rates in social impact valuations   319

11.3 Venture capital discount rates   320

12.1 Key variations in SIB models across the world   358

12.2 Value proposition of a SIB to some key stakeholders   373

13.1 Policy map: Global examples to illustrate the 'toolbox' applied to dynamics of the social finance market   416

15.1 Building the infrastructure   512

16.1 Crowdfunding platforms   525

16.2 Collaboration platforms   529

17.1 Bilateral and multilateral DFIs   544

17.2 Sample list of development impact and financial first funds   556

17.3 Sector preferences   559

17.4 Geographical analysis   562

17.5 Aligning sources of capital with investment strategies   566

18.1 Islamic finance products   580

While every effort was made to contact the copyright holders of material in this book, in some cases we were unable to do so. If the copyright holders contact the author or publisher, we will be pleased to rectify any omission at the earliest opportunity.

ABOUT THE AUTHORS

Rosemary Addis is a leading strategist and recognized global thought leader in social innovation and investment. She is Executive Director of Impact Strategist, and co-founded Impact Investing Australia. This builds on a career in senior roles across sectors, including leading creation of the Australian Government's first dedicated social innovation unit. Rosemary is the Australian representative on the Social Impact Investment Taskforce established by the G8, chairs the Australian Advisory Board on Impact Investment, is a member of the NSW Government Social Investment Expert Advisory Group, and a senior fellow of the Impact Investing Policy Collaborative. Her published works include *IMPACT-Australia: Investment for Social and Economic Benefit* (2013); *Inviting Investment in Social Enterprise* (2007) and contributions to *Laws of Australia* (1998).

Matthew Bishop is the US business editor and New York bureau chief of *The Economist*. He is the author of several books, including *Philanthrocapitalism: How Giving Can Save the World*, with Michael Green, about the new movement bringing an entrepreneurial approach to social innovation. *The Road from Ruin* (also with Green), about how to improve capitalism following the crash of 2008 and subsequent economic downturn, was published in 2010. He is a member of the World Economic Forum's Global Agenda Council on the Role of Business.

Jed Emerson is the originator of the concept of Blended Value and has played founder roles with some of the nation's leading impact investing, venture philanthropy, community venture capital and social enterprises. He is senior strategic adviser to five family offices with over $1.8bn in total assets and executing 100 per cent impact/sustainable investment strategies. Emerson is co-author of the first book on impact investing, and winner of the 2012 Nautilus Gold Book Award for *Impact Investing: Transforming How We Make Money While Making a Difference*. *The Impact Investor: Lessons in Leadership and Strategy for Collaborative Capitalism*, his second book co-authored on the topic, was released in October 2014. He is otherwise widely published and has given presentations at the World Economic Forum (Davos, Switzerland), the Clinton Global Initiative (New York City), the Skoll World Forum (Oxford, England) and countless conferences and professional meetings around the world. He is Chief Impact Strategist for ImpactAssets, a nonprofit financial services firm. He is Senior Fellow at the Center for Social Investment, Heidelberg University (Germany) and has held faculty appointments with Harvard, Stanford, and Oxford business schools.

Michael Green is Executive Director of the Social Progress Imperative. His books, written with Matthew Bishop, deal with the big economic trends in the world and have a particular interest in how capitalism can better serve people and planet. He was formerly a senior official in the British government where he worked in aid and development. Prior to that he worked in Poland, teaching economics at Warsaw University and as a freelance journalist. He is a graduate of St Peter's College, University of Oxford, and lives in London.

Dan Gregory has been lucky enough to gather a considerable range of experience of funding and financing voluntary, community, mutual, and social enterprises, through developing policy at the highest level and delivering in practice at the grassroots. He has worked for the UK Treasury and Cabinet Office, Social Enterprise UK, and the Social Economy Alliance. He now works as an independent adviser under the banner of Common Capital.

Jacob Harold is the President and CEO of GuideStar, the world's largest source of information about nonprofits. Harold's career has focused on two interrelated challenges: enabling smarter philanthropic giving and addressing climate change. He's worked as a grant-maker, strategist, and campaigner at the Hewlett Foundation, the Packard Foundation, The Bridgespan Group, Rainforest Action Network, Greenpeace USA, and Green Corps. Harold's essays have been used as course materials at Stanford, Duke, Wharton, Harvard, Oxford, and Tsinghua. He earned an AB summa cum laude from Duke University and an MBA from Stanford University.

Peter Hinton is CEO of Summit Development Group, which works with impact investors in sub-Saharan Africa. In 2003 he founded the Enterprise Banking Group, based in Botswana; it now has $120m in assets with operations in Kenya and Rwanda. Prior to that, he was Head of Development for the Africa Banking Corporation, he worked for CDC Capital Partners, and he ran Africa Trading in South Africa in the pre- and post-1994 election period. He began his career as a chartered accountant, and worked in strategy and development for BHS, the FT100 UK retailer. He is a non-executive director of Bean There Coffee Company (South Africa's first Fair Trade coffee company) and an associate fellow at Saïd Business School.

Rob John is Visiting Senior Fellow at the Asia Centre for Social Entrepreneurship & Philanthropy at NUS Business School, Singapore and an independent philanthropy consultant. From 2005 to 2009, he was a visiting fellow at the Skoll Centre for Social Entrepreneurship at Saïd Business School. He was the first executive director of the European Venture Philanthropy Association and co-founded the Asia Venture Philanthropy Network. Following a career spanning fifteen years in international development John directed the UK's longest-established venture philanthropy initiative, based in Oxford. His current research focuses on innovation in Asian philanthropy.

Clare Jones Before joining ClearlySo, Clare Jones worked in the impact space with social sector organizations, particularly with those supporting vulnerable women. Her Master's degree from the University of Cambridge focused on the British response to human trafficking. She is exploring how social enterprise can complement public and third-sector provision for survivors of gender-based violence.

Othmar M. Lehner is a professor of finance and risk at the University of Upper Austria and a visiting professor in social and sustainable finance at the University of Oxford. His research focuses on the motivations and interplay of the different players in the field, and the impact of public policy on its formation.

In this he works as adviser for public authorities and intermediaries in the UK and abroad. He is currently especially interested in the processes inherent to crowdfunding. Dr Lehner also serves as associate editor of the Routledge *Journal of Sustainable Finance & Investment* and of the *Journal of Social Entrepreneurship*.

Jonathan Michie is Professor of Innovation & Knowledge Exchange at the University of Oxford, where he is President of Kellogg College, Director of the Department for Continuing Education, and Director of the Oxford Centre for Mutual & Employee-owned Business. From 2004 to 2008 Jonathan was Director of Birmingham Business School. From 1997 to 2004 he held the Sainsbury Chair of Management at Birkbeck, University of London where he was Head of the School of Management & Organisational Psychology. From 1992 to 1997 he was at the Judge Business School in Cambridge where he was also a fellow and director of studies in economics at Robinson College.

Geoff Mulgan is Chief Executive of NESTA (the National Endowment for Science, Technology and the Arts), which is involved in social finance through investment, research, and grant programmes. Before that he was the first Chief Executive of the Young Foundation, which became a leading centre for social innovation. Between 1997 and 2004 Geoff had various roles in the UK government including director of the Government's Strategy Unit and head of policy in the Prime Minister's office. He was the founder and first director of the thinktank Demos and has been a visiting professor at LSE, UCL, Melbourne University, and a regular lecturer at the China Executive Leadership Academy. His latest book *The Locust and the Bee* was published by Princeton University Press in March 2013.

Alex Nicholls is Professor of Social Entrepreneurship at the University of Oxford. His research interests range across social entrepreneurship and social innovation, including: the nexus of relationships between accounting, accountability, and governance; public and social policy contexts; social investment; and Fair Trade. He has published more than sixty papers, chapters, and articles and four books. His co-authored book on Fair Trade (Sage, 2005) and edited collection of papers on social entrepreneurship (Oxford University Press, 2006, 2008) are the bestselling and most cited academic books on their subjects globally. He is the editor of the *Journal of Social Entrepreneurship*. He held lectureships at the University of Toronto, Canada and three UK universities before becoming the first staff member of the Skoll Centre for Social Entrepreneurship. Prior to his academic career, Nicholls held senior management positions at the John Lewis Partnership, the largest mutual retailer in Europe. He also a non-executive director for a major Fair Trade company.

Jeremy Nicholls is the Chairman of SIAA and the Chief Executive of the Social Return on Investment (SROI) Network since 2008. He started his working life as a chartered accountant in the UK. He has also lived and worked in Tanzania, Liberia, and briefly Nicaragua. His work has increasingly focused on understanding and managing the value of the impact of organizations' activities. He co-wrote 'There's no Business like Social Business' and the UK government-supported 'Guide to SROI'. He is a director of the FRC Group—a social business based in Liverpool—a member of the IRIS advisory committee, the London Social Stock Exchange admissions panel, and ICAEW Assurance Panel.

Anna Oleksiak is Vice President with Total Impact Investors and based in Washington, DC, focusing on the agriculture, healthcare, and education sectors. Her background is mainly in investment banking, but she has also held a senior position with a pharmaceutical company with operations in Ghana during the start-up and launch process. She takes an active role in developing capital structures and metrics that appeal to both financial and social investors. Anna graduated summa cum laude from the George Washington University with a double major, in finance and international business.

Rob Paton is Professor of Social Enterprise at the UK Open University. As a teacher, he pioneered the use of new learning technologies for work-based learning in management, leadership, and professional development. He was among the founding faculty of the OU Business School, and went on to lead major curriculum development exercises as well as research on new modes of learning. As a researcher, he has explored how value-based organizations can sustain both their social commitments and effective, enterprising forms of management and organization. He has served as Chair of the Trustees of the Scott Bader Commonwealth, and secretary of ARNOVA. He is Chair of the board of Still Green CIC, and of the Milton Keynes chapter of Citizens UK.

Aunnie Patton is a fellow at the University of Cape Town's Bertha Centre for Social Innovation and Entrepreneurship and at the University of Oxford's Saïd Business School. In addition to lecturing on social finance, she consults to a range of organizations including start-ups, financial intermediaries, investment funds, family offices, and foundations. She is closely involved with projects on Social Impact Bonds and Development Impact Bonds, impact investing, and sustainable philanthropy in Africa. Aunnie has experience in both the mainstream and the impact-oriented finance sectors in North America, the UK, Africa, and Asia. She has a BA in international political economy from DePauw University and an MBA from the University of Oxford's Saïd Business School.

Sweta Penemetsa is a finance professional with experience in principal investing, investment banking, and investor relations. She has previously written and presented on investment fund flows in emerging markets. While working at the European Bank for Reconstruction and Development, Bank of New York Mellon, and Fox-Pitt Kelton, Sweta covered markets as diverse as the USA, Central and Eastern Europe, Africa, and the Middle East. She holds a BA in mathematics from Rutgers University and an MBA from the University of Oxford.

Nicholas Sabin is Postdoctoral Fellow at the Saïd Business School, University of Oxford. His research draws on diverse types of empirical data for understanding advances in the microfinance field. He has conducted in-depth fieldwork and statistical analysis with microfinance institutions in West Africa. He previously served as a Kiva Fellow. Nicholas earned his PhD and MSc from the Saïd Business School, University of Oxford, and a BSc in Economics from the Wharton School. He also teaches graduate courses in research methods and statistical analysis at the University of Oxford.

Natalie Schoon is a financial consultant, specializing in risk management, anti-money laundering and Islamic finance. She worked as Head of Product Development at Bank of London and The Middle East plc; as a senior risk management consultant on the Basel II programmes for, among others, Barclays Capital and ABN Amro; and for a number of international financial organizations, such as Gulf International Bank and MeesPierson. She is a CFA Charterholder and an accredited trainer for the Islamic Finance Qualification, and a visiting fellow at the ICMA Centre, Henley Business School, University of Reading. Her books and articles include *Islamic Banking and Finance*, and *Islamic Asset Management: An Asset Class on Its Own?*

Rodney Schwartz started his career in 1980 at investment banks PaineWebber, Lehman, and Paribas in the equities arena, before starting venture capital firm Catalyst Fund Management & Research in 1997. It morphed into ClearlySo, which raises capital for organizations generating substantial social impact, and runs Clearly Social Angels. He has also served on the board of AXA Investment Managers and Winterthur Life (UK) and as Chair of Justgiving, Shelter, and Spacehive.

Roger Spear is Professor of Social Entrepreneurship in the Department of Engineering and Innovation at the Open University, where he teaches about organizations and innovation. He is also Guest Professor at the University of Roskilde Centre for Social Entrepreneurship. He conducts research on social entrepreneurship and social enterprise typically through European research projects, including for UNDP, OECD, the European Commission, and through the international research networks of EMES (where he is founder member) and CIRIEC (where he is a member of the Scientific Committee on the social economy).

Marieke Spence has a rich background in strategic philanthropy, programme planning, and impact investing. Some of her clients include the Ford Foundation, Unbound Philanthropy, the Wikimedia Foundation, and the Hartford Foundation for Public Giving. Spence is currently a consultant with the TCC Group and has provided strategic advice, research, analysis, planning, and programme design to various other clients including the Philanthropic Initiative and the Beijing-based Kaifeng Foundation. Spence has also served as a fellow at the William and Flora Hewlett Foundation. Spence serves on the board of Exploring the Metropolis (EtM), a New York City not-for-profit working to foster a vibrant and prolific performing arts community around shared resources of space and talent, to increase stability and growth within the artistic community, and to help broaden public access to the performing arts. Spence is a graduate of Brown University and the Fletcher School of Law and Diplomacy at Tufts University. Her executive education includes the Oxford Impact Investing Programme, Class of 2013.

Joshua Spitzer has served as an independent consultant to enterprises and individuals investing to create social, environmental, and financial value. The World Economic Forum, William and Flora Hewlett Foundation, Oxford University, and Stanford University Graduate School of Business have sponsored and published his work. He has also developed MBA curricula for the Center for Entrepreneurial Studies at Stanford University's Graduate School of Business. He is currently CEO of Schedulicity. He previously worked as a partner at Preservation Capital and as Director of the Sun Ranch Institute, where he led all Institute staff, contractors, and partners to accomplish measurable improvement in ecological and social value in the American West and beyond.

Richard Steinberg is Professor of Economics, Philanthropic Studies and Public Affairs at Indiana University. He coedited *The Nonprofit Sector: A Research Handbook*, 2nd Ed., co-authored *Economics for Nonprofit Managers*, and was Co-President of ARNOVA from 1992 to 1994. His research focuses on determinants of giving and volunteering, the theory of not-for-profit organizations, public policy, and not-for-profit managerial economics.

Emma Tomkinson is a social impact analyst living and working in Sydney, Australia. She is particularly interested in the role of impact measurement in evidence-based policy, including policy related to social investment. She created the Social Impact Bond Knowledge Box for the Centre for Social Impact Bonds at the UK Cabinet Office and also developed the Social Impact Bond concept for application in New South Wales, Australia. She works with a range of social purpose organizations to enhance their capacity for data-driven decision-making and storytelling.

Dennis R. Young is Professor of Public Management and Policy in the Andrew Young School of Policy Studies at Georgia State University and the founding editor of *Nonprofit Policy Forum*. A past president of the Association for Research on Nonprofit Organizations and Voluntary Action (ARNOVA), his awards include an honorary doctorate from the University of Liege and ARNOVA's Award for Distinguished Achievement and Leadership in Nonprofit and Voluntary Action Research.

Social finance

Capitalizing social impact

Alex Nicholls and Jed Emerson

Introduction

All organizations create economic, social, and environmental value. However, most organizations are not managed to optimize their social and environmental value creation potential (Emerson, 2003a). Yet, in recent years, a growing number of entrepreneurs and investors have focused on the intentional creation of social or environmental impact. Such activities require bespoke financial resources managed in alignment with the various stages of their development from start-up to growth to—in many cases—scale (Bloom and Chatterji 2009; Bugg-Levine and Emerson, 2011). Nevertheless, it is increasingly clear that conventional finance does not always offer the quantity or, perhaps more importantly, the *appropriate types* of capital required by this growing sector (Emerson et al., 2007; Nicholls and Pharoah, 2007; Nicholls, 2010a, 2010b).

Efforts to create mechanisms to allocate capital for social as well as economic value creation are not new. Indeed, there is a long history of faith-based, charitable, and mutual/co-operative finance organizations and models across many countries and numerous decades. More recently, over the past twenty years, a range of new organizations and financial instruments has emerged reflecting a set of significant institutional changes around the social contexts and objectives of finance (Emerson and Spitzer, 2007; Nicholls and Pharoah, 2007; Nicholls, 2010a, 2010b; Bishop and Green, 2010; SIITF, 2014). As a consequence, new institutions focused on supplying multiple types of capital have now emerged to fill this capital gap (Spitzer et al., 2007; J.P. Morgan and the GIIN, 2010, 2011, 2013; O'Donohoe et al., 2010; Brown and Norman, 2011; Cabinet Office, 2011; Brown and Swersky, 2012; Cabinet Office, 2012; Harji and Jackson, 2012; Addis et al., 2013; Nicholls, 2013; Clark et al., 2014; Nicholls and Lehner, 2014; Nicholls and Schwartz, 2014): such flows of capital constitute a new *social* finance market.

As of 2013, various estimates suggested that the narrower impact investing market amounted to between $40bn (Clark et al., 2012) and $89bn (Global Sustainable Investment Alliance, 2013) of assets under management. Several other reports have suggested the sector has the potential to grow to between $500bn (Freireich and Fulton, 2009) and $1trn (SIITF, 2014). It is important to note these figures do not in include charitable grants or co-operative and mutual investments, so are likely to be significant underestimates in terms of the overall social finance market.

This book will use the broad term *social finance* rather than the narrower alternative *social investment* for two reasons. First, an analysis of the capital allocation decisions that fund social purpose organizations demonstrates a complex blend of various logics and rationalities driven as much by personal or cultural values as rationalistic calculations of a specified set of return-on-investment expectations (Nicholls, 2010a). Thus, some of the funding activity in this sector resembles consumption as much as investment, effectively buying outcomes prioritized by the investor as opposed to building long-term capacity or increasing overall returns over time.

Second, using the term social finance allows this book to capture more of the full range of instruments, hybrid funding models, and structured deals blending various types of capital that are evident across this emergent sector.[1] These include: philanthropic donations; government grants; 'soft' return debt and equity; mutual finance; as well as 'finance first' and 'total portfolio' impact investing strategies. In practice, social finance includes a wide range of risk and return models from the 100 per cent loss capital allocation of philanthropy to the market—or above market—returns achieved by some social venture capital funds, such as Bridges Ventures.[2] The wide variety of types of capital available in social finance—and the complex set of risk and return calculations attendant on each type—offers opportunities for innovative structured deals and funds that do not exist outside of this sector. It is suggested here that only such blends of capital may offer the critical support needed by socially entrepreneurial organizations if they are to tackle the 'wicked problems' currently confronting the world (Rayner, 2006).

This book accepts that all notions of the *social* are culturally constructed and contingent on a range of institutional logics and legitimacies (Suchman, 1995) rather than being institutional absolutes. Nevertheless, the meaning of *social* presented here draws upon the well-established analyses that have been used to define civil society and the social sector as distinct from the public and

---

[1] Some are arguing for an extension of the term '(social) impact investment' to include any capital allocation for measurable social impact. This would include philanthropy and mutual models (SIITF, 2014). As of 2014, however, such an extended use of this term had not yet become widely accepted.

[2] The capital allocation characterized as social 'investment', on the other hand, typically involves, at a minimum, the return of an investor's capital and, sometimes, also an additional return. This is the definition preferred in the impact investing market and also by some significant new institutional players such as Big Society Capital in the UK: 'Social investment is the provision and use of capital to generate social as well as financial returns. Social investors weigh the social and financial returns they expect from an investment in different ways. They will often accept lower financial returns in order to generate greater social impact. Some interpretations of social investment include the provision of capital without any expectation of financial return. When we refer to social investment, however, we mean investment mainly to generate social impact, but with the expectation of some financial return' (BSC, 2012).

commercial sectors (e.g. Salamon and Anheier, 1999). Of particular significance here are: a public benefit focus (often taking the form of creating public goods or positive externalities); a significant attention to stakeholder voice and accountability; a distributive focus on the beneficiary rather than the owner (this is sometimes legally formalized as in the non-distribution constraint typical of charities). Given the contingent nature of the social, such distinctions can, of course, blur in reality, particularly with regard to issues of intentionality. Thus, the *social* component in social finance is taken here to include capital allocated to all projects or organizations giving a strategic priority to achieving outcomes that are socially positive in any given normative societal context.[3] This includes organizations whose social impact is exogenous via the production of goods of services and as well as those whose impact is endogenous via organizational structures and processes (notably work-integration social enterprises: see Nyssens, 2006). Social finance may also support the generation of positive 'social externalities' (perhaps better described as 'intentionalities') that are the deliberative consequence of socially entrepreneurial action. Finance that supports environmentally positive projects or organizations is also included here.[4]

In its simplest terms, social finance refers to the allocation of capital primarily for social and environmental returns, as well as in some cases, a financial return. The Social Investment Taskforce (established at the 2013 G8 Social Impact Investment Forum) defined a key part of this market as:

Social impact investments are those that intentionally target specific social objectives along with a financial return and measure the achievement of both. (SIITF, 2014, p. 1)

Others have referred to it as 'three-dimensional capital'—capital allocated according to conventional, financial, risk and return criteria plus optimizing a given social or environmental return. Such finance has also been referred to as 'blended value investing' (World Economic Forum, 2013, 2014). However, social finance goes beyond being just a new set of 'social' capital return opportunities for investors. As Nicholls and Pharoah (2007, p. 2) noted:

---

[3] Social value creation is best understood in terms of the outputs and impacts of organizational action identified as 'social' or 'environmental' in terms of normative (and often localized) assessments of their positive effects across five dimensions: geography and demography (Nicholls and Schwartz, 2014): who the target market or beneficiaries are and where they are located, for example a project working in a deprived area or within disenfranchised populations; organizational processes: how value is created within an organization for key stakeholders and beneficiaries, for example work integration social enterprises that aim to bring excluded groups into the labour market; goods and services produced: how mission objectives are achieved in terms of outputs, for example providing care services or low-cost irrigation pumps; sector: in which category of economic activity the organization fits, for example health, education, clean energy/green technology, clean water (the main areas of activity identified in the emerging impact investing sector); financial or organizational structure: who appropriates the value created, for example mutual or co-operative enterprises or dividend-capped or asset-locked legal forms (such as UK Community Interest Companies).

[4] See Harold et al. (2007), for example, and further below.

Social finance...is more than just the flow of money into social or environmental projects. It is conceived as an ethos about the way money is used...social finance can be seen as the discourse around such flows that is developing in concrete terms in the new institutions of supply, intermediation, and demand. This is a discourse in flux with competing perspectives driving the debate.

Social finance is, therefore, both a source of resources for social impact and a critique of the extant financial system as a market failure that drives social inequality and environmental failure. Thus, social finance internalizes the externalities of mainstream investment by setting social and environmental objectives as the first goal of its capital allocation strategies. It is both a positive generator of new social and environmental value and a corrective to the negative effects of conventional investing.

Moreover, social finance challenges the institutional logics associated with conventional investor rationalities by separating the logics of value creation and value appropriation (Nicholls, 2010a). In conventional investing, the assumption is that the owner of capital will appropriate all of the value created by her investment (minus fees and transaction costs), referred to as 'extractive investing'. The situation is quite different in social finance, wherein the social investor allocates capital knowing from the start that some of the value created will be appropriated by someone else (or something else in the case of environmental investment).

This separation of value creation and value appropriation logics allows social finance to focus on total *blended* social and financial outcomes (Emerson, 2000; Emerson, 2003a) across more than one interested party or stakeholder group. Of course, this has been the basic logic behind philanthropic grant-making from its inception, but today this approach has been expanded and developed further to embrace multiple types of capital, investment approaches, and financial instruments. Together these constitute the spectrum of social finance spanning a large number of diverse types of capital ranging from conventional grant-making and venture philanthropy via 'impact first' investments that may return some or all of the principal to the investor without other financial return to 'finance first' investments that return the principal and a return up to (and sometimes beyond) the risk adjusted market rate (see Figure 0.1) to the 'total portfolio' investors managing capital to optimize overall performance of a given portfolio of capital investments. Within this spectrum, the 'hot topic' has become impact investing: models capitalizing organizations that create social or environmental value with clear intentionality as well as returning invested capital to the investor (O'Donohoe et al., 2010; Bugg-Levine and Emerson, 2011).

The social finance spectrum is best thought of as a total portfolio that includes conventional financial assets of debt and equity, but also includes grants and bespoke asset types such as quasi-equity or upside revenue participation bonds (see Figure 0.2).

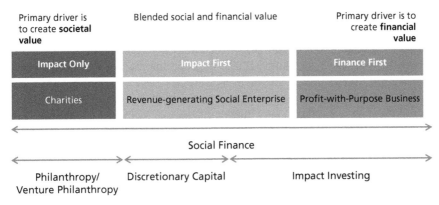

Figure 0.1. Spectrum of social finance

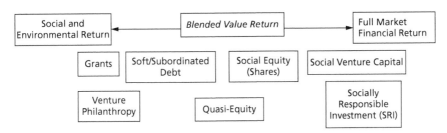

Figure 0.2. Spectrum of social finance instruments

Investees in receipt of social finance include charities, not-for-profits, social enterprises, companies limited by shares, companies limited by guarantee, limited liability partnerships, co-operatives and mutual organizations and, even, private, for-profit limited companies with a defined social mission (such as Fair Trade coffee companies and Benefit (B) Corporations.

Despite the fact that a significant practitioner literature regarding social finance now exists, particularly on the subset of this sector known as 'impact investing', the academic literature on this topic remains very limited (see Nicholls, 2010a; Nicholls et al., 2012). Practical research has largely focused on the extent of demand for, and availability of, such capital (Bank of England, 2003; OTS, 2006, 2008; Unwin, 2006; Bolton and Kingston, 2006; Emerson and Spitzer, 2007; Goodall and Kingston, 2009; NESTA, 2009; Wood, 2009; Freireich and Fulton, 2009; O'Donohoe et al., 2010; SITF 2010; Joy et al., 2011; Impact Investment Shujog, 2011; BCG, 2011; Cabinet Office, 2011, 2012; Thornley et al., 2011; Grabenwarter and Liechtenstein, 2011; Saltuk et al., 2011; Arosio, 2011; World Economic Forum, 2013; SIITF, 2014). In comparison, the scholarly literature on this subject is at a very early stage of development—with the exception of the well-developed sub-topic of microfinance (see, e.g. Sabin, in this volume). A scan of the research literature reveals only a small number of useful contributions focused on: investment structures (Brown, 2006; Edery,

2006; Scarlata and Alemany, 2012; Sunley and Pinch, 2012); the role of mainstream capital (Geobey et al., 2012; Moore et al., 2012); the motivations of social investors (McWade, 2012); the ethics involved in social impact investment (Eadery, 2006; Buttle, 2007); portfolio approaches for social impact investing (Ottinger, 2007). In addition, there has been a lively debate in print concerning the merits and disadvantages of 'philanthrocapitalism' between Bishop and Green (2008) and Edwards (2008: see, further, this volume). Yet, to date, Nicholls (2010a) still represents the most developed attempt to theorize the subject.[5]

The relative paucity of scholarly work on social finance may suggest the topic has yet to be recognized by mainstream scholarship as a distinct and legitimate field of research. Such a barrier to scholarly engagement with social finance reflects the fact that it is a field of praxis that has yet to develop clearly defined epistemological boundaries and institutional structures. As such, social finance lacks a normative narrative with which to build its wider legitimacy with scholars as a new 'paradigm' worthy of study (Kuhn, 1962; Suchman, 1995). Indeed, financial economists have proposed there is no such thing as 'social' investment at all, merely investment characterized by different investor appetites for risk–return options that do not (and, perhaps, should not) factor in social or environmental externalities or objectives per se (Hayek, 1944; Friedman, 1962, Harvey, 2005; Glyn, 2006). Moreover, within political science, state expenditure has been characterized by calculations based upon utilitarian cost–benefit analysis and models of Pareto efficiency rather than interpersonal, community and/or relative benefits, and wellbeing (see Offer, 2003, for an effective analysis of this approach). From this viewpoint, the idea of social investment is also redundant since policymakers might argue that all their spending is socially focused in accordance with their democratic mandate and responsibilities (see, for example, Moore, 1995). Finally, research focused on civil society or the third sector has typically viewed capital flows into the creation of public goods in charitable terms—namely as gifts or grants rather than investments (Clotfelter, 1992).

The prime purpose of this book is to address this substantial research gap. The chapters collected here provide the first attempt in the scholarly literature to take stock of this emerging market and to develop a set of underpinning theories, explore key research questions and issues, map its constituent elements, and provide a set of observations concerning its future trajectories, opportunities, and challenges. After more than a decade of development since the instigation of the world's first Social Impact Investment Taskforce in the UK, the social finance market is now sufficiently institutionalized to suggest that it will not prove to be just a fad or fashion. Social finance is not going away. Yet, the reality is that practice is moving much faster than research. This collection aims to provide a foundation of thinking and

---

[5] There has also been one special edition of an academic journal, the *Journal of Social Entrepreneurship*, 3.2 (2012).

evidence upon which subsequent research may be based. This too is a sign of the growing maturity of this market. Next, the section 'Drivers' in this chapter examines the drivers behind the emergence of modern social finance. After this, there is an overview, in the section 'Instruments', of the main financial instruments found in this market to date. An analysis of the basic market structure of social finance follows (see section 'Market structure'. The next section, 'Debates and issues', sets out some of the key debates and issues around the sector. The structure and contents of the book are summarized in 'Overview of book', and the chapter ends with some brief conclusions.

Drivers

The emergence of the modern social finance market has been driven by both demand and supply factors. On the one hand, social impact organizations wanting to move beyond a reliance on grant funding have struggled to access other sorts of finance to fund their start-up and growth, often due to their projected financial returns failing to match their perceived levels of riskiness. The social finance market has, therefore, partly developed in response to the growing capital needs of organizations with a clearly defined social impact. Two issues are relevant here—the overall size and growth of this sector and the shift from grant to contract or 'payment' funding models. These drivers have created the conditions in which social impact organizations have both a growing need for a wider range of capital beyond (but still including) grants and an increasingly capacity to take on board more diverse types of finance. The social sector is already substantial and accounts for more than 5 per cent of GDP and up to 10 per cent of employment in several countries, including Canada, Germany, the UK, and the USA (SIITF, 2014).[6] In a range of continental European countries (as well as in Francophone and Spanish-speaking countries elsewhere across the globe), there has been a long tradition of a lively and substantial social and solidarity economy that includes charitable associations, co-operatives, mutually owned organizations, and social enterprises. In France, for example, the social and solidarity economy employs 2.3 million people. Elsewhere, the social economy has developed more recently as many sources of funding have switched from grants to contracts—in the UK, for example, more than 80 per cent of government funding received by charities is now in the form of contracts for delivering services rather than grants to support their work, totalling over £11bn a year in 2011/12. In Germany, the welfare system includes legally guaranteed funding streams that have supported the growth of a large social sector tasked with delivering government-funded social welfare services.

---

[6] At one extreme, in Italy, the social sector accounts for more than 15% of national GDP and 10% of total employment.

On the other hand, there have been a growing number of owners of capital seeking to allocate their resources to generate social value as well as (or, sometimes, instead of) financial returns. Such action has a long history. Social finance as a model of capital allocation primarily for social value creation has its roots in the faith-based traditions of giving found in Judaism, Christianity, Islam, and elsewhere. By the Victorian period, these traditions became more formalized into a regulated charitable sector in the UK and beyond.

A second precursor of modern social finance may be seen in the co-operative and mutual sector. The co-operative movement had its origins in the radicalism of the Diggers movement in the mid seventeenth century in the UK and became institutionalized in the work of the Rochdale Pioneers in Lancashire in the early nineteenth century. A century and half later, the next precursor of social finance emerged as mainstream investors began to recognize capital allocated through conventional market processes often failed to value the negative externalities consequent from some investments. The result was the development of screened, or selective, equity portfolios under the umbrella heading of *Socially Responsible Investing* (SRI).[7] SRI aimed to deselect companies in 'unethical' sectors (defence, tobacco, alcohol, gambling) from portfolios according to investor preferences, whilst also maintaining (near) market-rate returns. Subsequently, the related clean/green energy sectors have also grown in the past decade.

In the foundation sector, innovations in the management of charitable assets have lead to a growth in mission-related or programme-related investment (Emerson, 2003b; Campanale, 2005), in which fund managers deploy a proportion of a charity's core assets towards mission-related objectives rather than in the conventional model of using such capital only to maximize financial returns to support grant-making. Changes in the shape and function of the state have also catalysed social finance as the public sector has retreated from the provision of some traditional welfare services under conditions of demographic or economic stress. This shift in the role of government from direct deliverer to commissioner or facilitator of welfare services has driven a range of new social finance initiatives from developing new contractual models, such as Social Impact Bonds (UK, USA) or Social Benefit Bonds (Australia), to market-building via direct support for new social finance intermediaries, such as Big Society Capital in the UK.

Finally, patterns of dramatic economic growth in many developing countries have also created new foreign direct investment (FDI) opportunities that increasingly go beyond the traditional 'hot capital' examples of short-term investment lacking significant local value creation. Instead, FDI into agri-funds and sustainable energy projects offers the opportunity to invest capital

---

[7] The definition of social finance used in this chapter excludes capital allocation to conventional businesses that simply employ people, pay corporate taxes, or that create other social value as incidental benefits of a central focus on maximizing financial returns to shareholders or other investors/owners. Thus, the majority of *broad* SRI is excluded here with only *core* SRI considered part of social finance.

for positive social and environmental impacts as well as attractive returns. The globalization of securitized microfinance debt products on mainstream markets has also driven the growth of a new sector increasing defined as *impact investment* (O'Donohoe et al., 2010).

As it has grown, the size and scope of the social finance sector has started to attract a wide range of interest across the public, private, and civil society sectors. For example, it is now estimated that the UK submarket of social finance that returns at least the principle to the owner of capital (the so-called *impact investing* part of the spectrum) could grow from £165m allocated in 2010 to £1bn by 2016, a 38 per cent per annum growth rate (Brown and Swersky, 2012).[8]

Moreover, mainstream players are now entering the market; for example Deutsche Bank became the first commercial bank to raise a social investment fund,[9] Goldman Sachs has invested in Social Impact Bonds in the USA, and the European Investment Fund has also made a direct investment into the UK social finance marketplace. However, despite the maturing of the social finance market over recent years, it is still far from completely institutionalized.[10] It is the purpose of this chapter to present this emerging landscape of social finance and present its key elements, major challenges, and future trajectories.

At the same time as the capital demands of the social sector have been growing, mainstream finance markets have become more socialized, largely as a response to client demand (and, sometimes, regulation). For example, by 2014, over 1,200 asset managers, managing assets of over $45trn, had signed up to the six United Nations Principles for Responsible Investment (PRI), thus committing themselves to incorporate environmental, social, and governance factors into their investment decision-making (SIITF, 2014). Simultaneously, the Socially Responsible Investment (SRI) market, that typically screens portfolios to avoid certain harmful or anti-social stocks and has more recently included 'ESG Integration' in which off-balance-sheet factors of environmental, social and governance issues, has now grown to over $13trn dollars in assets under management globally.

The charitable foundation sector also has substantial invested assets in its various portfolios, amounting to more than $450bn globally—though, somewhat ironically, very little of this is invested in the pursuit of social value creation since such assets are most often simply seen as the source of funds to give away as grants. Regardless, this is changing as the practice of programme-

---

[8] Though this is only about 1% of the value of all loans to small businesses in the UK.

[9] This is a £10m 'fund of funds' and is 'on balance sheet', i.e. the fund is financed internally and does not include external investors.

[10] The report particularly noted the continuing need for: social investors to accept higher levels of risk; more specialization of intermediaries in distinct sectors such as health or education rather than focusing on operational sectors; new types of 'value sponsorship' or purchasing of social goods by governments and foundations, rather than using block grants to build social enterprise cash-flows and profit and loss accounts.

related and mission-related investing has become more common—this is the allocation of a portion of a charitable foundation's invested capital to social impact organizations. Indeed some pioneering asset owners and foundations (such as the FB Heron Foundation, Gary Community Investments and Blue Haven Initiative in the USA, Felicitas Foundation in Europe, RS Group in Hong Kong and Small Giants in Australia) now allocate *all* the corpus of their investments for impact. In addition, the co-operative and mutual sector—the mainstay of the social and solidarity economy—owns assets amounting to over $2trn, although these are not typically investable outside of the organization itself due to its legal and ownership structure.

The development of the social finance sector, then, owes something to all of these trends. However, the expansion of social finance has also been driven in several countries by a proactive policy agenda (see, further, Addis and Nicholls and Spear et al., in this volume). In the vanguard has been the UK government with over ten years of policy development aimed at growing the social enterprise and social finance sectors. This included targeted fiscal policy (Community Investment Tax Relief; Social Investment Tax Relief), regulation (Community Interest Company legislation, Unclaimed Assets Act), direct investment (Futurebuilders, Investment and Contract Readiness Fund,[11] Social Outcomes Fund), and commissioning reform (Public Services [Social Value] Act; Social Impact Bonds), as well as a host of research and marketing support. Interestingly, this policy agenda bridged a change of government in 2010 and culminated in 2013 when London hosted the G8 Social Investment Forum, as a part of the UK convening that year's G8 Summit. This meeting lead to the establishment of a G8 (plus Australia and minus Russia) Social Impact Investment Taskforce that reported back in September 2014 with a range of policy recommendations agreed by the world's richest countries. The Taskforce also initiated four working groups to provide further support for an international social impact investment agenda exploring: asset allocation; social impact measurement; social mission lock-in; international development. Outside of the UK, important policy agendas have also developed in the USA, Canada, Australia, South Africa, South Korea, Japan, France, and India.

For example, many countries are now moving public capital into vehicles to support the evolving practices of social finance. In Italy, there is a Social Fund to finance impact-driven businesses. In Japan, the Government provided a $210m grant for social innovation during 2010–12 under the 'New Public' initiative, of which $86m went to support over 800 social enterprise start-ups. In France, the 2014 Social and Solidarity Bill facilitated the financing of social sector organizations and the Banque Publique d'Investissement (a state-owned bank) has

---

[11] In 2013, the UK Cabinet Office created a £10m 'Investment and Contract Readiness' fund to help social ventures access impact investment of at least £500,000 or to win contracts over £1m. In addition, a £10m 'Social Incubator Fund' was started to support social incubators to provide investment and support to early stage social ventures. In 2014, a further £60m was committed to future capacity-building funds for social sector organizations over the next decade.

launched a social innovation investment fund. In the USA, the Office of Social Innovation and Civic Participation within the Obama White House has used public money to catalyse additional private impact investment for entrepreneurs, particularly via existing social organizations and charities.

While having a perspective on the overall emergence of the field of social finance is important, the field itself consists of myriad investment instruments and strategies. These are considered next.

Instruments

GRANTS

In addition to government contracts, foundation and other charitable grants have been the main form of capital flows into social organizations. Such grants were typically used to fund operating income for specific programmes or mission-related outcomes rather than to build the capacity of grantee organizations to improve their performance or scale their activities. In recent years the effectiveness and efficiency of such funding has increasingly been questioned, with two consequences. First, there has been the rise of engaged or 'venture' philanthropy that attempts to use venture capital approaches to grant-making. Second, there has been an increased focus on generating earned income (the social enterprise or social business model) to replace grant funding.

Nevertheless, grant funding remains very important, particularly in terms of start-up capital for new social ventures that cannot access conventional bank funding. Grants also have the advantage, of course, of being non-repayable— this is important for organizations that are unlikely to achieve profitability with which to pay back capital to social investors. However, grants also have drawbacks, notably that they are often short term and can be inflexible, capricious, and narrowly programmatic. Moreover, as foundation assets have decreased and government cutbacks accelerated post 2008, grants have become increasingly difficult and competitive to access. Finally, raising grants can also be expensive for not-for-profit organizations—costing up to 30 per cent of funds raised—and grant reporting can be time-consuming.

DEBT

There are five basic debt options for social organizations: personal credit cards; personal bank overdrafts; mortgage finance; commercial loans and lines of credit from banks at market rates; commercial and semi-commercial loans from government and other social investors. Semi-commercial loans typically offer non-market interest rates, long repayment periods, and, sometimes, repayment 'holidays' that suspend interest—and, sometimes, principal—repayments for agreed periods (Joy et al., 2011).

Debt has the advantage that, assuming that the investee has collateral assets and/or sustained cash flows, it can often be quicker to obtain than grants. Terms may be flexible (short-, medium-, or long-term) and open to renegotiation over time. Debt is useful in bridging funding gaps and helping build for growth and scale. Debt contracts also typically attract fewer reporting requirements than grants and offer greater autonomy for the borrower. On the other hand, not-for-profits may not be able to access debt since it must repaid with interest and, furthermore, the need for collateral may put assets at risk in the case of default.

Micro-credit attempts to address this market failure for the un-collateralized individual or small organization. It has been a great success and now represents the most substantial and well-institutionalized sub-market of social finance. However, of the 365 to 445 *million* micro-, small-, or medium-sized firms in developing countries, 70 per cent need, but do not have access to, external financing. These firms are thought to generate 33 per cent of GDP and 45 per cent of employment in developing countries—a figure that is even greater if informal organizations are included. It is calculated that their unmet demand for debt credit is equal to $2.1–2.5trn or 14 per cent of total developing country GDP.

EQUITY

For the most part, equity in social finance is very similar, if not identical, to equity investments in mainstream companies. The main differences usually lie in the governance arrangements of the company. These might restrict the freedom of the board in some way in order to ensure the continuance of a social mission, or to provide for a certain percentage of any surpluses to be invested socially or retained by the company, or other socially oriented limitations such as an asset lock or 'golden share' that prevents a take-over.

Issuing 'social' public equity (sometimes known as an Alternative Public Offering: APO) can raise large amounts of capital on a permanent basis without the need for repayment. However, the social organization must give up some ownership and control when issuing equity and this is often either unattractive (for fear of mission drift) or impossible (because of legal limitations) for many social organizations. The absence of any full functioning 'social' stock markets—despite several important current initiatives in the UK, Brazil, South Africa, and Singapore/Mauritius—and the resultant lack of liquidity in social equity is also a major challenge to growing this form of social investment. O'Donohoe et al. (2010) noted that US impact investment to date has been dominated by private debt ($921m: 37.1 per cent of the total invested) and private equity ($836m: 33.7 per cent). Research by IIX Asia suggests this is also true in Asia, but that quasi-equity/mezzanine finance and guarantees are also important (Impact Investment Shujog, 2011).

QUASI-EQUITY

Quasi-equity was developed specifically for the social finance market. It aims to give investors returns that look like equity returns, with the feature of being tied to the organization's underlying performance. This is usually done by linking investor returns to the revenue growth of the firm or project invested in. Quasi-equity is, in fact, usually some sort of debt contract since the investee is typically a charity or other organization unable (or unwilling) to issue standard equity and grant investors any control over the organization's mission or operations. However, to secure investment capital for high-risk projects such organizations need to offer satisfactory returns to the investor. In this way investors receive equity-like returns, but without having any of the special rights associated with owning common shares.

EMERGING INSTRUMENTS

In addition to the examples outlined above, other instruments for social finance investment that are distinct from the mainstream have emerged. These include:

- *Revenue-based financing strategies* in which future returns to investors are based not on loan repayment or an ownership position in the enterprise, but rather through commitments to share future revenue on the basis of percentage growth in future enterprise revenue
- *Revenue redemption structures* that allow investors to purchase equity—with the company agreeing to repurchase shares out of a percentage of future revenue
- *Crowdfunding* strategies that enable potential investors to allocate capital at various levels to both not-for-profit and for-profit firms (see, further, Lehner, in this volume)
- *Direct public offerings* in which a company is able to raise capital on a crowdfunding basis from both accredited and non-accredited investors
- *Co-operative and mutual investment* that allow enterprises to be owned by employees, customers, or the local community
- *ESOP (Employee Stock Ownership Plan)* is a US example that has been actively used to offer employees an equity stake in the company for which they work.

Table 0.1 summarizes the key instruments.

Table 0.1. Social finance instruments and purposes

Financial instrument	Purpose of finance	Type of finance	Example
Private grant	Fulfilling mission	(Venture) philanthropy	Impetus Trust
	capacity building	PRI	FB Heron Foundation
		MRI	Calvert Foundation
Government grant	Regeneration	Community development loans	Community Development Finance Institution (CDFI)
	Market development	Unclaimed assets	Social Investment Bank
Government contracts	Outsourcing welfare services	Contractual exchange	Greenwich Leisure Ealing Community Transport
Debt	Economic and social development	Micro-finance	Grameen Bank CitiBank
Quasi-equity	Growth capital	Share of ownership	Bridges Community Ventures Catalyst
Sub-market equity	Growth capital	Restricted 'ethical' shares	Cafédirect Ethical Property Company
Market equity	Growth capital	Standard shares	London Bridge Capital Compartamos Bank
Joint equity	Start-up/Growth capital	Co-operative ownership (IPS)	Mondragon BayWind

STRUCTURED FINANCE

In the social finance sector it is frequently the case that different types or classes of investors have different risk and return plus social impact objectives. A government investor may have strong social impact objectives, but be far more tolerant of lower returns, higher risk, or longer payback periods. While the terms 'finance first' and 'impact first' are somewhat dated, a 'finance first' investor may be keen to participate, but be unwilling to sacrifice any risk-adjusted returns that may be indifferent to social impact. On the other hand, 'impact first' social investors may be willing to consider a host of financial–social return trade-offs. A structured finance deal in this sector typically seeks to balance and combine some or all of these in a single product or contract that tries to give everyone what they want, or at least enough of it so the deal can go ahead. Such transactions offer great scope for crafting the right overall cost of capital for an investment to work. However, because of the individualized nature of these instruments, they can be costly and inefficient to arrange.

Loan and other credit guarantees can also play an important part in making structured finance deals work. The presence of one entity willing to guarantee all or even a portion of the investment's risk can bring in other players, much as 'cornerstoning' does in conventional finance. Frequently governments or large grant-making organizations may have the capacity to underwrite a portion of the risk of an investment and, thereby, catalyse a far larger investment than may otherwise have been the case. For example, in 2011, Fair Finance—a UK-based micro-lender—raised a £2m loan from Societe

Generale and BNP Paribas that was underwritten by £750,000 of philan-thropic patient capital and a £350,000 soft loan from Big Society Capital. Guarantees or underwriting have also been important in structuring some social finance contracts, notably for Social Impact Bonds in the USA (where Bloomberg underwrote 70 per cent of Goldman's Sachs' investment in the Ryker's Island SIB) and Australia (where the New South Wales government underwrote a portion of the first Social Benefit Bond).

Having sketched out the range of investment instruments in social finance, this chapter now turns to the overall structure of social finance capital markets themselves.

Market structure

The Social Impact Investment Taskforce provided a nuanced market analysis identifying five key elements of the social finance sector (SIITF, 2014: 2):

- *Sources of impact capital*—to provide the investment flows needed
- *Channels of impact capital*—to connect investors to impact-driven organ-izations in situations where the sources of impact capital do not invest directly in impact-driven organizations
- *Forms of finance*—a variety of which are needed to address a range of different investment requirements
- *Impact-driven organizations*—all types of organizations which have a long-term social mission, set outcome objectives and measure their achievement, whether they be social sector organizations or impact-driven businesses
- *Impact-seeking purchasers*—these provide the sources of revenue that underpin investment in impact-driven organizations. Such purchasers can include governments, consumers, corporations, or foundations.

Such an analysis highlights the importance of the instruments needed for social finance and the sources of revenue through which social organizations could repay debt finance or issue dividends on equity. However, to put it simply, the social finance market, as in mainstream finance, is structured by three interlinked elements: supply, intermediation, and demand. Each of these elements will now be considered briefly in turn.

SUPPLY

On the supply side of social finance there are a wide range of owners of capital seeking different 'blended' returns on their capital allocation (Emerson, 2003a). These include: individuals, institutions, and governments. In the first group are individual philanthropists, social/ethical investors, commercial investors, retail investors,[12] savers that capitalize some microfinance institutions and community development finance institutions, and co-operative and mutual members. In the second group are charitable foundations[13] and, in some cases, corporations (for example, in India following the CSR Act of 2014).[14] In the final group are public funds, commissioners, and, indirectly, taxpayers.

Charitable donations and legacies constitute an important source of capital for social finance. In the UK alone there are assumed to be £60–80bn of endowment assets available for grant-making or investment (Nicholls, 2010a). In the USA this figure is estimated at £324bn (Nicholls, 2010a). Individuals also indirectly 'allocate capital' via the taxes they pay. All government spending is to some degree social finance since it capitalizes the production of public goods. But a subset of this capital allocation has been directed towards social finance specifically. For example, the UK government has been a global leader in capitalizing the social finance market investing over a £1bn of public money in the sector from 2001 to 2011 (Nicholls, 2010a).

To date, there has been only very limited work done on segmenting the supply side of social finance (Emerson, 1996; Hill, 2011; Saltuk et al., 2011; McWade, 2012). One segmentation approach is to separate this pool of capital into different categories according to the investment rationale of the owners of capital, on the one hand, and the type of value that the capital allocation is intended to achieve (Nicholls, 2010a). In the first case, investors can be seen as acting in either an instrumental (means–end) fashion that mimics standards investment behaviour by focusing on efficiency, analysis, and risk-adjusted returns or in an emotional, 'irrational' way driven primarily by personal values and preferences irrespective of absolute returns. In terms of value created, social finance can be directed toward primarily financial returns, toward primarily social returns, or toward blended returns that balance the two equally. Taken together, these dimensions offer one way to segment this growing pool of social finance capital.

There remain other challenges for the future development of the supply side of the market, including: better categorization of investment opportunities; new financial instruments that fit with multiple social and economic

---

[12] For example, since 1995, more than 13,500 people have invested over $1bn in the Calvert Foundation's Community Investment Note to support community development and social enterprise in the USA and around the world. In France, savers have the option to put their money into '*fonds d'investissement solidaires dits 90/10*', that allocate at least 10% to funding social enterprises typically with long-term loans at low interest rates. Retail investors can range from small-scale retail investors allocating capital via crowdfunding platforms such as Kiva or Buzzbnk or social finance institutions such as Charity Bank to High-Net-Worth Individuals investing via private banks such as UBS.

[13] Notable foundations active in social finance include: Bertelsmann Stiftung; Bill and Melinda Gates Foundation; Bloomberg Foundation; Case Foundation; Esmée Fairbairn Foundation; Kellogg Foundation; MacArthur Foundation; Omidyar Network; Pershing Square Foundation; Robin Hood Foundation; Rockefeller Foundation. The latter has played a leading role in developing the field of impact investing at a meeting it convened in 2007 at Bellagio.

[14] In Italy, Fondazione Cariplo, which holds more than €40bn in assets, is engaging in impact investing, while in Japan corporate foundations such as the Nippon Foundation and the Mitsubishi Foundation are starting to get involved.

objectives; increased performance transparency and information; more tailored investment incentives such as guarantees and underwriting.

INTERMEDIARIES

In terms of overall market structure, the area that has been subject to the greatest development has been in intermediary institutions (see, further, Schwartz and Jones, in this volume). Shanmugalingam et al. (2011) identified five crucial roles for market intermediaries in terms of developing the social finance market:

- to provide finance
- to provide access to people, networks, and expertise
- to provide market access and distribution (match-making)
- to provide support for innovation and start-ups
- to provide investment monitoring and performance information to investors.

Intermediaries linking supply and demand in social finance include: various sorts of private funds (including pension and venture philanthropy funds); microfinance institutions; credit unions; community development finance institutions; social stock exchanges and other 'matching' platforms; mainstream financial players such as investment banks and asset managers;[15] insurance companies;[16] specialist banks;[17] and wholesale institutions.[18] Associated with these is an emergent ecosystem of specialist professional service organizations that support the social finance market—for example, legal firms, consultancies, market-makers, and capacity-building organizations.

Alongside the investment managers, a new set of specialist social finance organizations has been particularly influential in the evolution of the sector over the past decade or so. These include: Social Finance (UK, USA, Israel); ClearlySo (UK, India); Imprint Capital (USA); Impact Assets (USA); Third Sector (USA); Société d'Investissement France Active (France); Institut de

---

[15] For example, Goldman Sachs and Bank of America Merrill Lynch have invested in Social Impact Bonds to tackle recidivism in New York City and New York State, and UBS has helped launch a Development Impact Bond to reduce drop-out rates from girls' primary schools in Rajasthan. Morgan Stanley created an Investing with Impact Platform for its clients that it aims to grow to $10bn in five years. Black Rock, one of the world's largest asset managers, has also developed impact investment products. J.P. Morgan has also committed almost $100m to Impact Funds.

[16] These include the Prudential (USA), AXA (France), and Zurich Insurance (Switzerland).

[17] This include Triodos Bank in the Netherlands, Italy's Banca Prossima, Banca Etica, Extrabanca, and Federcasse—the co-operative banks network—which are active in providing microcredit and funding for impact-driven businesses.

[18] In the UK, Big Society Capital was launched in 2013 as a provider of wholesale social finance. It was endowed with over £400m of unclaimed assets held by four high street banks plus £200m of equity from the same source. This model has sparked global interest with the Japanese and French governments considering similar legislation in 2014. This model could also be expanded to draw down not only the unclaimed assets of dormant bank accounts, but also dormant life assurance policies and pension funds.

Développement de l'Economie Sociale (IDES) and Credit Coopératif (France); Social Ventures Australia (Australia).

The development of the intermediary part of the social finance market has been rapid and is accelerating. It has been characterized by innovation and experimentation. It is also an increasingly global set of institutions spanning many countries. However, the intermediary space is far from fully institutionalized yet. The most obvious lacunae are performance (social *and* financial) data aggregators and analysts and well-developed secondary markets. The ongoing institutionalization of these two sets of activities will be vital for a fully functioning social market to emerge.

DEMAND

The demand side of the social finance market includes various investees such as social enterprises, charities, co-operatives, social 'profit-with-purpose' businesses, and hybrid organizations combining elements of the state, the private sector, and the civil society sector engaging in social innovation (Nicholls and Murdock, 2011). Many social investees have been in existence for a long time, for example, faith-based charities and mutual societies that are over a century old. Despite a large number of organizations seeking social finance capital, the demand side appears to be the least well institutionalized aspect of the market. Many investors complain that they cannot find many 'investable' social finance deals—such that, perhaps counter-intuitively, there appears to be an imbalance between an excess of supply and a paucity of demand (despite huge and growing social and environmental need).

There are a number of issues constraining the ability of the demand side to access social finance. The first is scale. Most social impact organizations are only able to absorb relatively small amounts of investment due to their size and turnover. The transaction costs of such investments are significant. As a consequence, there is need for more effective aggregation of investment opportunities, as well as a more assertive attitude towards providing risk and growth capital to such organizations.

This relates to a second set of issues—there are significant gaps in the funding options for social impact investees across their lifecycle of development, particularly between early-stage grants and large-scale debt or equity investments.[19] This 'missing middle' of social finance at the mezzanine round is partly a consequence of structural issues in many social enterprises—they are by design profit limiting since such funds may not be distributed to outside investors and are typically reinvested for social mission—and partly a result of poor data on the real risk and return performance of such investments. In the

---

[19] One response to the lifecycle challenges for investees has been a discussion of a new form of growth capital known as 'builder capital': <http://www.bigsocietycapital.com/blog/investable-social-entrepreneur-introducing-builder-capital>. Also, see the further discussion in the conclusions of this chapter.

absence of rigorous risk and return data the natural assumption is to allocate high levels of 'uncertainty' risk and demand high (and often, unachievable) returns as a result. Here greater co-operation between potential investors (sharing and structuring possible deals together) offers real promise.

Finally, there is an urgent need for vigorous capacity building particularly around financial literacy to enable potential investees to better understand which forms of investment best suit their structure and strategic mission object- ives. This can also support more successful approaches to public sector commis- sioners that, in turn, may grow their turnover and investment readiness.[20]

A report from Venturesome (Goodall and Kingston, 2009) noted that potential recipients of social finance require better support to:

- identify their own financial needs more thoroughly
- be aware of all available finance mechanisms and instruments and their pros and cons (and risks)
- be aware of the different capital providers available to them and their requirements
- have confidence to seek new finance from multiple sources and to structure deals blending investors with multiple risk and return profiles
- distinguish between income and capital both in their accounting and invest- ment plans
- understand that grants are not free money (they can cost up to 15–25 per cent of the capital raised: more than three times the typical cost of raising equity).

Furthermore, there is need for a more fully developed range of legal and contractual mechanisms (for example, asset locks) to protect investees against mission drift and take-over. These could reduce the investees' perceived *social mission* riskiness of taking social finance and help build incentives to diversify their funding base beyond grants. Building a robust pipeline of potential investments remains a major challenge for the social finance market, but is of central importance.

Having set out the basic market structure of the social finance sector, this chapter will now consider some of the key debates and issues within this emerging field.

Debates and issues

ASSET ALLOCATION

The question of whether or not social finance—and particularly impact investment—constitutes a separate 'asset class' has been much debated since

---

[20] See, for example, the UK government Investment and Contract Readiness Fund for such an initiative.

it was first suggested by O'Donohoe et al. (2010).[21] Clearly, the variety of instruments within social finance suggests that it would be quite unlike any other asset class if it were considered as such. Nevertheless, in practice significant innovation has emerged around this issue.

While much recent discussion regarding social finance has focused upon individual investment instruments, investment opportunities, public policy and related issues, in recent years a growing number of asset owners have approached investment strategies not from the perspective of individual deals or funds, but rather from an overall asset allocation perspective. These private and in some cases institutional asset owners are interested in managing asset allocation of their *total* portfolio on an ESG Integration and Impact basis. Building upon the concepts of Total Foundation Asset Management and new approaches to portfolio management (Emerson, 2002, 2003b; Bugg-Levine and Emerson, 2011; Christiansen, 2011), these investors seek to allocate their total asset base for impact, across traditional asset classes historically used to manage potential downside risk with various levels of projected financial return.

Within this total portfolio approach, asset owners and their advisors do not manage capital with reference to sets of trade-offs between 'impact first' and 'finance first' strategies, but rather seek to allocate capital across a portfolio of investments. Accordingly, they invest capital into a host of traditional asset categories (fixed income, private and public equities, real assets, cash and cash equivalents) and seek a competitive financial return for each strategy *together* with whatever form and level of impact is viewed as appropriate for any given strategy. Within this approach, public securities are invested for financial return commensurate with standard benchmarks (S&P 500, Russell 1000, and so on) while 'impact' is expressed through proxy voting and shareholder activism; whereas allocations to, for example, branded 'impact funds' seek competitive financial returns for that category of private equity or debt together with documented impact evaluated through various social impact metrics.

A growing number of wealth advisors (CapRock Capital Management, Veris Wealth Advisors, Sonen Capital, and others) are developing expertise at managing portfolios on a '100 per cent impact' basis, while new networks, such as The 100 per cent Impact Network discussed later in this book, and presently operating with over 50 ultra-high net worth asset owners as members, are being organized to offer peer-based support to such investors.

The rise in asset owners managing all their capital on an impact basis is a natural outgrowth of the positive experience early investors have had in

---

[21] The Social Impact Investment Taskforce identified four issues of particular importance and created subgroups to work and report back on them in late 2014. The reports are: *Allocating for Impact: Subject Paper of the Asset Allocation Working Group; Measuring Impact: Subject Paper of the Impact Measurement Working Group; International Development: Report of the Social Impact Investment Taskforce International Development Working Group; Profit-With-purpose Businesses: Subject Paper of the Mission Alignment Working Group.*

various discrete investment strategies (ESG Integration, microfinance, community development finance, and a variety of related approaches) who have concluded these discrete areas of investment are best managed from a total portfolio basis as opposed to being viewed as individual, unrelated allocations 'for impact'.

SOCIAL IMPACT MEASUREMENT

Today there is no standard unit of social impact nor any agreed methodologies or accounting regulations with which to capture and report it (see Nicholls, 2009 and, further, Nicholls et al., chapter 9, in this volume). This is widely seen as a drag on the future development of the social finance market since it makes the comparative analysis of various blended value deals and investments impossible. However, there has been some progress towards establishing a range of agreed impact accounting systems for social finance. Initiatives include: integrated ESG accounting; the Global Reporting Initiative (GRI); the Sustainable Accounting Standards Board (SASB); the Global Impact Investing Network's Impact Reporting and Investment Standards (IRIS) and the European Union 'Standard for Social Impact'. In the UK, the Cabinet Office supported the launch of 'Inspiring Impact', a ten-year project that aimed to build a coordinated and consistent approach to impact measurement. This included a commitment to explore the wider use of the Social Return on Investment (SROI) methodology that represents the nearest to a current industry standard for project or organization level social impact reporting.

The Global Impact Investing Ratings System (GIIRS)—developed by B Lab, the US organization behind the B-Corp certification—represents a leading example of an approach to creating standardized ratings and reporting of social impact. The GIIRS rating system uses IRIS metrics in conjunction with additional criteria to come up with an overall company or fund-level rating, as well as targeted sub-ratings in the categories of governance, workers, community, environment, and socially and environmentally focused business models. As of 2014, there were over 500 GIIRS-rated companies in 39 countries, each of which is scored up to a maximum of 200 points on criteria ranging from its commitment to a social mission and its land use to how it treats its workers and the community in which it operates.

INTERNATIONAL DEVELOPMENT

The potential role of social finance in international development became a 'hot topic' after it was debated at the G8 Social Impact Investment Forum in June 2013 (see, further, Hinton, in this volume). The evolution of the Development Impact Bond model, as a spin-off of Social Impact Bonds, represents one concrete example of this following on from this meeting. Moreover, many international agencies have invested in impact for decades and are exploring the possibility of doing more. Key initiatives include:

- In 2009, the French government launched the €250m FISEA (Fond d'investissement pour le soutien aux enterprises en Afrique) investment fund managed by CDC Group Proparco, the investment arm of the AFD. This Fund aimed to make equity investments in enterprises that have a high development impact in Africa through creating decent jobs and encouraging sustainable growth.
- In 2010, the Canadian Government created Grand Challenges Canada to make impact investments in low- and middle-income countries.
- In 2011, the German Development Bank KfW provided €5m of investment to the Aavishkaar India Impact Fund.
- In 2012, the UK's DFID, launched the £75m DFID Impact Fund, managed by CDC Group—a for-profit development finance institution (DFI) owned by the UK Government.
- In 2012, the US government's own DFI—the Overseas Private Investment Corporation (OPIC)—approved up to $285m in financing for six new impact investment funds.
- In 2013, DFID and the US international development agency (USAID) announced the joint creation of Global Development Innovation Ventures (GDIV)—an investment platform that aims to foster innovative solutions to the world's most difficult development challenges.
- In 2014, Italy approved a law on international co-operation to allow for funding based on public–private partnerships, making it easier to implement impact investment.

Models that link DFI activity with social finance structures and investors offer an opportunity to broaden the benefit of this sector outside of developed country contexts and to leverage real impact where it is most needed. There may also be an opportunity to tap into other, relevant, alternative finance systems that are significant in developing country contexts such as Islamic finance (see, further, Schoon, in this volume). However, there are issues concerning the lack of availability of local social finance capital in many developing countries that offer the prospect of development social finance being just another opportunity for developed countries to profit from poorer economies.

SOCIAL MISSION LOCK-IN

As has already been mentioned, taking social finance investment presents perceived risks to the investee (see, further, Nicholls and Tomkinson, in this volume). Chief amongst these is the risk of mission drift or, even, mission destruction in the case of a takeover (see, for example, Ben and Jerry's). Various strategies have evolved to protect the mission of a social organization including new legal forms such as the community interest company form in the UK that features an asset lock. Yet, no single agreed formula yet exists.

Moreover, while it may be expected that not-for-profit organizations should be committed to the pursuit of a social mission, for-profit companies are more challenged in executing mission-driven business models. This is due to an assumption that fiduciary obligation requires management to pursue strategies to maximize shareholder return on financial investment. Impact investors operating within the social finance ecosystem have managed this seeming conflict between shareholder and stakeholder interest in a variety of ways. To date, investors have sought to integrate impact into investment term sheets as one way to ensure alignment of impact and financial interest. New initiatives seek to document the specifics of these term sheets and make them available to other investors structuring new deals in the future (De Propper and Campbell, 2015).

B-Corp certification also seeks to lock in social mission through reframing the articles of incorporation of the company in order to give allowance to business managers creating ventures in pursuit of both market opportunity and social impact. Beyond enunciating an expectation of social and environmental impact within the articles of incorporation of a firm, mainstream private equity investors are also recognizing the value of embedding environmental considerations of performance and management within the business strategies of for-profit companies. Private equity firms such as Kohlberg, Kravis, Roberts and Co., Black Rock, and others are pursuing increasingly intentional strategies to manage companies within their portfolios on a sustainability basis—and documenting the financial benefits of doing so.

Finally, as described below, recent research also points to the reality that the highest performing impact investing funds often operate within a framework of 'impact DNA' or 'mission first and last'. In practice, this means that at the inception of a fund's life managers and limited partners set out a clearly defined impact thesis and then execute the investing practices of the fund with strict financial discipline in pursuit of that thesis. This approach integrates impact deep within the investment activities of the fund and creates a permanent social mission lock-in (Clark et al., 2014).

ROLE OF PROFIT-WITH-PURPOSE BUSINESSES

The primary contribution of the Social Impact Investment Taskforce subgroup exploring mission alignment was to explore a new style of business defined as fully profit-distributing organizations that had a long-term commitment to prioritize, deliver, and report on their social impact. Such organizations were given the title 'profit-with-purpose businesses'. Three features defined this type of organization: intent, duty, reporting. The intent must be to achieve social impact. The duty is to strive to achieve that impact. The reporting requirement is to demonstrate the impact created. Including a new category of profit-with-purpose organizations within the demand side of the social finance market is attractive for several reasons.

It would allow many existing firms to reclassify themselves as social investees and, thus, to gain access to often discounted capital. For social investors it would offer lower risk and more 'conventional' investments that lacked the measurement complexities of many social enterprises. These investments would also offer the potential for greater scale and scalability from the start, compared with many social purpose organizations. However, the devil must lie in the detail of any moves to develop a serious profit-with-purpose market. Absent clear regulatory guidelines, the opportunity for free-rider behaviour is considerable.

IMPACT INVESTING 2.0

While the academic community is demonstrating increasing interest in taking a methodical approach to researching emerging practices and experience within social finance, some of the most promising research is being executed at the practitioner level. The recent research initiative, Impact Investing 2.0 (Clark et al., 2012, 2013), sought to engage both investors and fund managers in an assessment of what practices made for not simply well-managed impact funds, but funds that were felt to have outperformed their peers on the basis of both financial and impact criteria. Beginning with a universe of over 300 branded impact investing funds, the researchers and their associates engaged in a series of interviews with both general and limited fund partners, exploring how investors understood outperformance and documenting investment best practice. On the basis of these interviews and their own analysis, the researchers then created a sub-set of twelve high performing funds that were then engaged in formal, deep, case-study analysis. In addition to these interviews, the researcher team benefitted from the input of scores of social finance practitioners who attended workshop sessions facilitated by the principals at such international gatherings of impact investors as SoCap (The Social Capital Markets Conference in San Francisco, described as 'Burning Man Meets Wall Street' and attended by over 2,000 participants annually) and The Skoll World Forum, held each spring at Oxford University.

The research team has produced several reports and a 2015 book exploring their findings and outlining how other impact investors might benefit from the practices of the leading funds included in the study. Four core themes that came out of the three-year research initiative include the concepts of:

- *Policy symbiosis*: Impact investing is grounded in deep cross-sector partnerships, including with the public sector. Impact investing intersects with all levels of government, consistent with the public sector's strong interest in maximizing social and environmental benefits to society, and the promise that impact investing can deliver these benefits at scale. (This finding contradicts the sometimes hubristic rhetoric of some impact investors who believe successful funds are a function of 'the free market' alone.)

- *Catalytic capital*: Investments that trigger additional capital not otherwise available to a fund, enterprise, sector, or geography can be transformative, generating exponential social and/or environmental value. Catalytic capital can be instrumental to a fund, from providing early funding to driving reputational benefits
- *Multilingual leadership*: Those responsible for making investments must execute with unshakable financial discipline, but successful fund leadership is about more than simply effective money management. It requires cross-sector experience and fluency both at the institutional and individual level.
- *Mission first and last*: As opposed to being 'finance-first' or 'impact-first', successful funds place financial and social objectives on equal footing by establishing a clearly embedded strategy and structure for achieving mission prior to investment, enabling a predominantly financial focus throughout the life of the investment.

ENVIRONMENTAL INVESTING

Environmental investing is an important part of social finance—since environmental degradation typically has profound human impacts (see, further, Harold et al., in this volume). Broadly speaking, environmental investing includes a wide range of investment strategies and instruments from conservation easements to land banking to conservation credits and carbon trading. Interesting initiatives have included:

- *The Vibrant Oceans Initiative*: a $53mm program of Bloomberg Philanthropies built upon a partnership of the NGOs Oceana and Rare who are working with the sustainable finance firm EKO Asset Management Partners to bring private capital to help finance the transition of local fishers and industrial fleets to sustainable fishing practices in critical fisheries around the world
- *The Nature Conservancy's Conservation Note*: through which asset owners may invest in fixed income notes at $25,000 levels with various terms. Capital raised through the offering is used to finance 'high priority' conservation projects around the world
- *The United Nations Environment Programme Finance Initiative*: that seeks to integrate consideration of environmental factors into the practices of mainstream finance firms. While a voluntary initiative, the UNEPF has played a significant role in raising the profile of sustainability within the mainstream financial services community and advancing practices of sustainable environmental investment at the institutional investor level.

The arena of environmental investing is not without controversy in that many of its practices involve efforts to 'put a price on the planet' and bring capital market innovation to the management and preservation of land, water, and animals. That said, it represents an important arena for researchers and practitioners exploring the intersects of finance and precious resources as we continue to seek solutions to both the growing needs of humanity and the paramount requirements of a healthy, diverse Earth.

RETAIL INVESTORS

Much of the present focus within the arena of social finance is centred upon funds, asset allocation by ultra-high net worth asset owners, institutional investors, and other initiatives standing well beyond the balance sheets of most individual investors who might be interested in placing smaller amounts of capital within a social finance strategy. Yet, if social finance is to attain real scale, it must be 'democratized' and become as accessible to those investing $250 as it is to those investing $250,000. At present, there are few investment vehicles available to those investing at lower increments, yet recent years have seen a variety of innovations that may be taken as an indicator of future possibilities. For example:

- The Calvert Foundation *Community Investment Note* has made it possible for individual investors to engage with social finance debt through their investment broker in coordination with the management of their retirement and other assets
- *TriLinc Global*, a type of 'impact mutual fund', offers smaller retail investors options for investing debt capital in a global strategy to finance small and growing enterprises in a variety of emerging markets, with job creation at the Bottom of the Pyramid as a primary measure of impact
- *Impact Assets*, a not-for-profit financial services organization, manages a donor-advised fund (a type of charitable-giving vehicle wherein individuals may donate as little as $500 into an account which is then used to make charitable gifts which the donor advises on) with $150m in total assets—80 per cent of which is managed on an impact basis. Furthermore, in early 2015 Impact Assets introduced two investment notes (one within micro-finance and a second targeting sustainable agriculture) available to investors in $25,000 increments
- Finally, as previously mentioned, various crowdfunding platforms offer new opportunities for individual investors (whether accredited or not) to make smaller investments in both for-profit and non-profit social ventures.

Each of these, together with various other initiatives are expanding the options available to investors at the retail level and opening up new channels for capital to move within the social finance capital market.

Overview of book

After this introduction, this collection contains nineteen chapters broken down into five parts. The first part, 'Contexts and Debates', sets up the background for the book as a whole with a series of discrete, expert, critiques and observations concerning the nature and development of different aspects of the social finance market. These four chapters serve to sensitize the reader to some of the key debates and issues in social finance thus far.

Part I opens with Mulgan's chapter that asks the fundamental question: does the 'investment' approach of social finance actually add any value? The chapter considers some of the origins of social finance and analyses eight different types of investment that are sometimes conflated under this title. It critiques some of the discourses that have evolved around social finance noting in particular the weak evidence base on the actual value added of bringing investment approaches and methods into the social sector. The chapter includes a detailed analysis of the development of the UK ecosystem for social finance drawing upon the author's own involvement in some key initiatives. This leads to a set of reflections on the development of 'pay-for-success' models that link financial flows to evidenced social impact (at least in theory). Next, four key challenges are highlighted around returns, definitions, impact, and scale. The chapter concludes with some observations concerning the likely future development of this sector.

The second chapter is by Steinberg and focuses squarely on the relationship between social finance and the not-for-profit sector. It asks the question: what should social finance invest in and with whom? This chapter considers two aspects of the question. First, it discusses the difference between societal needs that can be addressed through ordinary financial investments from those that require social investment. That is the 'what' part of the chapter. The 'with whom' part concerns investment targets, the organizations that use social investments to create social impact. The chapter starts by setting out the conventional rationales for social finance in terms of creating collective goods and addressing market failures, it then goes on to explore the specifics of social investment in not-for-profit organizations. The next section of the chapter considers the evolution of hybrid organizations that combine social and financial objectives—specifically it evaluates several key features such as their efficiency, sustainability, and access to capital. Conclusions summarize the various arguments and acknowledge limitations.

The third contribution to Part I comes from Young. This chapter explores social finance in terms of social enterprise investee types. This review empha-sizes that social enterprises are very diverse, multi-sectoral phenomena that seek capital through a variety of mixes of governmental, philanthropic, and market-based income and investment. As a consequence, the chapter goes on to build a cross-sectoral theory of social finance based on a *benefits* theory of not-for-profit finance. This benefits theory is extended so that, first, it can be applied to a variety of social purpose organizational forms not just not-for-profit organizations and so that, second, it can move its focus from the demand for the services of not-for-profit organizations to how social entrepreneurs finance their ventures. It is suggested that the latter involves them matching their mission interests with the potential sources of finance deriving from the mix of public and private benefits their ventures provide. The development and application of this benefit's theory exposes a series of challenges for social finance. Conclusions suggest that it seems likely that social enterprises will be perennially undercapitalized relative to the benefits they can potentially offer—*unless* compensatory entrepreneurial strategies and public policies are enacted.

Part I concludes with a contribution from Bishop and Green. Their chapter builds on their previous work on *philanthrocapitalism* to explore how this field of action has evolved. They suggest that, despite the financial crisis of 2008, engaged giving has expanded and become more institutionalized rather than withering away. Indeed, even governments are now advocates. The basic argument set out in this chapter aims to refute the normative assumption that there is an unavoidable antagonism between the pursuit of profit and the general well-being of society. The chapter functions as a set of debates addressing key critics of *philanthrocapitalism*—as such it is, itself, somewhat controversial. Yet, the chapter highlights several important issues that go beyond its particular perspective, such as the value of more diligent impact measurement and improved transparency and accountability in the grant-making sector. The chapter goes on to highlight some of the emerging innovations in this sector including philanthropic 'marketplaces' such as the Clinton Global Initiative. The authors conclude with a cautious reminder that taking risks can pay off, but demonstrable successes are important too.

The second part of this book focuses on the landscape of social finance. Four chapters provide in-depth analyses of the most well-developed sectors in social finance in rough chronological order: co-operative and mutual finance, microfinance, venture philanthropy, and impact investing. In chapter 5, Michie explores one of the very first forms of social finance—co-operative and mutual organizations. First, the author sets out a definition of this sector and its approach to investment and finance. Next, the chapter sketches in some historical background and puts co-operatives and mutual in their global context, including data about the (substantial) scale and size of the sector worldwide. After this, there is a section exploring the relationship between co-operatives and mutual organizations and public services reform. Michie goes on to argue that, post 2008, there is an increasing consensus that greater corporate diversity would reduce the overall riskiness of a national economy—in this context the growth of the co-operative and mutual sector offers macro-level benefits beyond the micro-benefits from the social value of individual membership and community embeddedness. The chapter then explores the possible shape and structure of a future market for mutual finance. Conclusions summarize the chapter as a whole.

The next chapter, chapter 6, examines another of the best-developed fields of social finance—microfinance. In this chapter, Sabin suggests that modern microfinance is a field 'in flux' facing a series of important challenges and issues despite over thirty years of practical action. The chapter opens with an overview of microfinance drawing upon the author's observations of changes in the field, as well as upon a review of a range of research studies. This section also establishes key terminology and explores two important historical predecessors: informal community associations and state-owned development banks. Following this, the chapter sets out how microfinance began in the mid 1970s and grew into its modern form, including a summary of the sector's scale, geographic coverage, institution size, and organizational type. The chapter goes on to consider three fundamental debates in microfinance: the critical features of the model, the appropriate role of commercialization, and the impact of microfinance. The chapter ends by reflecting on how the central debate concerning the profitability of microfinance has yet to be resolved. Sabin provides a series of vignette case examples throughout to illustrate key points and issues.

Chapter 7 explores venture philanthropy. John and Emerson start by defining this term and constituent elements and phases. Next the authors trace its development starting in the USA and the moving to Europe and, more recently, to Asia. These historical analyses demonstrate both how the field of 'engaged' philanthropy has changed over time, but also how important different socio-cultural contexts and traditions have been in its development. The chapter makes a clear connection with the work on 'philanthrocapitalism' earlier in the book. After the historical landscape analysis, the chapter goes on to discuss some of the criticisms that have been levelled at venture philanthropy. John and Emerson conclude by raising the key question of whether venture philanthropy will become the norm for grant-making or will remain an 'outsider' sector.

The final chapter in part two, chapter 8, gives an account of one of the most high profile sub-sectors of social finance: impact investing. The chapter begins by establishing a definition for this market and discussing the main contexts and trends that can be observed shaping its development. A section on key characteristics follows that covers such issues as geographical spread and diversity, sectoral spread, financial instruments, and risk and return profiles. Oleksiak et al. then discuss the emerging market structure of impact investing and give an account of the important role of policy in shaping and supporting the field. The chapter then moves on to consider future directions, opportunities, and challenges. The arguments and analyses of the chapter as a whole are finally summed up in a conclusion. Throughout the chapter short case examples provide important real world grounding to the analysis and commentary.

Part III of this collection, 'Models and Metrics', contains four contributions. Each provides new theoretical thinking and analysis around four key topics in terms of modelling and measuring social finance outcomes. The third part opens with Nicholls et al.'s chapter 9 on social impact measurement. The chapter opens by providing a definition of 'social impact' and then sets out some of the current debates and issues concerning how to measure it. Next the authors highlight the distinctive features of social finance in terms of the implications these have for metrics aimed at informing capital allocation decisions. Then the chapter introduces a critical issues framework that poses a series of questions to help orient and inform choices regarding the large number of available metrics for capturing social value creation and organizational performance. This leads to a discussion of the measurement methodologies relevant to social impact and an overview of the specific metrics and rating schemes now being offered for use in relation to social finance. The chapter then develops a contingency model to suggest the sorts of contexts in which social impact measurement (in its various forms) will and will not be appropriate. Conclusions summarize the chapter as a whole.

Chapter 10 engages with an important, but largely under-researched topic: risk and return in social finance. In this chapter, Nicholls and Tomkinson explore how far existing tools and frameworks for calculating risk and return parameters in mainstream finance can be applied to modelling the likely *social* returns to a given allocation of capital. First, the chapter examines risk and return in mainstream finance and establishes three distinct categories: probability risk, variance risk, and uncertainty risk. It then moves on to review the work to date (such as it is) on social risk and return. The three categories drawn from the established risk literature are then applied to social outcomes and suggestions are made as to how these can best be applied. The correlations between particular types of social risk and expected social returns are considered—the patterns of correlation are found to be complex. The chapter moves on to make some observations concerning how to measure and manage social risk in social finance. Conclusions suggest some of the opportunities offered to social investors by developing more rigorous conceptualizations of social risk and return.

The next chapter, chapter 11, builds on the work of Nicholls and Tomkinson to explore pricing and valuation in social finance. The chapter suggests that a significant challenge to the further development of the social finance market is the lack of consistent *blended* valuations and pricing that allow comparative allocation capital judgements to be made. The authors aim to address this issue by building a new framework—built upon the foundations of mainstream asset valuation—the projection-valuation-pricing (PVP) model. Each element of the model is then explored in detail with key observations being made concerning its distinctiveness in social finance contexts. This analysis highlights how existing models have validity for social finance, but will need to be adapted to a new context. The chapter then continues by exploring some of the key features needed to develop a distinctive social finance term sheet in terms of a range of investors. The chapter concludes by summarizing its contributions.

The final chapter in Part III, chapter 12, sets out in detail an example of one of the most important innovations in social finance: the Social Impact Bond (SIB). Nicholls and Tomkinson provide a detailed case analysis of the world's first SIB, based at Her Majesty's Prison in Peterborough, UK. This chapter starts by defining the SIB model and its key constituent parts. Next, the chapter sketches in the historical context that provides the background to the emergence of the SIB. The third section examines the Peterborough Pilot SIB in some detail. After this, the evolution of SIBs globally is discussed. Conclusions consider some of the issues that have emerged as the first SIB has been implemented. The chapter closes with a postscript reflecting on key issues that developed in 2014.

Part IV, 'Infrastructure', contains three contributions. The first two chapters reflect on the policy contexts and agendas that have shaped the ecosystem of social finance globally. Addis and Nicholls (chapter 13) focus particularly on how various public policy tools have been addressing building the social finance market around the world as a *catalytic* force. The chapter considers the rationale for policy interventions, looking firstly at a market-based analysis and then at arguments for a broader role for the state in encouraging innovation. The authors set out a new 'toolbox' for policy, drawing upon examples from around the globe. The chapter concludes with consideration of how social finance can provide a focal point for new collaborations across sectoral boundaries to shape a more productive generation of public–private partnerships going forward.

Whilst Addis and Nicholls focused on the issues and debates within the evolving social finance policy agenda globally, in chapter 14, Spear, Paton, and Nicholls examine three specific country contexts: UK, USA, and Canada. These choices of countries reflect both well-developed policy contexts and offer a contrast between liberal market economies (UK and USA) and a coordinated market economy (Quebec in Canada). The chapter addresses three basic questions: what governments have actually done; why governments became involved; how their policies and new institutions have developed. The chapter opens by summarizing key policy developments in the UK and considers the political and economic rationales used to justify such public action. The next section looks at the US context and then carries out a brief synthesis of action across these two liberal market economies. The next section shifts the focus to a coordinated market economy and sets out the relevant policy agendas in Quebec, Canada. The rationale here is that Quebec has developed an unusual, and unusually strong, infrastructure for the provision of social finance. The aim here is to move the discussion and analysis beyond the Anglo-American concerns that often frame discussions of social finance. Finally, the chapter draws some conclusions from its research in the form of a broad argument about how different policies in different jurisdictions may be evolving.

The third chapter in Part IV (chapter 15) explores the emerging infrastructure supporting the social finance market. Schwartz, Jones, and Nicholls, first, establish the wider background for their subsequent discussion by discussing in detail the basic requirements for the flourishing of a social economy. Building on this, the authors then go on to identify and explore four key types of infrastructure that support the development of the social finance market: governmental, facilitative, intellectual, and transactional. The chapter includes a range of international case examples to illustrate its analysis. Conclusions capture the key contributions of the chapter as a whole.

The fifth, and final, part of this collection, 'Future Directions', highlights four examples of emerging social finance markets that offer insights into the possible opportunities for the acceleration and broadening of the social finance market going forward. The first contribution from Lehner (chapter 16) examines crowdfunding (CF), particularly as it relates to financing social enterprise. The chapter suggests that crowdfunding offers a real opportunity to connect mass retail investors with social enterprise and also sets itself up to fill a significant research gap in this context. First, this chapter examines various business models for CF. Next it explores debt and equity-based CF models in terms of social finance. Finally, the chapter proposes future research themes and topics for CF scholarship in a social enterprise (SE) context.

Chapter 17 focuses on foreign direct investment (DFI) and private equity (PE) finance as a source of social impact. Hinton assesses the current investment landscape of DFIs and PE in the emerging markets with a special emphasis on the African and South Asian markets. He argues that DFIs have been providing a form of (largely unrecognized) social finance to emerging markets for many decades by dint of their impact mandates and ownership structures. Such finance stresses clear standards of environmental, social, and governance performance and aims to measure and account for them transparently. However, the chapter goes on to explore how various funds can be divided as being either 'finance' or 'impact' first with significant implications for their activities and structures. The chapter concludes by looking at a range of key issues with respect to DFI as social finance. Conclusions summarize the data and arguments presented throughout the chapter.

The next chapter, chapter 18, explores Islamic finance and suggests some linkages with social finance. The chapter opens with a brief overview of the history of finance to provide a context for some of the subsequent precepts of Islamic finance. Next, the most well known prohibition in Islamic finance— the prohibition on charging interest—is reviewed. This is followed by an overview of the different product types available in this market. The next section considers other, lesser-known prohibitions specifically focused on social responsibility within Islamic finance. Finally, conclusions draw the chapter together.

The final chapter of Part V, chapter 19, examines environmental finance. Specifically, the chapter sets out this intersection of households, the economics of environmental management and the environmental consequences of economic investment. The analysis is organized into four main elements: the first section begins by exploring the main themes in environmental economics. Next, it goes on to investigate the link between environmental investing and financial return and then proposes a framework for understanding the different forums in which environmentally oriented investment occurs. The second part proposes ten key propositions on how environmental concerns are connected to financial investment. Section three focuses on one particularly tangible domain—real estate—and includes three case studies to illustrate existing strategies for incorporating environmental value into real estate investment. The final section presents conclusions and recommendations for further research.[22]

The book as a whole concludes with a postscript from Gregory. This acts as provocation to the reader to imagine a future set of social relations and orientations—including those that define and operationalize financial markets—that moves from a focus on self-interest and the 'invisible hand' to co-operation and mutuality—a visible 'handshake'.

Conclusion

As reflected in this introduction and through this book, social finance represents a dynamic and multifaceted ecosystem of investors, entrepreneurs, and public policy actors. Yet, to be truly effective in continuing its movement from a fringe set of capital market practices to one that is truly embedded within the economic mainstream, social finance must overcome a host of challenges. Evenett and Richter (2011: 3) identified seven persistent challenges to the further institutionalization of the social finance marketplace:

- Fragmentation of capital supply and the absence of joined up and plural finance options. There is a need for more collaboration and co-investment in the sector as well as more players in the market to build competition. Furthermore, pooling demand-side investment opportunities could bring in players for whom the present market is currently too small
- Need for more bespoke business support with deeply embedded cultural and technical issues that need addressing
- No universally agreed metrics for social outcomes and no single 'silver bullet' solution to this. A pernicious consequence of this lack of accounting standards is high due diligence costs per deal and, therefore, high perceived risks in social investments (see further chapter 10)

---

[22] This paper draws heavily from two others by the authors, both published in 2007 by the Skoll Centre for Social Entrepreneurship at the Oxford Said School of Business: *Blended Value Investing: Integrating Environmental Risks and Opportunities into Securities Valuation* and *Blended Value Investing: Innovations in Real Estate.*

- No clear market signals: the mix of instruments in social investment noted above (i.e. including grants, soft loans, and so on) makes this a complex and difficult market for potential new entrants
- Restrictive regulatory and legislative environment for foundation assets
- Insufficient investor incentives such as tax breaks or government guarantees (though more creative structured finance deals can address this)
- Need for better deal brokering to address illiquidity of the secondary marketplace for social investment.

Whilst there has been progress on most of these issues in recent years, it is still the case that the social finance market remains fragmented and only partially institutionalized. However, partly as a result of the fluidity of this space, there has been a significant amount of experimentation and innovation that appears to be accelerating and moving across countries and continents. Learning and models are being shared and adapted across territories and in local contexts— an example is the multiple adaptations of the SIB model emerging around the world. The work of the Social Impact Investment Taskforce across the G8 states (plus Australia) combined with the work of other transnational institutions, such as the Impact Investing Policy Collaborative (IIPC), are providing important global infrastructure for fast-tracking successful developments across countries. The establishment of regional networks in areas such as venture philanthropy (EVPA, AVPN) is also helping to grow capital flows and share best practice (see, further, John and Emerson, in this volume).

Whilst it remains at an early stage of institutionalization, it is already possible to envisage some future patterns of the development of social finance. One of three future scenarios seems most likely: absorption, parallel institutionalization, institutional transformation.

SCENARIO 1. ABSORPTION

The first possible scenario for social finance would see it move into the mainstream of financial markets and, potentially, be absorbed by them. This scenario is predicated on social finance investment expanding its capacity to generate profit and then integrating with socially responsible investment as a mainstream portfolio option. The growth and success of clean energy investing may offer a precursor to such a trend. At present, however, it is unclear how many social investments offer the necessary scale for mainstream investment; at present, there is something of a capital absorption challenge in that there is potentially more capital 'sitting on the sidelines' than there are investible opportunities for mainstream investors seeking impact opportunities. Nevertheless, there is already evidence this scenario is moving towards becoming reality. Since the early development of modern social finance, actors from within conventional finance have played a leading role, bringing market/ business logics to its incipient institutionalization, particularly in the intermediary space. An important element within this transition has been a particular focus on 'professionalizing' social finance along mainstream investment lines in contrast to the traditions of gift-giving and grant-making.

The resources allocated to developing the quasi-mainstream impact investing market also demonstrate a desire to integrate social finance within conventional markets. There is also increasing evidence of mainstream capital asset managers looking beyond the traditional 'financial only' frame of analysis to consider the 'off balance sheet' risks and opportunities represented by social and environmental factors. Such managers have viewed environmental, social, and governance (ESG) integration and the related practices of social finance as *additive* to traditional financial analysis and have looked to integrate them into more holistic investment analytics (Clark et al., 2013).

SCENARIO 2. PARALLEL INSTITUTIONALIZATION

The second scenario suggests social finance would continue to operate on the margins of the mainstream intersecting with it where mutual interest makes this viable (i.e. around social enterprises that are at scale), but also working as a separate, parallel system supporting the wider social economy with a broad range of financial instruments, risk–return model, and hybrid deal structures. The logics of gift-giving and mainstream investment would be kept balanced (if in tension) by a larger number of new, hybrid organizations and financial instruments that would gradually gain wider normative and cognitive legitimacy and, thus, access larger pools of philanthropic and investment capital. In this scenario, venture philanthropy and collaborations between for-profit and non-profit organizations would play key roles in institutionalizing new relationships between formerly distinct investment logics and investor rationalities. A resurgence of mutualization would also be a distinctive feature of this scenario, seeing a return to regional stock markets, new local currencies, a new wave of friendly and building societies, and local co-operatives taking on significant roles in terms of public and private sector action (see, further, Michie and Gregory, in this volume).

SCENARIO 3. INSTITUTIONAL TRANSFORMATION

In the third scenario social finance would catalyse systemic change across all investment markets via radical and disruptive action seeking a broader or deeper transformation of society marked by more explicitly political, critical, and countercultural orientations (Davis et al., 2005). The rise of ethical consumption provides a possible template for this transformation. Whilst the market for ethical goods and services remains less than 1 per cent of all transactions in Europe (and less in the USA), its principles have proved to be far more influential. For example, in the North, the Fair Trade model has inspired consumers to demand both increased supply chain transparency and better supply chain practices across the entire retail industry (see Nicholls and Opal, 2005). In this scenario, social finance would act as both a viral symptom and a cause of a major realignment of capital investment that would demand that risk and return calculations are re-embedded in their social and environmental context, something that is already happening in terms of the carbon footprint of many industrial businesses and via ESG accounting. This transformatory social finance scenario would combine with the continued growth of ethical consumption and state regulatory responses post the 2008 global financial crisis to synthesize a new 'economy of virtue' (see Offer, 2006), 'after capitalism' (Mulgan, 2009) and an evolved form of 'Capitalism 3.0' (Emerson and Bonini, 2006) or 'collaborative capitalism' (Clark et al., 2014).

This process of transformation would not come about accidentally, but, rather, could be led by a new class of financial managers coming from both the mainstream and development/social finance communities. Research has shown (Clark et al., 2013) that the most effectively managed social impact investment funds are those led by teams and managers with *both* mainstream finance expertise and development finance experience. Therefore, this scenario could be driven by the evolution of new types of investment professionals operating within a 'both/and' investment framework.

Overall, these transformations of mainstream capital markets with social finance practices would respond to Sen's (1987) argument that ethics and economics have been theoretically separated for too long in an artificial representation of utility, rationality, and efficiency that has conspicuously failed to deliver maximum welfare and has, in fact, exaggerated inequality. An economy built upon the virtues of fairness and interpersonal regard may offer not only a new economy better suited to the cultural complexity of today's global trade but also a return to a more humanistic model of exchange and economic interaction that has—temporarily—been displaced in the past century by the rise of corporate power and marketing. From this perspective, Marshall's (1907) call for 'economic chivalry' may yet be realized by the simple power of shifting market forces.

It is, of course, as yet impossible to determine which of these future scenarios (or which others left unaccounted for here) may emerge as the dominant expression of this market. However, clearer directions and route maps are beginning coalesce. In this regard, 2014 was an important year in the development of social finance.

In response to a wide-ranging, year-long, discussion and analysis of the opportunities and challenges for the social finance market globally, the Social Impact Investment Taskforce, chaired by Sir Ronald Cohen, reported back in September 2014 with eight high level recommendations:

1. Set measurable impact objectives and track their achievement
2. Investors to consider three dimensions: risk, return, and impact

3. Clarify fiduciary responsibilities of trustees: to allow trustees to consider social as well as financial return on their investments

4. Governments should consider streamlining pay-for-success arrangements such as Social Impact Bonds and adapting national ecosystems to support impact investment

5. Consider setting up an impact investment wholesaler funded with unclaimed assets to drive development of the impact investment sector

6. Boost social sector organizational capacity: governments and foundations to consider establishing capacity-building grant programmes

7. Give profit-with-purpose businesses the ability to lock-in mission: governments to provide appropriate legal forms or provisions for entrepreneurs and investors who wish to secure social mission into the future

8. Support impact investment's role in international development: governments to consider providing their development finance institutions with flexibility to increase impact investment efforts. Explore creation of an Impact Finance Facility to help attract early-stage capital, and a DIB Social Outcomes Fund to pay for successful Development Impact Bonds (SIITF, 2014: 8).

This book engages with all of these issues in depth and adds a range of others to offer the most comprehensive account of the state of social finance globally yet published. It is hoped that the material contained in the following pages will make a substantive contribution to the future development of social finance research, policy, and practice. The need for a fully functioning social finance market is urgent—it is critical that it is both well capitalized but also that it is well designed. Only a capital market that recognizes the opportunities offered by creative combinations of value creation and value appropriation will be able to maximize social finance's capacity to address the most pressing global problems and to transform the lives of the most marginalized people who can otherwise seem very distant from finance and its potential for systemic change.

▓ REFERENCES

Addis, R., McLeod, J., and Raine, A. (2013). *IMPACT-Australia: Investment for Social and Economic Benefit*. Canberra, Australia: Department of Education, Employment and Workplace Relations/JBWere.

Arosio, M. (2011). 'Impact Investing in Emerging Markets'. Willow Tree Impact Investors/Responsible Research.

Bank of England (2003). 'The Financing of Social Enterprises: A Special Report by the Bank of England'. Bank of England, London.

Bishop, M. and Green, M. (2008). *Philanthrocapitalism: How the Rich Can Save the World and Why We Should Let Them*. London: A. & C. Black.

Bishop, M., and Green, M. (2010). 'The Capital Curve for a Better World', *Innovations*, 5(1): 25–33.

Bloom, P. and Chatterji, A. (2009). 'Scaling Social Entrepreneurial Impact', *California Management Review*, 51(3): 114–33.

Bolton, M. and Kingston, J. (2006). *Approaches to Financing Charitable Work: Tracking Developments*. London: CAF.

Brown, A., and Norman, W. (2011). 'Lighting the Touchpaper: Growing the Market for Social Investment in England'. Boston Consulting Group/Young Foundation, London.

Brown, A., and Swersky, A. (2012). *The First Billion: A Forecast of Social Investment Demand*. London: Boston Consulting Group/Big Society Capital.

Brown, J. (2006). 'Equity Finance for Social Enterprises', *Social Enterprise Journal*, 2(1), 73–81.

BSC (Big Society Capital) (2012). *What Is Social Investment?* <http://www.bigsocietycapital.com/what-social-investment>, accessed 5 May 2015.

Bugg-Levine, A., and Emerson, J. (2011). *Impact Investing: Transforming How We Make Money*. Hoboken, NJ: Jossey-Bass.

Buttle, M. (2007). 'I'm Not in It for the Money': Constructing and Mediating Ethical Reconnections in UK Social Banking', *Geoforum*, 38(6): 1076–88.

Cabinet Office (2011). *Growing the Social Investment Market: A Vision and Strategy*. London: HM Government, Cabinet Office.

Cabinet Office (2012). *Growing the Social Investment Market: Progress Update*. London: HM Government, Cabinet Office.

Campanale, M. (2005). *Mission Related Investing and Charities*. London: Henderson Global Investors.

Clark, C., Emerson, J., and Thornley, B. (2012). *A Market Emerges: The Six Dynamics of Impact Investing*. San Francisco, CA: The Impact Investor.

Clark, C., Emerson, J., and Thornley, B. (2013). *Impact Investing 2.0: The Way Forward—Insight from 12 Outstanding Funds*. San Francisco, CA: Pacific Community Ventures, Inc. (PCV), ImpactAssets, and Duke University's Fuqua.

Clark, C., Emerson, J., and Thornley, B. (2014). *The Impact Investor: Lessons in Leadership and Strategy for Collaborative Capitalism*. San Francisco: Jossey-Bass.

Christiansen, L. (2011). 'A New Foundation for Portfolio Management', RSF Finance and Portfolio 21.

Clotfelter, C. (1992). 'The Distributional Consequences of Nonprofit Activities', in C. Clotfelter (ed,), *Who Benefits from the Nonprofit Sector?* Chicago: University of Chicago Press, pp. 1–23.

Davis, G., McAdam, D., Scott, W., and Zald, M. (2005). *Social Movements and Organization Theory*. Cambridge: Cambridge University Press.

De Propper, D., and Campbell, B. (2015). 'Embedding Impact into Term Sheets', submitted for publication, Working Paper, Blue Haven Initiative, et al.

Eadery, Y. (2006). 'Ethical Developments in Finance: Implications for Charities and Social Enterprise', *Social Enterprise Journal*, 2(1): 82–100.

Edwards, M. (2008). *Just Another Emperor? The Myths and Realities of Philanthrocapitalism*. London: Young Foundation.

Emerson, J. (1996). 'Grants, Debt and Equity: The Nonprofit Capital Market and its Malcontents, in New Social Entrepreneurs: The Success, Challenges and Lessons of Nonprofit Enterprise', The Roberts Foundation.

Emerson, J. (2000). 'The Nature of returns: A Social Capital Markets Inquiry into Elements of Investment and the Blended Value Proposition', Social Enterprise Series Research Paper no. 17, Harvard Business School.

Emerson, J. (2002). 'A Capital Idea: Total Foundation Asset Management and Unified Investment Strategy,' *Research Paper Series*, no. 1786, Stanford University Business School.

Emerson, J. (2003a). 'The Blended Value Proposition: Integrating Social and Financial Returns', *California Management Review*, 45(4): 35–51.

Emerson, J. (2003b). 'Where Money Meets Mission: Breaking down the Firewall between Foundation Investments and Programming', *Stanford Social Innovation Review*, Summer 1(2): 38–47.

Emerson, J., and Bonini, S. (2006). 'Capitalism 3.0: Exploring the Future of Capital Investment and Value Creation', Blended Value Working Paper. <http://www.blendedvalue.org/capitalism-3-0/>, accessed 5 May 2015.

Emerson, J., Freundlich, T., and Fruchterman, J. (2007). *Nothing Ventured, Nothing Gained*. Oxford: Skoll Centre for Social Entrepreneurship.

Emerson, J., and Spitzer, J. (2007). *From Fragmentation to Functionality: Critical Concepts and Writings on Social Capital Market Structure, Operation, and Innovation*. Oxford: Skoll Centre for Social Entrepreneurship.

Evenett, R., and Richter, K. (2011). *Making Good in Social Impact Investment: Opportunities in an Emerging Asset Class*. London: Social Investment Business and The City UK.

Freidman, M. (1962). *Capitalism as Freedom*. Chicago: Chicago University Press.

Freireich, J., and Fulton, K. (2009). *Investing for Social and Environmental Impact: A Design for Catalyzing an Emerging Industry* New York: Monitor Group.

Geobey, S., Westley, F. R., and Weber, O. (2012). 'Enabling Social Innovation Through Developmental Social Finance', *Journal of Social Entrepreneurship*, 3(2): 151–65.

Goodall, E., and Kingston, J. (2009). *Access to Capital: A Briefing Paper*. London: Venturesome.

Global Sustainable Investment Alliance (GSIA) (2013). *Global Sustainable Investment Review 2012*. Washington, DC: GSIA.

Glyn, A. (2006). *Capitalism Unleashed: Finance, Globalization, and Welfare*. Oxford: Oxford University Press.

Grabenwarter, U., and Liechtenstein, H. (2011). *In Search of Gamma: An Unconventional Perspective on Impact Investing*. Barcelona: IESE Business School.

Harji, K., and Jackson, E. T. (2012). *Accelerating impact: Achievements, Challenges, and What's Next in Building the Impact Investing Industry*. New York, NY: The Rockefeller Foundation.

Harold, J., Spitzer, J., and Emerson, J. (2007). *Blended Value Investing: Integrating Environmental Risks and Opportunities into Securities Valuation*. Oxford: Skoll Centre for Social Entrepreneurship.

Harvey, D. (2005). *A Brief History of Neo-Liberalism*. Oxford: Oxford University Press.

Hayek, F. (1944). *The Road to Serfdom*. London: Routledge.

Hill, K. (2011). *Investor Perspectives on Social Enterprise Financing*. London: City of London/Big Lottery Fund/ClearlySo.

Impact Investment Shujog (2011). *Impact Investors in Asia: Characteristics and Preferences for Investing in Social Enterprises in Asia-Pacific*. Singapore: Impact Investment Shujog and Asian Development Bank.

Joy, I., de Las Casas, L., and Rickey, B. (2011). *Understanding the Demand for and Supply of Social Finance: Research to Inform the Big Society Bank*. London: New Philanthropy Capital/NESTA.

J.P. Morgan and the GIIN (2010). *Impact Investments: An Emerging Asset Class.* New York, NY: J.P. Morgan and the GIIN.

J.P. Morgan and the GIIN (2011). *Insight into the Impact Investment Market.* New York, NY: J.P. Morgan and the GIIN.

J.P. Morgan and the GIIN (2013). *Perspectives of Progress: The Impact Investor Survey.* New York, NY: J.P. Morgan and the GIIN.

Kuhn, T. (1962). *The Structure of Scientific Revolutions.* Chicago: University of Chicago Press.

Marshall, A. (1907). 'The Social Possibilities of Economic Chivalry', *The Economic Journal*, 17(65): 7–29.

McWade, W. (2012). 'The Role for Social Enterprises and Social Investors in the Development Struggle', *Journal of Social Entrepreneurship*, 3(1): 96–112.

Moore, M. (1995). *Creating Public Value.* Cambridge, MA: Harvard University Press.

Moore, M.-L., Westley, F. R., and Brodhead, T. (2012). 'Social Finance Intermediaries and Social Innovation', *Journal of Social Entrepreneurship*, 3(2): 184–205.

Mulgan, G. (2009). 'After Capitalism', *Prospect Magazine*, 26 April: 157–70.

NESTA (National Endowment for Science Technology and the Arts) (2009). *Capital Business: Risk Finance for Social Enterprises.* London: NESTA.

Nicholls, A. (2009). '"We Do Good Things Don't We?" Blended Value Accounting In Social Entrepreneurship', *Accounting, Organizations and Society*, 34(6–7): 755–69.

Nicholls, A. (2010a). 'The Institutionalization of Social Investment: The Interplay of Investment Logics and Investor Rationalities', *Journal of Social Entrepreneurship*, 1(1): 70–100.

Nicholls, A. (2010b). *The Landscape of Social Finance in the UK.* University of Birmingham: Third Sector Research Centre.

Nicholls, A. (2013). 'Filling the Capital Gap: Institutionalizing Social Finance', in S. Denny and F. Seddon (eds), *Evaluating Social Enterprise.* Basingstoke: Palgrave MacMillan, pp. 161–96.

Nicholls, A., and Lehner, O. (2014). 'Social Finance and Crowd-Funding for Social Enterprises: A Public–Private Case Study Providing Legitimacy and Leverage', *Journal of Venture Capital*, 16(4): 271–86.

Nicholls, A., Moore, M-L., and Westley, F. (2012). 'The Social Finance and Social Innovation Nexus', *Journal of Social Entrepreneurship*, 3(2): 115–32.

Nicholls, A., and Murdock, A. (eds) (2011). *Social Innovation.* Basingstoke: Palgrave MacMillan.

Nicholls, A., and Opal, C. (2005). *Fair Trade: Market Driven Ethical Consumption.* London: Sage.

Nicholls, A., and Pharoah, C. (2007). *The Landscape of Social Finance.* Oxford: Skoll Centre for Social Entrepreneurship.

Nicholls, A., and Schwartz, R. (2014). 'The Demandside of the Social Investment Marketplace', in L. Salamon (ed.), *New Frontiers of Philanthropy: A Guide to the New Tools and New Actors that Are Reshaping Global Philanthropy and Social Investing.* San Francisco: Jossey-Bass, pp. 562–82.

Nyssens, M. (2006). *Social Enterprise.* London: Palgrave Macmillan.

O'Donohoe, N., Leijonhufvud, C., and Saltuk, Y. (2010). *Impact Investments: An Emerging Asset Class.* New York: J.P. Morgan and Rockefeller Foundation.

Offer, A. (2003). 'Welfare Measurement and Human Well-Being', in P. David and M. Thomas (eds), *The Economic Future in Historical Perspective*, Oxford: Oxford University Press, pp. 371–99.

Offer, A. (2006). *The Challenge of Affluence.* Oxford: Oxford University Press.

OTS (Office of the Third Sector) (2006). *Social Enterprise Action Plan: Scaling New Heights.* London: Office of the Third Sector.

OTS (Office of the Third Sector) (2008). *Social Investment Pilots.* London: Cabinet Office.

Ottinger, R. (2007). 'Portfolio Philanthropy: How Philanthropists Can Apply Portfolio Theory to Make Wiser Social Investments', *Stanford Social Innovation Review,* 5(4): 25–6.

Rayner, S. (2006). 'Wicked Problems: Clumsy Solutions: Diagnoses and Prescriptions for Environmental Ills', Jack Beale Memorial Lecture on Global Environment, <http://www.scribd.com/doc/258818064/Rayner-Wicked-Problems-clumsy-Solutions#-scribd>, accessed 5 May 2015.

Salamon, L., and Anheier, H. (1999). *The Emerging Sector Revisited.* Baltimore, MD: Johns Hopkins University.

Saltuk, Y., Bouri, A., and Leung, G. (2011). 'Insight into the Impact Investment Market', J.P. Morgan Social Finance/GIIN.

Scarlata, M., and Alemany, L. (2012). 'Deal Structuring in Philanthropic Venture Capital Investments: Financing Instrument, Valuation and Covenants', in R. Cressy, D. Cumming, and C. Mallin (eds.), *Entrepreneurship, Governance and Ethics,* Springer, pp. 121–45.

Sen, A. (1987). *On Ethics and Economics.* Oxford: Blackwell.

Shanmugalingam, C., Graham, J., Tucker, S., and Mulgan, G. (2011). *Growing Social Ventures.* London: NESTA/Young Foundation.

SIITF (Social Impact Investment Task Force) (2014). *The Invisible Heart of Markets: Harnessing the Power of Entrepreneurship, Innovation and Capital for Public Good.* London: SIITF.

SITF (Social Investment Task Force) (2010). *Social Investment: Ten Years On.* London: Social Investment Task Force.

Spitzer, J., Emerson, J., and Harold, J. (2007). *Blended Value Investing: Innovations in Real Estate.* Oxford: Skoll Centre for Social Entrepreneurship.

Suchman, M. (1995). 'Managing Legitimacy: Strategic and Institutional Approaches', *Academy of Management Review,* 20(3): 571–610.

Sunley, P., and Pinch, S. (2012). 'Financing Social Enterprise: Social Bricolage or Evolutionary Entrepreneurialism?' *Social Enterprise Journal,* 8(2): 108–22.

Thornley, B., Wood, D., Grace, K., and Sullivant, S. (2011). *Impact Investing: A Framework for Policy Design and Analysis.* Insight at Pacific Ventures-Initiative for Responsible Investment at Harvard University/Rockefeller Foundation.

Unwin, J. (2006). *An Intermediary for the Social Investment Market?* London: CAF Venturesome/Futurebuilders.

World Economic Forum (2013). *From the Margins to the Mainstream: Assessment of the Impact Investment Sector and Opportunities to Engage Mainstream Investors.* New York, NY: World Economic Forum.

World Economic Forum (2014). *Charting the Course: How Mainstream Investors Can Design Visionary and Pragmatic Impact Investing Strategies.* New York: World Economic Forum.

Wood, A. (2009). 'Exploring a New Financial Paradigm in Social Investment', *Social Space,* 2: 113–15. Singapore: Lien Centre for Social Innovation.

Part I

Contexts and Debates

1 Social finance

Does 'investment' add value?

Geoff Mulgan

Introduction

This chapter looks at some of the origins of social finance and analyses the different types of investment conflated under this title. It describes some of the challenges (and in particular the weak evidence base on the actual value added by investment tools and methods) and, finally, it looks broadly at innovations around investing in social outcomes.

Like many fields before it, social finance combines real achievements with a fair amount of hype. Steady real growth has combined with a far faster increase in the quantity of media coverage and conferences. Hype has had some virtues: in particular, it has brought in talent and resources—and channelled enthusiasm. But it has also fuelled a fair amount of confusion and conceptual fuzziness and has encouraged a surprising lack of attention to evidence.

This chapter aims to provide an overview of what lies beyond the rhetoric. In particular it probes a central proposition of the social finance field: that the application of investment mind-sets and methods will achieve better results, more long-termism, and more clarity on the links between actions and results, than alternatives and that these advantages will outweigh any additional transactions costs.

At the moment the enthusiasts for social finance hope for very different things—some a world where much more money goes into grassroots organizations; others an almost opposite vision of more multinational non-governmental organizations with the accoutrements of a General Electric or a Google. Both may be achievable: but it's unlikely that the same means will work well for both.

Why now?

The mobilization of finance for social purposes is not new. Indeed the combination of social and financial objectives has been more common than purely financial investment over the past thousand years. Socially oriented investment institutions and funds are common in much of the developed world. In the Catholic countries, such as Italy, there is a clutch of Church-related banks—a tradition that gave birth to Banca Etica and Banca Prossima more recently. Germany has its regional small business banks, Spain has many regional and co-operative banks—some with very overt social goals like Caja Laboral in the Basque country—there is the Crédit Coopératif[1] in France, Triodos Bank in the Netherlands and Belgium, and Charity Bank in the UK. Moreover, there are also hundreds of state-owned banks across the world that have had more or less overt social missions, often to spread wealth to poorer regions and to create jobs.

Social finance appears new only because of the relatively recent dominance of a purely financial idea of investment: the idea that you only invest in order to achieve a gain in money, rather than to achieve status, recognition, or to please Gods or Kings. The narrowly financial view of investment became ubiquitous in recent decades mainly thanks to the boom in financialization and the spread of secondary and tertiary markets in the decades after 1970.

The current interest in social finance resulted from both the confidence, and the guilt, that followed this extraordinary surge in the financial sector that at one point left it accounting for 40 per cent of all corporate profits in the USA. The most successful investors were confident that the investment methods that had served them so well in business could be usefully applied to social problems. Thus, it was thought, venture-capital-type philanthropy might help fund a lot of high-risk social venture ideas—accepting that only a small proportion would come to fruition—with active involvement by investors helping to establish the right management teams with a sharp focus on results and social impact. The scaling of social innovations and social ventures invariably requires changes to structures, cultures, leadership, and accountability—because these are challenging, the default is often to spread rather than to scale. So, in principle, the presence of a tough, single-minded outsider might make it possible for far more good social ideas to achieve their full potential. Private equity methods made a similar promise: they could be used to restructure and grow charities and social enterprises—again helping them to achieve a degree of focus and attention to their marginal impacts, that might otherwise prove impossible. Social stock exchanges could provide liquidity for social enterprises and, in time, an outlet for public savings. This confidence that investment methods could contribute to better social outcomes was not based on hard evidence. But it provided a useful challenge and stimulus to civil society organizations that were often better at aspiration than results.

Guilt was the other factor. Even during the boom years it was obvious that many of the rewards flowing to finance had little to do with talent or merit—but were rather the result of the legal privileges afforded to banking (the right

---

[1] The bank is the first signatory of the Social Cohesion Fund, managed by the French public investor Caisse des Dépôts, and benefits from its guarantee for its personal microcredit programmes.

to create credit without matching responsibilities), the asymmetries in key markets (such as derivatives), and reward structures that gave investors a sizeable share of upside gains but no share of downside losses. This guilt became more intensive after the crash of 2008, as large parts of finance came to be seen as essentially predatory, sucking value out of the rest of the economy rather than creating it—privatizing rewards but socializing risks.[2] Not surprisingly, many of the most successful felt the need to make amends by committing some of their own time to socially oriented investment, while, at a more junior level, linking investment skills to social outcomes became a more appealing career option.

Different types of social finance

So, how should we understand what social finance is and what it could be? Much of the writing about social finance has essentially been advocacy and, to a lesser extent, pure description. There has been relatively little serious analysis and little testing of hypotheses, perhaps inevitably given the immaturity of the field. But the essential shape of the field is easy to describe. All forms of social finance connect:

- *Providers* of capital motivated to achieve social (and sometimes financial) returns
- *Users* of capital, who can deploy it in ways that will achieve social impacts and, sometimes, financial revenues
- *Intermediaries* who connect providers and users, and may in addition be able to improve the effectiveness with which capital can be used (through knowledge, skills, networks)
- *Environment* of law, regulation, tax incentives that enables or prevents the alignment of the motivations and rewards of each group.

As with any kind of finance, both investors and investees have to make judgements about risk (what is the chance of capital being wasted) and about potential reward (can a profit be made?) with the additional factor of judging both the scale and likelihood of social impact.

However, although that basic architecture is widely shared, there are at least eight very different types of social finance whose differences arguably outweigh their similarities:

1. Commercial investment to serve low-income markets (the 'Bottom of the Pyramid': Prahalad, 2004)

---

[2] See further Mulgan (2013).

2. Commercial investment in firms with some social or environmental object-ives as well as financial ones (most 'impact investment' in the USA is of this kind)

3. Investment in social enterprises—either equity or loans

4. Finance for other types of social organization—charities, mutually owned organizations—usually in the form of loans

5. Savings vehicles for the public which promise social outcomes as well as financial returns (and are then invested in 1–4 above)

6. Direct provision of personal finance for socially excluded individuals and families (low-cost micro-credit, affordable mortgages)

7. Procurement of social outputs and outcomes by governments and some-times foundations (often via grants)

8. Finance for high-risk social innovation.

This list is by no means exhaustive but it immediately shows the diversity that exists under the umbrella of social finance. The first few are, in principle, the most straightforward. Properly functioning financial markets should be able to develop products to meet these needs. In some cases—for example the 'Bottom of the Pyramid' market—the social outcomes may be doubtful: a fair propor-tion of the methods associated with this idea, from distribution of very small quantities of consumer products to commercial microcredit, have turned out to be damaging to poor customers. But investment markets have generally found it easy to finance commercial provision for large, low-income markets.

Economic activity with mixed motives is slightly more complex. The finan-cial returns of social enterprises may be lower on average than other enter-prises (though their attrition in recessions may also be less). But the usual methods of bank finance, or venture capital, are in principle relatively easy to adapt since these all have revenue streams and understandable markets. Where financial institutions are not serving these markets the reasons usually have to do with culture, lack of skills, and lack of adequate time series data to analyse risk and return properly. In these cases there may be a role for policy to help kick-start a 'social' financial market, but it would be unlikely to be justifiable long term.

The other types of social finance bring with them very different challenges. The creation of savings vehicles depends greatly on the maturity of institutions and markets for making use of the capital, and on the demand from the public. But there are many promising examples around the world, and a long history of specialist bonds that combine financial and other goals. Direct provision of finance for low-income groups also has a long history and, indeed, was one of the central roles of civil society in the nineteenth century, when microcredit, mutual savings, and building societies grew very fast in many countries. In more recent history, the Community Reinvestment Act in the USA helped to build up a strong infrastructure of community-based investment funds, pri-marily focused on housing: twenty years ago much of the discussion of social finance drew on these examples and the lessons to be learned from the network of Community Development Corporations (CDCs) and national bodies such as the Local Initiatives Support Corporation (LISC).

The procurement of 'pure' social outcomes is very different in nature again. Here social finance is a newcomer to a longstanding discussion about better ways of using public funds, and a forty-year effort better to purchase outcomes rather than just outputs. The jury is still out as to what works, and much depends on the detail. But this is a promising field in which genuine innovations are being tested out.

Finally, investment in social innovation is different again. Innovation will tend to be much higher risk than enterprise investment. That is why governments typically subsidize research and development through a battery of tools to take a large proportion of the risk in technology development. Banks play almost no role in innovation finance. Venture capital can play a part in funding innovation, and in some cases public policy proved very successful in galvanizing it (with Israel probably the best recent example). But venture capital is not well suited to very early stage finance, and works much better for Internet ideas than with other kinds of technology, let alone service, concepts. In the USA, venture capital accounts for barely 2 per cent of commercial investment in innovation, dwarfed by public subsidies, intra firm investment and business angels and in the UK it has tended to default either to Internet and digital technology ventures or to financing management buyouts. Innovation funding tends to come from 'friends, family, and fools', from philanthropy, or from public funds willing to accept a much higher level of risk than banks.

Any commentary on social finance needs to be clear which of these it is addressing. Otherwise there is inevitably confusion over what social investment is, its potential to grow, and the barriers it faces.

What works?

The relative youth of this field in its current forms also means that there is little hard evidence about what works. There is little certainty, for example, about which generic investment tools will work well or, conversely, how much specialized knowledge is needed to make the right judgements about risk and reward. There is little knowledge too about where the gains to be achieved from more 'rigorous' investment methods will outweigh the transaction costs.

The field has arguably not been helped by confusion over terms. Three examples of many: there are now several 'social stock exchanges' around the world, doing useful work—but none actually exchange stock. In political science, the terms social finance and investment are used to describe government spending on such things as early childhood interventions. Meanwhile, social finance continues to be confused with social innovation (such as in publications associated with the World Economic Forum). For the reasons mentioned above, social finance methods are often not at all well suited to radical innovation and, just as in business, no one would confuse finance and innovation, so in the social field it is important to understand their differences.

These examples all point to the need for clarity in how terms are used. The other crucial task for the field is accurate learning from other fields of finance, since much of its credibility depends on exactly which types of method will actually deliver superior results to the alternatives, such as traditional charity or public provision.

This is not always easy. Venture capital for example is often portrayed in misleading ways. It is true that venture capitalists often aim at very high rates of return on investment and across a portfolio aim for 20 per cent or more. But the returns actually achieved in the UK and USA have been far lower than these—indeed, venture capital in the UK has not made any positive average return across all investments.

Similarly, private equity is often portrayed as bringing unique rigour to bear on business strategy. But a significant body of opinion in finance sees it as largely an artefact of poor tax design in the USA and UK that gave very large implicit subsidies to private equity investors and, notoriously, also allowed the principals to pay lower tax on their income than their secretaries and cleaners.

The rigours of investment are undoubtedly useful in many cases, but they often come with a cost in the form of the added overheads of investment organizations (sometimes high, thanks to the inflated salaries of the financial sector). Just as venture capital has an uneven record, so is the jury still out on the virtues of tracker funds versus managed funds (the most that can be said is that a minority of managed funds outperform the market some of the time). Overall, there is surprisingly little serious evidence on exactly how to weigh up the costs against the gains in the many fields of commercial investment, let alone social finance.

A more positive conclusion is that while academic research continues to struggle to explore the true value added by different investment methods, a lot of 'craft knowledge' is being built up by practitioners of social finance, much of which mirrors the craft knowledge of fields like venture capital. This includes knowledge about assessment, deal structuring, exits, portfolio management, and, in particular, the handling of both financial risk and the risk of failing to achieve social outcomes. But, in the long run, it will only be through experiment and careful measurement that what actually works to create new value will become clearer.

Over the last few decades a high proportion of financial innovations destroyed more value than they created. This was partly the result of market asymmetries and partly the result of changes in financial markets that had increased the degrees of separation between decisions and resulting actions. The latter led to a degradation of knowledge (the widespread misjudgement of risk in particular) and a moral myopia (a lack of engagement with any of the effects of investment decisions). So, it matters greatly that the tools used for social finance are tested against demanding standards and avoid the risk that, like some innovations in other financial markets, they enrich the intermediaries but impoverish the investors and the intended beneficiaries.

Evolving an ecosystem of social investment in the UK

The UK, arguably, has one of the most evolved policy environments for social finance in the world. This provides a test bed for many of the claims surrounding social finance (Cabinet Office, 2014). The seeds of this were sown in the mid 1990s, when a cluster of new organizations, including the Community Action Network and the School for Social Entrepreneurs, sprang up to promote the idea of mixing business means and social ends. Little of what they proposed was entirely new. The tradition of socially focused business goes back at least to the nineteenth century. Britain has historically been rich in entrepreneurial charities, mutual organizations, co-operatives, industrial and provident organizations, and socially committed family firms. Robert Owen was one of many leading Victorian entrepreneurs who were convinced that enterprise could also have a social mission. Moreover, Daniel Bell dubbed the late Michael Young as 'probably the world's greatest entrepreneur of social enterprises' for his creation of dozens of new social-focused ventures in the 1950s to the 1990s.

But the climate of the 1990s was particularly propitious for social entrepreneurs and social investment. Parties of the left had lost their antipathy towards the language of enterprise, while those of the right were emerging from the extremes of Thatcherism and Reaganism. Anita Roddick had shown through the Body Shop that a mainstream business could have a social conscience and the Big Issue was a visible exemplar of social enterprise with an ethos of self-reliance at its core. City institutions with long philanthropic traditions became interested in bridging the gap between their core business, that used ever more sophisticated tools to assess, aggregate, and spread risk, and their charitable work that still defaulted to grants for good causes. The growing social enterprise sector became more vocal in making the case for new forms of finance—beyond contracts and grants—but found little suitable on offer from mainstream banks. A succession of governments saw political advantage in aligning themselves with the potential for social entrepreneurship, social enterprise, and social finance, and adopted policies to grow these fields, including: directly funding umbrella bodies; reforming legal forms; introducing tax reliefs; opening up public purchasing; creating new funds for very early-stage finance as well as growth finance; and backing certification schemes. Two decades on, the UK boasts a social enterprise sector worth more than £20bn a year, with strong and confident enterprises that range from

Divine Chocolate and People Tree to Greenwich Leisure and HCT Group (formerly Hackney Community Transport). The NHS alone claims to commission more than 30,000 charities and social enterprises, and many ministers (and every prime minister) compete to show enthusiasm.

Fuelling this enthusiasm was the push to open up UK public services to delivery by independent, non-state, organizations—with legislation to encourage spin-offs and spin-outs, following a trail blazed by organizations such as Central Surrey Health. A YouGov poll conducted in 2011 found that 43 per cent of the UK public thought that 'a community business that reinvests its profits to improve services' or a social enterprise would be best placed to run public services, compared with 36 per cent favouring central and local government and just 4 per cent favouring commercial firms.

Initially there was no comprehensive plan to create a UK social investment market. However, by the late 1990s there was a fairly widely shared view of the critical building blocks that would be needed, that was followed in a piecemeal and evolutionary way to result in a reasonably mature ecosystem for financing social projects today.

I was involved in this field development in four phases: first, working outside of government on the creation of the School for Social Entrepreneurs and Community Action Network and commissioning Demos publications, such as *The Rise of the Social Entrepreneur* (Leadbeater, 1996). Second, as a member of the prime minister's Policy Unit, I helped set up the Social Exclusion Unit, one of whose Policy Action Teams focused on social investment. I also became closely engaged with the National Community Development Initiative in the USA (a partnership of foundations and banks), which led me to draft the outline for what eventually became the Social Investment Task Force. Third, as Head of the Strategy Unit in the Government, I oversaw its work on the redesign of charity law reform in the early 2000s, that led to the introduction of the public benefit test for charities and the creation of a new legal form of incorporation—the Community Interest Company (CIC). Later, I co-chaired the Department of Health's panel on social enterprise and the third sector that helped push forward many practical reforms to overcome barriers to commissioning. And fourth, as Chief Executive of NESTA, I was involved in funding a range of social venture intermediaries, launching our own impact investment fund, and serving as a board member of Big Society Capital, the wholesale social investment bank.

This experience confirmed that a governments needs to align three types of intervention to achieve a coherent policy for social finance:

- *Creating enabling conditions*: one of the building blocks is legal—the creation of new legal forms to make it easier for social ventures to take investment, such as the CIC, which aimed to increase equity investment in social ventures. The spread of B-Corporations in the USA suggests another route for legal innovation. Another building block is tax treatment—to achieve some if not all of the incentives on offer for angel and venture capital investment that have lobbied for a remarkable battery of tax benefits in recent years

- *Enabling funding*: government in the UK tried to kick-start the field through a succession of significant funds, including the Phoenix Fund, Future-builders, the Adventure Capital Fund, and the Risk Capital Fund, all of which were intended to be transitional funds, demonstrating to commercial investors that good returns could be achieved in social finance. Some were more successful than others
- *Enabling demand*: through opening up public purchasing and commissioning, providing 'investment readiness funds' and other types of capacity building, the aim should be to provide more plausible and predictable revenue streams for social ventures.

With these as broad enabling conditions, the detailed challenge was to put in place forms of finance for every stage of the evolution of social projects and ventures, from the very high risk early stage, to finance to support growth or takeovers. These overlap substantially but broadly rise in scale with equivalent reductions in risk. Figure 1.1 below summarizes these, and the subsequent bullet points provide a rough hierarchy of types of finance:

- *Very early stage finance*: UnLtd provides small grants of between £500 and £10,000 to thousands of individuals with, in theory, very few strings attached.
- *Proof of concept funding*: often provided by foundations at a slightly higher level (e.g. £10,000–£40,000) to help innovators demonstrate their idea in a

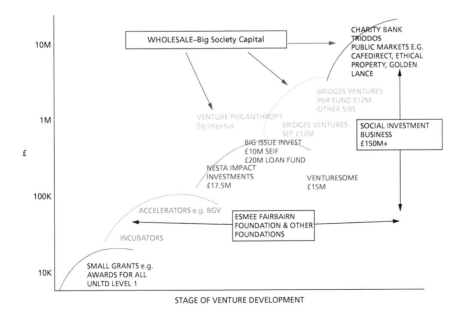

Figure 1.1. The lifecycle of social finance

real world environment. For example, Esmee Fairbairn Foundation provides finance at this stage as well as operating in several of the other categories listed below.

- *Accelerators*: these 'start-up factories' have become common in the technology sector supporting cohorts of start-ups with intensive support, initially under £20k—they are now spreading into the social field. Bethnal Green Ventures is a good example in the UK

- *Living Labs and social incubators*: a related approach has been the spread of Living Labs that test new ideas, often from NGOs, in real life conditions. The Global Living Labs network links many of these. Others include incubators such as Social Innovation Generation @ MaRS in Toronto, the Young Foundation in London or DenokInn Social Innovation Park in Bilbao

- *Early-stage investment funds*: at the next stage after incubators are various early-stage loan and equity funds such as Venturesome, the Department of Health's Social Enterprise Investment Fund, and the Scottish Social Investment Fund. These tend to fund more established ventures rather than innovations

- *Finance first funds*: at a somewhat larger scale there are commercial investment funds that prioritize financial return while also aiming to achieve social impact, these include: Bridges Ventures in the UK; PhiTrust in France; and BonVenture in Germany (Freireich and Fulton, 2009)

- *Social investment funds*: these are quite similar to finance first funds, but prioritize social impact while also seeking a financial return for their investors sometimes in order to 'recycle' funds into new investments, these include: CAF Venturesome, Big Issue Invest, and the Social Investment Business in the UK; the Hellenic Social Investment Fund in Greece; Fondazione CRT in Italy

- *Venture philanthropy funds*: such funds remain relatively small and aim to combine grants with intensive engagement. Examples include Impetus Trust and the Private Equity Foundation (now merged), the Social Business Trust, and the d.o.b. Foundation in the Netherlands

- *Innovation funds*: These are public funds explicitly focused on innovation, combining grants, loans, and equity. Many are primarily focused on technology, such as the Technology Strategy Board in the UK, SITRA in Finland, and Vinnova in Sweden but they are increasingly engaging in social issues and working with NGOs. The NHS Regional Innovation Funds in the UK were a good example, mainly focused on service innovations

- *Social banks*: such as Triodos and Charity Bank provide larger tranches of loan finance and often take deposits

- *Public offerings*: these are issues of equity, bonds, and other vehicles by large charities and social enterprises, such as Cafédirect, Ethical Property Company, and Golden Lane Housing

- *Wholesale and intermediary funding*: the best example is Big Society Capital in the UK that was capitalized with more than £600m, partly from unclaimed bank accounts and partly with equity for the major retail banks
- *Loans linked to contracts*: these are funds explicitly designed to provide working capital for social organizations signing up to payment-by-results contracts.

These types of investment are designed to cover the different stages of development of social ventures. Some social finance models do not fit so neatly into this framework—in particular ones providing products for the public (such as credit unions). But the aim of ensuring that there is finance available at each stage is a reasonable goal for any government.

NESTA has played a role in many of these stages: as a significant funder of other funds including Bridges Ventures, Big Issue Invest, Impetus Trust, the Young Foundation, Bethnal Green Ventures, and others, as well as through the creation of its own social finance fund that has placed a particular emphasis on evidence-based investing.

That experience has confirmed that, even with funds in place, the main barriers that stand in the way of greater impact are not so much particular laws or regulations, but rather the absence of capacities, skills, tools, and metrics. Traditional tools from finance remain too crude to cope with social realities; meanwhile the management and practice of most third sector organizations still do not fit well into the categories required by investors. These gaps have justified a significant investment in capacity-building including funds for investment readiness and programmes to develop common metrics.

As will be clear from this picture, although what has emerged is a complex social finance ecosystem (that remains not fully institutionalized), government played a leading role in filling key gaps. Philanthropy, led by a small number of active foundations, also played an active role, helped by regulatory moves by the Charity Commission to enable foundations to devote a share of their funds to mission-related and programme-related investment. By contrast, the private sector was much less involved than had been expected in the 1990s. It is possible that expectations then were unrealistic, partly an optical effect of the growth of corporate social responsibility that aims to make itself appear far larger than it is. But the fundamental point was that the investment opportunities simply did not look sufficiently attractive from a commercial point of view and that, as a consequence, public funding was required to kick-start market activity elsewhere.

Pay-for-success models

While most social finance has been focused on ventures, another important part of this landscape has involved experimentation around new ways of investing in social outcomes. There is extensive evidence on potential pay-backs to investment in early years programmes, or preventive measures in crime or health. But turning these into propositions for investment has proved hard. Incentives are misaligned: those who have the ability to improve social outcomes lack the incentive to act. For example, local authorities responsible for providing services to young people that divert them away from crime or worklessness do not share the savings from reduced prison numbers or reduced benefit bills.

Several developments accelerated thinking during the early 2000s:

- Steady advances within government in methods for assessing the impact of public investments on human capital bringing more systematic analysis of the links between spending and social outcomes such as crime reduction or health improvements
- The burgeoning debate about measuring social value and impact within civil society
- Widespread experience of private finance initiatives and public–private partnerships, and lessons about when these do and do not add value
- The development of markets for carbon reduction, prompted by the Kyoto Protocol and the European Union carbon trading market. Despite many complexities in terms of pricing and measurement these have led to the creation of new asset classes, and substantial trading. They have, thus, encouraged greater confidence in the potential to invest in social gains
- Experimentation in health around such initiatives as advanced market commitments—contingent revenue bonds—in which a payer guarantees a market will be available for breakthroughs such as vaccinations for malaria.

A family of different approaches to finance for social impact are likely to be tested out over the next few years. Some will be internal to the public sector—allowing either for investment within a public agency, with clear targeting of expected social outcomes and savings, or for contracts or arrangements linking different parts of the public sector, so that actions by one can deliver savings to another. Some will involve variants of payment-by-results and outcome-based commissioning. All aim to better align incentives, so that public spending has a better chance of achieving desired outcomes: payment for success.

Social Impact Bonds are one of the possible tools for achieving more for less. Work on their design and implementation has been in train since early 2008, when the UK City Leader's Group began work to identify new types of investment vehicles for social outcomes: the term 'Social Impact Bond' (SIB) was coined as a snappier alternative to contingent revenue bonds. Around the world, SIBs are known by various other terms including 'Pay-for-success Bonds' and 'Social Benefit Bonds'. Some of this work was taken forward by a new organization in the UK called Social Finance, which agreed the first SIB in the final days of the UK Labour government in May 2010.

Briefly speaking, under a SIB, a payer (often government, at a national, regional, or local level) agrees to pay for measurable improved outcomes of social projects and this prospective income is used to attract the necessary working capital funds from commercial, public, or social investors to offset the costs of the activity that will achieve those better results. This approach is possible where better outcomes lead to tangible public financial savings.

SIBs offer the potential to bring in new resources early and at scale, to focus attention on preventive action, and to provide new funding for civil society which has faced very sharp cuts in its funding from government. That said, SIBs are unlikely to be able to meet all of the expectations being placed on them and they face important challenges of which three stand out:

- *The relative weakness of the current evidence base.* This causes difficulties for any investors or banks wanting to judge the risk of a particular set of interventions, and the bodies being funded to carry them out. This is a key reason why commercial investment in SIBs has been very slow to materialize, unless it is heavily underwritten

- *Problems of overlaps with existing public programmes and spending.* In a world with no public spending, SIBs would be relatively straightforward. However, they depend on demonstrating a causal link between additional spending and outcomes achieved. This is hard for target groups already in receipt of public support, such as young people who are under 18 years old. To solve the problem, either contracts and measurement systems have to become complex—and require other public agencies not to cut or change existing programmes—or some form of partnership agreement is needed which ties in with other public providers

- *Issues of scale and transaction cost.* In practice, most public finance initiatives (PFI) under about £25m turned out to be uneconomic due to their high transaction costs. There may be a similar lower limit for SIBs, which is challenging given that a large majority of SIBs are on a significantly smaller scale to PFIs. In addition, SIBs face the challenge that also faces all new financing tools around public services, namely that governments always have a significantly lower cost of capital than other bodies. The key design issue for many SIBs is also the key issue for all kinds of social finance—how much value is added by the use of extra layers of management and oversight. In some variants of SIBs these layers are substantial and costly—perhaps a third of total costs in some early SIBs. In other variants, where a SIB is issued directly by a delivery organization, the transactions costs will be lower. But it is possible there will be fewer gains in terms of rigour. So far there has been no serious research on this fundamental question—and costs associated with SIBs have been heavily subsidized by philanthropic organizations such as Bloomberg Philanthropies and Rockefeller in the USA, and the Big Lottery Fund in the UK.

If these questions can be answered satisfactorily, the promise of SIBs is that, over time, methods of risk assessment could become sufficiently mature to allow investment organizations to assess both the risks and returns of particular interventions and of the organizations carrying them out. Here the analogy is with the evolution of markets for carbon and for pollutants.

The UK government has maintained its early commitment to growing the field. By 2014, over twenty SIBs had been agreed, covering issues ranging from children in care to homelessness. In 2012, the UK Cabinet Office launched the Social Outcomes Fund,[3] providing a top-up to outcomes payments for SIBs in complex areas and, in 2013, the Big Lottery Fund launched Commissioning Better Outcomes which will also offer top-ups to outcomes payments in SIBs. Together, these offer up to £60m of support available for SIBs tackling complex issues such as reoffending and drug addiction. The market is also beginning to take shape. In 2014, Bridges Ventures set up a dedicated fund to invest in SIBs supported by Big Society Capital as a cornerstone investor.

This scale of activity will generate plenty of evidence. By 2015, it should become possible to make sensible judgements about the success of early pilots such as the first SIB working with offenders from Peterborough Prison (see chapter 12), and by 2020 more general conclusions should be possible. Until then, however, this remains an important and interesting experiment, but one with limited proven results.

These uncertainties matter because SIBs, like other kinds of social finance, faces competitors. The idea of SIBs has also evolved in parallel with the much longer experience of commissioning for outcomes and 'payment by results' (PBR). Many governments have wanted to be able to contract directly with private or third-sector providers that could take the risk of achieving outcomes such as lower unemployment or reoffending. The UK government, for example, has put far more money into PBR contracts than into SIBs—and has shown a marked 'revealed preference'.

There is now extensive global experience of PBR, particularly in the field of 'welfare to work', but also in some areas of health. Any organization taking on a PBR contract faces the challenge of raising working capital. This is generally solved in one of three ways:

- Through large private firms raising money via normal capital markets (for example, firms like Serco or Capita in the UK)
- Through social organizations raising funds from existing lenders using property as security or, in some, cases borrowing against future contracts (though here they run into a lack of models for such borrowing in the banking world)
- Through commissioning agencies paying part of the contract upfront so as to minimize the cash flow risk.

---

[3] <https://www.gov.uk/social-impact-bonds#sources-of-funding-for-sib-projects>.

As a social investment wholesaler, Big Society Capital has also provided finance not only for a clutch of recent SIBs, but also for loans to social enterprises seeking PBR contracts.

With the prospect of new loans and overdraft facilities for social ventures some see SIBs as merely a transitional device towards more extensive outcomes-based commissioning or PBR contracts, since these avoid the need to pay for additional transactions costs. Despite the significant potential benefits of SIBs, a common response from government finance departments is that SIBs are an unnecessarily complex way of financing better social programmes. Since government's costs of capital are significantly cheaper than markets, they can finance outcomes-based projects more cheaply than the market (even if social finance seeks discounted returns). If there really are better approaches to cutting recidivism or unemployment, these should be directly funded by governments, rather than indirectly via SIBs. The counter-argument is that SIBs—like PFIs before them—help to bring in more rigorous management and performance measurement (as well as *additional* resources).

Another concern, mainly from philanthropists, is that SIBs risk diverting charitable funds to make up for public spending, essentially locking philan-thropic money into government welfare agendas. Or, alternatively, SIBs allow government to reduce its statutory provision of welfare services over time.

The best outcome would be for a range of variants to be tried, tested, and evaluated over the next few years with maximum openness on methods, legal forms, and results. This area of work has some parallels to the early experi-ments around private finance for infrastructure. A major error made at the time was the absence of proper evaluation or controls. PFIs were promoted as an article of faith, and very actively marketed by companies that directly benefited. When, belatedly, more thorough investigations were done, for example by public auditing bodies such as the National Audit Office in the UK, the models that seemed most promising turned out not to work or to be too costly. Indeed some estimates suggested that a large majority of projects were not economic, mainly because of very high transactions costs, and because risks were not fully transferred from government to the private sector contractor. Some methods, however, did become part of the mainstream, particularly around building and other capital projects, and where sufficient scale was achieved.

The promise of SIBs, and social finance more generally, is to introduce greater rigour, to redirect resources to the most effective interventions, and to allow for multiple resourcing methods beyond revenue funding. Here social finance needs to co-evolve with the field of evidence, including evidence-based policymaking and evidence-based practice and management. The creation of the Alliance for Useful Evidence (hosted by NESTA and supported by the ESRC and Big Lottery Fund) has provided a space for serious discussion about what evidence does and does not say. Likewise the establishment of six 'what works centres', covering issues ranging from ageing to early intervention, will provide a stronger shared understanding of what models achieve most impact.

Some of the rhetoric around social finance has suggested that investors need only to seek out the models that work and then to enable them to be scaled. In practice there is rarely enough evidence to make this feasible; how ideas are implemented matters as much as the ideas themselves and what works in one place and one time may not in another. These are, of course, all problems in business as well. Great improvements could be made in both the generation of evidence and its use. However, there are methodological problems involved in linking social finance investment to evidence, including: the relative weakness of available evidence; the uncertainties of social science methods more generally; the challenges of values as well as value; and the challenge of identifying appropriate discount rates (Mulgan, 2010). This led NESTA to propose a complementary approach that attempts to address the standards of evidence issue. Here the aim is to achieve a common language for describing the strength of evidence around particular interventions. This five-step ladder integrates many similar models developed around the world. The aim is to help organizations and funders move up this ladder—diverting some funds to support better evaluation, or trials with control groups. These need to be proportionate, since there is little point spending large sums evaluating very small or early-stage programmes. But when there is the prospect of serious scale, it is important to know that what is being scaled actually works.

Issues and challenges

Over next decade, there is likely to be a considerable inflow of money, skills, people, and political attention into social finance globally. There are some major challenges that are likely to come to the fore during this period of growth.

Returns. The most basic challenge is of achieving returns for different types of organization at different stages of development. This is in part a symptom of the over-aggregation of different types of investment, sometimes in the same funds. Some social purpose businesses can achieve good returns, as can many social enterprises. But most social organizations struggle to achieve even very modest returns, and may be unwise to take on debt finance. Genuine innovation is bound to be risky and requires suitable finance, with the right mix of grant funding and investment. The challenge of returns meant that a main focus for social finance is always likely to be housing—since housing is easy to understand using traditional investment methodologies, provides security for investors, and at least appears to meet social objectives. Over many decades regeneration policies have defaulted to investment in physical capital for these reasons—they were easier to measure and easier to manage. Yet experience repeatedly showed that this was not a wise way to achieve outcomes—better houses without better schools, lower crime, or more jobs, simply resulted in smarter ghettos. There are some fears that social investment could repeat this experience.

Definitions. As has already been pointed out, the social finance field suffers from blurred boundaries and confused labels. In itself this may not matter. But specific funds will need to clarify exactly what roles they are trying to play. They will also include better segmentation of the market and tightening of investment criteria and expectations.

Impact. There has been huge effort devoted to better understanding and measuring impact and linking this to social finance investment decisions. Some of this may have been over optimistic—in particular the search for measurable 'social returns on investment' is often difficult in practice. However, many investors are interested in finding a common language both to describe the levels of evidence available for particular projects or ventures and to explain what the evidence shows.

Scale. One of the main arguments for social finance is that it will enable great social ideas to grow big and have a large impact. Currently only a tiny proportion of social organizations grow big, far fewer proportionately than in business. Fifteen years ago, it was hoped that big social enterprise brands would emerge in fields such as food and transport, becoming in time as ubiquitous as Sainsbury's or Vodafone. Today, while there are some visible brands with a social or mutual dimension, including the John Lewis Partnership and the Co-operative Group, few social entrepreneurs have achieved the scale they hoped for. Most civic organizations find scale difficult and, although there are some very large NGOs, such as the Red Cross or Caritas in Germany, most are small. Some of this has to do with a lack of capital or skills, but there is also a legitimate fear that greater scale can corrode values, commitment, and stakeholder contact. When organizations do grow large, they tend to maintain small units of activity, either with federal structures that link hundreds of local branches—as in the case of Age UK—or with cellular structures—as in the case of Alcoholics Anonymous. Another reason why social enterprises have struggled to grow is that the very individuals who are adept at starting social organizations are often ill suited to growing and consolidating them and are even uncomfortable with what growth requires: a shift from freewheeling and informal cultures to structure, bureaucracy, and formal accountability to investors. Boards tend to dither over getting rid of charismatic founders or booting them upstairs into more honorary roles.

Some social finance models help overcome these barriers by driving a focus on what is scalable and pushing for the right strategies to build 'effective demand' and 'effective supply' (see Nicholls and Schwartz, 2014). Strong investors can also change or remove management and ensure that additional skills are brought in. But another problem is that many business models cannot be easily replicated. While some enterprises, including web-based organizations such as Kiva and Netmums, have thrived, others have struggled to grow. One of the UK's largest social enterprises, the Wise Group in Glasgow, tried to expand to cities in England and quickly amassed unsustainable debts. The Big Issue stumbled in some countries where the model simply did not work, while South Korean online newspaper Ohmy-News, one of the most exciting recent social enterprise models, has so far failed in its attempts to replicate its success elsewhere. Even the Grameen Bank model turned out not to work in India, where different models of microcredit have thrived, or in Europe, where the social conditions that helped microcredit succeed in the nineteenth century have largely disappeared. The lesson would seem to be that the conditions for success are often local and specific.

On a more optimistic note, the good news is that the social finance knowledge base is growing fast. The most developed fields of innovation benefit from a 'deep craft'—people building up experience in how to fit things together, what works, and how to turn ideas into reality. Social finance can only achieve impact if it is allied to skills of this kind, which is why initiatives to grow skills are so important. More narrowly, there is a clear need for more analysis of specific funds and the various stakeholders involved and training in how to make the most of different types of social finance.

Conclusion

The social finance field now has plenty of momentum. A notable moment was the Social Impact Investment Forum held in London in June 2013 alongside the G8 Summit hosted by the British Prime Minister David Cameron. This meeting announced the formation of a Social Investment Task Force spanning the G8 plus Australia (Russia was later disbarred). In September 2014, this Task Force published a set of wide-ranging reports packed with recommendations for the next, global, stage of the evolution of this field. There has also been extensive experimentation in the development of payment-for-success models, some using variants of SIBs. Many more players are now contributing to the craft of social finance.

In addition to the various enabling factors described in this chapter, some other policy choices could greatly affect the development of the field. One is the creation of stronger corporate forms. Another is the possibility, within Europe, of more open markets for public services and outcomes—so that social organizations providing eldercare in Finland could win contracts in Italy or vice versa. A third is the impact of new financial innovations such as peer-to-peer finance and crowdfunding models that offer alternatives to the social finance investment options of more established organizations. Finally, tax reform will also influence development: the UK government, for example, introduced Social Investment Tax Relief for retail investments in designated social sector organizations such as charities, community benefit societies, and CICs. Investors are able to claim back up to 30 per cent of their investment against their income tax or capital gains tax liabilities.

Each of the eight types of social finance listed in this chapter will evolve in different ways. Some will evolve incrementally and involve low risk—providing loan finance for social enterprises—while others are much better understood as radical and risky experiments.

The overall field looks well placed to become part of the mainstream landscape. The social economy in its various definitions accounts for between 5 and 10 per cent of GDP in many countries. It is reasonable to expect that social finance could, in the long run, grow to a comparable proportion of overall investment.

If it does so, a more fundamental question may come to the fore. This is the question of power. Will the movement of investors and investing institutions into the social field involve a weakening of the autonomy and values of civil society? Or will it provide a new basis for independence? Again the answers are likely to be mixed. The optimists argue that social organizations with their own sources of capital can better resist pressure from governments. Yet the more extreme advocates of venture philanthropy—who advocate that funders should be much more interventionist—can sound very undemocratic in spirit, threatening to extend the power of a wealthy elite from the economic sphere into the social sphere. Ultimately social finance will only be legitimate if there is a reciprocal relationship between the providers of finance and its users. The same is of course true in the wider economy. Finance should be seen as a vital input that exists to serve the economy—not unlike education, or electricity. Any society that allows finance to become a master not a servant, and one deserving of much greater rewards than other sectors, has only itself to blame when things go badly wrong.

■ REFERENCES

Cabinet Office (2014). *Growing the Social Investment Market: 2014 Progress Update*. London: Cabinet Office.

Freireich, J., and Fulton, K. (2009). *Investing for Social and Environmental Impact: A Design for Catalyzing an Emerging Industry*. Cambridge, MA: Monitor Institute.

Leadbeater, C. (1996). *The Rise of the Social Entrepreneur*. London: Demos.

Mulgan, G. (2010). 'Measuring Social Value', *Stanford Social Innovation Review*, Summer, pp. 38–43.

Mulgan, G. (2013). *The Locust and the Bee*. Oxford: Oxford University Press.

Nicholls, A., and Schwartz, R. (2014). 'The Demandside of the Social Investment Marketplace', in L. Salamon (ed.), New Frontiers of Philanthropy: A Guide to the New Tools and New Actors that Are Reshaping Global Philanthropy and Social Investing. Oxford: Oxford University Press, pp. 562–582.

Prahalad, C. K. (2004). *The Fortune at the Bottom of the Pyramid*. Pennsylvania: Wharton Press.

2 What should social finance invest in and with whom?

Richard Steinberg

Introduction

Social needs are everywhere. Increasingly, so are social investors—but there are too many needs and too little investment. What is a wise social investor to do with her limited capacity to make the world a better place? This chapter considers two aspects of that question. First, it discusses the difference between societal needs that can be addressed through ordinary financial investments from those that require social investment. That is the 'what' part of this chapter. The 'with whom' part concerns investment targets, the organizations that use social investments to, if all goes well, meet social needs. Is it better to invest in socially oriented for-profit or not-for-profit organizations with scarce capital? Or is there some third alternative, a hybrid organizational type that can blend the best of both sectors?

The road to the conclusions set out here is long and complicated. To motivate the weary reader, here are the basic impacts of the conclusions. First, social and economic goals are harmonious, but only up to a point that has been largely reached already. Beyond that point there are trade-offs—social goals require unprofitable investments. For-profit firms provide social goods when and to the extent that it is profitable to do so. Most of the remaining social needs will never be profitable unless social investors or governments pay firms to supply them. Second, social investors should help not-for-profits, rather than for-profits, whenever important elements of service quality are difficult or impossible to observe. Third, investor willingness to fund social ventures is limited, and would not automatically expand when new kinds of investment targets like the new hybrids are created. There is a risk of shifting money around without accomplishing any more than we already do. Thus, this chapter speculates on reasons why organizational structures might enlarge, or better direct, the pool of social investment. Fourth, the various kinds of new hybrid organizations will fall far short of combining the virtues of for-profit firms with those of not-for-profit organizations.

There is no consensus on critical definitions in the new field of social investment, so before proceeding further, there is a need for clarification of the use of terms here. Social investment is investment in social enterprise, but different authors have used that term differently. This chapter distinguishes neglected social investments in market niches that, once entered, are perfectly sustainable (through sales revenues, royalties, and rental payments) from those that are not sustainable. Social investors help the latter to germinate, but ongoing social investment is unnecessary because financial investors take over. This chapter concentrates on the latter, so it is appropriate to use Horton's (2006) definition of social enterprise:

Social enterprise provides, or tries to provide, things that society values but which for one reason or another are not usually provided by private enterprise. In most cases, this is because the social value of an activity is not easily captured by the price or financial return for the service or good offered.

This definition focuses on difficulties in capturing value, rather than the nature of the value that is created. The alternative, organizations with social purposes, leaves open the question of what is the difference between social and other purposes. Providing jobs and producing products that consumers want to buy are arguably social purposes, but by that classification every successful firm would be a social enterprise. Other classifications leave too many grey areas. For example, is the discovery, production, and marketing of various forms of insulin by Eli Lilly and Company a social purpose central to Lilly's operation? Hard to answer by some definitions, but the classification is clear by my chosen definition. Lilly is not a social enterprise because patents allow Lilly capture the value of insulin research, and revenues from insulin sales capture value for insulin production and marketing.

The social enterprise literature focuses on commercial activities, by not-for-profits and for-profits, that fund the provision of social goods. In contrast, this chapter focuses on the social goods themselves, including those financed by donations and grants. None of its analysis hinges on whether the social enterprise engages in commercial activity using business strategies.

The detailed definitions of for-profit firms and not-for-profit organizations vary across time and political jurisdictions, with a number of subtypes. The discussion here simplifies matters by focusing on pure organizational types defined by the rights of owners. Full owners have three property rights: the right to control the use of assets, the right to receive financial surpluses generated through use of assets, and the right to transfer the first two rights at a market-determined price (Ben-Ner and Jones, 1995). Investors own for-profits, possessing all three property rights. The for-profit form has subtypes defined by the type of owners: investor-owned, worker-owned, producer and consumer co-operatives, mutual insurance companies, and the like. To keep this chapter manageable, it is limited in its analysis to investor-owned for-profit firms, but the reader should keep in mind that it is neglecting some alternative social-investment vehicles.

Not-for-profits are owned by an appointed, elected, or self-perpetuating board of governors that has the right to control the use of assets but not the other two property rights. Not-for-profit corporations cannot distribute their surpluses to investors (donors) or those controlling the use of the organization's assets (directors) (Hansmann, 1980). Instead, not-for-profit investors accept dividends-in-kind (Wedig, 1994), enjoying their association with and satisfaction from the organization's accomplishments. In contrast to for-profits, not-for-profit organizations that fail to generate market rates of return are immune from the pressures of shareholders, derivative suits, and hostile takeover bids. This allows not-for-profits to sustain their nonmarket missions.

The next section of this chapter answers the 'what' question, detailing the kinds of social goods that cannot be sustained through ordinary market transactions. Then it considers private organizations as vehicles for social investment, with sections on not-for-profits and for-profits. More recently, societies around the world have experimented with not-for-profit/for-profit hybrid forms, such as Low-Profit Limited Liability Companies (L3Cs), Community Interest Corporations (CICs), and B Corporations in an effort to combine the advantages of each pure organizational form. The chapter discusses whether these efforts are likely to succeed in the penultimate section. Conclusions end the chapter.

What should social finance invest in?

Ordinary market transactions fail to capture value for collectively consumable goods and services (collective goods), non-verifiable attributes of goods or services (contract failure), goods that, in the judgement of some members of society, are undervalued by other members (merit goods), and essential goods and services that cost more than consumers can pay (affordability).

COLLECTIVE GOODS

Collective goods are those that, once provided, can be enjoyed simultaneously by many individuals. The literature often uses the terms 'public goods' instead of collective goods, because of scholars focus on government's role in correcting market failures. But it is clear that private, not-for-profit, organizations also provide collective goods and that governments also provide non-collective goods—so the older name is slowly disappearing. There are two kinds of collective goods—excludable and non-excludable—distinguished by the possibilities to restrict consumption to paying individuals. National defence is non-excludable—those who evade taxation are just as secure as those who pay taxes. It is senseless to charge a fee for non-excludable collective goods because payments are purely voluntary, more like a donation than a purchase. Non-excludable collective goods cannot be sustained through ordinary market transactions.

An opera performance or rock concert is excludable—the audience collectively consumes the show, but it is easy to charge admission and thereby exclude some consumers. Ticket-paying customers sustain performances through ordinary market transactions. Nonetheless, excludable collective goods present problems, because the restriction to those who can afford tickets excludes too many individuals. Because the performance is collective, there is no good reason to exclude anybody—it would not cost anything to let everyone in who wants to see the show and it would not hurt paying customers' enjoyment. Social value is lost because ordinary market transactions require over-exclusion.

CONTRACT FAILURE

Contract failure is a concept developed in its most general form by Hansmann (1980) and stems from difficulties observing the quality or quantity of a good or service. When applied to collective goods, the problem is with observing whether an individual purchase or donation actually increases the quantity of services provided. Purchasers may be able to observe the total amount of the collective good, but cannot observe how many other people have also purchased the good and this is the source of the problem. For example, suppose 100 people each pay an organization $1,000 to deliver food to the needy. If the organization delivers a total of $5,000 of food, it will be able to keep $95,000 in profits. Clearly most purchasers are cheated, but no individual purchaser could prove they did not get what they paid for. If one person doubled his payment, the organization could continue to spend $5,000, claiming another person reduced her purchase by $1,000. This illustrates what is now called 'marginal-impact contract failure', and shows why ordinary market transactions lead to underfunding of collective goods.

Contract failure also occurs for non-collective goods when it is difficult or impossible to observe critical aspects of quality. Even when quality is observable by the direct buyer and seller, it may not be verifiable by third parties and this makes it impossible to write an enforceable contract on the quality level. Consider hospital care. It is easy to observe some aspects of this service (like whether surgery was performed) but others are hard or impossible to observe (like whether adverse surgical outcomes were due to the doctor taking shortcuts). Ordinary market transactions provide no guarantees on quality for these attributes, reputation is not affected, and money-back guarantees are susceptible to false claims by the consumer.

MERIT GOODS

Merit goods are goods and services that consumers undervalue according to some external standard. This is an explicitly paternalistic matter, and controversy can be expected any time society overrules consumer sovereignty.

Aficionados think that opera is a merit good, something people have to learn to like and will not like unless nudged (say by school field trips to attend performances). Smoking, drinking, overeating, and risky sexual practices are things that consumers like more than they ought to, merit 'bads' that should be discouraged. Religiosity is a merit good for proselytizers. Ordinary market transactions focus on what consumers like, not what they ought to like.

AFFORDABILITY

Although social-welfare theorists think of distributional justice in terms of income and wealth, practical policymakers focus on the affordability of specified goods like medical care and housing. True, redistribution of income makes both affordable, but we do not like to give money to dysfunctional parents who choose not to spend that money on the medical and housing needs of their children. Instead, free clinics, housing vouchers, and the like are offered.

The case for social investment in not-for-profit organizations

This section discusses the extent of social investment in not-for-profit organizations, explaining why not-for-profits are often the best target for social investors. I discuss the disadvantages of the not-for-profit form in the following section, along with the merits of the for-profit form.

Social investors provide capital to not-for-profit organizations through their donations, grants, loans, and contracts. Volunteer labour is, in effect, donated and, sometimes, labour is partially donated to the not-for-profit in that workers are willing to accept a lower-than-market wage (Preston, 1989). Consumers sometimes overpay for not-for-profit products (like Girl Scout cookies or posters from the Metropolitan Museum of Art), in effect mixing a donation with a purchase. Members pay dues that often exceed the costs of goods and services received, again, mixing a donation with membership.

The extent of social investment in not-for-profits ($303bn donated to US not-for-profits in 2009 (Giving USA Foundation, 2010), plus the value of volunteering, cause-related marketing, and debt-like investments) is easy to understand. Not-for-profit organizations provide collective goods, avoid contract failure, provide merit goods, and offer financial aid, sliding-scale fees, and charity care at lower-than-market prices or for free. These socially beneficial activities are embedded in not-for-profit mission statements and organizational cultures. Social missions can endure because there is no market for the control of not-for-profits.

NOT-FOR-PROFIT PROVISION OF COLLECTIVE GOODS

Long ago, Weisbrod (1975) observed that not-for-profit organizations provide collective goods. Charities that help the needy do so, often in combination with non-collective (rival) goods. For example, the food provided in soup kitchens is a rival good, consumed by one person to the exclusion of others. But food provision collectively benefits all those who care about hungry people (either out of sympathy, empathy, or a concern with property value) in a non-rival way. Specific-disease philanthropies, like the American Diabetes Association, create collective knowledge that may provide a cure to specific sufferers (non-collective). Not-for-profit schools increase their students' lifetime earnings (non-collective), but also enhance later civic participation by their graduates (collective). Arts organizations provide a variety of excludable and non-excludable collective goods. Places of worship produce non-collective goods (depending on the theology), but also produce social capital by fostering repeated interactions between like-minded individuals. So it is clear that collective-good provision is a major activity of many not-for-profit organizations.

For-profits have the incentive and ability to deliver less than the promised quantity of collective goods. Unless a single social investor wants to fund the entire effort, purchases from (or donations to) a for-profit will not accomplish anything. In contrast, the not-for-profit form can be thought of as a standardized contract—a non-distribution constraint—that is enforced collectively by an entity (usually the State) that can observe total purchases, donations, and investments. This eliminates the possibility of marginal impact contract failure stemming from organizational decisions (Krashinsky, 1986). This non-distribution constraint also insures against marginal impact contract failure resulting from the reversibility of ordinary investments (Bilodeau and Slivinski, 1998). Finally, non-distribution implies that there are no shareholders encouraging opportunistic behaviour, and no possibility of hostile takeover to force such behaviour.

For-profit firms provide some excludable collective goods (like rock concerts) but not others (opera performances). When they provide excludable collective goods, they exclude too many individuals because to do otherwise would overturn their fee structures. The not-for-profit advantage here has not been as extensively studied, but theories suggest that not-for-profits provide such goods when for-profits do not, and use superior pricing strategies to reduce the exclusion problem (Hansmann, 1981a; Ben-Ner 1986; Bilodeau and Steinberg, 1997).

CONTRACT FAILURE IN COMMERCIAL MARKETS

Marginal-impact contract failure explains why for-profits do not provide non-excludable collective goods, why donors do not give to for-profits, and why donative not-for-profits are superior vehicles when social investors wish to increase the provision of collective goods.

For-profits have an incentive to shortchange the consumer on costly attributes that are difficult to observe and can succeed in doing so as long as the attributes are not third-party verifiable. Ethical for-profits that choose to deliver the promised level of quality face shareholder pressures to deliver the kind of profits that other (short-changing) for-profits realize. As a result, the quality of service delivered by for-profits is lower (in its unobservable attributes) than that contracted for, another kind of contract failure. In contrast, although not-for-profits offer low quality outputs on occasion (the soup at soup kitchens rarely wins Michelin awards), they deliver the quality that was promised. Theory does not predict which sector will deliver higher-quality goods and services, only that for-profit quality will be lower than represented.

Contract failure in commercial markets results from firms trying to cut costs in ways they can get away with in order to keep current and prospective owners happy. Not-for-profits cannot distribute any profits to those in control and so have less incentive to shortchange the social investor. That is the theory, anyway. But whether the not-for-profit form remedies contract failures is controversial. As has been summarized in more detail elsewhere (Steinberg, 2006), non-distribution removes one incentive but not all incentives for delivering less than the promised quantity of collective goods or quality of commercial goods. Further, it is difficult to enforce non-distribution, trustworthiness is not the same thing as trust, and many consumers don't even know whether the hospital, nursing home, or child day-care centre they patronize is not-for-profit, for-profit, or governmental. On the other hand, religious affiliation produces trustworthiness and trust (but not always), and religiously affiliated organizations are almost always not-for-profit. So the consumer does not have to know whether an organization is not-for-profit to benefit from reduced contract failure, as long as the choice is made based on characteristics that are absent from for-profits. Not-for-profits are less likely to take advantage of consumers and donors because they are governed by a volunteer board, have unpaid observers on site (volunteers) that would quit if they saw any devious behaviour, have a charitable mission and culture, pay lower salaries (but not always) and so attract workers and managers who receive part of their compensation in the form of a warm glow from helping to advance the organizational mission.

With strong arguments on both sides of the debate, it becomes an empirical question whether on balance not-for-profits are better than for-profits with respect to contract failure. Unfortunately, there are no direct tests for contract failure because we are dealing with unobservables. If the consumer, regulator, and courts cannot observe whether the promised quality is delivered, how can the researcher? But many indirect tests have been conducted, summarized in Steinberg (2006), and my personal opinion after reading the studies is that the average not-for-profit is more trustworthy than the average for-profit in markets for goods and services where contract failure is expected to be important. Thus, social investors should donate to not-for-profits rather than buying shares of for-profits when the target industry produces goods and services with important non-observable attributes.

NOT-FOR-PROFIT PROVISION OF MERIT GOODS

Sometimes the State provides merit goods, by banning the sale of large sugary drinks (changing the consumption of those who undervalue healthy eating), ticketing drivers who do not strap in (for those who undervalue their own safety), and imposing prohibitive taxes on alcohol and tobacco (for those who undervalue their own health and the well-being of others). Sometimes the State provides merit goods by taxing citizens to pay for free distribution. In both cases, the State exercises its coercive powers to address the issue, and therein lies the controversy: there is no consensus regarding whether this constitutes a legitimate exercise of coercive power.

Not-for-profits also provide merit goods, through social marketing campaigns, proselytization, and price subsidies (including free distribution). Social marketing is about sending messages that change the choices people make in such matters as unprotected sex, smoking, drinking and driving, and child-raising. Some religions seek to change not only the behaviour but also the beliefs of infidels, converting them to faithful followers on the path of true righteousness. Not-for-profit symphonies offer free performances for school-children, hoping to convert them to lifelong lovers of classical music. Unlike State provision, not-for-profit provision is voluntary and often at least partly financed voluntarily though donations and sales of goods and services.

For-profits generally prefer to give consumers what they want rather than what they ought to want. There are some exceptions—by investing in a company that produces a better nicotine substitute, social investors help to reduce smoking. Here the pursuit of profits leads to marketing efforts to persuade smokers to quit. But at the same time, unregulated cigarette manufacturers work in the opposite direction. In other cases, the for-profit label creates doubts about the truthfulness and sincerity of social marketing efforts, which are better conducted by not-for-profits. Rose-Ackerman (1986: 53) make this point in a slightly different context:

The not-for-profit form was chosen by the founders because their main objective was often not compatible with profit-maximizing behavior or even with the appearance of profit-maximizing behavior.... For proselytizing reasons, they may wish to present an image of service and dedication, rather than appear 'self-serving' and profit seeking. The non-distribution constraint conveys this image, at little cost to an organization which did not intend to make large profits anyway.

THE NOT-FOR-PROFIT ROLE IN AFFORDABILITY AND REDISTRIBUTION

Sometimes the goal of profit maximization aligns well with redistributive efforts. Thus, both for-profit and not-for-profit daycare centres for children offer sliding-scale fees; both for-profit and not-for-profit universities offer financial aid. Charging a single price neither helps the poor nor maximizes profits, so both sectors employ price discrimination, which means that different customers pay different prices. Price discrimination aids profits because organizations no longer have to decide between a high margin and low volume price versus a low margin and high volume one—they can do both. Price discrimination helps the poor, who are offered an affordable price while organizations collect sufficient revenues from their higher-priced sales to cover their costs.

The motivation is different, but the pattern of prices is similar for not-for-profit organizations that charge a higher price to some in order to have the resources to subsidize the price for others. However, there are at least two important differences in the pattern of prices between for-profit and not-for-profit price discriminators. First, they differ in the floor, the lowest price charged to any customers. For-profit floors must be higher than the cost of extending service to the last consumer (marginal cost); otherwise the last consumer would subtract from firm profits. Therefore, only those customers who can cover the cost of service will be offered prices they are willing to pay. Not-for-profit floors will be lower than marginal cost, and may be set at a price of zero, if the mission-target population requires subsidization. Second, for-profits set prices that maximize profits. In the limit, when for-profits know each consumer's maximum willingness-to-pay, individualized prices are set at each consumer's maximum. In contrast, because not-for-profits use price discrimination as a means to an end (subsidizing mission-target populations), the not-for-profit price schedule is lower in most cases (Steinberg and Weisbrod, 1998, 2005). Finally, the two types of organizations differ in their response to increased social investment: for-profits continue to exploit price discrimination to the maximum feasible extent whereas not-for-profits reduce the prices charged to high willingness-to-pay customers, reduce the price further for low willingness-to-pay customers, and increase the share of low willingness-to-pay customers allowed to purchase the good at a subsidized price (Steinberg and Weisbrod, 2005; Starke, 2012).

The case for social investment in for-profit organizations

Because this chapter defines social enterprise as encompassing things not ordinarily provided by markets, this ought to be an easy section to write. For-profits do not ordinarily provide non-excludable collective goods, overly restrict access to excludable collective goods, fail to deliver the promised quality in cases of contract failure, cannot effectively provide certain merit goods, and limit their redistributive efforts to those that add to profits. At least some for-profit owners want maximal profit distributions; others are constrained in their departures from profit maximization by the market for control. So it does not matter whether for-profits are more efficient and nimble because they don't engage in social enterprise.

But there are exceptions, cases in which for-profits provide collective goods and otherwise depart from the standard (neoclassical) model of for-profit behaviour. This section first describes the potential advantages of a for-profit social enterprise. Then it shows when and where social enterprise emerges in for-profit organizations, either because social production adds to corporate profits or because the market for control allows departures from profit maximization. This discussion is followed with one regarding limitations of for-profit social enterprise. The same forces that lead for-profits to engage in social enterprise erode the efficiency and capital advantages of the for-profit form. This section concludes with two case studies.

Although the literature on corporate social responsibility (CSR) has not stressed the point, much of this literature applies here. Kitzmueller and Shimshack (2012: 53) survey various definitions of CSR, concluding:

In essence, CSR is corporate social or environmental behavior that goes beyond the legal or regulatory requirements of the relevant market(s) and/or economy(s).

Like the definition of social enterprise used here, these authors allow exceptions, as they continue (p. 54):

In order to capture its complete economic relevance, this view emphasizes that CSR can be market driven or 'strategic' as opposed to McWilliams and Siegel (2001), who equate CSR only with social or environmental performance beyond market forces . . . CSR may be strategic but need not be.

CSR can be thought of as combining a small social enterprise with an ordinary private venture, but most of the results in this literature apply equally well to for-profits exclusively engaged in social enterprise.

THE FOR-PROFIT ADVANTAGE

Since Adam Smith, it has been understood that for-profits are sometimes guided, as if by an invisible hand, towards the common good. Progress since then has made Adam Smith's intuition precise as the First Fundamental Theorem of Welfare Economics, which for most purposes translates to the following: when all goods are produced and traded in perfectly competitive markets by for-profit firms under conditions of symmetric information, equilibrium is socially efficient. The impact of this theorem is often exaggerated, so each term can be expanded on. First, social efficiency is a specific kind of judgement based on the entire economy—production, consumption, and distribution of every good and service. An economy is socially efficient if there is no alternative economy that is unambiguously better, in the judgement of consumers. Put another way, starting from an efficient economy there is no way to make any individual better off without making at least one other individual worse off in their own estimation. There are no merit goods allowed in socially efficient equilibria because consumer sovereignty is fully respected.

The theorem is in 'if-then' form. There is no presumption that all goods *are* traded in the real world. In particular, non-excludable collective goods cannot be traded, and side effects of market transactions (externalities) are not separately traded in most cases. There is no presumption that information is symmetrically distributed—there is contract failure. Finally, there are many alternative efficient economies, differing in their distribution of income, and the theorem offers no reason to suspect that current ownership of resources will lead to a fair or just distribution of income or will make critical goods affordable to all. The advantages of not-for-profits come from each of these cases not covered by the theorem.

The First Fundamental Theorem offers many insights that do carry over to the real world, however. Profit-maximizing firms produce at the lowest possible cost (productive efficiency), seek to innovate, and pay attention to consumer preferences (allocative efficiency). This all works very well for private goods, whose characteristics are observable, in competitive industries. Now, the definition of social enterprise here rules out such cases, but perhaps productive and allocative efficiency carry over to for-profit social enterprise when social investment is needed.

Organizations need capital to grow and adapt to changing preferences. For-profit firms get the financial capital they need from investments by the founder, initial public offerings, and debt. Capital is plentiful (in normal times) and available for all projects expected to generate profits. But financial investors care little about activities that are not rewarded by the market, so capital is scarce for social enterprise. This is thought by many to be a particular problem of not-for-profits and one that for-profits address, but I argue here that not-for-profits have access to more capital than commonly thought, and later that for-profit sources of capital will dry up when used to finance social enterprise.

Hansmann (1981b) made the case for the for-profit advantage in access to capital. Non-distribution of profits rules out traditional equity capital—the sale of full-ownership shares. Absent risk-sharing by shareholders, banks and other financial institutions demand higher interest rates on loans to not-for-profits. Thus, it is asserted, not-for-profits are short of capital, occupy too small a share of the economy, and grow too slowly. But not-for-profits have sources of capital not available to for-profits, chiefly donations of time and money, but also, depending on the jurisdiction, special subsidies or the right to benefit from tax-exempt bonds. In addition, Hansmann argued, the difference between not-for-profit and for-profit entity taxation in many jurisdictions allows not-for-profits to grow more quickly through retained earnings.

Capital flows freely across for-profit organizations in search of the largest financial returns. In contrast, capital cannot easily flow out of not-for-profits, due to asset-lock practices that prohibit distribution to owners even when not-for-profits are terminated or converted to for-profits. Instead, not-for-profit assets must be sold at fair market value, with proceeds dedicated to some other not-for-profit organization whose mission is as close as possible to the original organization's mission. Capital does not flow across not-for-profit organizations in search of the highest social or financial returns, and this creates inefficiencies (Hansmann, Kessler, and McClellan, 2003).

PROFITABLE SOCIAL ENTERPRISE

The literature on CSR resulting from market forces finds four ways in which corporate philanthropy or direct social investment adds to the bottom line: enhanced revenue, reduced cost, increased investment, and reduced public regulation. Consumers will not pay more to buy identical products from profit maximizers or social investors, so the enhanced revenue models identify a reason why consumers do not regard the latter as a perfect substitute for the former. Corporate philanthropy models (e.g. Clotfelter, 1985; Navarro, 1988; Webb and Farmer, 1996) argue that a company's image affects willingness to pay for its products. Highly visible contributions to popular and noncontroversial charities improve that corporate image, leading to a higher equilibrium price.

In contrast, recent CSR models such as Bagnoli and Watts (2003), Kotchen (2006), and Besley and Ghatak (2007) consider CSR as the joint production of a private good and a collective one that serves to differentiate for-profit products. For example, when manufacturers choose a less-polluting technology, they jointly produce the private good they sell and the collective good of cleaner air and water. Coffee growers obtaining Fair Trade certification simultaneously produce a private buzz and collective benefits for those who care about working conditions and pay in the industry. Or light bulbs manufactured by persons with disabilities produce both glowing orbs and the warm glow of helping those in need. Consumers are willing to pay a bit more for private goods accompanied by collective ones. As long as the higher price covers the added costs stemming from joint production, CSR is a profitable activity. Another way CSR adds to revenues is by reducing the likelihood of boycotts by activists concerned with social performance (Baron, 2009).

Economies of joint production result in CSR by for-profit firms. But these economies do not provide for-profits with a comparative advantage over not-for-profits in most cases. Indeed, the joint production model was first used to explain the behaviour of commercial not-for-profits seeking to cross-subsidize their nonmarket activities (Posnett and Sandler, 1986).

Corporate philanthropy and other social investment cut costs in several ways. First, these activities can reduce recruiting and turnover costs, particularly for key executives that prefer to work for a company that makes social investments and is seen to be virtuous. Second, as pointed out on the revenue side above, CSR cuts costs when there are economies of scope between private and collective goods (where producing outputs together is cheaper than separately). Third, CSR can serve as a screening device, attracting morally motivated workers that will work for the interests of the organization without costly incentives and oversight (Brekke and Nyborg, 2004). Again, for-profits have no comparative advantage over not-for-profits in these sources of cost reduction.

Social investors buy shares of both profit-maximizing and CSR firms and also make direct donations to not-for-profits in the model of Graff Zivin and Small (2005) and subsequent extensions by Baron (2007). Profit-maximizing firms distribute all their profits as dividends, whereas CSR firms divert a share of profits to charities. Investors care about their consumption and their direct and indirect (via ownership of CSR firms) contributions to charity. But investors differ from each other in the relative value they place on a dollar donated directly vs. indirectly. This leads to diversity in shareholder portfolios, with some investing only in profit-maximizing firms and making personal donations and others buying shares in both kinds of organizations instead of donating.

Expected spending on CSR does not harm investors in these models because the price of a share of stock reflects the expected stream of future dividend payments. The CSR firm pays lower dividends, but it costs less to obtain the rights to those dividends. Baron quoted John Mackey (2005), the CEO of Whole Foods, and I reproduce that here:

I believe the entrepreneurs, not the current investors in a company's stock, have the right and responsibility to define the purpose of the company. It is the entrepreneurs who create a company,...and who negotiate the terms of trade with all of the voluntarily co-operating stakeholders—including the investors. At Whole Foods we 'hired' our original investors. They didn't hire us...We first announced that we would donate 5% of the company's net profit to philanthropy when we drafted our mission statement....Our policy...predates our IPO by 7 years. All seven of the private investors at the time we created the policy voted for it when they served on our board of directors....How can Whole Foods' philanthropy be 'theft' from the current investors if the original owners of the company unanimously approved the policy and all subsequent investors made their investments after the policy was in effect and well publicized?

When future social spending levels are known by investors, the costs of social spending are entirely borne by founding entrepreneurs. Firms that contemplate reduced profits as a result of CSR are not formed unless there are entrepreneurs willing to bear that burden. Social investors will buy shares, but organizations do not become responsible in order to attract more investment.

The most surprisingly results of these models are that, first, increases in corporate social spending come, dollar-for-dollar, at the expense of donations to charity and, second, despite this crowding-out of donations, corporate social spending increases total social spending. The discount price of CSR shares causes an increase in share ownership, resulting in more giving via share ownership than would occur if the only option were direct investor gifts to charity. However, social spending generally remains sub-optimal in the sense that average well-being would be higher if more were spent on collective goods.

Baron (2009) combines revenue and investment factors in a single model and concludes (as summarized in Kitzmueller and Shimshack, 2012: 67):

Equilibrium levels of CSR will vary across types and depend on the degree of substitutability between the various social contribution channels, i.e., invest, consume, donate or support an activist.

Finally, improvements in corporate image stemming from corporate philanthropy can forestall costly regulatory and legislative initiatives. The interested reader is referred to the formal analyses in Maxwell, Lyon, and Hackett (2000) and Calveras, Ganuza, and Llobet (2007).

SOCIAL INVESTMENT AND THE MARKET FOR CONTROL

For-profit ownership rights are for sale. In a stock corporation, shares are bought and sold and the largest shareholders have control. Generally, a shareholder gains a controlling interest with far less than half the outstanding shares; majority ownership is only required when other shareholders band together as one. Privately held for-profits also sell ownership rights through the transfer of shares, but there is less transparency as shares are neither traded on a public exchange nor subject to the reporting and regulatory constraints commonly placed on publicly held firms. It is harder to sell ownership rights in other forms of business enterprise (like partnerships and sole proprietorships in the USA), but all the organizational assets can be sold (including the name and goodwill) to a new entity.

In the canonical model of for-profits, the market for control limits behaviours that depart from profit-maximization. For example, Friedman (1970) characterizes CSR as the spending of stockholders' money by corporate executives and asks 'Will not the stockholders fire him? (Either the present ones or those who take over when his actions in the name of social responsibility have reduced the corporation's profits and the price of its stock)'. In the canonical model, CSR share prices are lower than they would be if the firm maximized its profits, and this difference in price motivates takeover bidders who gain control, return the firm to profit maximization, and then sell at a profit. More generally, Baron (2007: 705) concludes that: 'To be sustainable, CSR firms must be protected from the market for control.'

In more realistic models, firms are protected from the market for control, to varying extents, by laws, regulations, diversity of investor preferences, and informational asymmetries. If investors as principals want firms to maximize their profit distribution, managers as agents have other objectives. This principal/agent problem can be reduced by various costly measures, but not eliminated. At least some corporate philanthropy is motivated by the private and social interests of managers who advance their social status or further social welfare through the particular gifts they make. Most observers feel that this kind of philanthropy is shrinking when compared to profit-oriented 'strategic philanthropy' (e.g. Porter and Kramer, 2002). But to the extent that shareholders cannot control management behaviour, for-profits are free to pursue alternative missions, including social enterprise but also including cronyism, excessive compensation, and other less-desirable behaviours.

The rights of shareholders vary greatly from place to place and over time. Place enough constraints on shareholders and they will fail to discipline managerial departures from profit maximization, either because they cannot secure the necessary information or they cannot enforce their will on management. In addition, when ownership is relatively dispersed, individual shareholders would rather free-ride or simply buy stock in another firm than invest their time and attention to improving the quality of management. For-profits protect themselves from the threat of takeover bids with a variety of strategies like poison pills and golden parachutes. The laws regulating such practices vary over time and place and enforcement varies as well. Wikipedia's (2012) discussion of takeovers bemoans the lack of citations but has concluded since October 2006 that:

Corporate takeovers occur frequently in the United States, Canada, United Kingdom, France and Spain. They happen only occasionally in Italy because larger shareholders (typically controlling families) often have special board voting privileges designed to keep them in control. They do not happen often in Germany because of the dual board structure, nor in Japan because companies have interlocking sets of ownerships known as keiretsu, nor in the People's Republic of China because the state majority owns most publicly listed companies.

Takeovers do not occur if the owners value CSR more than the maximum financial gains (difference in share prices) that would be offered by takeover bidders. In summary, the market for control has less influence on for-profit behaviour when the number of owners is small, the firm is privately held, and the current owners have chosen to buy shares because of the high value they place on CSR.

LIMITATIONS ON FOR-PROFIT SOCIAL ENTERPRISE

Having made the best case I can for for-profit social enterprise, I conclude that the usual advantages of for-profits disappear when they engage in social enterprise, and in any case for-profit social enterprise is limited in volume and scope. Because of the diversity of definitions and a paucity of data, it is difficult to assess the true extent of for-profit social enterprise. One element of this is revealed by the volume of private social investments. A report by the Social Investment Forum Foundation (2010, Executive Summary p. 8) estimated that 'The total assets managed under policies that explicitly incorporate ESG criteria into investment analysis and portfolio construction (ESG assets) are valued at $2.51 trillion'. This compares with about $25trn in managed assets in the USA. Corporations devote a fraction of that sum to annual donations—$14.1bn in cash and in-kind gifts in 2009 (Giving USA, 2010). This is only about 4 per cent of total giving of $304bn. The Conference Board survey of major corporations found U.S. median contributions, as a percentage of pretax income, were only 1.55 per cent in 2008. Surveyed corporations gave an additional $2.59bn abroad in 2008, mostly in-kind (Cavicchio and Torok, 2009). A survey conducted by The Social Investment Consultancy (2010) finds that 'British business gives an estimated £1.4bn a year in revenue and support each year to good causes'.

Corporate philanthropy is also limited to noncontroversial causes. Those who support controversial causes risk boycotts and bad public relations, deterring some from giving and penalizing those who continue to give (Himmelstein, 1997). Thus, it is not surprising that Himmelstein concluded (as summarized in Galaskiewicz and Colman, 2006: 184):

> Giving officers in particular had a strong commitment to do something genuinely worthwhile for the communities in which their firms operated. Yet, doing good was difficult to defend in companies that were under attack by disgruntled shareholders, embroiled in cutthroat competition, or vulnerable to crises beyond their control. Because the function often did not directly contribute to the 'bottom line', to survive it had to have the support of the CEO or chairman of the board or it had to speak to the strategic interests of the firm. Yet, to ensure its integrity the giving program had to guard against becoming a 'plaything' of senior executives or an arm of the marketing/personnel/public relations departments. This is often a difficult tightrope to walk.

Social expenditures are encouraged when consumers are willing to pay a higher price for purchases from socially responsible firms. But in the joint production model of Bagnoli and Watts (2003) the level of private provision of the collective good varies inversely with the competitiveness of the private-good market.

Investors are willing to buy shares in CSR firms. But as Graff Zivin and Small (2005) and Baron (2007) show, corporate social expenditures come partly or entirely at the expense of individual donations. In the special case where all investors view corporate spending as a perfect substitute for individual giving, total social expenditures are unaffected by CSR. Every increase in corporate spending causes an equal and opposite decrease in personal donations. Further, because the costs of anticipated CSR are borne entirely by the founding entrepreneur in these models, the extent of CSR is limited by the scarcity of entrepreneurs willing to make the necessary sacrifice.

Although the market for control is far less effective in preventing departures from profit-maximizing behaviours than suggested by the canonical model, it is never entirely absent and so there are always questions regarding the sustainability of CSR spending. Current owners may have all bought-in to a social mission as Mackey (2005) suggested, but current owners die, preferences change over time, and those placing a lower value on CSR have the incentive to mimic their more socially responsible fellow investors. Rodgers (2005) commented:

Mackey spouts nonsense about how his company hired his original investors, not vice versa. If Whole Foods ever falls on persistent hard times—perhaps when the Luddites are no longer able to hold back the genetic food revolution using junk science and fear—he will quickly find out who has hired whom, as his investors fire him.

Even when the owners are somewhat in agreement, managers face the difficult problem described by Yunus (2010):

When you mix profit and social benefit and say that your company will pursue both goals, you are making life complicated for the chief executive officer. His thinking process gets clouded. He does not see clearly. In a particular situation where profit and social benefit need to be balanced, which way should the scales be tipped? ... What about in times of economic stress, such as a recession—is it all right to eliminate social benefits altogether in hopes of helping the company to survive? ... The idea of a "mixed" company offers no clear guidance on questions like these. In practice, profit tends to win out in struggles of this kind. Most often the CEO will lean—perhaps unconsciously—in favor of profit and exaggerate the social benefits being created. ... [T]he social goals will gradually fade in importance while the need to make money becomes more and more deeply ingrained in the company's culture.

The problem is magnified when for-profit social enterprises change owners. MacCormac et al. (2007: 97) conclude that 'Many socially oriented for-profits find that their social mission is dependent on founders' fervor, and when founders retire or sell, their social legacy is often lost as more traditional owners take over'. Katz and Page (2010: 96) view the problem 'as an intertemporal agency problem between an idealist founder (principal) and his older and perhaps more acquisitive self (agent)'.

Social expenditures by for-profits are only sustainable when the market for control is weak or absent. But this absence allows for-profits to sustain inefficient behaviours, so the efficiency advantage of for-profits is reduced or lost entirely when these firms engage in social enterprise.

For-profit access to equity capital is plentiful for profit-maximizing activities. But investor's purchase of CSR shares is, in the various models examined, the joint purchase of a stream of future dividends and donations. Although Baron (2007) showed that this arrangement may, under specified circumstances, increase total social investment relative to a pure private donations equilibrium, the increase is limited. Therefore, for-profit access to capital for social investment is not as bountiful as it is for profit-seeking investments.

None of the CSR models discussed above include informational asymmetry between purportedly socially engaged for-profits and consumers, donors, workers, and investors. For-profits have the same incentives here as elsewhere, and I believe contract failure is the most common result. It pays to exaggerate the degree of corporate social expenditures, as gullible consumers would overpay and gullible workers would accept lower financial compensation. One aspect of this informational asymmetry has become known as 'green-washing'—the selective disclosure of positive but not negative information about a firm's environmental performance (Lyon and Maxwell, 2011). There are private social-responsibility rating services and laws against fraud, but for collective goods marginal-impact contract failure is nonetheless likely.

TWO CASE EXAMPLES

Newman's Own, Inc. was founded by Paul Newman and privately held. Since its beginning, Newman's has successfully donated all after-tax profits to the Newman's Own Foundation, a grant-making not-for-profit. The founder strongly wanted all profits donated to charity, and got his way, a policy that continues after his death with donations exceeding \$350m (<http://www.newmansownfoundation.org>, accessed 30 June 2012). How did Mr Newman succeed in the face of the market for control in sustaining his mission for so long? The key is that Newman was the sole initial investor. He could have taken a distribution of profits at any time, but chose not to do so because he valued the social mission more than the potential profits he could receive as a distribution. Of course, the maximum takeover bid that could be advanced would be no greater than the potential distributable profits, so a mutually-beneficial transfer of ownership did not and could not take place. That is why Brakman Reiser (2009: 2451) concluded that 'social enter-prise companies are often small and controlled by owners who have a personal commitment to their social goals. A few have begun that way, but grew quite large as a result of their success'.

If Newman required investments exceeding his own ability to found the for-profit, ownership would be split among several investors. Perhaps Newman could have found a sufficient number of investors that shared his vision, and the for-profit would continue to operate charitably without pressure from the market for control. But if he guessed wrong, if he found investors that claimed to share his social mission but acted otherwise when the firm became profitable, then the market for control would make the social mission unsustainable. Prejudging investor motivations is difficult because greedy investors would pretend to share the social mission in order to vote for distribution at a later time.

Even if the original set of investors were sufficiently committed to escape the market for control, ownership shares would be transferred upon death and at any time there is no guarantee that those supporting Newman's original mission will continue to enjoy a controlling stake in the firm. Newman did not face the initial greed-revelation problem because he needed no other investors. But he did die, prompting an exchange of emails with Roberta Pearson of newmansown.com who wrote (12 May 2010):

When Mr. Newman became ill he formed the Newman's Own Foundation and the Foundation now owns Newman's Own, Inc. Now all royalties and after taxed profits from Newman's Own, Inc., go over to the Foundation and their board members disburse those monies to charitable organizations.

By making the for-profit corporation into a wholly owned subsidiary of the not-for-profit Foundation, there is a hybrid that cannot legally distribute profits. The same could be accomplished by merging the corporation into the foundation, which would then pay the 'unrelated business income tax' that applies to not-for-profits rather than the for-profit corporate income tax. In other words, for all intents and purposes, the corporation was converted to a not-for-profit, with all the comparative advantages and disadvantages of the form.

The conclusion is that for-profit social ventures are possible and will endure for a while if the founder has personal access to the requisite initial capital and remains committed to the social mission. But founders do not endure forever; eventually, like all mortals, they founder. Then, unless the venture is converted or effectively converted into a not-for-profit form, there will be a growing risk that the organization will revert to traditional profit-maximizing behaviour with distributions to shareholders. The larger the number of required investors, the smaller the chance that for-profit social ventures will be formed and if formed, the shorter they will endure as social.

Google.org (DotOrg) was created as a for-profit philanthropy by Google Inc. with an initial donation of 1 per cent of Google's equity and the transfer of grant management from the earlier, not-for-profit, Google Foundation. In addition, the corporation donates employee time and money to DotOrg. Like a traditional foundation, DotOrg makes grants, but has shifted most of its efforts towards developing engineering solutions for urgent world problems (Google.org, 2012). Unlike a traditional foundation, there is no asset lock—upon dissolution, assets would revert to the owner, Google Inc. This feature deters donations from outsiders. Unlike Google Inc., DotOrg does not issue shares to outsiders, so its access to capital is restricted by Google's admittedly deep pockets.

DotOrg is unique in taking this approach. They chose to forego the many advantages of the not-for-profit form (including tax exemption and the right to receive tax-deductible donations) because of the ways not-for-profits are regulated in the USA. As a for-profit, they escaped restrictions on investing in other for-profits, restrictions on direct access to the resources of Google, Inc., and restrictions on political activities stemming from federal tax law and state regulation (Brakman Reiser, 2009).

Because Google, Inc., announced plans to devote 1 per cent of profits to social investment prior to its initial public offering, Brakman Reiser (2009:

2468) concluded: 'Any shareholders disdaining such use of their capital could have looked elsewhere to invest....In fact, some shareholders may have purchased because of Google, Inc.'s philanthropic commitment, and would want to hold the company to its promises'.

The greed-revelation problem has no impact, and there is little pressure from the market for control because Google, Inc.'s contribution is only 1 per cent of its profits, an amount typical of traditional corporate donations. DotOrg is visible to the public, contributes to Google, Inc.'s corporate image, and so enhances marketing and reduces political will to impose costly regulations or pursue antitrust cases against the parent. Google, Inc.'s executives and key employees support the investment in social enterprise, so the investment reduces recruiting and turnover costs. All these factors combine to make Google, Inc. unattractive to hostile takeover bids that seek to end the investment in social enterprise.

Thus, Google.org's social mission is sustainable, at least for the short and medium term. But it is sustainable because it is like traditional corporate philanthropy, limited in size and scope. Perhaps a few firms that do not currently make corporate donations would be willing to make the kind of reversible donations embodied in the Google, Inc./Google.org partnership, so the model may increase social investment a bit, but it will not greatly transform the limits on corporate social investment stemming from the market for control.

New hybrid organizational forms

Is there a way to combine for-profit access to traditional equity capital markets and productive efficiency with not-for-profit trustworthiness, access to grants and donations, and mission sustainability? In the USA, a few such attempts have been made, but as Kelley (2009: 3) put it:

A few practitioners have learned to cobble together complex structures . . . that draw on a mix of for-profit and not-for-profit forms and doctrines to create legal scaffolding for hybrid ventures. But those complex structures, which involve corporations with multiple classes of stock and detailed shareholder agreements, or the creation of multiple interlocking entities, or the use of delicately drafted joint venture agreements, tend to be expensive to create, burdensome to maintain, and, due to their novelty, legally insecure.

That is why various US state and tribal governments, starting with Vermont, have enacted laws allowing for the incorporation of Low-Profit Limited Liability Companies (L3Cs) starting in 2008. In the UK, legislation took effect in 2005 providing rules for creating and operating another new kind of hybrid organization, Community Interest Companies (CICs). Alternative new hybrid forms continue to emerge (e.g., Social Impact Bonds, B Corporations, Benefit Corporations, and Flexible Purpose Corporations) in the USA.

The most flexible corporate form in the USA is called a Limited Liability Company (LLC). This form combines the structural features of a partnership with the limited liability of a corporation. LLCs have members, instead of shareholders. There can be multiple classes of members, each with distinct governance rights. Different member classes may require different financial contributions, and distributions of profit need not be split in proportion to member investments. LLCs are treated like partnerships for federal tax purposes in that income is taxed only when received by members. Hybrid organizations for social enterprise can incorporate with a variety of structures under the LLC designation, but legislation enabling distinct classification as an L3C was designed to create a 'brand name' company with standard features that stakeholders would recognize. To qualify as an L3C, the organization must significantly further one or more charitable or educational purposes (as defined by the federal tax code), not have the production of income or appreciation of property as a primary purpose, demonstrate that it would not have been formed but for the company's relationship to the accomplishment of one or more charitable or educational purposes, and not include influencing legislation or political campaigning among the organizational purposes.

Brakman Reiser (2010: 628, footnotes omitted) summarizes a tranched membership structure proposed by advocates of the L3C, designed to promote access to equity capital and incentivize efficiency while pursuing a sustainable social mission:

An equity tranche of members could be tax-exempt private foundations making program-related investments [PRIs]. Because the PRI regulations specifically bar foundations from contemplating a financial return as a motive for investment, this tranche of members would be given scant or very remote rights to distributions. A mezzanine tranche of individuals or entities could purchase L3C memberships as a type of socially responsible investment. This tranche of investors would agree to operating agreement terms that provided them with some access to distributions, but at a rate lower than market return, presumably doing so in return for the social or psychic value produced by the entity. The L3C's operating agreement could then provide for a market-like return to a senior tranche of individuals and entities seeking such returns, presumably doing so in competition with other market-rate investment opportunities. The structure of these provisions might be more debt-like or equity-like (though if the latter, more like preferred than common stock), providing either a guaranteed return or a return keyed to the L3C's profits.

The social mission is enshrined by giving equity-tranche members controlling or exclusive governance rights. This implies that conflicts between mission and profits would be decided in favour of mission and protects the organization from profit-seeking takeover bids. If, despite this structure, the social mission of the organization loses primacy, the statutes specify that the organization reverts to a regular LLC. There is no statutory asset lock preventing the accumulated assets from being distributed to members as a consequence of that reversion.

In the UK, CICs can be formed as a company limited by shares (analogous to US for-profit) or limited by guarantee (analogous to US not-for-profit), with additional requirements and variations such as an asset lock. In general, directors of companies limited by shares have a fiduciary duty to shareholders but can *consider* other interests. CICs limited by shares must place these other interests as primary goals. In general, companies limited by guarantee have one or more eligible charitable purposes. But if these companies chose to incorporate as a CIC, they lose the tax and certain regulatory advantages given to charities. Regardless of form, directors must preserve the organization's ability to pass the 'community interest test', which specifies that 'a reasonable person might consider [the CIC's] activities are being carried on for the benefit of the community' (Regulator of Community Interest Groups, 2009). The CIC must report its compliance with this test and must 'confirm that access to the benefits it provides will not be confined to an unduly restricted group' (Regulator of Community Interest Groups, 2009). Members, who may be shareholders, donors, or specified others have some governance rights, and have a duty to monitor that the company continues to meet the community interest test and fully involves the community in its activities and development.

The Regulator of CICs is empowered to limit dividends for CICs limited by shares. Initially the cap was set too low to attract investors, then the Regulator eased up and capped dividends at 35 per cent of distributable profits. In addition, the Regulator enforces an effective asset lock—the organization cannot sell its assets at less than fair market value except in pursuit of mission or when transferring assets to another charity or CIC. This lock includes distribution of assets following dissolution or conversion to a different structure.

Other emerging hybrids are described briefly, as the set of recommended alternatives is fluid and rapidly evolving. The US not-for-profit B Lab created the label B-Corporation form for for-profits that meet its certification standards. B-Corporation's website says:

B Corps, unlike traditional businesses: Meet comprehensive and transparent social and environmental performance standards; Meet higher legal accountability standards; [and] Build business constituency for public policies that support sustainable business. (<http://www.bcorporation.net/about>)

B Lab also successfully lobbied for legislation (passed in seven states, with more pending) to create a new corporate form, the Benefit Corporation (BC). Like L3C status, BC status is designed to create a brand name for social enterprise. BCs differ from other for-profits in that the enabling legislation uniformly and transparently specifies that the fiduciary duties of directors encompass interests beyond the shareholders. A corporation becomes a BC if approved by two-thirds of the shareholders. A supermajority is also required for mergers and conversions whenever the successor organization would not be a BC. Benefit corporations are required to have a purpose of creating 'general public benefit' and are allowed to identify one or more 'specific public benefit' purposes from a non-exhaustive list. BCs must produce an annual report on their economic, social, and environmental performance, with requirements to insure independent third-party evaluation of these claims (Clark and Vranka, 2013). Flexible Purpose Corporations began in California in 2011, as an alternative to BCs (Strom, 2011). These have more restricted purposes similar to not-for-profits, and unlike BCs, there is no requirement that a third party evaluate each stated special purpose.

Social Impact Bonds (SIB) are still a relatively new and unproven part of the social finance market, combining equity-like and bond-like tranched investment opportunities for social enterprise (Social Finance, Inc., 2012; Callanan and Law, 2012). Under this arrangement, government agencies ask consortiums of investors and donors to bid for a contract between the government and a service provider, for-profit or not-for-profit. The contract specifies detailed performance criteria, and the winning consortium (the bondholders) is responsible for funding and overseeing the project. Risk is transferred from government and service providers to bondholders because government payments to bondholders are only made when performance objectives are met. The first SIB was issued in the UK in 2010, and Massachusetts issued requests for proposals for SIB grants in 2012.

Evaluating hybrid organizations

Advocates of hybrid organization seek the best of both worlds—to combine the advantages of for-profits and the advantages of not-for-profits in a single entity. This section evaluates this claim. First, it looks at whether hybrids obtain the efficiency advantage asserted for for-profits. Then, it examines whether they are likely to secure more capital for social enterprise. Then, it asks whether hybrids are likely to avoid contract failure. Finally, it looks at mission-sustainability for hybrids.

HYBRID EFFICIENCY

Hybrids are profit-distributing organizations, so they are thought to provide the efficiency advantage of the for-profit corporate form. However, extension by analogy is logically dubious, and I do not find this argument to be persuasive. For-profits are efficient for three reasons: the owners want efficiency, the market for control eliminates inefficiency, and competition results in the death of inefficient for-profits. In hybrid organizations, there are various ownership structures but generally speaking, those investing in order to obtain financial returns (e.g. the senior tranche in L3Cs) are given little governance power (which rests primarily with the equity tranche in this example). So unlike regular shareholders, who have the choice of voice (demanding management change) or exit, financial investors have no choice. If they don't like the returns they are getting, they invest elsewhere. For this same reason, financially motivated takeover bids will not occur.

In addition, asserted for-profit efficiencies and not-for-profit inefficiencies have been exaggerated. Note first that the First Fundamental Theorem claims that *equilibrium* is efficient. There is no theoretical reason to think that this equilibrium is ever reached in the real world, because the underlying fundamental parameters (tastes and productivity) change and we still do not fully understand the dynamics of adjustment even under perfect competition. Second, the 'if' part of this 'if-then' theorem is not true in the real world. Markets are not fully competitive, some goods are untraded, and there are myriad principle–agent problems impairing efficiency. Firms employ costly strategies to immunize themselves from takeover (poison pills, golden parachutes), creating inefficiency and impairing the market for control. Third, efficiency is attained by the death or restructuring of *inefficient* for-profits. Unless this death is instantaneous, at any point in time there will be many for-profits that are 'Not dead yet' (Python, 1975), lowering the average efficiency of for-profits. In practice, corporate follies, particularly by 'too big to fail' firms, make it increasingly hard for me to believe that for-profits are generally efficient.

Conversely, claims of not-for-profit inefficiency are exaggerated and in some cases, not-for-profits are more efficient than for-profits. Money is not the only way to motivate people, and in areas of social enterprise, money is often not the best way to motivate people. True, not-for-profits are relatively restricted in their ability to use financial incentives to motivate their workforce. But Slivinski (2002) showed that worker enjoyment of the collective output of the firm (dividends in kind) can be the most efficient way to motivate team production by workers. True, not-for-profit directors do not have pecuniary incentives to instill efficiency in the organizations they control. But waste impairs mission accomplishment, which can powerfully motivate board members and top managers. True, potential takeover bidders do not search for not-for-profit inefficiencies, but there are many other agents who do. More details, and empirical evidence on these points are summarized in, for example, Steinberg (1987, 2006) and Schlesinger and Gray (2006).

Ironically, hybrids may be efficient *because* they, like not-for-profits, are controlled by those concerned with the social mission of the organization. But whether we are talking hybrid organizations or commercial not-for-profits, the clash of cultures between those charged to seek profits and those charged to pursue social objectives is a continuing source of inefficiency. Absent economies of scope, ongoing fights among stakeholders are costly to mediate and competing stakeholders devote considerable scarce resources to those fights.

HYBRID ACCESS TO CAPITAL

Do hybrids get more capital than for-profits? Advocates assert the leveraging power of social investment to attract profit-seeking investment. Again, this does not appear plausible on theoretical grounds. Some advocates are using different definitions, but because social investment is defined here as investment in things that are not ordinarily done by markets, the overall rate of return must be below market. In tranched investment structures like L3Cs and SIBs, the senior (market-return-seeking) tranche would need to be cross-subsidized by investors in the other tranches. The ability to do so is limited, and the desire of social investors to subsidize other investors is questionable. What is the point in paying investors to invest? This is particularly true for Social Impact Bonds, because profit-seeking investors will need a higher rate of return (to compensate for the risk that the bond will not be redeemed by government if the programme fails to meet performance criteria). Private foundations in the USA would face additional constraints if the IRS viewed cross-subsidization and risk transfer as a 'jeopardizing investment'.

Advocates for L3Cs believe that additional capital would come in the form of low-interest loans made by private foundations (programme-related investments or PRIs). Indeed the enabling legislation borrows language from the tax code permitting PRIs that meet specified criteria. To date, IRS guidance has been unclear, and few private foundations have been willing to make PRIs (e.g. Kelley, 2009; Doeringer, 2009–10). On 19 April 2012 the IRS proposed modifications to the Code of Federal Regulations that, if adopted, would reduce the legal uncertainties and encourage PRIs (IRS, 2012).

While no firm empirical evidence is available at this time, a non-random sampling frame consisting of applicants for Echoing Green Fellowships for early-stage social entrepreneurs was used to survey a random 3,500 members of that frame (Battilana et al., 2012). They found (p. 53) that 'most hybrid entrepreneurs we have encountered still experience difficulty in raising capital'. It should be noted, however, that during the great recession, many for-profit entrepreneurs also encountered difficulty in raising capital, and although the problem may be worse for hybrids, there is little evidence to prove it.

CICs limit dividend payments, and this restriction reduces their ability to raise equity capital. Doeringer (2009–10) notes how an early CIC success exhausted its credit lines after it was unable to tap the equity lines due to limited investor interest until it was forced to sell nearly all its assets to the private sector. He concluded (p. 315):

It remains to be seen whether the dividend restrictions will prohibitively limit CICs' access to capital, or whether creative social valuation metrics can nurture an active social-equity market. However, the rapid pace at which entrepreneurs continue to register CICs shows hope, at least, for the latter.

HYBRID CONTRACT FAILURE

To what extent do hybrids avoid contract failure? In theory, this depends on the hybrid's structure. Although both L3Cs and CICs are governed by parties whose primary goal is not profit distribution, profits can be distributed on dissolution or conversion of an L3C. This provides an incentive for profit-motivated agents to invest in the equity or mezzanine tranche, pretending to be mission-motivated. These mimics could then vote for dissolution, resulting in marginal-impact contract failure. Regular not-for-profits and CICs are constrained by an asset lock, making attempts to mimic mission-motivated investors less tempting.

Not-for-profit trustworthiness is always constrained by the need to secure adequate resources. In resource-scarce environments, not-for-profits may be forced to compromise or go out of business. Would hybrids become so reliant on market-rate capital that they would be forced to concede de facto control to these investors?

HYBRID SUSTAINABILITY

In theory, control by mission-oriented parties insures against takeovers or conversions that would shift the hybrid towards profit-maximization and hence away from social objectives. That control is weakest for certification hybrids like B-Corporations, and weaker for L3Cs than for hybrids constrained by asset locks. To sustain the social mission, asset locks are necessary.

However, some social missions do not require eternally sustained efforts. Katz and Page (2010: 98) pointed out that, 'a social enterprise can succeed by demonstrating that it is no longer necessary and that the market failure the not-for-profit undertook to address no longer exists'. But the eventual distribution of profits may attract investors who push for the kinds of behaviour that leads to contract failure, and perhaps would deter social investors.

Continued adherence to the social part of dual missions requires some form of oversight with teeth. Yet the power of stakeholders in benefit and flexible purpose corporations to enforce strictures against opportunistic boards and managers are limited (Brakman Reiser 2011, 2012; Munch, 2012). For both organizational forms, shareholders are the only parties with the authority to bring suit, and shareholders may be less focused on protecting the interests of other stakeholders. The laws requiring directors to merely *consider* the impact of their decisions on stakeholders other than shareholders make it unlikely that such shareholder suits could succeed. Directors can always defend their actions as consonant with the business mission of the organization. In any case, shareholders dissatisfied with the balance between business and social missions or with the zeal with which the social mission is pursued will 'almost invariably fail' in derivative suits alleging breaches of the duty of care

(Brakman Reiser, 2012: 16). The ratings requirement for benefit corporations could help, but with over one hundred raters listed on the B Lab website and more available elsewhere, less scrupulous directors could shop for the least-constraining ratings agency.

Conclusion

This chapter has argued that social finance investors should direct their resources towards collective goods, merit goods, and affordability. For-profit firms suffer from contract failure, implying that social investors should be wary of marginal-impact contract failure in collective goods, and that for-profits will take advantage of purchasers when important aspects of quality are unobservable or cannot be verified by third parties. Not-for-profits are protected from the market for organizational control, making their social missions more sustainable. Not-for-profits have a harder time raising capital through ordinary market transactions, but social investors have the opportunity to fix this.

For-profit firms provide considerable amounts of social goods, mostly because and to the extent that profits are enhanced through consumer good will, joint production, reductions in recruiting and turnover costs, and reductions in regulation. To a more limited extent, for-profits provide social goods at the expense of profit. But as long as the majority of investors seek market returns, further growth is limited by the scarcity of social entrepreneurs and investors. Further, there are good reasons to think that social investments in for-profits come at the expense of other donations and other social investments.

There is a variety of emerging legal structures that attempt to combine the advantages of not-for-profits (trustworthiness, sustainability, credibility) with those of for-profits (access to capital, efficiency). The details vary with the specific legal form, but hybrids to date suffer from unclear guidelines regarding the proper balance of market and social returns. Easy-to-measure market returns are balanced against imprecise social returns, which, along with survival pressures, pressures from the market for control, and untested enforcement, leads to difficulties in sustaining the social mission. Some observers are quite sceptical that this can ever work. In her article on failed hybrids, *New York Times* reporter Strom concluded (2011):

Like Dr. Dolittle's pushmi-pullyu, the animal that had trouble moving because its two heads could not agree on a single direction, the hybrid model for not-for-profits is proving problematic. On occasion, the need to generate returns for investors overwhelms the social mission. In other cases, the business falters altogether and cannot support the not-for-profit.

Although it is worthwhile to think about additional hybrid structures that might combine the best of both sectors, there is always the danger of combining the worst of both sectors. For-profits enjoy easy access to capital because the majority of suppliers of capital can obtain market rates of return. For-profits with blended missions or the new hybrids cannot offer market rates of return, or, in the case of L3Cs, offer market rates of return only if socially conscious investors subsidize market investors rather than subsidizing social goods. Alleged for-profit efficiency advantages stem from the seeking of market rates of return, and that too goes away when for-profits or hybrids pursue blended missions. This chapter, therefore, endorses the conclusion reached by Brakman Reiser (2010: 654–5) and cannot state it better than she did:

It is too soon to diagnose with certainty which, if any, of the extant hybrid forms will emerge as successful and which will fall by the wayside. One pattern that does emerge, however, is striking. The two invaluable contributions a hybrid form must make— expanding financing options and providing enforceable commitments to a blended mission—appear to trade off against each other.... It is possible that the impasse cannot be breached, and instead the creators of any hybrid model will simply have to choose a point at which they are willing to trade access to capital for enforcement of blended mission.

There may be several possible positive effects of social finance for for-profits and new hybrids. First, even if increased social finance investments in some organizations resulted in decreased investments elsewhere, the value of social investments could increase. It is clear that some purported social investments are no more than greenwash—if these investments were replaced by better ones, more would be accomplished without additional spending. Second, behavioural economics shows that financial decisions are not always rational. Thaler (1980) argued that people place their resources in mental accounts and are reluctant to invest resources in one account towards causes in another. The theory has blossomed, and there is evidence supporting it in a number of realms of economic decision-making, but there is, as yet, no evidence on mental accounting in social finance. If for-profit, not-for-profit, and hybrid organizations reside in differing accounts, it is possible that innovations in management and organizational form could enlarge the pool of social invest-ment. Of course, the reverse is also possible, and so, predictably, it is evident that more research is needed.

REFERENCES

Bagnoli, M., and Watts, S. G. (2003). 'Selling to Socially Responsible Consumers: Competition and the Private Provision of Public Goods', *Journal of Economics and Management Strategy*, 12(3): 419–45.

Baron, D. P. (2007). 'Corporate Social Responsibility and Social Entrepreneurship', *Journal of Economics and Management Strategy*, 16(3): 683–717.

Baron, D. P. (2009). 'A Positive Theory of Moral Management, Social Pressure, and Corporate Social Performance', *Journal of Economics and Management Strategy*, 18(1): 7–43.

Battilana, J., Lee, M., Walker, J., and Dorsey, C. (2012). 'In Search of the Hybrid Ideal', *Stanford Social Innovation Review*, Summer: 51–5.

Ben-Ner, A. (1986). 'Nonprofit Organizations: Why Do They Exist in Market Economies?' in S. Rose-Ackerman (ed.) *The Economics of Nonprofit Institutions: Studies in Structure and Policy*. New York: Oxford University Press, pp. 94–113.

Ben-Ner, A., and Jones, D. (1995). 'Employee Participation, Ownership, and Productivity: A Theoretical Framework', *Industrial Relations*, 34: 532–54.

Besley, T., and Ghatak, M. (2007). 'Retailing Public Goods: The Economics of Corporate Social Responsibility', *Journal of Public Economics*, 91(9): 1645–63.

Bilodeau, M., and Slivinski, A. (1998). 'Rational Nonprofit Entrepreneurship', *Journal of Economics and Management Strategy*, 7: 551–71.

Bilodeau, M., and Steinberg, R. (1997). 'Ransom of the Opera', IUPUI Department of Economics Working Paper, Indianapolis.

Brakman Reiser, D. (2009). 'For-profit Philanthropy', *Fordham Law Review*, 77(5): 2437–73.

Brakman Reiser, D. (2010). 'Governing and Financing Blended Enterprise', *Chicago-Kent Law Review*, 85(2): 619–55.

Brakman Reiser, D. (2011). 'Benefit Corporations: A Sustainable Form of Organization?' *Wake Forest Law Review*, 46: 591–625.

Brakman Reiser, D. (2012). 'The Next Big Thing: Flexible-Purpose Corporations', *Legal Studies Working Paper 331, Business Law Review*, pp. 1–21, available at SSRN: <http://ssrn.com/abstract=2166474>.

Brekke, K. A., and Nyborg, K. (2004). 'Moral Hazard and Moral Motivation: Corporate Social Responsibility as Labor Market Screening', University of Oslo Department of Economics Memorandum 25/2004.

Callanan, L., and Law, J. (2012). 'Will Social Impact Bonds Work in the United States?' McKinsey and Company, available at: <http://mckinseyonsociety.com/downloads/reports/Social-Innovation/Social-impact-bonds.pdf>.

Calveras, A., Ganuza, J.-J., and Llobet, G. (2007). 'Regulation, Corporate Social Responsibility and Activism', *Journal of Economics and Management Strategy*, 16(3): 719–40.

Cavicchio, C., and Torok, J. (2009). 'The 2009 Corporate Contributions Report', The Conference Board, Report Number R-1458-09-RR, New York.

Clark, W. H. Jr, and Vranka, L. (2013). 'The Need and Rationale for the Benefit Corporation: Why It Is the Legal Form that Best Addresses the Needs of Social Entrepreneurs, Investors, and ultimately, the Public'. White Paper, January, 18, available at: <http://www.benefitcorp.net/attorneys/benefit-corp-white-paper>.

Clotfelter, C. T. (1985). *Federal Tax Policy and Charitable Giving*. Chicago: University of Chicago Press.

Doeringer, M. F. (2009–10). 'Note, Fostering Social Enterprise: A Historical and International Analysis', *Duke Journal of Comparative and International Law*, 20: 291–329.

Friedman, M. (1970). 'The Social Responsibility of Business Is to Increase Its Profits', *The New York Times Magazine*, 13 September: 32–3, 122, 126.

Galaskiewicz, J., and Sinclair Colman, M. (2006). 'Collaboration between Corporations and Nonprofit Organizations, 'in W. W. Powell and R. Steinberg (eds), *The Nonprofit Sector: A Research Handbook, Second Edition*. New Haven: Yale University Press, pp. 180–98.

Giving USA Foundation (2010). *Giving USA*. Giving USA Foundation.

Graff Zivin, J., and Small, A. (2005). 'A Modigliani-Miller Theory of Altruistic Corporate Social Responsibility' *B. E. Journal of Economic Analysis and Policy: Topics in Economic Analysis and Policy*, 5(1).

Hansmann, H. (1980). 'The Role of Nonprofit Enterprise', *Yale Law Journal*, 89: 835–901.

Hansmann, H. (1981a). 'Nonprofit Enterprise in the Performing Arts', *Bell Journal of Economics*, 12: 341–61.

Hansmann, H. (1981b). 'The Rationale for Exempting Nonprofit Corporations from the Corporate Income Tax', *Yale Law Journal*, 91: 54–100.

Hansmann, H., Kessler, D., and McClellan, M. (2003). 'Ownership Form and Trapped Capital in the Hospital Industry', in E. Glaeser (ed.), *The Governance of Nonprofit Organizations*. Chicago: University of Chicago Press, pp. 45–69.

Himmelstein, J. L. (1997). *Looking Good and Doing Good: Corporate Philanthropy and Corporate Power*. Bloomington, IN: Indiana University Press.

Horton, R. (2006). 'Thoughts on the Meaning and Field of Social Enterprise'. Columbia, Graduate School of Business.

IRS (2012). 'Examples of Program-Related Investments'. Document IRS-2012-0015-0001, Posted online and in the Federal Register on 19 April 2012, available at: <http://www.regulations.gov>.

Katz, R. A., and Page, A. (2010). 'The Role of Social Enterprise', *Vermont Law Review*, 35: 59–103.

Kelley, T. A. (2009). 'Law and Choice of Entity on the Social Enterprise', *Tulsa Law Review* 84, available at: <http://works.bepress.com/thomas_kelley/2>.

Kitzmueller, M., and Shimshack, J. (2012). 'Economic Perspectives on Corporate Social Responsibility', *Journal of Economic Literature*, L(1): 51–84.

Kotchen, M. J. (2006). 'Green Markets and Private Provision of Public Goods', *Journal of Political Economy*, 114(4): 816–34.

Krashinsky, M. (1986). 'Transaction Costs and a Theory of the Nonprofit Organization', in S. Rose-Ackerman (ed.), *The Economics of Nonprofit Institutions*. New Haven: Yale University Press, pp. 114–32.

Lyon, T. P., and Maxwell, J. W. (Forthcoming). 'Greenwash: Corporate Environmental Disclosure under Threat of Audit', *Journal of Economics and Management Strategy*.

MacCormac, S., Glass, J., and Cooke, J. (2007). 'The Emergence of New Corporate Forms: The Need for Alternative Corporate Designs Integrating Financial and Social Missions', in A. White and M. Kelley (eds), *Paper Series on Corporate Design*, available at: <http://www.corporation2020.org/pdfs/SummitPaperSeries.pdf>.

Mackey, J. (2005). 'Putting Customers Ahead of Investors', *Reason*, available at: <http://reason.com>.

Maxwell, J. W., Lyon, T. P., and Hackett, S. C. (2000). 'Self-Regulation and Social Welfare: The Political Economy of Corporate Environmentalism', *Journal of Law and Economics*, 43(2): 583–617.

McWilliams, A., and Siegel, D. (2001). 'Corporate Social Responsibility: A Theory of the Firm Perspective', *The Academy of Management Review*, 26(1): 117–27.

Monty Python (1975). *Monty Python and the Holy Grail* (film). Relevant segment available at: <http://www.youtube.com/watch?v=dGFXGwHsD_A>.

Munch, S. (2012). 'Improving the Benefit Corporation: How Traditional Governance Mechanisms Can Enhance the Innovative New Business Form', *Northwestern Journal of Law and Social Policy*, 7(1): 170–95.

Navarro, P. (1988). 'Why Do Corporations Give to Charities?' *Journal of Business*, 61(1): 65–93.

Posnett, J. W., and Sandler, T. (1986). 'Joint Supply and the Finance of Charitable Activity', *Public Finance Quarterly*, 14: 209–22.

Porter, M. E., and Kramer, M. R. (2002). 'The Competitive Advantage of Corporate Philanthropy', *Harvard Business Review*, 80(12): 56–68.

Preston, A. E. (1989). 'The Nonprofit Worker in a For-profit World', *Journal of Labor Economics*, 7: 438–63.

Regulator of Community Interest Companies (2009). 'Frequently Asked Question 13', available at: <http://www.cicregulator.gov.uk/CICleaflets/FAQ>.

Rodgers, T. J. (2005). 'Put Profits First', *Reason*, available at: <http://www.reason.com/0510/fe.nf.rethinking.shtml>.

Rose-Ackerman, S. (ed) (1986), *The Economics of Nonprofit Institutions*. Oxford: Oxford University Press.

Schlesinger, M., and Gray, B. H. (2006). 'Nonprofit Organizations and Health Care: Some Paradoxes of Persistent Scrutiny', in W. W. Powell and R. Steinberg (eds), *The Nonprofit Sector: A Research Handbook, Second Edition*. New Haven: Yale University Press, pp. 378–414.

Slivinski, A. (2002). 'Team Incentives and Organizational Form', *Journal of Public Economic Theory*, 4: 185–206.

Social Finance, Inc. (2012). 'A New Tool for Scaling Impact: How Social Impact Bonds Can Mobilize Private Capital to Advance Social Good', available at: <http://www.socialfinanceus.org/sites/socialfinanceus.org/files/small.SocialFinanceWPSingleFINAL_0.pdf>.

Social Investment Forum Foundation (2010). 'Report on Socially Responsible Investing Trends in the United States 2010, Executive Summary', available at: <http://ussif.org/resources/pubs/trends/documents/2010TrendsES.pdf>.

Starke, C. (2012). 'Serving the Many or Serving the Most Needy?' *Economics of Governance*, 13(4): 365–86.

Steinberg, R. (1987). 'Nonprofits and the Market', in W. W. Powell (ed.), *The Nonprofit Sector: A Research Handbook*. New Haven: Yale University Press, pp. 118–40.

Steinberg, R. (2006). 'Economic Theories of Nonprofit Organizations', in W. W. Powell and R. Steinberg (eds.), *The Nonprofit Sector: A Research Handbook, Second Edition*. New Haven: Yale University Press, pp. 117–39.

Steinberg, R., and Weisbrod, B. A. (1998). 'Pricing and Rationing by Nonprofit Organizations with Distributional Objectives', in B. A. Weisbrod (ed.), *To Profit or Not to Profit: The Commercial Transformation of the Nonprofit Sector*. New York: Cambridge University Press, pp. 65–82.

Steinberg, R. and Weisbrod, B. A. (2005). 'Nonprofits with Distributional Objectives: Price Discrimination and Corner Solutions', *Journal of Public Economics*, 89: 2205–30.

Strom, S. (2010). 'Hybrid Model for Nonprofits Hits Snags', *New York Times*, October 25, available at: <http://www.nytimes.com/2010/10/26/business/26hybrid.html?_r=0>.

Strom, S. (2011). 'A Quest for Hybrid Companies that Profit, but Can Tap Charity', *The New York Times* (October 13).

Social Investment Consultancy (2010). Press release, March 23, 2010, available at: <http://www.tsiconsultancy.com/corporate-giving-to-be-cut-by-a-third/>.

Thaler, R. (1980). 'Towards a Positive Theory of Consumer Choice', *Journal of Economic Behavior and Organization*, 1: 39–60.

Webb, N. J., and Farmer, A. (1996). 'Corporate Goodwill: A Game Theoretic Approach to the Effect of Corporate Charitable Expenditures on Firm Behavior', *Annals of Public and Cooperative Economics*, 67: 29–50.

Wedig, G. (1994). 'Risk, Leverage, Donations and Dividends-in-Kind: A Theory of Not-for-profit Financial Behavior', *International Review of Economics and Finance*, 3: 257–78.

Weisbrod, B. (1975). 'Toward a Theory of the Voluntary Nonprofit Sector in a Three-Sector Economy', in E. S. Phelps (ed.), *Altruism, Morality, and Economic Theory*. New York: Russell Sage Foundation.

Wikipedia (2012). <http://en.wikipedia.org/wiki/Takeovers>.

Yunus, M. (2010). Excerpt from *Building Social Business: The New Kind of Capitalism that Serves Humanity's Most Pressing Needs*, as cited at: <http://www.businessweek.com/smallbiz/content/jun2010/sb2010067_884209.htm>.

3 Financing social innovation

Dennis R. Young

Introduction

Even after two decades, public understanding of social enterprise is limited and even those involved in the field argue frequently about what is and is not a real social enterprise. A basic issue is whether social enterprise necessarily involves new forms of organization such as social purpose businesses or social co-operatives or whether it also encompasses the activities of conventional forms such as commercial activities of not-for-profit organizations or corporate social responsibility programmes of business corporations. In short, there is no consensus on the boundaries between social enterprises per se and conventional businesses, government, or not-for-profit organizations. Nonetheless, a common view is that social enterprises are market-based ventures that balance financial success with social purpose but are nonetheless financed by income earned in the private marketplace. This view applies to both social enterprises pursued within the context of not-for-profit organizations and in newer forms including variants of social purpose (for-profit) businesses. In the former case, social enterprises are seen to contribute to a not-for-profit organization's social mission in part by generating profits that can cross-subsidize mainstream mission-focused programmes. In the latter case, social enterprises are viewed as successful businesses that have found market niches that are both profitable and socially beneficial.

In fact, most social enterprises are more complex than the stereotypes suggest. The various limited conceptions of social enterprise can easily lead to overly narrow views of what is needed for the financing and growth of the field as a whole. Not-for-profit market-based ventures may or may not be profitable, while social businesses may depend directly or indirectly on philanthropic or public sector capital and operating revenue. Moreover, many social enterprises consist of multifaceted partnerships of business, not-for-profit, and governmental agencies, and are sustained by a mix of different streams of operating income. This much has been recognized elsewhere (Depedri, 2010). What has received less attention is how these various initiatives are capitalized, and who provides the investment to set them up or to expand them when they have growth opportunities.

The fact that social enterprises finance themselves from sources other than earned revenue should be of little surprise. After all, these ventures are intended to produce public as well as private benefits; hence, it is likely that sources supportive of public benefits, such as government and philanthropy, would contribute to their support. Moreover, if socially motivated and pragmatic entrepreneurs drive social ventures, then there is no reason to expect that these entrepreneurs would ignore or avoid any legitimate source of support (Young and Grinsfelder, 2011). Indeed, it seems more likely that social entrepreneurs are agnostic to both sources of support and organizational vehicles (not-for-profit or business) through which to pursue their intended balance of social impact and material gain.

This chapter provides an overview of the varieties of social investment, and consider the challenges that those involved in this developing field face. To do so there is a need first to illustrate the range and rich tapestry of social enterprises and their funding, in order to make the point that social enterprise is a very diverse, multi-sectoral phenomenon that finances itself through a variety of mixes of governmental, philanthropic, and market-based income and capital investment. It follows that a cross-sectoral theory of social enterprise finance is required to understand both the complex patterns of finance of contemporary social enterprises and the kinds of financing strategies that can best support future social enterprise ventures.

Towards this end, the subsequent section of the chapter introduces the benefits theory of not-for-profit finance (Young, 2007, 2010). This theory was developed initially to explain and assist with the development of the operating income portfolios of conventional not-for-profit organizations—so it needs to be broadened if it is to encompass the challenges of the wider field of social enterprise.

That is the task of the following section where benefits theory is extended along two dimensions. First, the theory can be applied to a variety of social purpose organizational forms outside the arena of not-for-profit organizations alone. Second, the theory, which has focused to date on the demand for the services of social purpose (not-for-profit) organizations, can be extended to consider how social entrepreneurs finance their ventures by matching their mission interests with the potential sources of finance deriving from the mix of public and private benefits their ventures provide.

Finally, the development and application of the benefits theory leads us to explore the challenges of social enterprise finance. This research suggests that each prospective source for financing social ventures has its own serious limitations. Hence it seems likely that social enterprises will be perennially undercapitalized relative to the benefits they can potentially offer—*unless* compensatory entrepreneurial strategies and public policies are enacted.

Note that the discussion here focuses mostly, but not exclusively, on developments and examples from the USA. However, social enterprise is a worldwide phenomenon—its various interpretations and variations in form and focus inform and enrich the discussion. Indeed, the first use of the term social enterprise is said to emanate from Italy, and certainly developments in Europe are highly relevant to the full understanding of this topic in the USA and elsewhere (Defourny and Nyssens, 2008).

A thousand flowers are blooming

While Mao Tse Tung might not approve, the diversity of social enterprise is apparent at two levels. First, there is a variety of legal and structural forms through which social enterprise can be organized and this variety is growing—especially with new forms of social business. Second, within broad categories of social enterprise, such as not-for-profits, co-operatives, social purpose businesses, and various combinations thereof, there are widely varying approaches to the financing of social ventures. Indeed, the blurring of the borderlines between sectors and among sources of finance in the pursuit of social missions is so prominent that it has achieved its own almost iconic name—*hybridization* (Billis, 2010).

The blurring of sector boundaries and the mixing of sources of finance is testimony to the creativity of social entrepreneurs and their frustration with the capacity of conventional forms to accommodate imaginative social innovations, raise sufficient financial support for those innovations, or accommodate the mixed public/private motivations driving entrepreneurs, investors, and philanthropists. For example, some of the new business forms are intended to attract investors who seek investments that produce both financial returns and social benefits while protecting managers and directors from litigation by profit-maximizing shareholders. Other new business forms are intended to leverage greater levels of philanthropic investment by encouraging foundations to include programme-related investments in their endowment portfolios to supplement their conventional grant-making. Alternatively, commercial ventures, partnerships or profit-making subsidiaries of conventional not-for-profit organizations are intended both to generate new net revenues to support mainstream mission-focused activities but also to contribute to mission in new ways such as employing workers who are otherwise unemployable because of physical or behavioural challenges or other factors such as criminal records or skill deficits, and educating them with skills and habits required to succeed in the workplace. A few illustrations in the categories of not-for-profit organizations, new forms of business enterprise, and combinations of for-profit and not-for-profit forms, will demonstrate the richness of the present tapestry of social enterprise.

SOCIAL ENTERPRISES IN NOT-FOR-PROFIT FORM

A broad definition of social enterprise—ventures with a social purpose operating in the private marketplace—would include traditional not-for-profit organizations whether or not they engaged in commercial ventures or relied substantially on earned income. By this standard, it may be observed that these organizations rely on a highly varied mix of income sources. In the USA, overall, for reporting public charities (those with incomes exceeding $25,000 and excluding churches), approximately 46 per cent of revenues derive from fees for services paid from private sources while another 24 per cent derive from fees for services paid by government. Government grants account for another 8 per cent while private contributions and investment income constitute 12 per cent and 8 per cent of revenues, respectively (Wing, Roeger, and Pollak, 2010). This overall mix varies considerably by field of service, however. Combining fees from both private and public sources, reliance on earned (fee) income ranges from 88 per cent in the health-care field, to 56 per cent in education, to 53 per cent in human services, to 25 per cent for environmental organizations (Wing, Pollak, and Blackwood, 2008). Similarly, reliance on charitable donations ranges from 67 per cent for internationally focused not-for-profits, to 48 per cent and 41 per cent for environmental and arts organizations respectively, to 16 per cent and 4 per cent for human services and health-care organizations respectively. There is also substantial variation in income mixes within these broad fields as well. In all, the variety of income mixes among US not-for-profits demonstrates several key points: For this variety of social enterprise, earned income while important and even dominant in certain fields, is by far not the only important source of income. Moreover, the mix of income sources varies by the type of mission in which a not-for-profit is engaged.

Certainly, it is not surprising that not-for-profit charitable organizations rely on charitable and public sources of support as well as earned income. What may be more interesting, however, is that fact that ventures by these organizations, explicitly framed as social enterprises, also rely on more than just earned income, for both the short and long run. Consider a few examples:

- Goodwill of North Georgia, a not-for-profit whose mission is 'to put people to work', operates thrift stores, donation centres, career centres and a variety of job-training and employment services. It relies heavily for its operating revenues on the sale of donated goods sold through its thrift stores, but also receives (monetary) charitable donations and as well as government funding for its employment services
- College Summit is a not-for-profit whose mission is to increase the numbers of high school students from low-income school districts applying to college. It does this by working with public school districts and partnering with universities and colleges anxious to increase quality applications from these districts. The universities and colleges pay fees to College Summit, which also raises grant funds from foundations and secures substantial government funding as well
- The Georgia Justice Project (GJP) is a not-for-profit that provides free legal services and social and employment assistance to indigent criminal offenders. As an in-house for-profit programme, GJP operated the New Horizon Landscaping Company from 1993 to 2011 to provide jobs and job training for clients whose criminal records made them hard to employ. New

Horizon Landscaping provided some fee revenue to the Georgia Justice Project which relies most heavily on charitable donations.

In summary, social enterprise ventures undertaken within the traditional framework of not-for-profit organizations do not rely exclusively on market revenues or traditional investors to finance these enterprises. Nor do they necessarily generate profits to support the overall organizational mission. Experiences vary but it is just as likely that the ventures contribute directly to mission rather than simply serve as an earned income strategy.

SOCIAL PURPOSE BUSINESSES

Much of the recent interest in social enterprise has been focused on the engagement of for-profit business forms to pursue social goals. This line of development actually has a substantial history beginning with the development of corporate philanthropy (Burlingame and Young, 1996). In recent years, corporations have come to embrace the notion of 'corporate social responsibility' as a sensible strategy for long-run profitability. Now, however, there is broader interest by 'social entrepreneurs' and 'social investors' in employing the business form to achieve social purposes for their own sake, not just as a means to greater profits. This 'double bottom-line' thinking has resulted both in the establishment of conventional businesses devoted to certain social goals, and in new legal forms of business that explicitly balance social and financial goals. In some of these instances, the line between philanthropy and investment blurs as investor/donors seek to put their capital into organizations and projects that will result in some combination of financial and social returns to their investments. Consider the following examples:

- Newman's Own is a for-profit corporation whose owners have decided to donate all of its profits to designated charities
- Last Chance Thrift Store in Atlanta, Georgia, is a family-owned business that received donated merchandise from the not-for-profit AADD (All About Developmental Disabilities) and turned over a fixed percentage of gross revenues to AADD
- Ben & Jerry's is a well-known public corporation which embraced social (environmental, workplace, and other) goals. Unilever bought out the firm and there is some question about the degree to which the new owner maintains the social focus
- WCLV was a for-profit radio station in Cleveland, Ohio, devoted to 'keeping classical music on the radio'. When the owners retired they wanted to ensure that WCLV's mission was maintained. In a complex series of transactions the station was sold to the local (not-for-profit) public radio/television station IdeaStream that integrated WCLV with its existing public broadcasting stations

- Better World Books (BWB) is an online book retailer whose mission is to promote global literacy in an environmentally conscious manner by donating a portion of sales to over eighty domestic and international literacy organizations such as Books for Africa, Room to Read, Worldfund, and Invisible Children. BWB is organized as a 'B Corporation' which is essentially a conventional business that has met the standards established by B Lab, a not-for-profit organization that certifies that businesses meet their social goals.

These various cases illustrate a number of important points. First, it is clear that the management or ownership of a profitable for-profit corporation may pursue laudatory social goals if they so choose, assuming they have a profitable (or breakeven) strategy for doing so. However, as the Ben & Jerry and WCLV cases illustrate, there is also no assurance that a balanced approach to profits and social impact will continue beyond present ownership. Moreover, while balanced pursuit of social and financial goals may proceed relatively easily for sole proprietorships or firms held closely by a small group of investors who agree on their goals, the same does not apply to firms with a more diversified ownership base. In particular, if some investors in more widely held businesses insist on pursuing maximum profits, the managing directors can be held liable if they make decisions seen to compromise profit-making. This realization is what has led to the development of new (and still experimental) legal forms of business, such as Low-profit Limited Liability Companies (L3Cs), Benefit Corporations, and other variations which give legal sanction to such decisions. Furthermore, these new forms open the door to investment by philanthropic institutions. In particular, the L3C form offers the possibility to charitable foundations to invest part of their endowment portfolios in L3Cs, where they can finance so-called programme-related investments that provide a financial return and also advance a social purpose. As well, it is thought that the new forms of social business may attract new kinds of 'donors' who want some return on their invested funds but also value the achievement of a social purpose. In all, the variety of for-profit social businesses that have emerged suggest that the financing of social enterprise, even in this guise, may be broadly financed by more than just commercial income and suppliers of financial capital seeking the highest financial return on their investments.

CO-OPERATIVES AND OTHER FORMS

In Europe, Quebec, and elsewhere, the term 'social economy' is used to connote the 'Third Sector' outside of government and business, where associations, foundations, co-operatives, and other 'related not-for-profit private forms of enterprises' (Defourny and Nyssens, 2008: 204) operate to serve the needs of society or various needy or worthy groups and constituencies therein. It is within this general context that 'social enterprises' operate, especially in the form of co-operatives. It is interesting, however, that not all co-operatives are considered social enterprises. Indeed, 'social co-operatives' are distinguished from other co-operatives as 'serving a broader community and putting more emphasis on the ... general interest' whereas other co-operatives are 'primarily oriented toward members' interests' (Defourny and Nyssens, 2008: 205). Social co-operatives have been established as a separate legal type in several European countries including Italy, France, Portugal, and Greece. The membership of, and stakeholders in, these co-operatives is often (but not always) diverse and is generally reflected in their governance. Moreover, these co-operatives are restricted in the degree to which they can distribute financial surpluses to members. Social co-operatives support themselves through market sales but are also often substantially funded by government and tied to specific areas of public policy, notably integration of marginalized populations into the workforce and other areas of social service. There is an interesting parallel between social and conventional co-operatives on the one hand, and ordinary versus the new social business forms in the USA. In particular, the managers and directors of social co-operatives and social businesses are both legally protected from liability when they make decisions that do not maximize the direct interests of their stockholders or members. Thus, while all co-operatives inherently pursue the collective interests of their members (whether they are workers, consumers, or other such groups), the social co-operative form allows co-operatives to broaden their focus to the larger interests of society.

In the United Kingdom, the Community Interest Company (CIC) has emerged as another prominent form of social enterprise. CICs are an interesting hybrid between a not-for-profit and a business corporation. Established under law in 2005, more than 1,400 such organizations now operate in the UK. CICs are legally required to operate for the benefit of the community but may also pay limited dividends to external shareholders (subject to a dividend cap) and financially compensate their board members (Chertok, Hamoui, and Jamison, 2008). CICs may be publicly owned (by government) or privately owned. However, while CICs have investors (stockholders) they also feature an 'asset lock' that requires that their assets (including profits) be used for the benefit of the community and either retained by the company, sold for fair market value, or transferred to another asset-locked body (Regulator of Community Interest Companies, 2010).

SOCIAL ENTERPRISE COMBINATIONS

As discussed by Cordes, Poletz, and Steuerle (2009), social enterprise can be pursued in the context of various combinations of not-for-profit and for-profit forms arrayed together as different kinds of conglomerates. This strategy allows ventures to draw on alternative sources of public, private, and charitable income as well as providing flexibility and prospective clarity on the goals and strategies of the various sub-units. One common approach is to establish a not-for-profit holding company that controls some mix of not-for-profit and for-profit affiliates. For example: Manchester-Bidwell Corporation, which provides skills training to challenged youth and other groups, maintains a mix of not-for-profit and for-profit entities. The former include Bidwell Training Center, Manchester Craftmen's Guild, Manchester-Bidwell Development Trust (to establish and maintain an endowment) and the Denali Institute. The former include Harbor Gardens Park which owns and manages an office building and (until 2001) Bidwell Food Services. Overall, Manchester-Bidwell received over 28 per cent of its income from earned income in 2001 and some 64 per cent from government contracts (Cordes et al., 2009). Earned income sources included cafeteria sales, and fees from classes and catering, and jazz concert tickets and CD sales.

Another approach set out by Cordes et al. (2009) is called Corporate Quid Pro Quo. A simple example is Last Chance Thrift Shop's arrangement with AADD as described above. Another more complex example is First Book which distributes new books to low income children through a system of participating local literacy programmes, and which partners with publishing and media companies. First Book operates First Book National Book Bank, which offers publishers a way to efficiently donate large volumes of unsold books, and First Book Marketplace, where registered organizations may buy deeply discounted books.

In summary, the variations in form and organizational combinations for social enterprise seem limited only by the imagination. The same may be said for the financing of these ventures. While earned income appears to be a mainstay for the operating income of social enterprise in its various manifestations, it is by no means the only source of funding. In particular, government funding and philanthropy remain critically important. Capital financing of social enterprise is also a matter of blending alternative sources of investment, including philanthropic gifts and 'programme-related investments', retained earnings, government funding, and traditional (but socially sensitive) investment by venture capitalists and stockholders.

A benefits theory of social enterprise

The variegated pattern of financing for social enterprise raises several related questions—how can the observed patterns of finance for social enterprises be explained, and are the available strategies of finance sufficient to support social enterprise at an efficient level? If it is posited that engagement in social enterprise in part reflects efforts to expand social purpose programming beyond the levels possible through traditional governmental and philanthropic organizational forms and sources of finance, then what are the prospects for success, that is, for achieving a significant expansion of services or social impact?

To answer these questions, first requires a sense of what levels of support would be efficient by characterizing the potential demand for social enterprise; then an assessment of the potential for tapping into that demand through social entrepreneurship. This chapter uses 'demand for social enterprise' in the economists' sense here, that is, is how much society is willing to pay—through various means—for the outputs of these ventures? And it views social entrepreneurs as supply-side agents attempting to secure resources, subject to the limitations and constraints associated with the various manifestations of funding—earned income, philanthropy, government funding, etc.—through which demand can be expressed.

A benefits theory of social enterprise is a natural extension of the benefits theory of not-for-profit finance recently advanced by Young (2007) and colleagues, and confirmed in recent empirical papers that show that the public/private character of services produced by not-for-profit organizations in the USA correlate with the proportions of income derived from earned income versus philanthropy (Fischer, Wilsker, and Young, 2011; Young, Wilsker, and Grinsfelder, 2010; Wilsker and Young, 2010). The concept is straightforward:

- to the extent that not-for-profits produce private goods whose benefits accrue to specific individuals from which they can be excluded if they fail to pay (e.g. admission to a museum), they can charge fees to capture those benefits
- to the degree that not-for-profits produce collective benefits to specific target groups, for example, those vulnerable to a particular disease or alumni of a particular university, they can effectively appeal specifically to those groups for charitable contributions
- to the degree that not-for-profits produce society-wide collective benefits, they can appeal or qualify for governmental funding supported by taxation
- and to the degree that not-for-profits can engage in quid pro quo arrangements with sponsors (such as corporations who may benefit from association with the social enterprise), they can engage in exchanges of services for monetary or in-kind support with those sponsors.

In each of these cases, there is a specific source of demand (willingness to pay) and a particular mechanism through which demand may potentially be tapped. The challenge in each case is to overcome the transactions costs associated with identifying the beneficiaries and collecting income from them. Each of those mechanisms presents different challenges. (Nonetheless, as discussed above, a typical social enterprise would involve several of these sources of income.) It is the charge of the social entrepreneur to both identify the potential transactions and to find ways of addressing the challenges. These challenges vary from source to source.

Earned income requires the ability to exclude beneficiaries if they are unwilling to pay the stipulated price. This can be costly if the organization is not set up to market its services, process payments, and avoid mishandling of funds. More importantly, for a social enterprise the provision of a private good may be associated with a redistributive mission goal—for example, accessibility of pre-school education to children from low-income families. In this case, the social enterprise will want to design a sliding-scale price schedule to accommodate those who cannot pay high fees, and/or it may wish to offer scholarships to children from low income families. Those scholarships may be viewed as collective goods that could appeal to philanthropy or government for support. Thus, fee income in such cases, although feasible, may be intrinsically limited by the enterprise's social goals.

Philanthropy to pay for collective benefits for an identified group, such as alumni of a college or a group at risk for a genetic disease, is of course subject to the classical free rider programme. Since benefits are indivisible and not subject to exclusion, appeal must be made to altruistic motives, inevitably resulting in a shortfall between value received (potential willingness to pay) and actual contributions. Several strategies are available to overcome free riding, such as selective private incentives (e.g. calendars, tee shirts), and social pressure (e.g. listing of donors in programmes or annual reports or personal soliciting by peers), but the degree to which these can be effective varies from case to case.

Government funding requires identification of existing funding programs for which the social enterprise may be eligible and/or lobbying for new programmes or special projects. For small enterprises, political engagement may be out of reach, as might the capacity to manage and report on the expenditure of government funds. Moreover, existing programmes are likely to be limited to offerings that appeal to a large number of citizens so as to reflect majority rule or coalitions of active voting groups. Government funding also typically requires sophistication in grant-writing and reporting. All these factors will vary by field of service and will limit the degree to which government funding can be secured to support public goods dimensions of social enterprise activity.

Sponsorship by corporations or other forms of quid pro quo support depend on finding what analysts of barter call a 'double-coincidence of wants' (Ben-Ner, 1993). The social enterprise must identify some special benefit that it can offer to a sponsor in exchange for some resource or funding that it needs. The benefits may be related or peripheral to the mission of the organization. For example, the (not-for-profit) social enterprise called Ka-Boom! that constructs playgrounds for children in low-income urban neighborhoods, receives building supplies from Home Depot in exchange for the public relations value received by the company for its association with this initiative. Similarly, Timberland provides CityYear with cash and volunteers as well as boots, gear, and uniforms for CityYear corps members in exchange for substantial public recognition as well as morale benefits to Timberland employees who volunteer. On a more modest scale, docents who volunteer for arts organizations receive personal satisfaction and free access to collections and performances. The limitations on this source of finance derive from its intrinsic character as barter, requiring careful search for appropriate partners and matching of mutual benefits. This process can be expensive, risky, and tenuous. The wrong partners can do damage to a social enterprise's reputation, for example, if the corporation is involved in a scandal (e.g. Enron) or in a business antithetical to the social enterprise's mission (e.g. tobacco funding of a health-care organization). Corporate sponsors can be fickle or unreliable, especially if they are taken over, perform poorly in the marketplace, or their corporate headquarters are moved away from the social enterprise's local venue.

In summary, applying benefits theory, the social entrepreneur faces challenges on all fronts in his or her effort to construct a robust income portfolio since each generic source of income is subject to limitations and restraining factors that preclude taking maximum advantage of the potential willingness to pay of prospective beneficiaries. Moreover, this argument can be extended to sources of capital for the start-up and growth of social enterprise ventures.

Capital financing and benefits theory

Capital financing may be defined as funding gathered and accumulated for the purpose of spending on relatively large 'capital' projects such as buildings and art collections, or less tangible expenses such as start-up funds for a new venture; such funds 'are needed to move a project forward, and those funds are needed in relatively large amounts over a relatively short period of time' (Yetman, 2010: 59). The purpose of capital funding is investment in the future rather than current consumption of operating resources (Tuckman, 1993). Sources of capital funding for not-for-profits include debt, programme-related investments, gifts and grants from individuals, foundations, corporations, or government, and accumulated internally generated cash from operating surpluses (Tuckman, 1993; Yetman, 2010). Theory of capital formation for not-for-profit organizations is undeveloped (Yetman, 2010) and the same may be said of social enterprise more broadly. Here, this chapter applies the same benefits theory rationale to capital finance as to operating income of social enterprise, by associating prospective sources of capital for social enterprise with the nature of benefits provided, as follows:

- Private benefits accruing to individual consumers can undergird capital financing through retained earnings from earned income, borrowing (e.g. from banks) against future earned income streams and equity financing based on stock ownership keyed to future earnings
- Group collective benefits accruing to identifiable communities of interest can stimulate giving of capital gifts (e.g. endowments and other large donations) from donors associated with or sympathetic to those communities

- Public (and redistributive) benefits accruing to the general public or large segments of society can elicit capital grants from large (national or regional) foundations or capital grants or contracts from government
- Exchange benefits accruing to selected partner organizations, sponsors, or groups may elicit capital gifts (monetary or in-kind) from those partners or sponsors.

Capital gifts by definition are intended to provide start-up capital, invest in capital assets such as buildings and equipment, or finance expansion or other major initiatives. Particularly at the start-up stage, sources of capital are critical to efforts by social entrepreneurs to establish and nurture social enterprise ventures, especially those that will depend in the long run on future streams of earned income, annual giving or ongoing governmental payment for services. Start-up capital is just that—resources intended to get things started before operating income streams come fully on-line. Thus, capital gifts usually require business plans that demonstrate to resource providers how the venture will be financed once the start-up capital is expended.

Overall, Figure 3.1 depicts the benefits theory as applied to the start-up of a social enterprise, focusing on the central role of social entrepreneurs in gauging the prospective sources not just of operating income, but also of capital financing—and making the appropriate matches with the mission, services, and benefits of the venture.

Essentially, as the figure illustrates, social entrepreneurs are market makers or catalysts, simultaneously shaping their enterprises to appeal to suppliers of

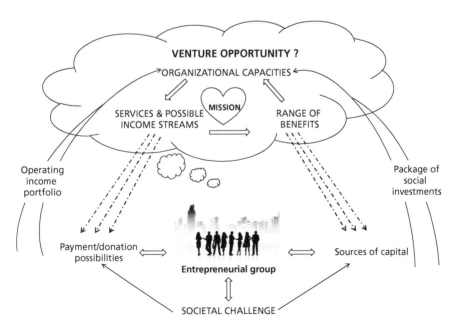

Figure 3.1. A benefits theory of social enterprise capital finance

capital while soliciting that capital to support their visions. As part of that appeal they must show that they can generate operating income to sustain and renew the enterprise. Their efforts presumably will succeed if they can match the promised benefits of their ventures with the interests of the sources of prospective capital, whether that is banks, foundations, individuals, government agencies, or corporate sponsors. At the same time, they will employ whatever organizational form or combination of forms will support the selection of the appropriate capital sources.

Thus, if for-profit investors are the likely source of capital then some form of business corporation would be favoured, whereas if philanthropy is the most likely source, the not-for-profit corporate form would more likely be chosen. Combinations of these forms, or possibly hybrid forms such as not-for-profits with for-profit subsidiaries or social purpose businesses, would accommodate multiple sources of capital funding.

Limits to the capital financing of social enterprise

The benefits theory analysis of capital financing of social enterprise reveals multifold limits for each prospective source that appear to preclude reaching the full potential of support for these ventures. These limits may be summarized as follows.

If social enterprises generate private goods and services that can be sold to individuals on a fee basis, then, through some form of business venture, they can create streams of future earnings that may permit capital financing through surplus accumulation, sale of stock, or borrowing against future earnings. However, this may be limited by the fact that some of these private goods and services may be intended to serve disadvantaged populations or, in order to enhance mission impact, should be produced in quantities exceeding the amount that would clear in a free market, thus constraining or even eliminating profits. Assuming positive but constrained profits, sale of stock or borrowing may still attract individual or corporate investors who seek some satisfying combination of personal and social return but it seems likely that the pool of such investment capital will be substantially smaller than that offered by investors who seek maximum financial returns at some given level of risk. This is, of course, an empirical question that the new forms of social business, such as L3Cs and Benefit Corporations are eager to test.

If social enterprises generate collective benefits limited to specific groups of beneficiaries, they can pursue capital gifts from those beneficiaries. Despite various compensating strategies, however, such as social pressure and selective incentives (e.g. naming opportunities) it seems likely that free rider tendencies will persist to some degree. It is possible that changes in millionaire/billionaire culture such as that preached by Bill Gates and Warren Buffet will alter this picture but in fact the number of major givers compared to the overall number of wealthy people is small. Thus, philanthropy (of all varieties) is likely to remain within its historical bounds around 2 per cent of national income, probably well below the value of collective benefits received by groups (such as university alumni, at-risk groups, faith-based communities, art-loving groups) to which wealthy individuals subscribe.

If social enterprises generate society-wide benefits or benefits to major population groups which are of general concern to the electorate or to viable political coalitions, then government start-up or other capital funding becomes another option. This requires a great deal of consensus as well as political skill and effort, especially in the current era of conservatism and preferences for limited government. Since social enterprises are often focused and idiosyncratic many would not qualify for existing government funding or find champions in government.

Finally, social enterprises often have something to offer to specific corporate or other partners in exchange for capital support. However, sponsorships and other partnering exchanges require finding the right match-ups in a thin, idiosyncratic marketplace. Moreover, these exchanges are often based on considerations outside the specific mission focus of a social enterprise—that is, it involves not so much selling of the enterprise's mission, services, and benefits as determining what the prospective partner requires and how that matches up with the capacities of the social enterprise venture to accommodate those requirements. Many social enterprises succeed in finding their ideal corporate partners but many do not, and it remains unclear whether there are logical partners for all such ventures.

Conclusion

This chapter has offered an overview of the varieties of social investment and considered the challenges faced by those involved in developing the field of social enterprise. It has illustrated the range and rich tapestry of social enterprises and their funding in order to make the point that social enterprise is a very diverse, multi-sectoral phenomenon that finances itself through a variety of mixes of governmental, philanthropic, and market-based income and capital investment. Social entrepreneurs themselves are opportunistic and often agnostic to sources and sectors from which they draw capital and establish income streams. Their activity can be seen as essentially transactional; support is exchanged for benefits received by the parties that finance social enterprises. As a result, successful social innovation requires entrepreneurs to find the appropriate mix of commercial investment, philanthropy, and governmental support.

Thus a cross-sectoral theory of social enterprise finance is required to understand both the complex patterns of finance of contemporary social enterprises and the kinds of financing strategies that can best support future social enterprise ventures. Accordingly, this chapter advances the benefits theory of social venture finance by examining the supply-side activity of social entrepreneurs. In so doing, it identifies the challenges that social entrepreneurs face in financing their projects. In particular, social enterprises often seek to provide private benefits to individuals with limited ability to pay, leading to limitations on private investment, retained earnings, and borrowing. Such enterprises also require philanthropic investments to finance the externalities, public goods, or redistributional benefits they offer to particular communities of interest, hence facing the free-riding limitations of this source of support. In addition, social enterprises produce community-wide benefits that can be financed by government but which are also constrained by majority preferences. Finally, social entrepreneurs can often identify 'exchange benefits' with corporate and other sponsors that offer special private benefits in return for support of public benefits, but these too are limited by the need to identify activities of mutual interest to social enterprises and their sponsors and the capacity of social enterprises to provide these additional activities.

The benefits framework tells us also that there are vast potentials for supporting social enterprise from a variety of sources, including the private marketplace, philanthropy, government, and exchange arrangements with corporate or other sponsors or partners. As such, the proponents of social entrepreneurship may be right, that there are many new combinations to be explored and hence many creative possibilities for supporting social enterprise work once the narrow boundaries of sector-specific thinking are breached. There has been a new surge of such creativity with the invention of new forms of social business and new approaches to social enterprise finance, such as programme-related investments and social impact bonds (Young, Salamon, and Grinsfelder, 2012).

Nonetheless, this chapter has argued that each of the basic sources of social enterprise finance is intrinsically limited by free-rider, political, or thin market effects and the extent to which these limitations can be substantially overcome remains unclear at this juncture. In the end, it may be that the combination of creative new forms of organization cannot overcome the intrinsic limitations of the four generic sources of social enterprise capital (markets, government, philanthropy, and exchange) and that a substantial degree of market failure and underfinancing of worthwhile social enterprise initiatives will remain.

Still, the benefits theory suggests that social entrepreneurs can do much to expand the support of social ventures by linking the sources of latent demand to the supply of services and benefits in creative ways. They can also add an evangelical element, perhaps creating demand through articulation of the benefits of their good works. At this stage in the development of social enterprise, it is not clear how far these entrepreneurial efforts can go towards creating social impacts well beyond the boundaries of conventional public and not-for-profit sector approaches.

Thus, it is important to ask what can be done at the policy level to address these issues. A possible approach would be to develop a societal consensus around the need for investment capital in social enterprise and a mechanism for government support of these ventures. Tax incentives already exist for encouraging charitable contributions to not-for-profits. These could be extended and amplified to apply to social enterprise more broadly defined. Start-up capital funds could be created, perhaps on a revolving basis with incentives for private as well as governmental contributions, so that prospective social entrepreneurs with new ideas or plans for building upon initial successes could be evaluated and supported. Rules for the management of earned income could be changed to encourage faster accumulation of operating surpluses so that social investments could be accelerated. And markets for ownership in social businesses could be structured to attract greater numbers of socially minded investors. The future will witness many experiments along these various lines, and others not yet anticipated.

■ REFERENCES

Ben-Ner, A. (1993). 'Obtaining Resources Using Barter Trade: Benefits and Drawbacks', in D. C. Hammack and D. R. Young (eds.), *Nonprofit Organizations in a Market Economy*. San Francisco: Jossey-Bass Publishers, pp. 278–93.

Billis, D. (ed.) (2010). *Hybrid Organizations and the Third Sector*. New York: Palgrave Macmillan.

Burlingame, D. and Young, D. R. (eds.) (1996). *Corporate Philanthropy at the Crossroads*. Indianapolis: Indiana University Press.

Chertok, M., Hammoui, J., and Jamison, E. (2008). 'The Funding Gap', *Stanford Social Innovation Review*, 6(2) Spring: 44–51.

Cordes, J. J., Poletz, Z., and Steuerle, C. E. (2009). 'Examples of Nonprofit-for-profit Hybrid Business Models', in J. J. Cordes and C. E. Steuerle (eds.), *Not-for-profits & Business*. Washington, DC: The Urban Institute Press, pp. 69–82.

Defourny, J. and Nyssens, M. (2008). 'Social Enterprise in Europe: Recent Trends and Developments', *Social Enterprise Journal*, 4(3): 202–28.

Depedri, S. (2010). 'The Competitive Advantages of Social Enterprise', in L. Becchetti and C. Borzaga (eds.), *The Economics of Social Responsibility*. Abingdon, Oxon: Routledge, pp. 34–54.

Fischer, R. L., Wilsker, A. L., and Young, D. R. (2011). 'Exploring the Revenue Mix of Nonprofit Organizations—Does it relate to Publicness?' *Nonprofit and Voluntary Sector Quarterly*, 40(4): 662–81.

Regulator of Community Interest Companies (2010). 'Information Pack: Community Interest Companies', BIS: Department for Business Innovation & Skills, March.

Tuckman, H. P. (1993). 'How and Why Nonprofits Obtain Capital', in D. C. Hammack and D. R. Young (eds.), *Nonprofit Organizations in a Market Economy*. San Francisco: Jossey-Bass Publishers, pp. 203–32.

Wilsker, A. L. and Young, D. R. (2010). 'How Does Program Composition Affect the Revenues of Nonprofit Organizations? Investigating a Benefits Theory of Nonprofit Finance', *Public Finance Review*, 38(2): 193–216.

Wing, K. T., Pollak, T. H., and Blackwood, A. (2008). *The Nonprofit Almanac 2008*. Washington, DC: The Urban Institute Press.

Wing, K. T., Roeger, K. L., and Pollak, T. H. (2010). *The Nonprofit Sector in Brief.* Washington, DC: The Urban Institute.

Yetman, R. J. (2010). 'Capital Formation', in B. A. Seaman and D. R. Young (eds), *Handbook of Research on Not-for-profit Economics and Management.* Northampton, MA: Edward Elgar Publishers, pp. 59–68.

Young, D. R. (ed.) (2007). *Financing Not-for-profits: Putting Theory into Practice.* Lanham, MD: Alta-Mira Press.

Young, D. R. (2010). 'Nonprofit Finance: Developing Not-for-profit Resources', in D. O. Renz and Associates (eds.), *Jossey-Bass Handbook of Not-for-profit Leadership and Management*, 3rd edition. San Francisco: Jossey-Bass, pp. 482–504.

Young, D. R. and Grinsfelder, M. C. (2011). 'Social Entrepreneurship and the Financing of Third Sector Organizations', *Journal of Public Affairs Education*, 17(4): pp. 543–67.

Young, D. R., Salamon, L. M., and Grinsfelder, M. C. (2012). 'Commercialization, Social Ventures and For-Profit Competition', in L. M. Salamon (ed.), *The State of Not-for-profit America*, 2nd edition. Washington, DC: Brookings Institution Press, pp. 521–48.

Young, D. R., Wilsker, A. L., and Grinsfelder, M. C. (2010). 'Understanding the Determinants of Nonprofit Income Portfolios', *Voluntary Sector Review*, 1(2): 161–73.

4 Philanthrocapitalism comes of age

Matthew Bishop and Michael Green

Introduction

As Lehman Brothers, one of the world's largest and seemingly invincible financial institutions, crashed to earth in 2008 triggering a global economic crisis on a scale not seen since the 1930s, we launched a book that set out an optimistic vision for what business, in general, and wealthy entrepreneurs, in particular, could do to solve some of the world's biggest problems. That book, *Philanthrocapitalism* (Bishop and Green, 2008) described the way that a new generation of entrepreneur philanthropists are using the tools of business to achieve impact on key global problems. Such approaches included charitable giving that drew lessons from the hedge fund and venture capital industries. It also included techniques that do not involve traditional grant making, such as social or impact investing. In a broader sense, it also looked at the reorientation of capitalism towards ways of making money that are socially and environmentally sustainable, embracing, but going beyond, corporate social responsibility.

Philanthrocapitalism clashed with the zeitgeist of the dark, frightening times in 2008. In the years since the crisis began, economic recovery has been fitful and business leaders, particularly in the financial sector, have struggled to reimagine themselves as socially useful. Yet philanthrocapitalism, as a quasi-movement, has continued to develop.

Giving by wealthy entrepreneurial donors did not cease, as some predicted (Mulgan, 2009). Indeed, led by Bill Gates and Warren Buffett, it has thrived, with more than ninety American billionaires having signed up by the end of 2012 to a 'Giving Pledge' to dedicate at least half their fortunes to philanthropy. And, as Bishop (2006) noted in the special report in *The Economist* in which he first coined the term 'philanthrocapitalism', these new philanthropists continue to apply insights and language drawn from the business world as they go about their giving. The spread of social media-based giving and crowdfunding platforms—such as Kiva—has continued to extend to the general public some of the direct engagement and greater accountability enjoyed traditionally only by wealthy donors. Innovation in using market-based solutions and social or impact investing tools to tackle societies' ills has boomed. Finally, a growing number of corporations are embracing the creed of 'doing well by doing good' and focus on 'creating shared value' (Porter and Kramer, 2011).

Perhaps the most significant measure of how philanthrocapitalism has moved into the mainstream is the way that governments are starting to engage with these 'new' actors in solving society's toughest problems. In part this reflects governments' diminished resources, the fiscal hangover of nationaliz-ing the private sector financial crisis. This new enthusiasm for partnering with private donors is most clearly seen in the field of international development, since aid budgets are often the first line in public budgets to fall under the axe. An interesting example of this can be seen in the changes over time in the language of the Organisation for Economic Cooperation and Development's club of aid donors, known as the DAC (Development Assistance Committee) before and after the financial crisis. The 2005 'Paris Declaration on Aid Effectiveness' of the DAC makes no reference at all to philanthropy and barely mentions the private sector at all. Six years later, the 'Busan Declaration' by the same organization is littered with references to private actors, and the G20 group of the world's largest economies even commissioned Bill Gates to come up with new ideas on funding the fight against poverty for its 2011 meeting in Cannes.

Governmental interest in philanthrocapitalism is more than just an attempt to compensate for cuts in public budgets, however. Politicians are increasingly seeing partnering with private actors as a way to drive innovation in public policy and service delivery. In *Philanthrocapitalism* we described New York City Mayor Michael Bloomberg's use of philanthropic rather than public money to test controversial initiatives to reform the school system, such as elite leadership training for school principals and payments to parents to get kids into classrooms. Bloomberg's decision to use his own philanthropy to underwrite Goldman Sach's investment in one of the first Social Impact Bonds in the US provides further evidence. Since then, the idea of public–private innovation has found its clearest expression in British Prime Minister David Cameron's vision of a 'Big Society'. This policy has largely failed as a political idea, crushed by the weight of becoming synonymous in the electorate's mind with Mr. Cameron's fiscal austerity measures, which have meant significant cuts in public spending. But the Big Society idea lives on in the work that the Coalition Government has done to move forward New Labour's earlier ini-tiatives around creating a social investment market in the UK. As societies grapple with fiscal consolidation over the next generation and confront the unsustainable cost of ageing populations, it is likely that more governments will look to partnerships with philanthrocapitalists as a way to meet their welfare obligations.

The other 'demand-side' driver of philanthrocapitalism has been the grow-ing public concern, sometimes anger, at inequality. As the philosopher Slavoj Žižek has pointed out, global economic stagnation challenges the assumptions that had legitimized capitalism over the previous thirty years or so of eco-nomic boom. Without the promise of a rising tide of prosperity to lift the quality of life of all citizens, the economic debate has been increasingly framed as a 'zero-sum' battle for a share of the pie between rich and poor. We see evidence of this in the growing concern about inequality and in the ideas of the Occupy Movement of 2011 that captured the sense of frustration at the privileged 1 per cent of the population by the 99 per cent of us who make up the rest. Significant philanthropy by the rich, together with more enlightened and responsible business practices will be a minimum requirement of a new social contract that is likely to emerge from the current stand-off. However, as is already the case, there is also likely to be a growing debate about how philanthropy is regulated and incentivized through the tax system, as part of this new social contract.

It is suggested here that philanthrocapitalism is coming of age, but the question remains: how will it evolve next? To answer this question, this chapter will look at three common critiques of philanthrocapitalism: that it is an oxymoron; that it ignores wider drivers of social change; and that it seeks to privatize social justice. The chapter will then examine and draw lessons from three areas where there have been significant divergences from what was first predicted in 2008: the risk appetite of philanthropists; the role of intermediaries in the capital market for good; and the relationship between big companies and social innovation.

Profit and purpose: Friends not enemies

Philanthrocapitalism challenges a widely held view that there is a fundamental antagonism between the pursuit of profit and the general well-being of society. This argument was most colourfully expressed by Žižek in a discussion of the philanthropy of Bill Gates and George Soros in the *London Review of Books* in 2006:

There is a chocolate-flavoured laxative available on the shelves of US stores which is publicised with the paradoxical injunction: Do you have constipation? Eat more of this chocolate!—i.e. eat more of something that itself causes constipation. The structure of the chocolate laxative can be discerned throughout today's ideological landscape; it is what makes a figure like Soros so objectionable. He stands for ruthless financial exploitation combined with its counter-agent, humanitarian worry about the catastrophic social consequences of the unbridled market economy. Soros's daily routine is a lie embodied: half of his working time is devoted to financial speculation, the other half to 'humanitarian' activities (financing cultural and democratic activities in post-Communist countries, writing essays and books) which work against the effects of his own speculations.

In other words, for Žižek, a contradiction is hard-wired into the concept of philanthrocapitalism: within his framework, profit is always a product of exploitation of labour value, hence it is impossible for a capitalist to be anything but an exploiter.

This may seem an extreme, marginal critique, yet it seems to influence several critics of philanthrocapitalism. Michael Edwards, the author of a pre-emptive strike on philanthrocapitalism entitled *Just Another Emperor?* (Edwards, 2008) argued that, 'systemic change has to address the question of how property is owned and controlled, and how resources and opportunities are distributed throughout society'. This is, 'the "means of production" question that takes us back to Marx, and not just Adam Smith'. In a similar vein, Kavita Ramdas, the former CEO of the Global Fund for Women, reflecting on a meeting between Gates and Buffett and a group of Indian billionaires to promote the Giving Pledge, argued that 'far too few in this elite club are willing to ask themselves hard questions about a model of economic growth that has made their phenomenal acquisition of wealth possible in a nation where more than 800 million people still languish in poverty'. More recently Mulgan (2013) has argued persuasively for a new focus on the notion of 'lived value' in exchange contexts that challenges some of the basic tenets of pure market theory.

Whilst it is not in dispute that the capitalist system can and should be improved to serve society better, such critiques may only offer a limited set of alternative solutions. A second book, *The Road From Ruin,* has argued that before the crisis of 2008, capitalism placed too much emphasis on short-term success, most obviously through an obsession with quarterly profits and daily increases in stock prices. Now a new, improved, capitalism needs to emerge from the ruins of the old, which if it is sustainably to bring about a more prosperous world must focus instead on long-term measures of success. In this context, philanthrocapitalism can be seen as a capitalism that, to its core, embodies a commitment to be socially and environmentally sustainable.

Such an approach is not necessarily a rejection of Friedman's view that the only social responsibility of business is to maximize profits, but is rather a growing realization that a more constructive attitude to solving society's problems may increase the profits of a company over the long term, through 'enlightened self-interest'. This is a revolutionary shift in how to value our institutions that was first heralded as 'blended value' by Emerson nearly a decade ago.

For Edwards, the idea that the winners in capitalism can or will be part of a process to transform our economic system is 'akin to the man who tries to pull himself out of a swamp by his own hair'. Instead, he argued, it is the countervailing power of civil society that must drive the reform of capitalism, and solve society's problems: 'civil society and the market are not just different—they pull in opposite directions'.

Civil society clearly is crucial—something fully endorsed by leading philanthrocapitalists such as Gates, Soros, and Jeff Skoll, who are using their philanthropy to build up civil society with the goal of making it a more effective partner in solving society's problems. But properly to reflect what is happening today the definition of civil society may need to be broadened from the widely held but narrow version used by Edwards.

Civil society is different from the market because its richness and diversity are important in their own right, not just in terms of the results they deliver. Better, Edwards argued, to think of civil society as an ecosystem where diversity itself is precious, rather than a market of competitors. This framing sets philanthrocapitalism in opposition to civil society since it tends to treat civil society and not-for-profit organizations as synonymous leaving for-profit organizations, by definition, outside of civil society. 'No great social cause was mobilized through the market in the twentieth century', Edwards asserted; there is no space in this system for capitalism to play a positive civic role. Philanthrocapitalism has been assumed to be negative from the outset.

However, it could be argued that such framing ignores the way that for-profit organizations can create social or civic value. A striking recent example is Vodafone/Safaricom business MPesa—the private business venture that has driven the explosive growth in cellular phones in Africa over the past decade, which has played a massive role in the economic and political empowerment of citizens. The International Center for Research on Women has similarly identified the motor scooter, created and disseminated by for-profit businesses, as one of the top innovations empowering women in recent years. These examples suggest that profit and social value are not necessarily in contradiction. Indeed, profit may even contribute to strengthening civil society, as the Africa Media Development Initiative, led by the BBC, showed when it highlighted the importance of commercial success as a crucial part of developing a robust and independent media in Africa. Then there are all the charitable activities that for-profits do.

Philanthrocapitalism demands a re-evaluation of how we understand and define civil society. Rather than falling into the business bad/civil society good dichotomy, we should rather be open to the possibility that both for-profit and not-for-profit organizations can be part of civil society. They are just different forms of organization that generate economic and social value in different ways.

This is not a new discovery. One of the things the philanthrocapitalism concept intended to do was to locate today's trends in their historical context. The book attempted to explain how modern philanthropy emerged as a product of the European Renaissance at the same time as capitalism. Sixteenth-century entrepreneurs, who, for example, created the first micro-credit schemes and established the first charitable foundations, were as interested in philanthropy as their peers in the twenty-first century. They shared the sense of responsibility for tackling society's problems, as well as a fear of the consequences if they failed. Four previous 'golden ages of philanthropy' can be identified: the Renaissance; the emergence of joint-stock capitalism in the eighteenth century; the Victorian era; and the age of Andrew Carnegie in America. A similar pattern may be discerned today as the fifth golden age: innovations in capitalism being used by a new class of entrepreneurs to take on social problems.

Power not performance

For those suspicious of business, a second critique of philanthrocapitalism is that it brings an obsession with metrics and measurement that is a potentially dangerous distraction from the real business of changing the world. There is certainly a revolution going on in development thinking, as books such as *Poor Economics* by Duflo and Banerjee have championed the idea of using randomized control trials to test whether development interventions actually work. Several philanthrocapitalists have been at the forefront of this work, not least by applying the metric-driven approaches of finance to their giving, such as the hedge-fund backed Robin Hood Foundation, Absolute Return for Kids, and Children's Investment Fund Foundation.

So what's wrong with evidence? Some think that measurement of philanthropy's impact is a fool's errand because the social sector has no single unit of value (unlike the business world, which uses measures such as profit to compare businesses operating across countries and across sectors). Edwards suggested that, 'markets work because they stick to a clear financial bottom line, use a simple mechanism to achieve it (competition), and require a relatively small number of conditions to make that mechanism work'. However, it may not be quite so simple in the business world. One of the important lessons of the financial crisis is that 'simple' measures of corporate success, such as quarterly profits or share prices (neither of which flagged up the trouble Lehman Brothers was in, for example), can be incredibly misleading. Better measurement is a challenge for the for-profit and not-for-profit worlds alike.

Social impact measurement certainly is difficult but that does not mean it is pointless. Without measurement, how is it possible to judge which interventions work and which do not? Rejecting measurement risks condemning philanthropy to a world where all grants can be believed to be a success. Perhaps that is why so much of the resistance to measurement is coming from established professional philanthrocrats, fearful of what rigorous analysis of their track record might reveal?

Gates devoted his 2013 annual letter on philanthropy to the case for measurement, and it seems likely that his analysis will increasingly become the conventional wisdom for many donors. Gates wrote that, 'you can achieve amazing progress if you set a clear goal and find a measure that will drive progress toward that goal'. When measurement has had perverse effects that may not always have been due to the measurement system itself being at fault. Rather, Gates argued, 'a lot of efforts fail because they don't focus on the right measure or they don't invest enough in doing it accurately'. The challenge for philanthrocapitalists, then, is to identify the right goals and measures that engage their beneficiaries and key stakeholders.

A more fundamental case against measurement was well captured in an online debate by development experts Rosalind Eyben and Chris Roche in 2013: 'arguably evidence-based approaches build an anti-political firewall.

Development assistance becomes a "technical" best practice intervention based on rigourous objective evidence, delivering best value for money to domestic taxpayers and recipient country citizens mostly without interfering in that country's politics'.

However, there is no inherent problem with the idea that the interventions of philanthrocapitalists or official aid agencies can be political, even overtly so. Soros, for example, presents himself as an avowed 'political philanthropist' in both the USA and Eastern Europe. Similarly, the Gates Foundation sees its support for the One/Make Poverty History campaign for more aid in 2005 as one of its biggest successes. The Mo Ibrahim Prize for African Leadership is another example of innovative, potentially high-leverage philanthropy working through politics.

It seems that philanthrocapitalism is all too often misunderstood or misrepresented as being exclusively about metric-driven, technical interventions. Yet, this chapter proposes that it is actually a movement as diverse as capitalism. Some capitalists make money through models and measurement; others by making big, visionary bets. Some philanthrocapitalists seek social impact through models and measurement; others through big, visionary bets. Ted Turner, for example, became a billionaire by betting big on the rise of cable TV news when he created CNN. He also kicked off the philanthrocapitalism revolution with his almost off-the-cuff pledge to give a billion dollars to the United Nations. His measure of the success for his support to the UN was simply defined: 'I just feel that it is stronger'.

Privatizing the good

'Figuring out how the plutocrats are connected to the rest of us is one of the challenges of the rise of the global super elite', argued Chrystia Freeland in her 2012 bestseller *Plutocrats*. In saying this, she echoed a question asked more than a century ago by Andrew Carnegie in his *Gospel of Wealth*, a book that has influenced many of today's philanthrocapitalists. When Carnegie wrote that '[t]he problem of our age is the proper administration of wealth, that the ties of brotherhood may still bind together the rich and poor in harmonious relationship', he was describing the challenges facing the industrial world of the nineteenth century, as rapid industrialization brought incredible wealth and disruptive social change to America. But he could equally have been writing about the world in the twenty-first century where the globalization of trade and labour markets has lifted more people out of poverty than at any time in history but at a cost in terms of equality and environmental sustainability.

Is philanthropy the answer to the divide between the rich and the rest, the 1 per cent and the 99 per cent, the 0.001 per cent and the 9.999 per cent? 'No', concluded Freeland. The rich, she asserted, have created an 'income defence industry' of advisors to protect their wealth from the taxman. Only fairer taxation to ensure that the broadest backs bear the greatest burden can build a just society.

Most would agree with much of this argument, which ironically is often wielded as an attack on philanthrocapitalism. Yet the book set out a clear three-part test of what makes a 'good' billionaire: her wealth must have been earned fairly; she should commit to effective philanthropy; and she should pay a fair share of tax. Many philanthrocapitalists agree that they should pay more tax, not least Buffett, who has railed against the inequity of a US tax code that has allowed him to pay a lower rate of income tax than his secretary. Indeed, the wealthy of a high tax country like Sweden (assuming that tax is not avoided completely) are in a stronger position to justify their fortunes than those of a lower tax country such as the United States.

Yet tax alone is not sufficient as the basis of a social contract between the rich and the rest. There is some evidence that at certain rates of tax wealth creation is deterred, to the detriment of society as a whole. The logic of this is that some inequality may have to be allowed if society as to prosper to its full potential in a utilitarian sense. Nevertheless, there should be an expectation and welcoming of philanthropy from the winners in society, not only because it is just, but also because of the potential to drive social progress. However, there needs to be careful account taken of the private nature of philanthropy in terms of its wider social accountability. Buffett may have noted that he would rather give his money to the Gates Foundation than the US Treasury because the Gates Foundation may be able to spend it more effectively, but this does not take account of any democratic process.

Nevertheless, this chapter suggests that philanthrocapitalists have the *potential* to use their resources in ways that, through giving, investing, and advocacy, could have a much greater impact for good than the equivalent amount of public spending. This is not to claim that charity is necessarily more effective than government. Rather, there exists—at least in principle—an effective division of labour in which philanthrocapitalists can do things of which governments may be incapable, by taking greater risks, being more innovative and by thinking longer term. By the same measure, there are tasks that only government can do, such as providing universal welfare coverage and public goods and ensuring equity of opportunity across a whole society. As Gates himself pointed out, compared to the resources of government and the private capital markets, even his multi-billion dollar foundation is a 'tiny, tiny organization'. It is in the smart use of that relatively small resource to influence and leverage other resources to achieve larger impact that provides the best case for philanthrocapitalism. Indeed, evidenced effectiveness is a key part of the test of 'good' philanthropy.

As a consequence, a key challenge in the years ahead is likely to be how to measure and otherwise demonstrate the effectiveness of philanthropy in ways that satisfy the demands for fairness of the population at large. There is likely to be a growing interest in improving the regulation of philanthropy too, which currently is light touch and mostly ineffective, and in whether and to what extent giving should be tax deductible. Transparency and public scrutiny is something that philanthrocapitalists will have to get used to, and ideally come to see as an ally; they should not expect in future to receive tax subsidies for activities that do not yield, or at least aspire to, a demonstrable public benefit.

The risk of risk aversion

A core concept in philanthrocapitalism is that people approach their giving in the belief that they are investing in building a better world. A philanthrocapitalistic investment mentality is essentially one that looks to maximize the social and environmental returns on the money the philanthrocapitalist is putting to work. This is far broader than venture philanthropy, which essentially focuses on social good start-ups (or pre-starts-ups). Indeed, that there is scope for social investors to mirror all aspects of the for-profit capital market along a 'capital curve' from debt to venture to private and public equity, and to go further to investments, such as grants, that aim only for social return and do not require any financial return (Bishop and Green, 2010). In 2012, the Omidyar Network, established by eBay founder Pierre Omidyar, published a useful set of articles, 'Priming the Pump for Impact Investing', presenting an alternative vision of this 'capital curve', using a matrix linking different levels of risk and potential social return.

As philanthrocapitalism has evolved, a major concern has been that the investor mindset that has been adopted is often conservative and risk averse, when what is needed more often than not is a willingness to embrace risk in pursuit of a breakthrough social innovation with the potential to be truly transformational.

In his analysis of innovation, *Adapt* (Harford, 2012), the *Financial Times* columnist Tim Harford pinpointed failure as a crucial ingredient in success. Harford gathered evidence from a wide range of topics from regime change in Iraq, through the global financial crisis, to the efforts to eradicate malaria. Across all of these problems he demonstrated that success requires the cultivation of lots of different potential solutions, many of which will fail, rather than single top-down strategies and a rigorous screening of the evidence to find out which of these solutions work. Yet, whilst the entrepreneurs of Silicon Valley love to tell war stories about past disasters and what they learned from them, failure is a word still seldom heard in philanthropy.

Philanthrocapitalism cited the Annenberg Challenge, a half-billion dollar effort to reform the US education system funded in 1993 by media billionaire Walter Annenberg, as a rare example of a philanthropic initiative that was widely acknowledged to have been a failure (albeit not by those responsible). It is to be hoped many more stories of failure from risk-taking philanthrocapitalists over the coming years will be heard, as a demonstration of a new found willingness by philanthropy to learn from failure that is inherent in the all innovation.

There have been a few exceptions. The Omidyar Network has admitted past mistakes, which has helped it to improve. The Gates Foundation has admitted to an overly technology-driven approach to global health issues in the past. As Harford described, philanthrocapitalists have also made good use of 'incentive prizes' as a way to encourage innovation, yet only pay for success, citing examples such as the X-Prize and the Gates Foundation's work on Advance Market Commitments.

But stories of positive failure by philanthrocapitalists remain rare. The creation of an annual risk-celebrating prize for 'Heroic Failure' could have a catalytic effect, not least by encouraging philanthropists to share their lessons from things that did not work, just as Silicon Valley entrepreneurs tend to do.

The philanthropic field is as ripe as any other for change by prize, as the Arizona-based philanthropist Jerry Hirsch has demonstrated. To encourage collaborations between not-for-profits, especially mergers, his Lodestar Foundation created a collaboration prize. The prize is awarded after the fact, as a celebration of success, not as an up-front incentive. First awarded in 2009, the inaugural $250,000 prize went to a merger between a Jewish Community Centre and YMCA in Toledo, Ohio. When the prize was awarded again two years later, it attracted a far larger number and broader range of entries. The prize seemed to have played a useful role in legitimizing and encouraging activities that have long been rare in philanthropy compared with business.

However, this chapter is not advocating recklessness but, rather, innovation that sometimes requires risky ideas that challenge and are challenged by the conventional wisdom. Philathrocapitalists are not typically cowed by expert opinion to simply follow received best practice. Some donors—especially living donors rather than endowed foundations run by professional managers who feel less empowered to be bold—can test the boundaries of their work. One such donor is Silicon Valley venture capitalist Peter Thiel. His offer of $100,000 a head to lure bright young things to drop out of Ivy League universities and start their own businesses sparked a fair amount of consternation. As did his programme of grants to 'garden shed' scientists (academics and corporate researchers need not apply).

Middling middlemen

Recently, there have been interesting discussions about the emergence of a philanthrocapitalism marketplace that brings together those with the money and those with the ideas—such as social entrepreneurs. Whilst this marketplace has continued to emerge, it has not done so exactly as might have been predicted, and still has some way to go.

Markets rely on good and plentiful information. Without information, or when information is spread unevenly, markets struggle to set accurate prices and fail to do their job in allocating resources efficiently. *Philanthrocapitalism* described a host of new intermediaries—so-called 'virtue's middlemen'—that promised a more efficient market for the creation of public good, ranging from market-making convenors (e.g. the Clinton Global Initiative—CGI), to advisory firms (e.g. Bridgespan), to analysts (e.g. New Philanthropy Capital), to social stock exchanges (London and Singapore). The story since has been one of both successes and failures.

Collaboration is an emerging theme among philanthrocapitalists, so convenors that can bring them together have largely done well. Bill Clinton's 'Philanthropy Oscars', the CGI, rolls on each September in New York City, attracting political leaders, corporate bosses, philanthropists, charities, and social entrepreneurs to make commitments to work together to make the world a better place. The glitz and glamour are not to everyone's tastes. Equally, the CGI has not, as some hoped, displaced the annual meeting of the World Economic Forum in Davos as *the* place for serious people to network. Yet, after wobbling in 2009 due to both politics and economic downturn, it remains a premier fixture in the giving calendar. President Clinton's ambitions to turn the CGI into a global movement had to be postponed because of the risk of his profile conflicting with his wife's duties as Secretary of State. Without that conflict, following Mrs Clinton's decision to step down from her Cabinet job, as of early 2013 those global ambitions were being resurrected.

At the same time, for the super rich, there has been the launch and growth of the Gates/Buffett 'Giving Pledge'. At the outset, the founders of this pledge were adamant that this was not an attempt to coordinate action or to twist the arms of their fellow billionaires to back their favourite causes. Nonetheless, many Giving Pledgers have found this group to offer a useful basis for getting together to compare notes and, sometimes, to collaborate. The annual meeting of the Pledgers is becoming part of the way the richest philanthrocapitalists do business.

On the other hand, late 2012 saw the collapse of a brand once as revered in advice and consulting as Lehman Brothers was in the investment banking business. The Monitor Group had been founded by one of the world's top management gurus, Michael Porter of Harvard Business School, and had grown into a major consultancy group offering strategy advice for competitive success. *Philanthrocapitalism* described how Monitor Group, like its rival, McKinsey Consulting, had started to diversify into low-cost and pro-bono advisory services for not-for-profits. This business model needed the for-profit part of the company to stay profitable. When that went under, due to the global slowdown, some loss of competitive edge and financial overstretch, Monitor's philanthropic arm was closed.

Consultancies focused entirely on the not-for-profit and philanthropic sector seem to have fared better. Bridgespan, a spinout from Bain Consulting led by Tom Tierney, has continued to play a leading intellectual role in the development of the not-for-profit sector. The Center for Effective Philanthropy (CEP) also appears to have found a robust business model, offering clear and honest feedback from grantees to foundation bosses.

However, Bridgespan's rigour and CEP's vigour may be exceptions to the rule played by much of the rest of the philanthropy advisory business, particularly private banks. This is an industry where the commercial imperative of keeping the client happy tends to act against more challenging conversations that might result in greater societal impact.

Life has not been easy for philanthrocapitalism's new breed of analysts, often wrestling with the challenges of measuring the impact of philanthopy. Credit for effort should go to the popular US website Charity Navigator, which had built up a following by measuring charities in terms of their administration costs but was trying, under the leadership of Ken Berger, to find a less meaningless but equally compelling way of measuring not-for-profit performance. Guidestar, a similar site, has also made significant efforts to measure the impact of the charities it tracks, but has failed to find a sustainable business model of its own.

Charity Navigator's struggle is largely down to the fact that it is trying to find a single performance metric that can be used across a vast array of charities, using publicly available data, with the minimum of expert input. Others have come at the problem from the opposite direction by trying to spot only the highest performing not-for-profits. A leading online example is GiveWell.org, who examine the randomized control trials and evaluations of charities working in overseas aid to tell the ordinary giver where their money can most effectively be used. GiveWell's analysis appears to be rigorous and transparent about its methodologies and evidence, but the intensity and cost of this research effort means that only a tiny proportion of all not-for-profits will ever get such treatment.

The highest profile advisory intermediary in the UK is New Philanthropy Capital (NPC). Created by senior partners from the investment bank Goldman Sachs, NPC was founded in 2002 to produce rigorous and comparable analyses of charities within and across sectors. It was always going to be a high-cost business but, it was hoped, a sustainable one once a new generation of donors, particularly among London City financiers, took it to heart. Yet even before the crash of 2008, NPC was struggling to find clients willing to pay, despite winning good reviews for its analysis. Today it appears to be moving away from targeting donors to offering advice to charities.

However, although NPC has not yet the found a sustainable business model, that is not to diminish its considerable achievements, particularly under the leadership of Martin Brookes. NPC challenged the complacency of some of the charity sector about measuring impact and was often criticized by the sector as a result. NPC aimed, 'to create a wider debate about what is performance in the charity sector'. In those terms NPC looks like a success. It has also left a legacy through the creation of a new Social Impact Analysts' Association (SIAA) that continues this work. Technology may also enhance the analysis of social performance, particularly the emergence of algorithms for analysing ubiquitous 'big data' to find evidence of impact.

In June 2013, a London Social Stock Exchange was launched, where businesses that publish an audited 'social prospectus' alongside the usual financial prospectus will be able to list their shares and match their capital needs with prospective investors. A similar exchange for social entrepreneurs also opened in Singapore in 2013.

Whilst measuring, analysing and marketing social performance has proved to be a difficult process, there has been faster progress in the effort to create an market for 'impact investments' that promise both a minimum financial and social/environmental return. The rapid growth of this sector is, in part, the result of social investment's similarities to commercial investment. If investors are risking their capital in the hope of a return (albeit some 'blend' of social and financial return) from backing social enterprises, this will require institutions like those in the mainstream capital markets. The role of the Global Impact Investing Network (GIIN) in focusing this emerging industry on finding common language and metrics has been essential in accelerating its emergence.

The other driver of the rapid growth of this sector is the strong backing it has received from governments, particularly in the UK (most recently in the launch of the Big Society Capital wholesale social investment bank), from major foundations, and from some banks. If this is enough to kick off a trillion dollar global impact investment class, as predicted by J.P. Morgan, then the future may be bright for intermediaries.

A broken keyboard

Philanthrocapitalism is as much about what businesses do while they are making money as what their founders do with their profits as they turn to private giving. *Philanthrocapitalism* heralded the rise of the 'good company' by, among other examples, highlighting the ambitious goals of Google.org, the for-good sibling of for-profit Google.com that was established in 2004. The Google founders, Larry Page and Sergey Brin, believed that Google 'dot org' (backed by 1 per cent of Google.com's equity, 1 per cent of its profits, and 1 per cent of its staff time) would some day eclipse the impact that Internet search giant Google 'dot com' had had on the world. Google.org's first CEO, Larry Brilliant, suggested that by setting up as a division of the company rather than a traditional grant-making foundation, 'dot org' could 'play with all the keys on the keyboard' to achieve massive impact. Yet, so far Google.org has failed to meet these lofty expectations.

What went wrong at Google.org is a complex story. By 2009, Brilliant had move on to run the Urgent Global Threats Fund for another prominent philanthrocapitalist, Jeff Skoll, where he has built on one of 'dot org's successes, using Google searches to track the spread of influenza, to create a wider epidemic tracking system. Google 'dot com' is also struggling to live up to its 'do no evil' motto with respect to Internet freedom in places like China.

Yet despite the failure, at least so far, of Google.org, the last few years have seen some remarkable developments in what it means to be a corporate philanthrocapitalist, spurred in part by the questions asked of business by the financial crisis of 2008. A crucial step has been the growing recognition that charity may be the least important part of what it means to be a good corporate citizen. Take Goldman Sachs, for example. Before the financial crisis it was one of the most revered companies in the world. Since, it has been widely used as an exemplar of what is wrong with capitalism, ridiculed by *Rolling Stone* magazine as a 'great vampire squid wrapped around the face of humanity, relentlessly jamming its blood funnel into anything that smells of money'. Goldman Sachs can still point to some terrific philanthropic activities, such as its '10,000 Women' programme to support female business leaders in developing countries. But this may be little more than a fig leaf if, as its critics suggest, the iconic investment bank is still making money in ways that are socially useless, or even socially destructive. Goldman's challenge is not to give more, but to make a convincing case to the public that what it does is in the interests of society at large.

A financial firm that has found a more concrete way of incorporating philanthrocapitalism into its business practices is the private equity giant, Kholberg, Kravis, Roberts (KKR). Twenty years ago, when the firm stunned the corporate world with a leveraged buyout of RJR Nabisco, KKR were seen as, according to a book about that deal, 'the barbarians at the gate'. Yet KKR has been greening itself in very un-barbarian ways. In 2007 the company acquired a Texas-based electricity business, TXU, which had been on the receiving end of attacks from environmental campaigners for plans to build eleven coal-fired power stations. KKR cancelled those plans and partnered with respected green not-for-profit the Environmental Defense Fund (EDF) to verify KKR's commitments and help find greener alternatives. By avoiding reputational damage and gaining valuable cost savings, KKR was, at least in this respect, 'doing well by doing good'.

The idea, which was set out in *Philanthrocapitalism*, that for-profit corporations can thrive commercially *and* contribute positively towards people and planet by behaving responsibly through their supply and distribution chains, has been crystalized in the notion of 'creating shared value' (Porter and Kramer, 2011). Porter and Kramer suggested that companies should pursue strategies that create a shared value combining social and environmental value as well as profits. In itself this was not an original idea, but it has helped to reframe corporate 'do-gooding' as a rational, competitive strategy rather than a sign of executive beneficence at the expense of shareholders. In 2013, a leading practitioner of the shared value approach was Unilever which has put social and environmental sustainability at the core of its 'Vision 2020' strategy, with bold targets such as halving its environmental footprint within a decade and helping half a million small farmers in its supply chain, whilst boosting profits by doubling the number of customers using its products.

However, the transformation of business into champions of virtue will only ever be partial, due to the need to turn a profit. Regulation will be essential to rule out certain socially harmful profit-making opportunities. Companies will often be good in some respects and bad in others. Wal-Mart, for example, continues to reduce waste in packaging and cut carbon dioxide emissions, yet still gets plenty of criticism over its restrictive labour practices and large-volume gun sales, not to mention getting caught up in scandals over alleged foreign corruption. It is likely to remain hard for a corporation to be legitimate to all of its stakeholders all of the time.

A new class of companies may be able to do better than most by embedding a social mission in their corporate DNA. The growing popularity in America of B-Corps, which are for-profit firms with an explicit social purpose, and experiments along similar lines elsewhere such as Community Interest Companies in the UK, may prove to be an exciting development for philanthrocapitalism.

Yet, shared value approaches may not be to the taste of shareholders, if pursuing them requires a cut in short-term profits. Richard Branson, who sees all his businesses as having a social mission, has been trying to rally CEOs to the cause of shared value (or long-term value, as he frames it) by creating the 'B Team' of enlightened corporate titans. But Branson has the freedom to pursue radical strategies because his Virgin group of companies is privately owned. If he wants to sacrifice some profit to achieve other aims, the only person he has to persuade is himself. For publicly owned businesses using other people's money, it is more complicated, as Friedman pointed out.

One of the major obstacles facing corporate philanthrocapitalism is the endemic short-termism of the institutionalized investing world. Short-termism is the result both of flaws in economic thinking about how to value companies and flaws in the structure and regulation of major investors such as pension funds. Without suitable reform of the financial sector, even enlightened CEOs will face an uphill struggle to maintain support from shareholders when trying to prioritize the long run over the short run—including when the more virtuous long-run strategy will ultimately prove more profitable. The financial crisis and its aftermath have created an opportunity to make the necessary reforms—though it is not clear it will be taken.

Conclusion

Philanthrocapitalism ended with a speculative gaze into a future when malaria had finally been eliminated. How likely is this? When Gates began his assault on that disease, which had already been eradicated in the rich world, it was still killing a million people a year, most of them children. By 2010 that number had fallen to 660,000, according to reporting by the World Health

Organization. Between 2000 and 2010, more than a million peoples' lives had been saved from this disease. Ending malaria by 2025, or even sooner, is now a realistic possibility.

Malaria is an important story for philanthrocapitalism. Gates has not achieved this success by acting alone. He has leveraged in other philanthropists, the pharmaceutical industry, the public, and, crucially, government donors to the cause. His capacity to create 'coalitions of the positive' to focus on a specific problem is a remarkable innovation in global governance in the twenty-first century.

Over the coming years it may be that more of these 'coalitions of the positive' form around specific issues. As well as health, Gates has focused on agricultural development in Africa with the aim of repeating the success of the 'Green Revolution' in Asia that boosted crop productivity in the decades after World War Two. Women's rights have also been a high profile issue for the Gates Foundation, with a particular emphasis on better reproductive health services. The Elders, a grouping of retired leaders interested in addressing global problems, has aimed to use its leverage to stop child marriage. One of the funders of The Elders, Jeff Skoll, has moved to focusing his efforts on 'urgent global threats' such as creating tools to spot and prevent epidemic diseases early.

By forming and leading such coalitions, philanthrocapitalists can be at the heart of global decision-making around addressing 'wicked problems'. But there will be risks to manage. The past golden ages of philanthropy all came to an end for reasons that show the obstacles on the road ahead for today's philanthrocapitalists.

The first risk is war and conflict that causes a breakdown of the basic economic and political institutions. In the sixteenth and seventeenth centuries in Europe this conflict was caused by the schism within Christianity between Catholicism and Protestantism. The great flourishing of the first golden age of modern philanthropy was stamped out by the paroxysms of religious conflict during the Reformation. Many of today's philanthrocapitalists are actively working to mitigate such risks, from nuclear proliferation, resource competition, and pandemics.

The second, more immediate, risk is a politically driven squeeze on wealth that undermines the resource base of philanthropy. Britain's transition from a world-leading role in philanthropy at the end of the nineteenth century to a country where charity is no longer the central model for providing public welfare was a product of the steadily expanding role of government over that period and funded by increased taxation. Today's philanthrocapitalists are partly the product of a switch in economic orthodoxy that began in the 1970s towards lower levels of taxation in general and the abolition of punitive rates of taxation on the very wealthy. As concerns about inequality grow, the orthodoxy could switch back. Philanthrocapitalism itself offers a way to reduce that risk for the rich.

Our final lesson is drawn from Britain's experience in the eighteenth century, which was a period of extraordinary innovation in capitalism and philanthropy. Yet this golden age of philanthropy petered out because of a crisis of confidence. 'The Age of Reason' of the eighteenth century brought new tools of empirical analysis for social problems. One of the most influential thinkers of that age was the demographer Thomas Malthus, who used statistical techniques to predict that humanity would eventually experience a nightmare of over-population. Malthus' pessimistic predictions played a crucial role in a debate about whether philanthropy and government welfare schemes were really helping the poor, or just exacerbating the population problem and trapping the less well-off in 'pauperism' (what is often called today 'welfare dependency'). The lesson that this teaches twenty-first century philanthrocapitalists is that success is crucial to keep the momentum behind philanthrocapitalism going and that success must be measured in terms of demonstrably solving problems, not simply more effective grant-making. Ending deaths from malaria within a decade—and, perhaps, polio even sooner—is a challenging goal but, if achieved, it will help create the optimism necessary to rally the next coalition of the positive to take on another problem. For the future development of the philanthrocapitalism revolution, demonstrable impact will be everything.

▓ REFERENCES

Bishop, M. (2006). 'The Birth of Philanthrocapitalism: The Leading New Philanthropists See Themselves as Social Investors', *The Economist*, 23 February, p. 56.

Bishop, M., and Green, M. (2008). *Philanthrocapitalism: How the Rich Can Save the World and Why We Should Let Them*. London: A & C Black.

Bishop, M., and Green, M. (2010). 'The Capital Curve for a Better World', *Innovations*, 5(1): 25–33.

Edwards, M. (2008). *Just Another Emperor*. London: Young Foundation/Demos.

Harford, T. (2012). *Adapt: Why Success Always Starts with Failure*. London: Abacus Books.

Mulgan, G. (2009). 'After Capitalism', *Prospect Magazine*, 26 April: 157–70.

Mulgan, G. (2013). *The Locust and the Bee: Predators and Creators in Capitalism's Future*. Princeton, NJ: Princeton University Press.

Porter, M., and Kramer, M. (2011). 'Creating Shared Value', *Harvard Business Review*, Jan./Feb.: 1–17.

Part II
The Landscape

5 Co-operative and mutual finance

Jonathan Michie

Introduction

Across the globe—as well as within most individual countries—there are a variety of corporate forms, including sole-traders, private individual owner-ship, family ownership, partnerships, companies limited by guarantee, companies limited by shares, publically traded shareholder-owned firms, state-owned firms (with ownership by national, regional, or local government), charities, and different types of co-operative, mutual and employee-owned companies. As discussed below, this chapter uses the term 'co-operative and mutual' to refer to the last three of the above list—namely, all member-owned organizations, whether the members are customers, employees, or a hybrid mixture of the two, possibly with other member owners as well, such as representatives of the local community. In some cases this member-ownership will be shared with other owners; in other words, there may be some degree of private ownership, whether direct ownership or via shareholdings, along with a degree of member ownership.

There are two types of co-operative and mutual finance, both of which are important to consider. Firstly, mutuality has been a long-standing corporate form for the provision of finance, especially to consumers, via various forms of credit unions, mutual building societies, and co-operative banks. This remains the case today, globally. Secondly, these co-operative and mutual organizations need themselves to raise finance for investment and expansion, and there are a variety of ways in which this is done, both via loan capital and by 'co-operative and mutual' share-capital. This chapter discusses both dimensions: finance raised and provided by co-operatives and mutual organizations.

The organizations being considered here are thus those companies that are neither owned by single individuals or families, nor by external shareholders, nor by government, but, rather, by their 'members', where the members are the customers, the employees, or some other stakeholder group, and in some cases with the ownership being shared across a hybrid combination of two or more such stakeholder groups. The clearest example of such a company is probably the co-operative, with a one-member one-vote governance structure, regardless of how much capital each member contributes. Such co-operatives tend to be of three types according to their membership—producer co-operatives, typical in farming; consumer co-operatives, common in retailing; and employee co-operatives, generally in small-scale production. The definition of a co-operative includes consistency with the seven principles of the co-operative movement, namely: voluntary and open membership; democratic member control; member economic participation; autonomy and independence; education, training, and information; co-operation among co-operatives; and concern for community—as set out and discussed on, for example, the website of the International Co-operative Alliance.

The first principle, of voluntary and open membership, is an important defining one, as many organizations are established for the benefit of their members or owners, but if such an organization restricts its membership, thus restricting who can benefit, it would fall foul of this principle. Democratic member control, the second principle, marks out co-operatives from most private or shareholder-owned companies, where such control is in the hands of the owners and their appointed directors and managers. Member economic participation, the third principle, means that all profits need to be controlled democratically by members and for their benefit. In the case of consumer co-operatives, an important way in which profits can be used for the benefit of the consumer members is by reducing the price of the goods and services being provided, which may then result in lower profits subsequently; so the distribution of profits may, to this extent, be less visible than is the case when they are reported as profits and then distributed as a 'co-operative dividend'. Co-operatives also need to be autonomous and independent, the fourth principle, even when they enter into agreements with their government or other organizations. The fifth principle means that the organization has to be committed to educating and developing their members as well as their staff (who may or may not be members). Co-operatives are also required—the sixth principle—to work together with other co-operatives to strengthen the co-operative movement as a whole. Finally, the seventh principle is that co-operatives also need to work to improve and develop the community, both locally and globally.

Consistency with these seven principles means that providing finance to such organizations would generally meet the definition and description of 'social investment', most obviously the seventh principle of 'concern for community', meaning that 'co-operatives work for the sustainable development of their communities through policies approved by their members'.[1]

However, in addition to co-operatives, there are other types of member-owned companies that would not necessarily meet the co-operative principles, most obviously, perhaps, companies that are either wholly or only partly employee-owned, where that ownership may take the form of individual share ownership, or ownership by a trust on behalf of the employees, or by some combination of both types of ownership, which may still be alongside part-ownership by private shareholders. Many such organizations are

---

[1] For a definition, description and discussion of social finance, see Nicholls and Pharoah (2008); and Nicholls (2010).

analysed and described by, for example, Kruse, Freeman, and Blasi (2010) for the USA. An example in the UK is the large chain of department stores, the John Lewis Partnership, selling clothing, furniture, and other household goods, along with their chain of food stores Waitrose, which is owned by a trust that operates in the interests of current and future employees of the company. This is a large organization with around 80,000 employees, and while the employees are consulted and involved, and have various rights—including the ability to vote out the chairman—nevertheless, it would not be considered to be a co-operative, and the same would be true of many other employee-owned organizations.

There is no generally agreed term internationally for all such member-owned organizations, although there has been a trend in some countries to use the term 'mutual' as such a generic term. Confusingly, though, the term 'mutual' has traditionally been used to denote only those member-owned organizations that are in the financial and insurance sectors, and in some countries (such as the USA) the term is used to denote investment funds that would have little relation to the 'member ownership' meaning of the term. In this chapter, therefore, the terms 'co-operative and mutual' are used together to denote this whole member-owned sector of the economy, regardless of whether the member-owned company happens to meet the definition of a co-operative or not.

The motivation for founding a co-operative or mutual, or for choosing such an ownership structure—whether for a new or an existing company—is generally to create an organization that consumer members will feel able to trust to deliver the products and services desired, without having to be concerned that the firm might cut quality in order to deliver increased financial returns to external shareholders (in the form of dividend payouts and increased share price); or to band together as producers, or as employees, with similar motivations in terms of governance. An additional motivation may relate to place, to contribute to the local economy and community, where a co-operative or mutual form may embed the endeavour locally through the membership, which might include local community organizations within the ownership and governance structure. The Fair Trade movement deals through co-operatives in order to give the small producers a degree of producer power by combining together; it thus combines a number of the above motivations concerning both trustworthiness of the product, and by seeking to contribute to local economies and communities.[2]

For these organizations, finance then arises as an issue, or problem, as and when the organizations wish to expand beyond what their internally generated financial surpluses will fund. So, the motivation for choosing a mutual corporate form is to benefit from the potential advantages of customer trust and satisfaction, or producer co-operation, or employee motivation and

---

[2] On the Fair Trade movement, see for example Ransom (2001); and Bowes (2010). See also <http://www.wfto.com>.

commitment, and access to finance then becomes an issue, of being required to support the organization's functioning and growth.

There is, though, an additional aspect to co-operative and mutual finance, which is that having banks and other financial institutions owned by their members may not only deliver the sort of benefits to those members as described above, but also, the whole financial sector—and hence the economy as a whole—may benefit from having a more corporately diverse financial services sector, which having a critical mass of co-operative and mutual financial organizations can help to deliver. Such potential benefits are three-fold. First, the member-owned mutual form may deliver benefits in itself, through the corporate incentives being to deliver the sort of services desired by the members, rather than engaging in risky speculative behaviour to try to deliver high financial returns to external shareholders, which may in turn be linked to financial bonuses for the decision-makers. This advantage will often be reinforced by regulatory restrictions that prohibit such member-owned organizations from engaging—at least to the same extent—in the sort of speculative behaviour that private banks are permitted to pursue.[3]

Second, the competitive pressure that a strong co-operative and mutual sector will provide to privately- and shareholder-owned banks will tend to make those banks more focused on delivering good quality financial products to consumers.[4] And third, a more corporately diverse financial services sector is likely to be more robust in face of the sort of shocks that the financial sector tends to face from time to time. Because co-operatives and mutuals have different ownership patterns, governance arrangements and incentive structures, their behaviours, policies, and practices will be concomitantly different. These differences in behaviours act as a break to the sort of financial contagion to which financial markets are prone (as analysed for example by Keynes, 1936). The importance of this factor has gained increased recognition following the 2007–8 global financial crisis and the consequent 2009 international recession—the first year since the 1930s when world income and output actually fell, as a result of failures amongst privately and shareholder-owned banks and other financial institutions.

Beyond the financial services sector, there may also be advantages in having companies with co-operative or mutual funding structures—as opposed to funding from external shareholders—for example for the delivery of public services where trust in the provider is regarded as a particularly important factor, and where the danger of quality being sacrificed—perhaps only at some point in the future—by managers seeking short-term financial benefits for external shareholders and, thereby, for themselves via bonuses is regarded as particularly serious, in terms of the potential damage to the service receivers. This is, perhaps, an area of growing importance globally, as governments are

---

[3] The arguments in this paragraph are discussed and evaluated in detail by Michie (2011a); see also the analysis of the Ownership Commission (2012).

[4] Evidence of this is reported and discussed in Michie and Blay (2004).

becoming increasingly interested in how public services can be made more accountable to their users via a stronger culture of employee engagement and organizational ownership, and in an economic environment where governments are looking for ways in which to reduce public spending. In its Promotion of Co-operatives Recommendation, 2002 (ILO Recommendation 193), the International Labour Organization recommends (amongst other things) the adoption of measures to promote the potential of co-operatives in all countries, irrespective of their level of development, for a range of purposes including the creation of income-generating activities and employment, the development of human resource capacities and knowledge of co-operation, the development of business potential, the increase of savings and investment, and the improvement of social and economic well-being. They also recommend the promotion of co-operatives as one of the pillars of national and international economic and social development, and propose that governments should facilitate access of co-operatives to support services, investment finance, and credit.[5]

Likewise, there are benefits in having corporate diversity, and hence a strong co-operative and mutual sector, across the economy as a whole, not just in the financial services sector.[6] This has been argued in detail by, for example, the UK's Ownership Commission (2012), and globally by the International Co-operative Alliance (2013). However, this chapter focuses mainly on the two key aspects of co-operative and mutual finance set out above: first, the benefits of having a corporately diverse and, hence, robust financial services sector, and second, the problem faced by co-operative and mutual companies in securing funds for investment and growth. The chapter starts by setting out the history of co-operative and mutual finance and considers some of its historic successes and failures.[7] Next, it addresses the international experience and landscape, before considering the potential for co-operative and mutual finance to increase the degree of corporate diversity and what benefits this may bring in terms of the resilience of economies overall. Finally, the chapter will review how a market for mutual finance might be further developed going forward and where the key challenges and opportunities lie.

The co-operative and mutual model

Co-operatives and mutual organizations generally access finance for their operations, and for investment and growth, from internally generated

---

[5] As reported and discussed in International Co-operative Alliance (2013).

[6] As *The Economist* notes: 'Just as an ecosystem benefits from diversity, so the world is better off with a multitude of corporate forms' (*Economist*, 2010: 58).

[7] For a description and analysis of the mutual sector in the UK, see Oxford Centre for Mutual and Employee-owned Business (2012); and globally, the International Co-operative Alliance (2012).

surpluses and from borrowing. There is also the option of issuing shares, to raise risk capital, although what is possible in this regard varies across jurisdictions. However, as discussed in the concluding section of this chapter, this is an area that is likely to see new models developed in the future, with a concomitant growth in this aspect of co-operative and mutual finance.

The key differential issues between co-operatives and mutuals on the one hand, and other corporate forms on the other, lie in ownership, governance, and profit distribution. These will tend to create other differences, related to culture and leadership, policies and practices, and behaviours and performance, although these latter factors do not follow automatically, and require conscious and persistent effort to sustain.

First, it is an interesting question as to whether members—as owners—of mutuals can benefit financially from profit distribution. The members of mutuals do expect the company to be able to charge lower prices, or lower premiums on insurance policies, and to pay higher interest on savings. This is the economic benefit of not having to pay dividends to external shareholders. But this is a different meaning to the term 'financial gain' from the one used in the context of shareholders who will receive a return on their investment—where the amount of money received will increase both with the size of their financial stake and with the profitability of the company. External shareholders, thus, have a direct material interest in the profitability of the company being raised, so as to increase the personal financial return that they as owners will receive. Stock options will often transmit such incentives to managers too.[8] In contrast, the purpose and objective of a co-operative or mutual is to make *sufficient* profits for the attainment of their other more fundamental corporate objectives—of serving and benefitting their members.

Second, in terms of governance, mutuals are generally run on a 'one member, one vote' principle, whereby each member has the same influence and say regardless of how much money they may have with the company. In the case of, say, a mutually owned bank where a member can invest savings, or in the case of any mutual that might raise capital by issuing a bond, which might enable members to invest in the company, the bond will pay a certain rate of interest which is unlikely to be linked to the profitability or performance of the company. Even were the bond to be designed to include any such link of interest payments to profitability, the ownership of that bond (or the relative size of the investment in the bond) would not bring with it any greater say in the governance of the organization, as does shareholding in a shareholder-owned company.

Third, with respect to ownership, in principle the members of a mutual may be able to 'cash in' the value of the company or organization, sharing the

---

[8] For example, 'Companies where executives are disproportionately compensated in stock options are more likely to report earnings that meet or beat analysts' forecasts' (Tabb, 2012: 48); the mechanisms whereby this is achieved and the evidence regarding the scale of such activity is provided by Tabb (2012: 48–9).

proceeds amongst themselves. This is what happened to many of the major mutual building societies in the UK during the 1990s following a change in the legislation governing such societies made by the Thatcher government. The members gained financially. So too, in general, did the directors of the mutual building societies who recommended demutualization to their members; and likewise the financial and other professionals who advised in favour of this course of action and who oversaw the sales. This process also led to the phenomenon of 'carpet-bagging', where people would join a mutual for the sole purpose of voting that it cease to be a mutual, so that they could benefit financially from the distribution of the proceeds from demutualization.[9]

The historical context

During the nineteenth century, mutuals as a corporate form arose in the UK as a response to the development of privately owned and shareholder-owned companies during and following the Industrial Revolution, where there was a mistrust of the quality of goods being delivered by the established for-profit companies. This was a consequence of some deleterious profit-maximizing behaviours, including cases of downright dishonesty, that negatively impacted poorer consumers. In general, this led to inferior products and services than would have been the case had the strategic aim of the companies been to maximize the quality of goods and services for the customer. Cox (2010), for example, detailed the various ways in which dishonest practice in the retail trade were commonplace in the pursuit of higher profits and financial returns.

This led to the emergence of the 'Rochdale Pioneers' in the north of England in 1844. These pioneers effectively founded the co-operative movement that led to the subsequent development of co-operative and mutual corporate forms owned by their customer members with the purpose of delivering good quality and trusted food and other commodities, including financial services. The first mutual building societies had actually already been established by then, as socially embedded financial institutions in which local people could entrust their savings, receiving interest payments in return, and from which they could then borrow money with which to purchase a house,

---

[9] Within the UK, mutual building societies continued to occupy a dominant role in the market for home loans until legislative change under the Conservative governments (1979–97) opened them up to demutualization, enabling current members to cash in on the value that had been built up in the companies over years and, indeed, across generations, starting with Abbey National which converted to a bank in 1989 and is now owned by Santander. Within ten years or so the majority of the market had been transferred from member-owned companies to being PLCs (public limited companies) owned by external shareholders. These demutualizations withdrew around 70 per cent of assets from the mutual building society and insurance sectors, thus substantially reducing their critical mass. By 2013, none of the companies that demutualized had survived as an independent entity: they were all either taken over, or had failed, or a combination of the two.

paying back in the form of a mortgage. Ketley's Building Society was the first in the UK, founded in 1775, and by 1825 there were more than 250. Such mutual building societies tended to be local, with a building society being formed to serve its members in the locality, with the names of the building societies often reflecting the town or locality in which they were formed and were based, such as the Barnsley Building Society, Bath Building Society, and so on. Receiving such a large loan—or a mortgage—was generally dependent on the individual having already been a member of the mutual building society and having saved with it over a number of years: that is, it was conditional on the risk mitigation of the lender being a proven, 'loyal' member.[10]

In 1862 Friedrich Wilhelm Raiffeisen founded the first credit union in Germany; these are member-owned financial co-operatives that are democratically controlled by their members and operated for the purpose of providing credit and other financial services to their members. This has since led to the growth of credit unions and other forms of financial co-operatives and mutuals globally. For example, a third of Canadians are members of credit unions, which have a growing share of the retail deposit markets and the residential mortgages markets—standing at 16 per cent and 19 per cent market share respectively in 2010.[11] In the USA and UK, community development financial institutions (or 'finance', in the UK, and in both countries referred to as CDFIs) serve a similar purpose but also supporting businesses and economic development, seeking to provide credit and other financial services in markets and to populations that are otherwise poorly served by the financial services sector.

The history of co-operatives and mutuals across most of the advanced capitalist economies has been as a relatively small, but resilient, sector of the economy—albeit generally overshadowed by the shareholder-owned limited liability corporate form.

Global developments

The United Nations has for some time argued that co-operatives contribute significantly to economies across the world, and has urged governments to encourage and facilitate 'the establishment and development of co-operatives, including taking measures aimed at enabling people living in poverty or belonging to vulnerable groups to engage on a voluntary basis in the creation and development of co-operatives' (UN Resolution 56/114 adopted in 2001).

---

[10]   For more detail on the history of mutual building societies, see for example <http://www.bsa.org.uk>, 'The History of Building Societies'. See also Price (1958); Cleary (1965); Ashworth (1980); and Boléat (1982).

[11]   As reported and discussed in International Co-operative Alliance (2013).

The UN declared 2012 to be the International Year of Co-operatives, with the goals of:

- increasing public awareness about co-operatives and their contributions to socio-economic development and the achievement of the Millennium Development Goals
- promoting the formation and growth of co-operatives
- encouraging governments to establish policies, laws and regulations conducive to the formation, growth and stability of co-operatives.

The International Co-operative Alliance built upon that year's activities by aiming to take the co-operative way of doing business to a new level by 2020, with the goals of having the co-operative form of business acknowledged as a world leader in sustainable finance, the model preferred by most people across the globe, and as the fastest growing form of enterprise (as detailed in ICA, 2013).

By 2012 the membership of co-operatives and mutuals had reached over one billion across ninety-six countries. The world's 300 largest co-operatives had (in 2008) a combined turnover of US$1.6trn a year (ICA, 2011). ICA (2012) reported on 2,190 co-operatives from sixty-one countries, whose turnover in banking was US$185.3bn, in insurance US$1,101.8bn, and in non-banking or insurance, US$1,155.1bn—so of the total US$2,442.2bn ($2.4trn), the majority ($1,287.1bn, or $1.3trn) was in banking and insurance. Restricted to co-operatives with a turnover of at least US$100m a year, the above breakdown becomes 1,478 co-operatives from forty-six countries, whose turnover in banking was $183bn, insurance $1,096.4bn, and non-banking or insurance $1,142bn. Of these, only one was from Africa, fifty-two from Oceania, seventy-two from Asia, 440 from the Americas, and 913 from Europe. For the top ten countries, these organizations represented the following combined turnovers: USA, $598bn; France, $361bn; Japan, $324bn; Germany, $303bn; the Netherlands, $110bn; Italy, $109bn; Switzerland, $81bn; the UK, $76bn; Spain, $67bn; Finland, $59bn; Canada, $51bn; Denmark, $48bn; Brazil, $36bn; Austria, $32bn; New Zealand, $29bn; Belgium, $28bn; Sweden, $24bn; Norway, $21bn; Australia, $15bn; and Republic of Korea, $11bn.

By sector, 30 per cent of these co-operatives (each with over US$100m turnover a year, in 2010) were in insurance, 28 per cent in agriculture and food industries, 19 per cent in consumer and retail, 8 per cent in banking and financial services, 5 per cent in industry and utilities, 4 per cent in other services, 2 per cent in health and social care, 1 per cent in housing, with 3 per cent in other sectors. Thus, almost 40 per cent of the activity was in banking and insurance.

Of the banks, the top fifteen by turnover were Groupe Crédit Agricole, France, $45.7bn; Groupe BPCE, France, $31.2bn; Groupe Crédit Mutuel, France, $19.7bn; Rabobank Group, Netherlands, $17.0bn; Desjardines Group,

Canada, $11.6bn; Federal Farm Credit Banks Funding Corporation, USA, $6.4bn; RZB, Austria, $5.7bn; DZ Bank, Germany, $5.1bn; Agribank, FCB, USA, $4.0bn; Navy Federal Credit Union, USA, $3.2bn; OP-POHJOLA Group, Finland, $2.3bn; Swiss Union of Raiffeisen Banks, Switzerland, $2.1bn; Ag First Farm Credit Bank, USA, $1.7bn; Shinkin Central Bank, Japan, $1.7bn; and US Agbank, FCB, USA, $1.4bn.

Of the insurance companies, the top fifteen were Zenkyoren, Japan, $71bn; State Farm Group, USA, $57bn; Nippon Life, Japan, $56bn; Kaiser Permanente, USA, $44bn; Meiji Yasuda Life, Japan, $38bn; Sumitomo Life, Japan, $35bn; Liberty Mutual Insurance, USA, $28bn; Achmea B.V., Netherlands, $27bn; Nationwide Mutual Insurance Company, USA, $26bn; Mapfre, Spain, $24bn; New York Life Group, USA, $28bn; Groupama, France, $20bn; Covea, France, $19bn; Farmers Insurance Group, USA, $18bn; and R+V Versicherung AG, Germany, $15bn.

For the economy as a whole, the proportion of national output generated by co-operatives in Sweden is 13 per cent, in Switzerland it is over 16 per cent, in New Zealand over 17 per cent, and in Finland 21 per cent (Worldwatch Institute, 2012).

As indicated above, the co-operative and mutual sector is relatively strong in the major Continental European economies of Germany, France, Italy, and Spain, and this includes within the financial sector. The different legal and regulatory traditions have a major influence both on the strength of the co-operative and mutual sector from country to country, and also the form that the sector takes—and this is true even between Continental European countries.

In countries with a civil (French) or Germanic legal tradition, advanced integration across co-operative and mutual organizations is common, while the opposite is generally the case in common-law countries. Thus, in Scandinavia and Continental Europe (with the exception of Spain), such integration is advanced to the level of being a strategic network. In contrast, in the USA, Canada, the UK and Commonwealth countries, such networks are much weaker, depicted by Cuevas and Fischer (2006) as 'consensual'. For Scandinavia and Continental Europe, these networks often represent the largest financial intermediary in the country, for example the Germany Sparkassan network, which 'controls 30 percent of the country's financial assets, the largest share of the market of any financial institution' (Cuevas and Fischer, 2006: 36). The Netherlands' Rabobank—reported above with a $17bn pa turnover—utilizes a strong network to provide and take advantage of 'back office' economies of scale and scope.

Public services reform

The UK's Coalition Government, formed in May 2010, aimed to extend the role of mutuals in delivering public services. The potential benefits of such a move have been discussed and analysed in Ham et al. (2010), including in particular the potential for generating additional employee commitment, motivation, effort, and innovation:

Employee ownership—when combined with opportunities for workplace participation—can deliver a range of benefits in terms of improved productivity and innovation, reduced absences and staff turnover, and higher levels of employee commitment and well-being. It achieves these outcomes by more closely aligning employee interests and goals with those of the broader organisation. The evidence suggests that employee ownership may help the NHS to engage staff and unlock their potential to drive service improvements. (Ham et al., 2012: 12)

This relates to the long-standing academic literature and history of corporate practice and public policy relating to employee commitment and motivation, and the role of a 'feeling of ownership'. In the literature, this relates to the idea of 'high commitment work systems'.[12] The evidence suggests that such policies deliver the best results when employees feel that they really do have an ownership stake. The effect of participatory management practices is also significant, and this is more likely to play a major and significant role if employees have a genuine ownership stake. Without such a stake there is also a greater risk that employees will regard any participatory management practices as just a fad, or not necessarily likely to endure when the current manager or managers move on (as reported and discussed in, for example, Michie and Oughton, 2003).

What are referred to as 'social co-operatives' exist to provide social services such as care for the elderly. In Italy these have been legislated for as either 'type A' where the members are both the providers and the beneficiaries of the social service in question, or 'type B' which aim to bring the unemployed into the workforce, where the members will be both existing employees and the unemployed whom the co-operative will be seeking to assist. There are around 7,000 of these social co-operatives—across both type A and type B—in Italy. Belgium and Poland have also legislated along similar lines, whereas in the UK and elsewhere there is no specific legislation for this area, but there are co-operatives and mutuals operating in the provision of such services, and indeed this is currently on the increase (as reported and discussed by Davies and Yeoman, 2013).

Co-operatives and mutuals are also playing an important role in welfare contexts in the developing world. Thus, for example, a study of farmers in the Yaqui Valley, Mexico, found that they were far more likely to gain information on implementing new technologies from their local credit union than from scientists; the researchers concluded that efforts to introduce new, more sustainable technologies into farming were more likely to succeed via participatory organizations such as co-operatives (see ICA, 2013). In 2009, the

---

[12] As discussed, tested for, and analysed by, for example, see Michie and Sheehan (2005).

Indian Government amended the constitution—through its Constitution (111th) Bill—to make the right to form co-operative societies a fundamental right.[13] In the case of developing countries, many of the same points apply as have been made above in relation to the USA and Europe. There are, of course, many co-operatives and mutuals operating across, for example, Africa—in agriculture, finance, and retail. But the size of the typical company in terms of turnover will in general be relatively small as compared to those operating in the larger developed economies. The opportunities and challenges are, however, quite similar. There are the potential benefits of achieving sustainable growth that will prove robust in face of global 'shocks' and other pressures. A degree of corporate diversity, with a critical mass of co-operative and mutual business, is likely to prove beneficial in this regard, including within the financial services sector, in order to reduce the danger of contagion to which the privately owned financial services sector is so prone. But the co-operative and mutual sector in the developing world faces the same challenges as elsewhere regarding the sources of capital for investment and growth. The International Co-operative Alliance (2013) highlighted this issue—of the need to develop co-operative capital—for the sector globally.

The potential for other aims and objectives of international aid and development bodies, and NGOs delivered through co-operatives and mutuals is an additional opportunity. Of course, prior to the development of the welfare state, much of the population did rely on co-operatives and mutuals to provide healthcare and other public services. So in this sense the current developments might be seen as a return to previous arrangements—as welfare states are rolled back as part of austerity measures—rather than the development of something entirely new. This also means that the use of co-operatives and mutuals for the delivery of public services is controversial, since while the contracts from government for the delivery of such services may go to such mutuals in the first instance, subsequent tendering may lead to those contracts going to private contractors, thus representing a form of privatization, which raises an issue of public accountability.

Corporate diversity

The Centre for European Policy Studies (CEPS) produced two in-depth studies of the European financial services sector, following the 2007–8 financial crisis, which concluded that there are important advantages in having a degree of corporate diversity in banking structures and models (Ayadi et al., 2009, 2010). These reports include case studies of several European economies

---

[13] See <http://agricoop.nic.in/cooperation/hpcc2009new.pdf>, cited in ICA (2013).

that the authors argued illustrate the advantages that derive from a degree of corporate diversity:

The most important conclusion is that the current crisis has made it even more evident than before how valuable it is to promote a pluralistic market concept in Europe and, to this end, to protect and support all types of ownership structures. (Ayadi et al., 2009: 3)

In the UK, the Bank of England Financial Stability Report noted:

Policy action is needed to reduce the structural problems caused by banks that are too important to fail (TITF). Larger UK banks expanded much more rapidly than smaller institutions in the run-up to the crisis and have received disproportionate taxpayer support during the crisis. That reflected a misalignment of risks on TITF banks' balance sheets, due to implicit guarantees on their liabilities. (Bank of England, 2010: 11)

The 2008 financial crisis left a substantial legacy problem which is still constraining bank lending in 2013—as predicted at the time by Llewellyn (2010). Alongside the macroeconomic costs, the interests of individual consumers were sacrificed by managers who were primarily focused on shareholder value. One of the champions of shareholder value, Jack Welch, in 2009 referred to the concept as 'the dumbest idea in the world'. Alan Greenspan, the former chairman of the Federal Reserve—and described by the *Financial Times* as 'a high priest of laissez-faire capitalism'—announced in 2008 that the financial crisis had exposed a 'mistake' in the free market ideology which had guided his eighteen-year stewardship of US monetary policy: 'I have found a flaw', Greenspan announced, referring to his economic philosophy, 'I don't know how significant or permanent it is. But I have been very distressed by that fact.'[14]

The financial crisis, which was largely caused by the activities of private sector banks, resulted in the UK Government providing them with a bailout amounting to around £80 bn. In addition, the Government borrowed in order to provide the fiscal boost that was coordinated internationally to prevent a slide into global depression. These costs, along with the additional hit to government finances that the recession caused, as tax receipts fell and unemployment benefits and other such payments rose, combined to create the fiscal deficit and accumulated debt. Given the financial, economic, and social costs of the financial crisis and concomitant recession, a key priority for policy has become putting in place measures to prevent a reoccurrence in the future. Otherwise such problems may well recur, whether that be in ten, twenty, or thirty years time. (And there is evidence that the incidence and frequency of bank crises around the world had already increased over time—see for example Eichengreen and Bordo, 2002.)

---

[14] See Andrew Clark and Jill Treanor, 'Greenspan—I was wrong about the economy. Sort of', *The Guardian*, 24 October 2008.

A major contribution to ensuring the necessary systemic stability would be to create a more diverse financial services sector. Diversity of ownership and business models promotes systemic stability and is also good for customers because of the resulting increased competition and choice, quality of service, and fairness. Andrew Haldane, Executive Director of Financial Stability at the Bank of England, describing the factors that lay behind the 2007–8 global financial crisis, noted that individual institutions had been diversifying, and that while this might be thought to reduce risk, it does not do so if all are diversifying in the same way, so instead the system becomes more concentrated (Haldane, 2009: 18–19). It is a classic fallacy of composition—what may be good for an individual institution acting alone, will not necessarily apply when considering all of them together. In addition to increasing risk through reduced diversity, this process also had the effect of shifting risk from the shareholder-owned banks that moved into investment banking, to the public sector, on account of the Bank of England's obligation to act as Lender of Last Resort and the UK government's obligation to support systemically important banks. Reflecting such concerns, the UK Coalition Government elected in 2010 was committed to introducing a greater degree of corporate diversity into the financial services sector, including through supporting mutuals:

We want the banking system to serve business, not the other way round. We will bring forward detailed proposals to foster diversity in financial services, promote mutuals and create a more competitive banking industry. (HM Government, 2010: 9)

The consultation document on 'financing a private sector recovery' that was issued jointly by the Department for Business, Innovation & Skills and HM Treasury stated that:

Mutuals play a strong role in local communities, building long-term relationships with members and often operating in areas of economic and social deprivation. The range of services offered by building societies and other mutuals has expanded as the legal framework has been updated, and in response to changes in technology and customer demand. The Government is interested in views on the role that mutuals could play in facilitating access to finance for businesses and providing greater choice in financial services. (Department for Business, Innovation & Skills, 2010: 32)

Likewise the Treasury White Paper on 'a new approach to financial regulation' stressed:

The need to maintain diversity in the financial services sector (for example, by removing barriers to entry where possible, and ensuring that its rules do not disadvantage mutually owned financial institutions). (HM Treasury, 2010: 32)

There have been similar moves globally to try to tackle the problem of 'too big to fail' banks, to deal with the relation between investment and consumer banking, and to ensure a degree of corporate and regional diversity in the financial services sector, with the response to the 2008 financial crisis in the USA including the Dodd-Frank Wall Street Reform and Consumer Protection Act (generally referred to as the Dodd-Frank Act), which was signed into law in July 2010. There are three main arguments in favour of having a significant co-operative or mutual sector of the economy, where by 'significant' is meant sufficient critical mass, in terms of market share, to be able to make a difference to how the economy as a whole functions.

First, there are certain potential advantages in the member-owned mutual form, as against the shareholder-owned or other corporate models, because of the trust that members can have that 'their' firms will operate in their interests, given that this is their corporate purpose. So having such member-owned organizations with which to do business is, in itself, in the interests of at least those customers who choose to become members. In addition, mutuals are often loyal to their locality, reflected for example in local sourcing; they sometimes deliver goods and services that would simply not otherwise be provided; and due to the social purpose inherent in many mutuals, they tend to give greater support to local charities.[15]

Second, customers who choose instead to do business with shareholder-owned firms will also benefit if there is a critical mass of mutual businesses operating in the market, as these will provide competitive pressure for the shareholder-owned businesses who may reduce their prices or improve their service in some other way in order to meet this additional competitive pressure. There is evidence that shareholder-owned firms do improve their performance in terms of customer service when faced with competition from mutual financial providers, specifically in terms of the spread between charges made for loans and interest rates offered on savings.[16]

Third, as mentioned above, mutuals have different ownership and governance structures, different corporate purposes and objectives, and different management structures and behaviour as compared with shareholder-owned companies. They therefore tend to behave differently, including in the face of new events or incentives, such as from an external shock to the system. Having different corporate models will thus tend to make the system as a whole more resilient, less likely to suffer from a domino effect, with all companies reacting in the same way to an external shock.[17]

Of course, co-operative and mutual financial institutions can take risks that go wrong, and they can be badly led and managed, and can fail. But their owners do not have the same incentive as do owners of private banks to engage in risky, speculative behaviour, and the regulation of the co-operative and mutual sector generally will not permit it to the same degree as is allowed for privately owned banks.

---

[15] For the evidence on these behaviours, see Michie and Blay (2004).
[16] This evidence is reported and discussed by Cook et al. (2003).
[17] The evidence for this is reported and discussed in Michie (2011a).

A market for mutual finance

Given these various potential benefits from having co-operative and mutual companies in the financial services market, what in practice is done in terms of promoting such corporate forms? A crucial factor is the legislative and regulatory regime for such companies, as compared to firms with different corporate forms such as shareholder-owned companies. Shareholder-owned companies will tend to lobby for their own interests. Given that this is the dominant corporate form in most economies, organizations generally will tend to favour such corporate forms by default, and will tend to oppose legislation or regulation that is seen as favouring some alternative corporate form such as co-operative and mutual companies. The result is that whether for this explicit reason, or just because shareholder-owned companies are seen as the norm, most legislation and regulation tends to assume that this is the 'natural' corporate form: legislation and regulation, thus, tends to be designed for such entities, often hampering the ability of mutuals to operate.

Ayadi et al. (2009, 2010) found that mutual and co-operative banks across Europe tended to have a lower risk appetite than shareholder-owned banks, due, in part, to the fact that mutual and co-operative banks cannot easily attract external capital. This lower risk appetite will contribute positively to the resilience of the financial services sector, both by lowering the overall level of risk, and by providing a greater spread of risk appetite across the sector as a whole.

The nature of corporate ownership was analysed in detail by the Commission on Ownership that ran from 2010 to 2012 in the UK, although taking evidence globally.[18] Their Report, published in 2012, argued that a more diverse ownership structure would indeed be beneficial for the economy as a whole, including for the financial services sector (see Ownership Commission, 2012).[19] That report argued that a single corporate form dominates the UK economy, namely the large shareholder-owned firm, to the detriment of corporate diversity. 'Plurality of ownership forms', the Commission's report argued, 'should be viewed as an economic good in its own right, increasing both choice and the variety of corporate forms available for varying business models and their investors while spreading risk more effectively' (p. 9). Gagliardi (2009) concurred:

A plurality of ownership types and business models creates a corresponding diversity in forms of corporate governance; risk appetite and management; incentive structures; policies and practices; and behaviours and outcomes. It also offers wider choice for consumers through enhanced competition that derives in part from the juxtaposition of different business models... Variety is the evolutionary fuel in economic development as well as in biology. Diversity is desirable across the economy, and diversity

---

[18] This was, unfortunately, just a UK initiative; it could be usefully repeated in other countries.

[19] Downloadable free of charge at <http://www.kellogg.ox.ac.uk/researchcentres/mutuals/activities>.

within the financial sector itself—both a variety of corporate forms and geographical dispersion, with stronger local presence—tends to support a broader variety of corporate forms in the rest of the economy which in turn enhances competition and consumer choice.[20] (p. 19)

The Commission was also concerned that short-term financial performance was increasingly influencing decision-making in private share ownership. The Commission, therefore, made various suggestions for reforming the PLC model to engender more long-term thinking and behaviour, but it also made recommendations for strengthening the operation of co-operatives and mutuals so as to enhance that sector and create a more corporately diverse economy.

In this context, Hesse and Čihák (2007) concluded:

The presence of diverse business forms is good for competition and choice for the consumer. More importantly perhaps, their existence acts to mitigate risk in our business economy…Yet regulators and policy makers have consistently failed to take seriously the mutual corporate form. At least in part, this is because of its inability to easily raise capital, despite the fact that this reduces their risk appetite and thus means that a financial services sector with a strong mutual sector will have a greater diversity of risk appetite, which is a positive outcome in terms of creating a stable and robust financial services sector—as reported in IMF and other research…There are many examples of the positive role that differently owned businesses can and do play in aiding a plurality of corporate forms, but these positive impacts could be greatly enhanced given the right environment and political goodwill. The benefits of creating a more diversified corporate sector include greater stability, more accountability to consumers, reduced systematic risk, and more competition. (p. 22)

At a systems level, two of the proposed reforms were particularly important: first, enhancing the ability of mutuals to raise capital; second, fostering the legal structures to create *permanent* mutuals so as to give voters and local citizens the confidence that transferring public services from the public sector to mutual organizations would not result in those services being taken over by profit-seeking shareholder-owned companies. Shareholder-owned firms can raise capital for investment and expansion by issuing additional shares. Indeed, this is often the reason that a company will become shareholder-owned in the first place. Mutuals, on the other hand, tend not to raise funds in this way, as they generally do not have private shareholders. Were they to issue shares, the shareholders would want a say in how the business was run, and they may want to maximize profits. This would enable the shareholders to enjoy financial benefits not only from the receipt of dividends but also from the capital gains realized from the sale of their shares in the future. Mutuals are thus largely constrained to raising funds through debt, with interest paid at some fixed amount or rate—perhaps varying according to some exogenous

---

[20] Gagliardi (2009).

factor or variable such as the bank rate, but not varying in relation to the profitability of the company itself, as this would inject into the business an incentive to focus on profitability rather than serving the trading interests of the members of the mutual. However, mutuals do need to raise capital for investment and expansion, and the requirement to use debt only—from bank loans, issuing of bonds, or other such mechanisms—can be a constraint. Whether and how this conundrum can be resolved is not a simple or straight-forward issue, but, nevertheless, there are ways in which progress could be made in terms of legislative and regulatory change—something that is advo-cated globally by the International Co-operative Alliance (2013). Certainly, there may be some investors who would be happy to provide 'patient' capital in return for some ownership stake, while still accepting some degree of safeguards to enable the mutual nature of the organization to be maintained. The downside is that the investor would not get an increased vote in relation to the size of their financial stake. Thus, new member and shareholder finance is an option, although what is available in this area does vary according to national legislative and regulatory frameworks.

There is another way in which a larger market for co-operative and mutual capital would strengthen the economy, and this is by providing an alternative—perhaps more robust and sustainable—option for business suc-cession. When the next generation of a family no longer wishes to devote their time and energies to continuing to operate the family business, what are the options for the owners to divest themselves of the company? Financial advi-sors will generally point to a trade sale, or floating on a stock exchange. However, there is another option, and that is to sell to the existing stakeholders—the employees, customers, suppliers, or local community—or possibly to some combination of these stakeholders. A famous example of such a sale was that of John Spedan Lewis transferring ownership to his workers of the chain of department stores that his father, John Lewis, had established. The mechanics in that case was for a Trust—that was established to own the company on behalf of its current and future employees—to pay the owner over time from the profits generated on an annual basis. But many owners—private or family—may want payment up front, rather than being prepared to wait, as Spedan Lewis was prepared to do. In that case, it will be important for funding to be made available for the Trust to borrow to pay the owner. But private and shareholder-owned banks will tend to be biased against such arrangements, and thus reluctant to assist.

So a stronger mutual finance sector could also create a more robust set of options for business succession: Davies and Michie (2012) argued for this in detail in the case of the Welsh economy. The general context is that many successful businesses fail each year because succession is handled badly, that there are serious economic and social costs associated with business succession failure, and that these costs could be avoided through more advanced planning of succession strategy, both financial and managerial. The dominant routes for small- and medium-sized enterprise succession at present are trade sales (to competitors) or family ownership (leaving the founder's equity in the business), both of which have deficiencies as a basis for sustainable competitiveness, reward to the founder, and employment. Family ownership is less sustainable than it appears, and in the UK typically fails to survive beyond the second generation and trade sales offer no continuity or security for the other stakeholders in the business. Employee buyouts avoid these risks, offering instead a model for succession that can often be sustainable, viable, and financially attractive to the exiting owner. This can involve indirect ownership via an Employee Benefit Trust, or direct ownership, via purchase of shares by employees. Such buyouts can be financed by debt, equity, or retained earnings.

Conclusion

This chapter has argued first, that there are benefits to the economy in having a degree of corporate diversity, and that having a critical mass of co-operative and mutual businesses is beneficial in this regard—most particularly in the financial services sector, but also more generally. And secondly, that the co-operative and mutual corporate form has some inherent benefits in terms of providing goods and services the quality of which the members of the organization feel they can trust; and in providing financial services, in particular, to markets and consumers that might otherwise be underserved. To expand the sector requires investment capital, but issuing this is not necessarily straightforward for co-operatives and mutuals. Safeguards are required to ensure that the introduction of ownership rights for external shareholders does not undermine the membership model of ownership and governance. This is an area for future policy globally—namely, the development of new co-operative and mutual financial instruments.

Given the minority status that co-operative and mutual finance has in most economies, it is not immediately obvious which phenomenon is in need of explaining—why mutuals hold only a minority market share, or why they have nevertheless managed to continue to operate for over a century without being squeezed out of the market entirely. With a market share of only a few percent, it might be expected that co-operatives and mutuals would be regarded with some suspicion, or, at least, with a degree of uncertainty by consumers. However, the most important transaction that most people will make in their lifetime is likely to be borrowing the money to purchase their house, and many people have for years been happy to deal with mutuals in this sector. The reason relates to the social embeddedness of co-operatives and mutuals, and their consequent legitimacy with their stakeholders, and concomitantly higher levels of trust.[21]

---

[21] For a detailed discussion of these issues of trust as regards co-operative and mutual firms in the financial services sector, see Michie (2011b).

As discussed above, this positive aspect of the mutual form is one of the reasons for wanting to encourage the growth of the mutual sector, along with the benefits delivered by the additional competitive pressure that is provided from a critical mass of mutuals, and the systemic stability arising from having a greater diversity of corporate forms, enriching the 'ecosystem'.

Of course, co-operative and mutual organizations may not be suitable for all types of financing, and large scale infrastructure projects, for example, may be better suited to publicly owned state or regional banks, or sovereign wealth funds. The key question is whether the members—or potential members—of the mutual organizations perceive a market need that they would like to have delivered by an organization that would be dedicated, through its corporate purpose, to focus on that market need for its members, whether these are savings, mortgages, or any other financial products. The ability of such mutuals to deliver superior outcomes will then depend in part on how well the country's legislative and regulatory system is at supporting such corporate forms.

Reference has been made above to the historic origins of co-operative and mutual finance—and the mutual form of ownership remains crucially important today as a counterbalance to the instability of conventional capital markets. Indeed, some would argue that the trend towards demutualization of the 1980s and 1990s contributed towards the 2007–8 global financial crisis:

The era of globalisation from the 1980s was one that prioritised the interests of private ownership of productive assets. It was fuelled by privatisation, demutualisation and deregulation. It was always a false dichotomy to suggest that the critics of such globalisation were opposed to international economic activities—it was not globalisation *per se* that was being contested, but rather the particular *laissez faire*, neoliberal form that was being promoted. This is not just being wise after the event. As noted above, Andrew Glyn had warned of this on the very eve both of his own death and of the global collapse of what proved to have been a massive Ponzi scheme—literally in the case of Bernie Madoff, and figuratively in the case of the UK and US 'greed is good' variant of capitalism.[22] (Michie and Labao, 2012)

Thus, in addition to the points made above about financial co-operatives and mutuals being appropriate for delivering products and services to their members, and providing healthy competition for the private and shareholder-owned sector of the economy, a strengthened mutual sector nationally and globally could be supportive of a renewed era of economic development on a more sustainable basis than that experienced since the 1980s.[23]

[22] Bernie Madoff is a former American businessman and non-executive chairman of the NASDAQ stock market, who admitted operating a Ponzi scheme that is considered to be the largest financial fraud in US history. In March 2009, Madoff pleaded guilty to defrauding thousands of investors of billions of dollars, estimated by the court at $18bn. He is currently serving a 150-year jail term.
[23] For a discussion of how new political settlements reshaped capitalism in the past and are likely to do so in the future, and for an argument that the fields of social innovation, enterprise, and investment indicate how capital could in the future be made more of a servant and less of a master, see Mulgan (2013).

These various points do require further research, as one of the problems facing current attempts to diversify economic activity, encourage a more corporately diverse financial services sector, and seek greater involvement of co-operative and mutual organizations in the delivery of public services, is precisely that this sector of the economy has been relatively neglected by academic researchers as well as by public policymakers, regulators, and others. Further research is required into how greater corporate diversity could be brought about and sustained—across the economy, as well as specifically to create a more robust financial services sector. Such research needs to look across industrial sectors and different areas of economic activity; across national boundaries, with their different legislative and regulatory regimes;[24] and across the different forms of corporate structures in the private, public, and third sectors.

Thus, there is a need to research the potential benefits to be had from exploiting—or taking advantage of—member-owned organizational forms, and how those potential benefits can best be realized. This includes the 'macro' issues of resilience. It also includes the nature and quality of competition, and how the competitive pressure on private firms to deliver can be enhanced by their facing competition from alternative corporate forms.

That is one collection of research questions and issues, with their concomitant policy implications. As flagged in the introductory remarks to this chapter, the other collection of cutting-edge research questions and issues relate to the need for the co-operative and mutual sector to raise investment capital—and how this can be done whilst maintaining the co-operative and mutual character of the organizations. This need for new research, policy advice, and concomitant regulatory and legislative action is an international one—as set out clearly by the International Co-operative Alliance in their new 'blueprint' for the future. The challenge is to create the circumstances for these organizations to have the technical and legal ability to attract such investment capital, by issuing share capital in return, while retaining the co-operative and mutual nature of these member-owned organizations in face of the introduction of shareholders alongside these member-owners. The key is to ensure that the governance structure does not change to make voice proportional to shareholding (as in shareholder-owned companies), and to provide 'lock-in' mechanisms so that the organization cannot be demutualized to anyone's financial benefit.

These are big questions and difficult issues. But they are not insurmountable. The co-operative and mutual sector across the globe has shown a new enthusiasm to innovate. This reflects a new confidence and ambition to grow the sector and enhance its global influence going forward.[25]

---

[24] Including, for example, the wealthy Emilia Romagna region of Italy which has long had a particularly vibrant network of co-operative enterprises, and the Mondragon Corporation in Spain which employs more than 83,000 through a co-operative network that includes industry, retail, and finance.

[25] As indicated by the International Co-operative Alliance (2011, 2012, 2013); and the Oxford Centre for Mutual & Employee-owned Business (2012).

▓ REFERENCES

Ashworth, H. (1980). *The Building Society Story*. London: Franey.

Ayadi, R., Llewellyn, D. T., Schmidt, R. H., Arbak, E., and De Groen, W. P. (2010). 'Diversity in European Banking: Why Does it Matter?' Centre for European Policy Studies (CEPS), Brussels.

Ayadi, R., Schmidt, R. H., Valverde, S. C., Arbak, E., and Fernandez, F. (2009). *Investigating Diversity in the Banking Sector in Europe: the Performance and Role of Savings Banks*. Brussels: Centre for European Policy Studies (CEPS).

Bank of England (2010). 'Financial Stability Report'. Issue No. 27, June, Bank of England, London.

Boléat, M. (1982). *The Building Society Industry*. London: George Allen & Unwin.

Bowes, J. (2010). *The Fair Trade Revolution*. London: Pluto Press.

Cleary, E. J. (1965). *The Building Society Movement*. London: Elek Books.

Cook, J., Deakin, S., Michie, J., and Nash, D. (2003). *Trust Rewards: Realising the Mutual Advantage*. London: Mutuo.

Cox, P. (2010). *Spedan's Partnership: The Story of John Lewis and Waitrose*. London: John Lewis Partnership.

Cuevas, C. E., and Fischer, K. P. (2006). 'Cooperative Financial Institutions: Issues in Governance, Regulation, and Supervision'. World Bank Working Paper No. 82, The World Bank, Washington, DC.

Davies, W., and Michie, J. (2012). *Employee Ownership: Defusing the Business Succession Time-bomb in Wales*. Cardiff: The Wales Co-operative Centre.

Davies, W., and Yeoman, R. (2013). *Becoming a Public Sector Mutual: Understanding Transition and Change*. Oxford: Oxford Centre for Mutual & Employee-owned Business, for the Co-operative Group and Mutuo.

Department for Business, Innovation & Skills (2010). *Financing a Private Sector Recovery*. London: The Stationery Office.

Eichengreen, B., and Bordo, M. (2002). 'Crises Now and Then: What Lessons from the Last Era of Globalization'. NBER Working Paper 8716, National Bureau of Economic Research, Cambridge, MA.

Gagliardi, F. (2009). 'Financial Development and the Growth of Co-operative Firms', *Small Business Economics: An Entrepreneurship Journal*, 32(4): 439–64.

Haldane, A. G. (2009). 'Rethinking the Financial Network'. Speech delivered at the Financial Student Association, Amsterdam.

Ham, C., Dixon, A., and Brooke, B. (2012). 'Transforming the Delivery of Health and Social Care: The Case for Fundamental Change', The King's Fund, London.

Ham, C., Michie, J., and Mills, C. (2010). 'A Mutual Health Service'. Oxford Centre for Mutual and Employee-owned Business, Kellogg College, University of Oxford.

Hesse, H., and Ĉihák, M. (2007). 'Co-operative Banks and Financial Stability'. IMF Working Paper No. WP/07/2.

HM Government (2010). *The Coalition: Our Programme for Government*. London: Cabinet Office.

HM Treasury (2010). *A New Approach to Financial Regulation: Judgement, Focus and Stability*. London: The Stationery Office.

International Co-operative Alliance (2011). *Global 300*. Brussels: ICA.

International Co-operative Alliance (2012). *World Co-operative Monitor*. Brussels: ICA.

International Co-operative Alliance (2013). *Blueprint for a Co-operative Decade.* Brussels: ICA.

Keynes, J. M. (1936). *The General Theory of Employment, Interest and Money.* London: MacMillan.

Kruse, D., Freeman, R., and Blasi, J. (2010). *Shared Capitalism at Work: Employee Ownership, Profit and Gain Sharing, and Broad-based Stock Options.* Chicago, IL: University of Chicago Press.

Llewellyn, D. T. (2010). *The Global Banking Crisis and the Post Crisis Banking and Regulatory Scenario.* Amsterdam: Amsterdam Centre for Corporate Finance, University of Amsterdam.

Michie, J. (2011a). 'Promoting Corporate Diversity in the Financial Services Sector', *Policy Studies*, 32(4): 309–23.

Michie, J. (2011b). 'Mutual Financial Firms', in J. Springford (ed.), *A Confidence Crisis? Restoring Trust in Financial Services.* Chapter 7, pp. 125–31, London: The Social Market Foundation, Chapter 7, pp. 125–31.

Michie, J. and Blay, M. (2004). *Mutuals and Their Communities: How One in Three Enjoy the Mutual Advantage.* London: Mutuo.

Michie, J. and Labao, L. (2012). 'Ownership, Control and Economic Outcomes', *Cambridge Journal of Regions, Economy and Society*, 5(3): 307–24.

Michie, J. and Oughton, C. (2003). 'HRM, Employee Share Ownership and Corporate Performance', *Research & Practice in HRM*, 11(1): 15–36.

Michie, J. and Sheehan, M. (2005). 'Business Strategy, Human Resources, Labour Market Flexibility, and Competitive Advantage', *International Journal of Human Resource Management*, 16(3): 448–68.

Mulgan, G. (2013). *The Locust and the Bee: Predators and Creators in Capitalism's Future.* Princeton, NJ: Princeton University Press.

Nicholls, A. (2010). 'The Institutionalization of Social Investment: The Interplay of Investment Logics and Investor Rationalities', *Journal of Social Entrepreneurship*, 1(1): 70–100.

Nicholls, A. and Pharoah, C. (2008). 'The Landscape of Social Investment: A Holistic Topology of Opportunities and Challenges'. Skoll Centre for Social Entrepreneurship Working Paper, Oxford.

Ownership Commission (2012). *Plurality, Stewardship and Engagement: The Report of The Ownership Commission.* London: Mutuo.

Oxford Centre for Mutual & Employee-owned Business (2012). *Mutuals Yearbook 2012.* London: Mutuo.

Price, S. J. (1958). *Building Societies: Their Origins and History.* London: Franey.

Ransom, D. (2001). *The No-nonsense Guide to Fair Trade.* Oxford: New Internationalist Publications.

Tabb, W. K. (2012). *The Restructuring of Capitalism in Our Time.* New York: Columbia University Press.

The Economist (2010). 'The Eclipse of the Public Company', *The Economist*, 21st August, p. 58.

Worldwatch Institute (2012). Membership in Co-operative Businesses Reaches 1 Billion, *Vital Signs.* <http://www.worldwatch.org/membership-co-operative-businesses-reaches-1-billion>, accessed 1 February 2014.

6 Microfinance

A field in flux

Nicholas Sabin

Introduction

Microfinance is often cited as the success story of the broader social finance movement. Financial access for poor and low-income clients has expanded dramatically over the last four decades to include over 3,500 microfinance institutions reaching over 200 million clients worldwide (Maes and Reed, 2012). The approach is often viewed as a clear example of using market-based principles to advance a social objective, in this case primarily the use of unsubsidized lending to alleviate poverty (Nicholls, 2006). The movement has also generated extensive public acclaim, such as the United Nations recognizing 2005 as the International Year of Microcredit and the Norwegian Nobel Committee awarding the Peace Prize to Dr Muhammad Yunus and the Grameen Bank in 2006.

However, to characterize the microfinance movement as an uncontested success story lessens our ability to understand the challenges of pioneering the social finance space. A more nuanced view of microfinance reveals a field in flux faced with unresolved debates and ongoing changes. The market structure is shifting, with organizations increasingly accessing commercial funding (Glisovic, González, Saltuk, and de Mariz, 2012). Some markets have over-heated, producing substantial criticism (CGAP, 2010). Recent impact evaluations are raising new questions about what microfinance actually can and should attempt to achieve (Bauchet, Marshall, Starita, Thomas, and Yalouris, 2011). Even the basic offering is being rethought in terms of products and services that will better suit the needs of the poor (Morduch, 2011). Amidst these developments, the global reach of microfinance continues to grow (Maes and Reed, 2012). In such a state of flux, it is increasingly important to understand both the unifying trends as well as the points of disagreement within the field.

The intent of this chapter is to provide an overview of microfinance by exploring both its historical roots, as well as the significant changes that have occurred over the last decade. To help place microfinance in context, the chapter begins with a brief introduction to terminology and a review of two key historical predecessors that were particularly relevant to the emergence of modern microfinance: informal community associations and state-owned development banks. The following section describes how the modern microfinance movement began in the mid 1970s and grew to its present form. The current landscape is then characterized in terms of scale, geographic coverage, institution size, and organizational type.

The remaining content of the chapter is structured around three of the most fundamental debates in microfinance. Not only have these questions shaped the course of microfinance to date, but they are still unresolved and will likely direct the future of the field. The first topic concerns the critical features of the microfinance model. For decades practitioners and researchers have grappled with understanding exactly what makes microcredit appear to work (e.g. Stiglitz, 1990; Attanasio, Augsburg, De Haas, Fitzsimons, and Harmgart, 2012). Some institutions are shifting their focus beyond credit, to include such products as microsavings and microinsurance (e.g. Dupas and Robinson, 2011; Karlan, Osei-Akoto, Osei, and Udry, 2011). The second topic addresses the appropriate role of commercialization in microfinance. This issue has become increasingly polarized as organizations have begun accessing capital through public stock markets and sometimes generating substantial profits for shareholders (CGAP, 2007). Whether commercial funding represents a much-needed capital source or a move in the wrong social direction, may be the most contested issue in microfinance (see e.g. Yunus, 2011). The third topic concerns the actual impact of microfinance. The publication of several randomized controlled trials suggests that the impact of credit on microenterprise growth is more modest than originally hoped (Bauchet et al., 2011). However, the upside of such studies is that microfinance programmes often produce other unintended benefits for the poor, such as risk reduction and better cash-flow management (Morduch, 2011). These findings are useful in that they suggest how microfinance might be reconceptualized to improve its social impact. The chapter concludes with implications for the broader field of social finance based on lessons learned from the microfinance movement to date.

Microfinance terminology

A basic definition of microfinance is 'financial services for poor and low-income clients' (Gonzalez and Rosenberg, 2006: 1). While this definition offers a good starting point, it is helpful to further clarify what is typically associated with the term 'microfinance.' Broadly, the idea and practice of financial services for the poor is not new. For example, informal savings and credit associations for impoverished communities have existed for centuries in many countries around the world (Helms, 2006). However, when the term 'microfinance' is used today, there is a general understanding in the industry that one is referring more narrowly to the movement that has taken shape over the last four decades built around a more specific financial model. It is common for this movement to be referred to as 'modern microfinance' (Trezza, 2006: 20) or the 'new microfinance' (Robinson, 2001: 224). In this chapter, usage of the term 'microfinance' will refer to this more narrow conception.

What are the primary features of the modern microfinance movement? The Grameen Bank, pioneered by Muhammad Yunus in Bangladesh during the 1970s, is often cited as the prototypical example of modern microfinance (Morduch, 1999). There are two key tenets to this type of model: (1) financial self-sustainability of the service provider and (2) targeting clients that are typically excluded from the formal financial market. While not all microfinance institutions achieve financial self-sustainability, the intent is generally to charge interest rates and fees that allow the provider to cover its operational costs. This can be contrasted with the model of many state-owned development banks during the 1950s to the 1980s that were built on the idea that credit to rural farmers had to be subsidized (Robinson, 2001). The second tenet of modern microfinance is social inclusion; this has typically been borne out by targeting historically excluded clients in developing countries, such as women and the poor (Yunus, 2003). As we shall see, new organizations are increasingly blurring the boundaries of what characterizes a microfinance institution.

A further aspect of terminology that is useful to clarify is the distinction between microfinance and microcredit. Microfinance is a more general term that refers to a variety of financial services; microcredit is a subset of microfinance that specifically refers to the provision of small loans. In addition to loans, microfinance can also include financial services such as deposits, insurance, payment services, and money transfers (Daley-Harris and Awimbo, 2011). Historically, the focus of microfinance has been on providing microcredit via group loans. Because of this, the majority of microfinance research to date has explored the features and effects of providing such loans. However, over the last decade there has been a substantial shift in attempting to provide a more complete set of services beyond microcredit (Armendáriz and Morduch, 2010).

Historical predecessors of modern microfinance

The idea of financial services for clients excluded from the formal market has a substantial history. In development finance, it has been a perennial question as to why certain populations seem to be cut off from the global credit market (see e.g. Braverman and Guasch, 1986; Stiglitz, 1990). In response to this question, several reasons have been suggested as to why providing loans in developing economies is difficult. Given the small loan amounts and high transaction costs, an institution needs to be highly efficient and maintain low default rates if it is to be financially sustainable. While this challenge is not insurmountable, a lender typically faces the additional difficulties of: scarce information on potential clients before issuing the loan; limited ability to effectively enforce the loan once it has been disbursed; and, a lack of collateral to rely on if the client goes into default (Besley and Coate, 1995). Taken together, these challenges create a daunting environment for an institution to be financially sustainable. Faced with such circumstances, what financial models have been used in the past?

Two types of predecessors are particularly important for understanding the current movement: community associations and state-owned development banks. Community associations, in particular rotating savings and credit associations (Roscas) and credit co-operatives, have been in use for centuries and are relevant for their use of group lending. These models are thought to have played a role in inspiring Yunus' ideas for the solidarity groups of Grameen Bank (Morduch, 1999). The role of state-owned development banks are relevant for their use of subsidized lending. They are of interest predominately because their failed attempts during the 1950s to 1980s provided such a strong impetus for the new microfinance model (Armendáriz and Morduch, 2010).

COMMUNITY ASSOCIATIONS

The roots of group lending can be traced to a type of community association known as the Rosca (Geertz, 1962; Besley, Coate, and Loury, 1993). Ardner defines a Rosca as an informal association 'formed upon a core of participants who agree to make regular contributions to a fund which is given, in whole or in part, to each contributor in rotation' (1964: 201). Roscas serve the function of allowing members to pool their money into lump sums without the involvement of formal institutions. If a member receives the lump sum earlier in the rotation, it can be viewed as that member having received a loan from the group. If a member receives the lump sum later in the rotation, the Rosca has functioned more as a savings device for the member. This basic arrangement is used extensively around the world with a high degree of similarity[1]. Since the nineteenth century, Roscas have been documented under different names; for example, in China they have been referred to as *hui hui*, in Nigeria as *esusu*, and in Scotland as *menages*. There is written evidence of Roscas being used in Japan as far back as 1275 (Ardener, 1964).

An important feature of Roscas is that the members typically know each other socially. They rarely start with a formal management or organizational structure, yet they typically have very high repayment rates. Many researchers have asked how the repayment rates are maintained. Roscas seem to avoid default problems by relying on the social cohesiveness of the group (Geertz, 1962; Ardener 1964; Besley et al., 1993). Not only can members provide positive support and solidarity, there can be significant social cost in terms of pressure, embarrassment, or exclusion. Such social mechanisms are key features of the modern microfinance model involving group loans.

A more formalized community organization for financial access is the credit co-operative. In contrast to Roscas, co-operatives often have a formal charter

---

[1] There are notable variations on the basic model including organizer fees, group size, fund amount, frequency of repayment, determination of payout order, and so on.

and some legal status (Armendáriz and Morduch, 2010). Loans also tend to be larger and are paid back over longer periods. In the co-operative model, the members are all shareholders, but not all the members are expected to take out a loan. The concept of community lending is still central to the model as members have a say in setting the terms of credit access and an ongoing interest in ensuring that the loans are repaid. Co-operatives emerged in Germany during the late nineteenth century and are now seen internationally in countries as diverse as Ireland, France, Kenya, Malawi, and India (Huppi and Feder, 1990).

STATE-OWNED DEVELOPMENT BANKS

While community associations are historically relevant for their often-successful use of local cohesiveness, state-owned development banks are relevant for demonstrating the limitations of subsidized credit programmes. During the 1950s to 1980s, there was a focus on development via government-mediated subsidies for the rural poor. Using external funding and formalized organizational structures, state-owned development banks hoped to scale up financial services to the poor. Subsidized credit for farmers was the most common approach. Despite positive intentions, the results of such pro-grammes were broadly deemed a failure (Morduch, 1999). See the following vignette 'India's Integrated Rural Development Programme' for a detailed example.

The programmes often failed to achieve their development goals and resulted in very high default rates. Most government-subsidized credit pro-grammes in Africa, the Middle East, Latin America, and South Asia produced default rates between 40–95 per cent during this period (Braverman and Guasch, 1986). Failure of these programmes is often attributed to an inability to enforce the loans, corruption within the institutions, and the diversion of funds to better-off clients (Braverman and Guasch, 1986). The experience of state-owned development banks led many to question whether such pro-grammes were a viable approach for extending financial access to the poor. By the 1980s, it was clear that a different approach was needed.

Vignette 1: India's Integrated Rural Development Programme

India's Integrated Rural Development Programme (IRDP) during the 1980s is an example of an ineffective attempt at development by means of government-subsidized credit. Approximately US$6bn in subsidies was directed to the rural poor throughout the decade (Armendáriz and Morduch, 2010). The Government's intentions were decidedly focused on social impact for farmers: 'The imperative laid down for the plan for rural areas of the country is increasing productivity through a strategy of growth with social justice...

More specifically, it involves a sharp focus on target groups comprising small and marginal farmers, agricultural labourers and rural artisans' (Rath, 1985: 238).

Given the amount of money invested, the results were startlingly unimpressive. Why did the IRDP fail to achieve its goals? Critics often blame the performance of IRDP on several factors: endemic corruption, lack of infrastructure, and poor administration (Dreze, 1990). Others more generally disagree with subsidized credit programmes, arguing that they are not sustainable and disrupt the financial market. The impact on poverty alleviation was a disappointment and default rates were over 40 per cent. 'More than any positive historical precedent, it is the repudiation of these negative legacies that has driven the microfinance movement to look to the private sector for inspiration' (Armendáriz and Morduch, 2010: 11–12).

The modern microfinance movement

Following in the wake of the disappointing subsidized credit programmes, the greatest accomplishment of modern microfinance has been the demonstration that poor clients can be reliable bank customers (Cull, Demirguc-Kunt, and Morduch, 2009). Some have described the rapid spread of the microfinance model as a financial 'revolution' (Robinson, 2001). What is different about the modern microfinance movement and where did this innovative model come from?

Accounts of the pioneering microcredit institutions suggest that the model evolved from real-world experimentation in low-income countries like Bangladesh, Indonesia, and Bolivia (Armendáriz and Morduch, 2010). Credit is often given to Muhammad Yunus for developing the prototypical design of the Grameen Bank in Bangladesh during the 1970s. In his own words, Yunus was not attempting to fix the financial market, but rather to address a social problem: 'I had no intention of lending money to anyone; all I really wanted was to solve an immediate problem ... the problem of poverty which humiliates and denigrates everything that a human being stands for' (Yunus, 1998: 12). The late 1970s was an experimental phase for Yunus and his collegues: 'We did not know anything about how to run a bank for the poor, so we had to learn from scratch. In January 1977, when we started, I looked at how others ran their loan operations, and I learned from their mistakes' (Yunus, 1998: 104).

Since the beginning, Yunus focused his lending scheme on female borrowers. He was particularly driven by their unjustified exclusion from the banking sector. Yunus began by providing small loans to groups of women. He thought that the group feature made the loans easier to keep track of for the bank. Furthermore, groups could provide positive support and social pressure to smooth out behaviour patterns. In terms of collection, he also experimented with very small and frequent repayment amounts, believing that lump sum repayments cause psychological hurdles for the borrowers. For a 365 taka loan (aproximiately UD$15) he would require the borrower to simply pay back one taka every day (Yunus, 1998). Building on these principles of female inclusion, group lending, and small frequent payments, Grameen was formalized as an independent bank in 1983.

Around the same time, institutions in other countries were pioneering similar approaches for providing microcredit. In Indonesia, the microbanking division of Bank Rakyat Indonesia (BRI) underwent substantial reform in 1983. Aided by the Government's major financial deregulation package, BRI was able to produce a large-scale commercially sustainable microfinance system with unusual quickness and success. By the end of the 1980s, both the Grameen Bank and BRI had demonstrated that microfinance institutions could reach over 1 million borrowers and maintain high repayment rates (Robinson, 2001). In Bolivia, BancoSol was established in 1992 to provide microfinance on a national scale (Rhyne, 2001). A substantial portion of BancoSol's funding was from international investment firms, further sparking global interest. There were differences in approaches taken by such pioneering organizations, but the common thread was an interest in developing financial methods to reach the poor without subsidy. Organizations were designing new financial products based on group and individual loans, reassessing appropriate interest rates to cover operational costs, devloping new management and information systems, and rethinking appropriate training and incentives for staff members. By the late 1990s, microfinance had transitioned from a collection of institutions to a rapidly growing industry (Robinson, 2001).

Accurately quantifying the growth of microfinance is a challenging task as many of the institutions are small and informal. However, several research organizations have made estimates of microfinance at the global scale. The largest primary-source collection of microfinance data has been produced by the Microcredit Summit Campaign (MSC). Figure 6.1 provides the number of registered microfinance programmes and their clients according to the MSC (Maes and Reed, 2012).[2]

In 2010, the number of microfinance programmes registering with the MSC was 3,652. These programmes reported reaching a worldwide total of 205.3 million clients with a current loan. During the period from 1997 to 2010, the number of total microfinance clients reported to the MSC grew on average by 23 per cent per year. A more conservative estimate of microfinance growth over the period from 1998 to 2004 was produced by the Consultive Group to Assist the Poor (CGAP) by accounting for pre-existing institutions that start

---

[2] For alternative estimates see CGAP (<http://www.cgap.org>) or Microfinance Information Exchange (<http://www.mixmarket.org>). Also note that the Microcredit Summit data includes growth based on existing programmes registering for the first time, so may inflate year-over-year growth. For further detail on the Microcredit Summit data, see: <http://www.microcreditsummit.org>.

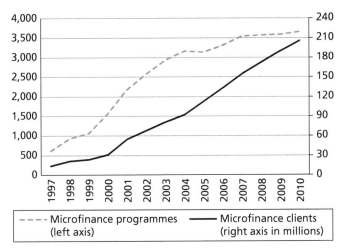

Figure 6.1. Growth of microfinance programmes and clients
Source: State of the Microcredit Summit Campaign Report 2012

reporting to the MSC for the first time. This approach resulted in a growth estimate of 12 per cent per year (Gonzalez and Rosenberg, 2006). For further detail on the diffusion of microfinance, see the extensive study by Banerjee, Chandrasekhar, Duflo, and Jackson, (2013).

The landscape of microfinance

Given the origins and growth of the industry, what does the landscape of microfinance providers look like today? The landscape is populated by a diverse set of institutions. To name just a few dimensions, organizations vary considerably in terms of mission, targeted clients, product offering, and funding source. As more varied actors continue to enter the microfinance space, what qualifies as a microfinance provider is becoming increasingly blurred (Helms, 2006). In this section, an overview of the landscape of microfinance is provided by examining three basic dimensions: (1) geographic coverage, (2) institution size, and (3) institution type.

Figure 6.2 summarizes the geographic coverage of microfinance based on the number of 'poorest' families reached in 2010. 'Poorest' refers to those living on less than US$1.25 a day adjusted for purchasing power parity (Maes and Reed, 2012). The figure provides an estimate of percentage coverage for each geographic region by comparing the number of poorest families accessing microfinance to the total number of poorest families. Microfinance in Asia and the Pacific is the most extensive both in terms of the absolute number of clients and in terms of the percentage of the relevant population

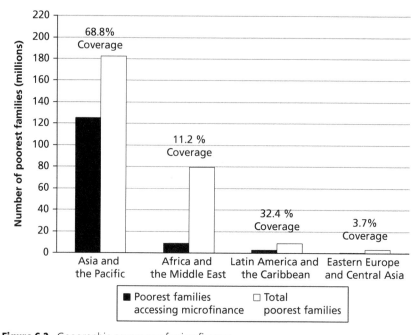

Figure 6.2. Geographic coverage of microfinance
Source: The World Bank and State of the Microcredit Summit Campaign Report 2012

that has been reached (68.8 per cent coverage).[3] Since the 1980s, as was described with Grameen Bank and BRI, many of the pioneering institutions of microfinance have been located in Asia.

A second key dimension of the microfinance landscape is the size of institutions. Currently, a small number of large organizations account for the majority of clients, producing a fairly concentrated market structure. See Table 6.1 for a breakdown of the market structure based on MSC data. Of the 3,652 microfinance organizations that registered with the MSC in 2010, the largest twenty-one organizations provided loans to over 75 per cent of the total poorest clients worldwide. In contrast, there were thousands of small organizations that each served fewer than 2,500 poorest clients and accounted for only 1.1 per cent of the global market.

Finally, what does the current landscape look like in terms of institution type? The Microfinance Information Exchange (MIX) provides a public source of institution types. Here the institutions are divided into five categories based on legal status:

---

[3] It is known that some clients have outstanding loans at multiple organizations. This results in some amount of overestimation of the number of microfinance clients and the coverage percentage. However, based on individual MFI data, it is currently not possible to accurately gauge the overlap of borrowers (Gonzalez, 2008).

Table 6.1. Microfinance market structure by institution size

Institution size–type	Number of institutions	Combined number of clients	Percentage of total
Networks	8	65,105,273	47.3%
1 million or more	13	40,267,670	29.3%
100,000–999,999	64	17,095,196	12.4%
10,000–99,999	361	10,877,810	7.9%
2,500–9,999	558	2,731,044	2.0%
Fewer than 2,500	2,648	1,470,448	1.1%
Total	3,652	137,547,441	100.0%

Source: State of the Microcredit Summit Campaign Report 2012
Note: Size refers to poorest clients below the US$1.25 a day threshold.

- *Bank*: a licensed financial intermediary regulated by a state banking super-visory agency
- *Co-operative—credit union*: a non-profit, member-based financial intermediary
- *Non-bank financial institution*: this category is often created specifically for microfinance composed of financial intermediaries that provide similar services to those of a bank, but may have lower capital requirements or restricted service offerings
- *Non-government organization*: an organization registered as a non-profit, typically not regulated by a banking supervisory agency
- *Other*.

Figure 6.3 provides the market structure in terms of the legal status of micro-finance institutions in 2011. NGOs are the most common institution type although they are relatively small and account for only 23.6 per cent of the borrowers. Historically, NGOs accounted for a larger share of the microfinance market. Currently, the increasing commercialization of the field is expanding the presence of banks and non-bank financial institutions. It can be argued that these different institution types are serving different segments of the microfinance market. An analysis by Cull et al. (2009) found that NGOs typically have a stronger focus on social objectives. NGOs tended to provide the smallest loans, target the greatest number of women, and reach the poorest clients. The arguments for and against commercial funding are discussed in greater depth later in this chapter.

Critical features of microfinance

So far in this chapter, an overview of microfinance terminology, historical growth, and current landscape has been provided. With that background, the focus now shifts to three central debates in microfinance. Focusing on unre-solved debates is useful for understanding a field currently in flux. The topics

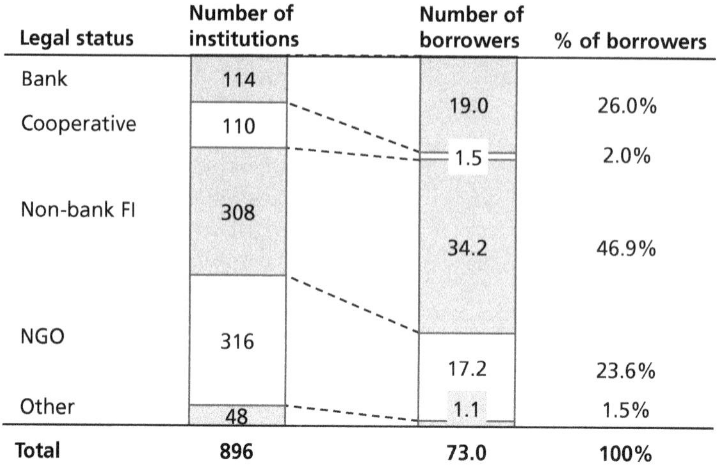

Legal status	Number of institutions			Number of borrowers	% of borrowers
Bank	114			19.0	26.0%
Cooperative	110			1.5	2.0%
Non-bank FI	308			34.2	46.9%
NGO	316			17.2	23.6%
Other	48			1.1	1.5%
Total	**896**			**73.0**	**100%**

Figure 6.3. Microfinance market structure by institution type

Source: MIX Market 2011

Note: The allocation is based on 896 institutions reporting to the MIX Market in 2011. The criteria used to define what qualifies as a microfinance provider can produce different characterizations of market structure. For an alternative view, see Helms (2006). Number of borrowers in millions.

highlight alternative views regarding what has worked to date and potential future directions for microfinance.

The first debated topic concerns the critical features of microfinance. Given the historical emphasis on credit programmes, much of the research to date has focused on loan features. Microfinance pioneers often innovated along multiple dimensions simultaneously. This produces a situation in which it is difficult to disentangle the factors that may have been most effective. Understanding the underlying mechanisms is particularly important when attempting to replicate the model in different cultural contexts. It remains an open question as to which features of microcredit are necessary, as well as how additional services and products should be incorporated in the microfinance offering. Here the debate around five features of microfinance is summarized: (1) group versus individual lending, (2) necessity of public repayment, (3) optimal repayment frequency, (4) impact of dynamic incentives, and (5) breadth of product–service offering beyond credit.

GROUP VERSUS INDIVIDUAL LENDING

One of the most discussed features of microfinance is the use of joint-liability group lending. Instead of offering loans to individual clients, microfinance institutions often offer loans to groups of clients, such that if a borrower defaults, the other group members are held financially responsible. Organizations have used a variety of group sizes and structures. On one side of the spectrum,

BancoSol provides loans to 'solidarity groups' as small as three borrowers. At the other extreme, 'village banking' models are based on groups of up to fifty borrowers. Such models were pioneered by the Foundation for International Community Assistance (FINCA). The Grameen Bank began with a nested structure between these two extremes: eight subgroups of five borrowers were linked as a forty-person group.

Why are group loans particularly relevant to the poor? The basic motivation is that financial institutions often lack information on potential clients, are unable to effectively enforce the loan, and have little collateral to seize if a borrower defaults. These problems often make traditional lending in such markets financially unsustainable. Group lending seems to overcome some of these challenges by leveraging the social relationships of the group. Researchers have suggested that group members are in a better position to screen, monitor, and enforce on each other (Ghatak, 1999; Stiglitz, 1990; Besley and Coate, 1995).

However, group lending has also been argued as placing too great a burden on borrowers. One issue is that group lending transfers some of the risk from the bank to the group members, even though the bank is often in a better position to bear the cost of a defaulting client (Stiglitz, 1990). A second concern is that group lending can produce substantial social costs for the borrowers as well. One can easily imagine how positive support to repay could turn into a harmful form of group pressure (Woolcock, 1999; Brett, 2006). Moreover, survey research indicates that when the question is posed to clients if they would prefer a group loan or an individual loan, most respondents strongly favour not being held jointly liable (Murray and Lynch, 2003; Ditcher and Harper, 2007).

Do the benefits of group lending outweigh the additional costs for the borrowers? A first step towards answering that question is in understanding the impact of liability type on repayment rates. If the institution's operational benefits from group lending are minimal, a case can be made that the social costs of group lending outweigh the marginal economic benefits. Studies that directly address this issue have been limited to date, but are beginning to gauge the effect of liability type on repayment. Giné and Karlan (2006) conducted an experiment in the Philippines in which the existing clients of a rural bank were assigned either to continue on with joint-liability contracts or to switch to individual lending contracts. They found no effect of switching on repayment rates, suggesting that individual lending can be as effective as group lending.

A recent experiment by Attanasio, et al. (2012) in Mongolia also found no difference in repayment rates, although other positive effects of group lending were noted. In their study, different villages were randomly assigned to receive access to group loans, individual loans, or no access. While they did not find a difference in default rates based on contract type, they did find that group lending produced an additional positive impact for the borrowers in terms of business creation and poverty alleviation. Attanasio et al. argue that group lending ensures greater discipline in borrower behaviour, notably better project selection, and long-term execution. A recent study conducted in Sierra Leone by Sabin and Reed-Tsochas (2014) found that variation in a microcredit group's social structure has a significant effect on its economic performance. The study shows that group features, such as average spatial density and fragmentation, help us to understand why groups behave differently in terms of repayment.

To date, it is still unclear how crucial group lending is to microfinance. However, a general trend in the field is a shift away from joint-liability contracts. Armendáriz and Morduch (2000) suggest that while group lending may be relevant in some situations, it is time to focus on other mechanisms that may be more important to microfinance and less socially costly.

PUBLIC REPAYMENT

One such alternative mechanism for microcredit is public repayments. Repayment in front of fellow community members leverages a social incentive without the full joint-liability contract. Research has found that the borrower's motivation to avoid embarrassment and social stigma can improve repayment rates (Rahman, 1999). Furthermore, public meetings can offer additional opportunities for training borrowers. Often viewed as an innovator in the field, Grameen Bank revised its group lending approach in 2001. Grameen no longer requires joint-liability loans but still administers loan collection in large public groups (Yunus, 2003). The importance of public repayment is also well illustrated by the practical example of recent innovations in mobile phone banking. See the 'M-Pesa and Group Lending' vignette for a more detailed account.

Vignette 2: M-Pesa and Group Lending

In 2007, Safaricom-Vodafone launched a new mobile banking platform in Kenya called M-Pesa. The platform allows clients to transfer money via their mobile phones. Within four years, M-Pesa had been adopted by over 14 million customers and over 70 per cent of households in Kenya (Suria, Jack, and Stokera, 2012).

Though no longer limited to microfinance clients, M-Pesa actually started as a pilot programme in 2005 to facilitate the loan disbursements and repayments of a microfinance institution called Faulu Kenya (Kumar, McKay, and Rotman, 2010). During the six-month pilot, Faulu realized that if borrowers could make their payments using their mobile phones, public meetings to collect payments were not necessary. However, the management and staff at Faulu were concerned that without these public meetings, group cohesion—a key component of their lending model—would deteriorate. Following the pilot, Faulu decided not to use M-Pesa for loan repayments.

Other MFIs have come up with a hybrid approach that integrates M-Pesa with public meetings. The Small and Micro Enterprise Programme pioneered an approach in which borrowers can make their payments via M-Pesa before group meetings, but attendance at the meetings is still required (Kumar, et al., 2010). This results in less meeting time spent on cash collection and leaves more time for discussion of business problems and financial education. Such an approach integrates the latest banking technology with the well-known benefits of public meetings for group cohesion.

REPAYMENT FREQUENCY

Another questioned aspect of microfinance is the appropriate frequency of loan repayment. The basic tension arises because more frequent repayments typically produce better loan performance but are more operationally costly. If payments are not frequent enough, borrowers are faced with the challenges of repaying a larger lump sum. Repaying a lump sum is difficult for practical reasons, e.g. borrowers often do not have savings accounts, as well as for psychological reasons, e.g. there is greater temptation to prematurely spend the money on consumption needs (Fischer and Ghatak, 2011). Furthermore, Rai and Sjostrom (2004) argue that frequent payments produce more opportunities to gain information on the status of borrowers' projects. This offers the lender greater insight to whether a defaulting borrower is truly unable to pay, or is simply unwilling to pay. Analysing empirical data, Silwal (2003) found that greater frequency of repayment (weekly versus monthly) is correlated with lower delinquency rates.

However, if payments are scheduled too frequently an unnecessary cost is placed both on the lender and the borrower in terms of time and resources. Grameen Bank initially experimented with daily payments, expecting these to be the easiest for borrowers to make. However, Yunus found that daily payment was logistically burdensome and eventually switched to weekly payment (Yunus, 1998). Lenders worldwide are still experimenting with credit products to achieve the right level of repayment frequency for their specific cultural context and the needs of their borrowers.

DYNAMIC INCENTIVES

Another feature that is often attributed to the success of microcredit is the use of 'dynamic incentives' or 'progressive lending' (Hulme and Mosley, 1996). This practice refers to a lender offering a progression of increasing loan amounts to the borrower. For example a progression of four six-month loans might proceed in the amounts of $100, $125, $150, and $200. With dynamic incentives, relatively quick access to a greater amount of capital can serve as a strong incentive to pay back the current loan (Tedeschi, 2006).

Programmes based on dynamic incentives make it clear to the clients from the outset that how they perform on their current loan directly affects the amount they can qualify for on the next loan. In the case of default, access to all future loans is typically cut off. This method has been used by microcredit providers of both individual and group loans. In group loan situations, if one member defaults and the other group members are not willing to repay, all the members lose access to future loans. Morduch (1999) notes that dynamic incentives may not produce an effective repayment mechanism if borrowers have easy access to loans from other organizations. For example, if a borrower can default on a loan and subsequently receive a loan from a different organization that does not know his or her repayment history, there is less incentive to repay the current loan. This suggests that without credit bureaus that can link repayment history across multiple lenders, the impact of dynamic incentives will decrease as the microfinance industry matures. An increase in the saturation of microcredit providers will make it easier for borrowers to strategically default and take another loan elsewhere.

BREADTH OF PRODUCT–SERVICE OFFERING

So far in this section the debated features of microfinance have focused on microcredit. This is reflective of the industry's historical focus on credit. However, during the 1990s a shift in terminology began in which 'micro-finance' replaced 'microcredit' as the standard industry descriptor (Helms, 2006). This shift was spurred by an understanding that the poor needed access to a fuller set of financial products. See Figure 6.4 for an overview of additional

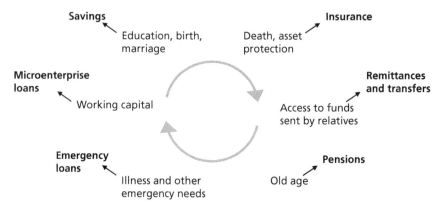

Figure 6.4. Need for broader range of microfinance products and services
Source: CGAP 2006

microfinance products. Though most microfinance providers are still credit-focused, today we see a greater number of providers offering a combination of credit, savings, insurance, money transfers, and 'plus' services. Pro Mujer based in Latin America, offers a clear example of the 'microfinance plus' model. In addition to providing microcredit, Pro Mujer offers business training and healthcare support for women.

Why has attention only recently broadened to a fuller set of financial products for the poor? In the case of microsavings, proponents have argued for its relevance for decades, referring to it as the forgotten half of rural finance (Vogel, 1984; Gonzalez-Vega, 1994). Microsavings can serve the dual purpose of providing the financial institution with an additional source of capital and offering clients a product that is critically needed. Resistance to offering savings is often driven by the perceived difficulty of administering small deposit accounts in developing countries. Financial institutions often expect such accounts would be unprofitable (Robinson, 2001). While there has been a realization that there is significant demand for complementary products such as savings and insurance, as of yet there have been no breakthrough innovations on the supply side of these products in the same way that the industry experienced breakthroughs regarding the implementation of the microcredit model (Armendáriz and Morduch, 2010). This may currently be changing as practitioners experiment with new banking platforms such as mobile money (Scharwatt et al., 2015).

The commercialization of microfinance

The second core debate of this chapter concerns the appropriate role of commercialization in microfinance. It is useful to clarify at the outset what is typically meant by 'commercialization' in this discussion. As most microfinance providers use market-based principles to reach their objectives, the polarizing issue is not so much an issue of organizational design, but rather the use of commercial capital, that is, funding with a profit motive (Armendáriz and Morduch, 2010). Opponents of commercialization argue that expectations of generating profits for investors will necessarily result in mission drift and ultimately harm the poor (see e.g. Bateman, 2010; Yunus, 2011). In contrast, proponents of commercial funding view it as a positive and much-needed source of capital, not incompatible with the social focus of microfinance. They argue that earning profits will attract more capital to the industry and enable institutions to better meet the global demand for microfinance (see e.g. Akula, 2010; Rangan, Chu, and Petkoski, 2011). Armendáriz and Morduch (2010: 10) describe: 'If there is one unresolved tension that animates those who spend their days working on microfinance, it entails how to navigate the trade-offs between maximizing social impact and building strong, large financial institutions. It is a healthy tension, but an inescapable one.'

Prahalad's (2004) conception of *The Fortune at the Bottom of the Pyramid* brought further attention to the idea that profits could be made while alleviating global poverty. The microfinance industry has leveraged commercial funding through debt for a considerable time. Much more recently, the industry has begun to be seen as an appropriate place for equity investments, private and public. To date, several microfinance institutions have made initial public offerings (IPOs) on stock exchanges: Bank Rakyat Indonesia (2003), Equity Bank in Kenya (2006), Banco Compartamos in Mexico (2007), and Swayam Krishi Sangam (SKS) in India (2010). The two latter IPOs, both approximately thirteen times oversubscribed (CGAP, 2007; MicroCapital, 2010), generated a significant amount of public controversy with critics claiming the organizations were unnecessarily profiting from the poor. These IPOs have received the bulk of attention, both positive and negative. However, a significant amount of equity has also been invested in microfinance through private placements (Glisovic, González, Saltuk, and de Mariz, 2012). Table 6.2 summarizes the growth of private equity transactions both in number and value. Those in support of increased commercial interest in microfinance see these trends as a natural progression. Michael Chu, former president of Accion, argues that worldwide demand for microfinance cannot be met unless profit-oriented capital is drawn in. Increased competition will eventually help bring interest rates and profits down to consumer-friendly levels (Rosenberg, 2008).

What is the argument against the commercialization of microfinance? Muhammad Yunus offers one of the clearest views as to why increased commercialization is the wrong direction for microfinance. He argues that expectations attached to commercial funding cause microfinance providers to act as a new 'breed of loan sharks' (Yunus, 2011: 1). It is argued that commercially funded institutions will need to raise interest rates and engage in aggressive loan collection to satisfy profit-oriented shareholders. The demands of ever-increasing profits will cause a shift in the mission of microfinance that ultimately defeats the purpose of improving the lives of the poor. For those sharing Yunus' views, the IPO of Banco Compartamos was a striking

Table 6.2. Historical private equity transactions in microfinance

Year	Transactions (number)	Value (US$ million)
2005	28	106
2006	37	20
2007	37	60
2008	63	144
2009	32	230
2010	37	205
2011	68	292
Total	302	1,057

Source: CGAP Research, Global Microfinance Equity Survey 2012

Note: CGAP-J.P. Morgan estimates that this sample covers 70–80% of microfinance PE activity.

example of his concerns. Leading up to the IPO, Compartamos was charging an average annual interest rate of approximately 100 per cent to its clients (CGAP, 2007). During the IPO, the owners of Compartamos sold 30 per cent of their stock for a total of US$458m. Critics claim that such interest rates and profits cannot be morally justified. Yunus argues that an additional downside of such transactions is that they further burden the poor with financial risk. Instead of creating funds based primarily on local deposits, organizations pursuing IPOs are accessing capital from volatile global markets and then transmitting this volatility to poor borrowers who are ill equipped to mitigate the risk (Yunus, 2011).

A middle-ground view on the commercialization debate starts with the perspective that commercial funding will inevitably increase. The primary concern then becomes how it can best be integreated into the industry. There have been multiple occurances of commercial funding causing micro-finance markets to overheat. For example, in Bolivia during the 1990s there was an influx of commercial funding and the market became so oversaturated that default rates soared and the market nearly collapsed (Rhyne, 2001). In more recent years, the microfinance market in India has struggled with instability. See the vignette 'The Crisis in Andhra Pradesh' for more details. However, some empirical analysis has suggested that high growth of micro-finance insitutions is not inherently detrimental to portfolio quality, except in the most extreme situations (Gonzalez, 2010). Portfolio deterioration can be mitigated if providers focus on growing *expansively* instead of *locally*. By looking to less-developed geographic markets, the risk of creating a locally saturated market can be reduced.

Another reason why commercial and non-profit funding may construct-ively coexist in the industry is that these sources of funding tend to focus on different social objectives and market niches. Commercial microfinance banks are more likely to involve individual lending, make larger loans, and target fewer of the neediest clients (Cull et al., 2009). Non-governmental microfi-nance organizations are more likely to involve group lending, make smaller loans, and actively target more of the neediest clients (Cull et al., 2009). Furthermore, even though the microfinance industry is populated by of insitutions of diverse sizes and types as described in a previous section of this chapter, commerical funding raised through IPOs and private equity investments to date has concentrated on the larger, more established micro-finance institutions (Glisovic et al., 2012). This suggests that while multiple sources of funding are entering the microfinance industry, they are often directed towards organizations with different and potentially complementary objectives.

Vignette 3: The Crisis in Andhra Pradesh

A microfinance market to recently struggle with oversaturation is the state of Andhra Pradesh in India. The Indian market had been one of the strongest areas of microfinance growth over the preceding five years, accounting for over 65 per cent of client growth worldwide (Maes and Reed, 2012). Andhra Pradesh was home to four of the largest microfinance institutions (MFIs) in India and many state-supported self-help groups (SHGs) providing similar microfinance services. Combined, the MFIs and SHGs were reaching over 23 million clients in Andhra Pradesh as of 2010. In July of that year, the explosive growth of the market was exemplified by the initial public offering (IPO) of India's largest MFI, SKS Microfinance. The IPO raised over US$155m and made substantial profits for its shareholders.

However, Andhra Pradesh was headed for crisis. Microfinance clients in the area were highly over-indebted, with upwards of 80 per cent of clients responsible for loans from multiple MFIs. Most of the MFIs did not have guidelines in place to gauge a client's level of indebtedness. The breaking point of the crisis occured in late 2010 when allegations were reported of suicides resulting from the coercive collection practices of MFIs. This ignited a political debate in which some politcal figures urged MFI clients not to repay their existing loans. The loan recovery rate dropped below 10 per cent. Many MFIs were unable to continue their operations and the microfinance sector in Andhra Pradesh was almost wiped out.

Some describe the crisis in Andhra Pradesh as a primarily political issue. Others see it as a case of over-aggressive growth fuelled by the interests of commercial profits. Following the crisis, legislators in India have been working on passing regulation aimed at stabilizing the market and preventing such occurrences in the future. (This vignette draws primarily on material provided in CGAP, 2010 and Maes and Reed, 2012.)

The impact of microfinance

The third debate concerns the actual impact of microfinance. In recent years, there has been increased attention placed on moving beyond the promise of microfinance towards rigorously assessing its effects. In general, research studies and the experience of practitioners suggest that microfinance can make a positive impact on its clients, but the magnitude of the impact is often less than expected and the manner in which it benefits the poor is often not as originally anticipated.

Given the strong growth and high repayment rates of microcredit, why is impact assessment a critical concern? First, the magnitude of the impact is important because investing in microfinance draws on financial and human resources that could be invested in other poverty alleviation activities. If the impact of microfinance is positive but weak, perhaps those resources could make a stronger impact on poverty alleviation if they were invested elsewhere, for example towards large, labour-intensive enterprises in developing countries (see Karnani, 2007). Second, understanding impact is increasingly important as a broader range of investors enter the microfinance space. The philanthropic Rockefeller Foundation in conjunction with J.P. Morgan have set an agenda focused on 'impact investing' (O'Donohoe, Leijonhufvud, and Saltuk, 2010). See the vignette 'Rockefeller Foundation and J.P. Morgan: Impact Investing Initiative' for more details. Such investors are often interested in measuring impact using a variety of performance indicators, both social and financial. Third, impact assessments will play a critical role in influencing the future of microfinance. Careful impact studies can provide insight into how the services need to evolve to better meet the needs of clients and the goals of the institutions.

Vignette 4: Rockefeller Foundation and J.P. Morgan: Impact Investing Initiative

'Impact investing' captures the idea that investors can pursue financial returns while simultaneously addressing social and environmental problems (Bugg-Levine and Emerson, 2011: 17). Investing for non-financial returns has a substantial history; however, an initiative was recently launched by the Rockefeller Foundation and J.P. Morgan aimed at defining and unifying this space. A report by the Monitor Institute on social and environmental investing found that the state of the market was fragmented, lacked widely accepted impact metrics, and had few platforms for intermediation (Freireich and Fulton, 2009). To begin addressing such challenges, the Rockefeller Foundation and J.P. Morgan produced *Impact Investments: An Emerging Asset Class* (O'Donohoe, Leijonhufvud, and Saltuk, 2010), in which they attempted to clarify and size the potential market. They estimated that the market offered the potential over the following ten years for invested capital of US$400bn to US$1trn.

How will the increasing momentum behind impact investing affect the microfinance field? Though not restricted to developing countries, impact investing targets the 'base of the pyramid,' defined by the World Resources Institute as people earning less than $3,000 a year. The 2010 Impact Investments report (O'Donohoe, Leijonhufvud, and Saltuk, 2010) identified microfinance as one of the key sectors in which the initiative is to be targeted. Impact investors come in a variety of types, ranging from private foundations such as the Esmée Fairbairn Foundation, to large-scale financial institutions such as Citigroup. There is significant variation in the return expectations of such impact investors, with financial aims ranging from competitive to concessionary. This points to the importance of effectively matching the interests of investors to the social-financial mission of microfinance institutions. As the infrastructure for impact investing continues to develop, the interests of investors will increasingly fuel the demand for additional performance measures of microfinance institutions.

CHALLENGES OF IMPACT ASSESSMENT

The fundamental question driving microfinance impact assessments is typically some variant of 'How are the lives of the participants different relative to how they would have been had the programme not been implemented' (Karlan and Goldberg, 2011)? However, reaching an informative answer to this question is challenging for several reasons. First, accurately gauging how the lives of clients might have changed even if they were not involved in microfinance can be difficult. During a study period, clients not involved in microfinance may also experience some improvement in their financial situation due to other factors, for example the macroeconomic environment in the country may have improved or there may have been increased investment in community infrastructure. In order to accurately determine what amount of impact should be attributed to involvement in microfinance versus other such factors, it is necessary to have a valid measurement of the counterfactual, that is, how lives would have been had the programme not been implemented (Karlan and Goldberg, 2011). Gauging the counterfactual is usually accomplished by comparing the change experienced by those involved in microfinance to the change experienced by those not involved.

This comparison raises a second basic challenge of microfinance impact studies: selection bias. Often the individuals that want to be involved in microfinance programmes differ systematically from those that do not choose to become involved. For example, those that choose to get involved in microfinance may already have stronger businesses and feel more confident that they will be able to repay the loan (Hashemi, 1997). A simple comparison of microfinance participants to non-participants may significantly over-inflate the effect of microfinance involvement by not accounting for this selection bias.

A third assessment challenge particularly relevant to microfinance is the necessity to account for individuals that drop out of the programmes (Armendáriz and Morduch, 2010). For example, under group lending contracts a borrower is often kicked out of the group for poor performance. In such a case, microfinance may have had a negative effect on that particular client's life, but he or she often drops out of the assessment that leads to an overestimate of impact.

Finally, defining the measures of impact is a challenging task because effects of microfinance may reach into many dimensions of a client's life. The most common measures of microfinance impact are related to enterprise income and household consumption (Karlan and Goldberg, 2011). However, there is wider interest in other social impact measures as well, such as consumption smoothing, healthcare, education, and female empowerment (Armendáriz and Morduch, 2010). Understanding the interaction of these different measures is important because they can often be interrelated, for example, an increase in one measure causes a drop in another (Karlan and Goldberg, 2011).

The challenges of assessment mentioned here are not minor concerns. If such issues are not appropriately addressed, they can affect the results of impact measurements by 100 per cent or even reverse conclusions (Armendáriz and Morduch, 2010).

RESULTS OF RANDOMIZED CONTROLLED TRIALS

To overcome the challenges of impact measurement, there has been increased attention in microfinance placed on the use of randomized controlled trials (RCTs) (Bauchet et al., 2011). An RCT mitigates some of the challenges listed above by comparing the effects of a treatment group (e.g. those that receive access to microfinance services) to a control group (e.g. those not offered access to microfinance). By drawing on a large enough sample and randomly determining the groups that are designated as treatment and control, the groups serving as a control population are expected to have on average the same basic characteristics of the treatment population and provide a clean estimate of the counterfactual (Karlan and Goldberg, 2011). While the RCT method poses several benefits for research, it is useful to keep in mind that it can raise important ethical issues by selectively offering access to some potential clients and not others, that may be equally in need.

Several RCT studies on the effects of access to microcredit have been conducted over the last decade in different cultural contexts. Banerjee, Duflo, Glennerster, and Kinnan (2010) studied the effect of offering access to microcredit in randomly selected slums in Hyderabad, India. Crépon, Devoto, Duflo, and Parienté (2011) conducted a similar study providing access to selected rural villages in Morocco. Karlan and Zinman (2011) studied the affects of offering microcredit to individuals in a peri-urban setting in the Phillipines. In what ways did these studies produce similar and differing results?

Generally, the studies suggest that access to microcredit can have a modest, positive impact on the financial state of recipients, but often not in terms of direct impact as expected, for example, business revenue. Banerjee et al. (2010) found that recipients of microcredit access were more likely to start a new business than those without access; but, they did not find a statistically significant improvement in profits. However, the studies indicate that access to microcredit can improve the welfare of clients through promoting changes in their financial behaviour. Though microcredit did not change the *amount* households spent on average, it did effect *how* households spent based on their business activity. If recipients had started a new business or had owned a business prior to receiving credit access, they were more likely to reduce their spending on consumption goods and direct more money towards business investment and durable household goods (Banerjee et al., 2010; Crépon et al., 2011). However, if recipients did not have a prior business or did not start a new business, they were morely likely to increase their spending on consumption goods (Banerjee et al., 2010; Crépon et al., 2011). This suggests that when microcredit is accessed specifically by business owners, it can shift a household's expenditures towards usages that should improve their livelihoods in the long run. However, none of these studies found any significant impact on broader dimensions such as education, healthcare usage, employing more workers, or female empowerment (Banerjee et al., 2010; Crépon et al., 2011; Karlan and Zinman, 2011).

The interpretion of the results from the RCTs can be grouped into three perspectives. A first interpretation is that microfinance is failing to meet its lofty expectations (e.g. Bennett, 2009). Accordingly, one should consider funnelling more resources to alternative approaches for poverty alleviation. A second interpretation argues that excessive weight should not be placed on such a small number of studies (e.g. Maes and Reed, 2012). Overgeneralizing these studies may be particularly risky because the cultural context of microfinance programmes has been found to strongly affect their success (Ahlin, Lin, and Maio, 2011). Also, these impact studies have all been relatively short term, between eleven and twenty-four months, and it is conceivable that the more significant effects of microfinance take longer to occur.

A third interpretation of the recent evaluation studies considers that though microfinance may not be revolutionizing microenterpriseses as expected, it is positively impacting poor households in a variety of unanticipated ways (Morduch, 2011). There is a growing body of evidence, drawing both on formal evaluation studies and other forms of descriptive research (e.g. Collins, Morduch, Rutherford, and Ruthven, 2009), that suggests the real impact of microfinance is not its effect on microenterprises, but rather on managing tight cash flows in poor households. The studies suggest that microcredit is more often used to cope with financial risk (e.g. pay for funeral expenses), to make household investments, or to pay for food, medical bills, and school fees (Morduch, 2011; Bauchet et al., 2011; Karlan and Zinman, 2011). Microcredit recipients are adapting the product to suit their own needs. Often business growth is not the most pressing issue.

Such evidence lends further credence to the idea that the basic microfinance model should move beyond credit to involve a broader range of products. Though the findings are still preliminary, impact evaluations focusing on other microfinance products, such as savings and insurance, have found stronger positive effects on the lives of clients (Bauchet et al., 2011). A study by Dupas and Robinson (2011) on microsavings in Kenya found that there was strong demand and usage of savings accounts. Women that receieved access to a savings account increased their business investment, had more money available to purchase food for their households, and were better able to deal with health shocks as compared to the control groups.

An evaluation of microinsurance for farmers in Ghana also found positive effects on household welfare, with members of the households that received access less likely to go without meals (Karlan, Osei-Akoto, Osei, and Udry, 2011). These studies suggest that though the rhetoric of microfinance has almost exclusively focused on the mechanism of microenterprise growth, there are substantial opportunities for improving welfare through products focused on cash-flow management and risk mitigation (Bauchet et al., 2011).

Implications for social finance

Over the last four decades, the pioneers of modern microfinance have wrestled with developing an effective means for extending financial access to the poor. The evolution from a handful of organizations to a worldwide industry has been shaped both by innovative advances as well as unfortunate missteps. What implications can be drawn from the experience of microfinance for social finance more broadly? Three implications present themselves based on the content reviewed in this chapter.

First, the history of microfinance suggests that the details of the financial model and product features are not minor concerns, but are at the core of the movement's success. Microcredit did not dramatically expand over the last several decades simply because there was demand for credit access and an available supply of capital. The generally unsuccessful attempts of government-subsidized credit programmes for the rural poor during the 1950s to 1980s demonstrated that good intentions and available funding are not enough. Rather, a key differentiator of modern microfinance was the early demonstration of a model for credit that was financially sustainable and scalable (Cull et al., 2009). Seemingly subtle innovations such as group lending, frequent repayment, and dynamic incentives, were at the heart of the new movement. For the broader field of social finance, this suggests that the details of the financial products and services will play a central role in determining success or failure. As illustrated by the growing interest in impact investing, it is likely that the available capital for social investment will continue to increase dramatically over the next decade (O'Donohoe et al., 2010). The challenge lies in developing innovative products and delivery systems uniquely suited to their objectives, rather than relying on loosely fitted adaptations of pre-existing models.

Second, several missteps of the microfinance movement offer a cautionary word against extreme growth fuelled by commercial funding. In various markets, such as Bolivia during the 1990s and India during the late 2000s, institutions leveraging commercial funding contributed to the markets' dramatic increase in scale. However, these markets also became so quickly saturated that they reached crisis points and nearly collapsed (Rhyne, 2001; CGAP, 2010). Social finance is particularly at risk of excessive growth because it often targets markets that are urgently in need of social change. Often these markets are less developed and lack significant infrastructure to mitigate system-wide risk. In the example of microfinance, Bolivia and India lacked independent credit bureaus for tracking a client's individual level of indebtedness across institutions. In such markets, it is easier for unrestrained growth to result in collapses that ultimately harm the intended beneficiaries of social finance.

Third, as the public awareness of microfinance has grown, impact assessment has played different roles. Early on, the story and promise of microfinance played a primary role in building global awareness. Once the microfinance model gained international attention, controlled studies have played an increasingly important role. Furthermore, the case of microfinance suggests that quality evaluation studies can do more than gauge impact. Rather, evaluation studies can also be effectively used to shed light on the specific deficiencies of a programme and how they should be revised. For microfinance, a combination of practitioner experience, qualitative research, and evaluation studies has reinforced the idea that the basic microcredit product for enterprise growth has not been meeting the most pressing financial needs of the poor (Morduch, 2011). Clients were using products in unanticipated ways to suit their own needs for cash-flow management and risk reduction, suggesting further advances in microsavings and microinsurance are needed. For social finance more broadly, this indicates that there may be substantial benefits in viewing impact studies as more than straightforward assessments of programme success or failure. A nuanced understanding of why a programme does not work as expected can in itself reveal alternative paths forward.

Conclusion

This review of the development and current state of microfinance illustrates the rapid change occurring in the industry. The field is in flux along several dimensions. Access to new commercial sources of funding are shifting the market structure. The landscape of microfinance institutions is becoming increasingly diverse in terms of organizational design and mission. Some microfinance markets have overheated in recent years, highlighting the risk of markets becoming oversaturated. Rigorous impact assessments are raising new questions about what microfinance can actually achieve. This is causing many to rethink how the standard microfinance product–service offering should evolve to better suit the financial needs of the poor.

Muhammad Yunus goes so far as to say that some of the new commercial institutions entering the industry should not be allowed to leverage the term 'microcredit' with their business models (Yunus, 2011). He argues that the term has been built up over the preceding decades to connote a certain level of commitment to social objectives, a way of dealing with the poor based on trust and respect, and that the term can now be easily used to misrepresent an organization's business activities. Whether one endorses or eschews Yunus' view, it is true that microfinance is increasingly a diverse space and distinguishing organizational objectives is not obvious. This tension exemplifies the flux occurring in the field and highlights the need for an awareness of the diversity of models that constitute modern microfinance.

▓ REFERENCES

Ahlin, C., Lin, J., and Maio, M. (2011). 'Where Does Microfinance Flourish? Microfinance Institution Performance in Macroeconomic Context', *Journal of Development Economics*, 95(2): 105–20.

Akula, V. (2010). *A Fistful of Rice: My Unexpected Quest to End Poverty Through Profitibility*. Cambridge, MA: Harvard Business Press.

Ardener, S. (1964). 'The Comparative Study of Rotating Credit Associations', *The Journal of the Royal Anthropological Institute of Great Britain and Ireland*, 94(2): 201–29.

Armendáriz, B., and Morduch, J. (2000). 'Microfinance Beyond Group Lending', *Economics of Transition*, 8(2): 401–20.

Armendáriz, B., and Morduch, J. (2010). *The Economics of Microfinance* (2nd ed.). Cambridge, MA: MIT Press.

Attanasio, O., Augsburg, B., De Haas, R., Fitzsimons, E., and Harmgart, H. (2012). 'Group Lending or Individual Lending? Evidence from a Randomised Field Experiment in Mongolia'. European Bank for Reconstruction and Development, Working Paper Issue No. 136.

Banerjee, A., Chandrasekhar, A., Duflo, E., and Jackson, M. (2013). 'The Diffusion of Microfinance', *Science*, 341: 363–73.

Banerjee, A., Duflo, E., Glennerster, R., and Kinnan, C. (2010). *The Miracle of Microfinance? Evidence from a Randomized Evaluation*. MIT Working Paper.

Bateman, M. (2010). *Why Doesn't Microfinance Work? The Destructive Rise of Local Neolibralism*. London: Zed Books.

Bauchet, J., Marshall, C., Starita, L., Thomas, J., and Yalouris, A. (2011). 'Latest Findings from Randomized Evaluations of Microfinance'. Access to Finance Forum Reports by CGAP and its Partners (No. 2).

Bennett, D. (2009). 'Small Change: Billions of Dollars and a Nobel Prize Later, It Looks Like 'Microlending' Doesn't Actually Do Much to Fight Poverty', *The Boston Globe*, 20 September, pp. 36–40.

Besley, T., and Coate, S. (1995). 'Group Lending, Repayment Incentives and Social Collateral', *Journal of Development Economics*, 46: 1–18.

Besley, T., Coate, S., and Loury, G. (1993). 'The Economics of Rotating Savings and Credit Associations', *The American Economic Review*, 83(4): 792–810.

Braverman, A., and Guasch, J. (1986). 'Rural Credit Markets and Institutions in Developing Countries: Lessons for Policy Analysis from Practice and Modern Theory', *World Development*, 14(10/11): 1253–67.

Brett, J. (2006). '"We Sacrifice and Eat Less": The Structural Complexities of Microfinance Participation', *Human Organization*, 65(1): 8–19.

Bugg-Levine, A., and Emerson, J. (2011). 'Impact Investing: Transforming How We Make Money While Making a Difference', *Innovations*, 6(3): 9–18.

CGAP (2006). 'Annual Report 2006', CGAP.

CGAP (2007). 'CGAP Reflections on the Compartamos Initial Public Offering: A Case Study on Microfinance Interest Rates and Profits'. Focus Note, No. 42.

CGAP (2010). 'Andra Proadesh 2010: Global Implications of the Crisis in Indian Microfinance'. Focus Note, No. 67.

Collins, D., Morduch, J., Rutherford, S., and Ruthven, O. (2009). *Portfolios of the Poor: How the World's Poor Live on $2 a Day*. Princeton, NJ: Princeton University Press.

Crépon, B., Devoto, F., Duflo, E., and Parienté, W. (2011). 'Impact of Microcredit in Rural Areas of Morocco: Evidence from a Randomized Evaluation'. MIT Working Paper.

Cull, R., Demirguc-Kunt, A., and Morduch, J. (2009). 'Association Microfinance Meets the Market', *The Journal of Economic Perspectives*, 23(1): 167–92.

Daley-Harris, S., and Awimbo, A. (eds) (2011). *New Pathways out of Poverty*. Sterling, VA: Kumarian Press.

Ditcher, T., and Harper, M. (2007). *What's Wrong with Microfinance?* Warwickshire: Practical Action Publishing.

Dreze, J. (1990). 'Poverty in India and the IRDP Delusion', *Economic and Political Weekly*, 25(39): A95–104.

Dupas, P., and Robinson, J. (2011). *Savings Constraints and Microenterprise Development: Evidence from a Field Experiment in Kenya*. NBER Working Paper No. 14693.

Fischer, G., and Ghatak, M. (2011). 'Spanning the Chasm: Uniting Theory and Empirics in Microfinance Research', in B. Armendáriz and M. Labie (eds), *The Microfinance Handbook*. Singapore: Singapore World Press, pp. 59–71.

Freireich, J., and Fulton, K. (2009). *Investing for Social and Environmental Impact: A Design for Catalyzing and Emerging Industry*. Cambridge, MA: Monitor Institute.

Geertz, C. (1962). 'The Rotating Credit Association: A "Middle Rung" in Development', *Economic Development and Cultural Change*, 10(3): 241–63.

Ghatak, M. (1999). 'Group Lending, Local Information and Peer Selection', *Journal of Development Economics*, 60(1): 27–50.

Gine, X., and Karlan, D. (2006). 'Group versus Individual Liability: Evidence from a Field Experiment in the Philippines'. Yale University Working Paper.

Glisovic, J., González, H., Saltuk, Y., and de Mariz, F. R. (2012). 'Volume Growth and Valuation Contraction: Global Microfinance Equity Valuation Survey 2012'. CGAP & J.P. Morgan. Access to Finance Forum, No. 3.

Gonzalez, A. (2008). *How Many Borrowers and Microfinance Institutions (MFIs) Exist?* Washington, DC: Microfinance Information Exchange (MIX).

Gonzalez, A. (2010). 'Is Microfinance Growing Too Fast?' MIX Data Brief No. 5.

Gonzalez, A., and Rosenberg, R. (2006). 'The State of Microcredit—Outreach, Profitability, and Poverty: Findings from a Database of 2600 Microfinance Institutions'. CGAP Working Paper.

Gonzalez-Vega, C. (1994). 'Stages in the Evolution of Thought on Rural Finance: A Vision from the Ohio State University'. Economics and Sociology, Occasional Paper No. 2134.

Hashemi, S. (1997). 'Those Left Behind: A Note on Targeting the Hardcore Poor', in G. Wood, and I. Sharif, *Who Needs Credit? Poverty and Finance in Bangladesh*. Dhaka: University Press.

Helms, B. (2006). *Access for All: Building Inclusive Financial Systems*. Washington, DC: Consultative Group to Assist the Poor, The World Bank.

Hulme, D., and Mosley, P. (1996). *Finance Against Poverty, Volume 2*. New York: Routledge.

Huppi, M., and Feder, G. (1990). 'The Role of Groups and Credit Cooperatives in Rural Lending', *The World Bank Research Observer*, 5: 187–204.

Karlan, D., and Goldberg, N. (2011). 'Microfinance Evaluation Strategies: Notes on Methodology and Findings', in B. Armendáriz, and M. Labie, *The Handbook of Microfinance*. Singapore: World Scientific Publishing, pp. 17–28.

Karlan, D., Osei-Akoto, I., Osei, R., and Udry, C. (2011). 'Examining Underinvestment in Agriculture: Measuring Returns to Capital and Insurance'. Yale University Working Paper.

Karlan, D., and Zinman, J. (2011). 'Microcredit in Theory and Practice: Using Randomized Credit Scoring for Impact', *Science*, 332(6035): 1278–84.

Karnani, A. (2007). 'Microfinance Misses its Mark', *Stanford Social Innovation Review*, Summer, pp. 34–40.

Kumar, K., McKay, C., and Rotman, S. (2010). 'Microfinance and Mobile Banking: The Story so far'. CGAP Focus Note, No. 62.

Maes, J., and Reed, L. (2012). *State of the Microcredit Summit Campaign Report 2012*. Washington, DC: Microcredit Summit Campaign.

MicroCapital (2010). 'SKS Microfinance IPO Experiences Strong Demand, Total Share Offer 13 Times Oversubscribed'. MicroCapital Brief.

Morduch, J. (1999). 'The Microfinance Promise', *Journal of Economic Literature*, 37(4): 1569–614.

Morduch, J. (2011). 'Why Finance Matters', *Science*, 332(6035): 1271–2.

Murray, I. and Lynch, E. (2003). 'What Do Microfinance Customers Value?', *Women's World Banking*, Focus Note 20(1).

Nicholls, A. (ed.) (2006). *Social Entrepreneurship: New Models of Sustainable Social Change*. Oxford: Oxford University Press.

O'Donohoe, N., Leijonhufvud, C., and Saltuk, Y. (2010). *Impact Investments: An Emerging Asset Class*. London: J.P. Morgan Global Research.

Prahalad, C. (2004). *The Fortune at the Bottom of the Pyramid: Eradicating Poverty Through Profits*. Philadelphia: Wharton School Publishing.

Rahman, A. (1999). 'Micro-credit Initiatives for Equitable and Sustainable Development: Who Pays? *World Development*, 27(1): 67–82.

Rai, A., and Sjostrom, T. (2004). 'Is Grameen Lending Efficient? Repayment Incentives and Insurance in Village Economies', *Review of Economic Studies*, 71(1): 217–34.

Rangan, V. K., Chu, M., and Petkoski, D. (2011). 'Segmenting the Base of the Pyramid', *Harvard Business Review*, 89(6): 113–17.

Rath, N. (1985). '"Garibi Hatao": Can IRDP Do It?' *Economic and Political Weekly*, 20(6): 238–46.

Rhyne, E. (2001). *Mainstreaming Microfinance: How Lending to the Poor Began, Grew, and Came of Age in Bolivia*. Bloomfield, CT: Kumarian Press.

Robinson, M. (2001). *The Microfinance Revolution: Sustainable Finance for the Poor*. Washington, DC: International Bank for Reconstruction and Development, The World Bank.

Rosenberg, R. (2008). 'Mohammed Yunus and Michael Chu Debate Commercialization'. Geneva: Accion Media Coverage, CGAP.

Sabin, N., and Reed-Tsochas, R. (2014). 'Social Collateral: Structural Embeddedness and Economic Performance in Microfinance'. University of Oxford Working Paper.

Scharwatt, C., Katakam, A., Frydrych, J., Murphy, A., and Naghavi, N. (2015). 'State of the Industry 2014: Mobile Financial Services for the Unbanked.' *GSMA Report*.

Silwal, A. (2003). 'Repayment Performance of Nepali Village Banks'. Public Policy Thesis, Swarthmore College.

Stiglitz, J. (1990). 'Peer Monitoring and Credit Markets', *World Bank Economic Review*, 4(3): 351–66.

Suria, T., Jack, W., and Stokera, T. (2012). 'Documenting the Birth of a Financial Economy', *PNAS*, 109(26): 10257–62.

Tedeschi, G. (2006). 'Here Today, Gone Tomorrow: Can Dynamic Incentives Make Microfinance More Flexible? *Journal of Development Economics*, 80(1): 84–105.

Trezza, S. (2006). 'Products and Services in Modern Microfinance', in M. La Torre, and G. Vento, *Microfinance*. New York: Palgrave Macmillan, pp. 20–37.

Vogel, R. (1984). 'Savings Mobilization: The Forgotten Half of Rural Finance', in D. Adames, D. Graham, and J. Von Pischke, *Undermining Rural Development with Cheap Credit*. Boulder, CO: Westview Press.

Woolcock, M. (1999). 'Learning From Failures in Microfinance: What Unsuccessful Cases Tell Us About How Group-Based Programs Work', *American Journal of Economics & Sociology*, 58(1): 17–42.

Yunus, M. (1998). *Banker to the Poor: The Authobiography of Muhammad Yunus, founder of the Grameen Bank.* London: Aurum Press Ltd.

Yunus, M. (2003). *Banker to the Poor: Micro-Lending and the Battle Against World Poverty.* New York: PublicAffairs.

Yunus, M. (2011). 'Sacrificing Microcredit for Megaprofit', *New York Times*, January 14, pp. 1–3.

7 Venture philanthropy

Development, evolution, and scaling around the world

Rob John and Jed Emerson

Introduction

Venture philanthropy is a highly malleable term that has found itself adopted, adapted, and rejected in equal measure over the last fifteen years (see, for example, Letts et al. (1997) and Letts and Ryan (2003)). To some it is an oxymoron that raises the suspicion of impact investors (who are troubled by 'philanthropy') and grant-makers (who perceive 'venture' as implying commercial motive). To bring some order to the language chaos, we can view venture philanthropy as primarily representing the grant-making end of the 'entrepreneurial social finance' spectrum. Entrepreneurial social finance is a growing number of financing models that focus on providing the combination of financial capital and non-financial support to social entrepreneurs and their entrepreneurial social ventures (John, 2012). Venture philanthropists are largely content to use grants as finance method of choice, as they are not primarily concerned with recovering their capital or making a financial return on their investments.

Venture philanthropy is best distinguished from traditional grant-making by the level of engagement, rather than the kind of finance (grant, loan, equity) or legal form of the organization being supported (non-profit or social enterprise). A typical private or corporate philanthropic foundation may disperse hundreds of grants each year, with each individual grant officer handling scores of grantee transactions, without any expectation of a detailed knowledge of each the grantee's day-to-day operations. By contrast, a venture philanthropy portfolio manager will most likely handle only three or four investments, usually maintaining each of the relationships over the investment lifecycle, which could be several years.

The operational principles of venture philanthropy funds, as set out below by the European Venture Philanthropy Association (EVPA), are an amalgam of good grant-making practice and a language more associated with venture capital (Balbo et al., 2010):

- Investment policy: venture philanthropy funds will need to decide the parameters and preferences for their investment policy. These will include:

- Investee type: non-profit (charity), social enterprise, social business
- Investee stage: personal support to an entrepreneur, early stage, start-up, growth and scale-up
- Investment sector: narrow and specialized, broad and agnostic
- Geography: local, domestic, international.

Table 7.1 illustrates the matrix of investment and organizational policies available to venture philanthropy funds (John, 2012).

Venture philanthropy capital allocation occurs in stages, each is considered next.

DEAL FLOW

Like venture capital firms, venture philanthropy funds tend to be proactive in searching for potential investees, rather than employing a reactive application process of established grant-making foundations. A pipeline of potential 'deals' is usually sourced from the fund's networks or referrals from other grant-makers.

INVESTMENT APPRAISAL

This is usually a three-stage 'funnel' process of primary screening involving desk research and sites visits, due diligence, and finally the investment proposal for the successful investee. Due diligence may take months and involve active assistance in designing a business plan, defining social impact objectives, assessing the management team, governance, and defining the fund's financial and non-financial contributions.

PORTFOLIO MANAGEMENT

The day-to-day relationship with the investee's management team distinguishes venture philanthropy from the traditional approach of most private foundations and other funders. Portfolio managers have a keener sense of how each investee is progressing (or not), with frequency of contact varying from several times a week to at least monthly (John, 2007). The portfolio manager curates non-financial, advisory, and consulting inputs as agreed in the investment proposal. These inputs may include advice with strategy and operations as well as coaching the lead social entrepreneur, and will be provided directly by the portfolio manager or other members of the fund's team, or externally through volunteer associates. Unlike traditional funders, venture philanthropists usually take an option for formal or observer places on the investee's board; a practice common in private equity investment, but highly unusual, if not frowned upon, in the funding of non-profit organizations by private foundations.

Table 7.1. Venture philanthropy matrix

Investee type	Non-profit, charity: Reliant on grants and public fundraising for revenue	Social enterprise with subsidy: Grant/ patient capital subsidy; any surpluses reinvested in business	Social enterprise without subsidy: Little or no grant subsidy; reinvests surpluses; capped returns to equity investors	Social business: Trading model to create social impact; distributes surpluses to investors and owners
Investee stage	Entrepreneur support: Personal financial/coaching support for social entrepreneurs	Start up, early stage	Growth, scale up	International scale up/replication/ franchising; M&A activity
Investment sector	Narrow focus (specialized: single sector e.g. health, exclusion, education, environment)	Broad focus (multi-sector; diverse portfolio)	Convenor (brings sector players together in collaboration)	
Financial tools	Grants: Mostly non-returnable but performance-based donations	Loans, underwriting, patient capital	'Quasi-equity' Possibly revenue participation	Equity
Return to investors	Only social impact (loss of capital)	High risk; looking for some capital preservation or recycling	Social-first impact investor (–15% to +5% return)	Finance-first impact investor (+5% to +10% return)
Non financial support	'Front loaded'— mostly help during pre-investment business planning	Ongoing support during whole period of investment	Support delivered in-house (staff, board, associates, partnerships)	Support outsourced to external consultants
Depth of engagement	Monthly contact with management team	Weekly contact with management team	Seat or observer on board	
Exit/ Graduation	No clear exit 'event'; aspiration to disengage after agreed timescale	Agreed package of support with hard end date	VC type exit event such as secondary sale or IPO	'Graduate Club'— externalize learning
Geography	Community	National	Regional	Global
Performance and impact	Performance metrics (e.g. Balanced Scorecard) by portfolio organizations and fund	Social impact metrics (e.g. SROI)		
Disclosure	The fund publishes full accounts of its internal operations and its investments	Fund publishes details of its investments	Limited or no disclosure of accounts	

Source: John, 2012

EXIT

This is another term borrowed from private equity, and appears at first sight to sit somewhat uncomfortably in the social sector's lexicon. After all, the kind of 'exit event' common in private equity, such as an IPO or secondary purchase, is not relevant for the non-profits and social enterprises supported by venture philanthropists. And 'exit' conveys a rather brutal end to the partnership decided by the point of maximum return to limited partners (a private equity fund's investors). Exit in a venture philanthropy investment is more about readiness of the investee to move on to its next round of development and growth, after meeting milestones in the current round of funding (Alter, Shoemaker, Tuan, and Emerson, 2001). Since an objective of venture philanthropy is to help build stronger organizations, a planned, phased withdrawal of finance and other services is agreed beforehand with the organization as part of the investment plan, even though the reality may change as the investment progresses. Some funds prefer to use the term 'graduation' to denote the next phase of relationship, which may no longer involve hard inputs, but the organization remains within the fund's 'family' and may contribute to others through shared experience of mentoring.

Origins and development in the USA

While it is an old saying, there is still some truth to the statement, 'When you've seen one foundation, you've seen... one foundation!' People may talk about private, family, and corporate foundations or describe various elements of seemingly diverse philanthropic strategy, yet the reality is every foundation is free to define its approach, its methods, and its practices as it sees fit. There is no formal instrument of accountability demanding any single set of practices be employed by those operating under the label 'philanthropy'. However, as one reflects upon the rise of venture philanthropy in the USA in the late 1980s, the strategies and practices brought together under that banner were, indeed, distinct from those of the majority of foundations operating at the time. In fact, if one agrees with those who have over the years claimed the practices brought together under the label 'venture philanthropy' were nothing more than sound, fundamental elements of good philanthropic practices—practices in place and being applied by foundation executives well in advance of the rise of venture philanthropy[1]—then perhaps the only conclusion one may draw is that by the late 1980s the majority of foundations active within the USA were, in fact, not applying sound, fundamental philanthropic practices in their work.

---

[1] Kramer (2002) as cited by John (2006) in *Venture Philanthropy: The Evolution of High Engagement Philanthropy in Europe* (2006).

While there were no doubt a good number of innovative and entrepreneurial foundations active in the late 1980s within philanthropy in the USA, the practices of the time were dominated by philanthropic managers—executives who viewed their role as one of managing philanthropic assets for disbursement of grants to not-for-profit organizations. The field was driven by an approach to philanthropy which was fundamentally transactive (focused upon the transaction of making a grant) as opposed to operating within an investor mindset (focused upon understanding philanthropy as an act of investing in building an organization's capacity to bring its intervention to scale in order to create sustained change and impact within its area of operation (education, job training, and so on).[2] The transactive approach to philanthropy is characterized by such practices as not-for-profit organizations approaching a foundation and submitting a proposal, a grant proposal being reviewed, a site visit being conducted, a grant being awarded (usually following the passage of an extensive period of time ranging from three to nine months) and finally with the grantee submitting a grant performance report at the conclusion of the grant's time period (usually one to three years). In contrast, the venture philanthropy practices enumerated above (grantees being identified by a foundation following market research, funding based upon business strategies, regular engagement with the grantee by staff, and so on) came from an approach to philanthropy grounded less in the mindset of charity than that of finance and investment.

While some have claimed venture philanthropy evolved in the San Francisco Bay Area in the late 1990s as a result of new philanthropic resources generated by internet entrepreneurs (Buckland, Hehenberger, and Hay, 2013), before the time of high-tech entrepreneurs and dot-com millionaires, there was a period in the late 1980s characterized by the rise and excesses of 'Go, go Wall Street.' LBO titans were king and stock traders ruled the headlines of the business—and increasingly, mainstream—press. For social workers and community activists, America's turn to such celebration of wealth and the new Gilded Age seemed a period of excess and waste—yet it also brought forward a new generation of philanthropists. While some of these kings of Wall Street gave back to society by the traditional philanthropic means of supporting the S.O.B.s (symphony, opera, and ballet) or having buildings named after them, a separate group took their investment lens and applied it to philanthropy and the not-for-profit sector. 'How', they asked, 'could the acumen, principles, and practices that had created such great wealth in markets be turned to the creation of community impact and value?'[3]

[2] For more on the concept of transactive versus investment approaches to philanthropy, see Emerson (2000).

[3] See, for example, 'The Funders Perspective: Grantmaking as an Investment Strategy', in Emerson and Twersky (1996).

These individuals had made their wealth in their lifetime and launched foundations and giving institutions they would not turn over to philanthropic managers to operate, but which they intended to run in alignment with how they made their wealth—namely, through free enterprise, a faith in markets and the idea that business acumen could be applied for the creation of not only market value but community value and the generation of social impact, impact such as the improvement of employment options for formerly homeless people, the performance of children in under performing schools or the effectiveness of social service programmes targeting poor people—to name but three of myriad areas of interest.

Attempting to identify who first gathered the practices of venture philanthropy under one strategy is like trying to decide who invented the internal combustion engine—accordingly, in the USA there were a number of actors working to put the concepts of what came to be called venture philanthropy into practice. The Robin Hood Foundation, funded by some of Wall Street's leading investors, was launched in 1987 and operated under the framework of a business approach to philanthropy. And Echoing Green, also founded in 1987, was chaired by the finance group General Atlantic's CEO, Ed Cohen, who believed that by identifying a portfolio of individual entrepreneurs (who would come to be called, social entrepreneurs), and providing them with not simply small, seed capital grants, but a network of support for development of their ventures, the promise of innovation and new ideas for addressing some of America's most intractable problems could be captured for the common good. In Cohen's words:

When we first began to think about Echoing Green, we wanted to create a foundation that adopted a venture capital approach to philanthropy. We wanted to give more than just money; we wanted to help the people we supported build their dreams. Our idea was to find talented risk-takers who were leaders or potential leaders and back their dreams—ride their energy and motivation. We wanted them to be a little crazy, like most of the private sector entrepreneurs we knew. We wanted to be activists in finding the people and groups we supported; we did not want to wait passively to receive grant proposals and respond. . . . For Echoing Green to do this work, we must continue to be the entrepreneurial, risk-taking, nurturing, connecting, spirited organization we have been. We succeed because we are *not* a traditional foundation.[4]

In 1989, out on the West Coast, George R. Roberts, managing partner of the private equity firm Kohlberg Kravis Roberts & Co., initiated the Homeless Economic Development Fund (later called the Roberts Enterprise Development Fund or REDF) which not only executed early practices of venture philanthropy but extensively documented its work, becoming the first venture philanthropy fund to publish extensively on the topics of social entrepreneurship and venture philanthropy. In 1996, the Roberts Foundation published the

---

[4] Echoing Green (1995). *Community Report.*

400-page book, *New Social Entrepreneurs: The Success, Challenge, and Lessons of Not-for-profit Enterprise Creation*,[5] which included chapters on 'The Funder's Perspective: Grantmaking as an Investment Strategy', with sections titled 'The Funder as Venture Capitalist', in which they first documented the emerging elements of a venture philanthropy strategy.[6] This body of work and documentation of practice by HEDF/REDF in turn informed that of many other venture philanthropy funds to come in later years, both in the USA, Europe, and elsewhere around the globe.

The mid to late 1990s saw the creation of a number of leading venture philanthropy funds. These included Venture Philanthropy Partners (created by the venture capitalist, Mario Morino) and Social Venture Partners-Seattle (Founded by AutoDesk founder Paul Brainer and former MicroSoft executive Paul Shoemaker). New Profit (Boston), New Schools Venture Fund (SF Bay Area) and The Draper Richards Foundation (SF Bay Area) all advanced the practices of venture philanthropy and brought new levels of performance to the field. Each of these funds took a unique perspective to the practice—for example, New Profit pioneered an approach which mobilized a broad group of limited partners to invest in the fund (in contrast to other funds which were seeded by individual high-net-worth founders) or in the case of SVP, which mobilized large numbers of new philanthropists to provide the management and technical advice offered to portfolio not-for-profit organizations. Yet all of these—and other funds—operated under the core practices of high, long-term engagement with not-for-profits funded not simply as individual grantees but as part of a portfolio of investments in change.

With the January 1997 publication of the Harvard Business Review article, 'Virtuous Capital: What Foundations Can Learn from Venture Capital', venture philanthropy went mainstream—and a major debate ensued with regard to two key points: Was venture philanthropy something new or simply old toys in shiny new boxes? And, were the practices espoused by this new breed of philanthropist truly effective in building greater capacity on the part of their not-for-profit partners or simply an inappropriate application of business and market-based ideas? In the years since the development of venture philanthropy as a distinct area of practice from that of traditional philanthropy, numerous articles have been published arguing various sides to these questions.

Evolution in Europe

When America sneezes, Europe catches a cold, it was said of the 1929 Wall Street Crash. Indeed in philanthropy, and much of social innovation, the USA

---

[5] Available on line at <http://www.redf.org>.
[6] This chapter's co-author, Jed Emerson, founded and operated the Homeless Economic Development Fund and was founding director of the Roberts Enterprise Development Fund.

has pioneered with the UK trailing some years behind, followed by Continental Europe. In 2000 Oxford University's first real modern fundraiser, Henry Drucker, kick-started a debate on venture philanthropy as part of his wider comparison of the giving cultures in the USA and the UK. The conversation was further developed by the UK's only explicitly self-described venture philanthropy fund at the time, World in Need,[7] set up in 1965 by a modestly successful business entrepreneur, Cecil Jackson Cole. The pioneering efforts of this Quaker-inspired businessman to bring business acumen into the sleepy English charitable world are still largely unrecognized today, despite him being arguably the UK's first venture philanthropist, who was instrumental in the creation of Oxfam, Action Aid, and other non-profit organizations (Black, 1992). As an entrepreneur, Jackson Cole viewed operational charities like start-up businesses, needing seed and growth capital coupled to commercial thinking to deliver their social objectives sustainably. Viewing philanthropy as an instrument of investment, rather than just the passive funding of worthy projects, was not unique to Jackson Cole. Historically, there had always been a minority of grant-making foundations and individual philanthropists in the UK that sought to provide risk funding for innovation, over extended periods, adding value beyond funding. Notably, Allied Dunbar Charitable Trust, Joseph Rowntree Charitable Trust and Barrow Cadbury Trust had, for decades offered long-term, institutional funding to risky and unpopular ventures as Carrington (2003) has pointed out. While such far-sighted and strategic grant-making is perhaps not venture philanthropy in the modern sense, it shares several of its characteristics, in particular, building organizations rather than just funding their projects, and adding value by offering advice on strategy and operations.

In the UK, and to a lesser extent in Continental Europe, two factors converged to give a significant push to the development of venture philanthropy in the first decade of the new millennium: the inexorable rise of social entrepreneurship and the philanthropic frustrations of private equity professionals.

Leadbeater's pamphlet (1997) on social innovation put social entrepreneurs at the heart of innovative and sustainable grassroots social development in Britain, influencing the agenda of Tony Blair's New Labour government. Leadbeater's analysis built on a longstanding tradition of 'misfits and mavericks' as agents of social change—individuals we refer to today as social entrepreneurs, part of a recognizable global brand promoted initially by Ashoka and since emulated by many others. Three of the social entrepreneurs profiled by Leadbeater went on to create Community Action Network (CAN) the first UK-wide network to support social entrepreneurs and their hybrid ventures. Over the last fifteen years, social entrepreneurship has become a

---

[7] World in Need was established in 1965 as the Phyllis Trust, and has since been renamed the Andrews Charitable Trust, to highlight the connection to the estate agency business it owns. One of the authors, Rob John, was its executive director from 2000 to 2004. See <http://www.andrewscharitabletrust.org.uk>.

mainstream activity, widely promoted throughout Europe, and globally, by support organizations, policymakers, academic institutions, funders, and even governments.

In 2004 five successful private equity professionals embraced the venture philanthropy model they had investigated in the USA and UK to form the European Venture Philanthropy Association[8] (EVPA), with a clear nod towards their own professional body, the EVCA.[9] The EVPA was a response to the frustration experienced by the founders to make their own personal giving have long-lasting social impact, and of non-profits that did not seem to have the levels of transparency, governance, and entrepreneurship in the businesses they invested in commercially. But also they envisioned the opportunity in venture philanthropy to mobilize the company-building skills of the private equity industry and encourage greater personal and corporate generosity by demonstrating a model they viewed as more effective than traditional, passive 'cheque-writing' philanthropy. The founders, all leaders in the development of European private equity, initially set quite modest targets for the association to be an informal network of investment professionals. But EVPA resonated with the zeitgeist in philanthropy in which a new narrative was emerging with its own language borrowed from venture capital. This new 'philanthrocapitalism' (Bishop and Green, 2008) spoke of entrepreneurial and scalable approaches to solving entrenched social issues, and sought to put the know-how of business into the hands of ambitious social entrepreneurs.

This convergence of social entrepreneurship and private equity is exemplified in the creation of the Breakthrough venture philanthropy fund in 2005,[10] a synergistic joint venture between Community Action Network and the private equity firm, Permira. Adele Blakebrough, CAN's co-founder, herself a resourceful social entrepreneur was convinced the only way for social enterprises to gain real traction and visibility was to showcase a handful which could demonstrate successful, sustained growth without compromising social mission. Permira was Europe's second biggest private equity buyout firm at the time, whose managing partner, Damon Buffini led the partners' search for a kind of corporate philanthropy that 'could harness the power of the firm, not just the power of money, to create real impact'.[11] After a long search to find a model for the firm's philanthropy, Buffini met Blakebrough

---

[8] The EVPA was formed as a company limited by guarantee with charitable status in 2004 in England. One of the authors (Rob John) was its executive director from 2004 until 2009. It relocated to Brussels in 2009.

[9] The European Private Equity and Venture Capital Association, <http://www.evca.eu>. The EVPA founders all had long-standing connections with EVCA, including two former chairmen and a CEO.

[10] Based in part on unpublished research by one of the authors (Rob John) while a visiting fellow at the Skoll Centre for Social Entrepreneurship, Said Business School, University of Oxford 2009. Unpublished and published interviews with Breakthrough and Permira staff, and Breakthrough's portfolio CEOs.

[11] Quoted from an interview with one of the authors (Rob John) in John, Davis, and Mitchell (2007).

and realized that social entrepreneurs were not so different from the kind of people Permira invested in commercially—individuals, who for Buffini 'believed in enterprise, could build a business and have a long term perspective' (John, 2007). Breakthrough provided £2.5m of direct grant funding and an estimated £1.7m in monetized consulting and advisory services to twenty-five social enterprises. The small Cambridge-based disability charity, Speaking Up, was transformed into a multi-site social enterprise through growth funding provided by venture philanthropy fund Impetus Trust over four years. Speaking Up's CEO, Craig Deardon-Phillips, turned to Breakthrough in 2009 to help achieve the next phase of development, a merger with Advocacy Partners. Breakthrough led on the merger feasibility planning and support during the critical 100 days following the merger. Much of this skill set came from Permira staff who volunteered their time to help Deardon-Phillips manage the merger process effectively. The commercial experience leveraged in from Permira by Breakthrough brought fresh thinking and know-how to a sector where mergers are relatively uncommon or poorly executed. The merged enterprise, renamed VoiceAbility, has continued to grow through further mergers and its acquisition of a for-profit advocacy company. Breakthrough targets small to medium social enterprises looking for significant growth opportunities. In a market that is beginning to segment, Breakthrough's backers, Permira, saw potential for supporting much larger social enterprises with the potential to operate on a national level. In a unique partnership with several leading financial service and consulting companies, Permira launched the Social Business Trust in 2010,[12] to bring an enhanced venture philanthropy model to ambitious, scalable social enterprises in the UK.

This new interest in venture philanthropy however, was not limited to private equity professionals, but also hedge fund managers and entrepreneurs running their own investment houses, converts to the 'give while you live' approach of the philanthropist at the top of their professional lives. When activist hedge fund manager, Chris Hohn, and his wife Jamie Cooper Hohn, decided to become more strategic about their own giving, it was clear to Hohn he could leverage his skills as an investment manager to generate philanthropic capital. In a bold move that did not deter potential investors, Hohn named his London-based hedge fund 'The Children's Investment Fund' (TCI) and structurally linked its performance to donations made to its eponymous Foundation. One third of the hedge fund's management fees and a half per cent of assets under management, triggered by agreed performance hurdles, were covenanted as annual donations to the Foundation. This well-performing hedge fund has enabled the foundation to build an astonishing asset base of over £2bn and charitable spending in 2010 of nearly £28m (see further examples in Table 7.2).

---

[12] The founding partners were Clifford Chance, Bain and Company, Credit Suisse, Ernst & Young, Thomson Reuters, each committed to providing grant capital and volunteer staff time.

Table 7.2. European venture philanthropy funds originated by private equity, hedge fund, or family offices (family or individually owned private investment houses)

Venture philanthropy fund		Industries connected to the founders	Website
Business Angels des Cities	France	Private equity	Na
Citizen Capital	France	Private equity	<http://www.citizencapital.fr>
BonVenture	Germany	Family offices	<http://www.bonventure.de>
Social Venture Fund	Germany	Venture capital and investment banking	<http://www.socialventurefund.com>
Stiftung Charite	Germany	Family office	<http://www.stiftung-charite.de>
The One Foundation	Ireland	Entrepreneur/family office	<http://www.onefoundation.ie>
Fondazione Oliver Twist	Italy	Alternative assets (hedge funds)	<http://www.fondazioneolivertwist.org>
Fondazione Paideia	Italy	Family offices	<http://www.fondazionepaideia.it>
Invest for Children	Italy	Family office	<http://www.investforchildren.org>
Oltre Venture	Italy	Private equity	<http://www.oltreventure.com>
dob Foundation	Netherlands	Family office	<http://www.dobfoundation.nl>
Noaber Foundation	Netherlands	Entrepreneur/family office	<http://www.noaber.com>
Ferd Social Entrepreneurs	Norway	Family office	<http://www.ferd.com>
Voxtra	Norway	Private equity	<http://www.voxtra.org>
LGT Venture Philanthropy	Switzerland	Family office	<http://www.lgt.com>
Beyond Capital Fund	Switzerland and UK		<http://www.beyondcapitalfund.org>
Absolute Return for Kids (ARK)	UK	Alternative assets (hedge funds)	<http://www.arkonline.org>
Children's Investment Fund Foundation (CIFF)	UK	Alternative assets (hedge funds)	<http://www.ciff.org>
Breakthrough Fund	UK	Private equity and social entrepreneurship	<http://www.breakthroughfund.org.uk>
Impetus Trust	UK	Venture capital and consulting	<http://www.impetus.org.uk>
Venture Partnership Foundation	UK	Private equity	<http://www.vpf.org.uk/>
Wood Family Trust	UK	Family office	<http://www.thewoodfoundation.org.uk>
Bridges Ventures (and Social Entrepreneurs Fund)	UK	Private equity	<http://www.bridgesventures.com>
IKARE Ltd	UK	Private equity	<http://www.ikinvest.com/IKare>
Private Equity Foundation	UK	Private equity	<http://www.privateequityfoundation.org>
The Artha Initiative (in collaboration with Rianta Capital)	UK	Entrepreneur/family office	
The Sutton Trust	UK	Entrepreneur/family office	

Source: EVPA Annual Directory 2011, <http://www.evpa.eu.com>.

Entrepreneurs who have innovated and built successful commercial enterprises have a hard-earned insight to the challenges faced in growing business ventures. Those who turn their attention to philanthropy, perhaps after a 'cashing-out' event, have a natural kinship to entrepreneurship in the social sector. The spectrum of motivations for successful business people entering the world of philanthropy is wide and interrelated, with family background, humanistic or religious beliefs, and personal connection with a cause being key factors (John, 2007). But at its broadest, the social sector is a puzzling environment for those whose entrepreneurial life has been focused on creating shareholder value through innovation, competitive advantage, and growth. Social entrepreneurship provides the segue from business to social worlds and lowers the entry barrier into meaningful philanthropy. Paul and John Baan, Dutch high-tech entrepreneurs created considerable personal wealth through the sale of their database software company. Strongly influenced by conservative Dutch reformism and a biblical sense of 'neighbourliness', Paul Baan created the Noaber Foundation in 2000, which today pioneers impact investing, termed as 'social venturing', in the Netherlands, by supporting entrepreneurs creating social businesses in healthcare, providing services for older people or children with autism.

Venture philanthropy developed rapidly in Europe from 2004 to 2012 fuelled by the rise of social entrepreneurship and investment-minded philanthropists who wanted to integrate their commercial and giving mindset. This powerful alignment was played out across Europe through the launching of venture philanthropy funds linked to investment professionals and their firms (see Table 7.1), and championed by the evangelical zeal of EVPA. This structured approach to building a field led to European venture philanthropy being highly networked, strongly connected to the private equity industry, and generally more comfortable with experimenting with finance other than non-returnable grants (John, 2008).

EVPA estimated in 2011 that venture philanthropy funds in Europe had collectively committed €1.04bn, predominantly supporting early stage ventures, particularly in health and education.[13] In 2012 EVPA revealed that sixty-one European venture philanthropy funds expended €278m and estimated there to be 80–100 active funds in the region (Buckland, Hehenberger, and Hay, 2013). A small minority of venture philanthropy funds has thrived in Central and Eastern Europe. Current members on EVPA span sixteen European countries, with only three organizations outside Western Europe—the Czech Republic, Hungary, and Estonia. These three are, however, innovative funds that have pioneered support for social entrepreneurship in a demanding, post-communist environment. The Media Development Investment Fund, based in Prague, provides equity and technical advice to small, independent media companies in countries where free

---

[13] Source: EVPA Press Release 16th November 2011 available at EVPA website <http://www.evpa.eu.com>.

media is under threat. NESsT, is a well-established fund investing in social enterprises in central Europe from its base in Budapest. In the small Baltic State of Estonia, Heateo SA was the first organization to develop organized support for the country's experimental social enterprise sector.

Attempts to launch and sustain funds in Russia, Poland, Slovakia, and the other Baltic States have largely foundered in challenging environments because of the lack of sustained philanthropic capital available locally. One venture philanthropy fund takes a creative investment approach by actively seeking innovations that have potential to be replicated across European borders. Social Venture Fund, based in Germany, but with investors in several European countries, offers growth financing and infrastructure support and particularly seeks cross-border social business models.

Asia: A new frontier for venture philanthropy

Beyond the USA and Europe it is in the countries of Asia-Pacific where entrepreneurial philanthropy will develop most rapidly in coming decades, its style and trajectory influenced by three interconnected factors (John, Tan, and Ito, 2013):

- rapid and sustained wealth creation in Asia, especially the high-net-worth segment
- globalization of philanthropy, social investment and social entrepreneurship
- the new generation of entrepreneurial philanthropists.

WEALTH CREATION

Wealth is being created faster in Asia than any other part of the world. The Capgemini RBC World Wealth Report (2012) reveals that despite a 1.7 per cent decrease in global investable wealth in 2011, there was a rise in the number of High-Net-Worth Individuals (HNWIs) to 11 million individuals.[14] For the first time, Asia Pacific is home to the largest population of HNWIs of any region, resulting from a 1.6 per cent expansion from 2010 to 3.37 million in 2011 (Europe has 3.2 million, North America, 3.35 million, with Latin America, Africa, and the Middle East the remaining 1.1 million). Total HNWI wealth held by Asians in 2011 stood at $10.7trn, roughly on par with Europe and slightly below North America's $11.4trn. Japan accounted for 54.1 per cent of the region's wealthy in 2011, China for 16.7 per cent, and Australia for 5.3 per cent. Asia-Pacific accounted for fourteen of the top

---

[14] HNWIs have investable assets in excess of US$1m (excluding primary residence, collectibles, and consumer durables); Ultra-HNWIs have investable assets of at least US$30m.

twenty fastest-growing HNWI populations in the world in 2009, and eight of the top twenty in 2010. In 2011, Asia-Pacific accounted for seven of the top. The number of HNWIs in Indonesia jumped 23.8 per cent in 2010, and rose another 8.2 per cent in 2011. The 2010 and 2011 gains were 16.0 per cent and 12.8 per cent respectively in Thailand, and 12.0 per cent and 5.2 per cent in China. Capgemini RBC predicts that the region's economic fundamentals will remain robust in 2012 and beyond, despite global contagion, weak export markets, inflation, and poor real estate markets. China and India are likely to remain the fastest-growing global economies, with China's GDP forecast to grow by 8.5 per cent in 2013, and India by 7.4 per cent. Asians occupy five of the top thirty places in the Forbes global billionaire Rich List. These are all hugely impressive wealth statistics.

The 'Golden Age' of American philanthropy envisaged by Havens and Schervish (1999), where accumulated wealth is gifted to good causes rather than passed to the next generation, is by no means guaranteed in Asia, where wealth creation, giving and family are complex and closely entwined. An estimated 80 per cent of all enterprise in Asia is family owned (Fock, 2009), so making family a critical factor influencing the development of giving culture amongst Asia's wealthy. Barclays Wealth (2010) survey revealed that while 41 per cent of America's wealthy place giving high on their agenda, the figures in Singapore (23 per cent) and Hong Kong (16 per cent) are significantly lower.[15] Even so, a significant amount of the wealth being created in Asia is in the hands of first-generation wealthy, for whom making money is new and giving it away even more novel. So with wealth creation offering the huge potential for philanthropy in Asia, what are the levers that control its pace, style, and direction in the coming two decades, and what is the particular role for venture philanthropy?

THE GLOBALIZATION OF PHILANTHROPY AND SOCIAL ENTREPRENEURSHIP

Ignorance is no excuse in today's globalized world. A wealth creator in Mumbai, Jakarta, or Shenzhen is today likely to be as exposed to concepts like social entrepreneurship, venture philanthropy and impact investing as their US and European counterparts were a decade ago. In today's world, if you create wealth you are increasingly expected to have a public position on giving and more importantly, expected to be an effective philanthropist amongst your peer group. The Giving Pledge, the campaign led by Bill Gates and Warren Buffett to encourage the world's wealthy to donate most of their wealth to philanthropy, has not been well received during its road shows in

---

[15] Such wealth survey are of dubious academic rigor—see the critique of Asian philanthropy data collection in John, Tan, and Ito (2013).

India or China, a reminder that many Asians want to map their own personal philanthropic journeys, rather than have them imposed or made under the media scrutiny accompanying high profile events. Only seven individuals of Asian origin are amongst the 114 who have signed the Giving Pledge.[16]

Conferences and networks that promote social entrepreneurship are now commonplace across Asia, with an increasing number of these attracting philanthropists. In a region that historically has had very little in the way of grant-maker networks or philanthropy support organizations, the recent growth in domestic and regional activity in philanthropy promotion is meeting nascent demand among the region's wealthy. EVPA established in London in 2005 with just twenty-two members. Its sister network in Asia, AVPN, launched in 2012 with ninety-two founding subscribers, with its first conference attracting over 300 participants a year later.

The Asian diaspora in Europe or North America are a globalized community influenced by the styles of giving in their adopted countries. They are setting up foundations in their home countries focused on supporting social entrepreneurs and using a venture philanthropy approach. Gururaj 'Desh' Deshpande is a Boston-based serial IT entrepreneur, creator of ten highly successful Internet network-infrastructure companies. Deshpande was born in the 'second tier' south Indian town of Hubli, and after creating his fortune in the USA, focused some of the family's philanthropy back in Hubli by setting up, in 2007, the Social Entrepreneurship Sandbox (Ghosh, Applegate, Ghosh, and Kumar, 2012). The Sandbox provides executive education for social entrepreneurs and an incubator to help them test their ideas and bring to scale the most promising. As an entrepreneur who understood how technological innovation could be nurtured, Deshpande adapted this approach to the very different needs and environment of social entrepreneurs in his hometown.

A NEW GENERATION OF ENTREPRENEURIAL PHILANTHROPIST

Rapid wealth creation in Asia and the globalization of philanthropy provide a fertile environment for a new generation of philanthropist. The newly wealthy, probably themselves entrepreneurs and business-builders, are naturally attracted to entrepreneurial giving. Those who have inherited wealth through family business are also seeking expressions of giving that respect the family's tradition but rise to the challenge of financing today's social entrepreneurs. Entrepreneurs who build wealth in Asia are looking with fresh eyes at how their giving has impact, aligns to their personal entrepreneurship, leverages their skills and networks, and connects with the new opportunities for supporting social entrepreneurs. Today, Edelweiss Group is one of India's

---

[16] The seven individuals/families originated from India, Malaysia, and Taiwan. Correct at October 2013 at <http://givingpledge.org>.

entrepreneurial success stories. A financial services giant, employing 2,900 professionals across 144 Indian cities. Edelweiss was built from scratch by Rashesh Shah and Venkat Ramaswamy. Rashesh's wife, Vidya Shah, was the company's CFO until it floated in 2007. She was instrumental in developing the fledgling company's giving and after the IPO was asked by the new board to 'do something impactful' that reflected the company's entrepreneurial values and deep-rooted sense of giving back to society (John, Tan, and Ito 2013). The result was EdelGive, the company's foundation, run by Vidya, that takes a venture philanthropy model to support entrepreneurial non-profits with a mix of development grants and skills leveraged from within Edelweiss Group. Since 2008, EdelGive has granted $3.5m to a portfolio of twenty promising organizations coupled to 6,000 hours of Edelweiss volunteer time. EdelGive has demonstrated that the professional skills inside a company can be adapted and utilized to serve non-profits with ambitious plans for growth.

In Hong Kong, ADM Capital Foundation uses grants to invest in high-potential non-profit organizations in Southeast Asia, India, and China, using a small team to carefully select those organizations most likely to succeed from an injection of growth capital and capacity-building advice. The Foundation was set up in 2006 by the partners of ADM Capital, an alternative assets investment advisor to fund innovative approaches to human development and environmental protection in Asia. The founders intuitively felt that greater, sustained impact would come from investing in organizations, rather than funding their projects. As investment professionals they also wanted a model that was aligned to the investment strategy as a company—applying risk management, insight into financial structures, and a substantial network of local contacts—and applying to non-profits in Asia. The foundation leverages its impact by encouraging its business partners and investors to co-invest, providing them with a philanthropic platform. ADM Capital Foundation does not describe itself as a venture philanthropy fund, but its model of providing financial capital plus strategic advice to build operational infrastructure places it inside the core venture philanthropy model.

Family-run businesses that are today passing control to a new generation provide an opportunity for the family's historical giving to be reviewed and informed by contemporary practices of philanthropy. The UBS-INSEAD study on family philanthropy in 2011, based on 200 surveys and 100 in-depth interviews of philanthropists and philanthropy professionals highlighted social entrepreneurship as an important, emerging trend in the focus of Asian philanthropy. This younger generation of family philanthropists are interested in global issues such as the environment and civil rights, coupled to a keen sense of the need to measure the impact of their giving. While much wealth and business interest will continue to be handed down the family line many of this new generation are taking a refreshing review of the family's giving to embrace innovation in philanthropy while remaining respectful of the family traditions.

James Chen is a Hong Kong-based entrepreneur and leader of his family's investment office. Chen's grandfather left China in 1948 to establish what was to become the family's successful ceramics business. Since the 1970's the family pursued many philanthropic activities in Hong Kong and mainland China. Chen was asked by his parents to take stock of the family's thirty-year tradition of giving, which they viewed as declining in effectiveness over recent years. With a wide international education and business exposure, Chen modernized the family's philanthropy to give it a sharper focus on impact, supporting entrepreneurial ventures, and moving beyond grant-making alone towards impact investing. Today the Chen Foundation focuses on literacy in China using a venture philanthropy approach. Chen's family now pursues innovative impact investments including economic development enterprises in Tibet and low cost prescription eyeglasses globally (Carlock and Florent-Treacy, 2009). Chen has recently launched Retail Solutions Inc., which invests in companies and projects, which have a high potential social impact while being financially sustainable and in Legacy Venture, a venture capital 'fund of funds' with philanthropic purpose. Retail Solutions Inc. has agreed to donate all principal and profits from its Legacy Ventures investment to selected charitable causes.

Also in Hong Kong, RS Group, the family office of Annie Chen, has been a leading promoter of social entrepreneurship and sustainability in the region. As the lead funder of Engage-HK, as well as an investor in Civic Exchange's Asian Cities Index, RS-Group is deeply involved in advancing new social capital market innovations in the region. As of this writing, the firm is also executing a total portfolio management[17] approach to its work, investing all its assets in an integrated set of strategies that make use of philanthropic, near-market and market-rate investment instruments. As a leading impact investor, RS Group is demonstrating how the fundamental concepts of venture philanthropy and impact investing may be applied in an Asian context and perspective.[18]

ENGAGED-GIVING CIRCLES

One of the most exciting developments in Asian engaged philanthropy is the development of giving circles (John, Tan, and Ito, 2013; John 2014a, 2014b). In a giving circle, a group of individuals pool their philanthropic capital and choose non-profit ventures in their community to support with funding and their volunteered time. This model is a variant of venture philanthropy, analogous to an angel-investing group in commercial investment. Such circles can be group or institutionally managed; they can be grant or investment

---

[17] Emerson, 'A Capital Idea: Total Portfolio Management and a Unified Investment Strategy', Research Paper #1786, Stanford Business School, January 2002.

[18] One of the co-authors, Jed Emerson is a Senior Advisor to RS-Group.

based; and they can add value through non-financial services directly by group members or through a third party. In practice, giving circles can mix these attributes to make a local model that its members are most comfortable with.

Such circle models were pioneered in the late 1990s by Social Venture Partners International (SVPI) and Silicon Valley Social Venture Fund (SV2) in the USA. In the USA, during 2009, there were at least 600 such circles engaging 12,000 individuals and donating $100m (Eikenberry and Bearman, 2009). SVPI has helped establish affiliates in Japan, India, China, and Australia. In India, Dasra has taken giving circle method to a new level. Dasra is a Mumbai-based venture philanthropy fund that supports social entrepreneurs through direct investment and an executive education programme, and promotes philanthropy amongst India's HNW community through the Indian Philanthropy Forum. Dasra Giving Circles emerged out of the Forum to become India's largest collaborative giving effort. A Dasra Giving Circle comprises ten individuals, each committing to donate 1m Indian Rupees ($20,000) per year for three years, creating a $600,000 pool in each Circle. Eighty-five per cent of this pool is deployed as expansion grant capital to the NGO. The remaining 15 per cent is used to cover the cost of Dasra servicing the circle and delivering 250 days of non-financial support, through mentoring and technical advice, to each investee over the three-year funding cycle. The general sector in which a circle will operate and the shortlisting of potential investees begins on a solid research basis. Dasra's advisory research team will intensively research a specific area of interest in the social sector, for example, the problems surrounding the education of girls in India, or urban child malnutrition. A Dasra Giving Circle is then formed around each sector analysis, by inviting philanthropists to participate. The mapping exercise suggests which existing non-profits have a track record of success and a potentially scalable model, as a starting point for members of the Circle to decide which non-profit to focus their support on. By 2014 Dasra had initiated seven Giving Circles in this way. The first Circles have focused on the education of girls, improving Mumbai's public schools, and tackling urban malnutrition. Dasra plans to increase the entry ticket to $25,000 per year, believing that demonstrating high social impact through collaborative action, based on quality research, will attract a steady pipeline of new donors to its circles.

CHINA: FRONTIER VENTURE PHILANTHROPY IN ASIA'S 'WILD EAST'

Before 1988 there were no regulations in China governing civil society organizations; the concept of a non-profit entity was virtually non-existent, apart from those organized by the Communist Party or State (so called 'Government-Organized Non-Government Organizations, GONGOs'). Amity Foundation was one of the first proto-foundations ever registered in China, after encouragement from government to experiment with charitable giving. Amity Foundation was established in 1985 by the authorized Chinese Church as a response to the widespread poverty resulting from the Mao Zedong's social and economic experiments of the Great Leap Forward and the Cultural Revolution, and today is one of the largest and most respected charitable foundations in China that operates its own programmes and is an advocate for a strong private foundation sector in China. In a typically Chinese way, this sector will move fast by adopting and adapting from Western experience and practice, within the constraints of the Chinese socio-political system. The foundation sector will have to grow up fast if it to match the challenges of wealth disparity and the environmental pressure of industrial growth. The China Foundation Center estimates the number of foundations in China to be 2,882 (at November 2012), split almost between 1,291 'public offering foundations' (that are permitted to raise money from the public) and 1,591 non public offering foundations (that are endowed by individuals and use investment income—effectively 'private foundations'). Eighty-five per cent of endowed foundations were registered after 2004, when new legislation came into force encouraging private foundations. Several of these are actively engaged in venture philanthropy in at least a part of their activities. Jet Li One Foundation, YouChange, Non-Profit Incubator's Lenovo Venture Philanthropy Project, More Love Foundation, and Narada Foundation are a few of the new philanthropies in China adopting the venture approach to support ambitious non-profits (John, 2012).

Criticisms of venture philanthropy

While some recent commentators on venture philanthropy are sanguine about its evolution and future (Grossman, Appleby, and Reimers, 2013), from the start the movement has not been without critics. Many of these criticisms were levelled by those leading traditional philanthropic institutions (see, for example, Bruce Sievers' piece, *If Pigs Had Wings*) who felt venture philanthropy was neither necessary nor truly innovative and, in some pundits' opinions, simply the 'wrong' way to go about philanthropy. While there are others who've criticized venture philanthropy, Siever's points in his original opinion piece are exemplars of the basic ideas that:

- It is inappropriate for philanthropy to make use of business/investor models since philanthropy is 'different' from business practices—and in some cases was meant to make up for the various shortcomings of 'the market'.
- There is no equivalent to return on investment in the social sector as a measure of success, so attempting to force the notion of investment returns on to not-for-profit organizations is inappropriate.
- The notion that we need a 'new' approach to philanthropy is based on the idea that philanthropy is 'broken' or needs to be fixed. While critical social issues remain, Sievers argued that significant improvements in the lives of

people and the health of the planet have occurred through traditional philanthropy and so it therefore needs tweaking, not replacement.

- Foundations are not investors—they are donors, contributing funds into a not-for-profit venture and supporting the leadership's vision. They do not 'own' the enterprise or have no right to be overly directive in the execution of its strategies.

Kania and Kramer (2011) have argued that venture philanthropy has contributed to what they call *isolated impact*—an orientation towards 'finding and funding a solution embodied within a single organization'. This emphasis on building single organizations of excellence, they suggest, competes with the *collective impact* approach of deep collaboration where multiple organizations address complex, multi-stakeholder social issues. Whether or not this criticism is merited, venture philanthropy funds should use their convening power to develop strategies that support multiple players around a complex issue—and often do just that. For example, REDF supports and convenes a portfolio of nonprofit social enterprises in the San Francisco Bay Area and Los Angeles offering transitional and supported employment to economically disadvantaged individuals.

While these opinions certainly have their place in a discussion about the role and purpose of philanthropy, what has perhaps been most striking about the evolution of the venture philanthropy discussion is that many of the practice's central premises (that it is important to develop and appropriately apply metrics in order to track performance; that evidence and 'proof of concept' should underscore philanthropic strategy; that by thinking of philanthropy as a form of capital investment could open up new ways to enhance not-for-profit capacity-building; that grants are only the starting place to considering financing options available to non-profits and social enterprises, etc.) have now become mainstream within the larger field of philanthropy and, in fact, impact investing. Today's practice of philanthropy reflects many of the lessons of venture philanthropy, and venture philanthropy's continued evolution—whether in Europe, Asia, or elsewhere across the globe—will no doubt continue to inform the work of philanthropy and social finance as a whole.

Conclusions

From its early days of development in the USA, to its evolution within a European context and its ongoing refinement across Asia, venture philanthropy has shown that while it shares elements with the past, it is fundamentally forward looking and continually innovating. However, regardless of on what continent it manifests itself, the core elements of venture philanthropy remain the same:

- an investment approach to philanthropy
- high engagement with investees

- a performance metrics orientation
- a focus upon capacity building
- a long-term investment horizon
- the anticipation of 'exit' as an outcome of achieving new scale.

It is not certain that venture philanthropy, as it continues to evolve over coming decades, will maintain its 'outsider' edge. Indeed, many of the topics and ideas promoted by venture philanthropists over the two and a half decades since it was first introduced have either been adopted by mainstream foundations or have been accelerated in their previous exploration by the not-for-profit sector as a whole. Regardless of whether one understands the fundamental newness of the practice or believes it is simply the latest iteration of ideas and strategies long forgotten by modern philanthropy, venture philanthropy has helped shape a dialogue and debate within the not-for-profit sector that will continue for years to come.

▥ REFERENCES

Alter, K., Shoemaker, P., Tuan, M., and Emerson, J. (2001). *When Is It Time to Say Goodbye? Exit Strategies in Venture Philanthropy*. Virtue Ventures, SVP and The Roberts Foundation.

Balbo, L., Hehenberger, L., Mortell, D. and Oostlander, P. (2010). *Establishing a Venture Philanthropy Fund in Europe*, 2nd edition. Brussels: EVPA.

Barclays Wealth (2010). *Global Giving: The Culture of Philanthropy*. <http://www.barclayswealth.com>, accessed 2010.

Bishop, M., and Green, M. (2008). *Philanthrocapitalism: How the Rich Can Save the World*. London: A & C Black.

Black, M. (1992). *A Cause for Our Times: Oxfam. The First 50 Years*. Oxford: Oxfam Professional.

Buckland, L., Hehenberger, L., and Hay, M. (2013). 'The Growth of European Venture Philanthropy', *Stanford Social Innovation Review*, Summer, 1(3).

Capgemini RBC Wealth Management World Wealth Report (2012). *Asia-Pacific Wealth Report*. <http://www.capgemini.com>, accessed 2015.

Carlock, R. S., and Florent-Treacy, E. (2009). *The Chen Family: Succession through Philanthropy and Social Entrepreneurship*. Paris: INSEAD.

Eikenberry, A. and Bearman, J. (2009). 'The Impact of Giving Together'. Forum of Regional Associations of Grantmakers, University of Nebraska at Omaha, and the Center on Philanthropy at Indiana University. <http://www.givingforum.org>, accessed 2009.

Emerson, J. and Twersky, F. (eds) (1996). *New Social Entrepreneurs: The Success, Challenge, and Lessons of Not-for-profit Enterprise Creation*. San Francisco, CA: Roberts Enterprise Development Fund, <http://community-wealth.org/content/new-social-entrepreneurs-success-lessons-and-challenge-non-profit-enterprise-creation>, accessed 2015.

Fock, S. T. (2009). *Dynamics of Family Business: The Chinese Way*. Singapore: Cengage Learning Asia.

Ghosh, S., Applegate, L., Ghosh, R., and Kumar, A. (2012). 'The Sandbox: Creating a Bottom-up Entrepreneurial Ecosystem'. HBS Case Collection, Harvard Business School, Cambridge, MA.

Grossman, A., Appleby, S., and Reimers, C. (2013). 'Venture Philanthropy: Its Evolution and Its Future', *Harvard Business Review*, May 2013, N9-313-111.

Havens, J. J. and Schervish, P. G. (1999). 'Millionaires and the Millennium: New Estimates of the Forthcoming Wealth Transfer and the Prospects for a Golden Age of Philanthropy'. Boston College, Boston, MA.

John, R. (2006). *Venture Philanthropy: The Evolution of High Engagement Philanthropy in Europe*. Oxford: Skoll Centre for Social Entrepreneurship, Said Business School, University of Oxford.

John, R. (2007). *Beyond the Cheque: How Venture Philanthropists Add Value*. Oxford: Skoll Centre for Social Entrepreneurship, Said Business School.

John, R. (2008). *Venture Philanthropy Takes off in Europe*. Die Stiftung, Berlin.

John, R. (2012). *The Emerging Ecosystem of Entrepreneurial Social Finance in Asia*. Singapore: Asia Centre for Social Entrepreneurship and Philanthropy, NUS Business School.

John, R. (2014a). 'Virtuous Circles: New Expressions of Collective Philanthropy in Asia'. Singapore: Asia Centre for Social Entrepreneurship and Philanthropy, NUS Business School.

John, R. (2014b). 'Giving Circles in Asia: Newcomers to the Asian Philanthropy Landscape', *The Foundation Review* 6(4): Article 9.

John, R., Davis, R., and Mitchell, L. (2007). *Give and Let Give: Building a Culture of Philanthropy in the Financial Services Industry*. London: Policy Exchange.

John, R., Tan, P., and Ito, K. (2013). 'Innovation in Asian Philanthropy'. Working Paper No. 2 in the Entrepreneurial Social Finance in Asia Series, Asia Centre for Social Entrepreneurship and Philanthropy, NUS Business School, Singapore.

Kania, J., and Kramer, M. R. (2011). 'Collective Impact', *Stanford Social Innovation Review*, Winter, 9(1): 36–41.

Kramer, M. R. (2002). 'Will "Venture Philanthropy" Leave a Lasting Mark on Charitable Giving?' *Chronicle of Philanthropy*, May 2.

Leadbeater, C. (1997). *The Rise of the Social Entrepreneur*. London: Demos.

Letts, C., and Ryan, W. (2003). 'High Engagement Philanthropy: What Grantees Say about Power, Performance, and Money'. *Stanford Social Innovation Review*, Spring, pp. 36–43.

Letts, C., Ryan, W., and Grossmann, A. (1997). 'Virtuous Capital: What Foundations Can Learn from Venture Capital', *Harvard Business Review*, 75(2): 36–44.

Mahmood, M., and Santos, F. (2011). 'Family Philanthropy in Asia'. INSEAD and UBS Philanthropy Services, <http://www.ubs.com/1/ShowMedia/wealthmanagement/philanthropy_valuesbased_investments?contentId=194353&name=Insead_Report.pdf>, accessed 5 May 2015.

Sievers, B. (1997). 'If Pigs Had Wings: It's Sexy to Compare Grantmaking to Venture Capitalism. It's Also Dead Wrong.' *Harvard Business Review*, November/December 1997.

Sievers, B. (2001). If Pigs Had Wings: The Appeals and Limits of Venture Philanthropy'. Issues in Philanthropy Seminar, 21st November, Georgetown University, Washington, DC.US

8 Impact investing

A market in evolution

Anna Oleksiak, Alex Nicholls, and Jed Emerson

Introduction

Of all the various sub-markets within the wider social finance spectrum, the sector with perhaps the highest profile is impact investing. Although there is some variation in practice across industry participants, O'Donohoe et al. (2010) set out the generally accepted definition of impact investing:

> Impact investments are investments intended to create positive impact beyond financial return...Impact investors provide capital, expecting financial returns, to businesses (fund managers or companies) designed with the intent to generate positive social and/or environmental impact. (p. 7)

They are, therefore, *investments intended to create positive impact beyond financial return*.[1] In its simplest form, the general practice of impact investing may be defined as the placement of capital to fund for-profit, social or environmental projects whilst seeking—at a minimum—the investor's principal back. Thus, impact investing is *deliberately* structured to deliver *both* financial and (positive) social returns (rather than generating social externalities as a byproduct of financial value creation). While some of the practices that make up the impact investing market have been around for decades, the emergence of this market unified under the label of 'impact investing' is more recent (Kramer and Cooch, 2006). It is clear that—particularly in times of austerity post the 2008 financial crisis—the resources available to government and philanthropy are no longer adequate to address the global challenges affecting billions of people, such as food insecurity, lack of access to quality healthcare, shortage of affordable housing, lack of access to potable water, and inadequate sanitation. Impact investing aims to help fill the gap. It creates mechanisms through which investors may participate and fund innovative, solution-oriented social and environmental projects. In short, impact investing aims to expand the pool of capital available to fund the creation of social

---

[1] It is also interesting to note that a growing number of impact investors are exploring 'total portfolio management' approaches that, in addition to the expectation of financial return, also include grants—viewed as philanthropic capital—in their definition of the portfolio of assets under management within an impact investing strategy.

and environmental value, bridging the gaps between philanthropy, public funding, and mainstream capital markets.

The notion of investing in businesses that provide solutions to social problems or mobilizing capital for public good is not new. The Commonwealth Development Corporation (CDC) in the UK (established in 1948) and the International Finance Corporation (IFC: created in 1956) have been investing in sustainable businesses in the poorest countries for decades, achieving both financial and social returns, and attracting other co-investors to participate in their transactions. In the USA, the Community Reinvestment Act (1977) that has supported the creation of the Community Development Finance field has resulted in millions of dollars of private capital finding its way into the financing of affordable housing and various economic development ventures. In 1998, Pacific Community Ventures, a community development venture capital fund was founded, while in the UK, Bridges Ventures launched in 2002. Making use of philanthropic capital to invest in various social ventures, the Acumen Fund has been successfully investing in Africa and India and other impoverished regions since 2001. These and other funds pioneered the way, serving as a platform on which the impact investing industry was built. In 2003, Emerson identified a set of capital management practices focused upon the goal of integrated or *blended* value creation (Emerson, 2003). This work offered early examples of innovations that represent important precursors to today's impact investing market.

The specific term 'impact investing' itself is relatively new. Despite an early use of the term to describe engaged philanthropy that did not develop further (Kramer and Cooch, 2006), the origins go back to two special meetings held in Bellagio, Italy. In 2007 and 2008, under the leadership of the Rockefeller Foundation, a number of prominent industry practitioners and thought leaders gathered in Bellagio to discuss ways of building a new worldwide industry for investing for social and environmental impact. It was at these events the term impact investing was first coined,[2] although the core concepts of impact investing are grounded in a host of related concepts of social capital markets, social investing, and venture philanthropy (Emerson and Spitzer, 2007). The Bellagio meetings set in motion a series of events that aimed to build a new 'asset class' of impact investing. After these meetings, a variety of new investors have begun to participate in this emerging investment practice, from development finance institutions and foundations to private wealth managers, pension funds, and commercial banks. These organizations have invested in developed and emerging markets across different industries including agriculture, healthcare, education, water, housing, and other sectors,

---

[2] Interestingly, the first suggested title for this new 'asset class', was 'social impact investing', but this was later felt to be inappropriate in the US markets and the 'social' was dropped. However, in Europe, 'social impact investing' came into use again after the term was used in the G8 Social Investment Forum held in London in June 2013.

using various financial instruments. The exact size of the industry is hard to estimate, but, in 2008, the Monitor Institute stated the industry could grow to $500bn within five to ten years, representing an estimated 1 per cent of global assets under management at that time (Freireich and Fulton, 2009). In 2010, a survey by J.P. Morgan and the Rockefeller Foundation projected the industry's invested capital to be in the range of $400bn to nearly $1trn in the next ten years (O'Donohoe et al., 2010). Overall, there has been an increase in commitments for impact investing, and there are positive signs to suggest even greater capital inflows and activity may occur in the future. However, as of 2013, another survey estimated total impact investing assets under management as amounting to roughly $8–$10bn (Jackson and Harji, 2012). This figure is challenged by other research focusing on just twelve impact investing funds which on their own totalled $1.3bn under management (Clark, Thornley, and Emerson, 2014). Also US-SIF reported that in the USA community development finance organizations had over $61bn under management in 2012 (US SIF Foundation, 2012).

This chapter serves as an introduction to impact investing. It provides an overview of the current state of the industry and its trends, and gives examples of the participants and industry developments. This chapter draws on the work completed by the Global Research Unit of J.P. Morgan, Rockefeller Foundation, the Global Impact Investing Network (GIIN), Monitor Institute, E. T. Jackson and Associates, Pacific Community Ventures Insight group, and many others. The first section describes the historical context and current trends moving the industry forward. The second section builds on this, providing further examples of specific developments to define the industry as being in the market-building stage of industry evolution. The third section gives a statistical and factual overview of the different sectors, markets, instruments, and returns expected in the market. It also includes a practical overview of the state of healthcare in sub-Saharan Africa and it gives an example of impact investing from the perspective of a potential healthcare investor. The next section organizes the different market actors into functional categories to sketch out the market's overall shape and infrastructure. The following section gives an overview of the current policy agendas of relevance to impact investing in developed and developing markets. The last two sections summarize the current challenges, and provide the chapter conclusion, respectively.

Context and trends

While economic poverty, lack of access to healthcare and affordable housing for the poor have been present during the course of all of modern history, over recent years the world has faced additional unprecedented challenges and there are signs this trend is going to continue. One of the phenomena driving this is a dramatic growth in the human population. In 2014, the global population was over seven billion, and it has more than doubled over the last fifty years. This is already causing water and food scarcity and a squeeze on welfare and education services, especially in developing countries. This increase in population coupled with an accelerated rate of industrialization has caused the degradation of the natural environment, including deforestation, increasing carbon emissions, and depletion of natural reserves, putting excessive stress on the planet.

To make matters worse, government aid has plateaued in the recent years. Of the total financial flows from developed to developing countries, private funding contributes over 80 per cent of the funds, and government aid contributes less than 20 per cent, which is the opposite of forty years ago (Hudson Institute, 2013). The Official Development Assistance (ODA) from all OECD DAC donor nations amounted to $134bn in 2011 (Hudson Institute, 2013). While, overall, the total amount remained steady, some countries decreased their aid contributions markedly—often as a result of the spending cuts required of governments following the effective nationalization of the private sector banking crisis. The largest drop was seen in Spain and Greece. Spain decreased its contributions from $5.9bn in 2010 to $4.2bn in 2011 (34.1 per cent decrease). Greece decreased its contribution from $508m in 2010 to $425m in 2011 (22.1 per cent decrease), respectively. In addition, 11 other countries decreased their ODA flows. These decreases were matched by an increase in contributions by other DAC countries, notably Italy, Sweden, and Switzerland. However, in 2011 as in previous years, only five countries reached the 0.7 per cent GNI ODA target. (Hudson Institute, 2013).

The apparent worsening of the global situation and these reductions in targeted finance prompted some pioneer impact investors to look for solutions. A good example of an early impact investor group is the Investors' Circle. The Investors' Circle is an angel investor network assembled by High-Net-Worth Individuals (HNWIs) that has been funding small, for-profit enterprises addressing social and environmental issues for many years. Since 1992, it has facilitated the flow of more than $130m into more than 200 companies (Bugg-Levine and Goldstein, 2009). Examples of other early impact investors include Prudential Insurance, whose social investing unit has allocated more than $1bn across the USA to date mainly into affordable housing and development finance organizations, as well as Citibank, which developed its 'EQ2' structure to more effectively capitalize community-based financial institutions.

Efforts by these and many other organizations have encouraged other investors to follow, with an increasing number of traditional investors considering adding impact investments to their portfolios. In the last few years, many dedicated impact funds have been created, with several of them exceeding $1bn in assets under management (Credit Suisse and the Schwab Foundation, 2012). Many of these funds are raising their second or third fund after delivering market-rate-or-above returns to their investors. ImpactAssets, a not-for-profit financial services venture, publishes an annual roster of leading impact investing funds called *The IA-50* that has documented both the growth of the field and breadth of themes to which impact investors are directing capital. In 2013, the IA-50 reported that the fifty funds included in the roster managed in excess of $10.8bn of capital.

Examples of successful impact investing structures are emerging across multiple asset classes.[3] A common model is a direct investment into small- and medium-sized enterprises (SMEs) that provide scalable solutions to a number of global problems. An example of a more innovative impact structure is International Finance Facility for Immunization (IFFIm), which uses long-term legally binding commitments by donors to issue bonds on the international capital markets. The sale of these bonds provides cash that can be used to fund different vaccination programmes (WHO, UNICEF, and The World Bank, 2009). Another, more experimental structure gaining in popularity is the Social Impact Bond (SIB). Pioneered by Social Finance in UK in 2009, the SIB is a financial contract with the public sector that rewards private investors for the achievement of specific, pre-defined social outcomes (Social Finance, 2010). Examples of different impact investments are shown in Table 8.1.

Table 8.1. Examples of impact investments

Examples of impact investment	
LifeSpring Direct Investment	LifeSpring is a joint venture between Acumen and Hindustan Latex Limited, a public sector company in India. Its model rests on building a chain of small-sized (25-bed) hospitals across India. The company has significantly increased hospital-supervised deliveries and reduced maternal and child mortality and morbidity rates, and it has grown from one hospital at the time of Acumen's investment to nine hospitals. LifeSpring is now the largest chain of maternity hospitals in South India—it has treated more than 300,000 patients and delivered 18,500 healthy babies to date.(Source: <http://acumen.org/investment/lifespring/>)
Root Capital Investment Fund	Root Capital provides senior debt to large co-ops servicing the rural poor, the 'missing middle', which are too large for microfinance and too small or risky for corporate banks. Using contracts with agricultural buyers such as Starbucks to mitigate the lender's risk, Root Capital provides access to funds and creates sustainable partnerships between farmers and buyers. (Source: Bridges Ventures/Parthenon Group, 2012)
IFFIm Bonds Structured Product	Launched to support the GAVI (Global Alliance for Vaccines and Immunization) Initiative, these bonds were issued at market rates to both commercial and retail investors, and they hold an AAA/Aaa rating. This offering allowed GAVI to frontload committed funds that have been guaranteed over a twenty-year time horizon. GAVI is using these funds for immediate vaccinations and thus preventing illness and saving more lives overall. (Source: Bridges Ventures/Parthenon Group, 2012)

---

[3] Although much of impact investment to date has been private equity or private debt (O'Donohoe et al., 2010), a 'total portfolio approach' (linked to SRI approaches) increasingly sees it as operating across the entire continuum of instruments and asset classes.

Several other distinct impact investing trends have emerged, for example:

- Philanthropists, who made their fortunes in business including John McBain, Bob Johnson, and Pierre Omydiar, saw an opportunity to apply business principles and capital to social issues. They saw investment as more disciplined and sustainable than grants and giving (Simon and Barmeier, 2009). They also rejected the notion that making money from markets that engaged the poor is a form of exploitation
- Growing impatient with the lack of funding for interventions to address major global crises, powerful actors such as prominent family offices of the world's wealthiest individuals, large pension funds, and insurance companies actively sought to source and execute impact transactions (Freireich and Fulton, 2009)
- On the retail level, clients of major banks demanded more options than the binary choice of for-profit investment or pure philanthropy when allocating their capital, forcing banks to consider offering different impact investment products
- Corporations developed an understanding that social and environmental issues are material to their business performance and bottom line. Consequently, they explored the idea that an investment could be a part of their Corporate Social Responsibility (CSR) agenda. The Shell Foundation, for instance, invested in GroFin, a SME finance vehicle, and ChevronTexaco established its own microcredit bank in Angola
- Governments also look for new ways to address growing social problems and participate in the trend. They do it by introducing policies and enabling the development of the impact market. Aside from the introduction of new policies, in the last few years, several new initiatives have been introduced, including the Impact Investing Policy Collaborative (IIPC), that connect policymakers to the private sector. Additionally, the 2013's G8 Meeting was used for the first time as a platform to discuss the importance of social impact investing.

At the societal level, the idea of investing with impact has gone from a niche idealistic idea to a mainstream focus. Business schools report oversubscribed classes on social enterprise, and mid-career professionals see attractive employment opportunities in roles that enable them to address key social challenges. An additional factor affecting the impact investing industry has been the aftermath of the 2008 financial crisis. Some researchers have described the effects as positive and others as negative. A positive outcome has been that it became clear that markets seriously mispriced investment risk: as a result, mainstream risk and return expectations have changed dramatically and impact investing looked less risky than before the crisis (Freireich and Fulton, 2009). Indeed, microfinance bond notes largely held their value throughout the downturn and helped decrease volatility in many impact portfolios. Additionally, the macroeconomic slowdown, especially in advanced economies, made impact investments more attractive to diversify investors' portfolios. On the downside, due to the crisis, investors also reverted to what were perceived to be more conservative modes of investing, avoiding new trends like impact investing—despite significant losses incurred by many asset owners with investments in traditional, mainstream vehicles and strategies.

A nascent industry

Although momentum has been building for many years, it was not until recently that the impact investing market has taken shape and common themes and trends have started to emerge. In the early years, several prominent reports were issued, and the first book describing the concept and practices of impact investing was published in 2011 (Bugg-Levine and Emerson, 2011). In 2008, the Monitor Institute looked closely at the emerging market and characterized it as being on the verge of passing from a stage of 'uncoordinated innovation' into one of 'marketplace building' (Freireich and Fulton, 2009) that was characterized by higher volumes of activity, infrastructure building, and developing a common set of goals and impact measurement standards. E. T. Jackson and Associates reported that the impact investing market had made significant progress to a sustained 'marketplace-building' phase (Jackson, 2012). Within this phase itself, the market has moved from a period focused on organizing itself and establishing an initial infrastructure to one much more focused on implementation (see Figure 8.1).

One of the characteristics of the market-building phase is unlocking capital and supporting higher volumes of transactions. In the impact investing space, several prominent transactions contributed to unlocking new capital around the world. In 2007, Compartamos Banco became the first Latin American microfinance institution (MFI) to offer equity through an initial public offering (IPO). The IPO was thirteen times oversubscribed and it was considered a huge success by any financial market standard (Rosenberg, 2007). While this can only be viewed as a market success, it was then followed by the significant devaluation of stock of SKS MicroFinance in India as well as widespread and pointed criticism of microfinance with regard to whether it encouraged borrowers to take on consumer debt as opposed to capital for business and economic development.

In the following year, the World Bank issued the first Green Bonds valued at SEK 2.325bn. A year later, the Bill & Melinda Gates Foundation committed $400m to impact investing, and California FreshWorks launched a $200m loan fund to invest in facilitating healthy food options for underserved communities. The governments of many nations also stepped in. For instance, the UK Government committed over £1bn to a range of funds supporting social enterprises, the Australian Government announced two Social

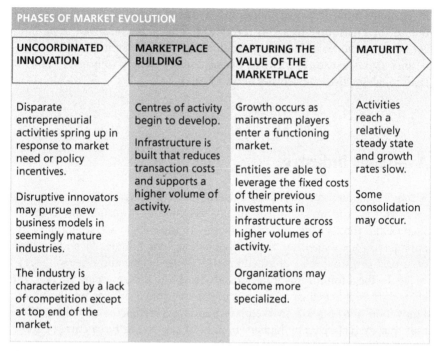

PHASES OF MARKET EVOLUTION

UNCOORDINATED INNOVATION	MARKETPLACE BUILDING	CAPTURING THE VALUE OF THE MARKETPLACE	MATURITY
Disparate entrepreneurial activities spring up in response to market need or policy incentives. Disruptive innovators may pursue new business models in seemingly mature industries. The industry is characterized by a lack of competition except at top end of the market.	Centres of activity begin to develop. Infrastructure is built that reduces transaction costs and supports a higher volume of activity.	Growth occurs as mainstream players enter a functioning market. Entities are able to leverage the fixed costs of their previous investments in infrastructure across higher volumes of activity. Organizations may become more specialized.	Activities reach a relatively steady state and growth rates slow. Some consolidation may occur.

Figure 8.1. Stages of new market development
Source: Monitor Institute (Freireich and Fulton, 2009)

Enterprise Development Investment Funds valued at A$20m, the Government of Hong Kong launched a $200m fund to support social enterprise development and the US Federal Government made a commitment to authorize $100m over five years in investments for pay-for-success projects targeting vulnerable populations.

As the flows of capital dedicated to impact investing strategies have steadily increased, there has been an increase in the number of impact-oriented funds targeting different sectors and regions. However, perhaps counter-intuitively, investing capital in the deals has in some ways proven more difficult than raising such capital. In response to this, a number of intermediaries have emerged, specializing in deal origination, structuring, and portfolio management. One prominent example is Big Society Capital (BSC) in UK that was founded in 2011 to help develop the social investment market, and in 2012 launched a £600m investment fund. Some mainstream institutions, such as Deutsche Bank, J.P. Morgan, and UBS, established bespoke divisions focusing on impact investing. Others, such as the Teachers Insurance and Annuity Association—College Retirement Equities Fund (TIAA-CREF) strengthened their existing in-house expertise.

On the investment side, the industry has experienced much less momentum. There seemed to be a belief that if more capital became available there would be more opportunities in which to place it. This was quickly proven to be inaccurate, with many private and institutional investors struggling to realize deal flow at scale. Contributing to these challenges were issues related to deal size (institutional investors require relatively large investment opportunities in order to move significant amounts of capital), high transaction costs due in part to the smaller overall deal sizes of many impact investments as well as a 'missing middle' of mezzanine finance to position growing social enterprises to move up the stages of development in order to be well positioned to take on new, larger amounts of capital.

This experience should not, however, be confused with a lack of demand for capital. On the contrary, the need and demand for capital is vast. For instance, in 2010, Hope Consulting reported there was a \$120bn market opportunity for impact investing, and Dalberg Associates projected that West Africa's high social impact sector alone would need an estimated \$65bn in investments (Jackson, 2012). In practice, producing deals that are investor ready and can achieve considerable scale has become one of the main challenges for the impact investing market going forward, with some newcomers to impact investing not recognizing the degree to which they would have to 'make their opportunities' as opposed to entering a fully formed market with defined actors and deal pipelines. Other challenges in the space include deal economics and high transaction costs, associated with smaller deals and with working across remote geographies. Additionally, most deals in the impact investing space require more than one type of capital, which often requires more than one investor to participate in the transaction.

One of the key areas of recent market development has been a focus on new metrics and standards designed specifically for impact investing (see section below entitled 'Achieving Impact'). A number of initiatives have been launched over the last few years to provide a common set of tools for investors to measure the social impact of investments. In 2008, the Impact Reporting and Investment Standards (IRIS) were launched that aimed to provide a standardized taxonomy and definitions for social, environmental, and financial performance. IRIS works closely with the Global Impact Investing Rating System (GIIRS), which conducts third-party social and environmental assessments of companies and funds.

Overall, the impact investing marketplace is only now emerging in a coherent, functioning manner. However, some sub-sectors, such as microfinance and community development finance have already moved to maturity and can provide valuable lessons (see Box 8.1).

Key characteristics

Impact investors span a wide range of sectors, geographical regions, and financial products. They can operate in developed as well as in emerging markets, depending on the investor's focus and preferences. Impact investments

---

BOX 8.1. THE GROWTH OF MICROFINANCE

Evolution of Microfinance

Microfinance, a subset of impact investing has moved through the early industry stages over the last few decades. The first microfinance institutions, including the Grameen Bank in Bangladesh, were funded in the 1970s, and operated as non-profits in the first years. They were slowly proving that microfinance can be a revenue-generating activity and provide a socially, as well as financially, sustainable model.

Over the next several years prominent organizations become involved in the field. In 1985 the Small Enterprise Education and Promotion (SEEP), a membership based international microfinance network was created and, in 1995, the Consultative Group to Assist the Poor (CGAP) was launched. CGAP is an independent organization that works to provide access to finance to the poor and consists of development agencies, financial institutions, and foundations. These and other organizations gave more visibility and increased the overall interest in microfinance that, in turn, led to building of the necessary infrastructure and attracted more capital to the sector.

In 1990s sophisticated measurements of performance and impact emerged with a greater emphasis on standardization. In 1996, MicroRate was launched, and in 1997 the first Microcredit Summit was held to share knowledge and best practices and to work towards reaching 100 million of the world's poorest families (Freireich and Fulton, 2009). In 2008 Standard and Poor's announced plans to provide global risks ratings for microfinance institutions. These activities attracted additional institutional investors, and the microloan volume had grown from \$4bn in 2001 to \$25bn in 2006 (Freireich and Fulton, 2009). In the mid 2000s, microfinance became more mainstream and started to move out of the market-building phase into the market value capture phase.

---

may be made in agriculture, healthcare, education, clean water provision, housing, and other sectors. They can also address environmental issues such as pollution and deforestation, and channel funds to enterprises working in clean energy and waste management, among many other environment-centred projects. The instruments used are closely aligned with the financial and social goals, and they yield various levels of financial return and types of impact to investors.

GEOGRAPHY AND SECTORS

Many impact investors choose to focus either on developing or developed markets. Part of the reason for this specialization is that there are significant regional differences that require local expertise and, often, presence on the ground. Another reason is investor preference. Some investors focus on their close neighborhoods to solve domestic issues, while others invest where they perceive the need to be the greatest.

It should be of little surprise that emerging markets are quickly gaining in popularity as an impact investing destination. They appeal to a wide spectrum of impact investors looking to achieve both social impact and a reasonable rate of financial return (or, at least, no overall loss of capital). In emerging markets, there are 2.5 million people that live on less than $2.5 a day—collectively referred to as the Bottom of the Pyramid (BoP) consumer market (Bridges Ventures and Parthenon Group, 2012). According to the World Bank, sub-Saharan Africa and South Asia have the greatest concentration of people living below the extreme poverty line, with over 50 per cent, and 40 per cent of the population, respectively, living on less than $1.25 a day.

From a macroeconomic perspective, many emerging markets have typically demonstrated higher and more stable GDP growth than developed markets over the last decade. Additionally, the rise of a new, developing-country middle class has built inviting markets for foreign investors. This has also created a new set of local investors. Although emerging markets can present a number of challenges, such as the overall business climate, political instability, and corruption, investing in emerging markets remains attractive to many.

In developed markets, many people benefit from impact investing as well. Although, low income populations in the US, Canada, and Western Europe earn substantially more than the poor in emerging markets, relative to the economies in which they live, they still live under the poverty level and can, therefore, benefit from impact projects. For instance, in 2010, FreshWorks in the state of California launched a $200m fund to facilitate healthy food options for underserved communities. Other social issues that are the focus of impact investing funds operating in the developed world include youth unemployment, recidivism, lack of affordable housing, and also arts and cultural preservation.

In January 2013, J.P. Morgan issued a report in which it presented findings from ninety-nine impact investors and other industry players. According to this report, the top regions of investor focus were sub-Saharan Africa, Latin America and the Caribbean, and the USA (see Figure 8.2).

The same group of respondents was asked to select their sectors of interest (see Figure 8.3). Looking at both, the developed and emerging markets, food and agriculture was one of the most important sectors to investors, with the healthcare and education sectors following closely. However, there is a big difference in the investor focus on microfinance and financial services in the

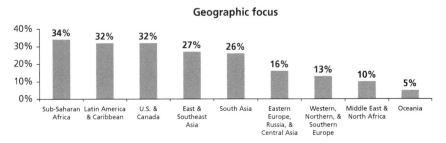

Figure 8.2. Geographic focus of impact investing

Source: GIIN/J.P. Morgan, 2013

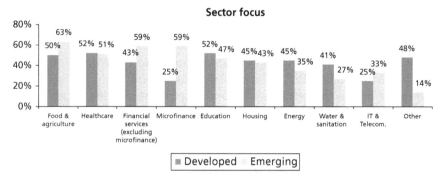

Figure 8.3. Sector focus
Source: GIIN/J.P. Morgan, 2013

developed versus emerging markets. While microfinance is very important to investors in emerging markets, it is much less so to investors in the developed world. However, according to an earlier J.P. Morgan (Saltuk et al., 2011) report that showed statistics on actual transactions, the food and agriculture category comprised only 15 per cent of the total transactions reported, second after microfinance. Healthcare represented only 3 per cent of the total investments reported. This could imply that given the current investor focus, there may be an increase in commitments to the food and agriculture, and healthcare sectors going forward (see Box 8.2 and Case 8.1). It is also worth noting that another J.P. Morgan (O'Donohoe et al., 2010) report predicted that affordable urban housing would be one of the most significant areas for impact investment over the next decade, and the potential invested capital required would be in the range of $214–786bn.[4]

ENVIRONMENTAL INVESTMENT

Environmental sustainability is a central theme addressed by impact investing. In the last few decades, the planet has suffered from the overuse of natural resources, increased carbon emissions, water and air pollution, and improper waste management. Heavy deforestation and logging in developing countries alone has caused great harm to local ecosystems. According to data from the Food and Agriculture Organization (FAO) of the United Nations, countries such as Indonesia, Nigeria, and Cambodia have lost a significant percentage of

---

[4] Big Society Capital (2013) noted that investments in capital intensive social sectors may be the most obvious way to leverage their assets to their greatest effect:

While not appropriate for all social sector organizations, social investment offers opportunities to finance at scale, particularly in the areas of greatest expenditure such as education and health, and capital intensive areas such as social housing and the provision of facilities for residential care.

BOX 8.2. HEALTHCARE IN AFRICA

Healthcare in Africa

In most of sub-Saharan Africa, healthcare provision remains the worst in the world. The region has about 11 per cent of the world's population, but carries 24 per cent of the global disease burden. Almost half the world's deaths of children under five take place in Africa, yet sub-Saharan Africa accounts for less than 1 per cent of global health expenditure and faces a severe shortage of medical doctors and staff. Only about 3 per cent of health workers globally are deployed in the region. Just as an example, every year, malaria alone costs an estimated $12bn in lost wages, and life expectancy in Swaziland is just 30 years, compared to 81 years in Switzerland.

The governments in many African countries lack the essential skills and resources to develop efficient healthcare systems. Additionally, corruption is still a major obstacle to investment, and the prospects for systemic reforms that could solve this issue vary considerably across the region. However, bilateral agencies, with a few exceptions, tend to provide support in the context of the public health system and the majority of international aid is deployed via the public sector.

Often, very little of this investment reaches the small-scale clinics and facilities that serve much of the poor populations—in both urban and rural areas. Local banks rarely lend to such facilities given their lack of experience in the sector and the limited balance sheets of the investees. Development finance institutions—that might be a source of capital for these small clinics—often find this sector challenging, due to regulatory issues and their own internal constraints.

Currently, there are still relatively few impact investing funds focusing on global healthcare. The IFC-backed Health in Africa Fund and the Dutch Investment Fund for Health in Africa are two private equity funds in the area, but they focus on large-scale investments only. Other impact funds, such as the Grassroots Business Fund and the Acumen Fund, have a portion of their portfolios in the healthcare sector, but also focus on other sectors, such as education and agriculture. There are several well-known venture funds in development such as Fanisi and FirstLight. However, as a rule, such venture funds are seeking high returns and only invest in sectors with a proven track record.

New financial structures such as Social Impact Bonds (SIBs) and Development Impact Bonds (DIBs) (which are similar structures, but used for development) are currently being developed to provide funding for some of the most needed interventions. For example, the Mozambique Malaria Performance Bond (MMPB) is designed to provide funding and increase efficiencies of interventions over the next ten years. The MMPB aims to prevent up to eight million new infections and reduce malaria prevalence in the targeted areas by up to 75 per cent. Other similar initiatives are underway.

Yet, the demand for healthcare in sub-Saharan Africa is growing. A study conducted by the IFC, with assistance from McKinsey & Company, estimated that, over the next decade, $25–30bn in new investment will be needed in health care assets alone, including hospitals, clinics, distribution warehouses, and other essential assets in the region.

Source: International Finance Corporation (IFC), 'The Business of Health in Africa.'; Han Lily, 'Malaria in Mozambique: Trialling Payment by Results.' Guardian Professional; TIA Analysis

---

CASE 8.1. IMPACT INVESTING IN CLINIC AFRICA, UGANDA

Impact Investment

Clinic Africa is a fast-growing network of primary-care clinics in Uganda. With demonstrated profitability at urban clinics, Clinic Africa's challenge is to build profitability among its rural clinics as it continues to grow aggressively.

DESCRIPTION	INVESTMENT CONSIDERATIONS
Two-year-old clinic network that opened five clinics (three urban, two rural) and served over 5,000, largely poor, patients in its first 1.5 years.	Urban clinics are quickly profitable
■ Clinics are centrally owned but individually operated by local physicians.	■ Profit margin about 5 percent for urban clinics with $30,000 in revenues. Rural clinics not yet sustainably profitable.
■ NGO oversees expansion and quality control for the network, but physicians retain most profits.	■ Typical clinic requires about $15,000 of seed capital from NGO, mostly for facility, working capital, and equipment.
■ Urban clinics are profitable within three to six months while rural clinics are unable to generate similar profitability.	Rapid expansion: Five clinics in 1.5 years
■ Typical facility characteristics:	■ Have demonstrated profitable urban model and ability to open new clinics.
√ Three to six physicians	■ Have not yet demonstrated self-sustainable rural model.
√ 2,600 pharmacy visits	Goal of 100 clinics in the region
√ 1,500 outpatient visits	■ Financing demand for continued rapid growth, potentially from donor, NGO or a private investor.
√ 1,400 laboratory tests	■ Strong urban growth opportunity.
√ 500 inpatient stays	■ Rural growth requires one of the following:
	√ Develop independently profitable model
	√ Expand rural network as social enterprise, subsidized by NGO funding and urban network profits

Source: IFC/McKinsey, 2011

---

their forests—31 per cent, 79 per cent, and 58 per cent, respectively—in the last fifteen years (Bridges Ventures and Parthenon Group, 2012).

Fortunately, sustainable forestry and other green models are becoming more profitable and gaining popularity among investors. For instance, the Global Environment Fund (GEF), established in 1990, with $1bn of assets under management (<http://www.globalenvironmentfund.com>) actively invests in environmental projects in both developed and emerging markets. The fund's portfolio includes an investment in Greenko Group, a clean energy production company in India, Saisudhir Infrastructure Ltd, which is a water sanitation, irrigation, and electricity distribution business in India, and Peak Timbers, a Forest Stewardship Council (FSC) certified pine and eucalyptus plantation company in Swaziland, among many other environmental investments.

Alternative energy models are also gaining popularity, especially in the Middle East and Africa. Solar power technology has greatly improved in the past few years, bringing costs down and increasing profits. However, solar may still represent a costly and unpredictable energy source when compared to other renewable and traditional energy sources. With constant technological advancements, investments in solar may become quickly obsolete and the returns are difficult to project accurately. There are several projects, however, that can prove an investment in solar to be worthwhile. For instance, the Renewable Energy for Affordable Living (REAL) Housing project in Israel provided affordable and sustainable housing, while lowering consumption and the cost of energy. The REAL Housing homes promised a potential 60 per cent saving on heating and cooling over comparable homes on the market (Spitzer, Emerson, and Harold, 2007).

FINANCIAL INSTRUMENTS

The choice of an impact investing instrument is dictated by the investors' preferences—since, as in traditional finance, different instruments carry different characteristics. In practical terms, to select the appropriate instrument investors look at several criteria, which include future cash flows, riskiness of the underlying business, the ownership structure, and exit strategies. In this sense, the investment process itself is very similar to the process that a traditional investment goes through. It is important to understand that impact investing is simply the augmentation of traditional investment practice with consideration of social and environmental value creation and risk management frameworks. While there are certainly innovations in financial structure (such as Social Impact Bonds or unique uses of philanthropic capital to provide loan guarantees) at its core impact investing builds upon traditional finance with new applications and vehicle structures.

Impact investors may invest in debt, equity, mezzanine capital—that has elements of debt and equity combined—or hybrid capital deals that can be structured to include elements of debt, equity, and grants. In addition to these traditional forms of capital, selected projects can be financed by straight grants. Grants do not have to be repaid, but they are often short-term and restricted to specific projects and activities. Table 8.2 shows a summary of various impact investing instruments.

In 2011, J.P. Morgan and the GIIN published a report based on an analysis of over 2,200 impact investments that suggested the most prevalent form of impact investing was debt. Out of $4.4bn in investments, 75 per cent took the form of debt investments, especially private debt (Saltuk et al., 2011).

One interesting evolution in discussions regarding impact investing practice has been the recognition of the important role played by philanthropic capital within the structuring of deals and markets. In the initial Monitor report on impact investing, published in 2009, grants—which do not return principal to investors—were not considered part of the impact investing toolkit. More recently, a growing number of impact investors are recognizing the critical role played by philanthropic capital in bridging the 'capital gap' between capital offering a return to investors and traditional charitable giving. Philanthropic capital can be used to 'buy down' or reduce perceived risk thereby

Table 8.2. Impact investing instruments

Instrument	Term sheet		Implications for social enterprise
Grants	Duration:	Short term	- Usually restricted use for predefined projects
	Annual Payments:	None	- High fundraising costs
	Repayment:	None	- Low entrepreneurial flexibility
Debt capital	Duration:	Long term (3–7 yrs)	- Annual interest payments require low-risk business model
	Annual Payments:	Interest payments	
	Repayment:	Yes	- No dilution of ownership
			- Far-reaching rights of capital providers in case of default
Equity capital	Duration:	Unlimited	- Dilution of ownership
	Annual Payments:	Dividend payments	- Investor receives control and voting rights
	Repayment:	No	- Profit participation for social investor
			- Potential impact on corporate culture
Mezzanine capital	Duration:	Long term (3–7 yrs)	- Annual interest payments require predictable cash flows
	Annual Payments:	Interest payments	
	Repayment:	Yes	- Dilution of ownership only if converted into equity
			- Mandatory repayment
			- Profit participation for social investor
Hybrid capital	Duration:	Long term (3–7 yrs)	- Inexpensive financing instrument
	Annual Payments:	None	- No dilution of ownership
	Repayment:	Depends upon structure	- Risk sharing with the social investor
			- Great structuring flexibility

Source: Schwab Foundation/Technical University of Munich 2011

making it possible for mainstream capital investors to participate in deals they would otherwise pass on.

As described in the recent UK Cabinet Office's 'Co-Mingling' report, foundations can leverage philanthropic funds and invest alongside commercially focused capital in a co-mingling investment fund, and thus tackle an issue at a scale that would not otherwise be possible to address (UK Government, 2013). For example, were it not for early stage, high-risk philanthropic investments in the field of microfinance, it would never have been possible for later stage, market-rate investors to enter. Indeed, in addition to philanthropy, the role of public capital has also been greatly undervalued within many impact investing discussions. Much of the appeal of impact investing for traditional investors is the notion that it is a 'free market' approach to addressing social issues. Yet, in truth, a recent study of the highest performing impact investing funds found that in each case public capital (either serving as an anchor investment, guarantor roles or other support of impact funds) was critical to attracting mainstream, traditional capital investors (Clarke, Emerson et al., 2014).

RETURN EXPECTATIONS

There is an ongoing debate with regard to return expectations in the impact investing arena. Several reports have been published showing these expectations range dramatically across a spectrum, with some investors setting up their portfolio to outperform traditional investments in the same category, while others expect to trade some of their financial return for increased social impact. For instance, E. T. Jackson and Associates gave an example of four distinct impact investors, expecting very different returns. The report puts Calvert Foundation with 0-2 per cent expected return at the lower end, and IGNIA, a venture capital firm active in Latin America, with 25 per cent return expectations at the higher end of the spectrum.

Several factors can affect the expected rate of return including the instrument type used and the geographical focus of the investment. Frequently, there is a difference in expectations for investments made in the developed versus emerging markets. The 2011 study by J.P. Morgan presented the following conclusions:

Developed markets: Debt investors in developed markets often expected lower than market returns. This could be partially explained by the fact that in many developed markets the regulatory framework and tax incentives encourage investment in social ventures that achieve lower financial returns. The results for equity investors were mixed, although it appeared that in developed markets equity returns were often concessionary.

Emerging markets: In emerging markets, expected debt returns appeared to be in line with the long-term realized index returns. Also, equity returns—benchmarked against 20–25 per cent gross or 15–20 per cent net—appeared to be in line with typical private equity or venture capital expected returns, measured in both developed and emerging markets.

There is a separate debate in the space about the simultaneous pursuit of social and financial returns. Some investors believe that financial performance and impact are inversely dependent, meaning that an increase in one variable will cause a decrease in the other. Other investors feel that the two are independent, which would imply that it is possible to have an increase in both at the same time. According to the J.P. Morgan report (Saltuk et al., 2011) about 60 per cent of surveyed investors believed that a trade-off is generally not necessary between impact and financial returns. About the same portion of total impact investors surveyed admitted that they would be willing to sacrifice financial returns for greater social impact if they were faced with that issue while contemplating an investment.

In general, impact investments can accommodate a wide range of impact goals and return targets. Some of the structures, for instance, mentioned above, co-mingling funds attract investors with different impact and returns expectations. They vary in structure and the risk–reward is designed to address the investors' mandates. Each co-mingling fund usually includes philanthropic capital coupled with commercial funding, and the risk–reward structure can range significantly. Foundations can take equal or more risk than other investors and receive equal or lower return compared to the risk taken.

This significantly de-risks the transaction allowing more conservative invest-ors to participate. Several case studies and analysis of this structure are presented in the recent 'Co-Mingling' report (2013) published by the UK Cabinet Office.

ACHIEVING IMPACT

Businesses may pursue impact objectives by many means, and investors can reference these means of impact in designing an investment strategy. In many cases, impact objectives are tightly related to the sector in which the investee operates. For instance, a newly built school should have a direct impact on local literacy rates and a hospital providing healthcare services, should improve the health status of the area. Other investments, such as investments in microfinance companies, are expected to generate indirect impact. They should provide capital to companies that, in turn, distribute that capital further to entrepreneurs, creating jobs, increasing incomes, and growing industries. Investing in companies working to improve the environment is also a clear example of investing for potential impact.

J.P. Morgan (Saltuk et al., 2011) categorized impact into 'process' and 'product'. Within process, a company may achieve some of its mission impact by hiring employees from a traditionally underrepresented or excluded group. In terms of products, on the other hand, a company producing solar lamps, for example, may deliver social impact by providing affordable access to light for people who lack access to electric grids. Targeting 'Bottom of the Pyramid' (BoP) customers can be considered an implicit part of the product method of impact (Saltuk et al., 2013). Several ways, developed by IRIS, that companies can achieve impact are presented below in Table 8.3.

Market infrastructure

The impact investing sector's market infrastructure has been growing signifi-cantly in the last few years, with many new investors and other players coming to the space. E. T. Jackson and Associates (2012) presented a widely accepted framework describing how market infrastructure forms (see Table 8.4). The framework classified different market actors into four categories: asset owners; asset managers; demand-side actors; and service providers. Asset owners and asset managers include High-Net-Worth Individuals, private foundations, impact investing funds, and institutional investors, including banks and pen-sion funds. The demand-side actors comprise investees that received and utilized impact investing. These include small and growing businesses, social enterprises, some corporations, cooperatives, and microfinance institutions. The final group of actors includes service providers, such as standard-setting

Table 8.3. Social and environmental impacts

IRIS Social Impact Objectives V3.0	IRIS Environmental Objectives V3.0
Access to clean water	Biodiversity conservation
Access to education	Energy and fuel efficiency
Access to energy	Natural resources conservation
Access to financial services	Pollution prevention and waste
Access to information	management
Affordable housing	Sustainable energy
Agricultural productivity	Sustainable land use
Capacity-building	Water resources management
Community development	
Conflict resolution	
Disease-specific prevention and mitigation	
Employment generation	
Equality and empowerment	
Food security	
Generate funds for charitable giving	
Health improvement	
Human rights protection or expansion	
Income/productivity growth	

Source: IRIS, 2015
Note: IRIS initiative is managed by the Global Impact Investing Network.

Table 8.4. Market actors

Actors in the impact investing industry			
ASSET OWNERS	**ASSET MANAGERS**	**DEMAND-SIDE ACTORS**	**SERVICE PROVIDERS**
■ High-Net-Worth Individuals/ families	■ Investment advisors	■ Corporations	■ Networks
	■ Fund managers	■ Small and growing businesses	■ Standards-setting bodies
■ Corporations	■ Family offices	■ Social enterprises	■ Consulting firms
■ Governments	■ Foundations	■ Cooperatives	■ Non-governmental organizations
■ Employees	■ Banks	■ Microfinance institutions	■ Universities
■ Retail investors	■ Corporations	■ Community development finance institutions	■ Capacity development providers
■ Foundations	■ Venture funds		■ Government programmes
	■ Impact investment funds/intermediaries		
	■ Pension funds		
	■ Sovereign wealth funds		
	■ Development finance institutions		
	■ Government investment programmes		

Source: Harji and Jackson, 2012

organizations, consulting firms, government bodies, and industry networks. It is worth noting that some actors, such as corporations can serve more than one function. For instance, some corporations can be the asset owners or investors, and other corporations can be the demand side actors or the recipients of the investment.

IMPACT INVESTORS

Asset owners and asset managers provide and allocate capital to impact projects. Just as in the traditional investment market, they vary in terms of their motivations, risk and return expectations, and social impact objectives (see Table 8.5). Within the impact investing market, it has been suggested that investors can be bifurcated into *impact first* or *finance first* investors, though, in reality, such neat distinctions do not always apply. Impact first investors have been defined as those who have a specific social or environmental return expectation above a minimum level of impact, but can accept a lower rate of financial return, which in most cases is predetermined at each organization (with a floor of zero return on capital). Impact first investors include some foundations family offices, and High-Net-Worth Individuals. Finance first investors, on the other hand, have a minimum financial return floor (sometimes below the market rate, sometimes not), and use impact outcomes as a secondary goal in their investment decisions. Some examples of finance first investors include banks, pension funds, sovereign wealth funds and some development finance institutions. There are many investors that have wide-ranging portfolios that touch on different approaches in relation to different specific investments. Consequently, the same investor may have deals that fall into the impact first and finance first categories.

Table 8.5. Examples of impact investors

EXAMPLES OF IMPACT INVESTORS	
Arm of major bank J.P. Morgan Social Finance	J.P. Morgan Social Finance was launched in 2007 and provides thought leadership through market research and reports. It also commits J.P. Morgan's capital to impact investing funds. A flagship investment includes the African Agricultural Capital Fund.
Institutional investor TIAA-CREF	TIAA-CREF is a leading financial services organization with over $440bn in combined assets under management. This US pension fund committed over $600m to impact investments across different asset classes.
Venture Firm and Family Foundation Omidyar Network	The Omidyar Network operates as a philanthropic investment firm, with both a grant-making foundation and a for-profit limited liability company. It deploys a range of capital toward impact investments.
Family foundation The Tony Elumelu Foundation	The Tony Elumelu Foundation, headquartered in Lagos, Nigeria was founded in 2010 by Nigerian businessman, Tony O. Elumelu. The Foundation is committed to the economic transformation of Africa. It supports small and mid-sized enterprises through start-up funding and business development services.
SME investment fund GroFin	GroFin is a leading provider of SME finance and business development focusing on developing sustainable enterprises in Africa and the Middle East. GroFin is present in thirteen countries, with an investment portfolio of 300 transactions and $300m investment capital across seven funds.
Development finance institution FMO	FMO is a Dutch development bank. It was founded in 1970, and it has Euros 5bn in assets under management. FMO supports private sector growth in developing and emerging markets. The bank focuses on sectors that it deems to have high long-term impact, including financial institutions, energy, housing, agribusiness, food and water.

Source: E. T. Jackson, 2012; Bridges Ventures/Parthenon Group, 2012

Since the initial introduction of the split between 'impact first and finance first' language, the impact investing field has recognized such a framing—while perhaps helpful on an interim basis—does not always reflect how impact investors operate when managing their investments. In the recent years, rather than an 'either/or' framing of this reality, many impact investors have moved to a 'both/and' understanding of capital performance. This is especially true of asset owners managing a portfolio of assets wherein each asset class (fixed income, private equity and debt, etc.) has various levels of impact and financial return which may be refined depending upon both the particular investment strategy and the intent of the investor creating a single portfolio managed for both financial returns and a variety of types of impact. Groups such as The 100% Impact Network engage in *total portfolio management* by seeking integrated financial, social, and environmental returns as *total* performance. Such an approach seeks to optimize financial returns appropriate to any given asset class while simultaneously seeking to maximize impact as appropriate for that same asset class. This is increasingly the approach taken by asset owners interested in executing impact investing strategies.

Although, in the past many impact investors have categorized themselves as impact or finance first, the current trend is toward investors managing for total performance. Clark, Emerson et al. (2014) described twelve impact funds that aimed to achieve both financial and social returns. These funds covered different sectors and regions, ranging from microfinance in India to sustainable property in the UK, and they demonstrated that the Pareto assumption that there should always be trade-off between social and financial returns may not hold in all cases. The research also stated that, going forward, the notion of achieving both financial and social returns will be regarded as standard best practice (Insight, Duke, and ImpactAssets, 2013).

Impact investors have different degrees of freedom in making their allocations. Some investors have a regulated, fiduciary duty to generate reasonable, risk-adjusted returns that compete with the returns of traditional investments. For instance, TIAA-CREF, a retirement fund manager, is required to invest in projects that generate competitive returns, and, therefore, it needs to prioritize a financial return over a social impact return in making its investment decisions. Foundations making impact investments from their endowments, such as the Kellogg Foundation and the Annie E. Casey Foundation, also typically seek competitive risk-adjusted rates of return, although this is less clear cut in so-called mission- or programme-related investments (MRI/PRI). One long-time pioneer in this work is the F.B. Heron Foundation of New York, which is perhaps the first American foundation to have a Bloomberg terminal in their offices to assist staff in tracking environmental and social performance of publicly traded companies, as well as executing a strategy which, over time, will use its entire corpus to advance the social mission of the institution.

In contrast, foundations such as the Rockefeller Foundation and the Bill & Melinda Gates Foundation make programme-related investments with the primary goal to advance a social mission, and, within these strategies, they invest for impact rather than a competitive rate of financial return. Interestingly, a number of the leading foundations promoting impact investing through their grant and PRI programmes do not actually engage in impact investing with their corpus. Ultra-High-Net-Worth Individuals typically have the greatest flexibility in their investment mandates. They can choose a particular social or environmental mission they wish to support, allocating part of their portfolio to projects yielding lower than a market rate of return. What is perhaps most interesting to observe in the evolution of these practices is the growing recognition that fiduciaries who do not take into account 'off balance sheet' factors such as global climate change or pandemics, may actually be operating in violation of their fiduciary responsibilities. It is for this reason many pension funds in the USA have taken the lead in exploring how to both protect their portfolios from the costs of climate change as well as position them to benefit from innovative investment strategies which seek to generate financial returns through investing in future climate-change solutions.

Additionally, different classes of investors can invest at various points in an investee's lifecycle to satisfy different risk–return–impact combinations. Impact investors, such as venture philanthropists, can provide early-stage finance that is more risky, but have high potential social returns, while other investors may position themselves to invest capital at later stages of the venture development when there are opportunities for growth and expansion. Follow-on investments can be made through a syndicate or a co-investment. For example, in the case of Husk Power (a sustainable energy social enterprise based in India), the Shell Foundation provided seed capital in the form of grants, which helped the company prove its concept and enabled it to access commercial capital when it was ready to scale up. Some of the subsequent investors in Husk Power included Acumen Fund, LGT Venture Philanthropy, Oasis Fund and, a later stage, the International Finance Corporation (Harji and Jackson, 2012).

DEMAND-SIDE ACTORS: DIRECT INVESTMENTS AND FINANCIAL STRUCTURES

As noted above, impact investments can take different forms and can be made across different asset classes, sectors, geographies, and financial structures. Frequently, impact investing takes the form of a direct investment into a social enterprise. These investments may be made into a wide range of sectors including food security, healthcare, and education. Especially, in emerging economies, SMEs are believed to be the backbone of social entrepreneurship and, if capitalized and managed properly, these enterprises can become a powerful force in poverty reduction, job creation, and economic growth. Several examples of successful models in emerging markets are shown in Table 8.6.

Table 8.6. Demand-side actors in developing countries

Company	Business model	Sector	Country
TeamLease	Connects students to the business community and provides the vocational courses required for their employability	Education	India
LifeSpring	Niche hospital chain providing affordable, high-quality maternal healthcare	Healthcare	India
Souk el Tayeb	Farmers' kitchen and market for local small-scale producers	Nutrition	Lebanon
Cambodian Business Integrated in Rural Development (CBIRD)	Provides access to loans for developing rural business activities	Microfinance	Cambodia
Zara Solar	Sells small photovoltaic solar devices to counter limited electrification	Infrastructure	Tanzania

Source: Arosio, 2011

Providing capital directly to social enterprises is just one way of delivering change through impact investing. There are many other financial structures that provide funding to create impact. A popular structure is an investment fund. Funds aggregate capital from investors and use it to invest in a number of enterprises that fit with their investment criteria and financial and social objectives. Impact funds can have just one type or multiple types of investors. In many cases, two or more types of investors, with different requirements and motivations can work together to combine different types of capital into one investment and create different layered-structure investments (Credit Suisse, 2012).

In the recent 'Co-Mingling' report by the UK Cabinet Office (2013), the authors explored the structures in more detail and presented case studies on several recent funds. These included the Deutsche Bank's Eye Fund, Bridges Social Entrepreneurs Fund, African Agricultural Capital Fund, and New York City Acquisition Fund among others. The report divided the investment structures into three categories: *pari passu*, meaning on equal footing, or sharing equal risk and financial return; *risk-reward* with social investors taking a greater risk and receiving a higher return; and *but-for* structures, in which foundations take a greater risk for a lower return. The fund structure is adapted to a specific situation and investors' motivations and risk appetite. Co-mingling funds, by combining different types of capital and providing attractive terms to commercial investors, can leverage philanthropic capital and provide significant amounts of investment available for social projects. A good example of this structure is the Deutsche Bank-sponsored Eye Fund presented below. In this structure Deutsche Bank attracted many investors with different objectives, and involved other industry participants to help with raising the fund (see Figure 8.4).

One popular, although still experimental structure, is the Social Impact Bond (SIB). The first SIB was launched in Peterborough, UK in 2010. The Peterborough SIB was designed to reduce the reconviction rates of short-

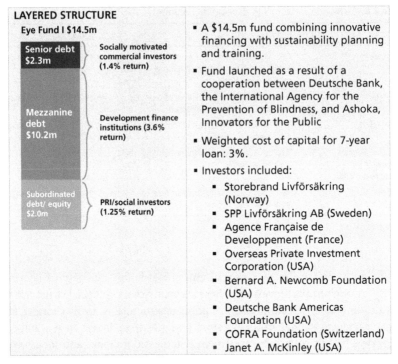

LAYERED STRUCTURE

Eye Fund I $14.5m

Senior debt $2.3m — Socially motivated commercial investors (1.4% return)

Mezzanine debt $10.2m — Development finance institutions (3.6% return)

Subordinated debt/ equity $2.0m — PRI/social investors (1.25% return)

- A $14.5m fund combining innovative financing with sustainability planning and training.
- Fund launched as a result of a cooperation between Deutsche Bank, the International Agency for the Prevention of Blindness, and Ashoka, Innovators for the Public
- Weighted cost of capital for 7-year loan: 3%.
- Investors included:
  - Storebrand Livförsäkring (Norway)
  - SPP Livförsäkring AB (Sweden)
  - Agence Française de Developpement (France)
  - Overseas Private Investment Corporation (USA)
  - Bernard A. Newcomb Foundation (USA)
  - Deutsche Bank Americas Foundation (USA)
  - COFRA Foundation (Switzerland)
  - Janet A. McKinley (USA)

Figure 8.4. A layered investment structure
Source: Deutsche Bank

sentence male prisoners leaving Her Majesty's Prison Peterborough (Nicholls and Tomkinson, 2013). It had an innovative approach to improving social outcomes within the community by incentivizing non-government investors to fund support programmes (Cave et al., 2012). There have been numerous SIB structures developed since then across the world. One of the more visible and the first SIB of this scale in the USA was the Rikers Island SIB announced in August 2012. This structure was a result of a close collaboration between Goldman Sachs, Bloomberg Philanthropies, the Osborne Association, MDRC, and the City of New York. A $9.6m loan from Goldman Sachs—guaranteed by Bloomberg Philanthropies—was structured to support the delivery of therapeutic services to 16–18-year-olds incarcerated on Rikers Island Prison. The loan will be repaid based on cost savings realized by the New York City Department of Correction directly related to any decrease in recidivism (see Figure 8.5: Olson and Phillips, 2013).

PERFORMANCE MEASUREMENT AND STANDARD SETTING

Establishing widely accepted performance measurement standards for impact investing remains a major challenge. Common reporting standards have the

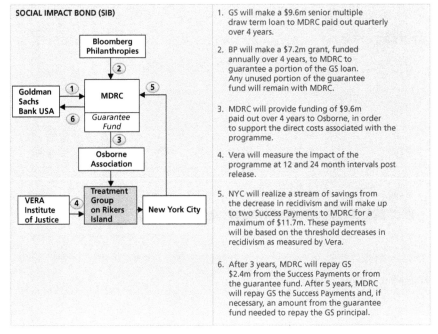

SOCIAL IMPACT BOND (SIB)

1. GS will make a $9.6m senior multiple draw term loan to MDRC paid out quarterly over 4 years.

2. BP will make a $7.2m grant, funded annually over 4 years, to MDRC to guarantee a portion of the GS loan. Any unused portion of the guarantee fund will remain with MDRC.

3. MDRC will provide funding of $9.6m paid out over 4 years to Osborne, in order to support the direct costs associated with the programme.

4. Vera will measure the impact of the programme at 12 and 24 month intervals post release.

5. NYC will realize a stream of savings from the decrease in recidivism and will make up to two Success Payments to MDRC for a maximum of $11.7m. These payments will be based on the threshold decreases in recidivism as measured by Vera.

6. After 3 years, MDRC will repay GS $2.4m from the Success Payments or from the guarantee fund. After 5 years, MDRC will repay GS the Success Payments and, if necessary, an amount from the guarantee fund needed to repay the GS principal.

Figure 8.5. The Rikers Island Social Impact Bond
Source: Olson and Phillips, 2013

potential of improving investment efficiency, lower due diligence costs, and enable performance benchmarking over the life of an investment (O'Donohoe et al., 2010). They can also provide real risk and return data to guide future investment, and improve the social impact of an investment by creating a clear set of guidelines before the investment is made. In recent years, several prominent projects have been developed to provide measurement standards for many different types of impact investing across the world. At the same time, many smaller, decentralized initiatives continue to exist, especially at the organizational level.

Particularly significant in this area is the work of the Global Impact Investing Network (GIIN) that developed a set of reporting standards called the Impact Reporting and Investment Standards (IRIS). The GIIN has overseen the development of IRIS since 2009. Prior to that, the Rockefeller Foundation, the Acumen Fund, and B Lab began the development of IRIS in early 2008 with support from Hitachi, Deloitte, and Pricewaterhouse Coopers.

IRIS works together with other measurement initiatives, specifically the Global Impact Investing Rating System (GIIRS), also developed by B Lab. Although these two systems work together, GIIRS is the more investor-focused tool. The GIIRS Ratings and Analytics platform is a set of third-party impact assessment tools on the performance of social enterprises, including companies, funds, and direct investments. Using the IRIS taxonomy

Figure 8.6. A GIIRS rating

of definitions and key performance indicators, GIIRS assesses impact investment funds on four performance areas: governance, workers, community, and
the environment. The assessments are intended to be comprehensive and easy
to compare across sectors and regions. GIIRS Ratings and Analytics was
launched in the second half of 2011, with fifteen GIIRS pioneer investors,
representing approximately $1.5bn in total assets (Jackson, 2012) and it has
grown significantly in size and popularity since then. A sample of a GIIRS
rating is presented in Figure 8.6.

It is worth noting that impact metrics data are proving to be very important
for investors. In a study published by J.P Morgan in early 2013, fund managers
confirmed that impact metrics are critical in attracting and raising capital. In
fact, the study found that 82 per cent of respondents believed that measuring
impact was necessary or important to attract and raise capital from investors.
About 16 per cent stated that measuring impact was important to all investors
and nobody said that measuring impact was not important at all.

INDUSTRY NETWORKS

There are several organizations that have played important roles in developing
the impact investing market infrastructure. The GIIN, mentioned above, has
become a platform for impact investors who want to learn more about the
industry and fund investment projects. With support from the Rockefeller
Foundation, J.P. Morgan, USAID, and many other prominent players, the
GIIN has become the leading international coordinating body for the market.
Its Investor Council serves fifty foundations, funds, and firms (Harji and

Jackson, 2012). Although, the majority of its early members have been based in the USA, more recently the GIIN began building links with partners in Europe and elsewhere, especially from the South, where a lot of the impact investing activity is taking place.

Other examples of industry networks include the Aspen Network of Development Entrepreneurs (ANDE), Toniic, and the previously mentioned 100% Impact Network. ANDE is a global network of organizations contributing expertise and investing money in small and growing businesses in developing and developed markets. In 2010, the network had 110 members and operated in 150 countries. The funds managed by ANDE members invested collectively $900m in 2,500 investments by 2013 (Harji and Jackson, 2012). Toniic, on the other hand, is an international investor network investing in social projects promoting a sustainable global economy. The network provides investment tools and deal process support to its members.

Impact investing is also prominent at conferences that focus on social and environmental issues around the world. Examples include the Skoll World Forum in the UK, the Social Capital Markets Conference (SOCAP) in the USA, the Sankalp Social Enterprise Awards Forum in India, the Good Deals conference held annually in the UK and the European Venture Philanthropy Association (EVPA) annual conference, amongst others.

Public policy

Government policy has played a very important role in building and growing the impact investing market. Effective policies, in several countries, have helped mobilize and direct the key resources needed to institutionalize the industry. Context has been important. In developed countries that experienced prolonged financial and fiscal stress from the 2008 economic downturn, impact investing offered to relieve some of these pressures. In these markets, policymakers saw impact investing as an opportunity to leverage private capital to achieve social outcomes in addition to (or in place of) public spending on welfare. This was not without controversy. In developing countries, on the other hand, the pattern has been different, with many demonstrating relatively high growth, creating a significant number of High-Net-Worth Individuals and large-scale investment pools, such as international corporations, and sovereign wealth funds. At the same time, these countries typically had large segments of the populations that lived in poverty. In these cases, governments chose to introduce polices directed at alleviating poverty and encouraging domestic and international investors to invest in projects providing jobs and services to their BoP populations (Harji and Jackson, 2012).

Regardless of the region and socioeconomic status, government policies can have a profound effect on this market and the actors within it. Indeed, research has found that of its pool of twelve high-performing impact investing funds, eight were identified as having significantly benefitted from public policies and capital leveraging private investment. Different policies can help build a supportive infrastructure, encourage innovation, and ensure the effective supply of impact capital. Clarke, Emerson et al. (2011) presented a range of ways in which government policies can positively affect impact investing:

- *Supply of impact capital*: This includes policies dealing with investment rules and policies that provide co-investment rules to increase the supply of impact capital, and invite more investors by enabling risk sharing with the government.
- *Demand for impact capital*: Policies that build demand include those that build institutional capacity, create enabling structures, and generally contribute to the development of impact related projects and capital recipients.
- *Directing impact capital*: These are policies that direct the way investments are made in the capital markets. They also encourage a shift towards impact opportunities. These policies can change the perceived risk and return characteristics of impact investments by adjusting market prices, and improving transaction efficiency and the availability of market information.

There have been numerous pieces of legislation in the USA, Europe, and also developing countries around the world that have contributed to the development of the impact investing market. One of the first was the Community Reinvestment Act (CRA) in the USA. Introduced in 1977, the CRA helped to stimulate the growth of the community development financial institution (CDFI) sector. This was matched by the Community Investment Tax Relief legislation in the UK in 2002. More recent legislation included the announcement of a Low-Profit Limited Liability (L3C) legal structure in 2008 in the USA, and the provision of an impact investing guide for charities in 2011 in the UK. In 2008, the European Social Investment Taskforce was launched, and the European Commission adopted the Single Market Act for funding of social business. In emerging markets, recent impact investing policies included Brazil's Clean Development Mechanism, Kenya's Microfinance Act, Regulation 28 in South Africa, and Malaysia's Corporate Social Responsibility (CSR) Disclosure Rule.

The UK Government has been especially active in the impact investing space, introducing programmes and legislation to grow the market and strengthen the UK's position as a worldwide hub. The 2012 report *Growing the Social Investment Market: 2012 Progress Update* gave an overview of key initiatives since 2005, centred on stimulating the demand and supply of capital and on improving the enabling environment by removing legal and regulatory barriers to impact investing. Notable actions included the passing of the Public Services (Social Value) Act that requires local authorities to take account of the social impact of all public service contracts during the procurement process, using the Red Tape Challenge to remove inconsistencies and omissions in the existing legal and regulatory framework that governs social investment, and the

---

BOX 8.3. THE LONDON PRINCIPLES

The IIPC 2013 conference, held in Oxford and London, aimed to develop The London Principles to serve as a resource and a catalyst for market development. Following four days of debate, the five principles emerged as:

CLARITY OF PURPOSE: Clarity of purpose allows governments to avoid inefficient use or misallocation of resources, insufficient policy support that impedes achievement of outcomes and disjointed policy regimes. According to this principle, governments should clearly identify the social objectives, identify why this impact investing strategy or policy may be appropriate to meet these objectives, and define realistic expectations for the results and time it may take to achieve them.

SHAREHOLDER ENGAGEMENT: Effective stakeholder engagement ensures that all actors are included. It also manages expectations and avoids the development of principles that are unfit for the purpose. This principle guides governments to identify and collaborate with key stakeholders, from concept implementation to revision of strategies and policies. It advises to support shared ownership of policy and guards against misaligned incentives and conflicting power structures.

MARKET STEWARDSHIP: Market stewardship ensures a holistic vision for impact investing strategies and policies. It focuses on a balanced development of investor interest, investment opportunities, and mechanisms to deliver intended social outcomes. This principle advises governments to identify the appropriate use of market interventions, and develop markets holistically, balancing capital supply, investment readiness, and support for intermediary infrastructure.

INSTITUTIONAL CAPACITY: This principle allows for the effective use of resources, adds value to existing policies, and creates the potential for developing innovative strategies that address key social problems. Following this principle, governments should determine cross-sector resources within the government currently available, or necessary to be developed for a successful policy implementation. It also talks about the need to measure and evaluate the impact of these policies against stated objectives.

UNIVERSAL TRANSPARENCY: Universal transparency mandates that stated objectives are clear, and progress toward their achievement is openly measured and reported to relevant stakeholders and the public at large. Governments should report on performance and develop a culture of transparency, engage in a process of shared learning, and commit to stated social objectives.

Source: IIPC, 2013

---

introduction of social investment tax relief in April 2014. Additionally, in collaboration with the Said Business School, the UK Government hosted the world's first International Symposium on Social Impact Bonds and other innovative financial products in 2012, and launched the Department for International Development (DFID) Impact Programme, with the goal to provide £100m of social investment to sub-Saharan Africa and South Asia to help transform the impact investing market in developing countries.

In addition, there have been several new initiatives in the last few years connecting policymakers to investors and other actors in the impact investing space in order to facilitate a dialogue and to help governments introduce effective policies. For example, in June 2012, the G8 Meeting platform was used for the first time to discuss social impact investing. The Social Impact

Investing Forum brought together 150 delegates including government officials, major philanthropists, business and finance executives, social entrepreneurs and academics, and provided an opportunity to discuss the steps needed
to enable the market to operate on a global scale (UK Government, 2013). One
of the main outcomes was the formation of the Social Impact Investing
Taskforce. The Taskforce's main goal was to oversee other initiatives, and
identify and propose future developments across the G8 plus Australia. While
in the United Kingdom, the 2014 introduction of the Social Investment Tax
Relief Act allowed for those investing in social ventures to receive a 30 per cent
tax break on their income tax filings.

Another prominent example of connecting government to the impact
investing market is the Impact Investing Policy Collaborative (IIPC), coordinated by Pacific Community Ventures' InSight team together with the Initiative for Responsible Investment at the Hauser Institute for Civil Society at
Harvard University. This initiative aimed to engage policy leaders in developed countries, such as the UK, USA, Canada, and Australia, as well as
partners from more than a dozen developing countries around the world.
The IIPC's mission was to grow the impact investing market by building a
global network to support policy research and innovation in this space. The
IIPC advised that impact-oriented policies should be designed and assessed on
the basis of six essential criteria: targeting, transparency, coordination, engagement, commitment, and implementation. These lead to the establishment in
July 2013 of the London Principles (see Box 8.3).

Future challenges

There is no doubt that the impact investing market has experienced significant
growth since the Bellagio Convenings. New investment models have been
developed, and many new investors have joined the trend. However, it appears
investors' perceptions are typically ones of 'cautious optimism' (Saltuk et al.,
2011) regarding the growth of the impact investing market in the future.
Despite positive developments, serious challenges remain. J.P. Morgan
(Saltuk et al., 2013) suggested that investors reported the 'lack of appropriate
capital' and 'shortage of high quality investments' as the main challenges to
future growth, but others can also be discerned. These are described below.

LIMITED SUPPLY OF INVESTMENT-READY DEALS

Whilst there has been a lot of emphasis on the supply of capital to this market,
there has, perhaps, been less of a focus on developing investment readiness on

the demand side (Harji and Jackson, 2012). Many funds continue to face challenges in deploying capital, and it is felt by some there are still too few examples of really successful investments, relative to the amount of interest and capital allocated to impact investing. Additionally, some regions appear to produce fewer investment-ready projects than others and some regions have very low ratios of projects that investors screen initially to projects that eventually receive capital. In the J.P. Morgan (Saltuk et al., 2013) study, respondents revealed the most robust investment pipelines were in the USA, Canada, South Asia, and Latin America and the Caribbean. On the other hand, sub-Saharan Africa, the region with the most interest from investors, had relatively few projects that were investment ready. The UK government has been a pioneer in recognizing the need for investment-readiness support—in 2013 it launched the £10m Investment and Contract Readiness Fund for this purpose.

CAPACITY BUILDING

Much of the activity in the impact investing arena has been focused on entrepreneurs that are at the seed or very early stage in their business evolution. Building capacity at these levels involves providing financial and managerial training, strengthening business models, and preparing the investment case. It is also important to educate entrepreneurs to understand the challenges and opportunities related to illustrating social and environmental impact while preparing to receive impact investing capital (Harji and Jackson, 2012). A wide range of models providing this type of technical assistance is required. After the early training, when entrepreneurs are able to manage the initial phases related to seed and start-up capital, often they are ready for additional, expansion capital and other more advanced types of technical assistance and training are needed. Thus, there is also a strong demand for programmes that are designed to transition entrepreneurs from a start-up phase to an early venture stage. Fortunately, there is an increasing interest in building entrepreneurs' capacity. IFC and Endeavor are examples of organizations that have developed such programmes.

CHALLENGING DEAL ECONOMICS

Several impact investing surveys confirmed that the majority of private debt and equity investments in this market were very small in comparison to average traditional private equity investments. However, the due diligence and other deal related costs are similar, which makes impact investments relatively more expensive to execute. In the case of a very small investment, the initial costs can be equal or higher than the future profits and, consequently, make the investment financially infeasible. According to IFC, on average, deals that were $2m and above were profitable, whilst deals below

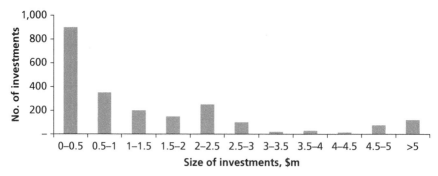

Figure 8.7. Individual deal size, $m
Source: J.P. Morgan 2011

this threshold in many cases were not (Wilton, 2011). To illustrate the case further, J.P. Morgan (Saltuk et al., 2011) analysed 2,211 impact investments and concluded that most of the impact transactions in the space were below the $1m mark (see Figure 8.7). Future opportunities could be realized if intermediaries aggregated small investments to lower the traditionally high execution costs and to make these investments both socially and financially attractive.

LIMITED TRACK RECORD

Another challenge facing impact investors, especially those focusing on emerging markets, is the lack of performance data and overall industry track record. It is difficult to get an accurate picture of the financial data mostly because the industry is still very young, and because most of the transactions are into private companies. According to J.P. Morgan's (Saltuk et al., 2011) study, investors reported that they had exited only about 10 per cent of their investments by this date. Most of the listed means of exit were through debt maturities and equity exits in the form of trade sale or buyouts. However, there are early success stories, mostly from the more mature sectors such as community development and microfinance, which have demonstrated successful exits. For instance, the Compartamos IPO in 2007 yielded original investors an internal rate of return of 100 per cent per year, compounded over eight years (Freireich and Fulton, 2009). This was, however, also controversial.

ALIGNING CAPITAL

Impact investments access a diverse range of capital sources that can include development finance institutions, private foundations, angel investment capital, and impact investment funds. Successful entrepreneurs are able to navigate these capital sources, and partner with investors whose different risk/ return appetites allow them to structure appropriate transactions and provide needed capital. However, aligning the right capital with the right opportunities continues to be a challenge. In J.P. Morgan (2012) report, survey respondents identified as the top challenges to the growth of the impact investment industry 'lack of appropriate capital across the risk/return spectrum' and 'shortage of high quality investment opportunities with track record'. These two challenges retained the two top spots from an earlier J.P. Morgan survey in 2011.

Another, related characteristic of the impact investment space is that the traditional cost of capital, or the yield curve in debt transactions does not hold very well. In traditional finance the interest is expected to increase with the tenor. However, in impact transactions, there is a fairly flat range of yields across all tenors (O'Donohoe et al., 2010). This trend is consistent with the perception that the highest risk is in the near term, as the young company is trying to establish itself and get traction in the market. After the initial period of uncertainty, the investment is considered less risky. Additionally, some foundations and government programmes are lending at subsidized rates, which could hold longer-term yields artificially low.

Given the above, in practice, the impact investing market has been characterized by a surplus of capital seeking the right investment opportunities. This capital is often looking for a different risk/return profile than that which is currently offered in the market (Harji and Jackson, 2012). This could also be referred to as a challenge of 'right deal, wrong capital' wherein entrepreneurs and funds are promoting strategies to asset owners who do not have the capacity to invest within the type of venture or fund being promoted. For example, entrepreneurs seeking early and start-up funding for social enterprises approach pension funds for direct investment support. However, the pension funds may want to invest in various types of fixed income instruments that could offer various types of impact (affordable housing, development finance, and so forth) and expect different levels of risk and return. This issue of attaining the right match between investment opportunity and investment capital is more a challenge of capital market intermediation than a lack of investible opportunity. In this case, investible opportunities simply try to connect with the 'wrong' type of capital.

INNOVATIVE FINANCING

Impact investments are made in a range of different asset classes, geographies, and market sectors. However, in the last few years, limited types of financial instruments have been used, comprising mostly equity, private debt (both secured and unsecured) in the form of loans, and deposits in community development institutions. There is an evident need for innovative financing options that are suitable for both the impact enterprise and the investors. In the absence of these, much of investment capital will remain on the sidelines, and the cost of capital for impact enterprises will remain correspondingly high (Huppé and Silva, 2013).

To provide more options to investors, it is common to see 'capital stacking' arrangements while funding an impact project. Such structures aim to achieve blended returns for different investors. Another method that can be used effectively to fund impact projects is securitization, which is a financial practice that pools different types of contractual debt. Although, diminished in popularity due to the financial crises and the controversy surrounding asset-backed securities, these securities can play an important role in impact investing. Securitization allows an efficient risk allocation, and this could solve the barriers for institutional investors looking for specific risk-adjusted returns, allocating the related risks to the most suitable participants, and achieving an optimal blended capital structure. A good example of this practice is a securitization of micro-loans in India by IFMR Capital and Equitas Micro Finance in 2009. The total securitization amount was $3m, and the underlying loan pool consisted of urban micro-loans with maturity in 2010 (Huppé and Silva, 2013). Another good example is Threadneedle, a UK social bond fund. Launched in late 2013 by Threadneedle Investments, the fund invests in a portfolio of fixed income securities issued by companies, associations, charities, and trusts in social outcome areas including affordable housing, community services, employment and training, financial inclusion, health and social care, infrastructure, and the environment. The innovative mechanism in this fund is that it provides daily liquidity, offering retail investors access to the social investment space (<http://bigissueinvest.com>).

While these are important considerations and strategies, risk remains an important issue for many impact investors. In 2014, Bridges Ventures of London (in partnership with Bank of America/Merrill Lynch) released their report, *Shifting the Lens: A De-Risking Toolkit for Impact Investors.* The reports outlined a variety of strategies for risk management within impact investing practice, ranging from how to structure downside protection to how to make use of technical assistance to decrease managerial risk exposure.

INTERMEDIATION CAPACITY

The lack of intermediation capacity is one of the major challenges limiting the ability of investors to find and place capital in impact opportunities (Freireich and Fulton, 2009). Intermediation is especially important for impact investors because traditional channels often do not meet their needs. Without effective and specialized intermediation many individual impact investors struggle to find investment opportunities that are at sufficient scale to justify the sourcing and due diligence costs. The lack of intermediation also makes the technical aspects of deals more challenging. Some investors are discouraged by impact investing because of the difficulties trying to structure deals that have layers of capital and different investors involved. Additionally, many investors require a very specialized approach. For example, in the case of institutional investors, they can consider deals of a certain size only, and require products that meet their existing fiduciary obligations while investing for impact.

The institutionalization of the intermediary space in the impact investing market has been subject to considerable development in the past decade. For instance, in the UK, Social Finance was launched in 2007 as an integrated advisory research and development specialist serving social sector clients in structuring and placing impact investing capital. Amongst other impact investing innovations, Social Finance created the first Social Impact Bond structure in the world. In the USA, Total Impact Capital helps connect investors in the United States and Europe with opportunities in Africa, Asia, and other regions. Similarly, in India, Unitus Capital is build-ing capacity around sell-side services for Indian firms (Bugg-Levine and Goldstein, 2009).

IMPACT MEASUREMENT

As noted above, developing common and agreed measurement standards for capturing the blended value performance of impact investments represents a central challenge for the ongoing development of the market as a whole. IRIS and GIIRS are currently the two leading systems for social impact measure-ment in the impact investing space. However other approaches such as social return on investment (SROI) or the emergent UK standards being developed by Big Society Capital (the Outcomes Matrix) and EngagedX are also proving to be useful tools for investors. Standardized metrics reduce transaction costs and help direct capital into the most effective projects. As better—and consistent—data sets are aggregated, it will also be possible to begin to calculate important ratios such as risk and return across sectors and types of investments. Additionally, developing a credible, independent rating and audit agency for impact investments would help unlock additional capital from investors (Bugg-Levine and Goldstein, 2009).

However, measuring impact continues to be a complex question for the industry. On the one hand there is a desire for standard approaches to measure-ment, while on the other hand there are important reasons why customized approaches may be more valuable. Sometimes, the objective of the measurement also creates a set of tensions. The measurements that are important to investors may differ from the practical measurements that can be applied by entrepreneurs on the ground. Also, investors and entrepreneurs may use these measurements in different ways and for different ends. It can also be difficult to achieve a balance between the amount and cost of data collected and the relevance of this data in practice to help impact investors make the right decision.

Conclusions

While the various components of impact investing have been in development for decades, impact investing as a coherent field of practice is in many ways still new and emerging; it is at an early stage of institutionalization with many gaps still to be filled in its overall market structure. However, there have been many innovative initiatives aimed at building the marketplace over the past decade and significant progress has been made. Such creativity has led to a strong increase in the overall investment activity across multiple asset classes addressing both, impact first and finance first investor preferences. The market has moved from the 'uncoordinated innovation' phase to a more sustained 'marketplace-building' phase (Harji and Jackson, 2012) with predictions of capital growth estimated to be in the range of $400bn to $1trn by 2020.

The emergence of this market is very timely. The world is facing unprecedented challenges such as food scarcity, lack of access to quality healthcare and education in developing countries, and the accelerated degradation of the natural environment. Whilst of continuing importance, conventional models of aid and development that are driven by government and philanthropy cannot provide sufficient resources to address all of today's global 'wicked problems' alone. Indeed, due to the financial crisis, government aid has plateaued in the recent years. While overall the total amount remained constant, some countries decreased their aid contributions in the recent years. As a consequence, additional capital is urgently needed.

Emerging markets have become a popular destination for impact investors. They appeal to a wide spectrum of impact investors looking to achieve both social impact and a decent rate of financial return. In emerging markets, there are 2.5 million people that live at the Bottom of the Pyramid on less than $2.5 a day. From a macroeconomic perspective, emerging markets have typically experienced higher and more stable levels of economic growth than developed countries creating a new middle class that serves as both an attractive new consumer market and a set of new investors. While this growth may be challenged in coming years, their development cannot be ignored—and in fact, may continue to create a host of new opportunities for both impact and traditional investors.

Impact investors have traditionally been divided into finance first and impact first groups. Impact first investors are defined as these who have a specific social or environmental return expectation and also have some flexibility related to their expected financial returns. Finance first investors, on the other hand, have a financial return floor, and use impact outcomes as a secondary goal in their investment decisions. This initial bifurcation of impact investing is now giving way to a host of asset owners managing their total portfolio for various levels of impact and financial return. On the level of deal structure, there are many examples of investors collaborating to create what are referred to as 'capital stacks' which combine different types of capital to satisfy different objectives and motivations of various investors.

The impact investing market has seen the emergence of bespoke networks and supporting organizations around the globe. A major challenge continues to be establishing agreed performance impact metrics and standards. However, several prominent projects have been developed to provide measurement standards for different types of impact investing. Particularly significant in this area is the work of the Global Impact Investing Network (GIIN) that developed a set of reporting standards called the Impact Reporting and Investment Standards (IRIS). IRIS is intended to co-exist with other measurement initiatives, such as the Global Impact Investing Rating System (GIIRS) that is a set of third-party assessed reports on the impact for companies, funds, and direct investments.

Government has played an important role as well. Through different policies governments have enabled the development of the impact investing market and helped channel private capital into models creating social and environmental benefits. In the last few years, there have been several initiatives facilitating better dialogue between the state and the private impact investing sector to help develop effective policies. The UK has been especially active in supporting the impact investing space with targeted fiscal policy, regulation, legislation, commissioning guidelines, and direct and indirect investment.

Although, the impact investing market has grown significantly in the last few years, some major challenges remain. In its first phase of development, the market focused largely on mobilizing and supplying capital, but it did not increase substantially the number of investment-ready projects. Additionally, deal economics were not always feasible. The majority of investments have been very small compared to average private equity investments, but with similar due diligence costs: making the impact deals proportionately less profitable or not profitable at all. Another challenge facing impact investors, especially those focused on emerging markets, has been the lack of performance data and overall industry track record.

The market has also been characterized by significant innovation. There are interesting exit structures emerging, giving investors more confidence in investing in impact projects. Structured products, such as vaccine bonds have attracted good amounts of capital, and new structures, such as Social Impact Bonds, and pay-for-performance bonds, have gained popularity globally. There has been an increasing range of innovations in structuring transactions and funds. One approach has been to create layered structures that allow investors focused on social returns to leverage their capital while reducing the risk to commercial investors.

The relative lack of institutionalization in the intermediation space has made the technical aspects of impact investing deals more challenging. Some investors have been discouraged from impact investing because of difficulties trying to structure deals that have positive social and environmental impact and, at the same time, have layers of capital and different investors involved. Fortunately, the market has seen several new firms emerge that provide bespoke deal sourcing and structuring services to bring different types of investors into one deal.

In conclusion, the impact investing market has made significant progress in recent years. However, it is only now emerging as a formalized marketplace. A stronger market infrastructure still needs to be developed before impact investing can become a stable and sustainable alternative for either traditional philanthropists or mainstream investors. As the market infrastructure builds further and more funds across different asset classes achieve attractive rates of blended return, impact investing may be able to bring mainstream capital into play as a powerful vehicle to address significant social and environmental issues, chart a new course for the financial services industry overall, and serve as an engine of social and economic growth for the poor and excluded billions. In order to successfully execute on this agenda, investors will need to become multilingual (having the ability to move easily between and among various silos of market-rate investors, development organizations, NGOs, and public actors), they will need to leverage the best public policy initiatives (in the form of a symbiotic relationship between impact investors and public sector actors), they will need to use capital in ways that allow private capital to be structured for public good and will need to drive mission 'first and last' as they develop and execute their impact investing strategies (Clark, Emerson et al., 2013). Truly challenges remain, but knowledge with regard to how to 'do' impact investing is also on the rise. And that expertise comes none too soon for the need is dire.

Perhaps Sir Ronald Cohen said it best at the closing ceremony of the Skoll World Forum in 2014:

We've heard a lot about the invisible hand of markets. Let's hear about the invisible heart of markets to help those whom the invisible hand has left behind. (Cohen, 2014)

■ REFERENCES

Acumen Fund. [online], Available: http://www.acumenfund.org/investment/lifespring. html [31 Aug 2014].

Arosio, M. (2011) *Impact Investing in Emerging markets*, Singapore: Responsible Research.

Barby, C., and Gan J. (2014) *Shifting the Lens: A De-Risking Toolkit for Impact Investors*, Bridges Ventures and Bank of America/Merrill Lynch, London: Bridges Ventures.

Bayon, R., Hawn, A. and Hamilton, K. (2009) *Voluntary Carbon Markets: An International Business Guide to What They Are and How They Work*, 2nd Edition, London: Earthscan.

Bernholz, L. and Richter, L. (2009) *MRI and Community Foundations Report*, Ford Foundation, New York: Ford Foundation.

Bertocci, B., Bolli, B., Friedman, A., Hudson, A., Khan, K., Reiman, K., Stiehler, A. and Zlotnicka, E. (2013) *UBS Research Focus: Sustainable Investing*, UBS CIO Wealth Management Research, New York: UBS Financial Services.

Big Issue Invest. *Social Enterprise Investment Fund LP: Threadneedle.* [online], Available: http://bigissueinvest.com/funds/threadneedle [2 Aug 2014].

Big Society Capital. (2013) *Social Impact Tests and Threshold*, London: Big Society Capital.

Big Society Capital. (2013) *Social Investment Compendium: Portfolio of Research and Intelligence on the Social Investment Market*, London: Big Society Capital.

Big Society Capital. (2013) *Social Investment from Ambition to Action: Annual Review 2013*, London: Big Society Capital.

Bishop, M. and Green, M. (2008) *Philanthrocapitalism: How the Rich Can Save the World*, New York: Bloomsbury Press.

Bolton, E. and Savel, L. (2010) *Towards a New Social Economy: Blended Value Creation through Social Impact Bonds*, Social Finance, London: Social Finance.

Bridges Ventures and The Parthenon Group. (2012) *Investing for Impact*, London: Bridges Ventures, Parthenon Group and GIIN.

Bugg-Levine, A. (2013) *Complete Capital*, Stanford Social Innovation Review, Winter 2013, Stanford, CA: Stanford Social Innovation Review.

Bugg-Levine, A. (2009) *Impact Investing Bold Models to Drive Development at Scale*, Beyond Profit Magazine, Inaugural Issue, May/June, pp. 17–21.

Bugg-Levine, A. and Emerson, J. (2011) *Impact Investing: Transforming How We Make Money While Making a Difference*, San Francisco, CA: Jossey-Bass.

Bugg-Levine, A. and Goldstein, J. (2009) *Impact investing: Harnessing Capital Markets to Solve Problems at Scale*, Community Development Investment Review, vol. 5, no. 2, August pp. 30–41, San Francisco: Federal Reserve Bank of San Francisco.

Cave, S., Williams, T., Jolliffe, D., and Hedderman, C. (2012) *Peterborough Social Impact Bond: An Independent Assessment*, London: Ministry of Justice Research Series 8/12.

Chung, A. and Emerson, J. (2013) *From Grants to Groundbreaking: Unlocking Impact Investments*, ImpactAssets Issue Brief No. 10, Washington, D.C.: ImpactAssets.

Clark, C., Emerson, J. and Thornley, B. (2013) *Impact investing 2.0: The Way Forward—Insight from 12 Outstanding Funds*, InSight, Center for the Advancement of Social Entrepreneurship, and ImpactAssets.

Cohen, R. (2014) *Keynote Remarks at the 11th Skoll World Forum*, April 9th, Oxford.

Conservation Finance Alliance. (2014) *Supporting Biodiversity Conservation Ventures: Assessing the Impact Investing Sector for an Investment Strategy to Support Environmental Entrepreneurism.* Washington, D.C.: Conservation Finance Alliance.

Cooch, S., Kramer, M., Cheng, F., Mahmud, A. Marx, B. and Rehrig, M. (2007) *Compounding Impact: Mission Investing by U.S. Foundations*, Boston, MA: FSG Social Impact Advisors.

Credit Suisse and the Schwab Foundation. (2012) *Investing for Impact: How Social Entrepreneurship Is Redefining the Meaning of Return*, Zurich: Credit Suisse.

EIRIS Foundation Charity Project. (2009) *The Value of Environmental, Social and Governance Factors for Foundation Investments*, London: EIRIS Foundation.

Elkington, J. and Hartigan, P. (2008) *The Power of Unreasonable People: How Social Entrepreneurs Create Markets That Change the World*, New York: Harvard Business School.

Elsen, T. and Yonavjak, L. (2012) *Scaling up Environmental Entrepreneurship in Emerging Economies—Framing the Discussion*, Next Billion. [online], Available: http://www.nextbillion.net/blogpost.aspx?blogid=2680, [31 Aug 2014].

Emerson, J. (2003) *The Blended Value Map: Tracking the Intersects and Opportunities of Economic, Social and Environmental Value Creation.* [online], Available at: http://www.blendedvalue.org/wp-content/uploads/2004/02/pdf-bv-map.pdf.

Emerson, J., Berenbach, S. and Freundlich, T. (2007) *Where Money Meets Mission: Creating a Unified Investment Strategy*, Washington, D.C.: Calvert Foundation.

Emerson, J. and Spitzer, J. (2007) *From Fragmentation to Function: Critical Concepts and Writings on Social Capital Markets' Structure, Operation and Innovation.* Alex Nicholls, Editor. Said Business School, Skoll Centre for Social Entrepreneurship, Oxford.

Emerson, J., Spitzer, J. and Harold, J. (2007) *Blended Value Investing: Innovations in Real Estate.* Alex Nicholls, Editor. Said Business School, Skoll Centre for Social Entrepreneurship, Oxford.

European Venture Philanthropy Association. (2013) *A Practical Guide to Measuring and Managing Impact.* Brussels: European Venture Philanthropy Association.

Eurosif. (2012) *High Net Worth Individuals & Sustainable Investment*, Belgium: Eurosif A.I.S.B.L.

Fitzgerald, N. and Cormack, M. (2007) *The Role of Business in Society: an Agenda for Action*, The Conference Board, Harvard University Kennedy School of Government, and the International Business Leaders Forum.

Fleishman, J. L. (2007) *The Foundation: A Great American Secret; How Private Wealth is Changing the World*, New York: PublicAffairs.

Forum at Google. (2007) *Creating Social Capital Markets for Fourth Sector Organizations: Opportunities and Challenges*, New York.

Freireich, J. and Fulton, K. (2009) *Investing for Social & Environmental Impact*, Monitor Institute, San Francisco, CA: Monitor Institute.

Fulton, M., Kahn, B. Ph.D. and Sharples, C. (2012) *Sustainable Investing: Establishing Long-Term Value and Performance,* Deutsche Bank Group, Frankfurt: Deutsche Bank.

Global Environment Fund. [online], Available: http://www.globalenvironmentfund.com/category/portfolio [9 Sept 2014].

Hammond, A., Kramer, W., Katz, R., Tran, J. and Walker, C. (2007) *The Next 4 Billion: Market Size and Business Strategy at the Base of the Pyramid*, New York: World Resources Institute and International Finance Corporation/World Bank Group.

Han, L. (2014) *Malaria in Mozambique: Trialing Payment by Results,* Guardian Professional. [online], Available: http://www.theguardian.com/global-development-professionals-network/2014/mar/31/malaria-control-payment-by-results [31 Aug 2014].

Hudson Institute/The Center for Global Prosperity. (2013) *The Index of Global Philanthropy and Remittances 2013*, Washington, D.C.: Hudson Institute.

Humphreys, J. (2007) *The Mission in the Marketplace: How Responsible Investing Can Strengthen the Fiduciary Oversight of Foundation Endowments and Enhance Philanthropic Missions*, Washington, D.C.: Social Investment Forum Foundation.

Humphreys, J., Solomon, A. and Electris, E. (2012) *Total Portfolio Activation: A Framework for Creating Social and Environmental Impact across Asset Classes,* Tellus Institute, Boston, MA: Tellus Institute.

Huppé, A. and Silva, M. H. (2013) *Overcoming Barriers to Scale: Institutional Impact Investments in Low-Income and Developing Countries.* Winnipeg, Manitoba: International Institute for Sustainable Development.

Impact Capital Summit. (2014) *Smarter Money: 2014 Primer.* Watershed Capital Group and Kellogg School of Management, Chicago, IL.

Impact Investing Policy Collaborative (IIPC). (2013) *Policy Innovation in Impact investing—The London Principles,* '3rd Annual IIPC Conference, Oxford and London.

Jackson, E. and Harji, K. (2012) *Accelerating Impact: Achievements, Challenges and What's Next in Building the Impact Investing Industry,* E.T. Jackson and Associates Ltd, New York: E.T. Jackson and Associates Ltd

Koh, H., Karamchandani, A., and Katz, R. (2012) *From Blueprint to Scale, The Case for Philanthropy in Impact Investing,* Monitor Group and Acumen Fund.

International Finance Corporation (IFC). *The Business of Health in Africa,* Washington, D.C.: International Finance Corporation.

Johnson, K. and Lee, H. (2013) *Impact Investing: A Framework for Decision Making,* Cambridge Associates LLC.

LaVoie, V. and Wood, D. (2009) *Handbook on Climate-Related Investing across Asset Classes,* Chestnut Hill: Boston College Center for Corporate Citizenship.

Kramer, M. and Cooch, S. (2006) *Investing for Impact: Managing and Measuring Proactive Social Investments,* Foundation Strategy Group.

Martin, M. Dr. (2013) *Status of the Social Impact Investing Market: A Primer,* Impact Economy, Geneva: Impact Economy.

Microfinance Banana Skins (2008) *Risk in a Booming Industry,* Tonbridge: Centre for the Study of Financial Innovation.

Nicholls, A. and Tomkinson, E. (2013) *The Peterborough Pilot Social Impact Bond.* Said Business School, Skoll Centre for Social Entrepreneurship, Oxford.

O'Donohoe, N. et al. (2010) *Impact Investments: An Emerging Asset Class,* J.P. Morgan, The Rockefeller Foundation and Global Impact Investing Network, London and New York: J.P. Morgan.

OECD netFWD (2014) *Venture Philanthropy in Development: Dynamics, Challenges and Lessons in the Search for Greater Impact,* Paris: OECD Development Centre.

Olson, J. and Phillips, A. (2013) *Rikers Island: The First Social Impact Bond in the United States,* Goldman Sachs: Community Development Investment Review. pp. 97–101, San Francisco, Federal Reserve Bank of San Francisco.

Parthenon Group and Bridges Ventures. (2009) *Investing for Impact: Case Studies across Asset Classes,* London: Bridges Ventures and Parthenon Group.

Robins, N., Clover, R. and Singh, C. (2009) *A Climate for Recovery: The Colour of Stimulus Goes Green,* HSBC Global Research, London: HSBC Global Research.

Population Services International and Zurich Insurance Group (2014) *Using Private Investor Capital to Increase NGO Impact: A Framework and Key Considerations to Facilitate Engagement,* Washington, D.C.: Population Services International and Zurich: Zurich Insurance Company.

Rosenberg, R. (2007) *CGAP Reflections on the Compartamos Initial Public Offering.* [online], Available: http://www.cgap.org/publications/cgap-reflections-compartamos-initial-public-offering [9 Sept 2014].

Saltuk, Y., et al. (2014) *Spotlight on the Market,* J.P. Morgan and Global Impact Investing Network, London and New York: J.P. Morgan.

Saltuk, Y., et al. (2013) *Perspectives on Progress*, J.P. Morgan and Global Impact Investing Network, London and New York: J.P. Morgan.

Saltuk, Y., Bouri, A. and Leung, G. (2011) *Insight into the Impact Investing Market*, J.P. Morgan and Global Impact Investing Network, London and New York: J.P. Morgan.

Schwab Foundation for Social Entrepreneurship & Technical University of Munich. (2011) *Social Investment Manual: An Introduction for Social Entrepreneurs*, Munich: Technical University of Munich.

Senge, P., Smith, B., Kruschwitz, N., Laur, J. and Schley, S. (2008) *The Necessary Revolution: How Individuals and Organizations Are Working Together to Create a Sustainable World*, New York: Doubleday.

Schwab Foundation for Social Entrepreneurship. (2013) *Breaking the Binary: Policy Guide to Scaling Social Innovation*, Switzerland: Schwab Foundation for Social Entrepreneurship.

Shanmugalingam, C., Graham, J., Tucker, S., and Mulgan, G. (2011) *Growing Social Ventures: The Role of Intermediaries and Investors: Who They Are, What They Do, and What They Could Become*, The Young Foundation and NESTA.

Simon, J. and Barmeier, J. (2009) *More than Money: Impact investing for Development*, Center for Global Development, Washington, D.C.: Center for Global Development.

Social Finance. (2014) *A New Tool for Scaling Impact: How Social Impact Bonds Can Mobilize Private Capital to Advance Social Good*, Social Finance, Boston, MA: Social Finance.

Social Finance. (2014) *Foundations for Social Impact Bonds – How and Why Philanthropy Is Catalyzing the Development of a New Market*, Social Finance, Boston, MA: Social Finance.

Social Investment Forum. (2008) *2007 Report on Socially Responsible Investing Trends in the United States*, Social Investment Forum, Washington, D.C.: Social Investment Forum.

Swack, M., Northrup, J., and Prince, J. (2007) *Expanding Philanthropy: Mission-Related Investing at the F.B. Heron Foundation*, Southern New Hampshire University, School of Community Economic Development.

Thornley, B., Wood, D., Grace, K. and Sullivant, S. (2011) *Impact investing: A Framework*, San Francisco, CA: InSight and Cambridge, MA: The Initiative for Responsible Investment at Harvard University.

UK Government. (2013) *Achieving Social Impact at Scale: Case Studies of Seven Pioneering Co-mingling Social Investment Funds*, London: Cabinet Office.

UK Government. (2013) *G8 Social Impact Investing Forum Outputs and Agreed Actions*, London: Cabinet Office.

UK Government. (2013) *Growing the Social Investment Market: 2014 Progress Update*, London: Cabinet Office.

UK Government and Design Council (2014) Social Finance in the UK—Designing the Experience for Ventures, London: Design Council.

Voorhes, M., Humphreys, J. and Solomon, A. (2012) *Sustainable and Responsible Investing Trends in the United States 2012*, US SIF Foundation.

Wilson, K. (2014) *New Investment Approaches for Addressing Social and Economic Challenges*, OECD Science, Technology and Industry policy papers, No. 15, OECD Publishing.

Wilton, D. (2011) *Private Equity, Public Equity, Risks & Opportunities,* Presentation.

Wood, D. and Hoff, B. (2007) *Handbook on Responsible Investment across Asset Classes,* Chestnut Hill, MA: Institute for Responsible Investment, Boston College Centre for Corporate Citizenship.

World Economic Forum. (2013) *From the Margins to the Mainstream Assessment of the Impact Investment Sector and Opportunities to Engage Mainstream Investors,* Switzerland: World Economic Forum.

World Health Organization, UNICEF, and The World Bank. (2009) *State of the World's Vaccines and Immunization,* 3rd Edition, Geneva, World Health Organization.

World Bank Development Indicators. (2011) [online], Available: http://www.google.com/publicdata?ds=wb-wdi&met=sp_pop_totl&tdim=true&dl=en&hl=en&q=world+population [22 Nov 2013].

Yunus, M. (2008) *Creating a World without Poverty–Social Business and the Future of Capitalism,* New York: PublicAffairs.

Part III
Models and Metrics

9   **Measuring social impact**

Alex Nicholls, Jeremy Nicholls, and Rob Paton

Introduction

It seems intuitively obvious that any social investor engaging in the social finance market would show a concern for proof that her investment is creating the value that it claimed it would—typically a blend of social and financial. Yet, the current metrics and data sets available in social finance remain some way short of providing such evidence. Nevertheless, investees and financial intermediaries seeking to raise funds for social start-ups and enterprises still make claims about beneficial outcomes, that may, or may not, be well founded. Indeed, innovative schemes to address major societal challenges may be based on simplistic thinking ('solutionism') and deliver far less than they promise (e.g. Morozov, 2013). Likewise, as microfinance has attracted mainstream finance, 'mission drift' in order to improve financial performance has been reported and not just in Andhra Pradesh (Arunachalam, 2011). Indeed, as an open letter from the Global Impact Investing Network (GIIN)—precipitated by the Indian microfinance crisis—made clear[1] the more social finance is accepted within financial markets the more serious such challenges are likely to become. When large sums of money are involved, hard-to-verify claims can boost interest in a scheme and put a premium on prices. Hence, social investors need to be able to distinguish between well-conceived projects and those based on wishful thinking, and between hybrids and fakes. Likewise, investees need ways to reassure potential investors that they are achieving what they said they would, that they are measuring and managing their own social performance diligently. Taking known risks and uncertainties into account as far as possible, both parties need to have a reasonable degree of confidence in claims about prospective (or continuing) social outcomes and impact. The challenge is to find a basis for such confidence.

It is a small step from here to the matter of metrics: how else can the claimed social benefits be demonstrated, not just in general or anecdotal terms, but in ways that can allow performance to be tracked over time, predicted in the future, and even compared with what has been achieved by others? However, this small step is a significant one—because posing the question in terms of

---

[1] 'This is increasingly important as impact investing is gaining prominence and becoming an attractive label for many entrepreneurs and investors, including some who are not committed to social impact'. Available on <http://www.thegiin.org/binary-data/MEDIA/pdf/000/000/13-2.pdf>.

metrics assumes that the underlying challenge can be best addressed through the *measurement* of social impact. It is not surprising that this assumption is widespread in social finance circles; performance measurement data of various sorts provide the fuel for the analysis and reporting on which mainstream financial markets run. Nevertheless, the assumption that social metrics are the answer to accelerating the growth of the social finance market may be open to challenge from several directions. One critical observation is based upon sixty years of accumulated research on the limitations and dysfunctions of per-formance measurement processes and mechanisms (see e.g. Blau 1963; or Austin, 1996, provides a good review). Another reflects key, practical, imple-mentation issues of proportionality and costs. Not always, but quite often, social impact is a multilevel, multidimensional concept, the measurement of which is challenging even in the context of funded (academic/policy) research programmes, let alone in routine reporting. Indeed, when highly respected bank regulators are arguing that the limits of measurement may have already been reached in financial accounting with respect to regulating banks (Haldane and Madouros, 2013), it seems cavalier to presume that the less familiar and more challenging dimensions of social impact can be convin-cingly and reliably captured in standardized, quantitative terms.

So, this chapter considers the circumstances in which social impact metrics can used to generate the *reasonable* confidence needed for social finance relationships to function effectively—the approaches that are likely to be appropriate and useful in measuring the *social* outcomes of *social* investments. Tackling this question could involve reviewing an extensive academic and professional literature. Although the investment relationship provides a par-ticular context, the general issue—how to establish whether intended social outcomes are being achieved—has been discussed in some depth in several disciplines, including performance measurement, development policy, NGO, and not-for-profit/voluntary sector studies (Sawhill and Williamson, 2001; Ebrahim and Rangan, 2010). Moreover, as Mulgan (2010) noted, 'literally hundreds' of potentially relevant products and mechanisms are available, offered by a growing army of professional evaluators. Some are variations of familiar approaches tailored to particular fields; others offer ICT tools to assist in data-gathering and analysis. But the last two decades have also seen the emergence and increasing recognition of methodologically distinctive approaches involving quite different evaluation logics (Ebrahim and Rangan, 2010; Patton, 2011; Hall, 2014). So the choice of approach and metric is not straightforward.

Central to the current debate concerning social impact measurement is the question of standardization. From the perspective of mainstream finance this is an essential for the social finance market to function effectively in terms of allocative efficiency. The path to standardization can be conceived of as the consequence of one of three possible processes of institutionalization. First, standardized data could be regulated into being, as it has been for financial data via waves of accounting regulations. Second, such data could come about via various self-regulated methods that emerge within the social finance industry—Social Return on Investment (SROI) represents one such market leader (Nicholls, 2004), as do the Global Impact Investing Reporting System (GIIRS) metrics. Finally, standardization could come about in an entirely laissez-faire manner as the market of social investors coalesces around one favoured approach (Mulgan, 2010). Whatever the pathway to standardization proves to be—if, indeed, consensus is established—it seems likely that more favoured ways of addressing social problems and favoured measurement practices will gradually emerge. Meanwhile, that evolutionary selection of measurement practices may work better, and faster, in the light of information on what different approaches actually involve and analysis that highlights choice criteria relevant to different settings.

This chapter aims to review the key issues and debates in social impact measurement for social finance capital allocation. It will present a critical issues framework for measurement to inform choices of methods and will set out the main approaches currently in play. It aims to offer a framework for social entrepreneurs and social finance investors to think about their measurement choices, one that identifies the main methods, indicating when each will be more and less appropriate. As such, this is a contingency framework akin to Ebrahim and Rangan's (2010). But where that research was concerned with *when* it is and is not appropriate to measure outcomes and impacts (rather than relying on activity levels, outputs, and intermediate outcomes), this framework concentrates on the *how* of appraising social outcomes in different contexts. As such, it views the investor–investee relationship in terms of information processing. The basic proposition is that as the complexity of decision-making increases, those involved have to choose between, or find ways of combining, two fundamental strategies: either increase the capacity for information processing or reduce the need for it.[2]

Of course, social impact has been measured for decades. Welfare economics has provided guidance via cost–benefit analyses of welfare outcomes to support policy decision-making for decades (see e.g. Feldman, 1980; O'Connell, 1982). Development finance institutions, charities and other not-for-profits, have been capturing and reporting their social impact for an equally long time. More recently, corporations and other firms have used corporate social responsibility reporting and, in some cases, internal measures of their economic social and governance (ESG) performance to highlight their social value creation. Finally, governments have been paying increasing attention to measures of national well-being or happiness. As a consequence, there are many well-established methodologies for capturing social impact including randomized control trials (common in development), approaches from behavioural science (including revealed and expressed preference models) and, as noted above, cost–benefit analyses in welfare economics.

---

[2] This draws on the key insight from J. R. Galbraith's classic on organization design (Galbraith, 1973) and adapts it to the investment context.

However, the emergence of *blended value* (Emerson, 2003) analyses of organizations and their impacts has brought new attention to the complex set of relationships *between* social and financial value creation that demands new frameworks that do not treat these two streams of value as separate and unrelated.

For the purpose of what follows, social impact in social finance is understood as:

Significant changes in the wellbeing of key populations, whether intended or unintended, brought about by the allocation of social investment capital, going beyond what would otherwise have been expected to occur.[3]

As is often the case, this definition offers scope for debate—arguably, for example, investees are interested in *net* positive changes (most change involves losers as well as winners). But hopefully this is enough for now and tolerably clear. Finer points are dealt with in the course of the chapter.

The chapter proceeds as follows. First, some key structural differences between conventional investing and social finance are noted, along with the implications these have for metrics aimed at informing capital allocation decisions. Then the chapter introduces a novel critical issues framework that asks a series of fundamental questions to help orient and inform choices regarding the large number of available approaches to, and metrics for, capturing social value creation and organizational performance. Following an exposition and discussion of this framework, the chapter explores the measurement methodologies relevant to social impact, linking these back to matters raised by the critical issues framework. Next, the chapter presents an overview of the specific metrics and rating schemes now being offered for use in relation to social finance. Finally, this work offers a contingency model to suggest the sorts of contexts in which social impact measurement (in its various forms) will and will not be appropriate—and what the alternatives to measurement are. Conclusions summarize the chapter as a whole.

The distinctiveness of social finance

Two major structural differences distinguish conventional investing and social investing. The first is that, in the mainstream markets, the person investing and the person hoping to get a value created from that investment are one and the same—value creation and value appropriation are linked in the person of the investor (Nicholls, 2010a). In social finance investing the person who receives the financial return is generally different from the person(s) that receive the social 'return'. This creates an immediate accountability gap. The

---

[3] Such impact could, of course, be negative as well as positive—though there tends to be a general, normative, assumption that social impact always benefits key stakeholders.

organization receiving the investment remains accountable for any financial return in the normal way. No return and the managers are accountable, through their salaries and their jobs. However, typically, neither the investor nor the investee is accountable to the person expected to benefit from the impact. This is a fundamental problem that would not be acceptable for the financial return but has become acceptable in social finance investing. It is usually acknowledged that accountability is a good thing, not just because it helps ensure that organizations do not delude themselves and do more harm than good, but also because it drives innovation and increases the value being created. But accountability is often uncomfortable and may be avoided if possible.

The second major difference concerns the nature of competitiveness and displacement effects in the two sorts of finance markets. In conventional finance, free-market logics apply—seeking a sustainable competitive advantage becomes a central strategic objective to ensure the best financial returns to a firm. Monopoly offers the best economic returns (though not for the consumer) and, as a consequence, sustainable competitive advantage is a key strategic objective for companies, even if it often tends to be market-distorting. However, social finance is concerned with more than an economic return—the social return from an investment can only be the *additional* social impact over and above what any competitor provides. There is no point in simply displacing existing social impact unless it can be created more efficiently or effectively—and this will often be hard to demonstrate given the accountability gap noted above.

Assuming that the social investor's interest in social impact is serious, understanding these two differences is critical to managing and measuring social impact. Usually, it will not be possible to make the investor or the investee organization accountable for its social impact using the same approach as exists in a competitive market (where beneficiaries are customers and can make free and informed choices to express their preferences). So, a different approach is needed for social investments. This approach has to reduce the risk that relevant value is omitted or irrelevant value included in an account of an investment's social impact. In the field, a strong presumption is that the information generated by such an approach will be made available to the other external stakeholders, not just managers and investors. This follows if one acknowledges the accountability gap; in addition, these other stakeholders (the customers/beneficiaries/clients) will typically have been involved in providing the data on which impact reports and judgements are based.

However, this can quickly lead to difficult issues concerning transaction costs (proportionality) and the level of detail and relevance provided by the performance data. Whereas financial accounts for public companies are audited and regulated, social impact measurement and reporting is not yet regulated—outside of the basic reporting typically required of charitable legal forms or community interest companies in the UK (Nicholls, 2010b). As a consequence, within the emerging, and competing, conventions of social impact measurement, no widely accepted standards or practices yet exist. The issues and approaches discussed in this chapter can be seen as a commentary on the incipient institutionalization of social finance and the challenges involved.

The critical issues framework

In accounting and reporting for the social impact of an investment, the overarching question that should be asked is not how much of a difference did my investment make but was the difference as much as could be expected. This naturally breaks down into a number of questions that need to be answered. Answering these reduces the risk that social impact will be missed out or misallocated in the measurement process. How much rigour is necessary depends on the level of risk that is acceptable to the investor, the transaction costs and the level of detail required to prove causality. In general the two distinctive features of the social finance market noted above mean that the level of risk that can be accepted by the investor is far higher than would be acceptable to the people expected to benefit from the impact. As a result each of the questions needs to be considered carefully regardless of the investor's perception of risk or need in order to protect beneficiaries. As a result, demonstrating the proper consideration of these critical framework questions represents the best assurance process for successful social impact measurement. These questions also represent the alternative to a competitive market mechanism in mainstream finance that serves to protect investors (in principle at least).

The most commonly accepted approach to capturing social impact performance has been in the logic model (Ebrahim and Rangan, 2010). This linear representation of performance identifies five stages between organizational (or programme) inputs (financial, social, intellectual capital) and the final impacts that result in terms of sustained or systemic changes (which will be dependent on the strategic focus of the intervention or action). The intermediary stages are: activities (what happens at the organizational or programme operations level), outputs (the immediate results), outcomes (the medium and long-term results). In the case of a poverty reduction programme, for example, inputs would be funding and expertise, activities could include skill, training. and enterprise development, outputs would be number of people trained, outcomes would include increases in income levels, whereas impacts would cover issues such as the effects on the families and children of those who increased their incomes. The logic model has, however, been widely criticized for being over-simplistic in its basic assumption that each of its five stages leads to the next—it may not be a reasonable assumption to make that one particular output leads to a specific outcome, let alone wider impact.

Of course, measuring the social effects of organizations is not a new phenomenon. Policymakers, development organizations, and charities have paid careful attention to the accounting for their social impact for years and there are many well-established methodologies (Mulgan, 2010; Ebrahim and Rangan, 2010) and theoretical traditions behind this, notably in welfare and development economics. However, the rise of social entrepreneurship (Nicholls, 2006) within the larger field of social innovation (Nicholls and Murdock, 2011) has provided new contexts for the measurement of social impact. Primarily, this sector has driven new attention to the impact of organizational/programme *processes*, particularly within a participatory mode of data collection (Nicholls, 2010c; see also Jacobs and Wilford, 2010). The emergence and growth of a social finance (Nicholls, 2010a) and impact investing (O'Donohoe et al., 2010) market has also altered the metrical approaches to social impact outcomes by demanding more convincing and rigourous methodologies that generate credible performance data for social investors, including government[4] (see for example, Social Impact Bonds: Nicholls and Tomkinson, 2013; Nicholls and Tomkinson, this volume). Increasingly, therefore, providing convincing social impact data is proving key to accessing and maintaining resources and public legitimacy, within and without the organization (Nicholls, 2008; Nicholls, 2010d). Good data can also drive improved efficiency and effectiveness, as well as increase stakeholder accountability. Nevertheless, despite these significant shifts, many challenges in social impact measurement persist, notably questions of standardization and comparability, materiality and attribution, counterfactuals and dead-weight calculations, as well as proportionality/transaction costs to the organization itself.

It is argued here that effective accounting and reporting systems are built on a series of critical questions: why measure; who measures and for whom; when to measure; what to measure; how to measure (Nicholls, 2009). At the heart of these questions lies the recognition that accounting and reporting systems mobilize and articulate power structures (Chua, 1986; Power and Laughlin, 1996; see also Lukes, 1974), as well as being mechanisms for a more positivistic capturing of organizational value creation (Hopwood and Miller, 1994). This approach acknowledges a more interpretive framing of accounting as reporting data that acts as a symbolic mediator for discussion between organizational practice and key stakeholders (Ryan et al., 1992; Gambling et al., 1993; Nicholls, 2009). Moreover, the use of a critical framework for establishing the optimal social impact measurement and reporting system demands a renewed attention to professional *judgement* in terms of the accounting process, since the answer to questions posed by the framework typically do not have clear-cut answers.

---

[4] For example, the introduction of the Public Services (Social Value) Act in the UK in 2013 will increase the demand for credible social impact data in terms of the competitive commissioning of service contracts.

The critical issues framework of questions can be grouped under several headings. Each is now considered in turn.

WHY MEASURE SOCIAL IMPACT?

There are three main—related—reasons for measuring and reporting the social impact of an investment: external accountability to investors; internal strategic planning and decision-making to maximize the value created by an investment; assessing the holistic impact of an investment. Accurate and proportionate measurement of the social impact of a given investment provides both a measure of mission success (for investor and investee) and it may inform future capital allocation. This may create some moral hazard since it often creates an incentive to be less than candid about shortcomings—'Campbell's law' comes into play (Campbell, 1976). Nevertheless, the moral argument still stands: investors and investees that claim to create social value and that attract additional support as a result (a tax break or government subsidy or wider public legitimacy and greater donations) have a duty to evidence their claims. Moreover, creating effective social impact metrics and reporting and sharing the resultant data can help create wider best practice and offer benchmarks for other investments (as may be an important externality of the social impact bond model, for example).

WHAT TO MEASURE TO CAPTURE SOCIAL IMPACT?

The question of what to measure to get an accurate picture of the social impact of an investment is more complex that it might first appear. First, is the focus solely on direct impacts or *all* impacts including externalities or accidental effects (which could be negative)? If the objective is only to capture direct impacts (which is often the most appropriate approach) there still remains the questions of whether the impact occurs at the input, process, output, or outcome phase of the standard logic model of social change (or in all four phases). Each phase may need a different methodology to capture social impact.

Next, the unit of analysis needs to be considered. Is the social impact best captured at the individual, family, community, sector, or societal level (or, again, at all of them)? After this, issues of context and contingency also come into play. Namely, are the social impacts that are reported referential or absolute, socially constructed or somehow positivistic accounts of 'reality'? Moreover, are the impacts dynamic or static—are they a product of the moment in time when they are measured?

In order better to understand the unit of analysis of a social impact measurement process (the 'what') two subsidiary questions need to be asked: Who changes as a result of the investment? How will they change? Both the investor and the investee will hopefully have an idea who they want to change, which group of people will benefit from the investment. However, there are two challenges here. The first is that other groups than the main intended beneficiary group may also change as a consequence of the investment. If this is a negative change then the investment will not be creating as much social impact as expected or may even potentially create a negative overall impact. Even where this change is positive it may be important to understand the range of populations effected by an intervention for the organization to be able to maximize its total social impact.

The second issue is that there may be several changes experienced by the intended beneficiary group and understanding the relative importance to these beneficiaries of each change will be important for the overall service design to be as effective as possible. There may be different changes for different subgroups within the main beneficiary group. Some members may not achieve the intended benefit and may be worse off as a result of the changes. Some subgroups may experience different outcomes and service design needs to take this into account. Some subgroups may experience the same outcomes but they may not value them in the same relative order as others. Again understanding these complexities and nuances is an important part of designing effective social impact metrics. In summary, attention to the role of externalities across populations is an important part of capturing social impact accurately as is care in determining appropriate attribution to a particular investment.

Determining who changed and what the changes are may require judgement calls. This corresponds to the principle of materiality in conventional accounting, but is likely to be focused more on user-generated data rather than producer-performance information. Stakeholder involvement will reduce the risks of missing material changes, whilst fixed and prescriptive theories of change may bias the data collection towards intended changes. Without robust accountability and stakeholder engagement and participation mechanism in place, there is always a bias toward reaffirming the perceptions and goals of the investors and investee. The main risk is that not all of the stakeholder group experience the intended changes and it is assumed they are no worse off than before (often without any evidence or even recognizing this assumption has been made).

Determining the 'what' in a social impact measurement process will likely also involve a consideration of the management context of collecting such performance data. This relates back to the question of accountability. Where an investor only wants information on the intended positive outcomes this question is easy to manage. However this represents a low level of accountability. Where the investor wants information on important positive and negative outcomes for all stakeholder groups, then there is a need for a decision process to determine which ones should be managed. This is the case in several existing approaches such as SROI or the Global Reporting Initiative (and other sustainability approaches) where this decision process is called materiality and is the most important decision to make. Which out-comes are *material enough* to be included, and which are not and can be excluded? The starting point is to consider whether the information would effect a decision made by a stakeholder in relation to their involvement with the organization. If the information were left out would it change the stake-holder's decision? If no, then it can be excluded: if yes, then it should be included.

This frames the decision for including or not including outcomes, but the decision will require judgement and will be informed by the organization's policy on materiality. In financial accounting the same decision is made but is informed by accounting standards, considerable practice, and the audit pro-cess. If the investor drives the decision, then it is framed by whether the information is useful to the investor. It is likely that summary information will be sufficient. If the investee drives the decision in order to maximize value creation, then the information will likely need to be quite detailed. It will be possible to summarize the latter for the investor but it will not be possible to disaggregate the former to make it useful to the investee's internal decision-making.

WHO MEASURES SOCIAL IMPACT?

As has already been noted above, both users (external stakeholders) and producers (the organization itself) can generate social impact data. Users can include the direct beneficiaries or clients of an investee project, but also other stakeholders including the wider community, partner organizations, government (through welfare cost savings), employees, society at large, and, even, the investor herself. These stakeholder groups may have very different perceptions of the social impact of the same intervention, so working out whose opinion counts is an important process. Table 9.1 demonstrates how complex this can be in terms of establishing who the 'customer' for a given social impact might be.

Identifying who is best placed to generate the most appropriate source of social impact data is a question of establishing materiality that, in turn, is a matter of the professional judgement of the investee. The SROI model is

Table 9.1. Who is the customer for social impact?

	User	Purchaser	Influencer
Clinical services	Patient	Donor	Government
Elderly services	Retiree	Clients' children	Competitors
Child health	Child	Parent	Parent competitors
Pharmacy	Patient	Insurance	Regulation
Laboratory services	Public clinic	State	Government policy

predicated on a set of principles that place the focal beneficiary as the key actor in establishing materiality:

- involve stakeholders (to establish materiality)
- understand change (from the stakeholder perspective)
- value things that matter (to key stakeholders)
- only include things that are material (to key stakeholders)
- recognize your contribution as part of the system.

In the process, the data collection and measurement process itself becomes a source of social impact—offering empowerment, participation, and voice to often-marginalized beneficiary/client groups (see Table 9.1).

Not unlike the market research that underpins a business plan, research based on a discussion and interviews with potential customers is as important as desk research on the level of demand. All these questions require judgements and there are risks of bias and wishful thinking. The investor and investee can reduce the risk of the social value not being created as a result of over-optimistic judgements by ensuring appropriate involvement of stakeholders throughout the social impact measurement design and implementation process. A process that starts with stakeholders' views and then mediates them with expert practice is likely to be more accurate than one that starts with expert views and then checks that this is correct with stakeholders.

Where more sustainable social change is being sought, such that the causes of the problem are reduced or where the investment shows that, if replicated at scale, the problem could be removed, then the investor and investee will need to be sure that all those organizations and groups that will contribute to the success are involved and that the scale of the intervention is appropriate. For the investor, it may also be necessary to carry out due diligence on all those organizations and groups that contribute to the outcome. Otherwise there is a risk that the social return will not be achieved because of one of the other critical organizations. The process of determining who should be involved and at what scale will be a matter of judgement. Involving stakeholders is one way of reducing the risk of missing a significant contributor to the desired outcome (see Jacobs, 2006).

WHEN TO MEASURE SOCIAL IMPACT?

Early interventions may often have a far greater total social impact than several interventions over time: the logic is of prevention rather than cure. This model provided the foundations for the contingent liability bond (Wood, 2010) developed to provide upfront loan capital for clean water projects. This model was subsequently adapted to develop the Vaccine Bond and also provided the basic logic of the Social Impact Bond model. The principle here is of a *social* net present value calculation that values investment in social impact today as being of significantly greater *social* value than investment deferred to future years. However, whilst Social Impact Bonds have begun to establish methodologies for making this connection explicit in financial valuation (by linking investor payments for early prevention to improved social outcomes in the future), some issues such as climate change necessarily operate on such long-time scales that hyperbolic discounting remains the norm in practice (how to calculate the value of an improved climate to future generations fifty years hence?).

Another set of temporal issues concerns have a more explicit investor focus. Some investors will be investing in organizations where the business model can generate a financial return for activities that are more focused on cure than on prevention. Both investor and investee recognize that the problems being addressed will continue but recognize that individual lives can nonetheless be significantly improved by specific interventions. Even where impacts are expected to be more long term there will be important questions concerning the attrition rate of an intervention in terms of its impact—namely, how long after an intervention has finished can subsequent social impact in a target population be demonstrated to be a direct consequence of its activities?

HOW TO MEASURE SOCIAL IMPACT?

Clearly, decisions will be needed about the particular techniques of data collection to capture social impact. These may not simply be technical questions: a participatory approach to social impact measurement can itself create additional 'process' social value for the external stakeholders. Less obviously, social impact measures will also need techniques to estimate the extent to which the outcomes and impact created would have happened anyway (often called 'deadweight calculations'). The terms and techniques that may be used to address this include estimating the counterfactual (what would have happened without the intervention?) and benchmarking (what do data sets from other, comparable situations suggest?). Many approaches are on offer, and usually a greater degree of confidence comes at a price. Nonetheless, if the managers of an investee are considering this question it could be seen as a positive sign boding well for success of the investment, both social and financial returns.

A related issue concerns the *attribution* of outcomes to the investee. This arises whenever the outcomes being created are the result of several organizations, interventions or actions—and not only the result of the work of the investee organization. This question is related to further questions about whether the changes (and outcomes) will be sustainable.

In summary, then, it is suggested here that asking these five critical questions provides a useful grounding and orientation *before* plunging down into data collection methods, or rising up into high methodological principles, or as may be even more likely, going into a noisy marketplace to buy measurement services (whether bespoke or off-the-peg). Together, they offer some reassurance that subsequent data collection and analysis will generate a rounded picture of the positive social changes brought about by an investment. Central to this—and what commonly distinguishes social from conventional finance—are processes of stakeholder engagement to establish the boundaries of materiality and other key issues such as estimates of attrition, attribution, and deadweight. How much rigour is then deemed necessary depends (usually) on the level of risk that is acceptable to the investor (just how *sure* do they wish to be about, say, the scalable efficacy of the proposed innovation?). But as has been noted, the risks in social investment are not spread equally. The investor may accept far higher social risks be than would be acceptable to the intended beneficiaries of the impact. Indeed, the critical issues may need to be considered carefully in order to protect beneficiaries.

Methodological approaches

As has already been noted, there is no shortage of methods with which to measure social impact. But every method has its sub-text—the assumptions it makes, the uses to which it is expected to be put. Bringing out those assumptions provides a convenient way of grouping similar approaches and highlighting what may otherwise go unnoticed.

To that end, it is useful to take the three main theories of accounting and apply them to the different approaches to impact measurement. The first takes a positivist view of accounting: it assumes that accounting data is and should be a representation of financial realities (Whittington, 1986). The second sees accounting from a critical theorist perspective suggesting that accounting processes are essentially about the enactment of power (Chua, 1986; Power and Laughlin, 1996; see also Lukes, 1974). The key issue is who determines what data are captured and reported and for what purpose— since it is well understood that what is to be measured attracts more management attention than what is not. The third theory reconstructs accounting as, ultimately, an interpretive activity—one that provides shared symbolic mediators (terms, codes, conventions) and institutional spaces (practices, formal occasions) for a discussion among interested parties about the nature and extent of value creation, and how best to capture it (Ryan et al., 1992; Gambling et al., 1993). These three approaches represent a spectrum of conceptualizations of accounting and reporting from being a scientific process to representing a set of framing principles for control and action. Taken together in relation to social impact measurement, the three perspectives throw further light on the challenges involved. Since these challenges are considerable, a fourth approach—one which essentially tries to reduce the need for additional impact measurement by using audit and certification—is also outlined. These four approaches are discussed in turn (see Table 9.2).

Table 9.2. Different approaches to social impact measurement

Epistemology	Focus	Logic	Example
Positivist	Truth	Measurement captures empirical reality	Audited accounts
Critical theorist	Power	Measurement enacts power mechanisms	Participatory methods
Interpretive	Dialogue	Measurement acts as a symbolic mediator for discussion between organizational practice and stakeholders	Stakeholder-driven data collection design

POSITIVIST METHODS

Central to the positivist measurement approach is an assumption that social impact proceeds in a linear fashion from a set of inputs and processes to a set of outputs and outcomes. This is usually known as a 'logic model' and is typical of many evaluation studies. The idea underlying logic models is a set of 'if..., then...' causal propositions that set out the thinking behind a social, economic, or development intervention. The evaluator's task is to clarify these linkages and to establish cost-effective ways of gathering the information needed in order to track whether or not the intended interventions are working as intended and are leading to the hoped for outcomes and social impact. The ways of gathering such information are many and varied—from operational records, from interviews, from surveys, from observation, from official statistics. But however many and complicated these may be, the underpinning rationale is the same.

Two points concerning the logic model approach are worth noting. First, it may be argued that for an impact study, the only information that really matters is whether or not the impact is realized. This may be so, but generally, those involved want to understand their results: if there is some impact, but less than one hoped for, why is that? Could the results be improved by improving the way the scheme is run? Or was the intervention based on flawed thinking? Many evaluators and educators will know this as the distinction between *formative* evaluation (aimed at improving a process) and *summative* evaluation (what has actually been achieved?). Typically, investors want a bit of both.

Secondly, if the investor wants to establish whether (say) some lasting community benefit has been achieved, the volumes of information required can become very large indeed. Moreover, the findings are often not clear-cut and, so, evaluators may feel professionally obliged to report on the uncertainties and ambiguities involved. As a result, data-rich evaluations often gather dust because they do not provide the categorical conclusions that time-poor decision-makers hanker after. Such reports do not provide information in standardized form for comparisons and/or aggregation and use by others, either. Nor, normally, would they relate the benefits to all the costs involved in achieving them.

Most methods of social impact measurement and reporting are based, explicitly often, on a logic model, and so they fall into the positivist category. This suggests above all that interested parties favour an approach that appears to offer 'certainty' or 'scientific rigour' with a strong focus on numerical abstractions. At its extreme, this approach also attempts to monetize and 'value' social impact in order to allow comparative analysis across projects and interventions by using financial value as a common unit of social impact.

Methods under this heading include: cost–benefit analyses or expected return models such as Acumen's best alternative charitable option (BACO); experimental methods of choice modelling and valuation such as randomized control trials (RCTs);[5] behavioural models, such as stated or revealed preferences tests; welfare economics models such as public value assessments (judging how much the public values a service), value-added assessments (in education, judging how much a school adds value to a student), quality-adjusted-life-years (QALYs) in health, life satisfaction assessments (how much extra income people would need to achieve an equivalent gain in life satisfaction); government accounting measures that used standardized 'pricing' of welfare interventions to account for government spending.

CRITICAL THEORY METHODS

Whilst the range of methods currently used to capture social impact is dominated by those predicated on positivistic logics, alternative approaches are available. The one currently attracting most attention (especially in the UK) is SROI. Over time, SROI has evolved from a positivistic focus on calculative accuracy (paying careful attention to discount rates and the best proxies to monetize impact) to a more general, principles-based, framework for how to choose the most appropriate sources of input data. The shift has been from technique to principles. Partly, this reflects a realization that the quest for ever-more accurate numerical models of social impact had not delivered robust, standardized, or comparable data sets. As a result, SROI had not been shown to improve the quality or quantity of capital flows to social projects. Nevertheless, the principles of SROI have offered a credible way of advancing stakeholder engagement for better and more rounded measurement. So SROI now goes well beyond its logic model origins to highlight a set of principles that acknowledge power relations and locate judgements of materiality in stakeholder consultation. It combines this with a cost–benefit model that uses the principles of net present value discounting

---

[5] The use of RCTs in social impact evaluation has increased markedly in recent years (Bannerjee and Duflo, 2011; Haynes et al., 2012). Nevertheless, controversy still abounds over the scope for using RCTs and their practical value, largely because science is a cumulative enterprise and so what can be established by a single RCT is often quite limited. Often, RCT results are puzzling, raising more and better questions to be sure, but not giving the clarity about 'what works' for which, understandably, busy investors long.

to monetize future *blended* value (financial plus social) outcomes. While controversial, this has the merit of embracing a central concept in accounting and finance; it may be metaphorical, but it is an attempt to gain additional legitimacy by expressing a goal in terms investors readily appreciate.

Other methods imbued with the sort of assumptions associated with critical theory are 'strategy approaches' (Ebrahim and Rangan, 2010). Typically these view decision-making in and around organizations as the outcome of pluralistic rather than monological processes, involving coalitions and alliances of internal and external stakeholders. For example balanced scorecard approaches—whose origin was precisely to offer a way of resisting the dominance in the corporate domain of (usually short-term) financial concerns—aim to hold in tension the data and interpretations on performance arising from different stakeholder perspectives across the range of actors directly affected by organizational action. Other versions present 'dashboards' that attempt to provide managers and funders with manageable summaries of performance across important dimensions, however disparate (e.g. Paton, 2003: chapter 8).

INTERPRETIVE METHODS

Methods that prioritize stakeholder participation, voice and dialogue also align closely with the interpretive theory of accounting practice. These relationship-based methods typically focus on outcome mapping based on deep engagement with relevant stakeholder or beneficiary groups (for example the outcomes star model)[6] and SROI. Such engagement often starts before an intervention begins and uses stakeholder consultation to design the intervention as well as to shape the appropriate units of performance measurement and the subsequent methodology used. Moreover, this approach usually has built-in feedback loops to test for the ongoing accuracy of data and the effectiveness of the method. It is, thus, iterative, dynamic, and adaptable. Interpretive methods work well to capture key social impacts in complex or integrative settings by embracing collaborative learning, inter-subjectivity and dialogue among those directly involved. And as already noted, measurement systems that prioritize stakeholder judgement and build beneficiary voice can generate additional social impact through the very process of measurement.

However, a focus on such deeper dialogue and learning as part of the social impact measurement process may not be easily achieved: much may depend on building up resilient trust relations (over, e.g. how the measures will be used), as well as managing power asymmetries. Indeed, what becomes clear by thinking in terms of these three broad theories of accounting and their associated approaches, is that each has strengths and weaknesses, but they cannot easily be combined to compensate for each other (and of course using

[6] <http://www.outcomesstar.org.uk>.

additional methods increases the cost of measurement). SROI does attempt this: it draws on, and tries to integrate, positivistic, power and interpretive perspectives. The result is an approach that is very flexible—which may or may not be considered an advantage in a form of accounting.

ASSURANCE, COMPLIANCE, AND AUDIT

Given these challenges, some investors and investees look to assurance processes instead of engaging in impact measurement directly. Essentially, the assurance process considers whether those involved in the organization or initiative in question have done what they said they would do in accounting for their impact, typically, by following some version of 'best' or 'good' practice (that is, what they have done is reasonable by comparison with a standard).

Some of the attractions are immediately apparent: the intermittent and selective checking that appropriate practices are being followed is effectively outsourced to a third party (sometimes a peer) so as to add legitimacy to investee claims of impact; and that a third party provides the results of its appraisal in a way that is credible and impartial. The presence of standardized assurance processes also offers the opportunity to compare investments (*ex ante* or *post hoc*) at the meta-level. Assurance may also be less intrusive ('lighter touch') than audit—albeit, as Power (1996) demonstrated, many of the costs become internalized as processes that have to be undertaken and documented in ways that are auditable.

Currently, however, there are no agreed standards for social impact measurement nor uniform units of analysis, nor regulatory requirements for public reporting (aside from some general social reporting required from charities and some other legal forms such as community interest companies in the UK). So it is unsurprising that there are no generally agreed audit guidelines or requirements for such data. Instead, various social and environmental certification schemes have emerged. These may concern the terms of employment (The Living Wage marque), environmental considerations (e.g. FSC certification) and engagement with stakeholders and the monitoring of outcomes in appropriate ways (e.g. Social Audit, SROI). However, they have generally been concerned to encourage ethical consumption—that is, they are intended to influence consumers in the first instance. It remains unclear how much additional legitimacy these schemes add, particularly for investors.

Bespoke social finance metrics

As a part of the proliferation of impact measurement tools and techniques, several have emerged that are specifically designed for social finance. The front-running examples are reviewed next.

THE IMPACT REPORTING AND INVESTMENT STANDARDS (IRIS)

IRIS[7] was designed to be the basis of standardized performance metrics with which impact investors can measure the social, environmental, and financial impact of their investments, as well as to evaluate future deals. In addition, IRIS was deliberately developed to grow the credibility of the impact investment sector more generally by combining social impact metrics with those usually used in financial performance measurement and reporting. The Global Impact Investing Network (GIIN)[8] designed and manages IRIS. GIIN is a not-for-profit organization focused on increasing the scale and effectiveness of the impact investing market. IRIS is available as a free public good to increase the transparency, credibility, and accountability of the impact investment sector. IRIS aims to align with other, established, reporting standards to reduce overall transaction costs so that investors can compare performance information across their portfolio, or within specific sectors or investment objectives. By 2014, more than 5,000 organizations were using IRIS to evaluate, communicate, and manage their social and environmental performance.

The IRIS suite of measures is built on more than forty existing metric taxonomies and third-party standards. It is maintained and updated with support from a formal Advisory Body comprising experts in impact measurement and other relevant specialties. Each IRIS metric is accompanied by a standardized definition and user guidance. The IRIS metrics have six areas of focus:

- Organization Description: indicators that focus on the organization's mission, operational model, and location
- Product Description: indicators that describe the organization's products/services and markets
- Financial Performance: commonly reported financial indicators
- Organizational Impact: indicators that describe the organization's policies, employees, and environmental performance
- Product Impact: indicators that describe the performance and reach of the organization's products and services
- Glossary: definitions for common terms that are referenced in the indicators.

IRIS measures are not a third-party certification nor does it provide a performance rating. Instead, IRIS metrics are designed to provide a standardized foundation for *other* impact measurement approaches.

THE GLOBAL IMPACT INVESTING REPORTING SYSTEM (GIIRS)

GIIRS[9] was developed by B-Lab[10] to support the growth of the impact investing market by providing investors with a standardized set of third-party impact

---

[7] <http://iris.thegiin.org>. [8] <http://www.thegiin.org>.
[9] <http://b-analytics.net/giirs-ratings>. [10] <https://www.bcorporation.net>.

ratings that are comparable, transparent, and easy to use. GIIRS assesses the social and environmental impact of developed and emerging market companies and funds with a rating and analytics approach analogous to Morningstar Investment rankings or Capital IQ financial analytics. GIIRS offers services and data analytics to investors, funds, and companies to support capital raising and allocation. In time, GIIRS aims to publish aggregated impact investment data to help build the basis for future market and sector benchmark analysis—as such it is a meta-level analytic tool rather than being a measurement system per se. GIIRS charges for its analytic services but is a not-for-profit entity that also publishes data for public use and offers transparent standards and an assessment tool that can be used by any organization for internal use for free.

GIIRS focused on performance metrics in five areas of organizational activity:

- Accountability: these metrics rate organizational governance, transparency and the overall breadth and quality of public reporting
- Employees: this set of metrics considers employee compensation and benefits, whether the organization has any employee ownership, and the overall work environment
- Consumers: these metrics report on how beneficial (or not) key products and services are to target customers; whether the production process generates positive social impact; whether the organization aims at serving those in need (such as Base of the Pyramid customers)
- Community: these metrics capture how locally embedded the organization is, whether it embraces diversity, and whether it is a charity and/or a direct service provider
- Environment: these metrics evaluate the environmental performance of corporate offices, transportation and—where appropriate—distribution and manufacturing facilities.

Notwithstanding the claim implicit in the name, many of these metrics capture processes and outputs rather than impacts. To date, it is unclear what effects GIIRS has had on the broader development of the impact investment market, but it has many supporters and—in a similar way to SROI at the measurement level—has become a market leader.

ENGAGEDX

The development of mainstream capital markets required good and consistent data sets to be aggregated and this, in turn, drove the emergence of specified indices of risk and return. This infrastructure stimulated mainstream investment flows, yet such information is not currently available to social investors. EngagedX, which was founded in 2012, aims to fill this gap.[11]

---

[11] <http://www.engagedinvestment.com/engagedx.html>.

Engaged X is not a methodology for impact measurement per se, but rather a framework designed to aggregate and present social investment data across the market as a whole. The data is anonymized from the portfolios of existing social investors, as a data series over time covering: principal invested; date invested; yield; maturity; write offs/specific provisions; simple product categorization; simple sectoral classification; and importantly their reported social impact and methodology used. The pilot data set drew upon UK-only data, but the framework would have the same utility in any market or as an aggregated representation of the entire global market. The 'core' index data will be offered as an open and free public good to all interested parties with index management and analytics run as a social enterprise with a licensing and subscription model similarly to Bloomberg.

The index contains both financial data and social impact data but the main focus is on the former. This is because accurate and aggregated financial risk and return benchmarks will potentially give more transparency to the implied pricing of *social* returns (as in the Social Impact Bond model). The data in the index will better enable professional investors, asset owners and investment consultants prudently to consider social investing as a part of their portfolios on a basis that is comparable with other markets and asset classes.

THE OUTCOMES MATRIX

Developed in the UK by Investing for Good and Big Society Capital,[12] the Outcomes Matrix[13] aims to capture the key changes and impact that result from a social finance investment for key beneficiaries—the key advantages and benefits that lead to enhanced well-being. These are categorized in nine outcome areas, which break down into more specific outcomes, and corresponding measures, both for the individual, and for communities and society as a whole. These are:

- employment, training, and education
- housing and local facilities
- income and financial inclusion
- physical health
- mental health and well-being
- family, friends, and relationships
- citizenship and community
- arts, heritage, sport, and faith
- conservation of the natural environment.

Each 'cell' within the matrix contains a list of the high-level outcomes that can be achieved within a specific outcome area for the defined beneficiary group.

---

[12] The Matrix was developed with further research input from New Philanthropy Capital, the SROI Network, and Triangle (the developers of the Outcomes Star).

[13] <http://www.goodinvestor.co.uk/outcomes-matrix>.

The matrix allows each high-level outcome to be broken down further into measures and, further, to the specific measurement points that can be used to create indicators and collect data.

This is essentially a taxonomy of outcome areas with signposting to relevant metrics. It is intended to offer investors, intermediaries, and front-line organizations a single tool through which to plan, measure, and learn about their social impact. Moreover, it aspires to develop a common language regarding impact assessment throughout the social sector. By situating an organization's outcomes within a larger 'map' of possible human and environmental outcomes, the matrix encourages organizations to think through what they are doing holistically. However, it does not support the aggregation of outcomes, since these cannot meaningfully be added unless truly like-for-like numbers and contexts are involved.

The pilot version of the matrix is relatively static, but a more dynamic web interface, including functionality to allow users to tailor the matrix to the specific beneficiaries they work with has been envisaged.

A contingency model

This chapter suggests that social impact measurement and reporting is a fluid and interpretive practice that lacks institutionalization or a clear regulatory framework. As such, best practice must be driven by experience, judgement, and principles rather than formalized methodologies. The purpose of the critical issues framework set out above is to shape and inform the process of exercising judgement in designing social impact measurement approaches: but what of the underlying principles?

So, to return to the question posed in the opening section of this chapter: given the measurement options available, how can investors and investees chose an approach that is appropriate to their concerns and context? Framed in these terms, this question calls out for a contingency theory—a model that relates different approaches to the sorts of contexts in which they will be most appropriate. The aim is to identify where the 'good fits' arise between the characteristics of different approaches and the sorts of impact measurement challenges associated with different contexts. This section sets out such a theory based on viewing the investor–investee relationship in terms of information processing (Galbraith, 1973), allowing that information processing is as much about interpretation and making meaning as it is about data handling.

The starting point is to conceptualize the contexts of investor-investee relationships in terms of their underlying characteristics, especially as regards the nature and volume of information that needs to be handled. Two considerations (or dimensions) are considered crucial. The first concerns the basis for trust in the engagement between investors and investees. Put crudely, is the engagement direct—based on a personal contact, relationships and observation? Or is it indirect—dependent upon the collation and interpretation of various sorts of reported (objectified) evidence? The second dimension concerns the level of uncertainty (or, inversely, knowledge) associated with the work of the investee's organization or programme: generally, the more difficult and ambitious the work, the greater the information and information processing that is likely to be needed to evidence worthwhile progress (and vice versa).

THE BASIS-FOR-TRUST DIMENSION

How can investors have trust—justified, defensible confidence—in the claims for social performance made by an enterprise? Clearly, performance measurement—in the broad sense of generating and interpreting a body of abstracted evidence—is one way of answering that question. In some contexts such data, particularly if it can be presented in a quantitative, standardized, form will be expected by investors—for example, in the context of accessing public funding as part of the growing pay-for-success or pay-for-performance contractual universe. Likewise, in the contexts of impact investment that aims to access more mainstream capital markets, the conventions of the mainstream will require investees to expend considerable effort on reporting, proactively interpreting, analysing and investigating claims not just about performance but about strategic developments in the investee organization and, sometimes, in the target sector/intervention overall. This is because the established financial markets and their supporting ecosystem of advisory services have been built upon detailed, quantitative, information processing and modelling. Indeed, the development of the IRIS and the GIIRS was designed to act as a data interface between the mainstream and impact investment to facilitate capital between them.

Nevertheless, building quantitative data sets that mimic those of the mainstream is only one way of establishing a basis for investor–investee trust. Indeed, when a fund manager or private equity house is contemplating a major investment they would not rely only on doing their analytic homework. At some point they will want to engage with the board and meet the senior management team face to face. They will want to 'look under the bonnet' of the enterprise and form judgements about the quality of the management team and the challenges and prospects facing the business. If satisfied, they may decide to become, to a greater or lesser degree, an 'engaged' investor. Broadly similar rationales underpin some approaches to social investment. In information-processing terms, this is a way of reducing the need for further, formalized information processing. Direct contact, observation and dialogue allow confidence to build up (or not) and reduce the need for the costly generation and processing of abstracted evidence and reports.

The need for information processing can be further reduced when the enterprise in question is embedded in a particular community, a social movement or field of professional activity. In such situations, a well-internalized normative order allied to extensive tacit knowledge mean that an acceptable level of confidence in claims about social/environmental performance is perfectly possible—*without* extensive measurement and reporting. This will be especially true when well-established practices or technologies are being employed. For an investor or potential investor in such situations, being involved in the community or in dialogue with someone who knows it well, reduces or even precludes the need for certain sorts of formalized information processing. This draws upon traditions of solidarity and social capital—for example in faith-based sectors—that emphasize the social embeddedness of social finance. This is in stark contrast to the logics of mainstream capital that have, over time, replaced social context with a formulaic reliance on the 'market', primed by a stream of analysts, as sole arbiter of value or worth.

Thus, at one end of the basis-for-trust spectrum there are investment relationships where justified confidence can arise because the activities and relationships are (to varying degrees) socially embedded, infused with field-specific tacit knowledge, direct and dialogical—other things being equal, these will have low requirements for formalized and quantitative information processing. At the other end, relationships may be more remote and impersonal and, thus, various forms of proxy-knowledge and data may be required as well as formal audit and verification mechanisms (such as specific certification models, the use of standardized data, showing conformance to expected processes and so on).

THE UNCERTAINTY DIMENSION

A second, contingent, dimension concerns the level of uncertainty around the likely outcomes/impacts of any given social investment. The factors affecting the level of uncertainty include:

- The organizational/intervention model—how innovative is it, and how complex? Multi-systemic interventions are likely to involve far greater uncertainty than simpler, linear projects. Or perhaps the aim is to take a promising new model to scale (introducing new levels of uncertainty as growth proceeds)
- The setting/context—perhaps the approach is proven but is now being adapted to rather different challenges, and/or the initiative involves collaborations or cross-sector hybridity (with all the additional complexity these entail)
- The existing performance information/data landscape, and the investor's familiarity (or lack of it) with the field and with those relevant knowledge bases.

Each of these can be seen along a continuum from very well established and evidenced to very novel and untried or tested. These dimensions also relate closely to the discussion of social risk and return set out elsewhere in this volume.

A CONTINGENCY FRAMEWORK

Taken together, these two dimensions create a contingency framework that can provide some guidance in terms of what may be appropriate impact measurement approaches for the different contexts in which social finance deals may be agreed (see Figure 9.1).

The contingency framework locates different methods in relation to the different requirements generated by the type of relationship being sought between social finance investors and investees, and the level of uncertainty they jointly face. Thus, in the bottom left-hand corner there may be no need for explicit processes beyond visits, dialogue, and good governance.

Other approaches are similarly easy to locate. Participatory approaches reduce the need for costly information processing and often help preserve or extend trust relations. This is also often the case with certification. Equally, where a considerable social distance between investors and investees is unavoidable (as with social finance closer to mainstream practices, or where considerable public funds are involved) *and* the investees approach to impact generation is not yet well established, then careful impact studies conducted with detachment (objectivity) are required—and the randomized

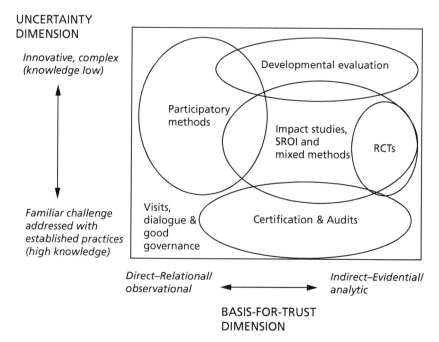

Figure 9.1. A contingency model for social impact measurement

control trial comes into its own. In information processing terms, this gathers, analyses, and uses the minimum necessary information to achieve maximum analytic effect.

Other 'spaces' in the contingency graph are less straightforward. In the top right-hand corner, no effective measurement approach may exist: even if the investor's wish is for evidence of impact, efforts to provide this may well be misdirected and will, almost certainly, be overtaken by events or advances in understanding developed elsewhere. Developmental evaluation (Patton, 2011, is seminal) was devised and articulated precisely as a response to situations where the uncertainty and ambiguity of the context required more complexity in measurement than could be accommodated through a predetermined logic model of outcomes and measures. It is informed by systems ideas and complexity theory and may be appropriate wherever attempts are being made to intervene in complex, rapidly changing, or otherwise poorly understood systems (most obviously, but not only, in post-conflict societies, or in the face of rapid environmental deterioration). For certain situations, it provides an intellectually robust alternative to the 'gold standard' of the RCT. Those situations are ones where those wishing to intervene are willing to accept that they do not yet understand enough (about the situation and what will 'work') to set out what their outcomes, targets, and impact should be.

In practice, this approach may lead to a series of rapid learning cycles as interventions are undertaken as much to learn about what is effective as to ameliorate a particular social problem. This method relies initially on immediate rather than longer term feedback and integrates action and measurement as a single, feedback-based, process of change.

The central area of the graph—where the uncertainty is considerable and the basis for trust is unclear—is the most difficult. Perhaps a scheme is modest in size and cannot sustain the cost of a heavily evidential approach—but certification and participative approaches will not be sufficient or appropriate for some stakeholders. In such settings the SROI model may well become a useful measurement tactic precisely because it is so flexible. It is not the only approach, by any means, but it readily combines (quantitative) evidence with participatory relationship building. It is highly pragmatic in trying both to reduce the need for information processing and increasing the capacity—as far as possible, in each case. Crucially, it focuses analytic attention on the *audiences* for social impact data and its relevance to clients and beneficiaries—stakeholders who typically have less power than funders or organizational managers. Attention to stakeholder materiality also allows a more nuanced sense of the potentially negative or perverse effects of well-intentioned action for some relevant populations. The SROI principles also acknowledge other key elements of wider best practice in terms of establishing the accuracy of the quantity of social impact claimed by a given intervention or project, these include issues of: attribution; deadweight calculations; attention to relevant counterfactuals; rates of attrition; proportionality in terms of the resources allocated to the measurement function with respect to its significance to the organization and its key stakeholders (ultimately a calculation of data risk vs data collection rigour).

Nevertheless, SROI also has definite limitations—especially its underlying linear, positivistic logic, and its controversial claim that to make better decisions between rival ways of creating social value, the social impacts can usefully be quantified and compared with the common yardstick of financial value. The lure of a single, standardized, and comparative unit of analysis based upon 'hard' numbers is often hard to resist. In fact, estimating the effects of the often 'clumsy solutions to wicked problems' (Grint, 2010) that are typically provided by social entrepreneurs may defy practical forms of quantification and, indeed, these effects may be misrepresented by an attempt so to do. Qualitative narratives and other accounts of value creation (photographs, mixed media, online, and so on) will always have an important role to play in providing the necessary depth of understanding of social impact in relation to contingency and context (albeit in non-comparative ways).

Conclusion

This chapter has presented social impact measurement and reporting as a fluid and interpretive practice that lacks institutionalization or a clear regulatory framework. Value is a negotiated commodity informed by both calculation and context—*values* also matter (Young, 2006). It has highlighted the essential differences between social and conventional finance, and—using the critical issues framework—some of the key considerations involved in planning social impact measurement for a specific context. The main methods and metrics currently on offer were set out, relating them to their use in negotiating investor–investee relationships and in informing social finance capital allocation decisions.

It is likely that the availability of good social impact measurement data will be critical to the continued advance of the social finance market, just as robust financial data sets have been important in growing the mainstream financial sector. Indeed, just as in the latter, social finance will need transparent and credible (perhaps, verified) social impact data sets. However, as has been suggested here, the creation and maintenance of such data will involve a series of important decisions. These will need to be carefully calibrated both to ensure the data really is informative and also transparently presented. The process by which an impact measurement methodology and its resultant data set are chosen and enacted is not a neutral process. Any measurement approach reflects key power relations and is, in effect, an act of control. In the case of conventional investment this has not so far been a matter for sustained controversy and challenge—for most of the actors involved, financial performance data is and should be generated, reported, and audited for investors as owners in line with the logic of the principal–agent relationship.

However, in social impact measurement the principal–agent relationship is more complex: the funders/investors may have the power to determine what constitutes social performance data, but if the exercise of that power is to be legitimate, the voice of the clients/beneficiaries also has to be heard. Different perspectives will produce very different measurement approaches and results—in society and politics, 'the good' is always contested. In principle, the 'disciplined pluralism' (Kay, 2003) of a well-functioning social investment market will allow rival conceptions of the good to be pursued and tested. But in the absence of regulation over social impact measurement and reporting, the necessary discipline will only arise if transparency about what will count as social performance becomes a fundamental principle of best practice and due diligence.

Today, it is well understood that conventional accounting and reporting have strong symbolic power (Hopwood and Miller, 1994; Power, 1994). In social finance, it may be that the symbolic power of social impact measurement is even more profound, since upon such data all claims of 'social' or 'impact' investment must ultimately be founded. As a consequence, being known for paying close attention to demonstrating the social impact of a given investment acts as a strong signal of the overall legitimacy and credibility of an intervention or organization. Indeed, demonstrating a robust approach to impact measurement may act as a proxy for achieving measurable impact—as is the case in the admission criteria for the London Social Stock Exchange, for example.[14]

Arguably, the influence of such symbolic power supports the argument for a standardized methodology for capturing social impact, as well as for a single unit of analysis—hence, the attraction of blended value models that monetize social value to combine with economic value as a single total impact figure. However, as has been argued above, this can lead to over-simplification and, ultimately, misleading data and analysis. In truth, social impact can only be meaningfully estimated in the context of careful attention to contingency and stakeholder voice. Currently, adherence to a set of workable (and auditable) principles based on contingency, materiality, stakeholder participation, and proportionality offers the guidance for effective social impact measurement practice and, as a consequence, the pathway towards the most accurate and useful data to guide social investment decision-making.

▧ REFERENCES

Arunachalam, R. (2011). *The Journey of Indian Micro-Finance: Lessons for the Future.* Chennai: Aapti Publications.
Austin, R. (1996). *Measuring and Managing Performance in Organizations.* New York: Dorset House.
Bannerjee, A., and Duflo, E. (2011). *Poor Economics: A Radical Rethinking of the Way to Fight Global Poverty.* New York: Public Affairs.

---

[14] <http://www.socialstockexchange.com>.

Blau, P. M. (1963). *The Dynamics of Bureaucracy*. Chicago: University of Chicago Press.

Campbell, D. T. (1976). 'Assessing the Impact of Planned Social Change'. The Public Affairs Center, Dartmouth College, Hanover, NH.

Chua, W. (1986). 'Radical Developments in Accounting Thought', *The Accounting Review*, LX1(4): 601–32.

Ebrahim, A. and Rangan, V. K. (2010). 'The Limits of Nonprofit Impact: A Contingency Framework for Measuring Social Performance'. Harvard Business School Working Paper 10-099, Boston MA.

Emerson, J. (2003). 'The Blended Value Proposition: Integrating Social and Financial Returns', *California Management Review*, 45(4): 35–51.

Feldman, A., and Serrano, R. (1980). *Welfare Economics and Social Choice* Theory. Boston, MA: Martinus Nijhoff.

Galbraith, J. R. (1973). *Designing Complex Organizations*. Reading, MA: Addison-Wesley.

Gambling, T., Jones, R., and Karim, R. (1993). 'Credible Organizations: Self Regulation vs. External Standard-setting in Islamic Banks and English Charities', *Financial Accountability and Management*, 9(3): 195–207.

Grint, K. (2010). 'Wicked Problems and Clumsy Solutions: The Role of Leadership', in S. Brookes and K. Grint (eds), *The New Public Leadership Challenge*. Basingstoke: Palgrave Macmillan, pp. 169–86.

Haldane, A., and Madouros, V. (2013). *The Dog and the Frisbee*. <http://www.bankofengland.co.uk/publications/Pages/speeches/2012/596.aspx>, accessed 11 May 2015.

Hall, M. (2012). 'Evaluation Logics in the Third Sector' *Voluntas*, 25(2): 307–36.

Haynes, L., Service, O., Goldacre, B., and Torgerson, D. (2012). *Test, Learn, Adapt: Developing Public Policy with Randomised Controlled Trials*. London: Cabinet Office Behavioural Insights Team.

Hopwood, A., and Miller, P. (1994). *Accounting as Social and Institutional Practice*. Cambridge: Cambridge Studies in Management.

Jacobs, A. (2006). 'Helping People Is Difficult: Growth and Performance in Social Enterprises Working for International Relief and Development', in A. Nicholls (ed.), *Social Entrepreneurship: New Paradigms of Sustainable Social Change*. Oxford: Oxford University Press, pp. 247–70.

Jacobs, A., and Wilford, R. (2010). 'Listen First: A Pilot System for Managing Downward Accountability in NGOs', *Development in Practice*, 20(7): 797–811.

Kay, J. (2003). *The Truth About Markets*. London: Allen Lane.

Lukes, S. (1974). *Power: A Radical View*. London: MacMillan.

Mulgan, G. (2010). 'Measuring Social Value'. *Stanford Social Innovation Review*, Summer, pp. 38–43. Stanford Graduate School of Business.

Morozov, E. (2013). *To Save Everything, Click Here: The Folly of Technological Solutionism*. New York: Public Affairs.

Nicholls, J. (2004). *Social Return on Investment: Valuing What Matters*. London: New Economics Foundation.

Nicholls, A. (ed.) (2006). *Social Entrepreneurship: New Models of Sustainable Social Change*. Oxford: Oxford University Press.

Nicholls, A. (2008). 'Capturing the Performance of the Socially Entrepreneurial Organisation (SEO): An Organisational Legitimacy Approach', in J. Robinson,

J. Mair, and K. Hockerts (eds), *International Perspectives on Social Entrepreneurship Research*. London: Palgrave MacMillan, pp. 27–74.

Nicholls, A. (2009). 'We Do Good Things, Don't We?: "Blended Value Accounting" in Social Entrepreneurship', *Accounting Organizations and Society*, 34(6–7): 755–69.

Nicholls, A. (2010a). 'The Institutionalization of Social Investment: The Interplay of Investment Logics and Investor Rationalities', *Journal of Social Entrepreneurship*, 1(1): 70–100.

Nicholls, A. (2010b). 'Institutionalizing Social Entrepreneurship in Regulatory Space: Reporting and Disclosure by Community Interest Companies', *Accounting, Organizations and Society*, 35(4): 394–415.

Nicholls, A. (2010c). 'The Functions of Measurement in Social Entrepreneurship', in K. Hockerts, J. Robinson, J. and Mair (eds), *Values and Opportunities in Social Entrepreneurship*. London: Palgrave Macmillan, pp. 241–72.

Nicholls, A. (2010d). 'What Gives Fair Trade It's Right to Operate? Organizational Legitimacy and Strategic Management', in K. Macdonald and S. Marshall, *Fair Trade, Corporate Accountability and Beyond: Experiments in Global Justice Governance Mechanisms*. Farnham: Ashgate, pp. 95–121.

Nicholls, A., and Murdock, A. (eds) (2011). *Social Innovation: Blurring Boundaries to Reconfigure Markets*. London: Palgrave Macmillan.

Nicholls, A., and Tomkinson, E. (2013). *The Peterborough Pilot Social Impact Bond*. Oxford: Skoll Centre for Social Entrepreneurship/Pears Foundation Case Study.

O'Connell, J. (1982). *Welfare Economic Theory*. Dover, MA: Auburn House.

O'Donohoe, N., Leijonhufvud, C., Saltuk, Y., Bugg-Levine, A., and Brandenburg, A. (2010). *Impact Investments: An Emerging Asset Class*. New York: J.P. Morgan, The Rockefeller Foundation, and the GIIN.

Paton, R. (2003). *Managing and Measuring Social Enterprises*. London: Sage.

Patton, M. Q. (2011). *Developmental Evaluation: Applying Complexity Concepts to Enhance Innovation and Use*. New York: Guildford Press.

Power, M. (1994). 'The Audit Society', in A. Hopwood and P. Miller (eds), *Accounting as Social and Institutional Practice*. Cambridge: Cambridge Studies in Management.

Power, M. (1996). *The Audit Society*. Oxford: Oxford University Press.

Power, M., and Laughlin, R. (1996). 'Habermas, Law and Accounting', *Accounting, Organisations, and Society*, 21(5): 441–65.

Ryan, B., Scapens, R., and Theobald, M. (1992). *Research Method and Methodology in Accounting*. London: Academic Press.

Sawhill, D., and Williamson, D. (2001). 'Measuring What Matters in Nonprofits', *McKinsey Quarterly*, 2: 98–107.

Whittington, G. (1986). 'Financial Accounting Theory: An Over-view', *The British Accounting Review*, 18(1): 4–41.

Wood, A. (2010). 'New Legal Structures to Address the Social Capital Famine', *Vermont Law Review*, 35: 45.

Young, R. (2006). 'For What It's Worth: Social Value and the Future of Social Entrepreneurship', in A. Nicholls (ed.), *Social Entrepreneurship: New Models of Sustainable Social Change*. Oxford: Oxford University Press, pp. 56–73.

10 Risk and return in social finance

'I am the market'

Alex Nicholls and Emma Tomkinson

Introduction

In mainstream finance, a central issue in capital allocation strategy is calculating risk.[1] Put simply, a calculation of financial risk aims to capture the likelihood of an expected financial return actually being realized. This can also be seen as the probability that the return will be achieved (Brealey and Myers, 2010). There are many reasons why this may not be the case including the potential for default, price and inflation risk in the case of debt, or unpredicted market variance in the case of equity. Numerous other market or operational factors may also determine risk. It is a convention in mainstream finance to link the level of expected (or required) return to a calculation of the risk of a given investment opportunity, such that the higher the perceived risk of an asset the greater the return on capital. However, it should also be noted that whilst there may be a normative assumption that these two variables have a positive linear relationship at the portfolio level, there is a high degree of variation at the individual investment level. In the latter, higher risk is also associated with a higher probability of low, or even negative, returns, since some high-risk investments will fail completely (Fiegenbaum and Thomas, 1988). In mainstream finance, it is assumed a fully functioning capital market will incorporate all available information into the price of an asset and that this will include—amongst other variables—its overall risk.

However, even in information-rich market settings, assessing risk accurately is a complex calculation that requires professional judgement as well as good data.[2] Three interlinked issues define the risk parameters around a given capital allocation decision: probability; variance; uncertainty. The *probability* of an investment attempts to the capture the likelihood of the actual future performance matching the predicted performance. This may be calculated

---

[1] The authors acknowledge the valuable comments of a number of reviewers, Dan Gregory in particular.
[2] Though, as the LIBOR scandal of 2012 demonstrated, the role of individual professional judgements in setting risk/return rates can be problematic in the absence of full transparency.

from historical data or, in the case of start-up investments, from prior equivalent or relevant data. The *variance* of an investment typically reflects the standard deviation of the historical returns of a similar investment compared to the total, historical, market average taking into account the 'risk free' rate typically offered by government bonds at the time of investment. This is usually calculated in the capital asset pricing model (CAPM).[3] In the CAPM the larger the variance (*beta*) of the asset's historical—or predicted—performance against the market average, the higher the risk or unpredictability of the asset. Finally, *uncertainty* recognizes that investment decision-making cannot incorporate all possible information because some relevant issues may be unforeseen or beyond quantification within risk calculations (Knight, 1921). Such information may still be significant in terms of capital allocation decision-making, however, and can only be 'managed' by a Bayesian approach that calculates probabilities in the context of incomplete information.

In mainstream capital allocation, the use of risk calculations is of central importance in valuing potential deals, capital allocation decision-making, and overall investment analysis. Not only do investors look for returns that match the perceived risk of their potential investment but a 'risk rate' can also be used to discount future returns—in addition to taking into account inflation—to calculate the 'net present value' or 'time value' of future predicted cash flows. This dual function of the financial risk rate—as a guide to expected returns and as a discount measure for the value of future cash flows—positions it as, perhaps, the single most important calculation in finance (*pace* estimates of actual future cash flows).

However, the financial crisis of 2008 demonstrated that historical market data do not offer a foolproof way of calculating the future risk of assets (Crouch, 2012). During this turbulent period, it soon became apparent that many important risk factors were not being priced into asset valuations.[4] At the same time, the emergence of a social finance sector focused on creating *blended value* returns (Emerson, 2003)—that combine discounted calculations of future social value creation with expected financial returns—has challenged the conventions of risk and return analysis developed in the narrow context of financial economics.[5] Taken together these trends suggest it is timely to reframe debates concerning risk and return in a more holistic context that

---

[3] The CAPM is only used to price equity investments. Debt calculations tend to use simpler historical/sectoral benchmarks with an added risk premium according to the individual investment opportunity.

[4] It may also be the case that the complexity of systemic risk in financial markets simply made accurate calculations impossible. In this context, another argument for social finance may be that it brings into risk calculations important data (particularly on social and environmental externalities) that will be significant for the future growth of robust financial markets more generally.

[5] There has been some pioneering work that attempts to take account of a larger set of data variables in calculating investment risk, but these are still rare and non-standardized (see, for example, O'Loughlin and Thamotheram, 2006; Gore and Blood, 2011).

takes account not only of the limitations of existing risk calculation approaches in capital allocation but also acknowledges the distinctiveness of *social* risk and return. This social risk represents a calculation of the likelihood that an intended *social* return will be realized in a given investment context. It is the purpose of this chapter to explore the distinctiveness of risk related to expected social returns separately from calculations of risk related to expected financial return. Such an analysis remains very unusual within the social finance market[6] and, it is suggested here, may also have relevance to the calculations of future value creation made in all capital allocation decisions.[7]

This chapter is structured as follows. Next financial risk and return are considered in the context of the emergent social finance marketplace. This analysis highlights social risk as a distinctive, yet under-analysed, issue in capital allocation decision-making in this field. Following this section, the specific features of social risk are explored separate from financial or blended risk. After this the correlations between social risk and social return are considered. The chapter then moves on to a discussion of the issues around measuring and modelling social risk and return. The chapter ends with a summary and suggests some future opportunities for social finance in terms of better assessments of social risk and return.

Financial risk and return in social finance

Over the past twenty years a range of new organizations and financial instruments has emerged that reflect some significant institutional changes around the contexts and objectives of capital allocation in financial markets (Emerson and Spitzer, 2007; Nicholls and Pharoah, 2007; Nicholls, 2010a, 2010b; Bishop and Green, 2010; Brown and Norman, 2011; Cabinet Office, 2011; Salamon, 2013). This emergent market has been variously characterized as an evolution of philanthropy (specifically in the neologism *venture philanthropy*: John, 2006), a mechanism of *blended value* creation (Emerson, 2003), investing focused on *social outcomes* or *impact* (i.e. in the increasingly dominant descriptor for this field, *impact investing*: O'Donohoe et al., 2010; Saltuk et al., 2011; Saltuk, 2012) or by its ownership structures (*co-operative* or

---

[6] The only other example of such an approach can be found in Hornsby and Blumberg (2013: 42), but here the analysis suggests a positive linear relationship between social risk and return. This chapter proposes a more complex set of correlations.

[7] Empirical evidence suggests that the conventional tools of analysis in mainstream finance over-estimate risk and undervalue returns in social finance investments. For example, the rapid development of the microfinance sector demonstrates that the normative assumptions behind the mainstream pricing of debt risk to the very poor were completely erroneous (see Sabin, 2013); the reality of the riskiness of this sector (as defined by the default rates) was far lower than had been predicted. Similarly, the emergence of a social enterprise equity market has shown that investors will price social value into the share price and expected yield as an additional return above the expected financial performance of an investment (see Hartzell, 2007).

mutual finance). In this book the range of capital allocated primarily for social purposes is simply called *social finance*.

Of particular importance in terms of conceptualizing social finance is a separation of value creation and value appropriation (Nicholls, 2010a, 2010b). In mainstream finance, the owner of allocated capital expects to benefit from an appropriate, risk-adjusted, proportion of the resultant value created.[8] This provides one of the underpinning logics of pure market theory extrapolated from Adam Smith's original conception of the benefits of the 'invisible hand' consequent from the actions of a rational, utility maximizing, individual. However, in social finance, the expectations of the owner of capital are typically more complex with respect to value appropriation. For example: a philanthropist will likely judge a grant by the value appropriated by a beneficiary not for herself; a dedicated social finance fund may be seeking a blend of financial value appropriated by the owners of capital with social value appropriated by another party; finally, an impact investor may be seeking primarily a 'mainstream' financial return appropriated by himself whilst still creating social value that may be appropriated by others, for example by buying equity in a microfinance company. Thus, a defining feature of social finance in practice is innovation in terms of the institutional norms that govern the relationships between its capital allocation logics (focused on the outcomes of placing capital) and investor rationalities (focused on the objectives of placing capital).[9] Whilst these two dimensions are typically aligned in the normative logics of mainstream capital allocation—namely to maximize value creation (outcome) appropriated by the owner of capital (objective)— they have a more complex set of interactions in social finance that challenge the conventions of both mainstream investing and traditional philanthropy.

The growth of social finance has been driven partly by a growing universe of social purpose organizations that cannot access mainstream finance due to their projected financial returns failing to match their *perceived* levels of risk (Joy et al., 2011: Shanmugalingam et al., 2011). At the same time, owners of capital are increasingly seeking to allocate their resources to generate social value as well as (or, sometimes, instead of) seeking financial returns (Hill, 2011).[10] This form of capital allocation is growing

---

[8] In social finance, a key issue is attribution in terms of *social* value creation. Often, there is no clear understanding of whether the investor should take credit for the social return of the investment, or whether a revenue stream generated off the back of the investment should take the credit. It is likely that some mix of these and contribution by other factors is involved, but calculating this remains largely beyond current metrics.

[9] In mainstream finance, revenue and investment finance are clearly distinguished. In social finance, many grants represent revenue for the investee, rather than investment, although the two are regularly elided in discussions of the social finance market.

[10] Social value creation is best understood in terms of the outputs and impacts of organizational action identified as 'social' or 'environmental' in terms of normative (and often localized) assessments of their positive effects across five dimensions (Nicholls and Schwartz, 2013): geography and demography—who the target market or beneficiaries are and where they are located, for example a project working in a deprived area or within disenfranchised populations; organizational processes—

across the world and attracting significant practitioner, policy, and academic interest. For example, it is now estimated that the UK social finance market could grow from the £165m allocated in 2010 to over £1bn by 2016, a 38 per cent per annum growth rate (Brown and Swersky, 2012).[11] Moreover, mainstream players are now beginning to enter this market such as J.P. Morgan, Deutsche Bank,[12] and the European Investment Fund as estimates of the global scale of the impact investment market suggest the potential for up to $500bn of assets under management (O'Donohoe et al., 2010).

The emergence of the social finance market over the past decade or so suggests that the current institutions of mainstream capital allocation and their attendant instruments and metrics have limitations in terms of financing organizations and projects focused primarily on social value creation (Nicholls, 2013). It is suggested here that this is a market failure that is largely the product of a lack of relevant information on the social as well as financial performance of organizations.[13] The result is that mainstream markets typically fail to account for the total value creation (or destruction) of a potential investment that incorporates an accurate and complete assessment of its entire risk and return profile. This also ultimately undermines the efficiency of capital markets in terms of their overall, long-term, return-on-investment calculations and appropriate discount rates. Such effects are already well recognized in terms of the historic failure to price the environmental impact of carbon emissions into share valuations in the energy and heavy industry sectors, for example.[14]

The response from the new institutions of social finance to this market failure has been to develop a number of corrective innovations notably a wider range of financial instruments (including bespoke innovations such as *quasi-equity* or *venture philanthropy*) and hybrid funding models that can structure deals reflecting multiple types of investor objectives and preferences balancing different blends of social and financial value creation and appropriation. Of particular significance in the latter is the financial risk and return spectrum evident across social finance investors from the '100% loss' capital allocation of

how value is created within an organization for key stakeholders and beneficiaries, for example, work integration social enterprises that aim to bring excluded groups into the labour market; goods and services produced—how mission objectives are achieved in terms of outputs, for example, providing care services or low-cost irrigation pumps; sector—in which category of economic activity the organization fits, for example health, education, clean energy/green technology, clean water (the main areas of activity identified in the emerging impact investing sector); financial or organizational structure—who appropriates the value created, for example mutual or cooperative enterprises or dividend-capped or asset-locked legal forms (such as community interest companies in the UK).

[11] Though this is only about 1% of the value of all loans to small businesses in the UK.

[12] This is a £10m 'fund of funds' and is 'on balance sheet', i.e. the fund is financed internally and does not include external investors.

[13] In addition, investment markets can be inefficient because they fail to account for relevant externalities. In contrast, analyses in social finance markets often focus on externalities related to value creation.

[14] This is the market failure exploited by the Generation Investment Management fund or the Carbon Tracker initiative: <http://www.carbontracker.org>.

Figure 10.1. Financial returns in social finance

philanthropic grants to the market—or above market—returns achieved by some social venture capital funds, such as Bridges Community Ventures (see Figure 10.1).[15]

This spectrum of financial returns has allowed the social finance market to innovate and evolve beyond grants alone. For example, traditional philanthropists, grant-making foundations and governments have underwritten the development of social finance products and deals by using both grant funds and sub-market return mission- or programme-related investments (MRI/ PRI) from their investment corpus (Patton, 2013).[16] In each case, the philanthropic capital is typically used to 'absorb' some of the financial risk of the product/deal to enable other investors to enter and achieve their desired risk-adjusted returns.[17] There are several different models of this risk mitigation including: taking the first loss of an investment; taking a subordinate position in the risk and return tranching; being the first mover or cornerstone investor; providing matching investments; offering a guarantee for part of the principle. In terms of taking a first loss or subordinate position within the financial structure or tranching of a product or deal, grant or sub-market capital can limit the overall risk for other investors by reducing the likelihood of loss of capital and by increasing the potential returns. Acting as a first mover or cornerstone investor increases overall investor confidence as it demonstrates that due diligence has already been carried out.[18] Matching investments also dilute the risk taken by the other investors and can increase aggregate returns

---

[15]   The capital allocation characterized as social 'investment', on the other hand, typically involves, at a minimum, the return of an investor's capital and, sometimes, also an additional return. This is the definition preferred in the impact investing market and also by some significant new institutional players such as Big Society Capital in the UK:

Social investment is the provision and use of capital to generate social as well as financial returns. Social investors weigh the social and financial returns they expect from an investment in different ways. They will often accept lower financial returns in order to generate greater social impact. Some interpretations of social investment include the provision of capital without any expectation of financial return. When we refer to social investment, however, we mean investment mainly to generate social impact, but with the expectation of some financial return (BSC, 2012).

[16]   In the case of the 100% loss grant capital, if an investment yields a return, then the grant can be recycled. In the case of MRI or PRI the foundation can argue that they are using their corpus to support their mission objectives rather than just the mainstream market, even if the financial risk is higher.

[17]   This is made possible by dividing products or deals into tiers or tranches, each with different risk and return profiles.

[18]   The UK government provided 50% of the funding for the first Bridges Community Ventures fund.

to all parties through scale economies. Guaranteeing or underwriting investments reduces the financial risk taken on by investors.[19]

A further interesting aspect on the above spectrum lies at the boundary point between philanthropy (equating to –100 per cent risk or guaranteed loss of all capital invested) and capital allocation that has some expectation of financial return. In the former scenario the grant-maker's social return is achieved the moment the grant is given, and thus they do not carry any social risk past that point. This is because once the financial transaction of grant-making has been completed, the foundation has typically achieved its primary social impact goal—to fund a social intervention or project in a third party— and the likelihood of an expected social return being achieved becomes, then, a function of the grantee's ability to operationalize the investment successfully. However, in the latter scenario (i.e. from –99 per cent loss to capital returned or beyond) the owner of capital is—at least at some level—an investor, rather than a philanthropist. Crossing this boundary fundamentally changes perceptions of social risk and alters decision-making behaviours as a consequence. One interpretation might be to say that as soon as an investor has a chance of receiving any of their capital back, they assume some of the ongoing social risk, although that is not to say that there is a direct correlation between the level of financial and social risk in the scenario. Elsewhere, this –99 per cent to 0 per cent loss is captured in the notion of 'grace capital' (Perry, 2011).

As has already been noted, recognizing the opportunities offered by the various levels of financial risk tolerance across the spectrum of social investors has been instrumental in driving the social finance market forward. However, these analyses are still primarily focused on conventional assessments of financial risk, albeit in the context of socially focused investment. Such analyses sometimes explore the relationship between financial risk and social risk, but do not typically consider the latter as a discrete set of variables.[20] Furthermore, these approaches draw their logic of risk analysis from conventional investment practice.

Mainstream finance assumes that risk and return correlate positively in a market of perfect information (i.e. have a correlation coefficient of +1). This means that, in theory, the market would be able to predict the likelihood of each possible return across the range and price the return of a product to accurately reflect this. An increase in risk would relate to a corresponding increase in return, in fact the two are often assumed be identical rates, interpreted differently, that is, a 1 per cent increase in risk would require a 1 per cent increase in return (see Figure 10.2).

---

[19] In the New York City Rikers Island Social Impact Bond (SIB), Bloomberg Philanthropies took more than 75% of the financial risk allowing Goldman Sachs to enter as a first mover investor bank in a SIB.

[20] Some element of idiosyncratic investor behaviour and preferences may still be maintained in the presence of rich information on social risk, as well as financial risk.

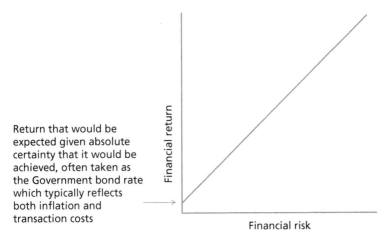

Figure 10.2. Risk and return across a portfolio in conventional finance

However, in social finance, financial risk and return do not appear to be so clearly positively correlated. Investments to date suggest a more mixed pattern of financial returns against financial risk in social finance. In some cases, such as Bridges' Venture Funds, social finance can match or beat the market in terms of finance returns without taking venture capital-like risk. On the other hand, in social enterprise investment there appears initially to be a positive linear relationship between financial risk and financial return that then plateaus at roughly 10–15 per cent financial returns irrespective of increased financial risk (see Figure 10.3). This may be explained by structural issues in the business models of many social enterprises that are rarely profit maximizing, as well as a general unwillingness in the sector to reward external investment with high financial returns. At higher still levels of financial risk—for example Esmee Fairbairn Foundation's investments in Venturesome—some loss of capital is actually expected (i.e. a negative correlation). These mixed patterns of risk and return correlation suggest that a missing variable is not being taken into account, it is suggested here that this is social risk.

There is only a small body of work that even acknowledges social risk as a distinctive variable in social finance. At the level of individual social investments, Emerson (2012) proposed that the judgements that need to be made to determine effective allocation of social finance capital run along three axes or dimensions: financial risk and return plus (social) impact. The intersection of these three dimensions provides 'an efficiency frontier' where financial risk and return are in balance with maximum social impact. However, this model considers social impact as unidimensional—a composite product of prior social risk and return calculations—and fails to explore the full complexity of social risk per se as a key component of projected social impact calculations.[21]

---

[21] Similarly, Puttick and Ludlow (2012) identified *impact risk* as distinct from financial risk in terms of the standards of evidence/data collection methods available to calculate social impact, but did not drill down into the components of social risk itself.

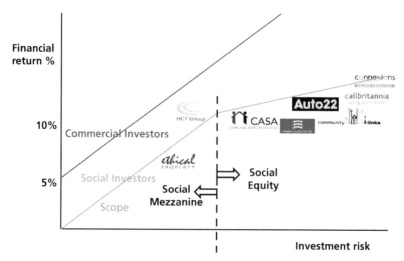

Figure 10.3. Financial risk and return in social enterprise investment
Source: Ross, 2013

In contrast to Emerson's three axes of social finance, Laing et al. (2012) identified social risk as a distinct variable within a *combined return framework* of social finance that followed blended value logics (i.e. the final value creation of a social investment reflects both its social and financial outcomes). However, the report restricted the definition of social risk to *the risk that an institution's investments might alienate key stakeholders and/or compromise the values of the organization* (p. 12). They also suggested that such a risk is not correlated to an increased expected return.[22]

Hornsby and Blumburg offered a more developed model of social risk by using 'indifference curves' to explore the relationship between 'impact generation' and 'impact risk', terms that are slightly broader than the definition of social return and social risk used here as they include environmental and cultural impact. Their report noted six categories of impact risk defined as 'a measure of the certainty that an organization will deliver on its proposed impact, as detailed in the impact plan' (p. 23). In their model, the assessment of impact risk interrogated six key qualities of an impact plan. Namely, to what extent it is:

---

[22] The report acknowledged that this definition was somewhat limited in a footnote:

Just as volatility does not capture all aspects of investment risk, social risk, as defined here, does not capture all types of social risks. For example, when making a social investment, there is the risk that the investment may not produce the desired social outcome (e.g., jobs may be lost rather than created). However, this social risk and others may be captured within the combined return framework. When an expected social outcome is not achieved, the ex post combined return would be lower than the expected combined return. (p. 12)

In this chapter, social risk is conceptualized as wider than either Laing's definition or a component of financial risk.

- *Explicit*: Is the impact plan explicit in all particulars?
- *Reasoned*: Does the impact plan present a compelling and well-reasoned theory of change?
- *Integral*: Is the generation of impact integral to the organization's business and operations?
- *Feasible*: Is the impact plan feasible?
- *Evidenced*: Is there evidence to support the impact plan's approach to impact generation?
- *Evidenceable*: Will the impact be evidenced by carrying out the impact plan?

The authors went on to assert that 'impact risk and financial risk remain separate parameters, with potential trade-offs between them' (Hornsby and Blumberg, 2013: 43).

Barby and Gan (2014) identified five categories of risk in impact investing: capital risk, exit risk, unquantifiable risk, transaction cost risk, impact risk. In terms of impact risk, the authors noted:

As with financial analysis, understanding the impact risk of an investment is as important as understanding its potential for impact return. Impact risks can take various forms. For example, there may be a lack of evidence that an intervention will lead to the desired outcome. Even if the intervention is successful, the investment could cause displacement, leading to reduced or no net benefit. Or, the investment may create positive change for its target beneficiary but a negative change for other stakeholders, which reduces or undermines its impact. In this respect, impact risk is directly linked to reputational risk.

For the asset owner providing concessionary capital, choosing between an impact investment product and another tool to create social outcomes (such as foundations making grants or the government allocating taxpayer money), the impact risk is greater still: the product needs to demonstrate that the investor's foregone financial return will generate equivalent or superior outcomes relative to an alternative approach to achieving the same impact. (p. 9)

The report then offers seven approaches to reduce risk in impact investing of which three relate directly to social risk: technical assistance, track record, and impact evidence. In terms of the latter, the authors comment:

A product with impact evidence has defined an impact strategy together with its stakeholders and worked collaboratively, using a credible methodology, to track progress against the expectations set. Impact evidence is most robust when the product's method of intervention is well understood and is supported by a randomised control trial (or other scientific study) that demonstrates the causal link between the investment's outputs and the asset owner's target social outcomes. (p. 15)

However, the report also acknowledges that this level of rigour may, in reality, be too expensive to be practical and that pre-existing scientific methods will not always be available anyway for every intervention.

Building on this pioneering work, it is argued here that an interrogation of social risk and return must be a *sine qua non* of effective social finance capital allocation separate from financial risk and return modelling. The variety of different financial risk and return tolerances evident across the risk spectrum in social finance (see Figure 10.1) suggests that there is a need for a deeper understanding of what lies behind these preferences and how this blends financial and social outcomes/impact expectations. Such investor preferences appear to operate beyond conventional market logics, incorporating complex combinations of value creation and value appropriation calculations, as noted above. Indeed, as one social investor quoted by Emerson (2012) made clear:

> My measure of return is not what the market may deem as an appropriate financial return, but rather a defined level of financial performance integrated with measurable social and environmental value creation. *I am the market* and I will determine what appropriate level of return I should seek. (p. 9)[23]

Social investors have often shown a willingness to accept a financial return below a comparable risk adjusted return expected in mainstream markets. Assuming that this behaviour is not completely irrational, this demonstrates that investors in social finance expect a compensatory value in social returns (Hill, 2011).[24] There are two elements to these variable investor preferences. First, there is the complex set of relationships between value creation and value appropriation already noted above. But second, there are the calculations of risk and return in social finance that combine assessments of financial risk and return with those of social risk and return. It is taken as a given that—with some caveats post the global financial crisis—methods of calculating financial risk and return are well established, broadly evidenced, and fully institutionalized in global markets. As a consequence, the remainder of this chapter focuses specifically on exploring the much less well-understood concept of social risk and return in social finance. This analysis will highlight social risk and return as a significant, but still inadequately conceptualized, issue in effective capital allocation decision-making in this inchoate field. Furthermore, it is proposed here that better social risk and return data will allow social finance investors not only to make better comparative choices based on projected social outcomes, but also to assess the likelihood of expected performance being achieved. Such data may also underpin more accurate projections of future social outcomes performance across potential investments. Both of these enhancements would significantly increase the allocative efficiency of the social finance market—something of great significance given the imbalance between demand-side social need and supply-side social finance capital.

---

[23] A wider interpretation of this is that investors in the social finance market simply make more transparent the inherent subjectivity of all capital allocation decisions, further refuting the standard models of *homo economicus*.

[24] *Contra* blended value assumptions, it is often suggested that the relationship between social and financial value creation may be a Pareto one where less of one equals more of the other. However, historical data shows this is only true in some cases and is not a given in social finance.

In summary, recognizing the opportunities offered by the various levels of financial risk tolerance across the spectrum of social investors has been instrumental in driving the social finance market forward. However, to date, these analyses have been primarily focused on conventional assessments of financial risk in the context of socially focused investment without isolating social risk as a discrete variable in capital allocation decisions. This must result in inefficient allocations of capital that aim primarily at driving social impact. The next section aims to address this by considering the nature and scope of social risk.

Social risk in social finance

This section falls into three parts. First, it sets out the distinctive features of social risk as a set of performance variables quite separate from those associated with financial risk. This analysis highlights the significance of individual investor preferences. Second, this section explores the relationships between social risk and social return in a variety of models and scenarios. Finally, some observations are made concerning measurement approaches to quantify and report social risk rates.

THE DISTINCTIVE FEATURES OF SOCIAL RISK

Put simply, social risk represents the likelihood that a desired set of social outcomes and impacts (social return) will be achieved as a consequence of the *deliberative* actions of a programme/organization whose objectives are to achieve these social outcomes and impacts. This excludes the socially positive externalities of other objectives. In terms of social finance, social risk is, therefore, the likelihood that a given allocation of capital will generate the expected social outcomes *irrespective* of any financial returns or losses. The complete separation of financial and social risk is important conceptually since, without doing this, the latter simply slides into the former or disappears completely within a less precise term such as overall social or blended impact. It is suggested here that—unlike financial risk and return—the relationship between social risk and return is unlikely to be linear in most social finance investments.

For example, a foundation can choose to invest either in low social risk, well-evidenced welfare programs that deliver predictable social outcomes per unit of investment, but that do not alter the underlying causes of a social problem, or it can aim to address more complex and systemic issues behind a welfare issue that may be high social risk with very uncertain outcomes but offer the potential of transformative impact.[25] In a more complex example, if a

---

[25] However, this is not to say that there is a *positive correlation* between less-well-evidenced interventions and greater expected social returns.

social investor wishes to address the social evil of malaria she has various options. She may choose what is apparently a low social risk option such as investing in the distribution of bed nets, where there would be an expected correlation between bed net use and reductions in malaria infection rates, but no opportunity to eradicate the disease. Or she can invest in research projects that aim to find a cure for malaria that are typically high cost and high risk: namely, the likelihood of a specific research project investment leading to a cure is small, but the potential social outcome impact huge. However, in this case, data suggests that the perceived social risk of the first option may be miscalculated, since there is field evidence that shows that bed net use is not always consistent with expectations—indeed, sometimes, bed nets are used for totally different purposes such as to function as fishing nets. Calculating social risk accurately, therefore, needs careful prior consideration and, preferably, evidenced data. Historically, many social finance investors have attempted a portfolio approach to their particular social objectives—attempting to combine low and high social risk projects. However, such portfolio strategies have been— inevitably, given extant data—poorly informed and somewhat hit-and-miss, at best.

While it is argued later that social risk will largely be driven by its own distinctive set of variables compared to financial risk, the former can still be mapped against the three broad types of risk noted above in mainstream finance.

The *probability risk* of a social investment is the likelihood that its social impact will be achieved. The social probability risk is determined by two factors: the reliability and extensiveness of the evidence base of historical data; differentiated populations potentially sharing similar outcomes.[26]

Figure 10.4 illustrates the perfect world of historical data on programme performance: here the data are assumed to be normally distributed along a single linear scale. The likelihood of the programme's social return exceeding a certain amount (called here 'k') is calculated as the proportion of previous similar programmes that also exceeded this level of social return (in this case, 73 per cent).

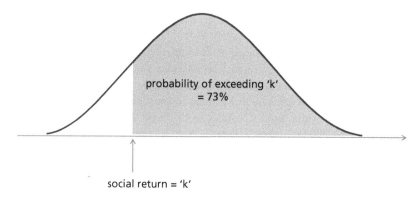

probability of exceeding 'k'
= 73%

social return = 'k'

Figure 10.4. Probability risk

---

[26] A lack of capacity or resources to perform rigorous social risk analysis at the organization, deal, fund, or market levels is a potential further risk factor.

Figure 10.5. Data availability and risk

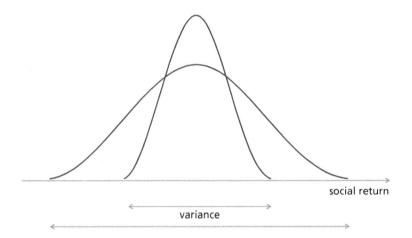

Figure 10.6. Variance risk

However, lack of either historical organizational data or equivalent/relevant data from other organizations and programmes makes it difficult for social purpose organizations to predict the effects of their programmes and for investors to verify these predictions. Probability calculations will, therefore, improve their accuracy as more deals are done and more social impact data, of higher quality, becomes consequently available (see Figure 10.5).

The *variance risk* of a social investment reflects the standard deviation of the social return that is predicted for that investment or the standard deviations of similar examples in historical data (see Figure 10.6). In Figure 10.8 there are two scenarios illustrated. Both have the same average or expected outcome. The wider bell curve represents an investment where there is a wider range of outcomes than the investment represented by the narrower bell curve. The variance of the investment with the wider bell curve is therefore greater than the variance of the investment with the narrower bell curve. The outcomes for the investment with the greater variance also have a higher likelihood of falling further away from the average or expected outcome: the greater the variance, the higher the risk of the investment. The calculation of variance can be informed by the range of performance results of existing or previous social programmes involving similar organizations, methods of service delivery, service users, measurement techniques, and financial structures: the larger the variance of historical performance from the average, the higher the risk of

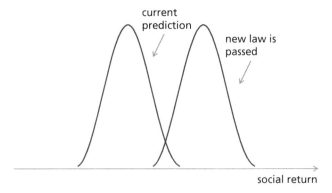

Figure 10.7. Uncertainty risk

subsequent analogous programmes is likely to be. If the variance of a social return can be calculated, then greater variance of predicted outcomes from this return represents higher risk. The smaller the variance, the higher the chance the actual return will be similar to the predicted return. Social variance risk is driven by three factors: financial structure risk, reputational risk, and organizational risk. Where there is a lack of relevant historical performance data, the track record of the organization and its management team, may act as a proxy for data-driven variance risk calculations.

The *uncertainty risk* of a social finance investment recognizes that not all risk factors can ever be fully understood or calculated and that there will always be unexpected or unpredictable exogenous influences on social outcomes and impact. Social uncertainty risk is related to contextual risk and responsiveness risk. For example, as with mainstream investments, the results of social programmes are sensitive to unforeseen changes in the economic, political, legislative, environmental, and social context.[27] Uncertainty risk can also be endogenous in terms of unforeseen organizational or managerial changes and stresses that can affect overall performance. Figure 10.7 illustrates the predicted outcomes for a programme that are altered markedly by an unexpected new law that was passed. In this case the law improves the outcomes, but legislative changes could impact the measurement of programme outcomes in either direction. For example, if a reoffending programme were measured by number of nights sentenced to custody, then a law increasing the length of sentences would make the measured result appear much worse. Responsiveness risk relates to the ability of an organization and its management to adapt and respond effectively to performance information ('strategic flex'), Constraints on strategic flex include rigidity of programme design, culture of resistance to change and constraints attached to funding.

---

[27] Though, of course, the particular PESTLE variables and their effects on social impact may vary from those affecting financial returns.

Table 10.1 sets out the key dimensions of social risk in social finance investing in terms of the main variables associated with each category of risk.

A further important factor in the calculation of social risk is the perspective of key stakeholders. This is most apparent in the important role played by investor preferences in terms of the perceived social risk of their social finance capital allocation. These calculations of social risk and return are typically idiosyncratic to an individual investor. For example, so-called, impact investors differ significantly in their assessment of social risk (i.e. social outcomes/impact risk) compared to philanthropists—with the former regularly investing in capacity building their investees and contributing to their administration costs in order to *reduce* the social risk of their investment (i.e. increase the likelihood of achieving their social impact and outcome objectives). Thus, social risk calculations are also partly a function of investor perspectives and expectations. In this regard, social risk has something in common with the private cost of capital model discussed elsewhere in this collection in the context of social finance valuation and pricing (Nicholls and Patton, 2013)—there appear to be distinctive *social* cost of capital calculations behind many social finance investment decisions.[28] The next section explores and models

Table 10.1. Social risk in social finance investment

Type of risk	Definition	Calculations	Drivers	Variables
Probability	Likelihood that social impact will be achieved	Calculated by the proportion of similar programmes that have achieved the intended impact in the past	More deals = better data = more accurate calculations	*Evidence base risk*: Presence–absence of relevant historical data *Population risk*: Focus on low–high risk populations
Variance	Standard deviation of the impact predicted for the programme	Calculated by the spread of deviations of intended impacts of similar programmes in the past	Higher standard deviation = higher risk	*Financial structure risk*: Higher–lower financial structure riskiness *Reputational risk*: Higher–lower organizational reputation risk *Organizational risk*: Experience–lack of experience of management team; stage of organizational lifecycle; size of organization
Uncertainty	Risk factors that cannot be known	Exogenous: PESTLE changesEndogenous: management and organizational change	Historical, political, and contextual volatility = higher risk	*Contextual risk*: Greater–lower volatility of PESTLE context *Responsiveness risk*: Greater–lower capacity to respond strategically to change

---

[28] Another element of the social risk calculation may involve beneficiary perceptions of the likelihood of a social return or impact being achieved. This aspect of social risk may be correlated to the social return expectations of different beneficiaries. Beyond this, other stakeholder perspectives on social risk may also be significant (government, service providers, other relevant third parties). Taken together these various perspectives on social risk represent an aggregated or composite social risk rate

some of the complex relationships between social risk and return in social finance in more detail.

THE CORRELATIONS OF SOCIAL RISK AND SOCIAL RETURN

As described above, the assumption in mainstream finance is that risk and return have a positive linear relationship. As was noted above, Hornsby and Blumberg (2013) suggested that social risk and social return have a similar relationship, however, there is little data by which to support this assumption and, when deconstructed, there is no logic to suggest that it should always hold anyway. There are many factors of social risk that could be considered by investors and a selection of these has been chosen to demonstrate the variability of the relationship between social risk and return. In some cases, if a risk factor increases as the potential social return increases, the relationship is positive. In others, if social return increases as a risk factor decreases, the relationship is negative. Finally, in some cases there appears to be no relationship between an increase in social risk and the potential social return at all. Each of these relationships will now be considered in turn with respect to the three categories of risk used throughout this chapter.

Probability Risk

The conventional method to assess the probability of a predicted return is to use the relative frequency of that return in similar investments in the past. The probability social risk of social finance investments is increased by two factors with respect to such assessments: a limited evidence base of historical data and differentiated populations sharing similar outcomes.

To reduce the probability risk of a social return, an evidence-based programme may be sought. Programmes that have a proven track record of delivering expected returns have a lower social risk based on evidence that results can be achieved. For example, multi-systemic therapy has been implemented in hundreds of locations over time to address a range of needs. It has not only been independently evaluated, but the results of programmes and evaluations have been published and are freely available. The social outcomes it routinely measures and achieves constitute an attractive social return that

in addition to the calculations that can be made under the headings of probability, variance, and uncertainty. Beneficiary perspectives on social risk are relevant for two main reasons. First, from an ethical point of view, their assessment of social performance and the likelihood of changes being achieved in their own lives should be taken into account. But, secondly, from an instrumental perspective, beneficiary assessments of social risk and return may well be the most accurate, as well as relevant.

investors can use to predict the likelihood of future programmes being suc-cessful. In comparison, many social programmes have limited evaluations that yield limited information as to their effect. This does not mean that their potential social return is less than a well-evidenced programme (Puttick and Ludlow, 2012), but it does mean that it is not only very difficult to predict their social return, it is also difficult to predict the likelihood of it being achieved. In fact, Hornsby and Blumberg argue that potential social return is greater for programmes that have yet to establish an evidence base (Hornsby and Blumberg, 2013). It should be noted that well-evidenced programmes are not spread evenly across areas of social need, thus reliance on evidence—or programme outcomes that are easily or cheaply evidenced—could create a bias towards investment in certain social issues (Patton, 2013: see also Puttick and Ludlow, 2012).

Social risk related to population risk is also uncorrelated to social return. High social returns may be achieved by working with both high- and low-risk populations. Populations are generally deemed higher risk when they are more likely to progress to worsening outcomes and less likely to respond to inter-ventions that prevent this progression. As is shown in Figure 10.8, however, the greater the potential social risk, the smaller the population and the greater the potential social return.

Programmes with a large, low-risk population will achieve social return at scale due to the incremental changes made in many peoples' lives. This will also involve spending a significant amount on people who would have made the change without the intervention or who do not fall into the target risk group to start with. An example of a programme that fits this description is a series of anti-drinking advertisements for teenagers, televised in the afternoons. Many people who see these advertisements will not be teenagers and the majority of teenagers who view the advertisements would not have developed a drinking

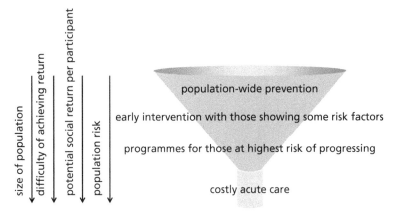

Figure 10.8. Population risk

problem had they not seen them. There will also be a proportion of teenagers who are at risk of developing a drinking problem who will not see the advertisements.

On the other hand, a small, high-risk population may generate high levels of social return due to the significant changes made to a few lives. Working with high-risk populations involves more cost per person, however, the proportion of people that would improve their own outcomes without intervention is much smaller and the potential change that can be made for each person is, therefore, greater.

Some social programmes may be criticized for creating incentives to focus only on low-risk populations. Social finance can encourage providers to work with high-risk populations by structuring payments such that it is more efficient to deliver an intensive programme to a small group of the highest risk people. For example, in the graph relating to criminal justice below (Figure 10.9), 6 per cent of offenders are responsible for 30 per cent of interactions with the system. Payments for achieving a reduction in offences may most efficiently be achieved by working with the highest risk population, while payments for achieving a reduction in offending population may most efficiently be achieved by working with the lower risk population.

The population risk of the staff of a programme is also uncorrelated to social return. Some programmes increase their social return by employing high-risk past participants. Other programmes employ only the lowest risk staff to increase the likelihood of social return with the highest risk programme participants.

Variance Risk

Social variance risk here reflects the spread of standard deviations around an average of past or predicted social impact performance. Financial structure

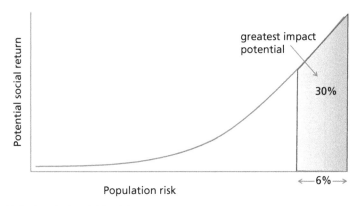

Figure 10.9. Population risk/social outcome

risk is a factor of social risk that may correlate to social return. For example, if a service provider takes on more financial risk to build its capacity to deliver services, there is an additional incentive to achieve a greater social return. The organizational willingness to accept more financial risk also demonstrates confidence in achieving a given social return. For example, in New South Wales, the Benevolent Society is investing in a SIB for which they will deliver services. As they are responsible for predicting the outcome targets from which investors will get returns, their co-investment gives other investors confidence in their predictions (Tomkinson, 2012a). This is similar to an approach seen in Massachusetts, USA, where the service delivery organization Roca took on 15 per cent of the financial investment (and, therefore, financial risk) of a Social Impact Bond, the services for which it will help deliver. In both these cases, investors and providers perceive a correlation between taking on more financial risk and a higher likelihood of delivering a social return.

All parties in a social investment deal face reputational risk and this increases with the media and community attention the social investment receives. The more reputational risk involved, the greater the incentive to deliver the social return. For a service provider, being involved in an outcomes-based contract in a social finance mechanism mandates unprecedented measurement and publication of results. As a consequence, they face the possibility of being 'proved' ineffective, which may be due in part to overestimating the effect that they can achieve with a new client group delivering a new programme with a new measurement regime. A government involved in a social investment may be held responsible for any number of ways a programme can be deemed a failure, including the way it is measured, managed, invested in, and observed in the community. A government that approaches the market with a request for social investment proposals takes on more reputational risk than one that agrees to a third-party proposal, as they are held more responsible for the outcomes of the programme. Investors face reputational risk should the programme fail to deliver to its service users or should social purpose organizations in it suffer as a consequence.

Organizational risk can take various forms but focuses on the leadership team, the organizational lifecycle, and other endogenous variables. Such risk is not related to social return. Key issues include whether the management team have experienced success delivering social returns in the past and can clearly demonstrate their capacity to understand and tackle the challenges of achieving the expected social outcomes. In terms of organizational lifecycle stage, start-ups are typically assessed as riskier than well-established organizations. Moreover, larger organizations may be assessed as less risky than smaller ones, particularly if the social investment funds only part of a wider and diverse portfolio of social value creation activities. Yet, in an emergent market, the social return of supporting new or smaller organizations can be significant.

Table 10.2. Social risk–social return correlations

Risk factor	Positive relationship	Negative relationship	Uncorrelated
Probability			Evidence base risk
			Population risk
Variance	Financial structure risk		Organizational risk
	Reputational risk		
Uncertainty		Contextual risk	
		Responsiveness risk	

Uncertainty Risk

Social uncertainty risk captures both exogenous (contextual/sectoral) and endogenous (responsiveness/organizational) factors. Contextual social risk is negatively correlated to social return. As has already been noted contextual risk corresponds to the multiple variables often summarized in the PESTLE acronym.[29] The greater the risk of change to the context in which the social return is delivered, the lower the social return that can be delivered. If the context of a programme changes, then there may be less incentive and capacity for continuous improvement, as lessons learnt under previous contexts may become unsuitable for application.

Responsiveness risk is also negatively correlated to social return. This form of risk represents the likelihood that the performance manager is either unable to collect performance data or to respond effectively to it. Inability to respond to information reduces capacity to deliver social return. For example, if a programme collects information that shows which components of its intervention are related to positive outcomes, it can optimize the delivery of these components to increase social return.[30] Likewise, if there are contracts or staff whose results are less than optimal, it is desirable that action be taken to change or terminate the contract before the impact becomes detrimental.

In summary, unlike in mainstream finance, the relationship between social return and different factors of social risk is not always a positive linear correlation but displays a much more complex set of relationships driven by distinctive variables. Table 10.2 summarizes the relationships between social risk and social return across the three main categories of risk set out in this section.

MEASURING AND MODELLING SOCIAL RISK AND RETURN

Following the example of the development of conventional capital markets, the expansion of the social finance market is likely to be reliant on the

---

[29] These are political, economic, social, technological, legal, environmental factors.

[30] Performance may be improved without data, albeit not so easily: for example, by operational changes such as filling vacant posts or hiring better qualified staff.

development of large and reliable performance data sets and related modelling by which its products can be analysed. An important component of this will be data and analysis that can quantify the risk and return variables specific to this market. In principle, investors in social finance could calculate the *financial* risk of their capital allocation using the methods and models by which conventional financial risk is usually quantified (with the caveats noted above). Indeed, this has been a normative feature of impact investing. However, this modelling is still hampered by a lack of credible and consistent historical data concerning financial performance of social finance investments. Social risk calculations suffer a similar shortage of data but, additionally, the methods and models by which this data can be collected and analysed have also yet to be standardized (Weisbrod, 2004, 2011; Foster and Bradach, 2005; Nicholls, 2009). Therefore, there are three related challenges in terms of building reliable (social) risk rates for social finance: developing appropriate metrics; building towards standardization across measurement systems; aggregating large and consistent data sets that are publicly available and transparent. In each case the first task is to account for social returns, before risk rates can even be calculated.

There are already a large number of social return metrics in use across the social sector (Ebrahim and Rangan, 2010; Mulgan, 2010). Many of these draw upon the established logics of public welfare economics. Input data include quantitative calculations of social return often monetized to allow for cost–benefit analyses as well as qualitative accounts of individual or group outcomes in the form of interviews or case studies within what has become known as 'social accounting'. Data collection methodologies vary from simple questionnaires or participant interviews to more complex models such at the social return on investment (SROI) approach (Nicholls, 2004). The latter uses a series of participative principles to support a stakeholder-driven model to, first, identify relevant social outcomes, second, establish measures of change, third, use financial proxies to monetize the returns and, fourth, compare return against input costs to develop a 'ratio' of social return. If the SROI calculation is predictive then the returns will also be discounted consistent with the conventional net present value approach. More sophisticated still are experimental methods that use revealed or expressed preference models to monetize the value of specific social outcomes to target populations. In some cases, randomized control trials may be used to attribute social return to a particular intervention.

In terms of quantifying social risk, effective metrics would include assessments of the overall risk of programme failure, incorporating risks associated with the evidence base and population. Risks associated with the organization, including its management, financial contributions, and reputation of all parties should also be considered. As noted above, it is also possible that measures of social performance risk could be developed that reflect the levels of uncertainty related to changing context and the ability of the programme to respond to those changes. In addition to understanding how these risks affect the likelihood of achieving a social return at the outset, investors would benefit from a longitudinal analysis of social risk that goes beyond a simple projection of the current state.

Partly as a consequence of the growing number of competing social return performance metrics in social finance, there remains a lack of agreed standards across the whole market. Such a lack of standardization creates a serious barrier to an investor's ability to compare social investment opportunities. Information on social outcomes is typically reported in a diverse and inconsistent manner across organizations and nations. Government regulation around social outcomes may encourage and standardize measurement, data sharing, and social value calculations on a wider scale. Successful standardization may, however, arise best from the continuing development of disparate methods that lead to an emergence of best practice through consistent adoption by those who measure social return (Ruff, 2012). An environment in which demonstrations of social return are valued can encourage the quality and strength of standards to improve. For example, the Social Value Act passed by the UK Government in 2012 encourages government officials to consider social value when commissioning a service. As more social purpose organizations develop the means to demonstrate the social value they are creating and more government officials develops the capacity to interpret this information, a conversation about standards can be had in a meaningful way. One aspect of this would be to establish benchmarks of performance by sector or type of organization. Within impact investing the IRIS typology and the related GIIRS standards are attempting to provide standardized data and benchmarks of performance at the organization and portfolio levels (Freireich and Fulton, 2009; O'Donohoe et al. 2010). A further possibility is that standardization may come in terms of frameworks rather than methods—for example the outcomes matrix[31] devised by Big Society Capital frames social impact measurement by a range of social welfare sectors ('housing and local facilities', 'employment, training, and education' etc.) and level of analysis ('individuals' and 'community, sector, and society') but is not prescriptive about the metrics used. Similarly, the underlying principles of SROI concerning stakeholder participation and materiality could provide a common framework (that can be audited or assured) for many different methods.

Finally, there are two opportunities in terms of developing useful social outcome data sets. First, existing data sets could be interrogated specifically to provide useful information. Second, new data sets need to be created that respond to the demand for social outcome information from investors and other key actors. In both cases such data would ideally be publicly available, free, and transparent. This would encourage the largest number of data analysts to enter the market and build relevant data subsets to address specific investor demand.

---

[31] See <http://www.bigsocietycapital.com/outcomes-matrix>.

With respect to existing data sets, the Government of the USA is looking to build its social investment market by making the data it currently collects on social purpose organizations more widely available. It has been suggested that should this data be made open source it could create an entirely new sector just as the Reagan administration's decision to make government meteorological data freely available created the weather forecasting industry (Patton, 2013). The Australian Government is also embarking on a process to make the data of its charities and other not-for-profits more accessible (Tomkinson, 2012b). Another example of this is the Open Data Strategy proposed by the UK Government in 2012. The release of specific administrative data to the public will be coupled with data on the social outcomes of government programmes more generally. Such open data initiatives also have the potential to correct the publication bias of social programmes. Organizations that purchase and deliver social programmes are understandably reluctant to publish information about programmes that do not achieve their expected social outcomes, yet this information is vital to allow the market to calibrate risk accurately.

Moving towards a robust ecosystem of data capturing social return is the first step towards quantifying social risk. However, even this is problematic in practice. Measuring and reporting social outcomes in a robust manner that can be interpreted by an investor requires expertise and resourcing that is beyond many small organizations. However, as the number and size of government and investor pools of funding that require evidence of social outcomes increase, more organizations are developing the skills to produce and report evidence. The rapid growth of the Social Impact Bond (SIB) market globally will also have a positive effect. SIB contracts are predicated on robust data collection that directly links social outcomes for beneficiaries with financial outcomes for investors. It is reasonable to expect that SIBs will provide benchmark methods and data sets for a range of social welfare interventions that can be used elsewhere—indeed, this may be the SIB's most important contribution to social finance (Social Finance, 2009; Nicholls and Tomkinson, 2013). Additionally, there is a growing number of specialist social accounting professionals emerging, although their costs may still prohibit the widespread use of their skills by many social enterprises.

Moreover, other professions that will be key to developing large data sets for the social finance market will include financial advisors, pension fund managers, accountants, and data custodians. Financial advisors and pension fund managers are essential for widening the investor pool and playing an educational role for potential social investors. Accountants and data custodians control many of the structures that collect data essential for the analysis of new investment products. In most public service and social purpose organizations, financial and (social) performance data is collected according to cost centres, so that managers can easily keep track of their expenses and activities. This does not, however, allow organizations to assess their expenditure or performance relating to one individual or group of people. For example, the ability to assess a social outcome in terms of the success of spending more on preventative services in order to reduce spending on acute care is very difficult in most government accounting systems. Furthermore, identifying the average length of time a service is delivered to an individual is often beyond the ability of data collection system related to social services. To enable the calculation of social risk and return, the manner in which data is produced needs to change significantly.

Finally, an important caveat around the development of data sets is that there is a danger of hampering the growth of a social finance market by requiring a level of information that exceeds that of other markets and potentially discourages innovation (Patton, 2013). Prescribing data and reporting requirements too early may not be the most efficient way of developing a standardized system. Good quality data that clearly demonstrate the case for a social finance investment may be sufficient for a decision to be made. The assumption that information must be comparable in order to be useful is one of efficiency, but perhaps not always a necessity. Questions to a social investor about their passions and preferences may be as valuable as information about the investments that they are considering. Whilst it remains difficult to quantify and compare social outcomes, it may be more straightforward to discover which ones represent greater value to a given social investor (see Hill, 2011). In this sense, reliable and usable social outcomes data may be more important than standardized or complete data.

Conclusions

This chapter has explored social risk as a distinct feature of social finance investment that has been poorly conceptualized to date. It has suggested that better understanding social risk represents one of the key opportunities not only to grow the flows of capital into social finance, but also to increase the outcomes that result from the capital allocated. Hill (2011) suggested that the owners of capital often perceive the level of risk involved in social finance to be too high, relative to the prospective blended social and financial returns. It is proposed here that this is, at least partly, because social risk and return calculations need further refinement and that this is symptomatic of a young market. A further attraction of more precision around social risk would be to avoid the sort of financial risk dumping that is now widely recognized as having been a major disadvantage in many private finance initiatives or public–private partnerships over the past twenty years. In many cases the eventual costs of these projects did not reflect the risks at all. As the market matures, a sharper understanding of how social dimensions of risk and return inform understanding of financial performance may emerge.

This chapter initially considered financial risk and return in the context of social finance and then went on to focus specifically on a detailed analysis of social risk. This is the first time that such an analysis has been carried out. The specific features of social risk were set out and the correlation between social risk and social return modelled. The chapter also addressed questions concerning the measurement of social risk.

At present the social finance market has barely begun to conceptualize, let alone calculate or report on, social risk in a coordinated fashion. Yet, the opportunities presented by such a process are considerable. Accurate calculations of social risk could provide a useful discount rate for assessing the comparative or absolute value of future social outcomes. Such net present *social* value (NPSV) could mirror the well-established discounting of future cash flows used in net present value assessments of capital allocation decisions in mainstream finance, but would calibrate the discount (risk–return) rate rather differently. For example, it is often the case that early and large programmes in welfare can produce better outcomes over time compared with consistent spending over several time periods. This means that the blended value creation resulting from upfront spending today may be much higher than that achieved by spending the same amount over time. A NPSV discount rate could be developed to capture this.[32] Alternatively, the future blended value of outcomes may be seen as higher than present outcomes if the perspective of subsequent generations is taken into account—for example in the case of programmes to address climate change.

Such approaches would also allow new *social* portfolio theory to emerge that reflects mainstream portfolio analyses but factors in some key differences between the outcomes of social finance and mainstream capital allocation. This new portfolio theory would be of great utility in guiding social finance allocation decisions across the multiple markets of social finance, both in terms of individual portfolios at the owner of capital level and in terms of structuring deals that blend multiple risk and return profiles—both financial and social—across owners of capital. Thus, impact first and finance first investors could structure optimum deals together to blend differential social and financial risk and return preferences, as could foundations and governments. Such combinations of risk and return profiles can be seen as a form of *social* weight adjusted cost of capital (WACC) in which the overall calculation of blended value returns is a composite of multiple preferences and perspectives across several owners of capital.[33]

Whilst social finance remains at a very early stage of institutionalization globally, a strategic emphasis on building reliable, transparent, and usable datasets covering all aspects of investment risk and return must be a priority to

---

[32] It should be recognized that net present social value may be subjective, i.e. NPSV will differ depending on the perspective from which it is calculated—social value calculated as positive from some investor perspectives will be negative from others. This will never be the case in calculations of financial return.

[33] It is interesting to note that one reason for the growing appeal of social finance to mainstream investors could be its low correlation with other asset classes. This low *social beta* is a consequence of the more diverse funding and income streams evident in organizations supported by social finance that makes them more resilient in times of market downturn.

drive the market forward. Without this the market will never go to scale and provide the much-needed capital with which to address the world's most challenging social and environment issues. A clear focus on social risk will not only drive more effective social finance capital allocation but will also serve as a constant reminder that the main purpose of social finance is not to make money but to bring about maximum social change.

■ **REFERENCES**

Barby, C., and Gan, J. (2014). *Shifting the Lens: A De-risking Toolkit for Impact Investment*. London: Bridges Impact+.
Bishop, M., and Green, M. (2010). 'The Capital Curve for a Better World', *Innovations*, 5(1): 25–33.
Brealey, R. A., and Myers, S. C. (2010). *Principles of Corporate Finance—Global Edition*, 10th edition. New York: McGraw-Hill Higher Education Edition
Brown, A., and Norman, W. (2011). *Lighting the Touchpaper: Growing the Market for Social Investment in England*. London: Boston Consulting Group/Young Foundation, London.
Brown, A., and Swersky, A. (2012). *The First Billion; A Forecast of Social Investment Demand*. London: Boston Consulting Group/Big Society Capital.
BSC—Big Society Capital (2012). *What Is Social Investment?* <http://www.bigsocietycapital.com/what-social-investment>, accessed 20 January 2013.
Cabinet Office (2011). *Growing the Social Investment Market: A Vision and Strategy*. London: Cabinet Office.
Crouch, C. (2012). *The Strange Non-Death of Neo-Liberalism*. London: Polity Press.
Ebrahim, A., and Rangan, V. (2010). 'The Limits of Nonprofit Impact: A Contingency Framework for Measuring Social Performance'. Harvard Business School General Management Unit Working Paper No. 10-099.
Emerson, J. (2003). 'The Blended Value Proposition: Integrating Social and Financial Returns', *California Management Review*, 45(4): 35–51.
Emerson, J. (2012). 'Risk, Return and Impact: Understanding Diversification and Performance Within an Impact Investing Portfolio'. Issue Brief 2, Impact Assets, New York.
Emerson, J., and Spitzer, J. (2007). *From Fragmentation to Functionality: Critical Concepts and Writings on Social Capital Market Structure, Operation, and Innovation*. Oxford: Skoll Centre for Social Entrepreneurship.
Fiegenbaum, A., and Thomas, H. (1988). 'Attitudes Toward Risk and the Risk-Return Paradox: Prospect Theory Explanations', *Academy of Management Journal*, 31(1): 85–106.
Foster, W., and Bradach, J. (2005). 'Should Nonprofits Seek Profits?' *Harvard Business Review*, 83 (February): 92–100.
Freireich, J., and Fulton, K. (2009). *Investing for Social and Environmental Impact: a Design for Catalyzing an Emerging Industry*. New York: Monitor Group.
Gore, A., and Blood, D. (2011). 'A Manifesto for Sustainable Capitalism', *Wall Street Journal*, 14th December. <http://www.wsj.com/articles/SB10001424052970203434040-4577092682864215896>, accessed 20 January 2013.

Hartzell, J. (2007). *Creating an Ethical Stock Exchange*. London: Skoll Centre for Social Entrepreneurship.

Hill, K. (2011). *Investor Perspectives on Social Enterprise Financing*. London: City of London/Big Lottery Fund/ClearlySo, London.

Hornsby, A., and Blumberg, G. (2013). *The Good Investor*. London: Investing for Good.

John, R. (2006). *Venture Philanthropy: The Evolution of High Engagement Philanthropy in Europe*. Oxford: Skoll Centre for Social Entrepreneurship.

Joy, I., de Las Casas, L., and Rickey, B. (2011). *Understanding the Demand for and Supply of Social Finance: Research to Inform the Big Society Bank*. London: New Philanthropy Capital/NESTA.

Knight, F. (1921). *Risk, Uncertainty, and Profit*. London: Dover Publications.

Laing, N., Long, C., Marcandalli, A., Matthews, J., Grahovac, A., Featherby, J. (2012). *The U.K. Social Investment Market: The Current Landscape and a Framework for Investor Decision Making*. Cambridge: Cambridge Associates Limited.

Mulgan, G. (2010). 'Measuring Social Value', *Stanford Social Innovation Review*, Summer, pp. 38–43.

Nicholls, J. (2004). *Social Return on Investment: Valuing What Matters*. London: New Economics Foundation, London.

Nicholls, A. (2009). '"We Do Good Things Don't We?" Blended Value Accounting in Social Entrepreneurship', *Accounting, Organizations and Society*, 34(6–7): 755–69.

Nicholls, A. (2010a). 'The Institutionalization of Social Investment: The Interplay of Investment Logics and Investor Rationalities', *Journal of Social Entrepreneurship*, 1(1): 70–100.

Nicholls, A. (2010b). *The Landscape of Social Finance in the UK*. Birmingham: Third Sector Research Centre, University of Birmingham.

Nicholls, A. (2013). 'Filling the Capital Gap: Institutionalizing Social Finance', in S. Denny and F. Seddon (eds), *Evaluating Social Enterprise*. London: Palgrave Macmillan.

Nicholls, A. and Pharoah, C. (2007). *The Landscape of Social Finance*. Oxford: Skoll Centre for Social Entrepreneurship.

Nicholls, A., and Schwartz, R. (2013). 'The Demandside of the Social Investment Marketplace', in L. Salamon (ed.), *New Frontiers of Philanthropy*. San Francisco, CA: Jossey Bass.

Nicholls, A., and Tomkinson, E. (2013). *The Peterborough Pilot Social Impact Bond*. Pears Case Study Series, Said Business School, University of Oxford.

O'Donohoe, N., Leijonhufvud, C., and Saltuk, Y. (2010). Impact Investments: An Emerging Asset Class. New York: J.P. Morgan and Rockefeller Foundation.

O'Loughlin, J. and Thamotheram, R. (2006). *Enhanced Analytics for a New Generation of Investor: How the Investment Industry Can Use Extra-Financial Factors in Investing*. London: Universities Superannuation Scheme.

Patton, A. (2013). The Social Investment Market: The Role of Public Policy in Innovation and Execution. Said Business School and Cabinet Office.

Perry, J. (2011). *The End of Charity—And Beginning of Welfare*. London: Panahpur.

Puttick, R., and Ludlow, J. (2012). *Standards of Evidence for Impact Investing*. London: NESTA.

Ross, A. (2013). 'Social Entrepreneurs Fund'. Presentation at Said Business School, Oxford, 30 April, Bridges Ventures.

Ruff, K. (2012). 'Developing a New Profession'. Presentation at the Social Impact Analysts Association Annual Conference, Berlin.

Salamon, L. (ed.) (2013). *New Frontiers of Philanthropy*. New York: Jossey Bass.

Saltuk, Y. (2012). *A Portfolio Approach to Impact Investment*. London: J.P. Morgan Global Research.

Saltuk, Y., Bouri, A., and Leung, G. (2011). *Insight into the Impact Investment Market*. London: J.P. Morgan Social Finance Research.

Shanmugalingam, C., Graham, J., Tucker, S., and Mulgan, G. (2011). *Growing Social Ventures*. London: NESTA/Young Foundation.

Social Finance (2009). *Social Impact Bonds: Rethinking Finance for Social Outcomes*. London: Social Finance.

Tomkinson, E. (2012a). *Social Impact Bonds: An Australian Snapshot*. Sydney: Centre for Social Impact.

Tomkinson, E. (2012b). *In Conversation with Susan Pascoe*. Sydney: Centre for Social Impact.

Weisbrod, B. (2004). 'The Pitfalls of Profits', *Stanford Social Innovation Review*, 2(3): 40–52.

Weisbrod, B. (2011). 'The Nonprofit Mission and Its Financing', *Journal of Policy Analysis and Management*, 17(2): 165–74.

11 Projection, valuation, and pricing in social finance

Alex Nicholls and Aunnie Patton

Introduction

Perhaps the most obvious challenge to growing the social finance market lies in the lack of consistent *blended* valuations and pricing that allow owners of capital to make comparative allocation judgements in this nascent market (Emerson, 2003; Nicholls, 2010; Nicholls, 2013; Nicholls and Schwartz, 2013). It is well understood that in order to function efficiently, capital markets require high levels of accurate, transparent, comparable, and relevant data to price allocation options efficiently and reduce transaction costs. Over many years, accounting standards have developed to support capital allocation decisions in mainstream finance, but in social finance the process of institutionalizing standards around blended performance data is still at an early stage (Nicholls, 2009). The consequence of this is a market characterized by high transaction costs, poor liquidity (and resultant difficulties with exit), and—often—capriciousness rather than rationality on the part of owners of capital (Weisbrod, 2004, 2011; Foster and Bradach, 2005). The main issue is not, however, a *lack* of blended performance metrics—there are many examples of this—but an absence of standardized processes for valuation and pricing across the whole market combined with limited mechanisms for verification and audit.[1]

This chapter aims to extend the current debates over social impact measurement beyond somewhat monological and solipsistic arguments concerning the best methods to capture absolute performance by exploring how investors value projections of the impact of social finance and how they can be priced in markets. Social impact valuation and pricing involves complex issues concerning the nature of performance information and the function of data collection models contextualized by investor preferences. To capture some of this complexity, this chapter develops a new, three-stage, model of the social

---

[1] The closest to an emergent standard globally is the social return on investment (SROI) model that has had significant policy support in the UK and beyond for several years, but whilst this has proved useful as an internal performance management and accountability tool it has yet to function as a market-making data set (Nicholls, 2004). Furthermore, SROI remains an absolute measure of monetized blended outcomes framed in a cost-benefit model. The more sophisticated data sets typical of mainstream capital allocation are unlikely to be driven by such a mechanism.

finance capital allocation process focusing on: social impact performance projections; the valuation of performance data at the organizational level; market pricing of investment options in the focal organization. The projection-valuation-pricing (PVP) model used here is built upon a critical examination of the utility of conventional projection, valuation, and pricing mechanisms found in mainstream finance when applied to social finance. The analysis below demonstrates both the utility and limitations of transferring existing models across these two markets. The main questions addressed here are:

- How can social value flows (SVFs)[2] be calculated to offer investors usable capital allocation information?
- How do different social investors value such SVFs?
- How are such valuations priced in the social finance marketplace?

This chapter aims to make several new contributions. First, it presents a unique analysis of the valuation and pricing process when applied to social finance. Second, it offers a framework that connects organizational level quantification of performance with investor preference valuation and market pricing that aims to be of significant practical value to each of the main groups of actors in the social finance market: investors, intermediaries, and investees. The chapter also develops new theory around market development, pricing, and reporting that aims to move the scholarly discussion forward with respect not only to social finance but also to mainstream finance more generally (see Nicholls, 2009).

The chapter is structured as follows. First, it develops its core framework of analysis that links social impact performance to investor valuation and market pricing drawn from mainstream finance. After this, each stage of the framework is considered in turn with respect to its utility and appropriateness to the distinctive features of social finance. Conclusions summarize the validity and limitations of the PVP framework as an analytic model to help accelerate the growth of the social finance market.

Projection-valuation-pricing (PVP) model

The PVP model aims to provide a three-stage framework of the analytic process that links performance measurement to market pricing in social

---

[2] Whilst acknowledging that an enterprise's *blended value* typically comprises its financial, social, and environmental value creation (or destruction), this chapter focuses on the integration of social value alone into the investment process. The pricing of, and accounting for, environmental impact is better developed than is the case for social impact (see, for example, carbon markets) and, therefore, this research contribution of this chapter is to focus on valuing and pricing social impact. For a detailed discussion of environmental impact in social finance see Harold et al. elsewhere in this book.

finance.[3] In mainstream finance, the capital allocation process typically omits social impact from its calculations and decision-making at each of these stages. For mainstream performance projections, this means using only single bottom-line projections that view financial results as the total sum of the value created by an investment. In terms of conventional investor valuations, risk and return calculations do not usually include an investment's potential positive or negative social impact or externalities. Finally, due to the absence of social impact from projection and valuation calculations, financial instruments in the market do not price the comprehensive risk and return of an investment. Thus, both in the allocation and management of capital, mainstream investors base their capital allocation decisions on calculations that are incomplete and fail to measure both the full upside (return) and the total downside (risk) of an investment.

The PVP model set out here aims to offer a process by which to correct the conventional mispricing of value creation at the organizational level. Although the focus here is on social purpose organizations within social finance, it is clearly the case that—post the global financial crisis of 2008—a more holistic approach to pricing value creation risk and return in all capital allocation decisions is widely needed. Each stage of the PVP model encapsulates a range of data points and decision-making frameworks and heuristics (see Figure 11.1).

The basis of the model draws its inspiration from mainstream finance. Each set of issues is then considered in the context of social finance. In conventional finance, in terms of projections, key issues include macro-level, exogenous factors such as macroeconomic conditions, competitors' forecasts, and industry/sector future performance, as well as micro-level/organizational, endogenous issues such as past (financial) performance, management projections, and funders' expectations. In terms of valuation, it is important to take into account projected cash flows, peer valuations, the views of current/existing shareholders/owners, projected exit multiples and the potential size of investment. Finally, pricing may be driven by control preferences, overall cost of capital calculations, risk–return expectations, and any covenants that may be

Figure 11.1. The projection-valuation-pricing model

[3] The PVP model is presented conceptually as a linear model, but, in practice, the process it illustrates will typically be more iterative and organic based on many assumptions and judgements across multiple data points.

required in term sheets. The next three sections elaborate each stage of the model in more detail.

Although the level of sophistication and detail of analysis varies based on the stage of the development of a given company and the availability of data, financial performance projections are an exercise in the amalgamation of macroeconomic, political, industry-, and company-specific forecasts and assumptions. Moreover, in evaluating such projections, funders add their own set of assumptions around growth, performance, and costs. It is, perhaps, interesting to note the prevalence of assumptions and individual judgement in the financial projection process making it rather less *objective* than is typically thought. The fact that assumptions and judgement are also required in calculating social impact projections needs to be seen in this context.

Performance projections

In mainstream finance the process of estimating future value creation has three components: defining the drivers of value; estimating the expected growth rates of these drivers; and calculating the costs associated with funding this growth (see Table 11.1).

However, when this approach is applied to projecting social impact perform-ance (or blended value performance) a range of additional factors need to be taken into account: conversion (how outcomes are represented); causality (how outcomes are attributed); integration (the blending of financial and social value flows); motivation (the incentives to take on the additional cost and complexity of social impact projection).

CONVERSION

For financial projections, the translation of performance projections into capital terms relies on calculating the conversion rates of customers or users

Table 11.1. Projection calculations in mainstream finance

Drivers of value	Growth rates	Costs of growth
Quantity of products sold		*Variable costs:* e.g.
Product price		costs of goods sold, acquisition cost per user,
Number of users		server costs
		Fixed costs: e.g.
User conversion rate	Revenue growth, conversion	employee salaries
Subscription price	growth	Rent
Advertising revenue	Margin growth	General and administrative costs
Number of contracts		

at specific price points for products and services. In financial projections, the point of sale is likely to be both the output and outcome and is expressed in monetized terms via metrics that are easily comparable across potential investments. However, for social impact projections, not only are outcomes as well as outputs typically taken into account, but explicit cost models cannot generally be used to determine the outcome's relative value (including the scale and depth of impact) to key stakeholders. This additional level of complexity coupled with the current lack of standardization across social impact metrics and lack of agreement over optimal units of analysis (*pace* the trend for financial proxies for outcome impact). Such issues make even this first stage challenging in terms of analysis and decision-making. The significance of outcomes with respect to calculating social impact performance also requires the participation of key beneficiaries or clients in the measurement process—since they are typically best placed to judge the degree of change affected by a given social intervention. Ensuring effective beneficiary participation demands sensitivity in terms of data collection design and implementation and can add significant transaction costs to the projection process.

CAUSALITY

Determining causality in social impact projections requires a careful process of attribution in terms of the impact claimed by a specific intervention or project being measured. In mainstream finance, the determination of the value that accrues to shareholders/owners is a product of calculating an organization's free cash flows (FCF). This calculation begins with the earnings before interest and taxes (EBIT) reported on the income statement and is then adjusted for non-cash items (e.g. depreciation and amortization that appear as expenses on the income statement, but does not represent cash expenditures), as well as cash affects that are not included on the income statement (e.g. changes in working capital, capital expenditure, and other long-term items, including minority interests). In social finance, the calculation of an organization's social impact also needs to be adjusted but according to deadweight and attribution calculations that determine how much of the social impact can be attributed to the specific organization as opposed to social impact that would have happened anyway as a product of other organizations' actions or more macro-level economic and social changes.

Deadweight (the percentage of the value flows that would have been created without the project) and attribution (the percentage of the value flows that could be attributed to other providers)[4] are two aspects of projecting social

---

[4] Note that the adjustment of duration (the drop off in benefits in future years) is not included in this discussion as this refers to the expected behaviour of value flows in future years, not the reconciliation of flows in the current year.

impact that the SROI model has particularly identified to establish the causality of social finance and its outcomes (Olsen and Lingane, 2003). Importantly, these adjustments are not discount factors, but rather adjustments to allow the SROI analysis to be more accurate in its initial data collection phase. Deadweight and attribution adjustments also play a significant role in making the process of conducting an SROI analysis instructive in itself, as it requires careful judgements to be made in concert with key stakeholders over the materiality and relevance of claimed impacts.

In the mainstream, capital flows are usually available in the form of cash to funders or owners. For social impact, these flows are generally made available to beneficiaries or clients (see Nicholls, 2010, for a discussion of the bifurcation between social value creation and social value appropriation in social finance).

INTEGRATION

The final step in building a social impact projection to inform the allocation of social finance is blending the financial and social value flows—or the economic and socioeconomic values—of an organization's performance. This task is also challenging since the financial and social impact of an organization may be closely linked and difficult to analyse separately—creating the potential for double counting (Olsen and Lingane, 2003).

This tension between holding the social impact and financial value separate during the projection analysis and, yet, acknowledging them as often intertwined, goes to the very core of the discussion of valuing social impact. On the one hand, the separation of social and financial can work against the industry moving towards an accurate blended valuation of an enterprise, preventing investors from recognizing this social value in their investment analysis. Yet, if the valuation of social impact is not transparent and subject to question or interpretation, it is unlikely that investors will accord blended analyses the same credibility given (rightly or wrongly) to traditional financial valuation techniques.

A final issue in the blending of financial and social projections is timing. While financial value flows are reasonably expected within the years they are projected, social impact may occur years or decades after an investment has closed. There remains an urgent need for further work on setting standards for what can realistically be measured in a particular time frame. Such work may allow the setting of 'social' discount rates and 'social' net present value calculations that will allow proper comparisons of the true social impact created by projects over longer periods of time—encouraging front-ended social investment where early intervention has higher long-term social impact than drip-feeding funding over years.[5]

---

[5] This is the principle behind the emergence of the social impact bond model.

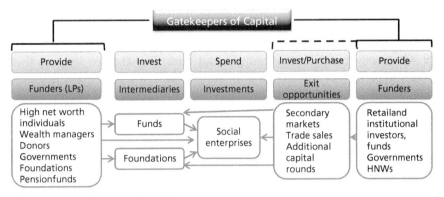

Figure 11.2. Gatekeepers of capital

GATEKEEPERS

Absent new government regulation, it will likely be the market demand for better and more standardized social impact data that will drive improved social impact metrics within integrated models of social valuation and pricing. The primary source of this demand will likely be the gatekeepers of capital that control the liquidity within social finance markets. As the field of social finance continues to develop, gatekeepers may increasingly demand accurate projections of their likely blended returns to establish both the financial and social impact of their capital. Qualitative presentations of social impact will not be sufficient to perform complex portfolio analysis. In addition, social enterprises may use such data to analyse prospective and current projects within their own organizations. Thus, whilst the extrinsic value of more accurate social impact data may push towards market stand-ardization in the short term (of value to gatekeepers), better performance data should be of significant value to investors and social enterprises too: creating a virtuous cycle, which will reinforce the use of social impact data projections as part of the valuation and pricing process.

However, just as financial projections do not accurately portray the full opportunities and potential of an investment, social impact projections will not offer the final word on the full social value of a social purpose organiza-tion. Rather, they will provide funders and enterprises with a mutually under-stood and standardized language and data set to underpin valuation calculations that can then be priced in the market.

Valuation

While many social investors have developed approaches to assessing the social impact of a potential investee, it is much less common to see such projections incorporated into their valuation calculations. The second stage of the PVP model considers how applicable current models of mainstream financial valuation are to social finance—namely the capital asset pricing model (CAPM), the cost of capital, and discount rates. This chapter proposes that social impact valuations have a distinct risk and return profile and that new models are actually needed to price this risk: in particular, it is suggested that there may be utility in adapting the private cost of capital model to create a cost of capital that incorporates both financial and social risk and return expectations based on individual investor preferences.

CAPITAL ASSET PRICING MODEL (CAPM)

The discount rate seeks to provide a net present value (NPV) of projected future value flows. For valuations, the discount rate is a proxy for both the riskiness of the asset and the return expected for assuming this risk. This rate can be calculated via the CAPM. The CAPM suggests that the expected return on an investment equals the risk-free rate of return (typically equated to the return on government bonds) plus the beta (or variance from the average market performance) of the investment multiplied by the expected market premium appropriate to a given sector, region, or size of organization (i.e. the expected market return—risk-free rate). This can be expressed as follows:

$$E(R_i) = R_f + \beta_i(E(R_m) - R_f)$$

The intuition behind this formula is that for any asset, investors expect a return that compensates for two factors: the time value of money (the risk-free rate); the risk of the individual asset.

In calculating the discount rate for social impact present values, there has been a tradition of setting a rate somewhere between zero (if the social finance is grant or grant-like) and the average rate of relevant municipal bonds. This approach has resulted in the value of social impact being typically more lightly discounted than the value of the financial impact of a social enterprise or social purpose organization that creates financial value. Thus, calculations of social impact value are not typically tied to the blended valuation of a social enterprise overall. Rather, they are a separate calculation of value that is created for beneficiaries or clients (Emerson, Wachowicz, and Chun, 2000; Emerson and Cabaj, 2000). Traditionally social discount rates are used to discount the benefits in future years to reflect the time value of money or the stakeholder's willingness to delay an outcome in a cost–benefit analysis (Zhuang, 2007). Though there is vigorous debate around the standards for social discount rates among development economists, there are guidelines for the public sector that include the UK government Treasury's Green Book's standard recommendation of

Table 11.2. Discount rates in social impact valuations

Discount rates		Discussion
0%	Cost of capital of philanthropic grants	Philanthropic grant capital is often cited as having a 0% cost of capital as donations do not require a return and grants do not provide any financial return.
3%	Rate carried by foundation program related investments (PRI)	PRIs are funds provided to charitable organizations or social business at a below-market rate of return. Foundations can 'use PRIs to leverage funds from ordinary investors who might otherwise be deterred by short-term market conditions, a lack of relevant data or experience, high transaction costs, or limited financial return.' (MacArthur Foundation)
9%	Average of standard, fully secured loan (in 2000)	The average interest rate of a loan that has assets worth as much as the loan that are pledged as collateral in case the borrower cannot pay (fully secured). This is the safest (least risky) type of personal loan.
15%	Rate charged by community development financing institutions (CDFI)	(CDFIs) lend money to businesses, social enterprises and individuals cannot access credit from high street banks and loan companies.
24%	Venture capital discount rate	The VC discount rate is discussed in Table 11.3.

Source: Emerson, Wachowicz, and Chun, 2000

3.5 per cent (2014). Other standards include 0 per cent in health and climate change, on the grounds that younger generations should not be disadvantaged relative to older ones (Freireich and Fulton, 2009) and '4% in drug criminal justice, and children and youth intervention policy areas' (Tuan, 2008). The range of discount rate options currently available for social impact value presents a further challenge to accurate or comparable valuations at the investor level (see Table 11.2). Moreover, though there is a long history of academic studies to determine these time preferences, this logic neglects the fact that stakeholders, like funders, face a menu of risk and return options (Chowdhury, 2012) in terms of a chosen enterprise delivering the outcomes promised. Thus, while stakeholder-specific discount rates certainly merit further research, the idea that a risk-free rate accurately represents the risk of social impact value creation needs to be seriously questioned.

As discussed above at the projection stage, despite the movements forward in the social impact measurement industry, there is still a great deal of uncertainty in the assumptions used to value and discount social impact. Thus, there is an underlying riskiness to such projections themselves and this riskiness can be priced into both the financial and social projections of a social purpose organization. In this context, venture capital (VC) discount rates for early-stage investment risk may be more appropriate for valuing social impact than rates used by foundations, community development organizations, or other social sector organizations.

Table 11.3. Venture capital discount rates

Type of finance	Discount rate	Cost of capital
Seed financing	Up to 80%	~10x
Series A (start-up) financing	50–70%	~8x to 5x
Series B financing	40–60%	~6.5x to 4x
Series C financing	30–50%	~5x to 3x
Series D to bridge financing	20–35%	~3x to 2x

VENTURE CAPITAL DISCOUNT RATES

The discount rate in a VC valuation represents the risk of the target achieving its financial projections (and, thus, its exit strategy) and the necessary annual return to achieve the target cash on cash multiple (CoC) for the funders. The CoC multiple is the amount of money returned to the funder upon exit of the investment divided by the amount of money invested. This number holds inherent portfolio risk as well—that is, venture capitalists do not just calculate the risk from the individual investment, but also the risk that others in the portfolio will not perform. A rough guide to VC return expectations is shown in Table 11.3.

However, O'Donohoe et al. (2010) reported that social investors expected lower rates of return than would be typical in similar VC investments: 15–20 per cent in developed markets and 12–15 per cent in developing markets. Notwithstanding the small number of data points that were available at the time of the report, this disparity between expected returns of VCs and expected returns of impact investors implies an inherent social discount. This is particularly striking since social impact valuations have several additional, distinctive risks above and beyond VC investments, including: impact risk, measurement and reporting risk, social enterprise/organizational risk, subordinate capital risk, and exit risk (Emerson, 2011). Additionally, the relevant investor set for social enterprises goes beyond just impact investors and VCs, as high-net-worth individuals, foundations, governments, and other social investors may also define the range of expected risks and return in this market. Therefore, whilst a VC approach to valuation offers some utility in terms of valuing social impact too, the calculation of relevant discount rates needs a different model.

PRIVATE COST OF CAPITAL MODEL (PCOC)

In mainstream finance, the weighted average cost of capital (WACC) model is used to determine the cost of capital for an enterprise. The WACC aims to combine the cost of capital of debt and equity within an individual organization's capital structure as a function of its overall riskiness. The WACC can be expressed as follows:

$$\left(\text{Pretax Cost of Debt} \times (1 - \text{Tax Rate}) \times \frac{\text{Debt}}{\text{Capitalization}} \right)$$

$$+ \text{Cost of Equity}^6 \times \left(\frac{\text{Equity}}{\text{Capitalization}} \right)$$

In mainstream finance, the WACC calculation relies on public securities data (beta, market premium, and small stock premium) to quantify the return expectations. The use of public market data for private return expectations creates the assumption that public and private markets are substitutes, an assumption that some scholars are beginning to question (Slee and Paglia, 2010). As a consequence, there has been an increased interest in generating more nuanced methods to calculate composite cost of capital rates.

One such approach is the Pepperdine private cost of capital (PCOC) model. This model is an example of a new approach to calculating the cost of capital that could be adapted for social impact valuation. The PCOC model rejects the notion that public and private market data are the same (Slee and Paglia, 2010). This rejection stems from the assertion that substitutability 'ignores market segmentation, investor return expectations, differences in access and cost of capital, and differences in how each market works, as well as distinctly different behaviour of players in each market segment who are guided by different market theories' (Slee and Paglia, 2010: 1). In order to capture the uniqueness of risk and return by market segment, the model undertook a survey that was the 'first comprehensive and simultaneous investigation of the behaviour of major private capital market segments, [examining] the behaviour of senior lenders, asset-based lenders, mezzanine funds, private equity groups, and venture capital firms' (p. 2). Using the result of this survey, the model proposed a cost of capital model that depended on the *private* cost of debt (PCOD) and the *private* cost of equity (PCOE), expressed as follows:[7]

$$\sum_{i=1}^{N} \left[(CAP_i + SCAP_i) x \frac{MV_i}{\sum_{i=1}^{N} MV_j} \right]$$

Focusing on the universe of investors who are reasonable candidates to provide funds to a particular investment rather than overall market data has the consequence that the cost of capital and expected return calculations can be more accurately calculated for a specific investment opportunity. A social

---

[6] Cost of Equity = Risk Free Rate + (Beta × Market Premium) + Small Stock Premium
[7] CAP_i = average expected return from survey for capital type i
   MV_i = specific capital risk adjustment for capital type i
   $SCAP_i$ = outstanding securities for capital type i.

impact valuation survey building on the work of the PCOC could be under-taken across the impact investing space to determine expected returns for both financial and social impact by type of investment or sector. The data collected could then be used to calculate a PCOC for the social impact value of an individual investment opportunity.

The social return methodology of the survey could go deeper than the current categories of impact first and finance first investment (O'Donohoe et al., 2010) and allow investors to create a cost of capital that specifically highlights their impact priorities. Such a survey would determine an average expected return for each type of investor and instrument, the specific capital adjustment would allow funders to determine the fit of the social impact value projected with the priorities of the fund, thus lowering the cost of capital and growing the capital pool for investments whose social impacts were projected to be greatest in areas the funder prioritizes. For this methodology to have both a stakeholder and impact area component will necessitate a grid-like approach, where funders rank their willingness to pay by both stakeholder and impact area.

Pricing

The final stage of the PVP model considers the pricing of social impact value. In mainstream finance, the price of a security will be set first by institutional intermediaries at the investment bank or fund level and, subsequently, by the supply and demand characteristics of secondary markets that are liquid and information rich. In social finance, the institutional landscape is much less well developed than in the mainstream and, as a result, approached to pricing social impact value are still emergent and, at times, capricious. This section outlines emergent practice across two sets of social investors and includes a note of the role of tranching risk and return pricing.

GOVERNMENTS AND FOUNDATIONS

Governments and foundations have established traditions of investing in social impact value creation. Both are typically judged on the delivery of their social outcomes and, as a consequence, have performance mechanisms and decision-making structures and protocols already in place to guide their social investments.

The pricing structure of some payment-by-results contracts, such as Social Impact Bonds (SIBs), offer examples of emerging government practice in this area. The approach to pricing SIBs and, thus, the pricing of social impact value to government can be characterized in two stages. First, a baseline or bench-mark is needed. This baseline should be how effective current spending is and how much the Government currently pays per unit of social/welfare outcome.

Unfortunately, in practice, an accurate portrayal of this baseline rarely exists, as metrics across programmes are not readily available and average outcomes are skewed by the survivor bias of successful programmes (Savell, 2012). Next, the premium over this baseline must be calculated and agreed across all the stakeholders in a SIB contract. In 2010, in the first SIB pilot scheme based at Peterborough Prison in the UK, for example, an intermediary—Social Finance UK—worked with the Ministry of Justice within the UK government to create metrics to demonstrate the social value *savings* created for the state by reducing recidivism rates. The contract was capitalized by private—mostly philanthropic—investors to provide upfront social finance for a partnership of social purpose organizations expert in reducing re-offending rates among ex-offenders. The social investors will receive financial returns in line with the social impact value of the project, which will range from 2.5 per cent to 13 per cent IRRs (Savell, 2012).[8] The SIB model is now being piloted in other projects in the UK and is also being developed in Australia, the USA, and Canada, with several other countries also showing considerable interest.

For foundations, a similar opportunity cost exists when looking at the benefits of a grant versus a social investment. For example, the Acumen Fund best alternative charitable option (BACO) method offers another approach to pricing social impact value. BACO evaluates the impact that a grant would have compared to that of an investment (Acumen Fund Metrics Team, 2007) and makes capital allocation decisions accordingly.

In both of these cases, the value of the social impact related to a baseline is a priority for the funders. For governments, some of this social impact value will result in reduced expenditure on purchased services such as foster care and, at scale, on block purchased services such as whole prisons (Savell, 2012). For foundations, it is the value of the social impact of an investment over and above that created through grants. In each case, the baseline, or the opportunity cost, is generally the amount that would have been spent anyway. This is significant because it implies that if governments and foundations are rational beings that choose the most efficient instruments for their money based on their priorities as investors, the argument for directing their capital towards social investments will grow as impact metrics evolve and the accuracy of baseline calculations are improved.

INSTITUTIONAL AND RETAIL INVESTORS

Currently, institutional investors are engaging with social finance either via bespoke funds—such as those created by Bridges Ventures—or via philanthropic or foundation mechanisms in terms of grants or programme/mission-related

---

[8] The pilot SIB employed a 'randomized control trial' approach to demonstrate its social impact on ex-offenders with a 1:10 ratio. This was designed to prove the social impact value beyond question—an expensive but necessary aspect of a pilot under considerable international scrutiny.

investment at the corpus level. The landscape of funds for institutional social investment is limited but expanding—one notable catalyst for this is the Big Society Capital (BSC) wholesale social investment bank established in the UK on 2012. BSC will mobilize up to £600m of capital—mostly from unclaimed assets in high street bank accounts—to leverage, via co-investment at the fund level, up to £2bn of new social finance capital. These funds typically price the 'extrinsic' social impact value of their potential investees as part of an overall financial analysis, typically in the form of a discount on the return expected from a particular risk profile investment. Alternatively, the social impact value is calculated as 'intrinsic' by means of secondary data on the particular investment's social performance—for example, Bridges Ventures's focus on investing in businesses in the most deprived areas of the UK relies on government data to determine the location of such opportunities, then assumes that the financial performance of such investments will move in lock-step with their social (largely economic/employment) local impact.

The opportunities for retail social investors are more limited, however, and represent a huge opportunity to expand and democratize social finance. To date, retail social investors have either used crowdfunding platforms—such as Kiva or Buzzbnk—to engage with this market or have had a small number of opportunities to engage in social equity share offers such as Ethical Property Company in the UK. In these cases, pricing social impact value has often been arbitrary and not subject to any market forces—the lack of liquidity, exit options, and transparent and comparable performance data have all contributed to this state of affairs.

As a result, the key next step in growing the retail market will be the creation of a public secondary market or social stock exchange that will price the social impact value of social equity and debt for retail (and, potentially, institutional) investors. For even if impact investors, government, and foundations standardize social valuation methods, the social finance market will not be mature until there is a capital market where prices can be set by supply and demand forces across multiple transactions. Several such projects are currently close to completion, notably the London Social Stock Exchange and Singapore-based Impact Investing Capital project.

TRANCHING

In traditional finance, deals regularly include capital from various funders in the form of instruments with different risk, return, and price profiles. Thus, a private equity investment might include a shareholder loan from the private equity firm, senior debt instruments from multiple major banks, and a mezzanine loan from another fund. Each of these instruments will be priced according to the overall riskiness of the investment, the risk associated with the level of subordination of the instrument, and the return required by the fund to be willing to take these compound risks. In social finance syndication of equity/debt investments among similar social investors has been more common than tranching. However, the last few years have seen social finance begin to experiment with tranching, for example in the case of Hackney Community Transport in the UK. This deal and others suggest that there is considerable opportunity creatively to blend different risk and return preferences across social investors at the deal or portfolio level, including philanthropists, foundations, governments, impact-first, and finance-first investors. Ultimately, such blended deals may create deal options for mainstream finance too. One aspect of successful tranching will be the development of social finance appropriate term sheets specifying the details of particular social deals—this is considered next.

PRICING CASE STUDY CAFÉDIRECT

Just as the PVP model provides a theoretical framework for a systematic analysis of the integration of social value into the investment process, examples of investors' willingness to incorporate social premiums or subsidies into transactions provide data points through which to assess how this willingness to pay for social returns is priced in the market.

The alternative public offering (APO) of Cafédirect PLC is one such example that offers a real-world case study through which to explore early market responses to social returns.[9]

In 1991, Oxfam, Traidcraft, Equal Exchange, and Twin Trading founded Cafédirect in response to a rapid decrease in global coffee prices, which was severely impacting small farmers worldwide. In addition to paying Fair Trade prices to farmers, a core component of Cafédirect's social impact is its Producer Support and Development (PS&D) (later called Producer Partnership Programmes (PPP)), which provides training and education for its producers.

Following turnover of £13.6m in 2003, the company launched a public share offering with a target of £5m. The investment firm Brewin Dolphin managed the raise, which was completed in less than four months. The raise was oversubscribed with a final count of 4,500 investors, 90 per cent of which were private investors.

In the prospectus, the stated uses of the funds included: brand building; repayment of borrowings; expansion of working capital; investment in computer systems; and to cover the expenses of raise.

The final capital table post-raise:

Shareholder	Shares	% Ownership
Founders	3,520,000	39.3%
Investors	5,000,000	55.8%
Growers	440,000	4.9%
Total	8,960,000	100.0%

In order to estimate whether a 'social premium' was paid for this investment and how that social premium was priced, two critical assumptions must be made. First, that the £1 per share price reflected the market's true judgement of the value of the company.[10] Second, that investors were

---

[9] In order to complete this analysis, a level of investor sophistication and access to information has been assumed that may not reflect the realities of the raise.

[10] That the raise was oversubscribed underpins both of these assumptions, but the authors acknowledge that the novelty of the issue may also have influenced investors to participate with little regard to price or value.

in possession of the information required to calculate the total value of the company and that they were also in a position to incorporate this information into their valuation of the shares.[11]

Building on these assumptions, the first step is to establish the *existence* of a social premium. Using the equation below, a social premium exists if the price paid per share by investors exceeds the estimated market value per share:

$$Price\ Paid\ per\ Share - Market\ Value\ per\ Share = Social\ Premium$$

First, to look at the price paid by investors. The shares were issued at £1 each (£5m raise for 5,000,000 shares), this implies a market capitalization of £9m (see table above). In order to compare this price per share to comparable share prices in the market, the price/earnings ratio must be calculated. A P/E ratio is a common representation of value in the financial marketplace and allows the relative prices of shares to be compared by dividing the price of a share by the net income per share of a company. Using the relevant information from Cafédirect, the implied P/E ratio is calculated below:

$$\frac{Implied\ Market\ Capitalization}{2003\ Net\ Income} = \frac{Share\ Price}{Earnings\ Per\ Share} = \frac{P}{E}\ Ratio$$

$$\frac{£8,960,000}{£369,045} = \frac{££1.00}{£0.04} = 24.3x = \frac{P}{E}ratio$$

Next, market value per share is estimated using traditional pricing calculations including historical and projected performance of Cafédirect and publicly traded comparables and liquidity considerations.

Below is a competitor chart of 2003 data from two sources: an index of five direct coffee competitors;[12] and an index comprised of data from thirty-five global coffee distributors.

	Top 5 Competitor Index	Global Competitor Index	Cafédirect
P/E (as of 2/1/2004)	19.6x	18.9x	24.3x
Difference	4.7x	5.4x	

It is evident that Cafédirect's P/E ratio is higher than both indices, suggesting a higher 'market' valuation relative to competitors. To determine if this valuation is appropriate, the other historical financial metrics must be examined:

Term	Discussion	Verdict
Gross margin	While the company outperformed the overall index, it underperforms the five selected competitors.	Neutral
Revenue growth	Cleary, the company outperforms both sets of competitors in one-year revenue growth.	Outperform
Net income margin	The company significantly underperforms both sets of competitors on net income margin.	Underperform

[11] One financial consideration not calculated in this analysis is EIS relief. EIS qualification varies by investor and could potentially apply to only a portion of the amount invested.
[12] Index includes Nestle, Tata Coffee, Farmer Brothers, Green Mountain Coffee Roasters, and Ten Peaks Coffee Company.

	Top 5 Competitor Index	Global Competitor Index	Cafédirect
Gross Margin	52.3%	34.5%	37.2%
Revenue Growth	(0.6%)	6.9%	31.8%
NetIncome Margin	12.5%	6.4%	2.7%

Examining these financial metrics based on historical performance provide mixed views on the relative value of Cafédirect shares versus competitors and do not substantiate the premium paid above competitor valuations. One remaining traditional explanation would be expected growth.

In the financial markets, valuations at IPO are comprised of both past performance and expected growth. In Cafédirect's case, the relative overvaluation could imply higher growth projections than its competitors. Indeed, in the prospectus, the company has illustrative revenue growth projections averaging 20 per cent annually for 2003–7, which exceeds growth projections for competitors. Importantly, this projection also exceeds Cafédirect's annual revenue growth from the prior four years and, as the company is not traded on a traditional market, there are no independent equity analysts to evaluate these projections. Thus, from the earnings side, while a portion of the premium paid for Cafédirect may have been due to expected growth, it is improbable that these expectations comprise the entire premium paid on 2003 net income (4.7x versus the top five competitor index or 5.4x versus the global competitor index).

In addition to this earnings premium, there is a liquidity premium to consider. In comparing Cafédirect shares to shares of publicly traded comparable companies, a similar liquidity to public markets is assumed, that is, investors in public markets can access their capital invested at any time by selling shares on the open market. Although Cafédirect shares can be traded through a matching system, this does not guarantee liquidity, particularly for large shareholders. Thus, it would be expected that investors would demand a liquidity premium to compensate for this additional risk. Using a conservative 15 per cent liquidity discount,[13] the multiples can be adjusted as shown below:

$$\frac{Price}{Earnings} - \left(\frac{Price}{Earnings} X\ Liquidity\ Discount\right) = Adjusted\ \frac{Price}{Earnings} Ratio$$

These adjusted ratios for the competitors can then be compared to the Cafédirect implied P/E ratio:

$$Cafédirect\frac{P}{E} - Competitor\frac{P}{E} = Difference\ in\ Multiples$$

	Top5 Competitor Index	Global Competitor Index	Cafédirect
P/E (as of 2/1/2004)	19.6x	18.9x	
Liquidity Discount	2.9x	2.8x	
P/E with Liquidity Discount	16.7x	16.0x	24.3x

---

[13] In *Liquidity as an Investment Style*, Roger Ibbotson quantified this 'illiquidity premium' from a study of 3,500 publicly traded U.S. stocks. From 1972 to 2011, micro-cap (low liquidity) stocks generated an average 15.36% annual return compared to a 2.24% annual return for growth (high liquidity) stocks.

With the liquidity discount included in the competitors' valuations, the premium paid for Cafédirect's shares is even more apparent.

Returning to the original equation for social premium, the terms can be filled in from the above analysis:

$$Price\ Paid\ per\ Share - Market\ Value\ per\ Share = Social\ Premium$$

$$24.3x - 16.7x = 7.6x$$

or

$$24.3x - 16.0x = 8.3x$$

This P/E premium can also be converted into pounds (in millions) and pounds per share:

$$Social\ Premium\ x\ Caf\acute{e}direct\ 2003\ Net\ Income = Premium\ in\ \pounds$$

$$\frac{Premium\ in\ \pounds}{Shares\ Issued} = Premium\ per\ Share$$

	Top5 Competitor Index	Global Competitor Index
P/E Premium	7.6x	8.3x
in MM£s	£2.8	£3.0
Per share	£0.31	£0.34

Assuming that investors acted rationally and the market has valued Cafédirect correctly, the price paid includes a social premium in addition to the market value of the investment.[14]

Establishing that investors are willing to pay a premium for social value is just the first stage of the analysis. The next stage is determining the relationship between the social value and the premium paid.

One proxy for the social value created by Cafédirect is the £400,000 spent in 2003 on Producer Support and Development (PS&D). PS&D is spent supporting and developing worldwide producer partners and is in addition to the £2.8m (in 2003) spent paying above market price to producers. This capital spend was featured in the prospectus and in interviews with management[15] was highlighted as the proxy for social value used during internal pricing.

Using this proxy, the relationship can be explored from two distinct pathways; blended valuation and separate financial and social valuation.

For blended valuation, the tax-adjusted[16] PS&D spend can be added to the reported net income to create an adjusted (or blended) net income:

[14] It is important to note that this calculation does not inherently imply a trade-off. Looking at the history of the company, investors could have projected that Cafédirect would continue to use its social value to market its products and take market share from traditional coffee distributors. They could also have assumed that consumers would be willing to continue to pay a premium for Cafédirect products due to this social value. Thus, a strong, demonstrable social value would be necessary for continued growth and profitability of the company.

[15] During the writing of this case, the authors spoke to management in charge of Cafédirect at the time of the APO.

[16] Whether or not to tax adjust the PS&D could be debated. If investors are viewing the spend as equal in value to financial net income, the tax adjustment treats the PS&D similarly.

$$2003 \ Reported \ Net \ Income + 2003 \ PS\&D \ Spending \ X$$

$$(1 - Tax \ Rate) = 2003 \ PS\&D \ Adjusted \ Net \ Income$$

$$£369,045 + £400,000 \ X \ (1 - 24\%) = £671,566$$

This blended net income would imply that the social spending is treated similarly to financial return. Using this adjusted net income, a blended P/E multiple can be calculated for Cafédirect:

$$\frac{Implied \ Market \ Capitalization}{2003 \ PS\&D \ Adjusted \ Net \ Income} = PS\&D \ Adjusted \frac{P}{E} Ratio$$

$$\frac{£8,960,000}{£671,566} = 13.3x$$

Calculating blended P/E ratio in this manner would imply that investors placed a 13.3x value on the financial bottom line (net income) and the social spending (PS&D). Thus, valuing the financial results of Cafédirect at the same level as the social value proxy.

As the blended P/E multiple is lower than either competitor index, a separate financial and social calculation may be implied. In that case, applying the top competitors' (liquidity adjusted) P/E multiple to the financial net income, a lower social P/E multiple is implied for the PS&D:

$$Market \ Capitalization = Competitor \frac{P}{E} Multiple \ X \ Cafedirect \ 2003$$

$$Net \ Income + Social \frac{P}{E} Multiple \ X \ 2003 \ Tax \ Adjusted \ PS\&D$$

$$£8.960m = 16.7 \ X \ £0.369m + Social \frac{P}{E} Multiple \ X \ £0.304m$$

Solving this equation, the social P/E multiple is equal to 9.2x. This evaluation raises several interesting questions.

Is the price paid for the social value created by Cafédirect high or low relative to the market? Although it appears that investors' relative willingness to pay for social value was less than the willingness to pay for financial value. It may be inappropriate to compare financial and social prices outright. The market value of the financial returns can be calculated based upon comparable public data (i.e. comparing financial P/E multiples to each other), but without comparable market data points, it is impossible to know whether the social P/E multiple is undervalued or overvalued.

What does this imply in regards to the risk of the social value? Paying market value for current financial earnings carries risk in that when the investor seeks to sell their shares the underlying earnings or the market multiples may have decreased. Paying for social value carries the risk that the social value will have decreased at the time of sale *and* that future investors may not be willing to pay for it (social P/E goes to 0). By paying for social value, are investors assuming that they will be able to sell their shares for a blended valuation in the future? Or are they willing to pay for the one-time social value?

Does this demonstrate a semi-pareto relationship? By paying for social value that they are unable to capture monetarily, the investors in Cafédirect have seemingly traded a portion of their financial returns for social returns. If the capital used for the transaction were to come from a traditional portfolio, this would likely be true. Anecdotal data from management suggests that many investors saw this as a portion of their social investment for the year. Thus, perhaps the financial value of shares could be seen as subsidizing or sustaining the social value being produced each year by Cafédirect.

It is evident that many more data points are needed to undertake a comprehensive analysis of investor's willingness to pay for social premia in public, as well as private, transactions. As this chapter has argued, the more investors and funders begin to explore the practice of integrating social value throughout the PVP process, the greater the ability to create comprehensive models accurately to price the blended value of these enterprises.

Term sheets

The term sheet, the legal document that lays out the valuation, ownership, option pool, board structure, closing conditions, and other key terms of an investment deal, is a powerful tool for both investors and entrepreneurs to outline the initial and ongoing relationship between funders and investee companies. In larger deals, an intermediary—often an investment bank—typically deals with the negotiation of the term sheet, explaining the terms and their significance to business owners. For start-ups, the majority of deals are completed without an intermediary. In social finance, there are funds that are being truly innovative in the creation of term sheet provisions that attempt to align the incentives of both social investors and their investees by codifying the values of each party within their financial relationship. Next, the key elements of term sheets are considered with respect to their applicability to social finance.

PRE-MONEY VALUATION

The pre-money valuation of an enterprise represents the value of the company just prior to the capital from an investment entering the capital structure. As discussed earlier, the majority of investments calculate this valuation based on financial projections and use a cost of capital that includes only financial expectations. A term sheet for social finance would need to include a social impact valuation pre-investment.

MILESTONES

Often milestones are used when an investment is made in various tranches, meaning that the investment is split into multiple investments over a specified time frame. Milestones are goals the company must hit in the form of revenue, users, profits, product design, patents, certifications, and so on, before the next round of funding is released. Milestones can equally be applied in social finance linked to agreed social impact outcomes and values. If structured correctly, such tranching of social finance can align the distribution of capital with the social impact objectives of the investee, for example by front-loading capital for early interventions in outcome-based payment-by-results contracts such as social impact bonds.

VESTING

In its simplest terms, vesting refers to an investor gaining ownership of an investee company over time. If an investor owns shares that have not yet vested, she has the right to own those shares once they vest. If an investor's own shares are vested, she controls those shares *ab initio*. In equity investment terms, reverse vesting is the powerful—and potentially controversial—practice of requiring entrepreneurs to relinquish control of their ownership shares to an investor with an agreement that ownership shares are returned to them along an agreed schedule. This practice allows investors to tie in entrepreneurs to a deal, because if they leave the company prior to the completion of the vesting schedule they only have a legal right to the ownership shares that have vested, with the rest returning to the investor. Vesting can also be used as a positive incentive, similar to milestones, promising entrepreneurs greater ownership if certain outcome goals are met. For social investors that may be less concerned with exit than with incentivizing investees to grow their social impact, vesting presents an interesting incentive: a deal could be structured to allow the social investees to earn back a portion of their ownership through achieving social impact goals over time.

OPTION POOLS

For fast-growing start-ups, the ability to hire and incentivize staff is an important priority. Option pools, which give the company the ability to compensate key employees with future equity ownership in the company, can be key to this process. For social entrepreneurs, buy-in to the organization's blended objectives may be even more critical. Offering future owner-ship/control or social equity share options (if appropriate) in a social enterprise or social purpose organization could be a powerful tool to help recruit talented and committed staff.

FINANCIAL INFORMATION

Investors typically require standard financial information from investees, such as audited financial reports, quarterly and/or month unaudited reports, annual budgets, and business plans. Social investors could also codify the type of social impact information about which they would like information, so that investees have an incentive to integrate effective and convincing social report-ing into their core organizational activities.

PROTECTIVE PROVISIONS

Protective provisions provide investors with protection from major changes occurring at the company without their consent. Often these terms include the liquidation, dissolution, and re-capitalization of a company, changes in the size of board, payments over a specified amount, and key employee changes. Protective provisions offer social investors and investees the mechanism by which the social objectives and outcomes of a social investment can be locked into a social finance deal. Two provisions from mainstream finance—material change and drag-along rights—may be particularly useful in social finance too. In traditional term sheets, the material change clause refers to any significant alteration in the investee's company structure or nature of its business. Social investors may use this clause to protect the social objectives of an investee through provisions that restrict any changes in mission focus (Stevenson, 2012). Drag-along rights state that if a preferred stock majority vote to accept an offer to sell all of their shares to a third party, the rest of the shares can be 'dragged along' as part of this deal. While this allows mainstream investors to make a return by selling to a third party that has offered a good price, for social investees the intentions of the proposed acquirer and how they plan to proceed with their organization will likely be more important. As a consequence, this term could be a key point at which social investees retain a right to block a sale if the social mission of the acquirer does not match that of the social purpose organization.[17]

Conclusions

This chapter has provided a systematic analysis of the applicability and appropriateness of the mainstream financial models to social finance. It particularly aimed to move the (important) debates on social impact measurement forward by linking this body of thinking to a practice-focused model of projection-valuation-pricing aimed at enhancing investment decision-making for social investors and investees.

The PVP framework used here had two purposes. First, it allowed an exploration of how far the conventions of mainstream finance can be translated to social finance. Second, it extended current thinking on social finance better to understand the role and nature of investor preferences in establishing the value of social investment and, then, to consider how such valuations may be priced in different market and deal structures and through established mechanisms such as term sheets.

This analysis demonstrates the potential for growth of social finance globally, but also highlights the significant under-institutionalizing of this space. The absence of transparent and credible performance data, well-functioning and liquid secondary markets, established investment structures, financial instruments, and risk and return profiles all make this a challenging environment for investors and investees. Nevertheless, this is also a space teaming

---

[17] Sometimes this can be locked into the financial structure of a social purpose organization by regulation, as with the social 'asset lock' in the community interest company form in the UK. This does not allow any investor that might acquire a CIC to realize the value of its social assets thus disincentivizing hostile takeovers.

with innovation and energy—witness Social Impact Bonds, for example—and there are considerable grounds for optimism that it will grow and flourish over the next decade.

■ REFERENCES

Acumen Fund Metrics Team (2007). 'Acumen Fund Concepts: The Best Available Charitable Option', January: pp. 1–5. <http://acumen.org/ideas/?search=best+avail able+charitable+optioncepts>, accessed 15 June 2015.

Emerson, J. (2003). 'The Blended Value Proposition: Integrating Social and Financial Returns', *California Management Review*, 45(4): 35–51.

Emerson, J., 2011. 'Risk, Return and Impact: Understanding Diversification and Performance within an Impact Investing Portfolio'. ImpactAssets Brief no. 2. <http://www.impactassets.org/files/downloads/ImpactAssets_IssueBriefs_2.pdf>, accessed 26 March 2015.

Emerson, J., and Cabaj, M. (2000). 'Social Return On Investment', *Making Waves*, 11(2): 10–14.

Emerson, J., Wachowicz, J., and Chun, S. (2000). 'Social Return on Investment: Exploring Aspects of Value Creation in the Nonprofit'. In REDF Box Set Volume 2, pp. 132–73.

Foster, W., and Bradach, J. (2005). 'Should Nonprofits Seek Profits?', *Harvard Business Review*, 83, February: 92–100.

Freireich, J., and Fulton, K. (2009). 'Investing for Social and Environmental Impact: A Design for Catalyzing an Emerging Industry'. Monitor Institute.

Nicholls, A. (2009). 'We Do Good Things, Don't We?' Blended Value Accounting in Social Entrepreneurship', *Accounting, Organizations and Society*, 34(6–7): 755–69.

Nicholls, A. (2010). 'The Institutionalization of Social Investment: The Interplay of Investment Logics and Investor Rationalities', *Journal of Social Entrepreneurship*, 1(1): 70–100.

Nicholls, A. (2013). 'Filling the Capital Gap: Institutionalizing Social Finance', in S. Denny and F. Seddon (eds), *Evaluating Social Enterprise*. Basingstoke: Palgrave MacMillan, pp. 161–96.

Nicholls, A., and Schwartz, R. (2014). 'The Demandside of the Social Investment Marketplace', in L. Salamon (ed.), *New Frontiers of Philanthropy: A Guide to the New Tools and New Actors that Are Reshaping Global Philanthropy and Social Investing*. Chichester: Jossey-Bass, pp. 562–82.

Nicholls, J. (2004). *Social Return on Investment: Valuing What Matters*. London: New Economics Foundation.

O'Donohoe, N., et al. (2010). *Impact Investments: An Emerging Asset Class*. London: J.P. Morgan Global Research.

Olsen, S., and Lingane, A. (2003). 'Social Return on Investment: Standard Guidelines', *California Management Review*, 46(3): 116–35.

Slee, R., and Paglia, J. (2010). 'Private Cost of Capital Model', *The Value Examiner*, March/April, pp. 23–32.

Tuan, M. (2008). 'Measuring and/or Estimating Social Value Creation: Insights into Eight Integrated Cost Approaches'. Final Paper. Bill and Melinda Gates Foundation.

Weisbrod, B. (2004). 'The Pitfalls of Profits', *Stanford Social Innovation Review*, 2(3): 40–52.

Weisbrod, B. (2011). 'The Nonprofit Mission and Its Financing', *Journal of Policy Analysis and Management*, 17(2): 165–74.

Zhuang, J. et al. (2007). *Theory and Practice in the Choice of Social Discount Rate for Cost-benefit Analysis: A Survey*. Metro Manila: Philippines: Asian Development Bank, Metro Manila, Philippines.

12 The Peterborough Pilot Social Impact Bond

Alex Nicholls and Emma Tomkinson

Introduction

Social Impact Bonds (SIBs) have become one of the most talked-about elements within the social finance market. Today there are multiple examples of SIBs under development across the globe and they have been highlighted in high-level policy briefings and in the work of the (G8) Social Impact Investing Taskforce. In 2014, the UK government announced that 'approved' SIBs would attract Social Investment Tax Relief. This chapter presents an in-depth case study of the world's first SIB in order to highlight the opportunities and challenges of the model.[1]

This case study[2] will examine the emergence, development, and global variations of a new financing mechanism for welfare services, the SIB. The case will define SIBs in their historical context and will explore the first pilot SIB in Peterborough in the UK in detail. In addition, it will consider innovations introduced by other examples from the UK, Australia, and the USA. Conclusions will set out the key innovations and contributions of the SIB form and will also consider obstacles and considerations in terms of the future expansion and development of this novel contractual model. Specifically, this case aims to enhance the reader's knowledge about:

- How an environment of government reform encourages the development of new contracting models.
- How social purpose organizations and social enterprises that deliver welfare services are involved in new relationships with government.
- How innovative social finance investment opportunities grow the social finance market.

---

[1] The case was intended to be used as the basis for class discussion rather than to illustrate the optimum contracting or financing model. Information in this case was collected from a site visit, interviews, presentations, and public sources. This case study was developed with support from the Pears Business School Partnership. The purpose of the partnership is to inspire future leaders to make a positive difference to society. <http://www.pearsfoundation.org.uk>.

[2] This case was made possible through the generous cooperation of Social Finance Ltd. The authors also gratefully acknowledge the valuable comments contributed by Dan Gregory.

- How social impact metrics can support new funding opportunities and improve organizational performance in terms of social outcomes
- How long-term contracts and flexible funding can enhance strategic flexibility in welfare services delivery that enhances overall performance
- How the involvement of several stakeholder groups in the pursuit of a single outcome creates a unique set of benefits and challenges.

This chapter starts by setting out a definition of the SIB model and its key constituent parts. Next the historical context that provides the background to the emergence of the SIB is sketched in. The third section examines the Peterborough Pilot SIB in detail. After this, the evolution of SIBs globally is discussed. Conclusions consider some of the issues that have emerged as the first SIB has been implemented. The chapter closes with a postscript reflecting on key issues that developed in 2014.

What is a Social Impact Bond?

The Social Impact Bond (SIB) model is an innovative method of financing welfare and other social services. It aims to improve a social outcome through the collaboration of government, service providers, and external investors. Put simply, a SIB involves a set of contracts, the basis of which is an agreement by government to pay investors for an improvement in a specific social outcome once it has been achieved. Service providers address the social outcome by delivering an intervention to a group within a target community. Investors provide working capital for service providers to deliver the intervention, thus assuming the financial risk. If greater improvements in the social outcome are made, government payments are larger and thus, investor returns are higher. Effectively, the SIB acts a social futures contract rather than a debt instrument.

The effective implementation of a SIB contract is underpinned by rigorous social impact metrics that measure relevant changes in the lives of service users. Unlike many public sector contract models, the measurement of social outcomes is a necessary component of a SIB, as a trigger for payments by government and repayment to investors. By enabling non-government investment to be utilized, SIBs aim to increase spending on preventative services, such that these interventions can have a direct impact on costly health and social problems, saving the state money over time without reducing the overall level of welfare services. SIBs also directly link financial rewards with social outcomes, something traditional government commissioning methods have struggled to do.

SIBs require innovative collaborations between government, investors, and service providers—something that occurs in the negotiation of the terms of the SIB, in its implementation, and in its management. The SIB structure also aims to align the interests of these key stakeholders around agreed and measurable social outcomes as follows:

- *Government commissioners*: SIBs ensure that payments are only made by the public sector if SIB-financed services improve outcomes for service users.[3] Government transfers the financial risk that funded interventions fail to improve outcomes to investors
- *Investors*: SIBs offer trusts and foundations, commercial and institutional investors, high-net-worth individuals, and retail investors an opportunity to generate a blended social and financial return on investment. The social and financial returns are aligned since investors receive higher financial returns for greater improvements in social outcomes
- *Service providers*: SIBs offer extra investment for service delivery. Providers are encouraged to innovate in order to maximize outcomes for their target populations. The focus is on collaboration and the social outcomes that service providers can generate together, rather than on the cost of services or outputs alone. Long-term contracts allow providers to employ full-time staff and gain the trust of service users
- *Intermediaries*: SIBs create a new market for intermediaries across a range of functions in their development and execution. For example, they can conduct feasibility studies, perform due diligence, negotiate the deal, establish a special purpose vehicle (SPV), raise capital, and manage performance
- *Service users*: services are delivered to a cohort of service users for whom outcomes could be improved. Payments by government are made on the basis of improvement of outcomes for this group of individuals. Services are flexible, responding to individual need rather than prescribed processes or units of time.

Each SIB is structured around at least one well-defined social outcome in an intervention area (e.g. youth offending, teenage pregnancy, young people not in education, employment, or training). Appropriate outcomes and success metrics are negotiated and agreed between government and the party responsible for delivering the outcomes. Investors may be involved in these discussions, or may be sought once the terms of the contract are established. These investors are asked to take on some or all the risk that the interventions lead to the target outcomes, but will make a return on their investment in the event that the intervention is successful. Due to the perceived riskiness of SIBs (they are novel and lack a track record of financial performance), social finance institutions—that are driven primarily by achieving social impact and will take more financial risk as a result—have typically funded or underwritten the first SIBs (Loder et al., 2010).

---

[3] The SIBs in New South Wales, Australia, called *Social Benefit Bonds*, are an exception to this. Even if no positive outcomes are achieved, government payments will be made and investors will be repaid a proportion of their capital.

The SIB model is different to other contracting models due to its use of both outcomes-based contracts and non-governmental investment to deliver social services.

The outcomes-based contract—a type of *payment-by-results* agreement[4]—between the government and the service provider is an innovative way of commissioning welfare services in two respects. First, it relates payments to measurable outcome change, for example a reduction in reoffending. This is in contrast to government contracts that have traditionally paid for services based on outputs, for example the number of people who completed a programme, or inputs, like the number of contact hours staff spent with clients. The outcomes-based contract also creates an incentive for the service deliverer to collaborate and sub-contract with effective local providers to achieve optimal outcomes for service users. Second, a SIB contract typically has a longer duration than most government contracts. For example, the Peterborough SIB has a payment-by-results contract with government that involves seven years of service delivery. It is unusual for government contracts to extend beyond allocations in the current spending review: for example, the UK government spending review typically occurs every three years or so. Payment on the basis of outcomes, combined with a longer contracting period, means that the service provider has more flexibility over how services are delivered and time to collect and respond to performance information. Thus the service is enabled, even required, to improve and adapt to performance information and changes in the delivery environment in a dynamic way.

External investors also have an outcomes-based contract with the service provider, by which they are ultimately repaid. Thus, the social and financial incentives of both providers and investors are aligned. The involvement of external investment shifts the financial risk of non-delivery and, therefore, responsibility for delivering the outcomes, to non-government investors. As a result, the service provider becomes focused on delivering the outcome for the investor, instead of the traditional model of delivering against a suite of non-outcomes metrics required by government commissioners. Moreover, traditional contracts with government can be highly prescriptive as to how a service is delivered. They deliberately restrict the flexibility the service provider has to deviate from the agreed process of service delivery by funding parts of the process, rather than the outcomes produced.

Investor involvement also enables social purpose organizations to engage in payment-by-results contracts with government, as the contract effectively provides working capital until payments are made.[5]

Social Finance—the pioneering developer of the world's first SIB—defined the model as follows:

---

[4] This model is sometimes known as 'payment by success', particularly in the USA.
[5] Smaller providers are, however, unlikely to be able to participate as the prime contractor due to prohibitive transaction costs, but may deliver services as a sub-contractor.

Social Impact Bonds are a form of outcomes-based contract in which public sector commissioners commit to pay for significant improvement in social outcomes (such as a reduction in offending rates, or in the number of people being admitted to hospital) for a defined population. Social Impact Bonds are an innovative way of attracting new investment around such outcomes-based contracts that benefit individuals and communities. Through a Social Impact Bond, private investment is used to pay for interventions, which are delivered by service providers with a proven track record. Financial returns to investors are made by the public sector on the basis of improved social outcomes. If outcomes do not improve, then investors do not recover their investment. Social Impact Bonds provide up front funding for prevention and early intervention services, and remove the risk that interventions do not deliver outcomes from the public sector. The public sector pays if (and only if) the intervention is successful. In this way, Social Impact Bonds enable a re-allocation of risk between the two sectors. (Social Finance, 2011a and 2011b)

The UK Cabinet Office has defined a SIB by four necessary criteria:

- A contract between a commissioner and a legally separate entity 'the delivery agency'
- A particular outcome or outcomes which, if achieved by the delivery agency, will activate a payment or payments from the commissioner
- At least one investor that is a legally separate entity from the delivery agency and the commissioner
- Some or all of the financial risk of non-delivery of outcomes sits with the investor. (Cabinet Office, 2013)

The key relationships and finance/outcomes flows in a SIB are summarized in Figure 12.1.

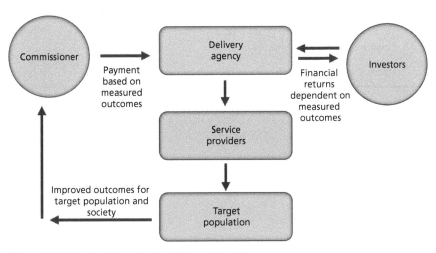

Figure 12.1. The structure of a Social Impact Bond

The historical context

Over the past thirty years—in many developed countries—there have been a series of significant structural and operational changes in the way the state aims to deliver its services to citizens. These changes have reflected both ideological and economic trends in terms of the role of modern government. These are typically characterized as representing the dominance of a neo-liberal agenda that prioritizes tax reduction and privatization over more centralized, 'tax and spend' models of the state. In purely economic terms this has been the consequence of a rejection of centralized, state-driven, neo-Keynesian economics in favour of more neo-liberal, market-based, Hayekian approaches.

Two key themes in this revolution have been identified as the 'new public management' approach to the internal functioning of the state and a broader 'reinventing government' movement (Osborne and Gaebler, 1995). In both cases, there has been a strong focus on reforming state bureaucracies and dismantling centralized government systems and structures in favour of more 'business-like' and enterprising models of welfare service delivery and internal operations. Although both sets of reforms have been very controversial (and strongly resisted at times by the civil service and others), these changes are now the norm in most modern governments (see Figure 12.2).

In addition to driving various systemic changes to government structures these agendas have also addressed other aspects of what were formerly exclusively state responsibilities. In terms of large infrastructure projects—schools, hospitals, roads—these reforms drove a series of new hybrid contractual models between the state and private, commercial companies, defined in the UK as public–private partnerships or private finance initiatives. In terms of service delivery, a series of key reforms aimed to introduce market—or

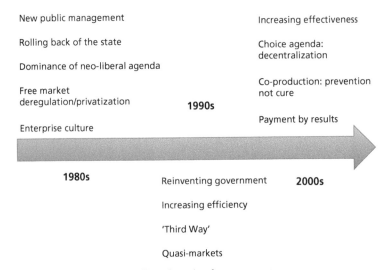

Figure 12.2. Innovations in modelling the role of government

quasi-market—models into public welfare that separate the (typically external of government) providers of services from the (internal government) commissioners. This market model introduced tendering processes into the provision of public welfare and was designed to be both more efficient and effective. As a result many areas of welfare are now delivered as out-sourced goods and services via contracts with third parties, often charities or third sector organizations. In the UK, this market has been of central importance to the development of the social enterprise sector.

SIBs fit into this tradition of change as part of a new wave of welfare reforms that have been largely driven by the deficit crises that many states faced following the effective nationalization of private sector bank debt in 2008–10. Many governments chose to address this crisis by introducing savage austerity programmes (rather than steep tax increases) that cut public spending by up to 40 per cent in some countries.[6] In conjunction, governments sought to increase the effectiveness of their remaining expenditure. In this context, several governments looked to payment-by-results models, or more specifically, an outcomes-based model of welfare services, which promised more effective services for key beneficiaries and were attractive within a broader policy focus on social innovation. The SIB model brings in third-party funding to scale or instigate welfare programmes with government only paying by results and—at least in theory—from savings over time. These features have made SIBs very attractive to cash-strapped ministers.

SIBs also fit into the context of a range of policy initiatives that aimed to develop the social finance market in the UK and beyond. The UK has been the market leader globally in such innovation and successive governments have developed policy approaches including: new fiscal policy (Community Investment Tax Relief); new regulation (the establishment of the community interest company legal form for social enterprises); direct investment (Futurebuilders); facilitating legislation for new social finance infrastructure (Commission on Unclaimed Assets and Big Society Capital); and changes to commissioning policy (the Social Value Act 2012). Policy enthusiasm for SIBs within this context represents a combination of new commissioning processes and direct investment.

The Peterborough Pilot Social Impact Bond

This case study focuses on the first pilot SIB that aimed to reduce reoffending by prisoners released from Her Majesty's Prison (HMP) Peterborough after serving a sentence of less than twelve months. It was launched in collaboration

---

[6] This was true in many OECD countries, but not all. For example, Australia did not experience the same banking crisis or subsequent deficit problems seen elsewhere in the developed world, yet there has been a long-standing policy enthusiasm for outsourcing models and New South Wales has developed Social Benefit Bonds that mirror SIBs (Tomkinson, 2012).

with the UK Ministry of Justice (MOJ) on 18 March 2010 and services were expected to be delivered over seven years (Strickland, 2010). The initial social investors were mostly charitable trusts and foundations, some of which represent individual or institutional wealth. The investment closed at £5m. The contract agreed that the MOJ would make payments to investors in the event that reoffending was reduced below an agreed threshold. Reoffending is an area where preventative work saves the taxpayer money: 60 per cent of the 40,200 adults on short-term sentences reoffend within a year of release in the UK. The pilot SIB offered intensive support to 3,000 short-term prisoners in HMP Peterborough over a seven-year period, both inside prison and after release, to help them resettle into the community. Social enterprise delivery partners included: St Giles Trust, Ormiston Children and Families Trust (Ormiston), SOVA, YMCA, Peterborough and Fenland Mind (Mind). If the SIB reduces reoffending by at least 7.5 per cent, investors would receive a minimum repayment of 2.5 per cent. The greater the drop in reoffending beyond this threshold, the more the investors would receive. The total payments by Government were capped at £8m (or £7m in real terms) and the return to investors was capped at 13 per cent annual IRR.[7]

DEVELOPMENT OF THE SIB MODEL AND ITS FIRST PILOT

In late 2007, the then Labour government in the UK established the Council on Social Action[8] 'to generate ideas and initiatives through which government and other key stakeholders can catalyse, celebrate and develop social action' (Cabinet Office, 2009). The Council became a platform through which key individuals and organizations connected according to four themes: social technology, social leadership, collaborative commitments, and new models for financing social action (Cabinet Office, 2009). The Council invited various organizations to generate ideas to contribute to its work. One of these was Social Finance, which was launched in April 2008 'to accelerate the creation of a social investment market in the UK' (Social Finance, 2008a; see also Social Finance, 2008b). The initial Social Finance board of directors included two members of the Council on Social Action.

At the same time, Arthur Wood, the former investment banker turned social investment specialist within the social entrepreneur network Ashoka, was developing a 'contingent revenue bond' focused on financing new

---

[7] According to an evaluation of a previous St. Giles Trust 'Through the Gates' by Frontier Economics, the economic benefits of preventing reoffending were ten times the programme costs.

[8] The members of the Council were: David Robinson, Community Links; Kay Allen, Royal Mail; Oli Barrett, Connected Capital; Shankari Chandran, Allen & Overy; Olga Heaven, Hibiscus; Geoff Mulgan, Young Foundation; Julia Ogilvy, Project Scotland; Rob Owen, St. Giles Trust; Tim Smit, Eden Project; Kevin Steele, Inspired Campaigns; David Thomlinson, Accenture; Sophi Tranchell, Divine Chocolate Ltd; Paul Twivy, Communications Consultant; Julia Unwin, Joseph Rowntree Foundation; Peter Wheeler, Investment and Philanthropy Specialist.

sanitation projects in developing countries. This instrument was funded by private investment linked to a repayment schedule contingent on outcomes.[9] In the contingent revenue bond funders would be split into for-profit loan providers of capital financing for work on the ground and charitable foundations that would fund measurable outcomes and, thus, repay the loans. This model became the basis for the SIB structure (Cabinet Office, 2013).

In 2008, David Robinson and Peter Wheeler—two members of the Council on Social Action approached Social Finance to explore whether they could develop a model of preventative activity that could be funded from savings made in acute services spending as a result of measurable outcomes. Robinson and Wheeler helped manage ongoing relationships with government for Social Finance as they developed the first SIB. They also connected Social Finance to Allen and Overy who later became their legal advisors, providing over 300 hours of pro bono legal support for the development of SIBs.

Also in 2008 Martin Brookes, then CEO of New Philanthropy Capital, invited Social Finance to join a meeting to consider whether financial structures could be developed to fund early intervention work. The meeting followed discussions with Graham Allen, MP for Nottingham, who posed the problem of how more resources could be devoted to early intervention initiatives. Social Finance were also introduced to Edmond Curtin, later of Cadwalader, Wickersham & Taft LLP, a derivatives lawyer who wrote the first draft term sheet for the pilot SIB, and Chris Egerton-Warburton, of Lion's Head Global Partners, who had structured the International Finance Facility for Immunization (IFFI) bond, and who helped with the vital work of getting support from the UK Treasury and an agreed accounting treatment.

Geoff Mulgan, of the Young Foundation, connected Social Finance to both senior policy makers and a range of previous research on outcomes-based commissioning that aimed to reduce perverse incentives across government departments. In early 2008, in response to ideas from the City Leader's Group and the work of Social Finance, the Young Foundation published a short paper and introduced the term 'Social Impact Bond' as one of several new social investment models (Young Foundation, 2008; Strickland, 2010; Bolton and Savell, 2010).

As the project moved forward, Social Finance looked at areas of social need where costs were high and there was potential to make a significant difference with new or increased preventative programmes. Criminal Justice was an obvious choice. Experts across the UK had highlighted the issue of short-sentenced prisoners (those who are imprisoned for less than twelve months) having very high reoffending rates: approximately 60 per cent are convicted of

---

[9] This model shares some similarities with the Global Alliance on Vaccine and Immunization (GAVI) model that uses future government development aid commitments to underwrite bonds in the capital market that, in turn, fund large scale early intervention and prevention programmes in developing countries. In addition the GAVI model works at sufficient scale to shape pharmaceutical markets and accelerate the development of drugs that are of particular utility in developing country contexts: see <http://www.gavialliance.org>.

at least one offence in the year after release. As a result, by late 2008, Social Finance was working closely with the MoJ and HM Treasury to build a pilot SIB in criminal justice. As part of this process, Social Finance engaged with a wide range of key groups including: prison staff, local stakeholders, voluntary organizations working in the field, other criminal justice experts, and potential investors (such as trusts and foundations).

In 2009, the UK Parliament provided further impetus to the pilot SIB project. First the Justice Committee advocated the development of a SIB within the criminal justice system in their December 2009 report *Cutting Crime: the Case for Justice Reinvestment* (Justice Committee, 2009). Second, in the same month, the White Paper *Putting the Frontline First: Smarter Government* stated that the Labour government would 'pilot Social Impact Bonds as a new way of funding the third sector to provide services' (HM Government, 2009: 32). In their response, Social Finance summarized the potential benefit of SIBs for the social sector, the public, and the Government:

The Social Impact Bond has the potential to unlock an unprecedented flow of finance for social sector organisations. By focusing returns on outcomes, these organisations will be incentivised to develop innovative interventions to tackle ingrained social problems which weigh heavily on our society and our national purse. (Social Finance, 2009)

In March 2010, two months prior to the May general election, the MoJ issued a press release announcing that the first pilot SIB in the world, developed by Social Finance, would begin in Peterborough that summer.

Taking a more systemic view, Toby Eccles, Development Director at Social Finance, positioned the launch as an important next step in the development of a social investment market:

These bonds can bring large amounts of new finance into the social sector, but first we need to build a track record of success. This first bond is likely to attract investors who are already experienced in this sector and we've been careful to choose groups with solid experience to deliver the services to prisoners. I'm confident that this first bond will be a success, offering excellent returns on investment. That will give other investors the confidence to invest in future bonds. SIBs could finance activities like enhanced support for foster carers, home care services for older people and nursing in the home for the chronically sick. (Macdonald, 2010)

During the May 2010 general election, the opposition Conservative party included SIBs within their manifesto platform *Big Society, Not Big Government*. As a part of this, the party promoted a social investment bank (later Big Society Capital) as a 'cornerstone investor in innovative products, such as Social Impact Bonds, that offer a blend of social and financial return that is attractive to socially responsible, mainstream investors' (Conservative Party, 2010).

After the election that installed a coalition Conservative-Liberal Democrat government, on 31 August 2010, the Big Lottery Fund announced that it would allocate £5m to Social Finance to develop SIBs as a tool for preventing social problems across the UK. They also agreed to co-fund the outcomes payments for the Peterborough Pilot SIB in partnership with the MoJ (see Social Finance 2010a and 2010b). Peter Wanless, Chief Executive of the Big Lottery Fund said:

The Big Lottery Fund's aim is to be an intelligent and innovative funder and it is our aspiration to seek out new ways to bring improvements to communities. At a time of tight public finances, Social Impact Bonds represent a new and innovative way of attracting investment from outside the public sector and by funding Social Finance's work we are hoping to pave the way for many more similar projects across the UK— this is a very exciting project for BIG. Prevention is better and cheaper than cure and there is a growing body of evidence that if preventative interventions are effective, we can all spend less money on services such as prisons, acute medical care and drug rehabilitation. (Big Lottery Fund, 2010)

On 9 September 2010, the new Secretary of State for Justice, Kenneth Clarke, visited HMP Peterborough and commented:

As part of our radical approach to rehabilitation we are considering a range of payment by results schemes like the Social Impact Bond. The voluntary and private sectors will be crucial to our success and we want to make far better use of their enthusiasm and expertise to get offenders away from the revolving door of crime and prison. (Ministry of Justice and Social Finance, 2010)

The press release on the day also included a quote from David Hutchison highlighting how innovative the structure was, but for the first time introducing the idea of aligning incentives:

The Social Impact Bond aligns the interests of government, charities, social enterprises and socially motivated investors around a common goal. We are delighted to be launching the first such structure in the world here at Peterborough. (Ministry of Justice and Social Finance UK, 2010)

STRUCTURE

Initial contracts for the Peterborough SIB were finalized in March 2010 with the formation of a new special purpose vehicle (SPV)—Social Impact Partnership (see Figure 12.3). The contracts agreed that the MoJ and Big Lottery Fund would make payments to the Social Impact Partnership in the event that reoffending is reduced for male, short-sentenced prisoners released from HMP Peterborough. Frontline services were to be managed by the One Service, an organization created by Social Finance specifically for this SIB.[10]

---

[10] For the purpose of this case study, 'the One Service' shall be used to refer to the management organization of the consortium of organizations delivering the services of the Peterborough SIB and the suite of services they deliver.

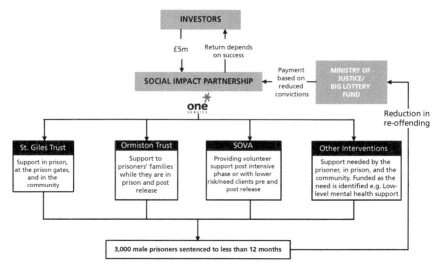

Figure 12.3. Structure of the Peterborough SIB

The One Service negotiated contracts to deliver services with social enterprise partners including St Giles Trust, Ormiston, SOVA, YMCA, and Mind. The RAND Europe (2011: 13) evaluation identified six key contractual relationships between:

- MoJ and Social Impact Partnership—the limited partnership set up by Social Finance which is the contracting entity in the SIB
- Social Impact Partnership and investors
- Social Impact Partnership and service providers (for example, St Giles Trust)
- MoJ and independent assessors
- MoJ and Peterborough Prison Management Limited[11]
- Social Finance and the Big Lottery Fund.

The investment pool in the SIB totalled £5m from seventeen investors including: the Barrow Cadbury Charitable Trust, the Esmée Fairbairn Foundation, the Friends Provident Foundation, the Henry Smith Charity, the Johansson Family Foundation, the Lankelly Chase Foundation, the Monument Trust, the Panahpur Charitable Trust, the Paul Hamlyn Foundation, and the Tudor Trust. The Director of the One Service, suggested that these investors were interested in two things: first, the reoffending results and their possibility of repayment; second (and not necessarily to a lesser degree) what the

---

[11] The MoJ negotiated a no-cost amendment to the private finance initiative contract to ensure that providers under the SIB could enter the prison, use prison premises, and access prisoners in order to deliver interventions (RAND, 2011: 16).

programme actually does and how it might change the lives of its service users. However, while the SIB contract agreed that investors would receive a quarterly report on the latter, the measure of the outcome by which their repayments will be triggered will begin to reveal information four years after SIB started to deliver services.

The One Service was available to male prisoners who were or would be discharged from HMP Peterborough after serving a sentence of less than twelve months. Sentenced prisoners at HMP Peterborough were all over the age of 21. These prisoners did not qualify for any other statutory support from probation services upon release from prison. Their engagement with the One Service was voluntary. The One Service was designed to be delivered to approximately 3,000 men, divided into three cohorts. The first cohort was set to close after the SIB had been in operation for two years, or when 1,000 offenders have been discharged—whichever happened first. The second cohort began when the first cohort finished, rather than a set point in time. It was expected that services would be delivered for approximately seven years. The Peterborough SIB began delivering services in September 2010. At the start of the programme, roughly 100 prisoners (from a total prison population of approximately 1,000) were eligible for the One Service. The One Service also aimed to interact with the roughly 30 per cent of remand prisoners sentenced to less than twelve months.

MEASUREMENT AND PAYMENT

The Peterborough SIB contract stipulated that if the SIB reduced reoffending by a threshold of 10 per cent for any of the three cohorts of 1,000 ex-prisoners—or 7.5 per cent across the entire 3,000—then a minimum payment equivalent to a return of 2.5 per cent per annum would be released by the MoJ and Big Lottery Fund to the Social Impact Partnership SPV and from this vehicle to investors (RAND Europe, 2011). If the SIB delivered a drop in reoffending below the threshold, investors would receive a corresponding increasing return capped at £7m in real terms, equivalent to approximately 13 per cent annual IRR. Payments to investors from the MoJ and the Big Lottery Fund were capped at a combined £8m (Strickland, 2010). If the SIB delivered outcomes below 7.5 per cent investors would lose their money.

The measure of reoffending used in the SIB contracts was the number of reconviction events resulting from offences committed in the twelve months following a prisoner's release from HMP Peterborough.[12] The number of reconviction events was compared to a control group of short-sentenced male prisoners from across the UK drawn from the Police National Computer database over the same time period and matched on the basis of factors like

---

[12] The reconviction event must occur within 18 months of release in order for it to be counted (RAND, 2011). This extends the measurement period to 18 months rather than 12.

criminal history, age, and ethnicity. Each Peterborough service user was compared to up to ten similar offenders. This strengthened the reliability of the measurement system to detect a statistically significant effect. The contract independently to assess the results of the Peterborough SIB was awarded to the University of Leicester together with private sector firm Qinetiq. The process of matching the Peterborough reconviction data with data in the Police National Computer database was expected to take up to six months and results were first available in summer 2014, four years after the first services were delivered (Ministry of Justice, 2012).

The outcomes-based contract for the Peterborough SIB related payments to one outcome only: the number of reconviction events from offences committed in the twelve months following release from HMP Peterborough. Using the number of reconviction events as the outcome measure had several advantages over using a binary measure like the number of prisoners reconvicted.[13] Specifically, the One Service had a greater incentive to work with more difficult offenders, from whom the state incurred far higher costs. There was also an incentive to continue working with offenders over the entire twelve-month period even if they had already been reconvicted. These two incentives do not arise from the seemingly simpler binary measure. Nick Leader, manager of HMP Peterborough commented: 'I think we've got the best monitoring process...compared to the binary measures' (see Figure 12.4).

Interviewees for the RAND Europe (2011: 35) report perceived the advantages of the measure as:

- a clear, single metric
- a metric that is already measured and for which good data is available

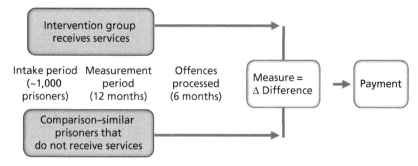

Figure 12.4. The measurement and payment system

---

[13] It is referred to as a 'binary measure', because there are two categories prisoners can fall into—either they are reconvicted or they are not. Measuring the number of reconviction events is referred to as a 'frequency measure'—it measures how often reconvictions are recorded.

- a measure that helps to prevent 'cherry-picking'—compared to a more simple yes/no reconviction measure, which could introduce an incentive to focus on those least likely to reoffend at all
- a measure that has the most direct link to costs.

Payments based only on one outcome meant that, while the One Service and their investors could not change how the outcomes were measured, they could change how they delivered services as the SIB progresses. Thus, as they collected performance information from their services, they could respond to this evidence strategically.[14]

THE ONE SERVICE IN ACTION

Connections Workers—Prisoner Engagement

On reception, prisoners eligible for the SIB programme were met by a Connections worker and shown a video about the One Service. Connections workers were prisoners serving long sentences that had volunteered and completed training to be peer support workers in the prison. Upon reception at HMP Peterborough, the Connections worker acted as an immediate point of contact and support. For example, as mobile phones had to be handed in upon arrival the Connection worker helped the new prisoner retrieve essential phone numbers for use throughout their stay. They also provided writing material should the new prisoner want to write a letter that night to 'get stuff off their chest', let the new prisoner know that there were education and training courses available, and gave them information about gym induction. If the prisoner was eligible for the One Service they went through an interview that formed the basis for individualized future service provision. This initial assessment was scanned and sent to a One Service caseworker prior to initial contact between the caseworker and the new prisoner. At the start of the SIB, there were four Connections workers specifically assigned to the One Service.

Connections workers were trained by other Connections workers and also completed the Level 3 NVQ Certificate in Information, Advice and Guidance, which took about three months and was delivered by St Giles Trust. They felt that 'because we're an inmate like them, we can ask questions better', particularly sensitive questions, for example 'What age did you first start offending?' The initial assessment included a discussion of the prisoner's expected needs at the point of release. This covered both what the new prisoner thought their needs were going to be as well as what the Connections worker thought. On leaving the prison, the main problems prisoners foresaw—and subsequently

---

[14] However, according to the One Service Director, the most difficult thing about the focus on a single outcome is not being able to tell staff how they were progressing against it until results come in several years into the programme.

asked for help with—were finding somewhere to live, obtaining identification documents, and opening a bank account.

Connections workers carried an information folder with them at all times. The folder contained all the application forms for the One Service and other prison services and systems. Some also carried pamphlets in up to twelve other languages for prisoners that did not speak English: some Connections workers at the prison also spoke multiple languages. Moreover, the local Polish community had been very supportive, providing magazines and conducting events in the prison for the Polish population.

Frontline Services

After the initial contact with a Connections worker, the One Service caseworkers provided by St Giles Trust conducted a more in-depth interview with the new prisoner and told them what help and support they could receive once they left prison. Caseworkers mostly provided knowledge, direction, advice, and support. If the prisoner was deemed suitable for a volunteer mentor managed by SOVA, they were introduced either at the initial caseworker interview or some time later. SOVA volunteers worked with lower-risk prisoners who had less complex needs, while St Giles Trust caseworkers typically took on higher-risk/need prisoners. Mentors and clients were matched on locality, interests, and other background factors and both had the opportunity to reject the partnership. Prisoners that did not live locally received a combination of a volunteer mentor from the SOVA national database, local services that were spot-purchased by the One Service or that were provided without any charge by pro-bono partners, and core support from the One Service itself.

However, in 2012, 63 per cent of the prisoners at HMP Peterborough lived in the local county (Cambridgeshire). The Director of the One Service noted the significance of this fact in terms of the delivery of services after the prisoner has left prison: 'I think that was a big factor in testing that 'through the gate' model'. The local distribution of HMP Peterborough's population may make the duplication of the One Service model more difficult elsewhere, where ex-offenders may be more dispersed after release. The Director of the One Service said, 'If it was rolled out with ten big prime contractors across the country you'd need to work hard to build real engagement, although we do currently manage a regular caseload of clients who are released to London. This is possible because St Giles Trust are based there and have a network of contacts.' One essential feature seemed to be location. The One Service and the 'through the gate' model would be difficult to replicate in other prisons as Peterborough had one of the largest local prison populations in the UK. Additionally, prisoners were often transferred between prisons in order to manage behaviour. The success of the 'through the gate' model may be a strong incentive to house more prisoners in the location in which they will live upon release. HMP Peterborough was also a relatively new prison, opening in

2005, and so had more 'general purpose' spaces for running workshops and other services than some older prisons.

In addition to casework and mentor support, the One Service commissioned Mind, a mental health support service, to offer services two days a week. Of this time, half a day was spent with prisoners still in the prison and the remainder with those who have been released. This was an unmet need identified after services began. Finally, Ormiston delivered the course 'Maintaining Family Ties' to clients of the One Service in the prison, as well as supporting their families on the outside.

The relationship between the four main service providers who worked for the One Service was designed to maximize efficiencies and offer a seamless and integrated service experience to prisoners. For example, an important design feature of the One Service was that all the service providers were based in close proximity to each other in a single building outside HMP Peterborough. They were also closely positioned within the prison. One Ormiston caseworker felt that it was very important that all the One Service partners were based under one roof to deliver their services outside the prison: 'they just say they're here for One Service'. A second important design feature was the decision to be completely transparent about sharing data.

The data system used by the One Service, 'Meganexus', was custom-designed to be client-focused, which meant that all information was attached to a client's personal record. All of the service providers used the same system and service users had to give them consent to share their data. That the data system operated seamlessly inside and outside the prison was an uncommon situation. An advantage of this system was that it saved the service user from retelling his story to every person he worked with, and facilitated collaboration between providers as they discussed support options for him. The use of evidence was an ongoing learning process and the development of this system was considered as much a tool that empowered caseworkers to do their job better, as it was a way for investors and managers to monitor performance. The system was not intended to track resultant savings for the MoJ, although it may be that the Meganexus data could be linked to the Police National Computer database to estimate costs avoided at some point.

Voluntary Engagement

An important feature of the One Service was that participation was voluntary: prisoners and ex-prisoners could opt in or opt out as they chose over the period the service was available. Service managers said that because the programme was voluntary there had been a far greater buy-in from participants. Managers said the participants also recognized and appreciated that the volunteers working with them have given up their own time and, therefore, put in more effort than they would have done for a mandatory programme. Some prisoners have said that the main reason that they engaged with the service was because it was voluntary.

When asked by his colleague how he would feel if the service he delivered for the One Service was mandatory, a Connections worker said, 'I don't think it would be very successful...Prisoners don't want to be told what to do.... I think if you told people they had to do it nine out of ten wouldn't want to.' His colleague added, 'It would destroy what we've built up...it would destroy what we're trying to do.' An ex-offender receiving services through the SIB said that if the One Service was mandatory, 'I don't think it would work...it's always about freedom of choice...I don't think many would turn up.'

However, crucially, the outcome results were to be measured for *all* prisoners eligible for the service, not just those who chose to participate. This created a significant incentive for the One Service to engage as many of the eligible prisoners as possible. More than 70 per cent of the eligible first cohort chose to engage with services, far more than was the case in many other social programmes in which participation was voluntary.

Contractual Flexibility

The One Service Director said the flexibility of their long-term, outcomes-based contract was an important strategic enabling factor: 'It's about trying to embed systemic change...people have talked about it and haven't had the freedom to do it.' The HMP Peterborough Prison Director agreed, saying: 'at the moment I'm paid for custodial services. Offender management services should be linked to reducing reoffending.'[15]

The One Service had one-year contracts with their service providers, reformulating contracts at each annual renewal and, sometimes, changing providers. The sub-contracted service providers saw the One Service as their commissioner and the SIB as their overall project. The One Service Director said, 'one of the good things is that you can commission in a very different way because of the way it's funded'. Despite the fact that the SIB was focused on delivering the same outcome from the outset, the providers and the services they delivered changed as the service has progressed. For example, the contract with the YMCA to provide local volunteers was not renewed, which may have seemed an unlikely decision considering the YMCA was also the landlord of the One Service outside the prison. However, the partnership between the One Service and the YMCA still continued and came to include payments for additional gym facilities and physical training as well.

Risks

The outcomes-based funding model was not without its risks. The One Service paid the full cost of services delivered by their providers. Service providers,

---

[15] All prisons currently have their performance scored against a raft of targets that include entering housing, education, and employment upon release (NOMS, 2012).

however, assumed significant reputational risk, heightened by considerable media attention on the Peterborough SIB as the pilot. A St Giles Trust manager said: 'Financially it's great for us, but I do say if it doesn't work we'll never work again.' Government was attracted to the accountability of paying only for results, but this came with reputational risk, as an ineffective programme for which government did not make payments would be widely viewed as a failure. The outcomes-based contract also held service providers to account as measurement of their results was published and scrutinized in a previously unprecedented manner.

Those against social investment sometimes argue that a profit should not be made from delivering services to address disadvantage. The investor's annual internal rate of return for the Peterborough SIB was expected to be 7.5 per cent and was capped at 13 per cent annual IRR (RAND Europe, 2011). Some investors expressed gratitude for this cap, as they felt uncomfortable with high returns. However, when asked what the users of the One Service thought about being 'invested in', the One Service Director said, 'I've been surprised how little people mind that the funding comes from social investors … They don't know who it is, they just think it's rich people and we just say it's seventeen investors, so they know it's very rich people. Some people give time as volunteers, some give money'.

Finally, outcome measurements relying on comparison with a control group cannot be rolled out nationally. Improved outcomes among the Peterborough cohort were measured by comparison to a matched control group that was not receiving the intervention. If every short-sentenced prisoner in England and Wales were part of a SIB, there would ultimately be no control group with which to compare the target population. Therefore, any future SIBs projects would have to test other ways of measuring counterfactuals or deadweight effects, for example, before-and-after measures (RAND Europe, 2011: see Box 12.1).

LEARNING AS THEY GO

Initially, the One Service intended St Giles Trust workers to be the service users' primary point of contact with prisoners, offering intensive support for four months at which point they would hand over to volunteer mentors. After beginning with this model, it became apparent that it was more effective for volunteer mentors to be involved from the beginning, with the intensive support provided by St Giles Trust left as an option if required. There was also a desire to involve ex-offenders as peer mentors, but it was realized that more support and screening would be needed when involving ex-offenders as mentors as the stability of the mentor relationship was essential. As time progressed, the service started taking on peer mentors that were on probation, but had already had some time out of prison and had adjusted well in this time. The service also employed ex-social workers.

BOX 12.1. KEY ASPECTS OF THE PETERBOROUGH PILOT SIB

The Peterborough SIB might be thought of as a 'proof of concept' of this form of PBR [payment by results] rather than a pilot, because there are some questions and issues which the Peterborough SIB will not be able to test. We identify the following five key areas in which the Ministry of Justice may be able to draw lessons from the Peterborough SIB for the wider roll-out of PBR models.

The SIB at HMP Peterborough provides an opportunity to test the concept of a PBR model which raises funds through, and shifts the risk to, private, non-governmental investors.

The Peterborough SIB tests whether and how, in this instance, stakeholders can develop feasible and suitable outcome metrics in the area of offender interventions, and agree upon a model to pay if outcomes are improved according to those metrics.

The Peterborough SIB may provide evidence of the performance of SIBs as a new kind of financial product, at least in the area of offender interventions. Developing this track record of investment will be crucial to building an investor base and improving understanding of outcome risk, all of which is necessary to open up a larger pool of capital.

The Peterborough SIB potentially involves a new commissioning relationship. In other payment-by-results arrangements, government has tended to maintain some control over the selection of providers, whereas in the Peterborough SIB the Government leaves the selection to an intermediary (such as Social Finance), and has no direct relationship with the service provider.

Although the intervention funded by the SIB at Peterborough (mentoring offenders) itself is not new, the SIB is an opportunity to test the impact of working intensively with short-sentenced prisoners. It is an opportunity to begin to build a robust evidence base on whether and how this was effective.

We identify the following as some issues which cannot be tested in the Peterborough SIB:

- The SIB at HMP Peterborough is not likely to result in substantial cashable savings to the Ministry of Justice or other government departments, which can be achieved only through significant reductions in the prison population or the number of court cases, and so on. Of course, there are other, non-cashable benefits to the public and victims if the Peterborough cohort reoffends less, in which the Ministry of Justice is interested. There is also the benefit of testing payment by results at a time of great pressure on public sector budgets.
- The SIB at Peterborough does not test whether and how different departments can share outcome payments.

Source: RAND, 2011: 7–9

A second point of learning was the One Service discovery that it was more effective to plan the endpoint of service after a particular goal has been achieved, rather than letting the relationship between service provider and prisoner peter out after essential needs had been met. It became clear that if the service ceased in a decisive way at a high point, the offender was more likely to re-engage if they needed future support, since they had a more positive previous encounter.

A third development flowed from a realization that prison staff could be just as institutionalized as the prisoners. As a result, the One Service organized for their providers and service users to come back and talk at full staff meetings. This both engaged staff to support the programme in prison and recognized the contribution of prison staff to prisoners' journeys. A member of the prison staff commented positively on this approach, 'before we only saw the failures, but now we see the successes. The One Service brings them back and it's really important to the staff to hear these stories'.

As the SIB progressed, collaboration with other services increased. Community partner organizations saw the One Service as having flexible, available funding that could offer benefits to their services, even if they were not direct providers. Some local organizations said that increased referrals from the One Service, from which they received no additional funding, has freed them up to focus more on service delivery and less on advertising their services to potential users. Moreover, the One Service Director sat on several boards across local community services and the One Service collaborated to help with issues faced by other organizations. For example, when the One Service forecast a local housing shortage for their clients, other local organizations including health, housing, and the police volunteered to assist in different ways to address the contributing factors.

Another important innovation achieved by the One Service in 2012 was the flagging of their service users' names on the Police National Computer database. This meant that when the police come into contact with an ex-offender, as they enter his name into the computer, the One Service phone number would automatically appear. This allowed the police to re-engage the person with the service, increasing their options for dealing with issues faced by ex-offenders and their communities.

The One Service delivery model initially had Ormiston relying on the St Giles Trust for referrals. However, after only a few referrals were forthcoming, it became apparent that service users were unlikely to disclose family support needs to St Giles Trust staff at a time when they were addressing crisis issues such as housing. In response, the One Service looked to create a separate opportunity for prisoners to engage with Ormiston to discuss family needs and arranged for Ormiston to offer new parenting courses in prison. These were so successful that the prison subsequently contracted the Ormiston to run parenting courses for other prisoners.

The introduction of mental health services through Mind was a further addition to the original programme. Mind had a business model offering appointments only to clients at their office in town on Wednesday and Thursdays. They also had a three- to six-month waiting list. The One Service worked with them to redesign this model and spot-purchased mental health visits to the prison, starting with a couple of hours a week. This soon increased to two days a week and Mind became an integral provider working out of the One Service premises and HMP Peterborough. Mind worked with clients in custody and in the community and played a valuable role in explaining to prison staff the journey and mental state of offenders. Prison management also commissioned Mind to provide services in HMP Peterborough for women and long-term prisoners. The flexible approach from Mind enabled clients who would otherwise not have visited Mind to access support at the One Service.

The One Service worked closely with the HMP Peterborough private management company, Sodexo (previously known as Kalyx). The prison resettlement manager stressed that it was not an easy partnership to enter into: 'the set-up process was really hard in terms of the way we had to collect data, share data work with prisoners, open our doors to different people.' However, the two management teams soon established fairly regular review meetings to work together to improve services. For example, the One Service provided the prison with a list of persistent reoffenders and asked them to think of ways of doing things differently for these men, even if it was just little things like rewarding an increase in the amount of time spent out of prison between sentences. The prison and the One Service were also able to work together to pool funding to test new services before either party commissioned them on a greater scale.

KEY INNOVATIONS

Long-term Contracts

The seven-year funding agreement was considered an important feature of how services are delivered on the ground. The One Service Director said, 'The long-term nature means the One Service can be taken seriously in the prison service space where so many services come and go frequently.' At their first meeting with Peterborough prisoners where the new service was explained, representatives of the One Service were surprised to be asked by a prisoner how the programme was funded. The prisoner later explained, 'I wanted to know how it was funded to know how long it's going to last.'

Long-term funding under an outcomes-based contract allowed the One Service to be flexible and adaptive as to how it spent money. Flexibility of funding means there were no fixed amounts directed at employment or housing, but, rather, spending could respond to what the service users needed as they needed it. If something was not working, the One Service could stop doing it. This flexibility allowed them to test out new services too, often in collaboration with other funders, before deciding whether to add them to the One Service. The flexibility of the initial budget for the Peterborough SIB was well demonstrated by the inclusion of an entry for 'unspecified expenses'. When asked what it was for, a Social Finance director simply said 'we don't know yet'. This became the 'innovation budget' to fund new work or address unexpected service gaps with community partner organizations.

St Giles Trust workers also experienced changes due to this flexibility. One worker commented, 'We're not being dictated to. We can shape the delivery model to meet needs.' For example, from handing over to volunteers, they later supported clients in parallel with volunteer mentors. St Giles Trust also found it easier to get spot funding for a particular service for an individual client than under previous contracts.

Single-outcome Contracts

Traditional government commissioning contracts were not necessarily a problem in all situations, however those involved with the Peterborough SIB saw several advantages in focusing their delivery on a single outcome rather than a prescriptive process. The One Service Director noted, 'It's about reducing reoffending, it's not just about finding a house, or focusing on one thing…it's a lifestyle change.' Lifestyle changes are what outcomes attempt to capture and measure, so it seemed that in this case the choice of outcome and measurement system produced an effective alignment. She elaborated, 'One of the real values of having one long-term outcome is…it just changes the whole dynamic, it's a different mindset…it's not competitive—if we want to pay for him to go see his mother's grave in Wales, we pay.' Those working with the One Service communicated a sense of a longer-term or more holistic goal: 'I've worked on other programmes that are focused on ticking the box, but they get someone a home and then what? Once you prescribe something and set targets for it, you lose the point.' The way an outcome is measured creates an incentive to work with people for the entire measurement period. An Ormiston worker commented, 'When you've got to work with people for twelve months, that's a lot of work, so you put more effort in.' Previously, she had been involved in contracts where she always worked with prisoners for six contact visits, regardless of need.

However, the outcomes-based contract introduced new risks to service delivery as well as new benefits. One risk was the change in location of prisoners. When the Peterborough SIB began, 63 per cent of the short-term prisoners released resided in the Peterborough area, with 10 per cent residing in London. The One Service was set up to cope with up to 20 per cent of the cohort resettling in London, but could find resources stretched if the proportion rose above that.

Collaboration

Collaboration with both providers and the community was one of the most difficult and rewarding aspects of the One Service. Collaborative working was not typical in welfare provision in the UK and the Peterborough SIB required a substantial culture change for the organizations involved. But benefits were realized. One of the workers involved in the One Service said that her other projects had become more 'outreach' focused, where she goes to work with clients on her own. Having been based in the same physical space as the other providers enabled her to offer her clients more support in handover to other services. She was also able to share vital information with other providers and prepare her clients to interact with new people, increasing the chance that they would successfully engage with other providers. She also spoke of the increased support available to her under the One Service, 'When you're thinking you don't have the answer, someone else might…as a social worker I've never had that before; I've always been on my own.'

Table 12.1. Key variations in SIB models across the world

Commissioner	How does it differ from Peterborough?
New York City, USA	Investment guarantee The $9.6m investment by Goldman Sachs in the New York City juvenile reoffending bond is underwritten by a $7.2m guarantee from Bloomberg philanthropies. This effectively reduces the risk of capital loss to $2.4m or 25% of total investment.
Essex County Council, UK	Early payments provide working capital Payments from Essex County Council, in their SIB for children on the edge of care, begin only nine months after services commence. Early cash flow is recycled into service delivery, with investor returns occurring at the end of the SIB.
Department of Work and Pensions, UK	A suite of new interventions The Department of Work and Pensions commissioned ten SIBs over two rounds, via their innovation fund, to improve the education and employment prospects of disadvantaged young people. Payments were made monthly as outcomes were evidenced. After the three-year pilot, a comprehensive assessment of the programme allowed for calculation of effect size and comparison between the interventions.
Greater London Authority, UK	Not about savings Improved outcomes for homeless people as a result of this SIB might reduce demand in some service areas, but it is expected that they will access additional health services with additional cost to government. This SIB is therefore not justified on the basis of savings, but on the basis of the value of improved outcomes.
New South Wales, Australia	No intermediary Australian not-for-profit organizations are directly contracting with the New South Wales Government, rather than through an intermediary, such as Social Finance in Peterborough. In Australia, very large not-for-profits have a long history of contracting with government for a range of services, and have, thus, developed the capacity for negotiating complex contracts directly.
Massachusetts, USA	Service provider as investor In Massachusetts, the service provider, ROCA, contributed 15% of the investment into the SIB. This reduced the risk for the other investors, by demonstrating their confidence in their ability to deliver outcomes, as well as share any financial upside.
Fresno, California, USA	Non-government commissioner An organization called the California Endowment, a private health foundation is funding the proof of concept for a pilot health-care SIB in California to improve the health of people with asthma.
Council for Voluntary Adoption Agencies, UK	Multiple commissioners and service providers The Council for Voluntary Adoption Agencies is bringing together 18 Voluntary Adoption Agencies to find successful adoption families for hard-to-adopt children, referred by local authorities across the UK. Payments will be made by local authorities in relation to the outcomes for the child(ren) they refer, and payments will be received by Voluntary Adoption Agencies as they effect outcomes for these individuals (see Bennett, 2012).

Notes: In the USA some SIBs are known as pay-for-success contracts (see Callanan et al., 2012). In Australia the SIB is known as a Social Benefit Bond (New South Wales) or Social Impact Partnership (Western Australia). The New South Wales Social Benefit Bond delivered by Uniting Care Burnside involves a Government guarantee of between 50% and 75%, dependent on time. The Benevolent Society is also another example of a service provider as investor.

Service Innovation

One of the early innovations of the One Service was to meet all prisoners at the gate as they were released, regardless of whether they expressed a desire for this or not. One prisoner said to a St Giles Trust caseworker, 'If you hadn't met me at the gate I would have been in custody by tonight.' The caseworker noted that sometimes preventing a reoffence is as simple as providing a prisoner with a lift to the train station so that they catch their train home rather than get distracted by the off-licence on the way.

Social Impact Bond models globally

As of 2014, there were approximately fifty SIBs or SIB-type contracts in operation or in development across the world. The early adopters were clustered in the UK, the USA, and Australia, with Canada and Israel also showing strong interest.[16] However, across these different jurisdictions a number of important variations in the structure and focus of the SIB model have appeared. These differences demonstrate the adaptability of the SIB model to local political, social, and economic contexts, as well as reflecting differences within countries in terms of the traditions of welfare service delivery, particularities of investor markets, and the landscape of service delivery organizations available for SIBs.

Table 12.1 sets out a number of the notable variants of the SIB model drawn from several examples across the world. These are presented in contrast to the Peterborough SIB pilot which for the purposes of this analysis is taken here as the archetypical model.

These variations of the SIB model emphasize its adaptability to different contexts and also underline the innovations that underpin it—namely the SIB model requires the agreement of several stakeholders of differing perspective and its many variables must be adjusted to suit their competing needs.

Conclusions

Since the launch of the first, pilot SIB programme in Peterborough in 2010, there has been an extraordinary amount of global interest in adopting this innovation elsewhere—interest that has preceded available evidence of the actual impact of this new model. There would appear to be a number of reasons for this.

---

[16] There is also evidence of interest in developing SIBs in Ireland, France, Germany, South Africa and South Korea as well as Development Impact Bonds (with development finance institutions or development-focused foundations as possible outcome funders) being explored in several other countries.

BENEFITS

First, for government, there are considerable attractions in engaging with SIB models that address the long-standing increased efficiency and increased effectiveness policy agendas mentioned above. These include:

Effectiveness

- *Outcomes focus*: focusing on evidenced outcomes (rather than outputs) based programmes to deliver improved results for service users and to increase the likelihood of delivering real and sustainable solutions to important social challenges
- *Evidenced effects*: adding discipline to measuring outcomes for government programmes and improving the evidence base for social services by mandating measurement and publication of outcomes
- *Enhanced social metrics*: building new data sets and performance benchmarks of value across other similar (non SIB) intervention and programmes
- *Scaling*: identifying effective innovations early to scale them more quickly.

Efficiency

- *New finance*: bringing in new private investment to fund welfare services[17]
- *Additionality*: expanding the range of effective interventions and make them available to more people funded by private investment
- *Innovation*: harnessing the innovative capacity of both investors and service providers to reform publicly funded service delivery models
- *Co-ordination*: facilitating coordination between organizations working on overlapping problems and aligning the interests of service users, service providers, private investors, and government
- *Early intervention*: exploiting the net present *social* value of welfare services by moving resources towards prevention and early interventions up front to achieve larger outcome impacts down the line
- *Transferring risk*: moving outcomes risk from state expenditure to private investment.

Accountability

- *Incentives*: outcomes are more likely to be delivered if there are incentives for every party to achieve them

---

[17] Thus allowing governments either to reduce existing spending for the same set of outcomes or to achieve more impact within existing budgets. The former policy position is more controversial than the latter in contexts where privatization agendas remain politically sensitive.

- *Adaptability*: flexibility to adjust model to reflect experience of delivery and needs
- *Rewarding success:* investors looking at new solutions to old problems encourages providers to innovate and demonstrate success.

In addition, the development of a significant number of SIBs will play an important role in growing the larger social finance market by unlocking new sources of capital to fund social issues. Growing the social finance market has been a significant policy objective in several countries over the past decade, notably in the UK, USA, and Canada. Moreover, at scale, SIBs may ultimately represent a new asset class within social finance that can harness private investment for the benefit of the community and enable investors interested in public welfare programmes to achieve financial returns and social impact simultaneously. Once a critical mass of SIBs has been established with a track record of successful performance and evidence of repayment, it is quite possible that a secondary market in SIBs could emerge that would be of interest to institutional—and ultimately retail—investors.

CHALLENGES

However, for all the optimism surrounding SIBs there remain a number of significant future challenges. These include:

- *Realizing actual—cashable—savings for government*: In reality, the early SIB models are not designed to allow government to make real budget savings in the short or medium term. In order for savings to be made, any reduction in demand due to a SIB must result in a reduction in the supply of services by Government. This is only likely to occur when the outcomes of a SIB are either directed at discretionary services bought in small units from third parties or when a SIB market is at such scale that its outcomes can lead to a systemic change, such as the closure of a whole prison (in the case of reducing reoffending). Indeed, even in the latter case such action could be so politically difficult—increasing unemployment, cutting public services, and so on—that it may still be avoided. It is also hard to imagine how an SIB could decrease spending on statutory services without major political consequences
- *Capturing cross-silo benefits within government*: Most government accounting structures make it very difficult to account for the savings and benefits accrued from a single project or intervention across several departments. In the UK, the Cabinet Office has set up the £20m Social Outcomes Fund to smooth across these issues by quantifying and then funding value creation from payment-by-results contracts that accrue across departments

- *Risks of distorting the social finance market*: There may be the potential for external investors to drive SIBs away from the more risky or innovative interventions that can lead to the largest social impact and, thus, narrow the potential impact of the SIB model in terms of addressing the most difficult welfare challenges, difficult to reach target populations, or hardest to measure outcomes

- *Reducing the legitimacy of government*: Transferring risk and therefore responsibility for welfare services to its citizens may diminish the role of the state and lead to a perceived 'democratic deficit'. In the UK, for example, the presentation of SIBs as a form of 'privatization by the back door' has already appeared in the public discourse

- *High transaction costs*: The costs of establishing the necessary metrics, baselines, legal arrangements, and financial calculations are sometimes so high that the SIB is infeasible without additional funding

- *SIB contracts are perceived to be complex* (RAND Europe, 2011): Efforts to simplify SIBs would result in greater understanding and take up

- *Allocating risk and return fairly*: There is clearly a need to price the risk of a SIB correctly to attract (social) investors, but there is also a need to avoid risk dumping on intermediaries and service providers

- *Early stage of outcomes measurement and data*: Few providers and public agencies have measured outcomes for the length of time and with the rigour to make confident predictions. This increases the scope of changes and length of time required for the development and implementation of a SIB

- *Procurement and optimism bias*: Service providers are optimistic about the outcomes they can achieve and the likelihood they will achieve them. At the same time, commissioners lack sufficient data to assess a bid as hopelessly optimistic. This can lead to outcome pricing that is too low and outcomes that are disappointing

- *High levels of public scrutiny*: Because of the structure and objectives (and novelty) of SIBs, such contracts may be expected to perform to a higher standard than other welfare service models. This offers the possibility of perceived failure or public cynicism over SIB outcomes

- *Political risk*: Due to the longer-term funding and contract structures of many SIBs, there is likely to be a need to consider how to transition across electoral cycles and between political ideologies—this could make SIBs vulnerable to political fashion

- *Innovating commissioning practices and systems*: If SIBs are to play a major role in delivering welfare services, there will need to be reforms across commissioning practices in many governments to acknowledge the unique requirement and opportunities of pay-by-results commissioning

- *Limited services and populations to which a SIB can be applied*: SIBs currently implement innovative programmes targeted at preventative 'service gaps' which are few and finite. SIBs have yet to be used to deliver services with a history of public funding and thus there may be limits to the size the SIB market can grow, limits that have not been explored to date

- *A means to an end or an end in themselves*: If successful, it could be assumed that there has been a funding shift to the preventative service introduced by the SIB, but it will need to be established whether SIBs best deliver impact if repeated in the same service area or whether they establish an evidence base for continued funding by other models.

LEGACY

The following section expands on this final issue concerning the legacy of, and exit from, a SIB contract. For key stakeholders, there is a need to evaluate whether the SIB achieved what was hoped and whether its legacy furthered or detracted from their strategic aims and objectives. For example, one key question of a SIB is when and why should it end? Other key questions to consider are set out below from the perspective of each stakeholder typically involved in a SIB:

Government

- How to institutionalize innovation into future welfare programmes and in the wider social services market?
- If early prevention is successful, how to maintain and fund preventative services after SIB ends? Do SIBs need to 'rollover' to produce sustainable change?
- How can SIB outcomes data (likelihood, effect size, cost of delivery, value or savings to tax payer, related externalities/proxy outcomes) drive better commissioning across government?
- How to achieve key outcomes post SIB?
- How to continue to grow the social finance market to fund welfare services?
- How to report on and share SIB learning and data more widely?
- How to calculate savings from SIB interventions?

Investors

- How to develop a secondary market exit?
- How to develop a follow-on SIB investment?
- How to adjust risk and return dynamically to the availability of new information from SIBs in the market?
- How to tranche investments in a single SIB according to different risk and return profiles and different personal costs of capital?

Service Providers

- How to ensure continuity of funding of increased capacity?
- How to institutionalize SIB performance data?
- How to build capacity to engage in future SIBs?
- How to manage ongoing collaborative relationships?
- How to disseminate learning?
- How to leave a community stronger when a service ends?

Intermediaries

- How to build a pipeline of SIB deals?
- How to build capacity in providers so that they are stronger for having worked on a SIB?
- How to continuously innovate?
- Where to apply SIBs and develop other models that build upon SIB learning?
- When are SIBs no longer necessary, if ever?
- How to build a business model, given high transaction costs?
- How better to segment the investor market to the real, rather than perceived, risk and return opportunities of SIBs?
- How to manage the involvement of commercial, rather than purely social, investors in terms of expectations of high returns and the potential for risk dumping?

Service Users

- How to access services and support with the SIB ends?
- How to sustain positive changes over time?

SIBs provide the opportunity to make significant changes to the way welfare or other social services are delivered. They introduce a contractual structure predicated on agreed outcomes that align incentives across all key stakeholders. At the early stage of its development the SIB market offered more in terms of promise and innovation than track record or evidence of success. But given the significant policy, media, and investor interest that has been evident in this new model, it seems likely that understanding the potentials and pitfalls of the SIB model will be an important skill within the social finance sector. This will be true for future entrepreneurs, policymakers, investors, and fund managers as SIBs appeal to interest groups in social finance, social policy, and social innovation.

Postscript: 2014

CHANGES TO THE PETERBOROUGH SIB

In April 2014, the Ministry of Justice announced that it would introduce an entirely new model of probation known as Transforming Rehabilitation (TR). This change outsourced the entire probation service into twenty-one areas that were offered to tender for non-governmental service providers. In addition, TR introduced a statutory responsibility for the provision of probation services for *all* prisoners, including short-term offenders for the first time. The effects of the introduction of TR were profound for the Peterborough SIB. First, since TR would offer probationary services to all prisoners, the control group for measuring Peterborough's impact disappeared. Second, as a new *universal* probation service, TR necessarily replaced the Peterborough SIB over time. On 24 April 2014, Social Finance issued the following statement:[18]

As announced today, the Ministry of Justice has proposed an alternative funding arrangement for Peterborough Social Impact Bond (SIB) in light of the expected introduction of a new approach to UK probation and rehabilitation services at the end of 2014. The proposal will enable the Peterborough intervention (the 'One Service') to continue but will change the way the service is funded and remove the outcomes payments for the third and last cohort of prisoners to be released from June 2014. Details of the alternative funding arrangement are still being discussed but the Ministry of Justice is keen to ensure that the same level of rehabilitation support continues to be provided to this group through until the new regime is established and a new provider is in a position to establish supply chain arrangements for rehabilitation. The support to prisoners in the second cohort will continue to be funded by social investors as anticipated until June 2015 and the investors will qualify for outcomes payments on the same basis as the first cohort.

The Peterborough SIB continued in its original form until June 2015 when the delivery of support for the second cohort ended: after this point the third cohort were not part of the SIB (as originally intended) though it was subject to statutory services under TR on a fee-for-service model. Moreover, in early 2015, it became clear that the One Service would not continue operating as part of TR and, as a result, would have to wind down. Nevertheless, the One Service's results and related outcomes payments for the first cohort were delivered in August 2014 and those for the second cohort were expected in the summer of 2016.

---

[18] <http://www.socialfinance.org.uk/social-finance-statement-peterborough-social-impact-bond/#sthash.AkSyDlut.dpuf>.

Despite the early ending of the SIB, Toby Eccles of Social Finance provided a positive assessment of its impact.[19] He explained that the SIB had several objectives and he took stock of its performance against them:

- *Enabling innovation: Success*, the model was implemented, when without the SIB structure the project would not have been put in place
- *Enable flexibility and focus on outcomes: Success*, as can be read in the RAND report, there are numerous citations from stakeholders that the model has enabled indeed required the service to adapt to the needs of service users and improve over time
- *Bring rigour to prevention: Success*, what other prevention pilot do we know of that has had detailed figures published while it was ongoing? Admittedly, actual results according to the payment metric aren't out yet, but this level of rigour simply isn't normally seen
- *Better alignment: Success*, investors in the pilot were keen, and investors in further SIBs have also been keener to fund the programme than they would have been had it been a traditional grant-funded project with no connection to government
- *Investment in social change: Still building*...We need more SIBs before we can claim that we have created a new investment community, though Bank of America Merrill Lynch distributing Social Finance's New York State SIB to their wealthy clients is a significant step in this direction
- And finally, most importantly, have we made a difference to short-sentence offenders? *YES!!!* There is a new statutory obligation to work with short-sentence offenders across the country. Whatever the merits or otherwise of the wider TR agenda, this is a very significant change on which many have been campaigning for a long time. Obviously it wasn't just the Peterborough SIB that caused this change, but it clearly played a significant role.

However, these changes were also subject to criticism.[20] Namely that the Peterborough SIB did not influence TR significantly and make the case for greater investment in rehabilitation, with the savings to come from the prisons budget not the probation budget. TR is mandatory, while the Peterborough SIB was voluntary. TR has a different payment metric than the Peterborough SIB, with a combination of frequency and binary conditions. TR was driven by a wider privatization and cost-reduction agenda, as well as rehabilitation. Moreover, the full resourcing of resettlement that the SIB made possible through its outcome payments structure is unlikely to be replicable under TR—short-sentence prisoners have been included in statutory provision without any new resourcing.

---

[19] 'Peterborough SIB: A Success or a Failure?' Posted on 25 April 2014 at <http://tobyecc.wordpress.com>.

[20] See, for example, Julian Corner, Chief Executive of Lankelly Chase Foundation and Peterborough SIB investor at <http://www.socialfinance.org.uk/transforming-rehabilitation-is-being-dressed-in-sheeps-clothing/#sthash.QaCFf8BG.dpuf>.

There was also concern about the wider effects of the early conclusion of the Peterborough SIB on the wider SIB market and, perhaps given its high profile, even on the social finance market more generally. Despite the provision of termination clauses, the investors in the first SIB were not able to see their investment through to its term and might, therefore, expect lower overall returns. Certainly, the One Service had imagined that the first cohort would return the poorest results due to it being a start-up without presence or track record in the prison. It was expected that the best performance would come from the second and third cohorts—with the former being particularly strong since the latter would have 'wind-down' issues. However, the putative 'best' cohort became the wind-down cohort post the announcement of TR, leaving the One Service potentially short of an absolute 'best' results group. Furthermore, the perceived riskiness for the potential investor of a SIB that is backed by the state could only increase after the Ministry of Justice's decision on TR. This could have the effect of either increasing the required return or cause investors to demand guarantees or other risk mitigation underwriting. In turn, this could hamper the evolution of future SIBs.

INTERIM RESULTS

On 7th August 2014, the results for the first cohort of prisoners that had gone through the One Service were released. The overall reduction was 8.4 per cent—there were 142 reconvictions per 100 prisoners at HMP Peterborough, compared with 155 reconvictions per 100 prisoners in the control group. This was less than the 10 per cent threshold required for investors to receive payments, but looked favourable in terms of a contribution towards the *average* figure of 7.5 per cent that was required to trigger payments across the whole SIB (though this would now only be two completed cohorts not the originally planned three). Social Finance published a letter from the Peterborough SIB investors on 8th August 2014:[21]

As investors in the Peterborough Social Impact Bond (SIB), we welcome the newly published results showing an encouraging 8.4 per cent reduction in reconviction rates among prisoners supported by the Peterborough One Service. Many of us have grant-funded charities and projects in the past to help fill the void in resettlement support for prisoners serving sentences of less than 12 months. In the SIB we saw an opportunity to demonstrate on a much more ambitious scale that support for these

---

[21] See more at: <http://www.socialfinance.org.uk/letter-from-peterborough-social-impact-bond-investors/#sthash.kbfhLaXO.dpuf>. The signatories were: Mark O'Kelly, Barrow Cadbury Trust; Danielle Walker Palmour, Friends Provident Foundation; Alexander Hoare, Golden Bottle Trust; Sir Michael Hintze, Hintze Family Charitable Foundation; Jerker Johansson, Johansson Family Foundation; Julian Corner, LankellyChase Foundation; Rob Bell, Paul Hamlyn Foundation; James Long, Tudor Trust; Mark Woodruff, Monument Trust; James Perry, Panahpur.

prisoners not only reduces crime and the numbers of future victims, it makes financial sense as well.

If the momentum built by the Peterborough One Service continues, there is a real prospect that we as investors will get our money back with a return. This is significant not only because we will be able to reinvest this money again in similar initiatives, but because under the terms of the SIB a financial return will only be paid to investors where HM Treasury calculates a net saving to the taxpayer. As the Government's plans for Transforming Rehabilitation move closer to implementation, we ask whether sufficient incentives to invest in the resettlement of prisoners serving short sentences have been reflected in the new providers' contracts. These providers, drawn mainly from the private sector, will face many competing pressures in designing and delivering their services. We now know from Peterborough that resettling people from prison, many of whom have very complex needs, only works with considerable and sustained focus, genuine flexibility, and proper resourcing. If the Government is determined to reduce reoffending, as it states, then the Peterborough One Service has set the bar for other services around the country. To emulate its results or improve on them, Transforming Rehabilitation needs to have the right contractual framework in place to ensure that new providers invest sufficiently in similarly effective approaches.

▨ APPENDIX A.12.1 SOCIAL FINANCE COMMENTARY

David Hutchison, CEO of Social Finance, describes how we must rethink the role of markets to enable social progress (September 2012):

When Social Finance launched the first Social Impact Bond (SIB) in October 2010, we were not anticipating the level of interest it would receive. The Peterborough Prison SIB is a £5m scheme that funds interventions for 3,000 short-sentenced male prisoners who are expected to leave the prison over the course of the subsequent six years. The scheme was oversubscribed by investors willing to take a risk on a project that would explore new ways of injecting funding into one of society's most pervasive problems: recidivism.

We wanted to provide increased funding for preventative services, with the dual aims of improving social outcomes and reducing long-term costs. Investors receive payments from the Ministry of Justice if—and only if—a measurable reduction in reoffending is achieved. The government will fund the payments with a proportion of the cost savings it can expect as a result of reduced criminal activity.

This small scheme has caught the imagination of world leaders: President Obama has allocated $100m (£65m) to fund better outcomes in areas such as recidivism and chronic homelessness through Social Impact Bonds. Social Finance has established a sister organisation in Boston to meet growing demand in the US. We are also working in partnership with other countries, including Australia, Ireland, Canada, New Zealand and Israel, to help them launch SIBs in their own markets.

And goes on to discuss investing in change:

Building a market from scratch is not easy; there may be high-profile failures, and products that lack any track record make for wary investors. However, with the launch of government-backed initiatives such as the Investment and Contract Readiness Fund and Big Society Capital, much-needed support to scale social enterprises into investable propositions is becoming more readily available.

It seems that people are waking up to the attraction of investing in this way. The bottom line need not always be to maximize profit at any cost, but instead what we at Social Finance call 'investing for a social and financial return'. In terms of delivering social outcomes and change, the investment model is harnessing this sense of accountability and provides the incentive for innovation. The investors in the first SIB were trusts and foundations, but retail products are the next step in enabling this burgeoning social investment market to grow. At a time when society's needs are increasing and public expenditure is declining, the concept of social investment is ripe to be more fully explored. (*Ethos Online Journal* at <http://www.ethosjournal.com/topics/the-economy/item/381-social-impact-bonds>)

▩ **APPENDIX A.12.2** DEFINITIONS OF SIBS

Social Impact Bonds are based on a commitment from government to use a proportion of the savings that result from improved social outcomes to reward non-government investors that fund the early intervention activities. (Social Finance, 2009)

A range of financial assets that entail raising money from third parties and making repayments according to the social impacts achieved. (Young Foundation, 2010)

Social Impact Bonds bring together government, service providers and investors/funders to implement existing and proven programmes designed to accomplish clearly defined outcomes. Investors/funders provide the initial capital support and the government agrees to make payments to the programme only when outcomes are achieved. So government pays for success. (Third Sector Capital Partners, 2013)

▩ **APPENDIX A.12.3** STAKEHOLDER PERSPECTIVES

An important feature of the SIB model is that—to be successful, indeed to even be agreed—it must align the interests and incentives of all its key stakeholders. These include: government, service providers, investors, and service users. Each will now be considered in turn.

GOVERNMENT COMMISSIONERS

SIBs may be attractive to government in terms of a range of policy agendas that will vary by context (see Jupp, 2011). However, some common drivers of state engagement in SIBs can be discerned.

Growing the Market for Welfare Services

It is beneficial to government to support a social sector that can both deliver services on behalf of the state and respond to the emerging or unmet needs of disadvantaged people. Disadvantage can be expensive for government and, therefore, the taxpayer voter. Social issues that remain unaddressed can escalate and governments worldwide are struggling to cope with current demands for acute services such as foster care, health services (see Loder, 2012), and custodial programmes. A stronger social sector arises both through the strengthening of the organizations and programmes they deliver, and the support of an emerging social investment market. SIBs can bring new capital into the social sector to grow existing programmes and start new ones.[22]

Shifting Funding to Prevention

SIBs can enable governments to shift funding from acute services to preventative services. Under increasing demand for acute services, accelerated in Western economies by ageing populations, governments have increasingly cut rather than grown preventative services despite the fact that they may ultimately reduce overall demand. Thus, SIB outcomes are particularly attractive to government if they have the potential to reduce the demand for acute care.[23]

Outcome Measurement

Governments worldwide are purchasing an increasing proportion of public services from external providers and moving to outcomes-based contracts can improve the effectiveness of this spending (Bolton and Savell, 2010). The basis of grants and contracts for services has traditionally been inputs or outputs. While most government grants or contracts require that providers report on the way they have spent money plus some operational information on a programme, they have typically not required providers to measure the change in the lives of the people they serve. Contracting by outcome allows government to quantify, as well as be held to account for, the real social value of state spending. A further benefit of the focus on outcomes data and evidence is that SIBs mandate rigour in measurement of the *effect* of services, so there is increased capacity for learning that can extend to wider services delivered by or on behalf of government (see Fox and Albertson, 2011). Moreover, payments dependent on proven outcomes also allow government only to fund programmes that have had a demonstrably positive effect. Finally, outcomes-based contracts mandate that results are measured and investor involvement increases the pressure for such measurement to be robust and results published. The data derived from SIBs may prove to have wider value in enhancing performance transparency and accountability in service delivery organizations. Such data can also support the development of the wider social finance market—since good information is the bedrock of all properly functioning markets.

Innovation

Governments may also be attracted to SIBs because they are innovative (Essex County Council, 2012). They are innovative because they change the nature of the Government contract with a service delivery body to one based on outcomes. They are also innovative because they involve government consideration of investor motivation, risk, and return. SIBs also often involve new relationships with and between organizations.

---

[22] The extent to which the delivery of public services by external organizations is acceptable to society will be, to some extent, dependent on political and cultural context.
[23] However, a reduction in demand for acute services is not necessarily a saving for government, as substantial savings can only be made when the supply of acute services is actually reduced (Bolton and Savell, 2010). As a consequence, SIBs are most attractive to government in areas where the supply of acute services can easily be reduced in response to a reduction in demand.

Wider Benefits

Due to the intensive resources required to develop SIBs and the media attention they have initially received, governments have so far invested substantial time and energy into making sure that they only invest in SIBs with a high likelihood of success. A benefit of this is that commissioners are developing skills that can be transferred to improve the purchasing and evaluation of services more widely.

INVESTORS

Investors may be attracted to SIBs purely on the basis that they offer a chance to make a financial return on investment. Indeed, the social element of a SIB (and its relationship to government) is likely to mean that an investment in such a model is not correlated to other mainstream investments—as such it offers a portfolio risk mitigation strategy. Furthermore, the involvement of government guarantees (New South Wales) or philanthropic underwriting (New York City) may make a SIB investment very low risk, despite its novelty and lack of track record. Indeed, even in the UK where no guarantees are in place, investments are likely to be low risk due to the high levels of due diligence done in advance of the first few SIB contracts. It does not benefit government or intermediaries to see a SIB fail.

Many investors in SIBs will, of course, also be motivated by the potential of a social return too. Social investors find SIBs attractive because they offer a blended social and financial return, where the financial return is dependent on the social return. In this way, SIBs offer a clearer measure of social return than some other social investments. Investors approaching SIBs from a philanthropic perspective also find them attractive as they offer a means to 'recycle' their grant or donation capital as 'investment', enabling them to contribute more over time. They also see their involvement as a means to support service delivery organizations to access increased government funding as well as helping to build the wider social investment market.

The RAND Europe evaluation of the Peterborough SIB (2011) referred to Social Finance saying that over half the value, and number, of investments was by organizations or individuals investing in criminal justice for the first time. The report listed several reasons given by investors for their involvement:

- *Desire to support a new kind of payment-by-results financial product*
- *Charities' desire to invest money more ethically*
- *Interest from some investors in funding programmes in the area of criminal justice*
- *Opportunity to learn about social investment was welcomed*
- *The idea of delivering upfront funding to providers was attractive*
- *An estimation by investors that there was a good chance of receiving a return. (p. 28)*

As the social investment market grows, it is likely that a secondary market for SIBs may emerge offering primary investors liquidity and exit and secondary investors, such as pension funds, a potentially attractive asset class within a diversified (and socially aware) portfolio.

The first example of retail investors having access to investment in a SIB was the Allia Future for Children Bond. The £1m bond offer opened 4 February 2013 and was withdrawn in April after failing to raise sufficient capital to cover costs. Eighty per cent of the bond was a low-risk loan to social housing provider, at 0 per cent return, and the remaining 20 per cent was a securitized portion of the original investment in the Essex

SIB, contributing an additional variable return. There was a minimum investment size of £15k. Allia stated, 'The applications received demonstrated that certain investors could be motivated to invest their capital for the purpose of creating social impact, even though for this product the expected financial return was unknown. The campaign also revealed however some of the challenges in the structuring and distribution of complex products for retail investors' (Allia, 2013).

SERVICE PROVIDERS

Service providers for a SIB fall into a three categories: the primary organization that holds the outcomes-based contract with government; a sub-contractor of the contract holder; an organization delivering services to SIB service users without receiving funds from the SIB. Each may be attracted to a SIB for different reasons.

A Service Provider that Contracts with Government

Service providers will find SIBs attractive if they offer new, longer-term, or more stable funding. Some social purpose organizations are effectively excluded from bidding for government contracts because they cannot access sufficient working capital to achieve results before payments are received. In a SIB, working capital is provided upfront by private investors that solves this problem.[24] Moreover, the length of time over which SIB funding is committed may be longer than government funding cycles tied to elections or spending reviews. This can mean greater funding stability for the service providers involved and the people they serve. Long-term funding is attractive to service providers as it allows them better to plan their budgets and resourcing.

Contracting by outcomes, rather than outputs, allows service providers more freedom and flexibility as to how their programmes are delivered. This can allow service providers to be more responsive to their service users' needs. It also allows them to innovate as a programme is delivered to improve services and also to capture these innovations to improve their other services and, even, set benchmarks for services delivered by other organizations.

A Service Provider as Sub-contractor

Service providers that sub-contract to deliver SIB services might be able to access longer-term, more stable funding too. This may allow them to expand the scope and scale of their work, thereby helping more people. Small organizations that find it difficult to access government contracts alone due to size, complexity, or lack of experience may find the role of the SIB sub-contractor opens the door to contracting.

Many sub-contractors will need to develop collaborative partnerships with other service providers. Collaborative service delivery can initially be difficult for organizations or employees that are used to working alone. However, it also offers additional benefits such as shared measurement systems and learning. Working with other service providers in a SIB can mean that learning is captured and shared more easily, allowing for greater or more rapid improvement in services.

---

[24] Some social purpose organizations may find a relationship with private investors problematic (or, at least, novel). The involvement of an intermediary may help to manage such relationships.

Table 12.2. Value proposition of a SIB to some key stakeholders

■ positive value proposition   ☐ neutral value proposition   ▨ negative value proposition

	Government	Service providers	Philanthropy	Investment
Shift outcome performance risk and upfront cost to investors	positive	neutral	positive	negative
Creation of outcomes not just outputs	positive	positive	positive	neutral
Improve lives of beneficiaries	positive	positive	positive	neutral
Expansion of preventative services	positive	positive	positive	neutral
Monetize cost savings of prevention	positive	neutral	neutral	positive
Uncorrelated return and diversification	neutral	neutral	neutral	positive
Risk-adjusted return on investment	negative	neutral	neutral	positive

Service Providers not Funded by the SIB

Service providers that are not funded by a SIB might still deliver services to SIB service users or collaborate with SIB service providers. SIB service providers might refer service users to other services in the community, allowing them to focus more on service delivery and less on attracting clients. SIB service providers might also advocate for their service users or provide vital background information to other stakeholders in a welfare ecosystem. Community organizations might partner with SIB service providers to pool funding for a new programme or find solutions to mutual problems. Incentives for SIB service providers to support other community service providers will depend on the design of SIB measurement systems.

SERVICE USERS

Service users targeted by SIBs may be attracted to their services since they aim at effective outcomes (rather than outputs) over the long term. In addition, long-term funding lowers the risk to service users that the services stop unexpectedly. If responsibility for engaging service users is transferred to providers, then providers also have an incentive to develop services that are appealing and tailored to the user. Thus SIBs

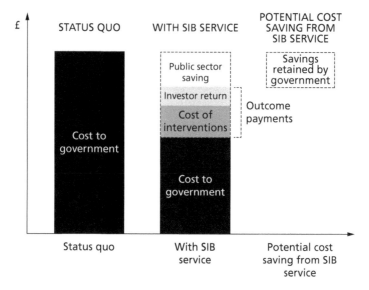

Source: Barclay & Symons, 2013

improve the likelihood of delivering real and sustainable solutions to important social challenges at the community and individual levels. Moreover, due to their emphasis on collecting and publishing rigorous performance data, SIBs should be more transparent and more accountable to service users. A focus on outcomes may also encourage SIB service providers to be more participative in terms of their key service users exploring co-production models and more embedded innovative practices.

Godeke and Resner (2012) set out the priorities and value propositions of some of the key stakeholders that engage in SIBs, or pay-for-success contracts as they are some-times referred to in the USA, though it excludes service users from this analysis (see Table 12.2).[25]

▨ APPENDIX A.12.4 THE THEORETICAL VALUE-FOR-MONEY CALCULATION BY GOVERNMENT

This figure summarizes the cost structure of a SIB to government. The 'Cost to Government' in the first column represents the costs of acute responses and care (for the Peterborough SIB this would include Police, court and prison costs). 'Cost to Government' in the second column shows that these costs are expected to decrease under a SIB, but government incurs an additional cost which is shown as the 'Outcome Payments'—'Cost of Interventions' plus 'Investor return'. The difference between the total costs to government in these two columns is shown as 'Savings Retained by Government' in the third column.

[25] This analysis does not acknowledge blended value returns that combine social and financial value creation as social investment/impact investment per se. Rather it ascribes social value creation only to philanthropy.

▨ **APPENDIX A.12.5** SIBS IN THE UK (2014)

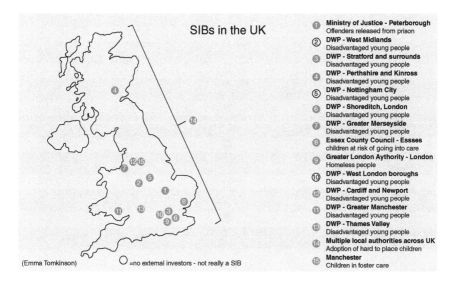

▨ **APPENDIX A.12.6** SIBS WORLDWIDE (2014)

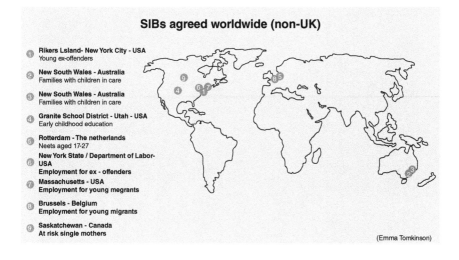

■ **APPENDIX A.12.7** SEVEN TESTS OF WHETHER A SIB IS AN APPROPRIATE
FUNDING MODEL

Source: Mulgan et al., 2010

APPENDIX A.12.8 THE PROCESSES OF NEGOTIATING AND DRAFTING CONTRACTUAL ARRANGEMENTS FOR THE SIB

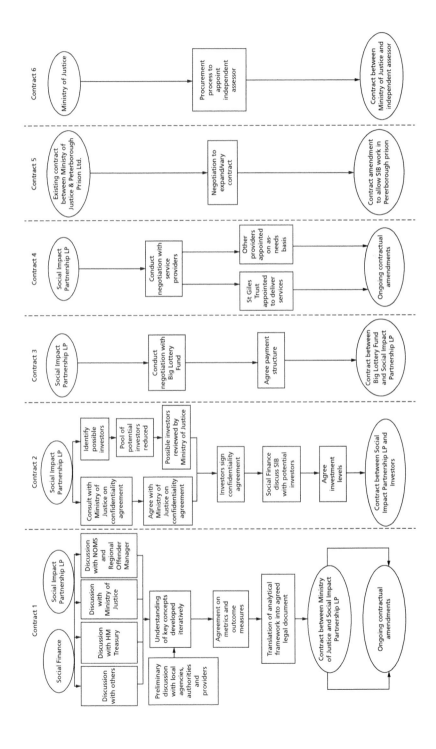

Source: RAND Europe (2011: 17) sourced from RAND Europe's analysis of interviewees' accounts

▥ **APPENDIX A.12.9** TIMELINE OF SIB DEVELOPMENT

Source: RAND, 2011: 70

▥ **REFERENCES**

Allia (2013). 'Future for Children Bond Offer Closed'. News release, 17 April.

Barclay, L., and Symons, T. (2013). *A Technical Guide to Developing Social Impact Bonds*. London: Social Finance.

Bennett, R. (2012). 'Adoption Bonds Will Provide Cash to Find Families for Children Languishing in Care'. *The Times*, 8 November.

Big Lottery Fund (2010). *BIG Paves Way forward through Social Investment*. London: BIG.

Bolton, E. and Savell, L. (2010). *Towards a New Social Economy: Blended Value Creation through Social Impact Bonds*. London: Social Finance.

Cabinet Office (2009). *The Council on Social Action*. London: Cabinet Office.

Cabinet Office (2013). *The Social Impact Bond Knowledge Box*. London: Cabinet Office.

Callanan, L., Law. J., and Mendonca, L. (2012). *From Potential to Action: Bringing Social Impact Bonds to the US*. New York: McKinsey and Company.

Conservative Party (2010). *Big Society Not Big Government*. London: Conservative Party.

Essex County Council (2012). 'First Local Authority to Award Social Impact Bond to Help Young People on the Edge of Care'. Press Release, 22 November, Colchester.

Fox, C., and Albertson, K. (2011). 'Payment by Results and Social Impact Bonds in the Criminal Justice Sector: New Challenges for the Concept of Evidence-Based policy?' *Criminology and Criminal Justice*, 11(5): 395–413.

Frontier Economics (2010). *St Giles Trust's through the Gates: An Analysis of Economic Impact*. London: Pro Bono Economics.

Godeke, S., and Resner, L. (2012). *Building a Healthy and Sustainable Social Impact Bond Market: The Investor Landscape*. New York: Godeke Consulting.

HM Government (2009). *Putting the Frontline First: Smarter Government*. London: HM Government.

Justice Committee (2009). *Cutting Crime: The Case for Justice Reinvestment*. London: House of Commons.

Jupp, B. (2011). *A Technical Guide to Commissioning Social Impact Bonds*. London: Social Finance.

Loder, J. (2012). *Social Impact Bonds in Health*. London: Young Foundation.

Loder, J., Mulgan, G., Reeder, N., and Shelupanov, A. (2010). *Financing Social Value: Implementing Social Impact Bonds*. London: Young Foundation.

Macdonald, K. (2010). *First Social Impact Bond Launched*. London: Philanthropy UK.

Ministry of Justice (2010). 'Scheme to Reduce Reoffending in Short-term Prisoners Launched'. Press release 18 March, Ministry of Justice, London.

Ministry of Justice (2012). *Peterborough Social Impact Bond: Propensity Score Matching Methodology*. London: Ministry of Justice.

Ministry of Justice and Social Finance UK (2010). 'Minister Launches Social Impact Bond Pilot'. Press release 10 September, Ministry of Justice, London.

Mulgan, G., Reeder, N., Aylott, M., and Bo'sher, L. (2010). *Social Impact Investment: The Challenge and Opportunity of Social Impact Bonds*. London: Young Foundation.

National Offender Management Service (NOMS) (2012). *National Offender Management Service Annual Report 2011/12: Management Information Addendum*. London: Ministry of Justice.

Osborne, D., and Gaebler, T. (1995). *Reinventing Government: How the Entrepreneurial Spirit Is Transforming the Public Sector*. New York: Perseus Books.

RAND Europe (2011). *Lessons Learned from the Planning and Early Implementation of the Social Impact Bond at HMP Peterborough*. London: Ministry of Justice.

Social Finance (2008a). 'Social Finance Launched to Accelerate the Creation of a Social Investment Market in the UK'. Press release 21 April, Social Finance, London.

Social Finance (2008b). *Social Impact Bonds: Rethinking Finance for Social Outcomes*. London: Social Finance.

Social Finance (2009). 'Social Finance Welcomes the Government's Initiative to Pilot Social Impact Bonds'. Press release 7 December, Social Finance, London.

Social Finance (2010a). 'Social Finance Launches First Social Impact Bond'. Press release 18 March, Social Finance, London.

Social Finance (2010b). *Peterborough Social Impact Bond*. London: Social Finance.

Social Finance (2011a). *Social Impact Bonds: The One Service, One Year On*. London: Social Finance.

Social Finance (2011b). *Overview of the Peterborough Social Impact Bond*. London: Social Finance.

Strickland, P. (2010). 'Social Impact Bonds—the Pilot at Peterborough Prison'. House of Commons Library: Standard Note SN/HA5758, 12 November, London.

Third Sector Capital Partners (2013). *Case Study: Preparing for a Pay for Success Opportunity*. Cambridge, MA: Third Sector Capital Partners.

Tomkinson, E. (2012). *Social Impact Bonds: An Australian Snapshot.* Sydney: Centre for Social Impact.

Young Foundation (2008). *Social Impact Bonds.* London: Young Foundation.

▣ KEY WEBSITES

<http://www.data.gov.uk/SIB_knowledge_box/>
<https://www.gov.uk/social-impact-bonds>
<http://www.socialfinance.org.uk/work/sibs>
<http://en.wikipedia.org/wiki/Social_impact_bond>
<http://mckinseyonsociety.com/social-impact-bonds/>
<http://nonprofitfinancefund.org/pay-for-success>

Part IV

Infrastructure

13 The roles of government and policy in social finance

Rosemary Addis

Introduction

Social finance intentionally seeks to create benefit for society as well as some measure of financial return.[1,2] This practice is developing in the context of broader questions about what how business and financial systems interact with and contribute to society and about the future role of governments. Those questions extend to how we measure social progress, achieve quality and performance in social services, and tackle societal issues rather than simply deal with their effects. In an environment of diminishing trust in institutions and changing world economies, these questions have acquired additional urgency.

The financial crisis of 2008–9 and its after-effects underscored calls for reflection on the role and functions of the established systems of finance. There has been renewed focus on capital and finance as means for enabling a range of activity, not ends in themselves. Some commentators have gone so far as to say: 'the capitalist system is under siege', that separating business and competition from social issues was a mistake, and *'that societal needs, not just conventional economic needs, define markets'* (Porter and Kramer, 2011: 1; Skoll 2013; Beinhocker and Hanauer, 2014).

These developments are challenging distinctions between public and private service provision and between public goods and private profits:

Do we really just have binary choices—between public and private provision of education, health and other social services; between aid agencies focussed on dire needs and corporations focussed only on maximising profits; between investors who

[1] The author wishes to acknowledge the encouragement, advice, and editorial suggestions provided by chapter editor Alex Nicholls.

[2] 'Social finance' is used in this chapter to refer to the field also called 'impact investment', that is, investments for social and economic benefit. Some commentators and literature draw a distinction between those terms, with the former referring to finance for the social or non-profit sector and the latter reflecting and expanded notion of finance that delivers social, environmental, or cultural benefit as well as some measure of financial return. The policy landscape for social finance is moving rapidly; the illustrations and examples in this chapter are a reflection of the picture in 2014. Further changes and additions and learning from them can and should be anticipated.

can choose only to maximise their returns or make philanthropic donations. (Schwab Foundation et al. 2013: 5)

Aspects of this are not new; a number of countries have rich histories of co-operatives and community enterprise and some companies historically undertook broad roles to support their employees and communities. Practice and language has differed across jurisdictions. For example, in parts of Europe including France and Belgium, a *'solidarity economy'* has strong roots; in the United Kingdom (UK) and the United States of America (USA) a range of socially focused innovation has developed within the context of 'non-profit ventures', 'social innovation', 'profit with purpose business' (Defourny and Nyssens, 2010). Some commentators argue that the post Friedman neo-classical economics has resulted in too narrow a focus on economic efficiency and short-term profit (Janeway, 2013; Nelson and Jackson, 2004). Others highlight the impact of the dynamics of public funding in constraining social service provision (e.g. Defourny and Nyssens, 2010; Adams and Hess, 2010).

A new, or renewed, focus on a variety of mechanisms to tackle social issues is evident across a range of settings (Eggers and Macmillan, 2013; Schwab Foundation et al., 2013; Social Impact Investment Taskforce, 2014). Whether captured as 'blended value' (Bugg-Levine and Emerson, 2011), 'shared value' (Porter and Kramer, 2011) or the 'solution revolution' (Eggers and Macmillan, 2013), the underlying shifts are consistent in their focus on creating societal as well as economic value. This goes deeper than debate about market mechanisms, for profit and not for profit, public or private service provision.

These shifts are challenging what have been the dominant neo-classical underpinnings of capitalism in developed economies with a more holistic approach that focuses on the nature of prosperity and sustainable growth. They suggest the real power in a well-functioning capitalist system is in creativity applied to deliver new solutions and better outcomes that can help tackle even the most difficult and pressing social issues (Social Impact Investment Taskforce, 2014; Beinhocker and Hanauer, 2014).

Rapid technological change and corresponding availability of information and communication is magnifying the impacts of these changes. Consistent themes are increasingly evident across geographies and political systems (Jackson and Harji, 2012; Eggers and Macmillan, 2013). Knowledge, data, and resources from entirely different fields and experience can be brought to bear on issues affecting society. This allows for new combinations and adaptations of approaches, a hallmark of social innovation (Mulgan et al. 2007; Adams and Hess, 2010) on a scale that was not previously possible.

These changing conditions are affecting citizens' expectations of governments more directly as well. Technology makes possible new channels for communication and for delivery of services. This increases contestability and enables ideas and approaches from one field to be adapted more readily to other situations or issues. Institutions of all kinds are beginning to harness and apply the masses of available data; the pros and cons of which are yet to be fully explored or even understood. (Eggers and Macmillan 2013; World Economic Forum, 2013; Mulgan, 2013) The World Economic Forum Global Agenda Council on the Future of Government made the point in a global survey:

Governments of the future will need to adapt and continuously evolve to create value. They need to stay relevant by being responsive to rapidly changing conditions and citizens' expectations, and build capacity to operate effectively in complex, inter-dependent networks of organisations and systems across the public, private and non-profit sectors to co-produce public value. (World Economic Forum, 2011)

Governments clearly have a stake in issues affecting society. Policy and programmes operate in the context of both social and economic conditions. Therefore, at a minimum, governments need to understand the shifts occurring, the underlying influences and their effects. This is critical context for governing and setting policy. The thesis of this chapter is there is greater potential, including a range of ways in which governments and policy-makers can actively engage and encourage more of the positive and highest value of these developments for society (Schwab Foundation et al., 2013: 7).

If the potential for innovation is embraced, it could fundamentally alter key aspects of the way in which the public sector operates and by which public goods are developed (Eggers and Macmillan, 2013; Shergold, 2013). This would be no small challenge. It remains to be seen if this potential can be realized in terms of positive change and better outcomes.

Many states are also experiencing significant resource constraint. This is increasing the scale and urgency of some social issues, for example youth unemployment, at the same time that resources for government action are scarce. It is also limiting available aid when billions of people still live in poverty and lack services to meet basic needs ranging from clean water to education and health care, to day-to-day financial services.

The reality of limits on public resources and the scale of need faced by many in society is a powerful rationale for examining the potential of different ways of working. In some cases, social challenges have lacked meaningful, practical solutions and, in some cases, have done so for generations. The alternative to exploring new ways of working is, in essence, to accept there are no better options.

Contrary to the fears of some, impact investment is not about government relinquishing responsibility for social issues, it is about government encouraging innovation, paying for successful interventions and driving down the cost of achieving a successful outcome. Nor is it about privatisation. Philanthropic investors are funding non-profits to serve governments on the basis of payment for outcomes. If government can pay for success, hold onto more than half the savings from innovative interventions funded by outside investors, increase the number of successful outcomes and improve citizens' lives in the process, this is an attractive model. At a national level, government is increasing the social capital of our country. It is improving our productivity, competitiveness and strengthening the values that bind our society. (Cohen, 2014)

Social finance has potential to be a critical enabler of these new ways of working. The practice developing around the field of social finance is one strand in the broader weave of affecting how value is created and how sectors work together. Some political leaders have taken up the idea that social finance *can really transform our societies by using the power of finance to tackle the most difficult social problems* (Cameron, 2013; Beinhocker and Hanauer, 2014). That view is not universally held. Some commentators are sceptical about motives, seeing the potential for cost and risk shifting away from government or even removal of government from services in key areas. Many governments are yet to explore the potential of social finance in any meaningful way at all. As questioning of performance of government services is also growing louder (e.g. Bridgeland and Orszag, 2013) this is fuelling debate about value for public spending and accountability for results.

Active debate about the role of government and the role of social finance is entirely appropriate. The question of real alternatives also needs to be clearly in frame; notions of what governments *should* do need to be tempered with practical consideration of the real limitations on what they can do and can resource. Social finance will not be a silver bullet, but it can be part of the toolkit.

Developments in social finance are having a positive effect internationally in catalysing new markets and encouraging entrepreneurship and innovation for sustainable solutions to social issues. Capital is already being deployed to resource communities, create jobs, and finance initiatives across areas including aged care, health, social housing, education, clean water and sanitation, microfinance, and sustainable agriculture.

To realize the potential, more needs to be done to communicate effectively to governments and policymakers what is happening, why it matters, what they can do and how it will contribute to delivering solutions to the issues they are tackling. Beyond theory, capability needs to be developed, demonstrations created and practical lessons drawn to provide guidance about what to do and how to do it. Good policy needs to be complemented by leadership and communities of practice (see Addis and Koenig, 2014).

In this chapter, the current policy context and case for policy action is outlined. This includes the rationale for policy interventions, looking firstly at a market-based analysis and then at arguments for a broader role for the state in encouraging innovation. A toolbox for policy and action is proposed, drawing upon examples from around the globe. The chapter concludes with consideration of how social finance could provide a focal point for new collaborations across sectoral boundaries and play a role in shaping a more productive generation of public–private partnerships to tackle the challenges and opportunities of the twenty-first century.

A role for government: The case for policy action

CONTEXT

There is emphasis in the commentary on the demands and expectations on government. Much of this focuses on changing citizen expectations, the need to increase productivity from all sectors and capitalize on new tools and models to tackle significant issues affecting society (Eggers and Macmillan, 2013; Schwab Foundation et al., 2013; Social Impact Investment Taskforce, 2014).

The trend lines reveal a confluence of factors: decreasing government expenditure and greater emphasis on evidence based interventions, growing consciousness among investors and a new generation of talented social entrepreneurs who are pushing boundaries and developing disruptive solutions. This points to a window of opportunity that cannot and should not be missed. (Schwab Foundation et al., 2013: 6)

Some commentators call for a new style of government that is more open and collaborative; government for the future (e.g. Osborne and Gaebler 1992; Shergold 2013). Calls for 're-inventing' (Osborne and Gaebler 1992) or 're-imagining' (Shergold, 2013) government tap into a sense of both the current limitations and bureaucracy and the opportunities for a public sector 'at the collaborative centre of a new public economy, actively encouraging flexibility, diversity, choice and innovation' (Shergold, 2013: 13). Others argue that focus on means or ways of working does not address the real questions of what we want governments to do (e.g. Winnick, 1993). Both 'what' and 'how' are important questions; both need to be asked in service of a further question: 'To what end?' This question is particularly pertinent in relation to outcomes for the people governments are intended to serve.

While the issues play out differently based on local context, and in particular based on the level of social and economic development in different countries, the need and opportunity to expand the toolkit is universal.

Governments in developed economies increasingly face a critical funding challenge to meet growing demand for services; the total bill appears to be more than they can afford. Across the G8, the 'gap' is estimated to be more than US$1.5trn by 2025 (Accenture and Oxford Economics, 2013). These governments face a range of social issues that have defied resolution over time, such as chronic homelessness and entrenched, inter-generational disadvantage. They are also confronted by the emerging realities of meeting the cost of ageing populations, and in many cases growing income inequality and high youth unemployment, the effects of which could carry through generations. At the same time, governments are tackling real economic challenges that require productivity growth to create employment and contribute to prosperity (Hajkowicz et al., 2012).

For a significant proportion of the world, basic social needs remain unmet. Millions of people live in poverty without clean safe water and sanitation, energy, health services, or education. The World Bank and United Nations agencies estimated the cost of delivering health services across forty-nine countries to meet Millennium Development Goal targets by 2015 at between

US$67.46bn and US$226.6bn, over 60 per cent of which was expected to be recurrent spending (World Bank et al., 2009). Other estimates have placed the cost of meeting Millennium Development Goals at between US$40bn and US$60bn annually, even if dramatic improvements in local institutions and infrastructure are achieved (Devarajan et al., 2009).

Domestic government spending and international aid and philanthropy are proving insufficient to meet these needs. Development institutions have been focused on innovative financing options to meet development needs for some time. The challenges they face include poor targeting of resources and limited scope for prevention and innovation (Centre for Global Development and Social Finance, 2013). In the current environment, opportunity for and interest in market solutions to solve these major challenges is growing. Examples ranging from solar power companies to mobile technologies, and micro-insurance to new distribution platforms for consumer goods are demonstrating the potential of large-volume, low-margin market opportunities.

There is growing recognition that future economic growth depends on solving difficult social issues (Mulgan et al., 2007). In developed nations, social services are overtaking other industries as growth drivers and require different forms of innovation from those that supported manufacturing and technology in the past. Citizens are increasingly asking Governments to look beyond economic growth to increased prosperity and well-being (Watts et al., 2009; Porter, 2013). Commentators on the practice of government are pointing to shifts from standardized to personalized services and to focus on place and community, shifts from public management to improved efficacy, innovation, and collaboration and from incremental efficiencies to public sector productivity (e.g. Accenture and Oxford Economics, 2013; Deloitte, 2013; Shergold, 2013).

Indicators of social progress are being developed that go beyond traditional economic measures such as gross domestic product to capture human needs, foundations of well-being, and economic opportunity on a country-by-country basis.[3] The Sustainable Development Goals, due to be introduced in late 2015, will be universal in their application. The significance of the availability of capital and financial services in building social cohesion, productivity, and participation has begun to be understood. For example, the UK Social Investment Task Force found that enterprise and wealth creation are vital to building sustainable communities and investing in them can be vital to a 'move away from a culture of philanthropy, paternalism and dependence towards one of empowerment, entrepreneurship and initiative' (United Kingdom Social Investment TaskForce, 2000: 4). Similarly, the Canadian Task Force on Social Finance (2010) emphasized the role of finance in tackling complex societal problems, creating jobs, and strengthening communities. Growing practice across Asia and parts of Africa and Latin and South America is also demonstrating that previously overlooked communities can offer new markets (Eggers and Macmillian, 2013; Schwab Foundation et al., 2013).

---

[3] For more information, see, for example, <http://www.socialprogressimperative.org/>.

Thanks to the explosion of mobile telephony, microfinance, and retailing in emerging markets, 3 billion previously excluded people are now on the grid. For the first time in history, the majority of humanity is reachable ... The dominant story that we are told about poverty is that these people live hand-to-mouth—a storyline that leads us to treat people as passive beneficiaries rather than agents. In fact, 85% of low-income people are emerging consumers, willing and able to pay for essential *products and services, if only offered, to help them to rise out of poverty and into the middle class.* (Leapfrog Investments, website accessed 2013)

By definition, social finance involves encouraging more capital to finance activity that will intentionally address issues for society and create positive outcomes. For governments, encouraging a social finance market has a number of potential benefits, including to:

- provide opportunity to more effectively target limited public resources
- stimulate creativity and innovation in the market focused on addressing social issues
- leverage private capital for public purpose in appropriate policy areas
- grow the pool of capital available to finance creation of social as well as economic value, including by addressing unmet needs and creating new public goods.

Some commentators have argued that a greater focus on social and economic factors will open up (and require) governments to think of business and market actors as key collaborators in delivering social value (Zadek, 2001; Porter and Kramer, 2011). They argue that focusing on expanding the total pool of economic and social value enables governments—and other actors—to move beyond trade-offs and redistribution to realize a more relational and systems based approach to creating value.

Many firms have taken the broader context in which they do business as a given. Solving social issues has been ceded to governments and non-government organizations. Governments, for their part, have often regulated in a way that makes shared value more difficult to achieve. Implicitly, each side has assumed that the other is an obstacle to pursuing its goals and acted accordingly. The concept of shared value, in contrast, recognizes that societal needs, not just conventional economic needs define markets; it is about expanding the total pool of economic and social value (Porter and Kramer, 2011: 2).

Systematic exploration of the policy dimensions and role of government in social finance is still in relatively early stages.[4] The Social Investment Taskforce in the UK was an early mover in 2000 and its work over a decade played a critical role as one of a number of factors that had a direct influence on policy, primarily in the UK but also beyond (United Kingdom Social

---

[4] Community investment and enterprise have traditionally been a greater feature of the policy landscape in some jurisdictions than others, for example there is deep history of the cooperative movement in France, but less so in the US although there have been targeted regulatory initiatives there to increase community development investment for nearly 5 decades. The commentary above focuses on relatively recent global developments in social finance.

Investment Taskforce, 2000; Emerson and Spritzer, 2007; Nicholls and Pharoah, 2008; United Kingdom Cabinet Office, 2013a).

Since 2010, a more concentrated focus has been brought to the role of policy and government in the development of social finance (Jackson and Harji, 2012). This is reflected in dialogue and action across more jurisdictions and more actors. The Rockefeller Foundation's Impact Investing Initiative included a focus on the central role of policy in taking the field of social finance to scale (Jackson and Harji, 2012). Aside from analysis and practice, this initiative seeded new forums and institutions, including the Impact Investing Policy Collaborative (IIPC) and the Harvard Kennedy School Social Impact Bond Technical Assistance Lab.[5]

By 2013, things had accelerated further. The building momentum is reflected in a range of developments including initiatives of the World Economic Forum and Schwab Foundation on the role of policy and future of government (World Economic Forum, 2011, 2013; Schwab Foundation et al., 2013) and the UK government elevating the discourse to global platforms through the 'G8 Social Impact Investment Forum' in June 2013.[6] The establishment of the Social Impact Investment Task Force[7] involving a majority of G8 countries, the EU, Australia, and development finance institutions[8] marked an acceleration of momentum toward developing the policy commitment to a global market for social finance. The effort brought together over 200 leaders from across sectors and had a galvanizing effect as well as producing a substantial body of research and practical recommendations to inform practice about what social finance is and the role it might play (Social Impact Investment Taskforce, 2014 and related working group and national reports). Collectively this contribution set an ambitious vision for the market and underscored that 'policy matters greatly' in stimulating and shaping markets (Social Impact Investment Taskforce, 2014; Addis and Koenig, 2014: 16).

Other indicators by 2014 that social finance was gaining traction included:

- Social finance forums convened in Asia, Latin and South America, India and South Africa[9]
- The publication of The London Principles, by the IIPC in June 2013: principles specifically tailored to inform the design and evaluation of social finance policy[10]
- The rapid spread of interest in and activity to develop Social Impact Bonds (SIBs), which has increased from a single SIB in the UK to a significant

---

[5] For more information, see <http://www.iipcollaborative.org> and <http://hks-siblab.org/>.

[6] For information on outcomes, see <https://www.google.com.au/#q=g8+impact+investmetn+forum>.

[7] For more information on the Social Impact Investment Taskforce and its work, see <https://www.gov.uk/government/groups/social-impact-investment-taskforce>.

[8] See Social Impact Investment Taskforce 2014: Appendix 1.

[9] For more information, see <http://www.rockefellerfoundation.org/our-work/current-work/impact-investing/events>.

[10] The principles are considered in more detail in a later section of the chapter focusing on policy design; for more on the principles, see <http://iipcollaborative.org/london-principles/>.

volume of activity in the UK and US and in jurisdictions as diverse as Mozambique, Columbia, Australia, Israel, Belgium, Italy, Germany, New Zealand, and Canada

- A growth in the number of leaders from across countries and sectors contributing to mobilizing the market, particularly through contributions to the Social Impact Investment Taskforce, its working groups, and national advisory boards in each of the participating countries
- Increasing numbers of impact funds operating in the market and attracting capital (Clark et al. 2012)
- Growing participation in benchmark surveys, for example the leading JP Morgan and Global Impact Investment Network Survey marked a 26 per cent increase in participant numbers in 2014 (Saltuk et al., 2014) and a further 17% in 2015 (Saltuk et al., 2015), albeit under expanded criteria

Developments beyond the social finance movement underscore the broader shifts occurring. Social economy legislation was passed in Portugal and in the Canadian Province of Quebec[11] was enacted in the Quebec province of Canada in 2013 and the French government introduced a framework law for the 'social and solidarity economy' in 2014.[12] These legal frameworks bring a focus in policy and regulation to recognition, support and development of 'social economy organizations' echoing similar developments in recent years in Spain, Greece, Mexico, and Ecuador.[13]

While momentum is clearly building, achieving critical mass for social finance is not a given. It remains a strategic challenge that will require many actors to play a role. Bringing together actors capable of meeting that challenge will require genuine engagement with a mindset for problem-solving, clarity of objectives, and commitment to measurement and evaluation. Consciously developing the mix of skills and resources needed to deliver will also require collaboration beyond the notions and practice of public–private partnerships that have built brick and mortar infrastructure (Zadek, 2001; Eggers and Macmillan, 2013).

There is a legitimate and important role for the state. Government is an important actor in many countries in both markets and the delivery of social services. The social finance market is likely to develop to scale more quickly where government is an actor, and will be richer in substance and outcomes in many countries if the experience of policymakers and data held by governments plays a role in its shaping and development (Social Impact Investment Taskforce, 2014). This is *not* to say other actors should wait for governments to

---

[11] Portuguese Social Economy Law 68/XII (13 March 2013); Social Economy Act, Bill 27 (2013, chapter 22), passed and assented to 10 October 2013.

[12] For further information, see <http://www.economie.gouv.fr/ess/loi-economie-sociale-et-solidaire-au-second-semestre>.

[13] Spanish Law on Social Economy (Law 5/2011); Greek Social Economy and Social Entrepreneurship Act 4019/2011; Ecuador Official Register No. 444, 10 May 2011; Mexico Official Journal, 23 May 2012. For an overview of the different legal regimes introduced, see Peels, R. (2013) *Legal Frameworks on Social and Solidarity Economy: What Is the Role of Civil Society Organisations in Policy Making?* United National Research Institute for Social Development, <http://www.unrisd.org>.

act or that it will be sufficient for government to act alone, or for other sectors and actors to rely on government action and policy. Governments have a critical stake in delivery of improved social outcomes.

A ROLE FOR GOVERNMENT

Much of the initial focus of the policy dialogue has centred on targeting and leveraging increasingly limited public resources: 'The scale of our global problems far exceeds the resources currently allocated to solve them. By tapping the power of the markets, impact investing has strong promise of unlocking new capital sources that can complement existing philanthropic and government funds' (G8 Social Impact Investment Forum, 2013: 9). Beyond more money, social finance is clearly about improving lives and encouraging creativity and innovation to enable greater scale and more diverse solutions that work to solve social issues.

For some, the rationale for action concentrates on the size of the opportunity. There is not yet definitive data on the quantum or potential of social finance activity or the impacts it is generating. The Monitor Institute, J.P. Morgan and the GIIN have all done analysis (Fulton, 2009; Saltuk et al., 2011, 2014, 2015) and arrived at estimates of at least US$60bn in social finance assets under management in 2013. US$400bn and US$1trn by 2020; the Social Impact Investment Taskforce (2014) also set the aspiration for a US$1trn global social finance market. Research taking into account broader community investing suggests a significantly higher figure, estimated at US$89bn in assets under management in 2012.[14] While it is not helpful to overreach on estimates of the potential scale for the social finance market, the potential for growth has been recognized. The estimates range from US$400bn and US$1trn by 2020; the Social Impact Investment Taskforce (2014) also set the aspiration for a US$1trn global social finance market.

Questions of scale are also relative. The potential for social finance to play a role needs to be considered in context, not just in relation to the global financial markets, but also in relation to government expenditure on social services, international aid and development, the scale of social sector activity, and, some argue, corporate investment in activities that have benefits for society. For example, estimates of the social finance capital under management in 2013 in excess of US$46bn (see Saltuk et al., 2014) is over two and a half times the estimated combined public and private humanitarian aid for the same period (US$17.9bn, Global Humanitarian Assistance Report, 2013). Over 18 per cent of the social finance assets under management identified in the most recent market survey are managed by development finance institutions (Saltuk et al., 2015).

Financial leverage alone is a narrow conception of the potential of social finance for policy. Other aspects of social finance contribute value. This is important and influences both the case for government taking a role in developing the social finance market and the nature of that role. New sources

---

[14] For more information, see analysis in Appendix 4, Addis, McLeod and Raine (2013).

and structures of capital intentionally targeting positive benefit for society, when provided on appropriate terms, have the potential to deliver significant public good, and at greater scale than can be achieved with public and philanthropic funding alone.

Beyond that, the mechanisms of the financial markets can also enable government to direct capital to new or existing ventures better placed to deliver community-based solutions. Availability of capital can encourage community organizations to boost their productivity by more efficient capital allocation. Engaging in new ways of financing services and with different actors that brings to the table can build capacity in the public sector to innovate and partner for the effective delivery of public services.

The case for policy action has a broader foundation. From a market perspective, it draws upon a relatively well-accepted role for the state in overcoming barriers to the emergence of growth and new industries:

The financial system has a central role in fostering innovation and growth. Policies and reforms of financial institutions and markets can facilitate financing of entrepreneurial firms ... Often the regulatory system is complex and/or has hidden disincentives for young innovative firms and/or investors. (OECD, 2013: 30)

There is significant body of precedent for action by the state to stimulate new investment. Examples can be drawn from fields including venture capital, pharmaceutical research and development, green and renewable technology, and business model innovation for structural adjustment. The OECD has recognized the role of government in enabling access to finance for seed and early stage investment:

Government intervention can play a catalytic role both in facilitating the functioning of the ecosystem and targeting actions to trigger its further development. However, these actions should provide incentives for the engagement, not the replacement, of the private sector and should be conducted in a manner conducive of the market. (OECD, 2013: 14)

Historically the pursuits of economic, social, and environmental objectives have been treated as quite separate. Creating social or public value has generally been seen as the domain of 'social policy' departments such as health, education, and welfare within government and of the third sector outside. Only recently has the social dimension of innovation been gaining increased attention as part of the innovation narrative within policy agendas (for example, Nicholls and Murdock, 2011; Australian Innovation Statement 2011, 2012).

Policy interventions intended to promote economic goals through support for venture capital and firm growth have recognized 'spillover' effects that contribute to broader productivity, in particular job creation. Some jurisdictions have begun to adapt these policy measures for environmental objectives, including by targeting incentives for venture capital and other investment for renewable or clean energy.

There is a case that government is not using these policy tools to best effect if the majority of benefit accrues to individual firms and actors, and benefits to society accrue only as spillover effects (Adams and Hess, 2010).

Some commentators argue that traditional sources of policy:

Economic innovation, social capital, community strengthening and regional development, together contribute the old ideas which come into new associations in what is being termed social innovation. (Adams and Hess, 2010: 3)

This highlights a third rationale for government and policy action: as standard setter and steward for the prosperity of society, and the related goal of stimulating more effective solutions to social issues:

The period in which social innovation practices are moving into policy, business and community sector activities is characterised by an inter-sectoral interest in new ideas and ways of doing things that create social value. The view underpinning this is that increasing social value has impacts in areas as diverse as sustainability, employment creation, physical security and personal health. At this practical level, social innovation can be defined as mould-breaking ways of confronting unmet social need by creating new and sustainable capabilities, assets or opportunities for change. (Adams and Hess, 2010: 4)

The analogies with economic innovation in terms of a role for government and policy are significant given that social finance is grounded in utilizing private capital and market based mechanisms to deliver solutions that government cannot achieve alone:

Just as the formation of the venture capital industry ushered a new approach and mindset toward funding innovation within the private sector, impact investment has started to bring opportunities to harness entrepreneurship and capital markets to drive social improvement. This, in time, will bring much needed change to the social sector. (Cohen and Sahlman, 2013)

Government is accepted as having a role and policy approaches well developed to encourage innovation and finance for economic development. It is difficult to argue that role should not extend to (social) innovation and (social) finance that intentionally target positive benefit to society.[15]

GOVERNMENTS' ROLE IN OVERVIEW

The importance of government as an actor in social finance is coming through in the most recent literature, recognizing the impact of productive relationships with government and constructive utilization of policy on performance

[15]   This proposition was accepted by the Australian financial System Inquiry, 2014; see http://fsi.gov.au/publications/final-report/: Appendix 1. Note: There is not scope in this chapter to debate whether the distinction of 'social' enterprise, 'social' innovation and 'social' finance is useful to the longer term if actors can be encouraged to take an approach that includes more intentional and integrated focus on positive benefit for society.

of social finance initiatives (Clark et al., 2013) and enabling social innovations (Thornley et al., 2011; Schwab Foundation et al., 2013).

Carrying forward the analogy with the role of governments in stimulating innovation and economic development, the argument is that governments have a role to play in relation to social finance as a market actor, and as market builder and steward to create the conditions for significant value creation for public good (Social Impact Investment Taskforce, 2014):

- *Market participant*: This role involves capturing new ideas and ways of doing things and adapting old ideas and practices that provide better solutions to social and economic problems; identifying opportunities more effectively to target and leverage public spending by attracting private capital.
- *Market Builder*: This role involves catalysing the field of social finance to encourage the market to grow, enabling new or existing ventures better placed than government to develop and deliver community-based solutions, and enlarging the pool of capital seeking to achieve positive benefits for society
- *Market steward*: This role involves stewarding the field of social finance, ensuring appropriate regulation, removal of barriers to action, and creating the conditions for replication and scale of what works.

Examples of governments as market participant typically relate to a particular social issue or problem such as social housing, environmental sustainability, or financial exclusion. Executed well, this approach can assist government to target scarce resources and leverage private capital to deliver improved outcomes or achieve greater reach.

The need for market development is increasingly in frame. There is a growing acknowledgement of the necessity for scale, which will require 'infra-structure' to accelerate development. This is a challenge for practitioners as well as for government seeking to move beyond a focus on deal-by-deal, firm-by-firm approaches to growing the field (Nicholls and Pharoah, 2008; Addis, McLeod, and Raine, 2013; Social Impact Investment Taskforce, 2014).

Increasingly, government is recognized as a critical actor in sector and infrastructure development to develop the potential for social finance (e.g. Thornley et al., 2011; Bannick and Goldman, 2013; Drexler and Noble, 2013a; Social Impact Investment Taskforce, 2014). The UK government has explicitly recognized market 'stewardship' as a formal part of its role. This reflects the culmination and adaptation of more than a decade of active policy engagement through successive governments.[16] The Social Economy Act in Quebec (2013) requires the Government to adopt a 'social economy action plan' identifying actions to 'support the development and promotion of the social

---

[16] The policy frameworks in the UK have evolved in tandem with development of policy to encourage social enterprise and other mechanisms for utilizing market-based mechanisms to deliver social outcomes. See, for example, discussion of the policy frameworks that underpinned significant elements of the Blair government's approach in Powell, M. (ed.) (2008) *Modernising the Welfare State: The Blair Legacy.* University of Bristol: The Policy Press.

economy' (Chapter IV, section 8) by April 2014. To what extent that will include a focus on the actions to develop finance for social economy activity is not yet clear. The central role of policy was highlighted in the work of the Social Impact Investment Taskforce in its report (2014) and in each of the subject papers and National Advisory Board reports. The US National Advisory Board on Impact Investing focused its work almost exclusively on federal policy and the role of government in scaling effective solutions and driving talent and capital to focus on tackling social and economic challenges at scale (US National Advisory Board on Impact Investing, 2014).

A number of commentators have argued that government signalling and the shaping of the policy environment will be among the key factors that determine whether or not social finance reaches its potential (Thornley et al., 2011; Schwab Foundation et al., 2013). Growing activity and focus on social finance globally may also be a factor that encourages policymakers to better understand developments and test the market. Exploring the potential of these actions and interactions is important not only for its financial dimensions but also for understanding the dynamics for productive partnerships between different actors.

Governments have scope to access not just more, but different resources and experience, and in new combinations. Importantly, they can also channel resources (directly and indirectly) to particular issue areas. The goal for social finance should be additive not just in terms of the amount of capital, but also in terms of outcomes. Capital can be a powerful focus to link government, community, and markets. This is not an argument for cost and risk shifting between the public and private sectors. The vision goes beyond matters of degree to new ways of working that go beyond what government or other sectors can achieve alone, in terms of funding, reach and efficacy. Social finance goes beyond what either grants or current capital markets can achieve alone.

Realizing that potential will require all actors to move beyond 'presumed trade-offs between economic efficiency and social progress' (Porter and Kramer, 2011: 1). That means going beyond 'efficient' market analysis of neo-classical economics. It will also require frank assessment of embedded experience and cultural expectations of 'public–private partnerships' to move toward more interest-based alliances (Zadek, 2001; Eggers and Macmillan, 2013). The 'risk/return' evaluations will be different and the nature of the incentives required to achieve greater efficacy for society will require more effective and reciprocal exchange of value between actors. Fundamentally, the change introduces a focus on impact and the value it creates (Social Impact Investment Taskforce, 2014).

A broader conception of value creation draws on the work of economists who have argued that growth and innovation depend on the state taking a role that goes beyond neo-classical views of government as 'condition setter' and market 'fixer' to develop a richer role of agenda setting and 'market making' in the national interest (Mazzucato, 2012; Janeway, 2013) and creative solutions to very human problems (Beinhocker and Hanauer, 2014). This case centres on an active role of the state in enabling transformative breakthroughs for the public good.

The following sections examine the frameworks and rationale for policy to develop social finance through the lens of both market economics and innovation economics, including consideration of the developing policy frameworks internationally.

Market dynamics: Policy agendas to develop social finance

Markets develop where there is the willing involvement from a range of actors prepared to act and interact to build the enabling environment within which a range of activities and transactions can occur.

Government is acknowledged as an important actor in economic market development. Policy levers are used routinely to shape markets, correct for market failures, create incentives for investment and disincentives for harm, and influence where capital is directed. In modern democracies, the role of government as regulator is generally well developed and some commentators argue good regulation furthers good governance and co-operation that enhances market effectiveness (Thornley et al., 2011; Beinhocker and Hanauer, 2014). Well-crafted policy is considered an important factor to facilitate for ordered capital flows, clear prudential standards and mandate disclosures to keep the market and investors informed. Governments set market conditions through legislative and regulatory oversights including remedies and penalties.

The financial crisis in 2008–9 brought a renewed focus on financial market regulation in developed economies. These events also served to emphasize the importance of sound financial systems in emerging markets (Masahiro and Prasad, 2011). In developing economies, the role of regulation can be less well established. Some markets lack developed institutions, reliable governance and/or regulatory capacity and this may present a variety of issues for attracting investment and operation of the market.

The regulatory environment and fiscal policy can be important drivers, or disincentives, for development of social finance (Thornley et al., 2011). The lessons from microfinance and community development finance demonstrate the central role policy can play in encouraging and directing capital to social finance and influence potential and pathways for achieving critical mass (Jackson and Harji, 2012). Lessons from development of venture capital and early stage finance for growth enterprises also underscore the influence of policy (OECD, 2013).

Work led by Venturesome (Goodall and Kingston, 2009; Cheng, 2011) identified four 'pillars' for effective social finance markets:

- creating confident and informed demand
- efficient matching of supply and demand
- variety of investment mechanisms
- resilient supply of finance.

These broad pillars are consistent across a global market. They require effective operation of supply, demand, and intermediation situated within an enabling environment of policy and market settings. Those essential components are fundamentally the same for social finance as for other capital and investment markets (Figure 13.1; Koenig, 2014).

Developing the potential for social finance will require careful design within the existing policy, regulation, and market frameworks of individual jurisdictions (Wood et al., 2012; Drexler and Noble, 2013a; Addis and Koenig, 2014). Local differences can be significant and are a critical consideration in policy design and implementation which must be tailored for context to be effective. In social finance, local context goes beyond usual financial and economic conditions to social context and the role of the state in social service delivery. For example, the strength and constitutional framework of the welfare system in Germany is a defining feature for development of social finance in that country (German National Advisory Board on Impact Investing, 2014; Benford, 2014).

Social finance is already emerging within existing institutional contexts, including evolving from the established capital market and philanthropic traditions (Thornley et al., 2011). Recent research indicates that in some areas the market for social finance is already operating with some depth and sophistication (Clark, Emerson, and Thornley, 2013, 2014). However, some areas of practice and in some jurisdictions, developments remain fragmented (e.g. Jackson and Harji, 2012; Addis, Mcleod, and Raine, 2013). To reach scale, this progress already made will need to accelerate and extend to mobilizing capital from the mainstream investment markets (Jackson and Harji, 2012;

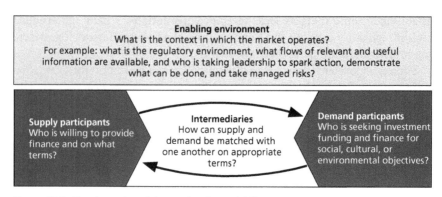

Figure 13.1. The dynamics of the market for social finance
Source: Addis, Mcleod, and Raine, 2013

Wood et al., 2012, Drexler and Noble, 2013a; Social Impact Investment Taskforce Asset Allocation Working Group, 2014).

Also, the distinguishing features of social finance require explicit focus on the societal as well as financial dimensions of transactions. This highlights potential limiting factors as to what can be achieved within the established frameworks as the current market conditions do not promote, and may prevent, investments with explicit social or environmental benefits (Thornley et al., 2011). However, some commentators argue that narrow conceptions of value creation focusing on financial performance alone are outdated (Emerson, 2000; Emerson and Spitzer, 2007; Porter and Kramer, 2011). And that not only can financial markets can play a significant role in encouraging enterprise and initiatives to tackle social and environmental challenges (Thornley et al., 2011), but the future of markets and economic growth depend on a broader approach to value creation (Porter and Kramer, 2011).

To address these challenges for development of social finance, clear and intentional focus on the particular conditions, market signals, and policy levers to encourage social finance is likely to be required. The rationale for such action can be underpinned by a market analysis as the next section illustrates. Beyond that, there is a case for a more expansive role for the state to develop social finance as a source and enabler of innovation for the public good is considered. Viewed another way, even through a relatively narrow lens that the role of policy should be contained to correcting market failures, there is a case for policy intervention to support and encourage social finance. And there is a case for a more expansive role for government and policy.

THE MARKET LENS

The market-based approach commonly starts with an analysis of market failure as the rationale for policy intervention. In determining whether and what policy intervention is justified considerations typically include (Goodall and Kingston, 2009; Thornley et al., 2011; see also OECD, 2013):

- structural barriers to investment
- information asymmetry
- uncertainty and other constraints on market development
- appropriate balance between stimulus and free market operation
- support for individual initiatives relative to sector development
- whether interventions will distort the operation of the market or result in other 'harm'.

The greater the likelihood that an investment will enable an important demonstration of models unlikely to attract finance on their own, enable the refinement of successful models that can be scaled and replicated for high impact, or contribute important public good for an industry sector, the greater the case for a catalyst or subsidy.[17]

In the social finance context, analysis of market failure often starts with information asymmetries between potential borrowers and potential lenders pointing to a need for greater knowledge and data infrastructure (Goodall and Kingston, 2009). This analysis is similar to that regarding policy interventions for seed and early stage capital where information asymmetry between entrepreneurs and investors is also common and promising innovations often do not reach market (Denis, 2004; OECD, 2013). It often builds on consideration of the extent to which markets currently externalize negative effects on society and whether government action can assist in overcoming short-term risk or lack of track record (Thornley et al., 2011; Drexler and Noble, 2013a). Issues of subsidy and support for overall market development also receive attention (e.g. Bannick and Goldman, 2013).

Thornley et al. (2011) proposed a framework for social finance policy within a market setting (Figure 13.2). That framework locates policy actions within market elements and dynamics identified in Figure 13.1. Examples of the types of policy interventions that can play a role in supporting development, in particular supply, demand, and directing capital toward particular areas of social need, are placed within that framework.

Building on well over a decade of foundation policy, pilots, and initiatives by successive governments of different political persuasions and a significant body of work from outside government, the UK was the first jurisdiction to have in operation a policy framework for social finance. There are still very few such policies.[18]

The Social Impact Investment Taskforce explored policy levers to support the establishment of an effective social finance market that could apply across multiple countries. A number of the National Advisory Boards on Impact Investing looked specifically at the policy settings and regulatory frameworks in their countries. This work contributed to an understanding of where there might be common ground and also highlighted areas where local variances were particularly significant (Addis and Koenig, 2014). So far, this analysis has been informed by the systems of a relatively small number of countries. Over time, it will need to be tested across a broader range of political and policy contexts, particularly in emerging and developing economies (Addis and Koenig, 2014).

---

[17] For more information, see Bannick and Goldman (2013).

[18] *Growing the Social Investment Market: A Vision and Strategy*, see <http://www.gov.uk>. The policies have also drawn upon the work, experience, and advocacy of a range of other actors in the market including but not limited to the National Endowment for Science Technology and the Arts, Charities Aid Foundation, and social enterprise groups from around the UK. Some of this rich body of practice and policy thinking has deep roots indeed. See, for example: the Institute for Social Entrepreneurs' Evolution of the social enterprise industry: A chronology of key events at <https://www.se-alliance.org/upload/Membership%20Pages/evolution.pdf> that provides additional background on the rich history of social enterprise and related developments. The New South Wales State Government in Australia introduced a policy framework in February 2015; see http://www.dpc.nsw.gov.au/programs_and_services/social_impact_investment/nsw_policy

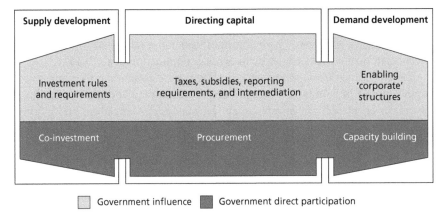

Figure 13.2. A framework for policy design and analysis
Source: Thornley et al., 2011

A full examination of the UK platform and its development is beyond the scope of this chapter. The salient point is that much of the policy analysis in the UK, past and present, has been framed in terms of correcting for a market failures and drawn upon parallels with economic innovation and entrepreneurship (e.g. United Kingdom Social Investment Taskforce, 2000–10). And the focus on market mechanisms, while not without its critics (e.g. Slocock, 2012; Bassett et al., 2012), has sparked debate about the blurring lines between public and private provision of services, even from left-leaning think tanks (e.g. Wind-Cowie 2012). The current policy platform explicitly recognizes the role of government as market steward, described as follows:

Government has an important role to play in the development of this world-leading market, not least in the creation of public goods that support social investment. However, a sustainable market is one which isn't dependent on Government investment. Our job is to highlight best practice, identify where barriers remain, and take action to enable wider participation in the market. (UK Cabinet Office, 2013a: 9)

In some developing countries, the strategies being employed for social innovation echo closely some industry development and innovation policies that have been utilized in OCED countries. Specifically, they include support through loans, grants, guarantee schemes, and tax incentives as well as a building focus on development of entrepreneurial capacity. An example that has featured in the social finance literature is the Indian National Innovation Council and India Inclusive Innovation Fund (Schwab Foundation et al., 2013; Bannick and Goldman, 2013). These initiatives are designed to harness the potential of entrepreneurship and enterprise in India.[19] The early results indicate that the policies have stimulated economic development (estimated at US $4bn in business revenue to poor communities), job creation, and attracted new investment capital (see case study in Schwab Foundation et al., 2013).

There is some debate about what distinguishes economic policy and social finance policy in countries where poverty is widespread and many communities experience multiple disadvantage (Jackson and Associates, 2012). Some argue the key difference is between investments designed to create positive impact in areas of social need and investments that have positive impact as a by-product but are designed based on financial considerations alone. This reinforces the distinguishing feature of social finance as its intentional design for positive benefit for society. Since 2013, a number of development finance institutions in particular have undertaken a process of making these distinctions across their portfolio.[20]

In a number of jurisdictions, specific areas of need have shaped the starting point for policy rather than a more general focus on encouraging a market for social finance. Within the market framework (Figure 13.2) these initiatives come within the rubric of 'directing capital'. Examples range from 'green' or 'clean' energy to affordable housing to addressing financial exclusion. In each of those cases, early initiatives have demonstrated feasibility for market-based mechanisms to contribute to the delivery of public goods. In each case, scale has developed as policy action and capital markets came together to create infrastructure that enabled a dramatic increase in the volume of capital being mobilized. (see, e.g. Cheng, 2011; Jackson and Harji, 2012).

Governments have an opportunity to create incentives and create investment opportunities relating to areas of particular policy importance. This approach, when well designed, can serve dual goals of increasing the supply of capital on appropriate terms to address a particular social need and contributing to the overall development of the market for social finance. In a range of areas there is confluence of need and market dynamics that indicate scope for governments to design policy to 'direct capital'. These include employment generation, directing capital to underserved communities, or building new community infrastructure, aged care, disease prevention, education, housing, and economic development and job creation (see for example, Burkett, 2012; Jackson and Harji, 2012).

The next section expands on the argument that governments have a role that goes beyond setting the conditions for the market and addressing market failures. The argument is for governments to take further their role as market builder and catalyst based in the potential for social finance to play a role in achieving transformational goals including alleviation of poverty and sustainable development.

---

[19] For more information, see <http://planningcommission.nic.in/reports/genrep/rep_eco2708.pdf>.
[20] For example, see Overseas Private Investment Corporation <http://www.opic.gov>.

THE VALUE INNOVATION LENS

There is a school of economic thought and research that promotes the role of the state as economic actor and market 'creator' and 'shaper' (Mazzucato, 2012; Janeway, 2013). Proponents of this view contend that where the state has invested with an ambitious 'mission-orientation' to promote innovation it has led to transformative developments:

It has been mission-oriented State investments that have, time after time, and over national boundaries, proved effective in driving individual sectors in the innovation economy ... writ large, the strategic State interventions that have shaped the market economy over generations have depended on grander themes—national development, national security, social justice, liberation from disease—that transcend the cultures of welfare economics and the logic of market failure. (Janeway, 2013: 231)

These commentators have suggested that 'arguments for state intervention to address market failures have proved only marginally compelling' and that 'efficiency is the enemy of innovation at a systemic level':

Innovations that have repeatedly transformed the architecture of the market economy, from canals to the internet, have required massive investments to construct networks whose value in use could not have been imagined at the outset of deployment. (Janeway, 2012: 1)

The proponents of this view argue that trial and error is a necessary hallmark of the innovation economy and that it is impossible to know the full economic value of innovations mid-stream. Therefore, every stage of innovation fundamentally depends on sources of investment that are decoupled from a narrow focus on (short-term) economic returns. While neo-classical economics would focus on the costs and risks of subsidy, particularly with respect to market distortions, this alternative approach suggests that there will be waste in any event and uses a more value-based analysis considering the overall benefits relative to the costs.

These arguments challenge some fundamental tenets of efficient market theory. The central thesis is that neo-classical economics has misunderstood the dynamics of the innovation economy and led to generalized and over-simplified propositions that 'markets are efficient' and 'governments are inefficient'. The 'proof' is in state investments that have financed and encouraged successive waves of innovation that fuelled productivity and improved quality of life across societies. They also point to waste identifiable in even the most 'rational' market effects once impacts such as unemployment and underutilization of assets are taken into account. Proponents of 'shared value' also point to costs to society and the environment that have been treated as externalities in economic and competition theory and practice. They argue that this 'narrow' conception of capitalism overlooks both true costs and opportunities for growth (Porter and Kramer, 2011). At the core is a central theme that over-reliance on neo-classical efficient market theory cannot underpin the future prosperity of everyone within a society.

In the social finance context too, commentary on the developing market includes perspectives that there is 'systematic under-investment':

In creating the conditions under which innovations—and entire new sectors—could be sparked and scaled. (Bannick and Goldman, 2013)

These strands of analysis have a common focus on the importance of policy settings that support innovation and the potential for transformations to occur that radically alter the market economy to create significant new value. Social innovation practitioners consider the developing economic commentary to:

Give credibility in economics to social factors in general and particularly to the agency of people and place as significant in creating the enabling conditions for innovation ... precisely two of the distinguishing features of social innovation. (Adams and Hess, 2010: 2)

The value innovation approach also recognizes that waste from more traditional economic policy approaches often includes socially expensive externalities, such as loss of jobs and cycles of under-investment in communities. The social innovation approach acknowledges the imperative to find new ways to address social issues that have defied resolution:

It is our contention that social innovation has a major role to play in the contemporary development of public policy and management. The major reason for this is that traditional ways of addressing social issues are not working. Several generations of highly professional dedicated public policy makers and managers have worked their way from welfare state to contracting out of social welfare provision but persistent and intractable social problems remain unresolved and have arguably gotten worse. Levels of poverty, for instance, remain at best relatively stable.

As a result of the contemporary trends in the community sector and in how government relates to communities, the need for innovation in social policy areas can now be addressed using new ideas about the enabling conditions for successful social innovation. (Adams and Hess, 2010: 6)

These entrenched issues are among the areas where (social) innovation, and (social) finance can play a role (e.g. United Kingdom Social Investment Task Force, 2000; Freireich and Fulton, 2009; Burkett, 2012; Social Impact Investment Taskforce, 2014). Pressing need for poverty alleviation, disease prevention, improved sanitation, clean water, and sustainable agriculture globally could provide the basis for renewed *mission-oriented* justification for policy action to support the development of social finance.

The Schwab Foundation for Social Entrepreneurship and their research partners (2013) proposed a Framework for Government Action to scale social innovation (Figure 13.3).

This research was initiated, in part, in response to increasing demand from policymakers to understand developments in social innovation and how governments can engage; it highlights the central role for social finance. The framework is not a prescriptive formula. Rather, it distils from practice some proposed entry points for 'policy-makers interested in developing

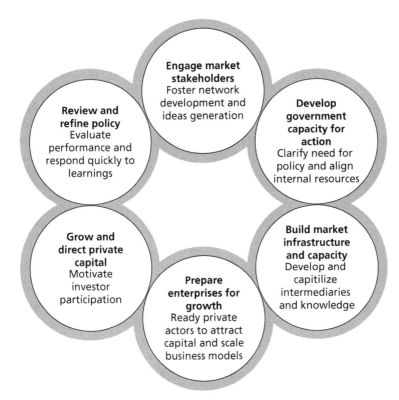

Figure 13.3. Framework for government action
Source: Schwab Foundation et al., 2013

opportunities for social enterprise in their own political, cultural and economic contexts' (Schwab Foundation et al, 2013: 7).

Social finance is an innovation story in its own right. It brings together new combinations and structures for capital and a new conception of how capital markets can function integrating social purpose and financial rigour. It is also an enabler of innovations, providing the capital to finance new models, infrastructure, and entrepreneurs focused on addressing issues affecting society. It can also be expected that realizing its potential will require 'some struggle against vested interests; the 'contagious courage' that persuades others to change; and the pragmatic persistence that turns promising ideas into real institutions' (Mulgan et al., 2007: 4).

The challenge remains in many jurisdictions to develop that interest in policymakers and other public leadership. Encouraging governments to take an active role as catalyst could be an essential element in realizing the potential innovation and its social and economic value:

If we have a broader theory of what the state is actually doing, value creation, the next period of growth will not only be smart, not only be green, but also inclusive. (Mazzucato, 2013)

Beyond scoping the role for government in social finance markets and the different rationales for intervention, lies the issue how to translate theory into practice. In the following sections, that is considered through four lenses. The next sections explores the practical dimensions of what to do and how to do it inherent in translating the potential role for governments into practice, including a proposed toolbox for policymakers. The following three sections focus on: stewardship of the market and its relationship to the development of market infrastructure; government as a market participant and, specifically, as catalytic investor; and the influence that market involvement could have on shaping the way in which government works with other sectors to solve social issues.

Translating policy into practice

Government action and policy are often considered as one. However, there are key distinctions between policy design and its implementation, and between policy and politics. Policy is a broad domain with a range of levers and options for implementation, some of which can be fluid, or even contradictory. Moreover, policy development and implementation occurs within a dynamic context, both within government and in the interactions between government and other actors.

There can also be an ideological dimension with practical and relational implications. The politics of social finance and of developing an agenda in particular jurisdictions is beyond the scope of this chapter, save to acknowledge that it is an important consideration (see Bannick and Goldman, 2013; Addis and Koenig, 2014).

Also, governments do not act in isolation. Policy and programmes affect where they live and work. Market participants engage with governments and with the policy and regulatory environment in a variety of ways.

Commentators analysing successful social finance funds identified that they all had productive collaborations with government that enabled them to utilize and benefit from policy and to do so in relation to a number of aspects of their fund management and investments. This work further identified that this 'policy symbiosis' can take a number of forms. Clark, Emerson, and Thornley (2014):

- *foundational*—with the origins of the fund integrated with policy at a fundamental level
- *financial*—in the sense that there is direct government investment in the fund
- *regulatory*—with various aspects of the fund structure, its investments and operations being influenced by regulation

- *advocacy-driven*—based on a direct relationship to shape the policy environment
- *opportunistic*—in leveraging discrete, individual policies and regulations.

Whether the focus is on particular areas of social need or broader market development, those with resources (supply-side actors) need to be able to connect with those who know where the need is and have solutions to offer (demand-side actors), and to do so in appropriate terms. That may require working across traditional sectoral boundaries and conscious design to achieve the objectives involving the different actors affected and involved.

EXPANDING THE TOOLBOX

The roles identified for governments in connection with social finance are linked with models for innovation and collaboration. This points to a suite— or toolbox—of policy options (Figure 13.4) that governments have at their disposal.

The 'toolbox' approach acknowledges the role of government as standard setter and funder, but also recognizes that there is more than money and regulation to contribute. In Australia, the Senate Economics References Committee recognized:

That Government can facilitate the development of the market through a number of means, such as providing a supportive environment; taking a longer-term view of its development; convening and encouraging collaboration across sectors; and designing and implementing innovative policies to challenge both social economy organisations and investors to take up new financing options. (Senate Economics References Committee, 2012: 3)

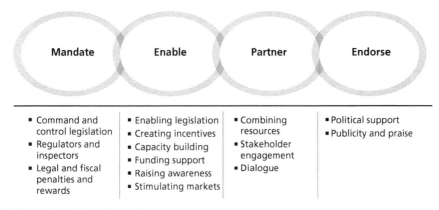

Figure 13.4. The policy toolbox

Source: Australian Departments of Education, Employment and Workplace Relations and Prime Minister and cabinet 2011, adopted by Senate Economics References Committee, 2011a

Government has a range of high-value (sometimes low-cost) contributions to make, such as experience, data, and research that are sometimes overlooked. Developing a more dynamic policy toolbox and using it effectively will be critical for governments to realize the societal, fiscal, and policy benefits of social finance.

The purpose of the framework is to point explicitly to a broader range of ways in which governments can contribute to and influence market development. Governments can be more explicit and intentional about the tools that they utilize as well as their intended effect. That said, the two are interrelated: being explicit about intention or purpose contributes to making good choices between the different tools on a 'fit for purpose' basis. The following examples focus on how some of the less traditional roles have been utilized in the social finance context.

GOVERNMENT AS CONVENOR

Governments are well placed to act as a convenor to bring parties together and generate dialogue and action. Simply indicating government interest can send powerful market signals. Effective strategic use of this convening capacity can demonstrate leadership that gives others greater confidence to act.

In the USA, the White House Office for Social Innovation and Civic Participation utilized convening as a key element of its strategy, creating a focus on sector development through dialogue on the *impact economy* and by creating momentum for social finance tools, particularly Social Impact Bonds ('pay for success'). The US Department of State used its global convening capacity to generate a shift in the development context from aid to investment with a Global Impact Economy Forum.[21] The UK Government and Cabinet Office utilized the prerogative for agenda setting during its presidency of the G8 to convene a global audience and elevate local policy and action to the global agenda through the G8 Social Impact Investment Forum.[22] In Australia, a government department utilized convening as part of an engagement strategy for the IMPACT-Australia initiative (Addis, Mcleod, and Raine, 2013) which brought stakeholders together and contributed to setting sector priorities for action. When focused on particular policy priorities such as health or education, such approaches can be effective in directing capital to those issues and translating dialogue to action (Shanmugalingam et al., 2011). Governments can frame the issues to promote sector-level development (see Bannick and Goldman, 2013).

---

[21] See <http://www.state.gov/s/partnerships/impact/>.
[22] For more information, see G8 Global Impact Investing Forum, London, June 2013 <https://www.gov.uk/government/uploads/system/uploads/attachment_data/file/225547/G8_Social_Impact_Investment_Forum_-_Outputs_and_Agreed_Actions.pdf>.

Governments and policymakers can also commission research to stimulate debate and action. Discussion and policy papers are commonly used. In the social finance context examples include a strategy paper on impact investing and the social and solidarity economy released by the French Premier Ministre's Department (Guezennec and Malochet, 2013), the IMPACT-Australia initiative of a department of the Australian Government (Addis, Mcleod, and Raine, 2013), and the UK Cabinet Office analysis of 'co-mingling' investment funds (UK Cabinet Office, 2012), and related 'Structure Note' to shortcut the process of design for other organizations.[23]

ENABLING AND ENDORSING

Government signalling is also an important driver of behaviours. Enabling activity can encourage and make it easier for participants to enter the social finance market by providing incentives or removing barriers. Endorsing and recognizing good practice also sends strong market signals and social finance and enterprise award programmes can highlight good practice (see, for example the recommendations of the Social Impact Investment Taskforce, 2014).

Governments can use their purchasing power to influence the development of markets too. The economists advocating for a more active role for the state in stimulating innovation place significant weight on the role of government as 'creative consumer' (Janeway, 2013).

Appropriately deployed, this can be a very practical means of shifting the way in which services are commissioned by requiring commissioners to take into account a broader approach to value creation. In 2014, the Council of the European Union adopted a package to reform public procurement, including to provide for 'common societal goods' in the assessment and selection processes. This includes consideration of environmental protection, social responsibility, innovation, climate change, and public value. All member states are required to enact corresponding laws by April 2016. Some states have already taken steps in this direction. The UK Social Value Act (2012: 11) is another example that requires public commissioners to consider:

- How what is proposed to be procured might improve the economic, social, and environmental well-being of the relevant area
- How, in conducting the process of procurement, it might act with a view to securing that improvement.

These developments are not confined to Europe. The Social Economy Act in Quebec[24] also requires Ministers to: 'take the social economy into consideration

---

[23] To access the structure note, see <http://www.gov.uk> 'Co-mingling Fund: Structure Note'.
[24] Social Economy Act, Bill 27 (2013, chapter 22). Passed and assented to 10 October 2013.

in measures and programmes, when updating those measures and programmes, and in developing new tools for enterprises' (Explanatory Notes and chapter III, section 7).

Whether achieved through social procurement, catalytic funding, or direct investment, government can act as a consumer for both social finance and the organizations and models that it finances. This can encourage new approaches to develop with the confidence that there will be a market for new products.

Government action can be as straightforward as highlighting practice. For example, the Social Economy Act in Quebec (2013) required Ministers to 'promote social economy initiatives carried out in Quebec and at the international level' (chapter III, section 7). Governments can go further and provide a focus on practice and a clearing house for what works. For example, the UK Cabinet Office developed tools to inform feasibility assessment and design of social impact bonds (SIBs) and the New South Wales Government in Australia has published model documentation.

POLICY AND INITIATIVE DESIGN

The challenge remains to develop policy and make use of the 'toolbox' in individual jurisdictions to have the desired effect of stimulating social finance, particularly in the context of a globalizing economy.

Other fields of activity with much longer history than social finance recognize there is still more work to be done to understand what works and why (OECD, 2013). Learning from early-stage finance for growth firms (an area of policy for economic innovation), for example, suggests:

Policy interventions should not be seen in isolation but as a set of interacting policies. Evaluation and periodic adjustments of the specific policy instruments as well as the full policy mix would be optimal, but is challenging in practice. (OECD, 2013: 5)

That process of developing data and evaluation to inform good policy design for social finance can be expected to be no less challenging in practice. This is not only because the field and policies are less developed, but also because social finance has the additional dimension of social, environmental and/or cultural impacts of the investments clearly in frame. Integration of these factors into either policy design or market practice has not yet occurred in any systematic way. However, it is not a blank sheet. There are practical tools to draw upon from available practice across a range of areas including responsible investment. More targeted measures of the social and environmental impacts of social finance are being developed and a principles based framework was developed by the Social Impact Investment Taskforce Working Group on Impact Measurement.

The IIPC proposed principles to inform policy analysis and design (Thornley et al., 2011). These principles intended 'to assist governments considering impact investing as a tool to address social objectives' provide useful guide-posts for testing policy and evaluating its impact and focus across six key areas: targeting, transparency, coordination, engagement, commitment, and implementation.

A French government policy paper identified three 'guiding principles' to be taken into account in framing policy and regulations for the financing of the social and solidarity economy sector, which reflect these elements (Guezennec and Malochet, 2013: 35):

- *inclusiveness:* in the definition of structures and types of finance and funding
- *transparency:* to promote accountability for projects being on track, protect investors, and preserve the underlying social and environmental objectives of the social economy
- *consistency:* between local and international policy directions, particularly in the European context.

Some commentators have suggested that more and better use could be made of theory of change principles in the design and evaluation of social finance initiatives (e.g. Jackson, 2013a).

The principles based approach is further developed in the IIPC London Principles—these were drawn from a range of political, economic, and cultural contexts, and have been developed to address different countries across varying stages of impact investing ecosystem development. The London Principles were designed to support a reflective approach to policy that drives learning and innovation over time to achieve important social objectives (IIPC, 2013). The key elements of the London Principles:[25]

- *Clarity of purpose:* focusing on integration of policy measures into existing policy and market structures, clear targeting of specific social objectives and definition of the role for social finance in achieving those objectives
- *Stakeholder engagement:* focusing on institutionalizing dialogue and feed-back with stakeholders as part of the policy design process, including for the additional legitimacy, discipline, and insight this can bring to the process and policy effectiveness
- *Market stewardship:* focusing on balanced and strategic development of policy and strategy across the elements of the market; advocating for 'appropriate' levels of regulation and against 'unnecessary management' of market activity
- *Institutional capacity:* focusing on creating institutions and capacity to facilitate resilient markets, deliver on policy intent and avoid mixed signals to the market

---

[25] The full text of the London Principles is available at <http://www.iipcollaborative.org/london-principles>.

- *Universal transparency*: focusing on clear and open communication of objectives and progress.

It is too early to assess whether any of these principles based approaches will be utilized broadly to serve their stated aims. There is also a question of how the effectiveness of policy measures can be evaluated, at the initiative and the market level (Addis and Koenig, 2014). The design principles may prove useful over time to inform this process as well as comparisons across jurisdictions, provided the high-level statements are developed by reference to a range of experience which can inform like-for-like comparisons and build content to inform future government and policy action.

GLOBAL THEMES ADAPTED FOR LOCAL CONTEXT

Common themes can be drawn from the international experience. The learning from one jurisdiction to another can provide valuable insights into what works and shorten the runway to design and implementation. Recent developments, in particular the Social Impact Investment Taskforce, have begun to paint potential for a global market.

Customization of policy design and implementation for local conditions is essential. For any given jurisdiction, the local environment will impact on what is required and what is possible and policy design needs to be fit for purpose in the local conditions taking into account existing regulatory frameworks and what levers are available and to whom. This helps to explain the variation already evident across policy approaches relating to social finance in different jurisdictions.

The work of the National Advisory Boards to the Social Impact Investment Taskforce highlighted how policy issues are manifested in individual markets and how action can and should be tailored for country conditions. How measures can and should be implemented also reflects structural, cultural, and philosophical underpinnings, including whether the country in questions has free market origins or underpinnings of a social or solidarity economy (Addis and Koenig, 2014: 15).

Global platforms that 'can connect people, ideas and resources in order to share best practice and build the impact investing market' (Social Impact Investment Taskforce, 2014: 10) are likely to be increasingly important to developing capability and accelerating developments and problem-solving to overcome barriers to market development. The emergence of communities of practice such as the IIPC (launched in 2012) and the Global Learning Exchange (announced in 2013 and trialled in 2014) to convene, curate, and disseminate knowledge and learning are promising recent developments. That could be evolved to build broader global praxis.

TOWARDS A POLICY MAP

Despite local differences, meaningful themes can be identified across policies developed and adapted for social finance around the world. These can be organized to 'categorize' areas for policy design and action in a 'policy map'.

The organizing framework for the 'policy map' (Table 13.1) is constructed with the 'toolbox' for government action (Figure 13.4) on one axis and the market elements for policy design and analysis (Figure 13.1) on the other to provide a matrix of categories for policy action. Examples of categories include: catalytic funding; enterprise and incubator development to stimulate demand; mandating disclosure of responsible investment practice; certification of social purpose organizations; focused procurement; and clarification of duties of fiduciary investors. The categories have been populated with examples from the global experience.

There is, no doubt, room for further debate and elaboration on the examples selected and their placement. The intention is to provide a starting point for the dialogue and illustrate a range of ways in which implementation has worked in various jurisdictions. Of course, the policy mix and local context remain central considerations (OECD, 2013). The positive story is that policy design and analysis for social finance is far from a blank slate, whether the policy intent is to correct for market failures or catalyse innovation and market development.

The next sections explore examples of government action and policy in more detail in the context of key factors for development and acceleration of social finance.

Infrastructure and investment for catalytic effect

This section focuses on two themes for government and policy action: market infrastructure and investment. In each case, with a particular emphasis on key areas where available commentary and experience suggests often relatively modest government action can create a catalytic effect in market development for social finance.

INFRASTRUCTURE: PROVIDING FOUNDATIONS AND SCAFFOLDING FOR SOCIAL FINANCE

Infrastructure is critical to develop social finance as a field of activity in the market (Freireich and Fulton, 2009). In 2013, the World Economic Forum highlighted the lack of clear and mature infrastructure for social finance as a significant barrier for institutional investors (Drexler and Noble, 2013a; see also Wood et al., 2012). In areas of economic policy, the significance of infrastructure development has been recognized:

It is important to focus on development of the market, rather than solely on provision of financing. This requires creating proper incentives and supporting the development of the necessary quality, skills and experience in the venture firms and angel investors to match international norms. (OECD, 2013: 36)

The likely development trajectory of a market for social finance (Figure 13.5) was articulated in the seminal report of the Monitor Institute (Freireich and Fulton, 2009). It shows the progression through uncoordinated innovation, principally through initiatives of individual leaders and firms, to development of a functional market, through to capturing the value and potential of the field toward greater maturity and stability.

In social finance, as in any emerging field, industry players often have common needs that are most effectively met through collective resources (Freireich and Fulton, 2009; Jackson and Harji, 2012; Addis, Mcleod, and Raine, 2013; Bannick and Goldman, 2013). Government is one of the actors that can lead this development. While concerns about market distortion and inhibiting competition are legitimate and should be considered, this should not be at the expense of the system view:

We would also note that LACK [original emphasis] of infrastructure can disrupt an otherwise burgeoning sector, and that many times infrastructure needs to be developed at a national level. (Bannick and Goldman, 2013: 10)

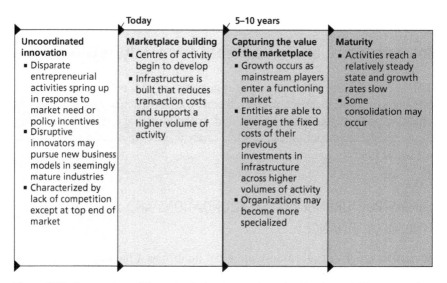

Figure 13.5. An overview of the systemic development required for the social finance market
Source: Freireich and Fulton, 2009

Regulatory and Social Environment that encourages and supports the adoption of enterprising solutions to social problems and the development of supporting services and markets

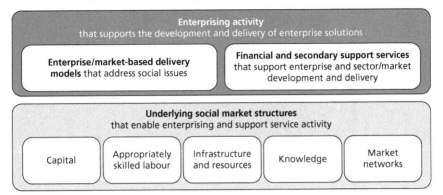

Figure 13.6. The elements of the enabling market infrastructure for social finance
Source: Hill, 2010

Governments are uniquely placed to take a systems-level view and to play an active role in laying foundations and providing the scaffolding for market activity and growth. The aim is not for government to replace private action, but to set the conditions that will enable more actors to place themselves in an emergent field and have confidence that the systemic conditions justify translating interest to action. Thoughtful attention to market infrastructure has potential not only to accelerate development of social finance, but also to assist in developing sectors of activity which social finance enables (Bannick and Goldman, 2013).

'Market infrastructure' encompasses a range of areas and activity (Figure 13.6), including the following that collectively populate the 'enabling environment' element of the market (Figure 13.1):

- regulation and standard setting
- metrics, measurement, and benchmarking, including analysis and comparison of performance
- awareness-raising, network development and brokering of connections to accelerate action
- capability development, including specialist intermediary organizations and financial advisors, analysts, and brokers and industry associations
- development of products, track records of investment performance, and secondary markets to promote liquidity
- development of a base of research and learning.

A number of initiatives across jurisdictions have already contributed or supported enabling infrastructure for social finance. Common themes are identified in the 'policy map' in Table 13.1.

Table 13.1. Policy map: Global examples to illustrate the 'toolbox' applied to dynamics of the social finance market

Mandate	Enable	Partner	Endorse
A. Supply-side development			
Government procurement rules to support impact investment	Tax incentives and subsidies	Public co-investments, including funds	Cluster investment institutions for incubation effect
Examples:	Examples:	Examples:	Examples:
Broad-Based Black Economic Empowerment Act (South Africa)	Social Enterprise & Investment Tax Incentives (UK)	Bridges Ventures Funds I and II (UK)	City of London development as impact investment hub (UK)
Social Value Act (UK)	Community Investment Tax Credit (UK)	Community Asset Fund (UK)	
	Social Investment Tax Relief consultation (UK)	CDFI Fund (US)	
	National Rental Affordability Scheme (Australia)	OPIC Impact Investment Funds (US)	
	Low Income Housing Tax Credit (US)	New York City Acquisition Fund (NYC; US)	
	New Market Tax Credit (US)	Impact Investment Fund—Small Business Administration (US)	
	Solar Energy and Business Energy Investment Tax Credit (US)	Social Enterprise Development and Investment Funds (Australia)	
	Community Economic Development Investment funds (Canada)	GoodStart Early Learning (Australia)	
	Green Funds Scheme (Netherlands)	Renewable Energy Equity & Venture Capital Funds (Australia)	
		Community Economic Development Investment Funds (Canada)	
		Venture Capital Trust Fund (VCTF, Ghana)	
Mandate bank/other institutional investment in underserved communities	Clarifying fiduciary duties for institutional investors	Initiate Social Impact Bonds (SIBs) and other innovative financial instruments for impact	Demonstrate and disseminate examples of social finance
Examples:	Examples:	Examples:	Examples:
Community Reinvestment Act (US)	Private and public pension funds, insurance companies, endowments (USA)	Peterborough Social Impact Bond (UK)	IMPACT—Australia initiative (Australia)
Priority Sector Lending (India)			SIB Centre of Excellence (UK)

Policy lever	Examples	
Regulation of 'fiduciary' investments	Aggregation of smaller investments to appeal to large asset owners	Highlight areas of policy priority where new solutions are needed or demand exceeds available supply to stimulate targeted innovation
Examples:	Examples:	Examples:
Disclosures recommended by UK Social Investment Taskforce (UK)	Build America Bonds (US)	Social Benefit Bonds for out of home care Newpin/UnitingCare (Australia)
Review of IRS regulation for mission-related philanthropic investment (USA)	National Equity Fund allocation of New Market Tax Credits (US)	New York City Rikers Island Prison/Goldman Sachs Social Impact Bond for Juvenile Recidivism (USA)
Regulation 28 Pension Fund Act Revisions (2011) (South Africa)	Micro-Credit Company Pilot Program (People's Republic of China)	New York State Centre for Employment Opportunities recidivism and employment Social Impact Partnership (USA)
	Multi-fondos (Peru)	For more on Social Impact Bonds see UK Cabinet Office Centre for Social Impact Bonds; Pay for Success Learning Hub and Harvard Kennedy School Social Impact Bond Technical Assistance Lab

Policy lever	Examples	
Mandate foundation allocation recommended Canadian Taskforce (Canada)	Innovative contracting	Showcase foundations increasing investments from the corpus of their funds in social finance
Programme-related investment category of investment for foundations (US)	Examples:	Examples:
Require institutional investors to disclose responsible investing practices	Department of Work and Pensions Innovation Fund (UK)	Encourage foundations to continue to innovate and make the strategic and cultural shifts necessary to apply full range of their assets to mission recommended Global Field Scan (international)
Examples:	Cross-sector development of new financial products	Highlight and disseminate financial product innovation
Regulation 28 Pension Fund Act Revisions (2011) (South Africa)	Examples:	Examples:
	Community shares (UK)	UK Cabinet Office Achieving Social Impact at Scale (UK)
	Affordable housing (various jurisdictions)	Impact Investing Document du Travail (France)

(continued)

Table 13.1. Continued

Mandate	Enable	Partner	Endorse
A. Supply-side development			
Reserve Fund Regulations (Norway)	Outcomes Finance Fund (UK)	Increase the variety of products that address the risk/return profile of a wide range of investors recommended Global Field Scan (international)	
Loi Pensions Complementaires (Occupational Pension Law) (Belgium)	European procurement package (EU)		
Mandate pension fund disclosure recommended Canadian Taskforce (Canada)		Develop new bonds and bond like instruments recommended Canadian Taskforce on Social Finance (Canada)	
Require CSR disclosure	Government credit guarantees and first loss positions	Encourage cross-sector collaborations and solutions	
Examples:	Examples:	Examples:	
Listed companies 'comply or explain' disclosure (Malaysia)	Small Business Loan Guarantees (US)	Joint European Support for Sustainable Investment in City	
Article 225 (France)	US Aid Development Credit Authority (US)	Areas (JESSICA) (EU)	
	Social Enterprise Development & Investment Funds (Australia)		
	Joint European Support for Sustainable Investment in City Areas (JESSICA) (EU)	Development of risk assessment and due diligence tools	
	Publicly funded safety nets recommended in Global Field Scan (international)	Examples:	
		Strengthen investor understanding of various dimensions of performance management recommended Global Field Scan (international)	

B. Demand-side development[26]

Federal government requiring outcomes-focused initiatives from state and local government.	Social enterprise strategy and support	Encourage cross-sector collaborations and solutions	Recognize diverse business models supporting social impact
Examples:	Examples:	Examples:	Examples:
Social Impact Bond Act (US) (still in progress in US Congress as at December 2014)	Social Enterprise Strategy (UK) Opening up public services (UK) Mi Chacra Emprenedora (Peru)—Social Enterprise Facilitation Project (Tasmania, Australia) Recommendations for access to mainstream enterprise support services (Productivity Commission Australia)	Memorandum of Understanding between Office of the Regulator of Community Interest Companies and Social Enterprise Mark (UK) National High-Tech R&D Programme (People's Republic of China) Unit cost data availability (UK)	Memorandum of Understanding between Office of the regulator of Community Interest Companies and Social enterprise Mark (UK) Co-sponsor action research on emerging hybrid and scalable social enterprise models recommended Global Field Scan (international)
	Organizational forms that legitimize mission-driven operating models		**Showcase and encourage philanthropic contributions to social finance**
	Examples:		Examples:
	Benefit Corporation (B Corp) (US) Low-profit limited liability company (L3C) (US) Social Cooperatives (EU) Community Interest Company (CIC) (UK) Certification including environment and social enterprise 'marks'		UK Cabinet Office Achieving Social Impact at Scale (UK) Sponsorship for Philanthropy Australia Impact Investment Education Series (Australia)
	Examples:		
	Energy Star Program (US) CDFI certification (US) Support for investment readiness and incubation capacity		

(continued)

26 No mandated aspects have been identified for demand-side development; some may argue that social procurement policies or aspects of cooperatives or other regulation could be included here. The author has not adopted that view.

Table 13.1. Continued

B. Demand-side development[26]

Examples:	Social stock exchanges
Investment and Contract Readiness Fund (UK)	Examples:
Mutual Support Program (UK)	Impact Investment Exchange Asia (Singapore)
Social Incubator Fund (UK)	
Mi Chacra Emprendedora (Peru)	Social Stock Exchange (UK)
EU investment in prototype and pilots (EU)	Bolsa de Valorous Socioambientais (Brazil)
National Innovation Council (India)	South African Social Stock Exchange (South Africa)
Funding and strategic partnerships School for Social Entrepreneurs (UK, Australia)	
Expand Enterprise Connect recommended Productivity Commission (Australia)	Impact Exchange Board (Mauritius)
Supporting cost-effective approaches to improving management capacity of social entrepreneurs recommended Global Field Scan (international)	
Government grant funding for the 'pioneer gap'	
Examples:	
Social Incubator Fund (UK)	
Department for International Development (UK)	

C. Intermediary development

Establishing dedicated financial institutions	Support intermediaries through investment
Examples:	Examples:
Big Society Capital (UK)	Big Society Capital (UK)
Venture Capital Trust (Ghana)	Big Society Capital investment in the Social Stock Exchange (UK)
Recommendation for Fund of Funds (Taskforce on Social Finance, Canada)	CDFI Fund Pilot (Australia)
Microfinance Act (Kenya)	Social Enterprise Development and Investment Funds (SEDIF, Australia)
Mobilization of multi-year grant funds to deepen public goods infrastructure recommended Global Field Scan (international)	Create intermediaries and strengthen existing ones recommended Global Field Scan (international)

D Infrastructure and Enabling Environment for market development

Market development policy strategies and frameworks	Review regulatory barriers to social investment	Encouraging impact measurement	Supporting leaders and champions across sectors to promote social investment
Examples: Growing the Social Investment Market: A vision and strategy (UK)	Examples: G8 Social Investment Taskforce (International) Social Investment Taskforce (UK) Impact Investing Working Group of the Presidential Investment Council (Senegal) Senate Economics References Committee *Investing for Good* (Australia)	Examples: Inspiring Impact cross-sector measurement initiative (UK) Strengthen investor understanding of various dimensions of performance management recommended Global Field Scan (international)	Examples: Social Investment Taskforce (UK) Impact Investing Working Group of the Presidential Investment Council (Senegal) Investment in the GIIN by US Aid (USA) and DFID (UK) Engagement with educational institutions to develop professional development content and pathways recommended Global Field Scan (international)
Regulatory bodies including for social sector organizations	Support for peak bodies	Participate in bodies to harness expertise and information across sectors and set direction	Creation and endorsement of social finance networks
Examples: Charities Commission (UK) Australian Charities and Non-profit Commission (Australia)	Examples: Community Development Financial Association (UK) GIIN (UK and US)	Examples: Impact Investing Policy Collaborative (International) Global Learning Exchange (International) MaRS Centre (Canada) Facilitation of open exchange among governments recommended Global Field Scan (international)	Examples: Facilitation of open exchange among governments recommended Global Field Scan (international)
Examples: Centre for Social Impact Bonds (UK) (International)	Centres of excellence and hubs to promote practice and connect investors and enterprise with opportunities Examples: Centre for Social Impact (Australia)	Support educational institutions to develop specialist social investment study programs Examples: Centre for Social Impact (Australia)	Support market analysis and research Examples: IMPACT—Australia (Australia)

(continued)

Table 13.1. Continued

D. Infrastructure and Enabling Environment for market development

Create new options by matching investor risk/return profiles with investee businesses	UK Cabinet Office and Said Business School Oxford Symposium on Social Impact Bonds 2012 (UK)	Australian Housing & Urban Research Institute research on financial products for affordable housing (Australia)
recommended Global Field Scan (international)		Encouraging business engagement (EU)
		UK Cabinet Office sponsored research (UK)
Establish dedicated government social finance capability to design policy, drive collaboration, and contribute to field building		Co-sponsor action research on emerging hybrid and scalable social enterprise models recommended Global Field Scan (international)
Examples:		
Department for Social Prosperity (Colombia)		
UK Cabinet Office Social Investment & Finance Unit (UK)		
White House Office of Social Innovation and Civic Participation (USA)		
Thai Social Enterprise Office (Thailand)		

Categories of potential policy action 'mapped' across different modes of government action (mandate, enable, partner, and endorse) across one axis and market dynamics for social finance (enabling environment, supply, demand, and intermediation) on the other axis. Adapted from Australian Government Department of Employment 'Impact Investment Policy Map', 2013

Note 1: For source material, see also: UK Social Investment Taskforce (2000, 2003, 2005, 2010); Canadian Taskforce on Social Finance, 2010; Thornley et al. (2011); Wood et al. (2012); E. T. Jackson & Associates (2012); Jackson and Harji (2012); Schwab Foundation et al. (2013). Adapted and updated with research for this chapter.

Note 2: The intention of this table is not to provide a comprehensive catalogue of policy for impact investing but to provide examples that illustrate the policy action taken across different jurisdictions, highlighting the consistent themes in terms of approach and areas of market focus. Only areas of government action have been highlighted; market- or sector-led initiatives have not been included unless specifically endorsed or adopted as policy or in other formal government actions. The information is current to 2014.

Note 3: The policy examples could also be mapped on to other frameworks. For example, the recent guidance on the policy drivers for social innovation (Schwab Foundation et al., 2013) could be utilized. That framework is similar in concept to the approach taken here in that it includes both a focus on how governments can operate (engagement of market stakeholders, development of government capacity for action, reviewing and refining policy) and a focus on market dynamics (building market infrastructure and capacity, preparing enterprises for growth, growing and directing private capital) to take innovations to scale.

REGULATION

Potential regulatory barriers to social finance are an important area for policy consideration. This is an area that requires each jurisdiction to look to existing regulatory measures and gaps and engage with stakeholders to identify whether regulatory aspects are acting as disincentives or creating barriers in practice and why.

The regulated duties of investors—fiduciary duties—are a particular area of focus. They impact on where organizations place their capital and set foundations practice at firm and industry level that govern investment decisions. These duties have particular significance for mobilizing philanthropic and institutional capital (Australian Productivity Commission, 2010; Heaney, 2010; Wood et al., 2012; Drexler and Noble, 2013a; Charlton et al., 2013; Social Impact Investment Taskforce, 2014).

Governments not only regulate these (fiduciary) duties, they also provide clear policy and practical signals and guidance for their exercise. There is a significant amount of (context-specific) debate, about whether regulatory changes are required to permit or enable investment in social finance (e.g. Wood et al., 2012; Charlton et al., 2013). The conclusion is often that existing regulation does not preclude social finance provided caution is exercised. Some practitioners have adapted asset allocation frameworks to specifically include impact considerations (e.g. see J.P. Morgan *A Portfolio Approach to Impact Investment,* October 2012 and analysis in Charlton et al., 2013).

Beyond the letter and interpretation of the law, signalling from government can influence practice and mobilize capital (Wood et al., 2012, Drexler and Noble, 2013a). In some jurisdictions, guidance material about what is permissible within current regulatory regimes is already available. In the UK for example, the Charity Commission published a detailed guidance note on the duties of trustees and the potential for funds to make mission-related investments.[27] A similar approach has been taken regarding institutional investment by state pension funds in some US jurisdictions (Wood et al., 2012) and in Peru (Thornley et al., 2011). Such guidance can clarify the boundary between regulatory constraint and practice norms and alters the perceived risk relative to return on investment decisions. Over time, such action can affect the culture and behaviours of investment decision-making.

One of the high-level recommendations of the Social Impact Investment Taskforce called for clarification of fiduciary duties to put beyond doubt that trustees can consider social impact as well as risk and return in investment decision-making (Social Impact Investment Taskforce, 2014: Recommendation 3). A number of the National Advisory Boards to the Taskforce gave this

---

[27] For more information, see Charity Commission <http://www.charity-commission.gov.uk/about_us/about_the_commission/char_invest_legal.aspx>. Further steps in the UK are under consideration.

issue particular attention (see reports of the National Advisory Boards on Impact Investing in participating countries, 2014).[28]

Some social finance commentators and practitioners call for clear regulatory change, often referencing the impact of changes to the 'prudent man' rule under the USA Employee Retirement Income Security Act (ERISA) in 1979. In that case, regulation was amended explicitly to state that pension fund managers could invest up to 10 per cent in venture capital assets. The change is seen as a critical step in opening the gateway for new investment into the venture capital industry (e.g. Wood et al., 2012; US National Advisory Board on Impact Investing, 2014).[29] Some have called for mandated allocation of investment capital from philanthropic foundations into social finance (e.g. Canadian Taskforce on Social Finance, 2010). The World Economic Forum recommended 'cautious' revision of regulation that may 'restrict willing capital' (Drexler and Noble, 2013a).

In France, legislation for 'socially responsible employee savings schemes' has been in effect since 2001. This legislation mandates that employees with access to a *Plan d'Epargne Entreprise* must have the opportunity to invest in funds that place between 5 and 10 per cent of their capital in organizations and activities certified with the 'solidarity label'.[30] Capital invested in these Solidarity Investment Funds is reported to have grown from €404m in 2006 to €2.6bn in 2012, although in keeping with the '90/10' allocation, at least 90 per cent of the capital under management is reported to be in listed equities selected primarily on responsible investment principles (Guezennec and Malochet, 2013). Nonetheless, the policy is considered to be a factor in both demonstrating a demand for social finance deals and, as a result, creating new social deals in France (Dupuy and Langendorff, 2014).

Other jurisdictions have introduced disclosure requirements with the intention of influencing investor behaviour. While there are not yet examples that focus on social finance per se, a number of jurisdictions have requirements for pension funds to disclose their responsible investment practices. Regulation provides for varying degrees of disclosure in countries from Australia to Malaysia to Norway, New Zealand, and South Africa (Richardson, 2008; Boersch, 2010; Mercer, 2012; Charlton et al., 2013). The objective of these measures is to bring focus and scrutiny to socially responsible investment practice. By targeting institutions that invest at scale, regulation can be expected to have a wider effect on other parts of the investment ecosystem from financial advisors to analysis, reporting, and capability development.

However, it is interesting to note that some industry surveys have identified public opinion and stakeholder activism as more significant drivers of investment decision-making than regulation (e.g. Boersch, 2010). This indicates that

---

[28] See <http://www.socialimpactinvestment.org>.
[29] For an overview of the ERISA regime for venture capital, see Gompers (1994).
[30] The solidarity accreditation is overseen by Finansol, a non-profit organization and is based on the criteria in the French Labour Code.

the emergence of a range of initiatives providing more information to the market[31] could prove an important development. Such tools can contribute to more informed community and shareholder positions regarding social finance investments and their performance, which may in turn influence the market. Government is one of the parties that has the power to encourage and fund the development of these tools, for which it can be difficult to attract private investment (Bannick and Goldman, 2013).

Regulation has also been in frame in the context of reducing financial exclusion and stimulating community investment. In the USA, regulatory measures providing both 'carrot and stick' for community investment have been a linchpin of the Community Reinvestment Act and related initiatives.[32] This regime initially responded to manifest discrimination in lending practices and has evolved over more than four decades into a relatively complex framework underpinning the US community development finance sector. This effectively makes regulatory approval of certain activities for financial institutions contingent upon their community investment contributions and provides a range of incentives through tax relief and co-investment for community investment. The Community Reinvestment Act has contributed to significant bank engagement in low- and moderate-income communities and generated employment and affordable housing outcomes across the USA (see the analysis in the US National Advisory Board on Impact Investing, 2014). If passed, the proposed US Social Impact Bond Act[33] would include investment by institutions in Social Impact Bonds as a factor to be considered in assessing their community reinvestment activities.

Arguments have been made in some other jurisdictions for a similar approach, or adaptation of the approach for local conditions. In Australia, the US community re-investment regime was considered by both the Productivity Commission (2010) and the Senate Economics References Committee (2011), though in each case concerns were raised based on the considerable differences in local conditions in the banking sector. In the UK, the Social Investment Taskforce (2000–10) recommended policy to mobilize bank capital for 'under-invested' communities and overcome perceptions that such communities are enterprise 'no-go areas'. This recommendation has not yet been taken up by UK governments. However, other policy initiatives to support and stimulate community development finance have been introduced.[34]

---

[31] Examples include Ethex, EngagedX, Impact Base, and the recent partnership between IIX and the Stock Exchange of Mauritius, some of which are considered in relation to exits and liquidity for social finance later in this section.

[32] There is a significant body of literature examining the Community Reinvestment Act, its operation, efficacy and impacts; see for example Campen (1997); Olson et al. (2009); Lindsey (2009); Essene and Apgar (2009).

[33] See <https://www.congress.gov/bill/113th-congress/house-bill/4885>.

[34] These measures include tax incentives and guarantees, considered in the context of investment below; for information on policy pertaining to community investment tax relief, see <http://www.hmrc.gov.uk/specialist/citc_guidance.htm> and regarding the enterprise finance guarantee, see <https://www.gov.uk/government/policies/making-it-easier-to-set-up-and-grow-a-business%976>.

Regulation can also have an enabling effect. This is evident in innovations such as B-Corporations.[35] Legislation to enable organizations to explicitly embed public benefit in their constitutional governance was first introduced in the US state of Maryland in 2009 and in less than five years has been enacted in over thirty US states and is in progress in a further nine. B-Corporation global partnerships are in effect in the UK, Europe, South America, Europe, Canada, Australia, and New Zealand. The Social Impact Investment Taskforce Mission Alignment Working Group (2014) recommended an international framework based on model laws. They concluded that regulating to enable (not mandate) social purpose organizations to embed their mission in new corporate forms could allow both more transparent accounting for the impact of social finance investments and could provide a system of recognition of the legitimacy of such organizations across global boundaries.

Some new models with application for social finance are challenging exiting regulatory frameworks. Crowdfunding is a prime example. Crowdfunding is the term used to describe a range ways in which funds are raised directly from the public, generally in relatively small individual amounts. This form of capital-raising has gained currency in microfinance through platforms such as Kiva and is becoming an important source of capital for a range of enterprises. There is overlap with fundraising and capital-raising and the existing regulatory regimes in those areas.

In most jurisdictions, the regulatory environment does not match the agility and pace of developing platforms for crowdfunding. Also, web-based plat-forms tend to operate across geographic borders, increasing complexity for those raising funds to navigate multiple regulatory regimes. In 2013, a number of jurisdictions, including Australia, France, Italy, the US, UK, and the EU considered whether and how to regulate crowdfunding and consulting stake-holders (see e.g. European Commission, 2013; CAMAC, 2013; Securities & Exchange Commission Fact Sheet, 2013). However, most of the regulation introduced or in contemplation is yet to be tested in practice.

Beyond this there is a broader retail market of investors: citizens seeking investment options that will enable more direct connection between their investments and society. Evidence suggests that the number of these investors seeking social finance options is growing but their needs are not being met (Triodos Bank, 2014). Furthermore, adapting the regulatory environment for retail social finance investment will be a crucial factor in increasing the supply of deals to meet this demand (Triodos Bank, 2014). While there must be prudent regulation to protect investor interests, practitioners point to examples of existing retail funds including the French '90/10' Solidarity Investment Funds and Dutch Green Funds that suggest retail impact fund models can succeed and illustrate how both objectives can be satisfied (Triodos Bank, 2014).

---

[35] Background on B Corporations is available at <http://www.bcorporation.net>.

LIQUIDITY AND EXITS

Another significant issue for market development is liquidity and the development of exit markets for investments. Financial returns and aspects of effective risk management are predicated on available exits. They can also facilitate greater transparency and provide a clearing-house role enabling investors to identify and vet a range of investment opportunities. The range of common exit mechanisms includes trade sales, public offerings on stock markets, and exchanges or sales to other investors. Well designed, such measures also provide a gateway for enterprises to access capital. The role of government here is not well defined and in the related context of early-stage finance for growth ventures, it has been noted that: 'The importance of exits and exit markets is often not fully appreciated by policymakers' (OECD, 2013: 40).

Exploring the operation of the range of exit mechanisms in social finance is beyond the scope of this paper. Exits are occurring, as funds mature and through private arrangements. However, there are not yet developed systems or dedicated channels for social finance capital and investment opportunities. The World Economic Forum recently identified social stock exchanges as one of the innovations that could unlock mainstream capital for social finance:

The Social Stock Exchange is a mechanism for opening up impact investing to retail investors, as well as making it more attractive to mainstream investment. A supportive environment for issuers and investors, along with an ecosystem within which they can interact, are important requirements for creating a vibrant public impact investing market. (Drexler and Noble, 2013b: 5)

Social finance exchanges are emerging internationally. In most cases this has not been a result of direct government action or engagement, although in some cases government has played a facilitating role. For example, the Social Stock Exchange UK launched in June 2013 that connects listed social impact businesses with investors was announced at the G8 Social Impact Investing Forum and the City of London is listed as a key supporter, but it is not a government initiative.[36] The initiative launched in June 2013 as a collaboration between the Stock Exchange of Mauritius and Impact Exchange Asia (developed from the Nexii initiative[37]) operates within the existing regulatory regimes but is not a policy or government-led initiative.[38] Exchange initiatives

---

[36] For more information, see <http://www.socialstockexchange.com>. Big Society Capital is a cornerstone investor in the exchange which is also supported by the London Stock Exchange and City of London. The Big Lottery Fund has capitalized a 'kick-starter' fund supporting enterprises seeking admission to the Exchange to develop necessary capability. The initiative was launched by the Right Hon. David Cameron, MP at the G8 Social Impact Investment Forum, for Social Stock Exchange announcement 6 June 2013, see <https://www.gov.uk/government/uploads/system/uploads/attachment_data/file/225547/G8_Social_Impact_Investment_Forum_-_Outputs_and_Agreed_Actions.pdf>.

[37] See <http://www.impacttrust.org.za/nexii/>.

[38] For more information, see <http://www.asiaiix.com>.

are also at various stages of development in jurisdictions as diverse as Brazil, Canada and Kenya, where the work is also sector led.[39]

The fact that government is not at the centre or leading these initiatives does not reflect on their importance. In most jurisdictions where they exist, stock exchanges operate within a regulatory framework and it is important this provides a robust and transparent environment for the transactions facilitated by the exchange. A key question to be tested over time is whether and to what extent separate mechanisms are necessary and useful to trade social finance instruments. In the early stages, clear principles regarding assessment of social and environmental impact appear to be the central distinguishing feature. Third parties are generally carrying out these assessments. It is too early to say as yet whether any specific adjustments to the regulatory environment will be required to accommodate the particular features of social finance exchanges.

Other policy mechanisms that can facilitate liquidity include credit enhancement such as loan guarantees, considered in the context of indirect investment.

MEASUREMENT AND METRICS

Metrics and measurement are another key component of the market infra-structure for social finance, enabling investment performance to be measured and compared. Progress in effective social impact measurement will be a key driver of growth in the social finance market (Social Impact Investment Taskforce, 2014). Measurement not only contributes to accountability for performance, but also provides inputs for benchmarking risk and return. Over time measurement enables the market to move beyond fragmented, bespoke deal generation to build critical mass. As the distinguishing feature of social finance is intentional design for positive benefits to society, it is critical that assessments can be made about the effectiveness of the organiza-tions and initiatives financed to contribute positive benefit.

It is fundamental that the social return is not an incidental or even 'nice to have' by-product of a financial investment, but is a primary purpose and expectation of the investment. (Evenett, 2012: 1)

Taxonomies and measurement have begun to develop for social finance. These developments have generally been sector led, for example development of the Impact Reporting and Investment Standards by the GIIN and of EngagedX by Engaged Investment.[40] Governments have begun actively considering and

---

[39] For an overview of the differences between and learning from these exchanges, see the work undertaken by SSHRC-CURA on Responsible Investing at Concordia University: <http://www6.carleton.ca/3ci/ccms/wp-content/ccms-files/mendell-EBVwebinar.pdf>.

[40] See <http://www.iris.thegiin.org> and <http://www.engagedinvestment.com> for more detail on these measurement frameworks.

experimenting with ways in which the efficacy of social and environmental programmes can be measured. However, practice has not yet developed in any systematic way to set performance benchmarks in terms of impact on and for communities or to inform funding decision-making. Also, governments have not yet adopted the developing social finance impact frameworks in a coherent way to inform their own decision-making.

The Social Impact Investment Taskforce embedded in its definition of 'social impact investment' intentional design for both positive social outcomes and financial return and attention to the measurement of both. One of the key recommendations of the Taskforce was to 'set measureable impact objectives and track their achievement' (Social Impact Investment Taskforce, 2014). The Social Impact Investment Taskforce Impact Measurement Working Group examined the current state of measurement practice and noted the need for the 'availability of material, reliable, comparable, additional, and universal impact data' to underpin robust impact measurement along with the need for all participants in the social finance market to take accept 'impact accountability' (Social Impact Investment Taskforce Impact Measurement Working Group, 2014: 1).

Like other areas of the social impact value chain, progress in social impact measurement is unlikely to be made by in isolation from governments. Measurement is a vital contribution to building the confidence of investors and identifying the benchmarks for good decision-making needed for the social finance to develop. In this context governments have a clear stake in development of sound metrics in their capacity as market steward.

Beyond that, governments have a direct interest in measurement and metrics. Improved measurement of the social impacts can help them understand what works and contribute to the evidence and practice base that informs policy design. They also have a significant contribution to make. Governments often have data and research to contribute, including about where the need is and what approaches have been tried before. This is not an argument for government control or direction, simply that governments have a stake in and an opportunity to inform and contribute to the development of measurement and metrics for social finance. Taking a proactive role can put governments and policymakers in a position to identify appropriate opportunities to leverage additional or different forms of finance.

If governments are not involved in the development of social measures, social finance and service delivery more generally may be the poorer for it. If they are not involved, it may be much more difficult for governments to engage with market opportunities or to apply any metrics that address the efficacy of their own policies and initiatives. It is also an opportunity missed if the significant bodies of data and information held by governments do not inform the development of metrics and measures.

Social finance products can provide a mechanism that focus on the shared or overlapping interest of government and the market in effective impact measurement. Some social finance innovations, particularly social impact bonds, are beginning to demonstrate this effect.[41] Social impact bonds are structured with clearly articulated and evaluated programme efficacy as a central feature. This creates a shared interest between the parties, of which government is usually one, in the outcomes and how they are measured. The challenges and opportunities of this practice are beginning to emerge as a focus for academic analysis (e.g. Jackson, 2013b; Nicholls and Tomkinson, 2013; Gustaffson-Wright et al., 2015).

In addition, government data can send powerful signals to the market. The UK has made available costing data for a range of social services through the unit cost database.[42] This cost information—drawn from academic studies and government data—covers a range of social service areas from education to justice and provides a reference point for anyone. It can be used by existing or new enterprises to inform service design, operating models, and evaluation. It provides a starting point for dialogue and further work to refine frameworks and costings. The Social Impact Investment Taskforce encouraged other governments to make this kind of data more available to enable more organizations to make assessments of their potential to 'deliver better outcomes more innovatively and cost-effectively'. The Taskforce noted:

> Greater transparency about the fiscal value of achieving specific social outcomes would help enormously, by showing social innovators where opportunities exist to do better. We would like to see other governments consider doing something similar to the UK's. (Social Impact Investment Taskforce, 2014: 15–16)

More generally, governments' role may involve support for or enabling market actors that can take a lead role in developing measurement infrastructure. For example, US Aid and DFID both support the work of the GIIN. In the UK, successive governments played a role in creating what is now Big Society Capital, which has developed an outcomes matrix[43] that has potential to streamline aspects of social impact reporting across a range of initiatives. Governments can also help increase the visibility of and access to available information by the expectations they set for performance. This can start with services governments provide and those they commission from others (e.g. Shergold, 2013). Governments are also one of the bodies well placed to invest in information, platforms, and infrastructure and in organizations willing to develop and provide these as a public good (Bannick and Goldman, 2013).

The next section explores the potential for governments to stimulate the market and demonstrate the potential of social finance through a range of direct and indirect investment.

---

[41] The interplay between social finance, and Social Impact Bonds in particular, and reform directions in public service is considered in more detail in the final section of the chapter.

[42] See <http://neweconomymanchester.com/stories/832-unit_cost_database>.

[43] For more detail about the Big Society Capital outcomes matrix, see <http://www.bigsocietycapital.com/outcomes-matrix>.

Catalytic investment

Government has substantial capacity to signal interest in a market area and stimulate investment by providing seed capital. In the early stages of financial market development, transactions are vital to demonstrate that investment is credible and establish deal flow.

Unfortunately, relatively few appear willing to step up to the hard and uncertain work of sparking and nurturing the innovations that ultimately generate a robust flow of investible, high-return impact investments. It is as if impact investors are lined up around the proverbial water pump. waiting for the flood of deals, while no one is actively priming the pump. (Bannick and Goldman, 2013: 1)

Strategically targeted, government leadership can fill this gap and have a powerful signalling effect that provides confidence to other actors and generates market development that would not otherwise have occurred.

CATALYTIC CAPITAL

The availability of 'risk' capital as a critical element for market development has received significant attention (Freireich and Fulton, 2009; Ludlow and Jenkins 2011; Burkett, 2012; Addis, Mcleod, and Raine, 2013; Impact Assets Issue Briefs #2, 3, 5, 8, UK Cabinet Office, 2012; The Global Impact Investment Network (GIIN) Issue Brief October, 2013; Social Impact Investment Taskforce, 2014):

Without some catalytic, risk-taking funding … the deals may not provide sufficiently attractive returns for social investors; without commercial investors, it may be more challenging to invest the volume of funds required to make a difference. (Freireich and Fulton, 2009: 8)

Social finance can draw lessons from initiatives promoting economic innovation and development. In particular, there is track record of government intervention to stimulate seed and early-stage funding and encourage nascent markets to scale. For example, most OECD countries have some form of investment partnerships with the private sector and and/or funds of funds to support increased investment in small and medium enterprises (OECD, 2012, 2013). This body of literature and research also indicates that well-designed co-investment strategies and policies have potential to leverage private investment and drive development, growth, and performance of the market (OECD, 2012, 2013).

'Co-mingling' of funds from different types of investors is one innovation identified by the World Economic Forum and others as critical to the development of social finance (Impact Assets Issue Brief #10, 2012; UK Cabinet Office, 2013a; Addis, Mcleod, and Raine, 2013; Drexler and Noble, 2013b).

Commingling funds serve as innovative forms of partnership among previously isolated capital providers. Set up correctly, they can multiply the impact of capital while preserving their contributors' interests. (Drexler and Noble, 2013b: 5)

Catalytic funding is typically seed funding and often involves providing subordinated capital to reduce the risk for return for other investors (Impact Assets Issue Brief #10, 2012; UK Cabinet Office, 2013a; The Global Impact Investment Network (GIIN) Issues Brief October 2013). The UK Cabinet Office (2013a) undertook a study of seven funds combining different kinds of capital and found three typical groupings of the terms on which catalytic capital is provided:

- *pari passu* or capital on equal footing
- *risk–reward* where the investors took different levels of risk based on motivation for social relative to financial outcomes
- *but-for* where investors seeking to catalyse impact accepted greater risk to attract mainstream or more commercially focused capital that would not otherwise have been invested.

Figure 13.7 illustrates the characteristic way in which the latter two categories of catalytic funding operate; layers two and three of the diagram shows the role of different types of risk capital.

A number of initiatives have demonstrated the potential for governments to generate positive market impacts with thoughtfully designed catalytic capital for social finance. This need not always involve new funding. Measures can be designed to reorient existing funding to leverage other capital and increase the reach and impact of the public monies involved.

The GIIN identified 'leverage for impact' and 'market development' as key scenarios suitable for providing first loss capital (Global Impact Investment Network (GIIN) Issue Brief October, 2013; see also, Impact Assets Issue Brief #10). In some of the existing social finance initiatives, the relevant government

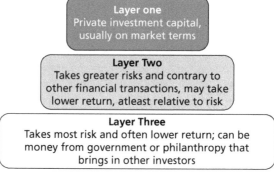

Figure 13.7. Layered capital structures for investment in social finance
Source: Addis, Mcleod, and Raine, 2013, adapted from Burkett, 2012

has identified these same policy objectives as drivers. For example, the SEDIF initiative in Australia identified two key policy objectives: greater access to capital for social enterprise; and development of the social finance market in Australia (Cullen and Addis, 2013).

Early research on performance of social finance funds across a range of jurisdictions suggests that the most successful funds have made effective use of available government investment and developed productive relationships with government (Clark, Thornley, and Emerson, 2012 and Clark, Emerson, and Thornley, 2013). Indeed, the most recent research suggests that catalytic capital and strong relationships between government and fund managers are key success factors for such funds (Clark, Emerson and Thornley, 2013).

There is a range of illustrative examples of government providing catalytic investment for social finance. These government-led initiatives take a range of forms. The body of practice in development finance has been growing for some time. Prominent examples include the US Overseas Private Investment Corporation and Global Development Innovation Ventures joint venture between the UK and US. Other government investments have targeted provision of capital for social enterprise on appropriate terms. Prominent examples in this category include the Scottish Social Investment Fund[44] and the Australian Social Enterprise Development and Investment Funds.[45] Other government investments have been into equity funds such as the Social Investment Fund in Ghana and Bridges Community Ventures Sustainable Growth Fund in the UK which target job creation and local economic development in communities experiencing entrenched disadvantage.[46] Other initiatives are emerging. Portugal has work underway for a €150m Social Innovation Fund to be capitalized with European structural funds and designed to stimulate transformation of social service provision.[47]

Some common themes and lessons can be drawn from this collective experience to inform future policy design:

- Provision of catalytic funding can mobilize both investors on the supply side and enterprises on the demand side. For example, the Scottish Social Investment Fund and SEDIF in Australia mobilized a range of investors from mainstream institutions and also contributed to demonstrating and generating demand (Cullen and Addis, 2013)

---

[44] Established in 2001 with funding from the Scottish Government and financial institutions including RBS, Bank of Scotland, Lloyds, and Clydesdale Bank; the focus of the fund is to support growth of Scotland's communities with a range of financial products, see <http://www.socialinvestmentscotland.org>.

[45] The Social Enterprise Development & Investment Funds combined Government grant-funding with private investment to seed three new investment funds in the Australian market offering financial products to social enterprises; see <http://deewr.gov.au/social-enterprise-development-and-investment-funds>.

[46] For more information, see <http://www.bridgescommunityventures.com>.

[47] Materials on the current debate on development of civic economy in Portugal are available at <http://youngfoundation.org/events/public-debate-strategy-civic-economy-portugal/>.

- Strategically designed government investment can moderate risk for other investors that might otherwise limit the development of a new market. The availability of subordinated capital, including from government has been identified as a key factor in mobilizing capital. For example, the investment by the Christian Super pension fund in one of the SEDIF funds (Cullen and Addis, 2013) and capital invested by banking institutions in the New York City Acquisition Fund (Bridges Ventures et al., 2010; UK Cabinet Office, 2013a)

- With appropriate conditions in place, a range of investors can and will participate, and in new combinations. The SEDIF initiative in Australia, for example, attracted investment from individual philanthropic foundations, a pension fund, a global sustainable bank, and local institutions (Cullen and Addis, 2013; for other examples see Bridges Ventures et al., 2010; UK Cabinet Office, 2013a)

- Government investment can direct capital to issues that are policy priorities. There are numerous examples in clean and renewable energy; New York City Acquisition Fund is an example attracting investment to affordable housing (Bridges Ventures et al., 2010; UK Cabinet Office, 2013a); Bridges Community Ventures and the Ghana Social Investment Fund are examples directing capital to under-invested communities to generate jobs and local economic activity

- The terms on which the capital is offered are a critical element in it providing a stimulus to other investment. See, for example, the analysis by the UK Cabinet Office (2013a), Impact Assets (Issue Brief #10, 2013) and the GIIN (Issue Brief October, 2013). Early research on top-performing social finance funds suggests that catalytic capital can be targeted to stimulate private investment into particular priorities such as areas of market failure or particular social need

- Jurisdictions can learn from, and adapt, initiatives and ideas from other countries for their own context (Schwab Foundation et al., 2013). See for example, the process analysis that underpinned design of the SEDIF funds in Australia (Cullen and Addis, 2013)

- Building the deal (or demand) pipeline is a necessary condition for funds to build a critical mass of social finance opportunities. In the UK for example, the experience of social enterprise funds has led to the development of demand-focused initiatives including the Social Incubator Fund and Investment and Contract Readiness Fund (Gregory et al., 2012).

Other lessons from the field include that governments should be cautious about putting too much money into the market at any one time or into any single initiative. The Futurebuilders[48] and Social Enterprise Investment

---

[48] For more information, see <http://www.futurebuilders-england.org.uk> and <http://www.sibgroup.org.uk/the-social-investment-business/>.

Fund[49] initiatives of the former UK government generated mixed reviews in terms of the level and nature of funding and the targeting of government investment in the early stages of market development.[50] Advocates argued that the availability of capital had a positive effect on encouraging social sector organizations to seek capital and diversify their funding and financing streams. Critics argued that there was a lack of clarity of objectives and that too much capital from government offered on 'soft' terms entering the market too quickly had a distorting effect which set back development of the retail social finance sector.[51]

Creating wholesale institutions or fund of funds is another method by which governments can seek to mobilize capital and enable intermediaries. This involves creating a portfolio of investments in third-party funds. Based on available data for policy to encourage capital for early stage growth ventures:

Experience suggests funds of funds and co-investment, both of which seek to leverage private investment might be more effective than direct public equity funds. While there is limited evidence, it is clear that design, management and incentive structures play a determining role. (OECD, 2013: 27)

Examples from the social finance context include the Venture Capital Trust Fund in Ghana, UK-based Big Society Capital wholesale social finance institution, and the European Social Impact Accelerator.[52] The Canadian Task Force on Social Finance (2010) recommended a similar approach. The different structures share the same policy intention of making available capital at a scale that can support the development of retail funds and products. This type of approach can provide 'anchor funding' for market builders, which was one of the policy measures recommended recently by the World Economic Forum to mobilize more mainstream investment capital for social finance (Drexler and Noble, 2013a).

The next section considers the levers beyond direct investment that can have a catalytic effect on mobilizing capital for social finance.

---

[49] For more information, see <http://webarchive.nationalarchives.gov.au> and <www.dh.gov.uk/en/ Managing. yourorganisation/Socialenterprise/SocialEnterpriseInvestmetnFund/index.htm>.

[50] For more information, see Wells, Chadwick-Coule, Dayson, and Morgan (2010); Wells (2012); Brown, Behrens, Schuster (2015).

[51] See for example, the evaluation of the SEIF <http://www.tsrc.ac.uk/LinkClick.aspx?fileticket= dIISde27qNA%3D&tabid=969>.

[52] See <http://www.bigsocietycapital.com> for background on Big Society Capital and <http://www. unclaimedassets.co.uk> and National Social Investment Wholesale Bank consultation for background on the genesis of the initiative. The Social Impact Accelerator is a fund of funds established in May 2013 with the stated aim of 'providing the first step in the EIB Group's (European Investment Bank and EIF) strategy to pioneer the impact investing space and respond to the wider EU policy aim of establishing a sustainable funding market for social entrepreneurship in Europe'; see <http://www.eif.org>. For information on the Venture Capital Trust Ghana, see <http://www.venturecapitalghana.com.gh/>.

BEYOND DIRECT INVESTMENT

Not all catalytic policy will involve investment of capital. Other incentives and risk reduction measures may affect the public balance sheet, but as revenue foregone or contingent liabilities, but do not involve direct funding. Appropriately designed, this type of approach can also mobilize capital. Commonly used mechanisms include guarantees and tax incentives.

Tax Incentives

Tax incentives have been utilized by policymakers across a range of areas to encourage investment or direct capital. The first principles of tax incentives or other subsidy through a market efficiency lens focus on cost–benefit analysis, often on the basis of estimating the effective rate of subsidy to correct market failures. That said, tax incentives remain a common feature of Western policies to increase access to early stage capital for growth ventures, for example, with a significant majority of OECD countries indicating in a recent survey that they increased such programmes in the past five years (OECD, 2013).

In recent decades there has been robust economic argument about whether and in what circumstances subsidies can contribute to a boost in productivity, for example by increasing the skills and well-being of the population enabling people to earn more income and contribute more to the tax system (Grossman, 1972; Bleakley, 2010). In the social finance context, the policy argument would be that enabling more activity that improves social outcomes in targeted areas improves productivity and so enables an overall increase in the tax revenue base.

Whatever the policy argument, design matters; an analysis of policy initiatives aimed at early-stage funding for growth-firms suggests that:

Tax incentives can be a 'blunt' instrument (i.e. difficult to target effectively) so careful design, monitoring, evaluation and adjustment is necessary to ensure that the intended results are achieved. (OECD, 2013: 21)

Long-term consistency and practical implementation are often identified as significant factors in the effectiveness of tax and other indirect incentives. Investors may have time horizons to realize the benefit of their investment of seven to ten years. Where the risk/return evaluation for investors depends upon policy initiatives, significant prospect of policy change creates uncertainty. This can affect both the effectiveness of the measure as an incentive to mobilize capital and the price. This issue of consistency has been identified as sufficiently important in the context of social finance to be included as one of the London Principles (IIPC, 2013). Policies still need to be monitored and adjusted for their effectiveness (e.g. OECD, 2013); a consistently poor policy will not achieve the desired impact either.

Indirect incentives need to be considered in context and are often not isolated interventions, but part of a set of interrelated policies (OECD,

2013). For example, initiatives related to the Community Reinvestment Act in the US have developed over decades and now involve a complex mix of interacting 'carrot and stick' incentives.[53] A change to one part of the system may affect the others, or the overall effectiveness of the policy mix.

The landscape already includes examples of tax incentives to direct (social finance) capital to particular policy priorities, adaptation and extension of existing tax incentives for social finance, and isolated examples of tax incentives developing specifically to encourage social finance more generally.

Tax incentives for particular types of activity such as clean energy and affordable housing have so far tended to gain traction on the basis of specific industry analyses or areas of social need rather than more general support for social finance (Thornley et al., 2011).[54] For example, the Green Funds scheme in the Netherlands and tax incentives designed to encourage investment in green energy operating in the a range of jurisdictions (see analysis across jurisdictions in KPMG, 2012). Schemes such as the Clean Development Mechanism in Brazil and in Tokyo the cap and trade mechanism use different designs to provide tradable credits for emissions reduction (Thornley et al., 2011). Tax incentives have been utilized to target community renewal and investment, for example the US Government New Markets Tax Credit and UK Community Interest Tax Relief.

Affordable housing has also been an area of focus; examples of incentives include The National Rental Affordability Scheme in Australia[55] and the Low Income Housing Tax Credit in the USA. Both are intended to attract investment for affordable housing. These measures have received mix reviews (see for example Heaney, 2010; Thornley et al., 2011; Stankiewicz and Rubin, 2012). The learning from this commentary and analysis has tended to focus on the room for improvement in design and implementation, in particular, how incentives are targeted with a focus on earlier engagement with key investors (e.g. Thornley et al., 2011).

There are examples where practical steps have been taken to maximize potential for existing tax incentives to be utilized for social finance. The Social Impact VCT established in the UK in 2011 is an example of a structure designed within the existing venture capital tax regime to promote social finance opportunities. Some argue that further change is needed to existing frameworks and incentives to create the interface for social purpose organizations and social finance transactions (e.g. Hill, 2011). However, tax systems are often complex with many interrelated parts, so this is an area that requires careful examination in the context of local conditions.

---

[53] There is a significant body of literature examining the *Community Reinvestment Act*, its operation, efficacy, and impacts; see for example Campen (1997); Olson et al. (2009); Lindsey (2009); Essene and Apgar (2009).

[54] A range of examples are included in the 'policy map' in Thornley et al. (2011 Appendix 1).

[55] Changes intended to phase the scheme out were announced in the Australian Federal Budget 2014–15.

The World Economic Forum identified tax incentives as one of the key levers for government to mobilize mainstream capital for social finance (Drexler and Noble, 2013a). Research in the UK found that the lack of specific incentives for social finance relative to the incentives for philanthropy and venture capital acts as a barrier to attracting capital. Further, it was estimated that appropriately designed tax incentives could unlock £480m over a five-year period, and that availability of tax incentives could be expected to enhance other sector development initiatives (Hill, 2011).

In the UK, the Treasury initiated a public consultation on the tax treatment of social finance in June 2013. Incentives targeting social enterprise and social finance (specifically SIBs) were implemented with effect from April 2014. They provide tax concessions for individuals investing in prescribed social organizations and initiatives on a basis broadly equivalent to other tax incentive policies operating in the UK to stimulate investment in enterprise and venture capital (Hill, 2011; UK National Advisory Board on Impact Investing, 2014).[56]

Other countries have considered the issue but not yet acted further on policy analysis and design. For example, in Australia, both the lead government economic advisory body, the Productivity Commission (2010), and the Economic References Committee of the Federal Senate (2011) recommended further consideration be given to tax treatment and potential for tax incentives for aspects of social finance. As Australia already has relatively sophisticated tax regulation in place for not-for-profit organizations and to encourage philanthropy, both bodies found the impacts of any policy change should be given detailed consideration in the context of broader tax and social systems.

Guarantees

Guarantees can provide another mechanism for risk sharing and promoting liquidity. In some parts of government, guarantees are perceived as high risk. In some cases policy debate may also benefit from greater relative analysis; that is risk relative to which alternatives. For example, if funding currently expended on grants could be utilized to leverage much greater capital by providing a guarantee pool, would that be a better or worse outcome even if some of the funding was eventually expended in calls on the government guarantee?

The capacity to bring private sector experience as well as leverage and achieve greater reach and efficiency of public spending are generally central to the policy case for guarantees (see, for example UN National Advisory Board on Impact Investing, 2014). As for other incentives, much depends on effective design (Thornley et al., 2011).

---

[56] For further information on the UK tax incentives, see guidance notes at <https://www.gov.uk/government/publications/social-investment-tax-relief-factsheet/social-investment-tax-relief>.

As with tax incentives, some jurisdictions have adapted or extended existing policies to social finance by specifically targeting social goals as part of the policy framework. One example is the US Small Business Administration 2012 initiative to direct capital to communities in need of more jobs and local economic activity with a US$400m guarantee fund for investments in qualifying enterprises. Early evaluation of these programmes suggests that restructuring existing funding streams can deliver social as well as economic impacts without necessarily involving greater risk (see Mills and Greene, 2012; Dilger, 2013). Another example is guarantees available in the UK to stimulate investment in affordable housing, which operate in conjunction with grant programmes and other initiatives.[57]

International development agencies also use guarantees to encourage investment and mobilize bank finance. Guarantees in this context have been operating for some time and they sometimes operate to mitigate a broader range of risk than financial and commercial risk, including the impacts of political risk. For example a number of states are members of the Multilateral Investment Guarantee Agency, a member of the World Bank Group specializing in guarantees that reduce the political and non-commercial risks of foreign direct investment into developing countries. Over twenty-five years to 2013, the agency is reported to have provided over US$30bn in guarantees for over 700 projects in over 100 countries.[58] State-based organizations like the US Overseas Private Investment Corporation and French Development Agency also utilize guarantees and insurance as part of their policy and programme repertoire.[59] As with direct investment the intention is bridge the gap of risk, real or perceived, without which capital will not be deployed where it is needed.

The next section considers the role government can play to stimulate demand and intermediation for social finance.

CATALYSING DEMAND AND INTERMEDIARIES

Potential for catalytic action is not confined to the supply-side of the market. Demand development and facilitating productive intermediation to connect those seeking capital and those with resources is critical to market development (e.g. OECD, 2013). Without attention to this aspect of social finance, there will not be a robust pipeline of transactions and organizations in which to invest. The significance of policy for these aspects of market development is increasingly being recognized (e.g. Mason and Kwok, 2007). The significance

---

[57] For more information on these initiatives, see: Australia—<http://www.dss.gov.au>; US—<http://portal.hud.gov/hudportal/HUD>; and UK—<http://www.homesandcommuities.co.uk> for details of the Affordable Homes Guarantees Programme.

[58] See <http://www.worldbank.org>.

[59] See for example <http://www.opic.gov/what-we-offer/political-risk-insurance>.

extends beyond developing the deal pipeline to 'social capital' developed through networks and other connections gaining focus as drivers of market development and dynamism (e.g. OECD, 2013).

This also applies to social finance (see e.g. Koh et al., 2012; Burkett, 2013). Unless there is support to translate promising ideas and innovations to solve social issues into propositions that can attract investment, the potential of those innovations and of social finance is unlikely to be realized at any scale (Koh et al., 2012; Burkett, 2012). Social finance is unlikely to develop without support to enable social sector organizations to utilize a broader range of funding and financing options (Australian Productivity Commission, 2010; Burkett, 2012; Koh et al., 2012; Gregory et al., 2013).

Demand Development

Initiatives to develop enterprises for investment are relatively new across all markets (Mason and Kwok, 2007) and have only recently begun to receive focused attention for social finance (Koh et al., 2012; Gregory et al., 2012). At a systems level, there has been a renewed focus on firms that combine social purpose and a revenue-generating business model, whether or not intended to be profit making. This is reflected in legislative frameworks proposed or enacted in countries including France, Spain, Portugal, Ecuador, Mexico, Greece, and in the Canadian province of Quebec[60] to promote and encourage social enterprise, co-operatives and other 'social economy' organizations. The UK introduced community interest company[61] structures in 2005 and refreshed co-operatives regulation in 2013.[62] In the USA, the growing number of states that have enacted or are considering regulation to enable B-Corps,[63] which can embed public benefit in their constitutional governance, is an indicator of the shifts underway.

Calls have been made for an international framework of regulation on the basis that it would support and encourage more purpose-driven organizations and provide transparency and market tools that could be applied across jurisdictions (Social Impact Investment Taskforce Mission Alignment Working Group, 2014).

Much of the commentary centres on developing social enterprises and the initiatives of socially motivated entrepreneurs to reach a point where they are ready to take on finance and where their offering will be attractive to investors. Growing numbers of these are creating for-profit business models that

---

[60] Spanish Law on Social Economy (Law 5/2011); Portuguese Social Economy Law 68/XII (13 March 2013); Greek Social Economy and Social Entrepreneurship Act 4019/2011; Ecuador Official Register No. 444, 10 May 2011; Mexico Official Journal, 23 May 2012; Quebec Social Economy Law Bill 27 (2013, chapter 22):

[61] See <http://www.gov.uk/government/organisations/office-of-the-regulator-of-community-interest-companies>.

[62] Co-operative and Community Benefit Societies Act 2010 and Co-operative and Community Benefit Societies Bill 2013.

[63] Background on B Corporations is available at <http://www.bcorporation.net>.

produce public goods or embed social mission (Eggers and Macmillan, 2013; Social Impact Investment Taskforce Mission Alignment Working Group, 2014). At a firm level, the research indicates that enterprises seeking finance from more mainstream commercial markets and those seeking social finance have more issues in common than points of difference (Mason and Kwok, 2007; Burkett, 2012; Gregory et al., 2012). That said, the degree of difficulty can be magnified in the context of social organizations. In some cases this is because they are seeking to satisfy dual aims of social and economic performance. In other cases it reflects transition from grant dependence or a lack of familiarity with navigating the institutions and products of the finance sector.

'Capacity building' and 'investment readiness' are terms often used to describe the process of developing enterprises and initiatives to a point where they are ready for finance. Broadly speaking, these terms are shorthand for a variety of skills and capabilities, such as the quality of organizational leadership, skills and skill development, and fluency in the language used by other disciplines. Financial skills and literacy are often a focus for those organizations seeking finance. Familiarity with the dynamics of social issues and the social economy for investors are rarely discussed. This is not surprising as even in more traditional markets available evidence suggests training for investors and finance professionals is often overlooked (OECD, 2013).

Commonly, policy on the demand-side focuses on support for individual enterprises with a focus on building capability within the firm to become ready and able to take investment. A number of jurisdictions have enterprise development programmes (OECD, 2012). In some jurisdictions it has been suggested that these be extended to work with social entrepreneurs (e.g. Australian Productivity Commission, 2010, although this has not yet been implemented).

Initiatives such as the UK Social Incubator Fund and the Contract and Investment Readiness Fund are designed to provide a more structured approach to building a pipeline of investable social enterprises. These UK government programmes provide funding and support designed to assist enterprises prepare for investment through social finance and to compete for government contracts. The structure and governance of the programmes are designed to assist organizations in identifying appropriate sources of advice and, in the process, develop networks of advisors. The approach is being adapted for other jurisdictions including Australia and Portugal. Recent research that emphasizes the role of experience with the process of seeking funding plays in building capacity (Mason and Kwok, 2007; Burkett, 2012, 2013; Gregory et al., 2012) supports this type of approach.

Two elements are often overlooked in the commentary on demand development: issues posed by the dominant behavioural paradigms between social purpose organizations and their funders; and latent demand for finance in the social sector if those cultural barriers can be overcome.

Where social innovation fails it is often because of financing. Community enterprises have the potential to address this because they can integrate sustainable finance from the earliest stages of the development of new ideas. By contrast in some parts of the community sector there has traditionally been an ethos that government has a responsibility to adequately fund good new ideas. If this was ever the case it is certainly so no longer. The growth in community enterprises is, however, uneven and often subject to very local factors—especially the capacity and willingness of communities to support innovative activity (Adams and Hess, 2010: 6).

Many social organizations operate as not-for-profit entities. However, this often belies the reality that they must generate a surplus of income over expenditure to remain viable. Most non-profits must source their revenue from a diverse range of sources, mostly grant-oriented. As a result, the leadership often 'go where the money is' rather than pursue a clear strategic plan targeting impact. The conditions placed on funding compound this dynamic and make it difficult to chart an impact-focused strategy or to plan over the long or even medium term. This creates a paradox because generating demonstrable social returns usually requires a consistent approach over an extended period:

> If business entrepreneurs had come to me at Apax with business plans that involved investing nothing on overheads I would have shown them the door. The combination of unpredictable funding and lack of investment capital has prevented almost all charitable organisations from realising their potential effectiveness and scale. (Cohen, 2014: 3)

The second area is the latent demand for capital to finance the activities of the not-for-profit sector. Many countries have diverse and dynamic and economically significant not-for-profit sectors. Significant potential is often not realized because not-for-profit organizations are constrained in practice or in culture from making the most effective use of their assets and resources.

A third factor in the social innovation approach is the recognition that the community sector is actually an industry with a full set of industrial characteristics including risk, opportunity, investment, management, evaluation of performance, and outcomes. The social value outcome of community sector activity is seen by many of its practitioners in the creation of social justice without which the sector loses much of its *raison d'être*. This focus can have a limiting effect as it may prevent those in community-based organizations appreciating the necessity for practical instruments that can improve sustainability and effectiveness (Adams and Hess, 2010: 6).

Changes affecting all sectors require diversification of funding and financing sources. This will require expanding the utilization by social sector organizations of a much broader range of funding and financing options along the spectrum from grant funding to mainstream financial products. This will require developing the capability of organizations, attracting a broader range of experience to the social sector to engage with finance, and for the finance sector to develop an understanding of social issues. It will also require growing the pool of capital available for social finance.

A roundtable hosted by Harvard Business School's Social Enterprise Initiative in 2011 reached a consensus that to garner the capital necessary to foot the bill for social change, not-for-profits need to think less about traditional grants and more in terms of innovation, and so do the organizations that fund them.[64] Governments have the capacity to influence this practice, not least through their own commissioning and funding practices (e.g. Australian Productivity Commission, 2010; Shergold, 2013; Bridgeland and Orszag, 2013).[65]

Developing Intermediaries

Efficient intermediation is recognized through the literature as an important component of market development (Shanmugalingam et al., 2011). Developing the market for social finance will require developing professionals and organizations with skills in finance and related disciplines who have a genuine understanding of the social economy to contribute to the workforce, financial providers, and the intermediaries in the market (Addis, Mcleod, and Raine, 2013; Burkett, 2013).

Without this, those with capital for social finance and those with investment propositions or organizations in need of investment capital may not be able to connect effectively, efficiently, or on appropriate terms. Intermediaries also play a valuable role in education and advice necessary to inform legal and business structures in order to support investment and identify appropriate types of investment for an organization at its stage of growth and also sources of capital.

Incubators and accelerators of the type seen in other fields such as technology are starting to develop with a focus on social enterprise.[66] Support among OECD countries for the development of networks and accelerators for entrepreneurs and investors is reported to have increased in the past five years (OECD, 2012, 2013). The commentary on these policies suggests that the features most commonly associated with accelerators— providing active and tailored support for enterprises and their leadership add significant value over and above simply providing shared resource platforms (OECD, 2013). Similar approaches in the domain of social finance could encourage organizations, with an intentional focus on creating social as well as economic impact. Some field-building work is already underway to develop innovations that will accelerate the growth and scale of social enterprises for social impact (e.g. see Rockefeller Foundation and InSight at Pacific Community Ventures, 2012).

From a government perspective, a focus on accelerators and incubators has a number of advantages. It avoids the complexity of direct delivery and enables

---

[64] Nobel, C. (2011). 'Social Investing: Emerging Trends in a Changing Landscape', Harvard Business School Social Enterprise Initiative.

[65] See also <http://www.moneyballforgov.com>.

[66] There are a range of examples including the School for Social Entrepreneurs with franchises in several countries and incubators attached to a number of business schools.

the development of specialists in the market, which in themselves can contribute to broader skill development and play a role as intermediaries. This can attract interest from investors and deliver outcomes beyond what has been the experience with direct grant funding from government. Incubators can be developed as resource and knowledge hubs that make a broader contribution to sector development. Appropriately skilled management with experience across sectors can offer greater depth of experience than government can for enterprise selection (e.g. Shanmugalingam et al., 2011; Burkett, 2012, 2013).

The significance and role of specialist social finance intermediaries has also begun to receive more attention (e.g. Shanmugalingam et al., 2011; Burkett, 2012, 2013). Organizations surveyed in the UK that been supported by a social venture intermediary reported significant improvements in their revenues and beneficiaries and ability to raise additional investment (Shanmugalingam et al., 2011).

Effective targeting of policy can encourage intermediaries directly and indirectly. New funds and incubators can develop as intermediaries in the market. Delivery agents for investment readiness programmes can develop as intermediaries sourcing both enterprise potential and bespoke advisers. Incubators and accelerators can provide sector development through focus on particular communities or with specific sectoral, impact, or outcome areas. Government can invest in stimulating this activity; like other infrastructure measures, there is not ready funding available from other sources yet there is significant potential for quality initiatives to contribute to market and sector development (Bannick and Goldman, 2013):

Innovators and industry-specific infrastructure firms often struggle to raise necessary funds and to get human capital support often so critical to success. Indeed, capital appears to be thinnest precisely where it is needed the most: to prime the pump of innovation and deal flow. (Bannick and Goldman, 2013: 13)

Intermediaries play a role in developing the frameworks and education for the market. Centres developing research, evidence, and thought leadership for social finance include the Case i3 initiative at Duke University, Center for the Study of Financial Innovation and Initiative for Responsible Investment at the Hauser Centre for Non-profit Studies at Harvard University in the US, National Endowment for Science Technology and the Arts and the Skoll Centre for Social Entrepreneurship at Oxford University in the UK, the OECD in Europe, and the Bertha Centre for Social Innovation in South Africa. Governments can facilitate this work through their funding choices and commissioning research as well as specific initiatives.

The following, and final, section of the chapter considers another dimension of the potential of social finance—specifically, the opportunity to look seriously at the commissioning of services and accountability for results and to re-imagine the nature of public–private partnership.

Innovation at the Intersection of the Public Sector, the Community Sector and the Market

There is another dimension to social finance policy and practice. That is, the potential to drive new and productive collaborations with a focus on improved outcomes in areas of significant social need.

In the economic domain there has already been some acknowledgement that 'the financial system has a central role in fostering innovation and growth' (OECD, 2013: 36). There is increasing recognition in this context also of the importance of social capital and networks (OECD, 2013; and the British Council references to 'collaborative economics' in the context of social enterprise and innovation).[67] The dynamics of engaging business and the finance sector in addressing social needs is already clearly part of the discussion about value creation for the future Emerson, 2000; (Zadek, 2001; Porter and Kramer, 2011).

The changing dynamics are not just about business. The social and public sectors are facing new challenges shaped by calls for greater agility and responsiveness, for evidence-based practice, greater transparency, and accountability for results (e.g. Australian Productivity Commission, 2010; Adams and Hess, 2010; World Economic Forum, 2013).

In the 21st century all governments are facing very challenging issues around the need for infrastructure, an ageing demographic and climate change...In order to find solutions, they need to understand they don't hold all the levers for job creation—and working together with industry and the private sector is an important mindset and the starting point.

(UK *Financial Times*, 27 March 2013, quoting Dr Uschi Schreiber, Global Head of Government and Public Sector, Ernst & Young)

Dialogue about the role and future of government (e.g. World Economic Forum, 2013; Shergold, 2013) and changing conditions for the social sector has brought into the frame the limitations of conventional approaches to government contracting and commissioning. Some governments have been experimenting with more open approaches to sourcing ideas and approaches from across sectors and disciplines. For example the US challenge.gov platform (<http://www.challenge.gov>, accessed January 2014) publicly solicits new solutions under the banner 'a partnership between the public and the government to solve important challenges'. The gap between available funding and the demand for services and changing paradigms for service delivery have started to challenge social sector organizations to re-examine operating models and increase diversification of funding and financing sources:

---

[67] See, for example, comments of Dr Mairi Mackay, Director for Society, British Council Beijing, at <http://www.gle.iipcollaborative.org>, webinar, 16 January 2014.

The relationship between what is being done, that is the drivers and character of activity, and how it is being done, that is, the instruments which operationalise the activity, is particularly significant for understanding the changing role of the community sector. During the 1990s a new stage began to emerge with social investment capturing the character of activity and social innovation becoming a major instrument. This has impacted upon both community sector organisations and government agencies ... it is at this stage social innovation merges [sic] as a usable public policy model because of its capacity to address complexity and sustainability. (Adams and Hess 2010: 3)

Commentators have suggested that what is occurring represents a significant shift in the dynamics for tackling social issues (Adams and Hess, 2010, Eggers and Macmillan, 2013).

Social innovation then is about a new level of capability that changes the framework within which issues are addressed. (Adams and Hess, 2010: 5)

Old certainties based on tightly defined roles for government, the social sector, and business are being tested and challenged (Shergold, 2013; Eggers and Macmillan, 2013; Social Impact Investment Taskforce Mission Alignment Working Group, 2014). There is increasing pressure for governments to 'make meaningful progress in tackling the social problems facing their countries' (Social Impact Investment Taskforce, 2014: 1). These trends are reflected in a move away from 'purchaser–provider' models employed by governments to a focus on commissioning where government is a catalyst and aggregator of resources (Addis, Bowden, and Simpson, 2014).

The point is that social finance is about much more than money. Social finance transactions often come together at the intersection of government, community, and markets. These transactions provide one means, and a structured approach, for exploring where appetite exists from other actors in the market to work with government to develop solutions to social issues. Each transaction or initiative requires a combination of actors to come together.

Impact investing is a multi-stakeholder issue. It engages governments as impact investments offer more opportunities for efficient delivery of public services. It engages civil society from non-profits that design and implement projects to individual recipients of social programmes. And it involves businesses, ranging from entrepreneurs to lawyers to consultants and investors. Clearly for impact investing to reach its potential, it must be considered from the perspective of all stakeholders (Drexler and Noble, 2013a: 1).

Critically, this is not just about finance; it is about the quality of services and improving outcomes. For example, addressing the challenges of an ageing population requires looking beyond facilities to the nature and quality of services and structural options to reduce the cost of ageing and supporting the aged. Social finance is the enabler and not the end. Innovative product development will requires a multi-disciplinary approach to problem-solving and design and this is likely to go beyond what any one sector can deliver on its own.

Recent research on the top-performing social finance funds internationally relates two of the four key success factors to productive cross-sectoral engagement

(Clark, Thornley, and Emerson, 2012; Clark, Emerson, and Thornley, 2013). 'Multi-lingual' leadership is one of those factors; it relates to the breadth of experience of the leaders, often in cross-sector disciplines. That skill-base equips these leaders to work across a diverse range of stakeholders. Taken as a whole, each fund team exhibits fluency in the vocabularies, networks, and unwritten norms of the private, public, and non-profit sectors (Clark, Emerson, and Thornley, 2013).

AN ILLUSTRATION: SOCIAL IMPACT BONDS

Perhaps the most powerful illustration so far is the emergence of SIBs (sometimes called 'pay for success' bonds). It bears underscoring at the start that these are only one instrument in a much larger social finance repertoire. They will not be appropriate for all situations. However, the experience with SIBs can provide some lessons with broader application for how social finance tools and processes develop. The first SIBs were designed through experimentation with a multi-disciplinary team focused on how to finance the investment requirements for innovation to address social issues and achieve better outcomes (Cohen, 2014).

Anecdotal evidence suggests that even early experiences of developing SIBs are delivering positive benefits in practice and learning. Parties to transactions report material learning and process improvements as a function of the design and negotiation process, including better understanding of available data, what the gaps are, and ways in which the parties can contribute from their different skills and experience.[68] The first analysis of the field and lessons from its development is starting to come through (e.g. Gustaffson-Wright et al., 2015) and also suggests some critical learning from early experience.

These innovative financing mechanisms (Figure 13.8) drive quite different working relationships between public sector commissioners, social sector service providers, and private investors. The structural elements of SIBs centre on actionable opportunities to improve social outcomes for a particular target group. Third-party investment provides the working capital for the provision of services. A commissioning party, often government, agrees to repay investors capital and a yield based on the improvement in outcomes achieved, in some cases linked to the cost savings the product–service will represent. The original design was for investors to assume the risk that outcomes are not achieved. Practice has rapidly developed to include a number of different approaches to risk and return.[69]

---

[68] For example, 'Proceedings of the NSW Forum on Social Impact Bonds', 2 December 2013 (unpublished).

[69] Detailed examination of the different SIB structures is beyond the scope of this chapter; see the literature referenced, including Social Finance (2010); Nicholls and Tomkinson (2013); Jackson (2013b).

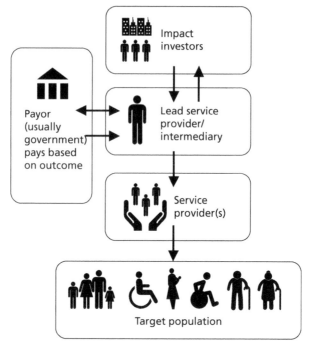

Figure 13.8. Structure of Social Impact Bond contract
Source: Australian Department of Employment, 2013

SIBs can be seen as one form of a broader range of payment-by-results and outcomes-based contracts. Some of these approaches have been the subject of debate, particularly where smaller and more local service providers may have limited capacity to take significant financial risk (e.g. Edwards, 2012). The focus here is on their particular design components as an illustration of how social finance can provide useful and practical responses to the challenges and opportunities ahead for governments and the social sector.

This potential is reflected in the rapidity with which SIBs have captured the collective imagination of a range of actors. Since the first SIB was launched in the UK in 2010, others are being developed and trialled in jurisdictions as diverse as the USA, Canada, Italy, Pakistan, Israel, Mozambique, Germany, Swaziland, Australia, and Columbia.[70] By August 2014, twenty-five SIBs had been commissioned in seven countries (Social Finance, 2014). There is already an emerging body of literature and research on SIBs (Social Finance, 2010; Nicholls and Tomkinson, 2013; Jackson, 2013b) and, more recently, the potential for development impact bonds (DIBs) (Centre for Global Development & Social Finance, 2013).

---

[70] For global picture, see Centre for Global Development & Social Finance (2013); to see the spread across the US, see <http://www.payforsuccess.org>.

While SIBs are still at an early stage of their evolution, there are encouraging signs that they are promoting new and productive collaborations across sectors. The developing practice appears to reinforce relatively consistent themes:

- a focus on issues a range of actors care about, but nobody owns with a contractual framework that provides for shared risk around a common cause
- new sources of capital that allow service providers to test and demonstrate innovations and focus on outcomes rather than 'follow the money'
- a better spend of limited financial resources including the potential to save public monies through improved efficacy
- greater clarity on agreed milestones with public accountability based on social outcomes
- an emphasis on performance, building the evidence base for what works and expanding the options for taking solutions to scale
- flexibility for delivery to meet need on the ground rather than pre-determined contract requirements
- capacity to show serious concern for global challenges married with local action
- harnessing the creativity and resources of a range of actors, particularly at the field level (Social Finance, 2010; Nicholls and Tomkinson, 2013; Australian Government Department of Education, Employment and Workplace Relations, 2012; see also UK Cabinet Office Centre for Social Impact Bonds, Pay for Success Learning Hub and Harvard Kennedy School Social Impact Bond Technical Assistance Lab).

It remains to be seen whether SIBs will fulfil the aspirations in practice. They could also play an important role in building the social finance market globally both as a means of attracting new private capital into delivering social outcomes and, as a recognized asset that can be traded on secondary markets. If the interest and discussion is not matched by a critical volume of transactions and improved outcomes, they may be dismissed as hype and that could damage development of broader social finance markets. Limited capability to work differently across sectors could also impede progress. Strong and generative governance and relationship management will be required to avoid devolution into more familiar practice, particularly if governments seek to restructure interventions as government programmes. Risks remain, including that fragmented experiments will fail to deliver because they are not informed by broader or more developed policy frameworks.

Judicious management of the risks will be required in the short and medium term to allow time for models to be developed, implemented, and come to maturity. Much will depend on delivery and the social outcomes achieved. As of 2014, the Peterborough SIB, which was the first in the world, had recorded improvements for the people receiving services (UK Ministry of Justice, 2013; Joliffe and Hedderman, 2014). In Australia the 'Newpin' social benefit bond met outcome hurdles required for investors to receive their first payments. While many SIBs are in development around the world, only a handful of other SIBs have yet been executed and meaningful results are yet to come in.

Government's role is critical, not only because in many cases it is an actor in the SIBs, but because this is an area where utilizing the broader toolbox can have a significant impact. In particular, the signalling and convening capacity of government can be used to encourage dialogue and action, bring new combinations of actors together, identify areas of policy priority, and contribute critical data to inform design and measurement.

The UK government has been one of the most active in this realm and was also the first to develop a SIB. They have led public dialogue, convened different actors, developed resources such as the UK Cabinet Office Centre for Social Impact Bonds,[71] and, more recently established a fund to promote SIBs in their jurisdictions.[72] Other governments have played an active role, including the current US administration which has initiated several policies to encourage SIBs, although 'pay for success' funds proposed in the 2013 and 2014 budgets to encourage state and local governments to develop pay-for-success models have not been approved by Congress. Notwithstanding that, US states have been exploring pay-for-success options, with initiatives in a number of states and cities.[73] And in June 2014, the Social Impact Bond Act was introduced to the US Congress and was referred to the Committees on Ways and Means and on Financial Services.[74] If passed, this legislation would require the US Treasury to seek SIB proposals targeting a range of social issues from state and local governments and prescribe process and funding for the development of proposals.

Other institutions can also play a role in developing the field in ways which inform future potential and practice. Centres focusing specifically on SIBs such as the Pay for Success Learning Hub of Non-profit Finance Fund and Harvard Kennedy School Social Impact Bond Technical Assistance Lab[75] are emerging.

No one instrument will be a silver bullet and there is much yet to learn in relation to SIBs. However, with a commitment to action and a developing body of examples and practice, SIBs and DIBS may add valuable tools and spur next generation products that embed collaborative problem-solving with a clear focus on quality and performance of social outcomes.

---

[71] <https://www.gov.uk/social-impact-bonds>.

[72] The UK Social Outcomes Fund is a GB£20m fund administered by the UK Cabinet Office <https://www.gov.uk/social-impact-bonds#sources-of-funding-forsib-projects>. The fund is designed to address challenges of aggregating benefits and savings that accrue across different public sector agencies if improved outcomes are achieved.

[73] See information on the spread of pay for success across the US at Pay for Success Learning Hub and Harvard Kennedy School Technical Assistance Lab.

[74] See <https://www.congress.gov/bill/113th-congress/house-bill/4885>.

[75] See <http://www.payforsuccess.org> and <http://hks-siblab.org/>.

A ROLE FOR SOCIAL FINANCE IN SHAPING NEXT GENERATION PUBLIC–PRIVATE PARTNERSHIPS

In many jurisdictions, the concept, and even the term, 'public–private partnerships' has become weighed down by expectations and precedent. This has history in a range of, mainly infrastructure-based, arrangements and the allocation, or shifting, of the risks and costs they entailed. These types of arrangements have usually been framed primarily through a lens of economic interests (Zadek, 2001; UN Economic Commission for Europe, 2008).

Social finance can provide a powerful focus on key elements: contract and the flow of money—which can centre other conversations regarding collaboration, performance, and outcomes. That is, social finance products are developing with characteristics identified as lacking or under-developed in some past models for public–private partnerships (Zadek, 2001; UN Economic Commission for Europe, 2008). Social finance appears to be providing some of the enabling conditions for cross-sector collaboration that proponents have argued for some time could deliver outcomes beyond what can be achieved by any one sector or silo alone (Adams and Hess, 2010):

What distinguishes these partnerships from those previously described is that the business partners enter the relationship with an explicit interest in achieving social and environmental aims that goes beyond short-term fee-for-service or goods-for-sale strategies. Commercial interests, in these contexts, have more to do with the participating businesses' broader licence to operate, which they see as having to be earned and sustained through demonstrable participation in addressing public policy objectives... The challenge is to find innovative means for rewarding commercial partners for their real contributions to addressing the public good. (Zadek, 2001: 17)

The difference embedded in this new breed of cross-sector collaborations is not a matter of degree. It is functionally redefining the terms on which organizations engage with government and society. The shifts embed a 'break from the orthodoxy of community, business and government sector activities' (Adams and Hess, 2010: 4). They enable the actors to combine new and old ideas and ways of working to achieve different ways of thinking and acting for social benefit (Mulgan et al., 2007; Adams and Hess, 2010). As such, they bear the hallmarks of social innovation. However, the categorization is far less significant than the potential for what could be achieved by consciously utilizing the opportunity and appetite to engage differently. Even if that opportunity arises only in targeted areas or between particular groups it can enable demonstration of the concrete potential from which learning can be distilled and applied.

To realize the potential will require placing social finance within the more generative context that commentators such as Emerson (2000) and Zadek (2001), and more recently, Porter and Kramer (2011) have encouraged. It will also require frank assessments of the ways in which government interacts with other actors and the development of capability by all actors to engage in new forms of partnership that focus on shared interests in improving social outcomes and delivering public good (Zadek, 2001; Eggers and Macmillan, 2013).

Conclusion

Certain points in history present a confluence of circumstances that make possible new opportunities for meeting the most pressing social needs. A number of trends point to such a 'moment of attention' currently enabling willing participants from public, private, and social sectors to combine ideas and resources differently and address pressing and persistent social issues. Social finance is an important and rapidly developing feature of this landscape. Governments can be not only funders, but also have a unique position to contribute to enabling and encouraging the market by using the tools available well beyond regulation and direct funding alone.

The opportunities are great; so are the challenges. Working differently is not a soft proposition. There are risks; not everything will work. It will take time to develop the skills and capabilities, the market scaffolding and infrastructure, and the robust market data and investment opportunities that can attract both investors and organizations seeking investment.

Leadership is critical, especially from governments and policymakers. The Social Impact Investment Taskforce (2014) called for all governments to appoint a champion, ideally a minister or other senior figure, to spearhead the formulation and implementation of effective social finance policy. The leadership challenge extends to engagement, collaboration, and practice-building to encourage the development of the social finance market (Addis and Koenig, 2014).

This is not a blank slate. There are many ideas and lessons to adapt and combine from what is already known and tested, including in other policy areas. Social finance is developing as a field and there is significant practice developing to inform design and action. Building critical mass and the process of government engagement is and should be gradual and deliberate.

Generative and appropriate government action and policymaking can have a powerful influence on realizing the potential of social finance. The signals it sends can go well beyond individual initiatives to encourage and give confidence to other participants in the social finance market. Social finance can provide new tools to assist governments and policymakers shape an innovative public sector to realize better outcomes for the people they serve.

■ REFERENCES

Adams, D. and Hess, M. (2010). *Social Innovation and Why It Has Policy Significance*. Australia: Economic and Labour Relations Review.

Addis, R., Bowden, A., and Simpson, D. (2014). *Delivering on Impact: The Australian Advisory Board's Breakthrough Strategy for Catalysing Impact Investment*. Australia: Impact Investing.

Addis, R., and Koenig, A. (2014). *G8 Taskforce and the Global Market—Why the Social Impact Investment Taskforce Work Matters and What Comes Next; Impact Investing*

Policy in 2014: A Snapshot of Global Activity. Impact Investing Policy Collaborative, <http://globalpolicy.iipcollaborative.org>, accessed 30 November 2014.

Addis, R., Mcleod, J., and Raine, J. (2013). *IMPACT—Australia: Investment for Social and Economic Benefit*. Australia: Australian Government Department of Education, Employment and Workplace Relations and JBWere.

Australian Government Department of Education, Employment and Workplace Relations (2012). *Social Investment: Social Enterprise Development and Investment Funds (SEDIF)*, online video, December, <https://employment.gov.au/videos/social-investment-social-enterprise-development-and-investment-funds-sedif-december-2012>, accessed 1 November 2013.

Australian Government Department of Employment (2013). 'Impact Investment Policy Map'. Social Innovation, Australia.

Australian Government Department of Prime Minister and Cabinet 2012, *Australian Government Response, Senate Economics References Committee Report—Investing for Good: the development of a capital market for not-for-profit organisations in Australia*, Australian Government Department of Prime Minister and Cabinet, viewed 1 November 2013, <http://www.dpmc.gov.au/publications/docs/government-response-investing-for-good.pdf>, accessed 1 November 2013.

Australian Innovation Statement (2011, 2012). *AusIndustry*. <http://www.ausindustry.gov.au/INNOVATIONAUSTRALIA/IA-ANNUALREPORT2011TO2012/Pages/default.aspx>, accessed 1 November 2013.

Australian Productivity Commission (2010). *Contribution of the Not-for-Profit Sector*. Australian Government. <http://www.pc.gov.au/projects/study/not-for-profit/report>, accessed 8 November 2013.

Bannick, M., and Goldman, P. (2013). *Priming the Pump: The Case for a Sector Based Approach to Impact Investing*. San Francisco: Omidyar Network.

Bassett, D., Cawston, T., Haldenby, A., Majumdar, T., Nolan, P., Seddon, N., Tanner, W., and Trewhitt, K. (2012). '2012 Reform Scorecard'. London: Reform.

Beinhocker, E., and Hanauer, N. (2014). 'Redefining Capitalism', *McKinsey Quarterly*, September.

Benford, J. (2014). *Social Impact Investing in the German Context, Impact Investing Policy in 2014: A Snapshot of Global Activity*. Impact Investing Policy Collaborative. <http://globalpolicy.iipcollaborative.org/>, accessed 30 November 2014.

Bleakley, C. H. (2010). 'Malaria Eradication in the Americas: A Retrospective Analysis of Childhood Exposure', *American Economic Journal: Applied Economics*, 2(2).

Boersch, A. (2010). '"Doing Good by Investing Well?" Pension Funds and Socially Responsible Investment: Results of an Expert Survey', Allianz Global Investors International Pension Paper, 1/2010.

Bridgeland, J., and Orszag, P. (2013). 'Can Government Play Moneyball?' *The Atlantic*, 19 June.

Bridges Ventures, The Parthenon Group, and the Global Impact Investing Network (2010). *Investing for Impact: Case Studies across Asset Classes*. Rockefeller Foundation. <http://www.rockefellerfoundation.org/uploads/files/d666caa9-9093-4f75-8502-9017a89a5dc7.pdf>, accessed 1 November 2013.

Brown, A., Behrens, L., and Schuster, A. (2015). *The Tale of Two Funds: The Management and Performance of the Futurebuilders-England Fund*. London: The Boston Consulting Group.

Bugg-Levine, A., and Emerson, J. (2011). *Impact Investing: Transforming How We Make Money While Making a Difference*. San Francisco, CA: Jossey-Bass.

Burkett, I. (2012). *Place-based Impact Investment in Australia: Building Blocks for Action*. Australia: Australian Government Department of Education, Employment and Workplace Relations, NAB Australia, Mission Australia, and JBWere.

Burkett, I. (2013). *Reaching Underserved Markets: The Role of Specialist Financial Intermediaries in Australia*. Commissioned by Social Traders and Foresters Community Finance, Australia.

Cameron, D. (2013). *G8 Social Impact Investment Forum, 6 June 2013*. <https://www.gov.uk/government/speeches/prime-ministers-speech-at-the-social-impact-investment-conference>, accessed 1 November 2013.

Campen, J. (1997). *The Community Reinvestment Act: A Law That Works, Dollars and Sense*. <http://www.dollarsandsense.org/archives/1997/1197campen.html>, accessed 1 November 2013.

Canadian Taskforce on Social Finance (2010). 'Mobilizing Private Capital for Public Good: Canadian Task Force on Social Finance'. MaRS, <http://www.marsdd.com/wp-content/uploads/2011/02/MaRSReport-socialfinance-taskforce.pdf>, accessed 1 November 2103.

Centre for Global Development & Social Finance (2013). *Development Impact Bond Working Group Report*. Centre for Global Development & Social Finance, <http://www.cgdev.org/sites/default/files/DIB_WG_REPORT.pdf>, accessed 1 November 2013.

Charlton, K., Donald, S., Ormiston, J. and Seymour, R. (2013). *Impact Investments: Perspectives for Australian Superannuation Funds*. Australia: Creative Commons.

Cheng, P. (2011). *The Impact Investors Handbook: Lessons from the World of Microfinance*, 1st edn. Charities Aid Foundation (CAF) Venturesome.

Clark, C., Emerson, J., and Thornley, B. (2013). 'Impact Investing 2.0: The Way Forward—Insight from 12 Outstanding Funds'. InSight at Pacific Community Ventures, ImpactAssets, and Duke University's Fuqua School of Business.

Clark, C., Emerson, J., and Thornley, B. (2014). *The Impact Investor: Lessons in Leadership and Strategy for Collaborative Capitalism*. San Francisco: Jossey-Bass.

Clark, C., Thornley, B. and Emerson, J. (2012). 'A Market Emerges: The Six Dynamics of Impact Investing'. The Impact Investor Project Research Collaboration.

Cohen, R. (2014). 'Revolutionising Philanthropy: Impact Investment'. Speech delivered at the Mansion House, London, 23 January.

Cohen, R., and Sahlman, W. A. (2013). 'Social Impact Investing Will Be the New Venture Capital', *Harvard Business Review*, <blogs.hbr.org/cs/2013/01/social_impact_investing_will_b.html> accessed 1 November 2013.

Cullen, A. and Addis, R. (2013). *Social Enterprise Development & Investment Funds: Lessons from the Implementation Process*. Australia: Australian Department of Education, Employment and Workplace Relations.

Defourny, J., and Nyssens, M. (2010). 'Conceptions of Social Enterprise and Social Entrepreneurship in Europe and the United States: Convergences and Divergences', *Journal of Social Entrepreneurship*, 1(1): 32–53.

Deloitte (2013). *The Future of Productivity 2013*. <http://www.deloitte.com/view/en_CA/ca/insights/insights-and-issues/the-future-of-productivity-2013/index.htm>, accessed 1 November 2013.

Denis, D. J. (2004). 'Entrepreneurial Finance: An Overview of the Issues and Evidence', *Journal of Corporate Finance*, 10(2): 301–26.

Devarajan, S., Miller, M., and Swanson, E. (2009). 'World Bank Policy Working Paper Development Goals: History, Prospects and Costs'. Washington, DC: World Bank.

Dilger, R. J. (2013). *Small Business Administration 7(a) Loan Guaranty Program.* Washington, DC: Congressional Research Service.

Drexler, M., and Noble, A. (2013a). 'From the Margins to the Mainstream: Assessment of the Impact Investment Sector and Opportunities to Engage Mainsream Investors'. A report to the World Economic Forum Investors Industries, prepared in collaboration with Deloitte Touche Tohmatsu, World Economic Forum 2013.

Drexler, M., and Noble, A. (2013b). 'From Ideas to Practice, Pilots to Strategy Practical Solutions and Actionable Insights on How to Do Impact Investing'. A report to the World Economic Forum Investors Industries, World Economic Forum 2013.

Dupuy, G., and Langendorff, C. (2014). 'Bringing Mass Retail to Impact Investing—the French '90/10' Solidarity Investment Funds, Impact Investing Policy in 2014: A Snapshot of Global Activity'. Impact Investing Policy Collaborative, <http://globalpolicy.iipcollaborative.org/> accessed 30 November 2014.

Edwards, J. (2012). 'Retrieving the Big Society', 1st edn, *Political Quarterly Special Series.*

Eggers, W., and Macmillan, P. (2013). 'The Solution Revolution: How Business, Government and Social Enterprises Are Teaming up to Solve Society's Toughest Problems'. Harvard Business School.

Emerson, J. (2000). 'The Nature of Returns: A Social Capital Markets Inquiry into Elements of Investment and the Blended Value Proposition'. Social Enterprise Series No. 17, Harvard Business School.

Emerson, J., and Spitzer, J. (2007). *From Fragmentation to Function: Critical Concepts and Writings on Social Capital Markets' Structure, Operation and Innovation.* Oxford: Skoll Centre for Social Entrepreneurship.

Essene, R. S., and Apgar, W. C. (2009). *The 30th Anniversary of the Community Reinvestment Act: Restructuring the CRA to Address Mortgage Finance Revolution.* Federal Reserve Bank of San Francisco. <http://www.frbsf.org/community-development/files/30th_anniversary_cra1.pdf>, accessed 1 November 2013.

Evenett, R. (2012). *Impact Investing: Going beyond SRI,* Your SRI: Socially Responsibly Investment. <https://yoursri.com/responsible-investing/newsletter/topic-of-the-month-november-2012>, accessed 1 November 2013.

Freireich, J., and Fulton, K. (2009). *Investing for Social and Environmental Impact: A Design for Catalysing an Emerging Industry,* Monitor Institute.

G8 Social Impact Investment Conference (2013). <https://www.gov.uk/government/speeches/g8-social-impact-investment-conference>, accessed 1 November 2013.

German National Advisory Board on Impact Investing (2014). *Wirkungsorientierte Investieren: Neue Finanzierungsquellen zur Lösung gesellschaftlicher Herausforderungen.* German National Advisory Board on Impact Investing.

Global Humanitarian Assistance Report (2013). Bristol: GHA. <http://www.globalhumanitarianassistance.org/wp-content/uploads/2013/07/GHA-Report-2013.pdf>, accessed 9 January 2014.

Global Impact Investment Network (GIIN) (2013). *Issues Brief: Catalytic First-Loss Capital,* Global Impact Investment Network. <http://www.thegiin.org/binary-data/RESOURCE/download_file/000/000/552-1.pdf>, accessed 1 November 2013.

Gompers, P. (1994). *The Rise and Fall of Venture Capital.* Newcomen Prize Essay, Graduate School of Business, University of Chicago.

Goodall, E., and Kingston, J. (2009). 'Access to Capital: A Briefing Paper'. Charities Aid Foundation.

Gregory, D., Hill, K., Joy, I., and Keen, S. (2012). *Investment Readiness in the UK.* London: Big Lottery Fund.

Grossman, M. (1972). 'On the Concept of Health Capital and the Demand for Health', *Journal of Political Economy*, 80(2): 223–55.

Guezennec, C., and Malochet, G. (2013). *Impact Investing: A Way to Finance the Social and Solidarity Economy? An International Comparison.* Document du Travail, Premier Ministre, France.

Gustafsson-Wright, E., and Gardiner, S., Putcha, V. (2105). *The Potential and Limitations of Impact Bonds: Lessons from the First Five Years of Experience Worldwide.* Washington DC: The Brookings Institute.

Hajkowicz, S., Cook, H., and Littleboy, A. (2012). *Our Future World: Global Megatrends That Will Change the Way We Live.* Australia: CSIRO.

Heaney, V. (2010). *Investing in Social Enterprises: the Role of Tax Incentives.* London: NESTA and the Centre for the Study of Financial Innovation.

Hill, K. (2011). 'Investor Perspectives on Social Enterprise Financing', London: City of London/Big Lottery Fund/ClearlySo.

Impact Assets (2013). Impact Assets Issue Brief nos. 2, 3, 5, and 8. <http://www.impactassets.org/impact-investing/issue-briefs/>, accessed 1 November 2013.

Jackson, E. T. (2013a). 'Interrogating the Theory of Change: Evaluating Impact Investing Where It Matters Most', *Journal of Sustainable Finance & Investment*, 3(2): 95–110.

Jackson, E. T. (2013b). 'Evaluating Social Impact Bonds: Questions, Challenges, Innovations, and Possibilities in Measuring Outcomes in Impact Investing', *Community Development*, 44(5) Special Issue: Innovative Measurement and Evaluation of Community Development Practices.

Jackson, E. T., and Associates (2012). *Accelerating Impact: Achievements, Challenges, and What's Next Building the Impact Investing Industry.* New York: Rockefeller Foundation.

Jackson, E. T., and Harji, K. (2012). *Unlocking Capital, Activating a Movement.* New York: Rockefeller Foundation.

Janeway, W. H. (2012). 'What I Learned by Doing Capitalism'. London School of Economics and Political Science. <http://www.lse.ac.uk/publicEvents/pdf/2012_MT/20121011-Janeway-Transcript.pdf>, accessed 1 November 2013.

Janeway, W. H. (2013). *Doing Capitalism in the Innovation Economy: Markets, Speculation and the State.* Cambridge: Cambridge University Press.

Joliffe, D. and Hedderman, C. (2014). *Peterborough Social Impact Bond: Final Report on Cohort 1 Analysis,* QinetiQ University of Leicester, Prepared for Ministry of Justice

Kasturi Rangan, V., Appelby, S., and Moon, L. (2012). Unpublished. *The Promise of Impact Investing,* Harvard Business School.

Koenig, A. (2014). *Creating Social Impact Investing Markets—where are we now and where do we want to go? Impact Investing Policy in 2014: A Snapshot of Global Activity.* Impact Investing Policy Collaborative. <http://globalpolicy.iipcollaborative.org/>, accessed 30 November 2014.

Koh, H., Karamchandani, A., and Katz, R. (2012). *From Blueprint to Scale: The Case for Philanthropy in Impact Investing.* New York: Monitor Group and Acumen Fund.

Leapfrog Investments (2013). *Profit-with-Purpose.* <http://www.leapfroginvest.com/lf/about/profit-with-purpose>, accessed 1 November 2014.

Lindsey, L. B. (2009). *The CRA as a Means to Provide Public Goods.* Federal Reserve Bank of San Francisco. <http://www.frbsf.org/community-development/files/cra_means_provide_public_goods.pdf>, accessed 1 November 2013.

Ludlow, J., and Jenkins, J. (2011). *Twenty Catalytic Investments to Grow the Social Investment Market*. London: National Endowment for Science Technology and the Arts (NESTA), Panahpur, and UnLtd.

Masahiro, K., and Prasad, E. (2011). *Financial Markets Regulation and Reform in Emerging Markets*. Asian Development Bank Institute and Brookings Institute Press.

Mason, C., and Kwok, J. (2007). 'Facilitating Access to Finance: Discussion Paper on Investment Readiness Programs'. Brussels: European Union.

Mazzucato, M. (2012). *The Entrepreneurial State: Debunking Public vs Private Sector Myths*. London: Anthem Press.

Mercer (2012). 'The ABC of ESG: An Introduction to Responsible Investment'. Mercer Investments, Australia.

Mills, K., and Greene, S. (2012). 'The Small Business Investment Company (SBIC) Program: Annual Report FY 2012'. Small Business Administration USA.

Mulgan, G. (2013). *The Locust and the Bee: Predators and Creators in Capitalism's Future,* Princeton, NJ: Princeton University Press.

Mulgan, G., Tucker, S., Rushanara, A., and Sandars, B. (2007). *Social Innovation: What It Is, Why It Matters, How It Can Be Accelerated*. London: Young Foundation.

Nelson, J., and Jackson, I. (2004). *Profits with Principles: Seven Strategies for Delivering Value with Values*. New York: Broadway Business.

Nicholls, A., and Murdock, A. (2011). *Social Innovation: Blurring Boundaries to Reconfigure Markets*. London: Palgrave Macmillan.

Nicholls, A., and Pharoah, C. (2008). *The Landscape of Social Investment: A Holistic Topology of Opportunities and Challenges*. Oxford: Said Business School and the Skoll Centre for Social Entrepreneurship.

Nicholls, A., and Tomkinson, E. (2013). 'The Peterborough Pilot Social Impact Bond', University of Oxford Case Study.

Olson, J., Chakrabarti, P., and Essene, R. S. (2009). *A Framework for Revisiting the CRA*. Federal Reserve Bank of San Francisco. <http://www.frbsf.org/community-development/files/revisiting_cra1.pdf>, accessed 1 November 2013.

OECD (2012). *Financing SMEs and Entrepreneurs 2012: An OECD Scoreboard,* OECD. <http://www.oecd.org>, accessed 1 November 2013.

OECD (2013). 'Policies for Seed and Early Stage Finance: Summary of the 2012 OECD Financing Questionnaire', Directorate for Science, Technology and Industry Committee on Industry, Innovation and Entrepreneurship.

Osborne, D., and Gaebler, T. (1992). *Reinventing Government: How the Entrepreneurial Spirit Is Transforming the Public Sector*. New York: Plume Publishing.

Porter, M., and Kramer, M. (2011). 'Creating Shared Value: How to Reinvent Capitalism and Unleash a Wave of Innovation and Growth', *Harvard Business Review*, Jan–Feb 2011.

Richardson, B. (2008). *Socially Responsible Investment Law: Regulating the Unseen Polluters*. Oxford: Oxford University Press.

Rockefeller Philanthropy Advisors (2009). *Solutions for Impact Investors: From Strategy to Implementation*, Rockefeller Foundation, viewed online 1 November 2013, <http://www.rockefellerfoundation.org/uploads/files/7ad1e157-82ca-4e09-8770-543f4e9e6226.pdf>.

Saltuk, Y., Bouri, A., and Leung, G. (2011). *Insight into the Impact Investment Market: An In-depth Analysis of Investor Perspectives and over 2,200 Transactions*. London: J.P. Morgan and the Global Impact Investing Network.

Saltuk, Y., El Idrissi, A., Bouri, A., Mudahar, A., and Schiff, H. (2014). *Spotlight on the Market: The Impact Investor Survey*. London: J.P. Morgan and the Global Impact Investing Network.

Schwab Foundation for Social Entrepreneurship and World Economic forum in collaboration with InSight at Pacific Community Ventures, the Initiative for responsible Investment at the Hauser Centre for Nonprofit Organisations at Harvard University and SK Group (2013). *Breaking the Binary: Policy Guide to Scaling Social Innovation.* Cambridge, MA: The World Economic Forum.

Securities & Exchange Commission (2013). 'Eliminating the Prohibition on General Solicitation and General Advertising in Certain Offerings', Fact Sheet. <http://www.sec.gov>, accessed 15 June 2015.

Senate Economics References Committee (2011). *Investing for Good: the development of a capital market for the not-for-profit sector in Australia.* Australia: Committee Hansard.

Senate Economics References Committee (2012). *Response: Capital Markets for Social Economy Organisations.* Australia: Committee Hansard.

Shanmugalingam, C., Graham, J., Tucker, S., and Mulgan, G. (2011). *Growing Social Ventures: The Role of Intermediaries, What They Do, and What They Could Become.* London: The Young Foundation and NESTA.

Shergold, P. (2013). 'My Hopes for a Public Service for the Future', *Australian Journal of Public Administration*, 72(1): 7–13.

Slocock, C. (2012). *The Big Society Audit 2012.* London: Joseph Roundtree Charitable Trust and Calouste Gulbenkian Foundation, UK.

Social Finance (2010). *A New Tool for Scaling Impact: How Social Impact Bonds Can Mobilize Private Capital to Advance Social Good.* New York: The Rockefeller Foundation. <http://www.rockefellerfoundation.org/uploads/files/655fab01-83b9-49eb-b856-a1f61bc9e6ca-small.pdf>, accessed 1 November 2013.

Social Finance (2014). *The Global Social Impact Bond Market.* <http://www.socialfinance.org.uk/wp-content/uploads/2014/08/Social-Impact-Bonds-Snapshot-2014.pdf>, accessed 30 November 2014.

Social Impact Investment Taskforce (2014). 'Impact Investment: The Invisible Heart of Markets'. Social Impact Investment Taskforce established under the UK's Presidency of the G8.

Social Impact Investment Taskforce Asset Allocation Working Group (2014). 'Allocating for Impact Subject Paper'. Social Impact Investment Taskforce established under the UK's Presidency of the G8.

Social Impact Investment Taskforce Impact Measurement Working Group (2014). 'Measuring Impact Subject Paper'. Social Impact Investment Taskforce established under the UK's Presidency of the G8.

Social Impact Investment Taskforce Mission Alignment Working Group (2014). 'Profit-with-purpose Subject Paper'. Social Impact Investment Taskforce established under the UK's Presidency of the G8.

Thornley, B., Wood, D., Grace, K., and Sullivant, S. (2011). 'Impact Investing: A Framework for Policy Design and Analysis'. InSight at Pacific Community Ventures and the Initiative for Responsible Investment at Harvard University, supported by the Rockefeller Foundation

Triodos Bank (2014). *Impact Investing for Everyone: A Blueprint for Retail Impact Investing.* New York: Triodos Bank produced for the Social Impact Investment Taskforce.

United Kingdom Cabinet Office (2013a). *Growing the Social Investment Market: 2013 Progress Update.* London: United Kingdom Cabinet Office. <https://www.gov.uk/government/uploads/system/uploads/attachment_data/file/205295/Social_Investment_Strategy_Update_2013.pdf>, accessed 1 November 2013.

United Kingdom Ministry of Justice (2013). *Peterborough Interim Figures—31 October 2013*. London: Social Finance. <http://payforsuccess.org/sites/default/files/peterbor ough_interim_figures_october_2013.pdf>, accessed 1 November 2013.

United Kingdom National Advisory Board on Impact Investing (2014). *Building a Social Impact Investment Marketplace: The UK Experience*. London: United Kingdom National Advisory Board on Impact Investing.

United Kingdom Social Investment Taskforce (2000). *Enterprising Communities: Wealth beyond Welfare*. London: Social Investment Taskforce. <http://www.so cialinvestmenttaskforce.org/downloads/SITF_Oct_2000.pdf>, accessed 1 November 2013.

United Kingdom Social Investment Taskforce (2003). *Enterprising Communities: Wealth beyond Welfare: 2003 Progress Report*. London: Social Investment Taskforce. <http://www.socialinvestmenttaskforce.org/downloads/SITF_July_2003.pdf>, accessed 1 November 2013.

United Kingdom Social Investment Taskforce (2005). *Enterprising Communities: Wealth beyond Welfare: 2005 Progress Report*. London: Social Investment Taskforce. <http://www.socialinvestmenttaskforce.org/downloads/SITF_July_2005.pdf>, accessed 1 November 2013.

United Kingdom Social Investment Taskforce (2010). London: *Social Investment Ten Years On*. London: Social Investment Taskforce. <http://www.socialinvestmenttaskforce.org/ downloads/SITF_10_year_review.pdf>, accessed 1 November 2013.

United Nations Economic Commission for Europe (2008). 'Guidebook on Promoting Good Governance in Public Private Partnerships', UN, Geneva.

United States National Advisory Board on Impact Investing (2014). *Public Capital, Private Good: How Smart Federal Policy Can Galvanize Impact Investing—and Why It's Urgent*. New York: United States National Advisory Board on Impact Investing.

Watts, B., Vale, D., Mulgan, G., Dale, M., Ali, A., and Norman, W. (2009). *Sinking and Swimming: Meeting Britain's Un-met Needs*. London: Young Foundation.

Wind-Cowie, M. (2012). *Rebalancing Risk and Responsibility*. London: Demos.

Winnick, L. (1993), 'Is Reinventing Government Enough? A Critique of David Osborne', *City Journal*, Summer: 1–21.

Wood, D., Thornley, B., and Grace, K. (2012). *Impact at Scale: Policy Innovation for Institutional Investment with Social and Environmental Benefit*. InSight at Pacific Community Ventures and the Initiative for Responsible Investing at Harvard University and Rockefeller Centre.

World Bank, UNICEF, UNFPA, Partnership for Maternal, Newborn and Child Health (2009). 'Health Systems for the Millennium Development Goals: Country Needs and Funding Gaps'. Background document for the Taskforce on Innovative International Financing for Health Systems.

World Economic Forum (2011). 'Future of Government: Lessons Learned from Around the World'. WEF, Geneva.

World Economic Forum (2013). *Global Agenda Council on The Future of Government*. WEF, Geneva.

Zadek, S. (2001). *Third Generation Corporate Citizenship: Public Policy and Business in Society*. London: The Foreign Policy Centre.

14 Public policy for social finance in context

Roger Spear, Rob Paton, and Alex Nicholls

Introduction

There is a view that the involvement of the state in the development of the private finance markets represents, on the one hand, an unwelcome and unnecessary distortion or, on the other, a mechanism for facilitating neo-liberal retrenchment of government provision of welfare services. However, whatever the particular ideological perspective taken, history demonstrates that markets rarely institutionalize effectively or efficiently when government retreats; rather, it usually takes the interventions of a strong activist state to create fully functioning markets (Crouch, 2004). Nor does social finance refer only to finance that is independent of government: it also refers to schemes that combine public, private, and philanthropic capital. In any event, like it or not, governments of all complexions, on both sides of the Atlantic, have been active agents supporting the development of new financial architectures.

These points are demonstrated by a review[1] and a comparative analysis based on the evolution of social finance policies, of what is a rapidly evolving terrain in several jurisdictions under contrasting forms of capitalism. This chapter aims, above all, to answer several basic questions concerning government involvement in social finance:[2]

- *What* governments have actually done—by reviewing the emergence of social finance policies in different jurisdictions, and thereby effectively collating the *main policy instruments* that have been created or adapted to facilitate social finance?
- *Why* governments have become involved—by considering the problems they have been addressing, and the terms, that is, the *policy narratives and discourses,* by which they have they justified their interventions?
- *How* their policies and new institutions are developed—that is *processes and networks* that have supported these developments?

---

[1] The review draws extensively on Westall (2010).
[2] The authors acknowledge and thank the involvement of Margie Mendell and Ben Thornley in the preparation of this chapter.

The analysis will set out the similarities and differences as regards policy instruments, rationales and ideologies, and policy processes. Based on this analysis it will highlight issues that are unresolved (and likely to remain unresolved) concerning different conceptions of social finance, and what might constitute a 'mature' market.

The second aim is to reflect on these developments and in particular to consider whether social finance is developing from being an assortment of separate responses to different political claims and issues, and may be becoming recognized not just as a fashionable label for this assortment, but as a suite of distinctive institutions, a field of financial activity with continuing public oversight and involvement.

The approach adopted here draws on institutional theory to argue that markets are socially embedded (Polanyi, 1945), and socially constructed (Weber, 1930; Kay, 2003), and it examines the role of the state as well as other stakeholders in constructing social finance policies and a market. It notes, drawing on Stiglitz et al. (1993), that the role of the state is particularly prominent in financial markets that are far from being idealized neo-classical markets—for example, the protection given to local banks in the USA. Thus different contextual and historical factors shape the kind of markets that are developed, but path dependency is not the complete story, since different varieties of capitalism[3] emerge across different jurisdictions, but moderated by global similarities. The two varieties of capitalism from which our country/regional experiences are drawn are: liberal market economies (USA, UK) that are contrasted with a coordinated market economy (Quebec). Social finance is a market in the process of becoming social, constructed and institutionalized, but clearly strongly influenced and subject to incorporation pressures towards mainstream financial markets. But on the other hand it may be able to maintain a hybrid distinctiveness—thereby posing the alternatives of financializing the social versus socializing the financial or a mix of these two (cf. Nicholls, 2010). Actors, networks, organizations, and institutions shape the emerging social finance market through processes of institutional entrepreneurship (Battilana, Leca, and Boxenbaum, 2009), within governance networks. Central players in this process are the state and politicians negotiating and legitimizing policy networks, and together with field actors (institutional entrepreneurs), shaping the policy agenda and legitimizing developments according to political ideologies.

The shift from government to governance in the UK (particularly with New Labour developing a partnership relationship with the third sector under the title of 'The Compact') has changed the role of the state from leading to enabling and shaping, employing private/third-sector policy advisors, funding and shaping cross-sector spaces/bodies for policy formulation, structuring stakeholder dialogue, coordinating wider consultation, and setting up intermediary bodies

---

[3] Hall and Soskice (2001).

which implement many policies. Theories of institutional entrepreneurship help model these processes.

While the variety of capital influences the general development of financial policy, path dependency at a more detailed level is apparent—thus it is no accident that in the UK, with its strong financial services sector, social finance has been particularly well developed. And the participation of high-profile people from financial services (such as Sir Ronald Cohen) has ensured both a high level of expertise in policy development and also legitimation both to politicians and the City. Policy also seems to have been driven by a small number of individuals and network organizations from the third sector/civil society—Demos, the Young Foundation, NESTA, and the Scarman Trust. And these institutional entrepreneurs both drive policy and are well positioned to benefit from it by taking leadership roles in intermediary bodies.

The structure of the chapter is as follows: it starts by recounting developments in the UK, a country where government activism over at least fifteen years has created a *relatively* mature suite of arrangements in support of social finance. In what sense mature? What would constitute 'maturity' is part of the debate and a topic that is addressed in the final section. Suffice to say at this point that the landscape of social finance in the UK is now characterized by a range of specialist institutions that have at their disposal an increasing array of products and instruments.

Having summarized recent UK experience, the following sections of the chapter reconstruct the cascade of initiatives in terms of the policy instruments that were deployed, the political and economic rationales used to justify public action, and the processes through which policy emerged. The gradual process of constructing a social finance market proceeds through shifting policy agendas, but remarkably similar policy network processes, within network governance processes shaped by the state. Each of these sections uses snapshots of the policy experience in other jurisdictions to suggest extensive commonalities as well as some significant differences between countries, as regards the patterns and trends in policy development in different countries. The jurisdictions used in these comparisons are the USA and Quebec.

The USA was an obvious choice given its early prominence in this field and the high profile that venture philanthropy and social entrepreneurship enjoy there. That said, the variety of experience at state level is enormous; discretion being the better part of valour, this comparison is limited to the federal level of government in the USA.

Quebec has developed an unusual, and unusually strong, infrastructure for the provision of social finance. It has been developing for fifty years and continues to take new forms. It is rooted in the co-operative and trade union movements and also in strong community organizations. These have developed a combination of political muscle and economic credibility such that governments at federal, state and local levels have chosen to be active partners in creating new financial funds and institutions.

Hopefully, by including a coordinated market economy alongside two liberal market economies (Hall and Soskice, 2001), the discussion will go beyond the Anglo-American concerns that often frame discussions of social finance.

Finally, the chapter reviews and draws some conclusions from the information and analysis presented—in the form of an over-arching argument about how the patchwork of measures apparent in different jurisdictions may be evolving, albeit, the measures are still unevenly spread and institutionalized and their further development remains unclear. In the absence of systematic studies to review and integrate, and even limited to three jurisdictions (and excluding transitional and emerging economies), the scope of the chapter is recklessly ambitious: thus, it can only be presented as exploratory.

Liberal market economies: UK

Since 1997 the UK[4] government has pursued a wide range of initiatives to encourage, facilitate, or provide what is now called social finance. These initiatives flowed thick and fast—Kendall (2009) described the New Labour government's style of policy as hyperactive—and this section can only offer a summary account. This activity may be more easily understood in terms of three overlapping phases, distinguished by the main concern motivating the policymakers in each case.

PHASE ONE: SOCIAL FINANCE AS COMMUNITY INVESTMENT (1999–2002)

One of the first initiatives of the New Labour government was the creation of a Social Exclusion Unit within the Cabinet Office. It set up eighteen policy action teams to work on the issues facing people in disadvantaged areas. In 1999, Policy Action Team 3 on Enterprise and Social Exclusion,[5] recognized the role of community development finance institutions (CDFIs) in helping existing and start-up businesses and community and social enterprises access finance on appropriate terms. Catching the mood, third-sector bodies established the Social Investment Task Force. Their continuing flow of recommendations led directly to government implementing several policies for cross-sector partnerships:

---

[4] The idiosyncracies of the British political system mean that the actions of the UK government discussed here are, in fact, mainly about *England and* Wales; Scotland and Northern Ireland have had different policy developments.

[5] The Policy Action Team 3 was a group of civil servants, business, voluntary sector, and local government who consulted widely about issues concerning business in deprived areas.

- A Community Investment Tax Relief (CITR), implemented in 2002 encouraged mainstream investment in 'under-invested' areas by giving tax relief to investors in community development finance institutions (CDFIs) providing funding and support (mainly) to micro- and social enterprises. The tax relief, available to individuals and companies, amounts to 25 per cent of the value of the investment and is spread over five years[6]
- The Charity Commission sought to enable the development in the UK of programme-related investment (PRI)[7] by giving greater latitude for investment in community development initiatives by charitable trusts and foundations
- Support for CDFIs was improved and part-funded by the UK government through the establishment of a Community Development Finance Association as their trade body in 2002[8]
- A community development venture fund (Bridges Community Ventures Ltd) was set up in 2002 as a hybrid structure—the first community development venture company with investment from government as well as the private sector to deliver both financial returns and social and environmental benefits, focusing on disadvantaged areas
- The launch of the Phoenix Fund in 2000 which included three elements: a development fund supporting business and social enterprise in disadvantaged areas; a challenge fund and loan guarantees for CDFIs (2003); and a national network of volunteer business mentors. This development fund represented a new way for government to intervene since it accepted the risk of failure.

PHASE TWO: SOCIAL FINANCE AS SOCIAL ENTERPRISE INVESTMENT (2002–2010)

The main focus of social finance policy gradually shifted to the financing of third-sector organizations, not least social enterprises. It was driven by the Government's desire to renew public services, and the hope that private capital could be attracted in to assist. Institutional developments began in 2001, when the Social Enterprise Unit (SEU) was set up in the Department of Trade and Industry. It specifically considered access to finance (both working and investment capital) as well as appropriate organizational structures. The Treasury's 2002 Cross Cutting Review into the role of the voluntary and community sector in public service delivery may also have played a role in distributing policy initiatives across government departments, as did the establishment of the Social Investment Taskforce and industry bodies such as UnLtd.

---

[6] <http://www.hmrc.gov.uk/specialist/citc_guidance.htm>.
[7] The current guidelines for charity investment are set out in *CC14 Investment of Charitable Funds: Basic Principles* <http://www.charity-commission.gov.uk/publications/cc14.asp>. The Charity Commission distinguishes social investment from ethical or socially responsible investment.
[8] <http://www.cdfa.org.uk>.

In 2002, the Social Enterprise Coalition was formed, again with some government support, to provide a broadly based representative body for the growing social enterprise sector. The SEU developed a social enterprise strategy with three themes that informed policy, including social finance, for many years and aimed to:

- create an enabling environment for social enterprise (including legal, regulatory, and procurement)
- make social enterprises better businesses (business support, capacity building, finance)
- establish the value of social enterprise (research, recognizing achievement, quality).

This led to legislation for a new business form—the community interest company (CIC)—introduced in 2005. This new legal form included a number of social value-focused aspects including: dividend and debt interest repayment caps, an asset lock, a community interest test, and the requirement to submit an annual stakeholder report.

The CIC can either be set up limited by guarantee or by shares—the latter option aimed to encourage social investment;[9] but this has proved less popular than anticipated, and after a further consultation the dividend cap was later raised to improve its attractiveness.

During this period, several capacity-building measures combining finance with developmental support were introduced in response to the growing marketization of state/third-sector relations—increased contract opportunities from the public sector, shifts from grants to contracts by government, and an increased pressure for earned income strategies. In 2002, the Government provided £14.4m funding for the Adventure Capital Fund (ACF) that was, in a new policy departure, delivered by third sector organizations. It was set up in order to develop capacity and increase the impact of medium-sized community organizations through the development of either physical assets or social enterprise activity and experimented with mixes of support, grants, patient loans, and various forms of (quasi-)equity. Later, an evaluation of the ACF demonstrated its efficacy in enhancing growth and organizational capacity of charities. It also stressed the important role of strategic advisors and of small grants to enable business development that were additional to the main investments.[10]

However, concern over undercapitalization and fragility amongst such organizations continued and led to the creation of Futurebuilders.[11] This

---

[9] Dividend payments are capped and, together with the asset lock, place limits on, as well as opportunities for, social investment forms and returns. A consultation as to the appropriateness or otherwise of the dividend limit was undertaken by the CIC regulator in 2009 <http://www.cicregulator.gov.uk>.

[10] Thake and Lingayah (2009) *Investing in Thriving Communities: The Final External Evaluation Report on the Adventure Capital Fund*. London Metropolitan University.

[11] <http://www.futurebuilders-england.org.uk>.

extended the model of the ACF, using loan financing, often combined with grants and professional support, to build up third-sector organizations the better to deliver public services.

Meanwhile, the importance of economic development in disadvantaged communities had not been forgotten, and in 2005 the Treasury established the Financial Inclusion Taskforce. In due course a £120m Financial Inclusion Fund was set up which included a £36m Growth Fund to support credit unions and social lending in disadvantaged areas.

In 2006 support for the third sector was rationalized: the UK Government combined the social enterprise and voluntary and community responsibilities in the Office of the Third Sector (OTS) located centrally in the Cabinet Office.

In 2007, the Department of Health replicated the approach of the Adventure Capital Fund with their own Social Enterprise Investment Fund (SEIF). This provided start-up funding and longer-term investment to emerging and existing social enterprises in the health and/or social care sector with a view to their sustainability. The finance offered by the SEIF took the form of development grants to cover start-up costs such as business planning, legal advice, and market research, together with a mixture of loans, loan guarantees, grants, and equity capital. The SEIF aimed to 'invest' £100m over a four-year period (minus management fees) and was administered by the Social Investment Business that already managed the Futurebuilders funds.

In 2007, an OTS consultation on a risk capital fund for social enterprise was undertaken in recognition of the need to fill the equity gap for organizations at critical stages of development and growth. This led to a number of initiatives to address this market failure, including the launch of the Bridges Ventures Social Entrepreneurs Fund in 2009. This fund aimed to provide investments in scalable social enterprises delivering high social impacts but at a sub-market rate of financial return.[12] A similar fund was developed by NESTA in 2012: the £25m Social Investment Fund.

Other government departments adopted similar social finance approaches, without labelling them as such. For example, in 2008 the Department for Children, Schools and Families launched a £100m Youth Sector Development Fund that promoted and supported growth and capacity in third-sector organizations that deliver effective services and activities for young people in England (particularly the most disadvantaged).

Likewise, the Department for Communities and Local Government together with the OTS established the Community Builders £70m investment fund in 2009 to strengthen larger community organizations with both financial and advisory support. In 2011 this fund was passed on to the Adventure Capital Fund, and its loan book became managed and recycled by the Social Investment Business.

---

[12] <http://www.bridgesventures.com/>.

Meanwhile, Regional Development Agencies together with the OTS worked on financial awareness training as well as enabling access to mainstream business support. In 2009 OTS and NESTA (National Endowment for Science, Technology and the Arts) launched a Social Enterprise Access to Investment (SEATI) programme to broker advice to social enterprise.

Capacity building also included asset transfer policies to increase the 'resilience' of local communities. The Quirk Review of community management and ownership of public assets in 2007 had attracted government attention. In 2009 the Department for Communities and Local Government set up and funded a new Asset Transfer Unit.[13]

This policy agenda focused on building the institutional landscape of social finance in the UK and was complemented by research activities exploring the demand for different types of government finance, including:[14]

- Two OTS-sponsored Action Research Pilots aimed at addressing issues of market-making in equity and quasi-equity finance for social enterprise
- These were led by Community Innovation UK and Charity Bank, and aimed to increase private sector finance, and improve the range of finance available for social enterprises. Outcomes included projects to create the UK's first social business angel network, alongside an investment readiness support service[15]
- Sponsoring and financing two Good Deals conferences on social investment as well as the Social Investment Almanack, part-funded by the OTS and described as a comprehensive guide to the world of social investment
- An OTS-initiated review of Social Return on Investment, as well as a set of guidelines on how to measure the value created by social enterprises and how to communicate this to finance providers and government[16]
- Other research commissioned on a Social Stock Exchange (in response to concerns about the lack of exit routes for finance in the development of social ventures) and on possible tax incentives to encourage investment in social enterprise that led to the introduction to Social Investment Tax Relief in April 2014.[17]

---

[13] The Assets Transfer Unit is being run by the Development Trusts Association (DTA), Community Matters, and the Local Government Association.

[14] *Finance for Small and Medium-Sized Enterprises: Comparisons of Social Enterprises and Mainstream Businesses* by Dr Stuart Fraser of Warwick Business School in 2007, based on data from the 2004 *Small and Medium-Sized Enterprise Finance Survey* and from the 2006 *Social Enterprise Finance Survey*.

[15] Attempts to move beyond these projects eventually bore fruit in 2012, when ClearlySo launched the first UK Social Business Angel Network, and when the Big Venture Challenge, a programme assisting twenty-five ambitious social entrepreneurs achieved a 'co-investment' of £1.1m from Big lottery Funding and external investors including eight 'angel investors'.

[16] The project is being run by a consortium of SROI UK, New Philanthropy Capital, New Economics Foundation, Charities Evaluation Service, and the National Council of Voluntary Organisations. <http://www.thesroinetwork.org>.

[17] *Real Help for Communities: Volunteers, Charities and Social Enterprises* <http://www.cabinetoffice.gov.uk/third_sector/real_help_for_communities.aspx>; <http://www.nesta.org.uk/library/documents/Investing-in-Social-Enterprise.pdf>.

PHASE THREE: SOCIAL FINANCE FOR SOCIAL INNOVATION (2010–2015)

In this phase government strategy became more concerned with leverage and brokerage rather than direct fund creation. This partly reflects the influence of social entrepreneurship and innovation practice involving cross-sector finance solutions to investment in public policy and social need.

In 2007, the Commission on Unclaimed Assets[18] made proposals to use funds that had been dormant for fifteen years or more in high street bank accounts as capital to leverage finance into social investment. The following year, the UK government published the Dormant Bank and Building Society Accounts Act (2008) to enable the use of such money for public purposes, including a Social Investment Wholesale Bank. This initiative was eventually launched in April 2012 as Big Society Capital (BSC) funded with over £400m from dormant bank accounts and £200m as equity contributed by the high street banks. BSC aimed to collaborate with other financial intermediaries to provide third-sector organizations and social enterprises with long-term investments via debt, equity, and quasi-equity. As a wholesaler, BSV aimed to leverage private capital through brokering co-investments,[19] syndication, and active collaboration. By the end of its first two years of operation BSC had made commitments of £150m to social finance intermediaries that invest in social enterprises.[20] By the end of 2013, there were about 140 such intermediaries (SIFIs) listed in BSC's directory.

BSC was one of several examples of policy continuity on social finance across the change of government in May 2010, when a coalition of the Conservative and Liberal Parties ousted Labour. New Labour had given a high profile to the third sector, with increased support and capacity building, but also with increased levels of contracting. In contrast the new government's 'Big Society' agenda presented itself as an alternative to Labour's 'Big State' and emphasized closer links between the community and third sectors. To do this, policy was oriented to reducing red tape to encourage voluntary action, and making it easier to set up voluntary organizations, facilitating the flow of appropriate resources (including through philanthropy and volunteering), and improving their working relationship with the state. The new government also renamed the OTS as the Office for Civil Society (OCS) and charged it with

---

[18] CUA (2007) *The Social Investment Bank, Its Organisation and Role in Driving Development of the Third Sector.* <http://www.unclaimedassets.org.uk/downloads/CUA_report_FINAL.pdf>.

[19] Matthew Pike (of Social Finance, <http://www.socialfinance.org.uk>) articulated the concept of co-investment as a way to mix government guarantees, tax reliefs, grants or payments with different investor risk-return profiles and demands to create a 'funding sandwich'. Such packages could better enable appropriate returns for different investors, as well as meeting public sector needs and increasing levels of public investment.

[20] Big Society Capital (2014), *Social Investment: From Ambition to Action. Annual Review 2013.* See also HM Government (2013) *Growing the Social Investment Market: 2013 Progress Update.*

pursuing a Big Society agenda. The new OCS echoed the previous government's view of social investment as:

The provision of finance to achieve social outcomes and gain a financial return. It is about harnessing the power of financial markets to help effect positive social impact. Our ambition is for social investment to become a third pillar of finance for the social sector, alongside traditional philanthropy and government grants. Critical to achieving this is the establishment of Big Society Capital to help grow the 'supply' of social investment capital to the sector.[21]

The new coalition developed Labour's policy interest in the blurring of boundaries around third-sector/social enterprise forms of organizations and their role in welfare provision. Thus, a report on mutual spin-outs of public services[22] claimed mutuals as a new business form and focused on a new hybrid form 'the public service mutual' as a mix of types including traditional mutuals, co-operatives, and worker-owned trusts like the John Lewis Partnership.[23] One strong narrative focused on a continuation of a strong social enterprise role in public procurement.[24] However, this raised the criticism that social enterprise was acting as a cover for a wider welfare privatization agenda under conditions of austerity and state retrenchment (see Teasdale, 2013, for a review of the fluidity of the use of the term 'social enterprise').

During this time the concern with capacity building continued, though with an increased interest in the socially innovative dimensions of social finance. The Treasury's 'Invest to Save' initiative was opened up to the third sector because of the belief in its ability to link up different departmental priorities. The last round of funds was disbursed in June 2009, but it was replaced partly by an Innovation Exchange for the third sector in areas of public services. The Transition Fund, launched in 2010, provided more than £100m to help civil society organizations delivering public services adapt to changing contracting regimes. Capacity building was also extended to the entrepreneurial process of spinning out mutual organizations from the public sector: in 2011 the Cabinet Office launched a £10m Mutual Support Programme (MSP) for business and professional services provided by a consortium of experts coordinated by PA

---

[21] <http://www.cabinetoffice.gov.uk/content/big-society-overview>.

[22] Mutuals Taskforce (2012).

[23] John Lewis is an interesting model worth promoting more widely; it is a trust-owned structure with substantial employee participation and profit sharing; but it is not a traditional mutual that like a cooperative is democratically owned and controlled by its members. John Lewis is a company owned by a trust on behalf of all its employees, who are known as Partners, who receive a share of profits. Each employee-partner can influence business through branch forums relating to each store's business. They also elect 80% of the representatives on the Partnership Council that is responsible for social and charitable activities. Commercial activities are governed by the twelve-person Partnership Board, with five directors elected by the Partnership Council, five directors appointed by the chair, and the chair and deputy chair make up the other two board members.

[24] This agenda was further enhanced by the introduction, in 2013, of the Public Services (Social Value) Act that required commissioners to take account of the social value created by tenders for government contracts.

Consulting. In a similar vein, in 2011, a £30m fund to modernize third-sector support organizations was launched with a further £20m pledged. The Transforming Local Infrastructure Programme aimed to develop some of the 2,000 infrastructure organizations that provided advisory and support to social enterprise and charities. This emphasis on capacity building was well-judged, since questions had long been be raised about the investment readiness of the social enterprise sector: in 2011, a report commented, 'It was felt that many social enterprises only had a weak understanding of the implications of taking on external finance.'[25] A 2013 review noted the biggest constraints on growth in the sector were identified by SIFIs as: high transaction costs—largely due to issues with investment readiness, variable commissioning practice by government, and a lack of attractive investment opportunities.[26]

In addition, a £10m Social Incubator Fund was set up in 2013, and four incubators for social enterprise start-ups have been funded. High growth potential social enterprise can receive grants to build capacity, from the Investment and Contract Readiness Fund. Fiscal and legislative work also continued under the coalition government including changes to industrial and provident society legislation that would enable increased social investment in a draft Co-operative and Community Benefit Societies Act, which after public consultation was enacted in August 2014. In order to raise the profile of social value in procurement, the Public Service (Social Value) Act was passed in 2013 requiring commissioners to take into account the social impact of each tender bid as well as its finances when offering public sector contracts. The suitability of charity law for facilitating engagement with social finance markets has also been addressed through the Hodgson Review (2012) that summarized the current difficulties faced by charities in these terms:

My first conclusion is that charity law (along with general trust law and prevailing accounting and financial regulation), while not actively prohibiting social investment, is certainly not set up to support it. There is no clear legal basis for investments of this type, causing nervousness among trustees and their advisors. This lack of clarity extends further, into the accounting and reporting processes that underpin investment. In this situation, social investment will always be the difficult option, discouraging those with a flicker of interest from pursuing the project further and presenting serious barriers to even the highly committed. (para 9.21)

Subsequent Charity Commission advice[27] differentiating between financial investment, programme-related investment, and mixed motive investment aimed to address some of these concerns.

---

[25] Brown and Norman (2011).
[26] ICF GHK in association with BMG Research (2013). The Cabinet Office acknowledged this with the introduction in 2013 of the Investment and Contract Readiness Fund to support capacity-building in social enterprises tendering for government contracts.
[27] Charity Commission (2013).

However, perhaps the most important development bringing together social investment and social innovation has been the policy agenda around social impact bonds (SIBs).[28] The first UK SIB was launched at Peterborough Prison in 2010 (See Nicholls and Tomkinson, chapter 12, this volume), a Centre for Social Impact Bonds was set up within the Cabinet Office in 2012 including an online resource, the SIB Knowledge Box; progress is good with fifteen UK SIBs having been set up by 2014 and a further ten internationally. In order to fund successful outcomes from SIBs, a £20m Social Outcomes Fund was set up at the end of 2012. In the same year, Bridges Social Impact Bond Fund was also set up to offer investors a route to a SIB.

The coalition government moved to position the UK as a world hub for social finance, building on the City's leading role in financial services.[29] In 2012 it sponsored an International Symposium on Social Impact Bonds to help support inward investment; and to transform the social finance market in developing countries, it launched an Impact Programme with £100m over thirteen years. And in 2013, as one of the events to mark the UK's G8 presidency, it hosted the G8 Social Impact Investment Forum. This event established three key themes with associated actions:

- The need to build a global social impact investment community that is collaborative and open to new actors. This will be supported by a new Social Impact Investment Taskforce and a working group of development finance institutions focusing on social impact investment and international development

- The need to create common frameworks to understand the potential of the market and move towards standardization in impact measurement. This will be supported by an OECD report on global developments in social impact investment and a working group of experts on impact measurement

- The need to develop and share best practice, both in governmental policy and more broadly amongst market actors. This will be supported through the Global Learning Exchange on social impact investment and the identification of a set of principles for policymakers in this market.[30]

The Forum led to the creation of a Social Impact Investment Task Force spanning all of the G8 countries plus Australia. In addition to country-level National Advisory Boards, the Task Force convened four expert topic groups focused on: social impact measurement, asset allocation, development contexts, mission lock-in. Each of these groups reported back in June 2014 and contributed to a series of reports issued later in the year.

---

[28] <http://www.socialfinance.org.uk/work/sibs>; see also the Young Foundation who developed this tool in collaboration with Social Finance.

[29] This echoed New Labour's earlier attempts to develop the role of the UK financial services sector in global sustainable development leading to the London Principles for sustainable finance. Three years later, progress on this project was reviewed in Johannesburg—with findings that more needed to be done in the areas of finance for eco-innovation, and finance for developing countries.

[30] Social Investment and Finance Team (2013). *G8 Social Impact Investment Forum: Outputs and Agreed Actions.*

Running in parallel to this significant policy work, the Impact Investing Policy Collaborative (IIPC)—a global network of policy experts—developed the London Principles for social impact investment. These included principles of stakeholder engagement, supporting market stewardship, building institutional capacity, transparency, and accountability.

Liberal market economies: USA

The origins of social finance policy in the USA—and formative influences upon it—can be traced back to the 1950s when the Small Business Administration's programme to support small business investment companies set important precedents (these would be drawn on fifty years later). Then, influenced by the work of the Ford Foundation, the term 'programme-related investment' was formally recognized by Congress in the Tax Act of 1969. In the same year, President Richard M. Nixon established what became The Minority Business Development Agency (MBDA). Two years later he signed an Executive Order to expand its minority business programmes by authorizing grants to public and private organizations to provide technical and management assistance to minority business enterprises (MBEs).[31]

The pace quickened in the 1970s as the issues around (in-)equitable lending by banks gained attention. By 1977 the Community Reinvestment Act had passed through Congress and Title VII Community Development Corporations were being formed. Criticisms notwithstanding, as one commentator put it, 'at the least CRA has served as a catalyst, inducing banks to enter underserved markets that they might otherwise have ignored. At its most successful, the CRA may have had a multiplier effect, supplementing its direct impact by stimulating new market-based, profit-driven economic activity in lower-income neighborhoods.'[32]

By 1989 the CRA had been reformed through the Financial Institution Reform and Recovery Act of 1989 (FIRREA). This required public disclosure of institutions' data, ratings, and performance evaluations, which allowed groups to advocate more effectively for their communities. As market failures were corrected, government and others involved realized that lending to underserved communities could in fact be profitable if properly underwritten and managed.

This led to the emergence of specialized community development institutions, combining small loans with technical assistance and business-advising.

---

[31] <http://www.mbda.gov/main/mbda-history>.
[32] <http://www.federalreserve.gov/newsevents/speech/bernanke20070330a.htm>.

In 1991, ACCION a micro-lending network brought international experience and strategy to the USA and began expanding. In 1994 the Community Development Financial Institutions (CDFI) Act created the CDFI Fund at the US Treasury. Its programmes encouraged demand for social finance and increased supply, using CDFIs (and others) as intermediaries.

During this time, the scope of policy began to broaden, perhaps partly in response to the emerging idea of social entrepreneurship. The community equity industry was also bolstered by the expansion of Community Development Loan Funds into equity and by individual states embracing the promise of venture capital as a way to stimulate economic growth in low-income communities.[33] CRA-related tax credits were introduced. And the Labor Department attempted to bring similar progressive incentives to mainstream fiduciaries, moving beyond core CDFI investors (foundations, CRA-motivated banks, and individuals). The first legal structure for social enterprises (the L3C corporate structure) was introduced in Vermont (2008) and others followed (B-Corps (spreading rapidly), and the Flexible Purpose Corporation).

From 2000 onwards, ideas—social entrepreneurship, impact investing, social innovation—and new environmental priorities led gradually towards a more holistic conception of social investment. This was reflected in diverse government initiatives including:

- the introduction of more enterprising approaches in US foreign policy assistance and aid (where 'Making Markets Work for the Poor' was challenging old orthodoxies)
- social impact bonds in New York and Massachusetts
- the White House creating an Office of Social Innovation and Civic Participation. One of its guidelines is to increase investment for innovative solutions that demonstrate results, noting: 'We will work with federal agencies to create tools, such as innovation funds, prizes, and other social capital market structures to drive resources toward community solutions that are demonstrating success'
- further efforts to enable programme-related investment.

At the same time the original focus on providing access to capital for smaller businesses was given sharply increased attention following the financial crisis. The primary policy instrument was a SBA Impact Investment Fund. The SBA worked with institutional investors to expedite the licensing and capital for qualifying fund managers to organize and operate impact investment SBICs. Then in 2011, as part of the Startup America Partnership, a co-investment vehicle was launched providing $1bn to funds that invested growth capital in companies located in underserved communities. The SBA aimed to provide up to a 2:1 match to private capital raised by these funds, partnering with private investors to target impact investments.

---

[33] Rubin (2007) *Financing Low Income Communities: Models, Obstacles and Future Directions.*

Liberal market economies: Synthesis

In trying to stimulate, enable and institutionalize social finance, public policymakers in both the UK and USA have drawn freely on the wide range of instruments at their disposal. These initiatives can be seen as directed towards the supply-side (supporting the provision of funds), the demand-side (stimulating the demand for social investment), or as 'field-shaping' interventions working more broadly and indirectly.

SUPPLY-SIDE MEASURES

In the UK, the principal measures used to increase the funds available for social investment have been:

- the provision of special funds directly by government (e.g. The Adventure Capital Fund, SEIF)
- initiatives to facilitate Programme Related Investment by charities
- the use of tax incentives (e.g. CDFI tax relief)
- providing loan guarantees or otherwise structuring special funds to draw in private capital (e.g. Bridges Community Ventures Ltd, Phoenix Fund, and latterly Big Society Capital)
- changing public procurement arrangements to facilitate social investment (Social Impact Bonds); so far SIBs have emerged internationally predominantly in liberal market economies—particularly Australia, USA, South Africa, and in similar public service areas like prisoner recidivism, support for NEETs, and so on
- Legislative action requiring the banks to provide funds for social finance (from dormant bank accounts).

The US experience is summarized above and all these supply-side interventions are apparent there as well. Both countries have attempted to innovate so that the full lifecycle of business start-up and growth is covered. Arguably, though, the US federal government through the Community Re-investment Act and later FIRREA acted more robustly towards the banks.

DEMAND-SIDE MEASURES

In the UK, the principal means of stimulating demand for social investment by social entrepreneurs and enterprises have been:

- creating a new legal form (the community interest company—or CIC) to enable equity investment and profit-making for social purposes in controlled ways

- funding capacity-building initiatives to support financially excluded communities (encouraging CDFIs)
- funding capacity-building initiatives targeted on the third sector organizations (e.g. Futurebuilders, support for the Social Enterprise Coalition)
- normative interventions—to raise awareness (media events, seminars, ministerial statements, and so on).

Again similarities with the USA are apparent—but also differences. The USA has also introduced new legal forms aimed at drawing in more mainstream finance into social investment. But the decentralized nature of the US government federal/state system has meant greater variation in form and take-up of these innovations. Moreover, the CIC aimed to enable the use of equity-based investment, while the L3C model was oriented to bond-based PRI finance (Hodgson, 2012).

Likewise, the federal government also invested in capacity building—by providing technical and management assistance through the Minority Business Development Agency. The USA clearly led the way here by establishing community development corporations as early as the 1970s, and these initiatives influenced developments in the UK. In both countries these community-based intermediaries acted as instruments of government policy, with a high degree of independence, so that they can draw in non-government money and act innovatively on behalf of the sector and their client base.

However, as noted above, a major focus for the UK's capacity-building efforts has been the third sector—encompassing both charities and social enterprises—in the context of a broader strategic compact between government and third sector. Indeed, the UK government has helped support new leadership in the sector (through the Social Enterprise Coalition). Similar initiatives in relation to the not-for-profit sector have not been apparent in the USA—possibly because the not-for-profit sector has for many years been economically stronger there.

FIELD SHAPING

In the UK, field-shaping activities[34] have taken the following forms:

- supporting or undertaking R&D—for example, the action research pilots and the promotion of Social Return on Investment on a developmental basis
- market-making initiatives—such as the Social Investment Almanack and the Funding Gateway, supporting work on the Social Stock Exchange
- legitimation and extension—through high level policy-governance mechanisms and cross-cutting initiatives, social finance has become a strategic

---

[34] Nicholls (2010).

theme, with a much broader scope across different departmental areas (e.g. on health and social care, local government, renewable energy)

- development of a variety of intermediary organizations: for capacity-building support, to minimize risk, and manage investments; with service provision frequently combined with engagement in policy networks and advocacy.

In this area the differences between the UK's activism and the USA's more focused effort are clearer. Nevertheless, this may be as much about timing as anything: in recent years, the USA has seen a broadening of interest across government departments linked to the wider interest in social innovation, as well as to foreign policy strategies which have been informed by social entrepreneurship partnerships between USAID and the Skoll Foundation, and the Global Impact Investing Network.

RATIONALES

In the UK, government interest in social finance began as a concern for community regeneration. As in the USA, intervention could be justified in order to correct market failures in the provision of financial services. However, in this as in many other areas, the language of enterprise and business suffused New Labour rhetoric and practice. This was echoed, or translated, into calls from within the third sector for more 'bottom-up' citizen-led activity whether in regeneration, or in society in general. Third-sector actors used the notion of 'enterprise' in a broad way to refer to 'self-help' and 'can-do', as opposed to top-down, government-led initiatives.[35] In the USA, where the notion of enterprise was more firmly lodged in the national psyche, rhetoric of social entrepreneurship—everyone a change-maker—has been used in a similar way.

But while the federal government's interest in social finance remained focused on improving the prospects for disadvantaged groups and communities, the UK government gave increasing priority to building up the capacity within the third sector as part of a drive to reform public services. This introduced social finance into more and more government policy areas, each one bringing in its own particular financing issues. These included assisting with the start-up financing of social enterprises being spun out of the National Health Service; asset transfer policies on the part of local authorities wishing to endow community anchor organizations with underutilized public assets; the need for appropriate social finance in contracting and subcontracting for work integration.

What lay behind this public sector reform narrative? Why was it considered important to build the capacity of third-sector organizations to compete in

---

[35] This approach was particularly promoted by the Scarman Trust, now part of the Novas Scarman Group <http://www.novasscarman.org>.

quasi-markets in service delivery? Arguably, the private sector was already engaged and had the capacity to deliver these services. Perhaps for some in government the answer was simply that the presence of third-sector providers legitimized the entry of the private sector into the new public services markets. But for many, the answer lay in some version of economic pluralism, the view that a mixed economy would work better than one dominated by a single sector. Social enterprises might not have the same commercial focus as private businesses, but they did not suffer from the misalignment of incentives that corporate providers were prone to display. Hence a robust third sector could restrain the private sector's rent-seeking proclivities—as well as being, on occasion, a source of innovation. Given that the development of a strong and business-like third sector was integral to the reform of public services, it was a small step to the use of loan funding instead of grants to incentivize the third sector. These made business planning de rigueur—and also reduced the cost to the Exchequer.

The role of government here was to address market failures in finance provision. There was an orientation of government policy towards disadvantage, linked to private sector engagement informed by corporate social responsibility (CSR).

During this time too, social enterprise had an increasing cachet and social finance was an obvious counterpart. Thus, initiatives in corporate social responsibility were often trying to shift from short-term project funding towards more sustainable models of social enterprise. And venture philanthropy became a *mot du jour*—much discussed, even if fiscal measures to support it were not forthcoming in the UK (cf. the US).

While the interest in public sector reform continues, the main focus of government attention has shifted, latterly, to a more strategic role (a social investment wholesale bank), and to justifying its efforts in terms of support for social innovation and impact. Similar trends are apparent in the USA—in the SBA Impact Investment Funds and the support for social impact bonds.

However, taking a more critical perspective, it could be argued that the Big Society narrative in the UK (Alcock, 2012) provided cover for a growing wave of back door privatization, and that the gradual reduction in the level of universal benefits, was rapidly destroying a safety net, leaving the disadvantaged at the mercy of a still fragile market which would inevitably develop not on the basis of need, but on the vagaries of consumer and donor preferences. In addition, the multidimensional nature of social enterprise interventions give pay-offs differentially to different government ministries—which reinforces the justification for a silo mentality, since cost savings for socially effective interventions would not necessarily be realized to the investing ministry; thus positive externalities are not easily funded.

The inequalities inherent in such risk–reward nexus problems are not limited to classic multidimensional or wicked problems, but are a feature of innovation generally, as Lazonick and Mazzucatto (2013) argued in relation to the unequal distribution of risk–reward for different stakeholders in conventional innovation. They proposed a number of measures to address such inequalities, such as constraining corporate resource allocation, orienting capital gains tax to innovators rather than value extractors, rewarding innovative labour, differentiating between productive and unproductive risk, and improving returns to state supported innovation. This risk–reward nexus framework is worth extending, since there may be parallels here for social innovation and social finance.

Coordinated market economies: Quebec

How does the UK and USA experience compare with what can be observed in more coordinated market economies? As a contrasting example, a summary of the policy developments in Quebec is provided below. What is striking is the similarity in terms of the policy instruments that were developed and deployed—the concerns with financial exclusion, the combination of numerous targeted funds and specialist business support, the range of products to meet business needs across the life cycle, the efforts to draw in mainstream finance—but also how different the political and economic rationales that underpinned these policies were.

In Quebec *solidarity finance* refers to investment in collective (social economy) enterprises; *development capital* refers to investment with social and economic objectives whether in private enterprises or in the social economy (what might now be called impact investment, elsewhere). Mutual aid societies emerged in Quebec in the mid-nineteenth century. The history of the co-operative movement, however, began with the establishment of the first credit union at the turn of the century, which was to become the large *Mouvement des caisses populaires et d'économie Desjardins*, a federation of independent institutions. Today, this federation includes the *Caisse d'économie solidaire* established in 1971 and more recently *Capital régional et coopératif Desjardins* (development capital with a commitment to invest in co-operatives).[36] Even if it has in some respects become a mainstream financial institution,[37] the *Mouvement Desjardins* is still active in every sector of the social economy and is central to its legacy and development in Quebec. Co-operatives exist in many sectors throughout Quebec society.

The recession of the 1980s stimulated a new wave of activity. Strong trade unions and local community organizations shaped Quebec's response to mounting rates of unemployment. The *Fonds de solidarité des travailleurs* (FTQ) was established by one of the three large labour federations to create

---

[36] The latter has invested $442m in more than 2,500 socially engaged enterprises. Its total assets today are C$690m.

[37] In 2012, total assets of the *Mouvement Desjardins* were C$196.7bn. <http://www.desjardins.com>.

and maintain jobs. The *Fonds* provided development capital by investing in enterprises with social and economic objectives. These were validated in obligatory social audits. The *Fonds* created a diversity of financial tools, including regional, local, as well as sectoral funds.[38] The local fund, the *Fonds locaux de solidarité* (FLS), expanded its investments to collectively owned enterprises. The *Fonds* are an example of the many hybrids that existed in Quebec through partnerships. For example, the FLS included the participation of the *Fédération québecoise des municipalités*, a federation of municipalities across Quebec. Total investment by this local fund in 2011, was C$91m, creating or maintaining 27,418 jobs. Both the federal and provincial governments agreed to provide tax credits for investors in the *Fonds de solidarité* as well as additional credits given to investments in registered retirement funds.[39]

In addition to the establishment of the *Fonds* in the early 1980s, economic recession in communities mobilized social movements to collaborate with the labour movement and the private sector to create Community Economic Development Corporations (CDECs) with the support of all three levels of government. Financial innovations that emerged in these early experiences inspired the creation of numerous solidarity finance and development capital institutions and instruments in successive decades. For example, the *Fonds de développement de Montréal* (FDEM) was created in 1988 by the CDECs with:

- the City of Montreal
- the *Fonds de Solidarité* (FTQ)
- the *Société de développement industriel du Québec* (now *Investissement Québec*, a public investment fund).

All three levels of government—municipal, provincial, and federal—participated in the initial capitalization of this fund. The FDEM provided capital to small enterprises with demonstrated capacity to contribute to local development and vitality and to create and/or maintain local jobs.

Micro-credit in Quebec was also an expression of collective action. In the late 1980s, community organizers fought to gain access to credit for local micro-enterprises ignored by the mainstream banks. They established the Montreal Community Loan Association (MCLA), the first micro-credit institution in Canada, to provide finance for initiatives embedded in a socio-economic development strategy. By 2013, this had developed into a network of micro-credit institutions—*the Réseau québecois du credit communautaire* (RQCC)—representing twenty-three community-based funds and loan circles across the province. By 2012, members of the RQCC network had invested $10m and had created or maintained 4,210 jobs.

---

[38] <http://www.fondsftq.com/>. Total assets of the *Fonds de solidarité* in 2012 were $8.5bn (2012). The *Fonds* has invested $5.7bn in 2,239 enterprises and has created or maintained 168,577 jobs.

[39] In 2012, the total assets of the *Fonds de solidarité (FTQ)* were C$8.5bn. They have created and/or maintained approximately 170,000 jobs in Quebec.

In 1995, the *Confédération des syndicats nationaux* (CSN), the second largest workers' federation in Quebec, established a fund—*Fondaction, le Fonds de développement de la CSN pour la coopération et l'emploi*—to promote economic development in Quebec. The *Fondaction* prioritized investment in enterprises with participatory management, distributed control, and environmental stewardship. In 2000, it also created *Filaction* to meet the need for smaller loans (between C$50,000 and C$500,000) and to invest in community funds. In 2012, the assets of *Fondaction* were C$940.8m; it had invested approximately C$620m in more than 100 small- and medium-sized enterprises (SMEs) and funds. Since its establishment, *Fondaction* has maintained or created, directly or indirectly, 27,848 jobs.[40]

Prior to a Summit on the Economy and Employment convened by the Government of Quebec in October 1996, a Social Economy Working Group was established to propose how the social economy could contribute to job creation and economic development in the province. Following the Summit, the Working Group was invited to continue its work for another two years. Its initial mandate, which it surpassed, was to identify twenty social economy projects that would create 20,000 jobs in three years. In 1996, the Working Group was incorporated as the *Chantier de l'économie sociale* and in 1999 it became a not-for-profit organization, providing a strategic voice and leadership ever since.

In 1997, the *Chantier* created an investment fund for the social economy, the *Réseau d'investissement social du Québec* (RISQ). Initial capitalization came from the Quebec government and a few private sector enterprises. RISQ invests exclusively in the social economy through loans and loan guarantees up to C$50,000. The Quebec government also introduced complementary state funds and established 120 *Centres locaux de développement* (CLD) across the province to promote economic development including the development of the social economy. The CDECs, created by activists in the 1980s, provided the template. Later, the Quebec government designated C$5m for RISQ to provide *pre-start-up loans* for social economy enterprises, acknowledging the importance of this kind of support.

In 2003 the need for long-term capital for social economy enterprises inspired the creation of a patient capital fund, the *Fiducie du Chantier de l'économie sociale*. The *Fiducie* provided access to patient capital or quasi-equity that was repayable after fifteen years. The federal government provided the initial capitalization with a C$22.8m grant by Economic Development Canada. In 2013, the investors (trustees) in the *Fiducie* were the two labour solidarity funds (the *Fonds de solidarité*—C$12m, and *Fondaction*—C$8m) as well as the Québec government (*Investissement Québec*—C$10m). To 2013, the *Fiducie* had invested C$30m in 106 enterprises and has created 1,689 jobs.[41] Subsequently, a new fund,

---

[40] *Fondaction* was also affected by the decision of the federal government to reduce and eliminate the 15% tax credits, noted earlier discussion on the *Fonds de solidarité* <http://www.fondaction.com>.

[41] <http://fiducieduchantier.qc.ca>.

Co-Investissement Coop, was established with C$30m in capitalization to provide access to patient capital to co-operatives. This was a partnership between:

- *Capital Regional et Coopératif Desjardins* (CRCD)
- the federal and the provincial government
- networks of regional economic development intermediaries. The CRCD and the federal government's Development Bank of Canada have each also contributed C$10m; the Minister of Finance and the Economy, Quebec, C$4m; the networks themselves contributed C$6m.

Finally, since 1997, the Government also invested directly in the social economy principally through *Investissement Québec* (IQ). In 2001, IQ created *la Financière*, designating C$15m for collective enterprises—co-operatives and not-for-profits. In 2003, IQ created the Capitalization of Social Economy Enterprises Programme (*Programme pour la capitalisation des entreprises de l'économie sociale*), providing loans between C$25,000 and C$500,000 and a moratorium on the repayment of the capital and interest for two to five years. IQ created independent investment products that often complemented other sources of finance, and it also entered into partnerships with solidarity finance, the cooperative movement, *Desjardins* and intermediaries, such as the CFDCs.

Clearly, the landscape of political institutions and ideas is very different in a coordinated market economy like Quebec when compared to the USA or UK. An entrenched welfare state culture limits the disengagement of government and a history of dialogue among principal social actors—labour, government, business, and more recently, social movements and community organizations—distinguishes Quebec from the political culture of the USA and the UK and, indeed, from other regions across Canada. In particular, the co-operative and labour movements still command respect and along with new social movements have been able to appeal to norms of mutuality and solidarity in campaigns to defend livelihoods and communities. They have been able to engage the attention of government and to sustain a policy narrative around the role and contribution of the social economy. Indeed, given the history of investment with social impact and the creation of numerous innovative financial tools and institutions, since the beginning of the twentieth century, the idea of 'impact investing', now making its way into Quebec much as micro-credit did in the early 1990s, has been greeted with some perplexity. It remains to be seen whether in Quebec 'impact investing' will lead to a further surge of capital, and what forms of enterprise and areas of business activity will benefit.

Above all, the Quebec experience demonstrates that social finance is a 'roomy' concept—one through and around which diverse agendas can be pursued, and actors with different political and business outlooks can combine. As Gregory[42] pointed out, policies towards social finance can be presented in either or both of the following ways:

---

[42]   Dan Gregory, Office of the Third Sector presentation to the social investment seminars at Open University Business School 2009. <http://www.open.ac.uk/oubs/socialinvestmentseminars/p2.shtml>.

- as efforts to *socialize the market*—to make private enterprise and markets more effective (sustainable, fairer, democratic, transparent so that firms have less negative and more positive externalities)
- as efforts to *marketize the social*—to make social enterprise and the wider third sector ready for and part of the market and subject to its disciplines.

But if social finance is, indeed, 'roomy' and can encompass disparate ideas, it remains another matter as to whether governments take up or sideline a particular policy proposal.

Conclusion

So far the discussion has proceeded as if government was a tolerably single-minded entity able to determine its aims and means in accord with its political orientation. Such conceptual 'shorthand' can be convenient but is also mis-leading. In fact, governments only get clear what they want to do through engagement with other key actors and, especially in this context, through building close relationships with the third sector and social economy. Current office-holders in government may hold some trump cards, but they always depend on the co-operation of others; the government function is necessarily, in significant measure, shared and distributed. In other words, public policy in relation to social finance emerges from governance systems rooted in each country's economic and political institutions and traditions.

Moreover, these are *multi-level* systems of governance, with responsibility shared up and down as well as outward—they operate at local, state/provincial and inter-state levels. In the UK, the creation of institutional spaces for policy dialogue around social enterprise and social finance was one of the hallmarks of New Labour, attracting important third-sector players (some representing apex organizations, some speaking as successful innovators on the ground), representatives of socially responsible investors (e.g. the UK Social Investment Forum), and policy researchers from universities and think tanks (e.g. the Joseph Rowntree Foundation).[43] Particular business leaders such as Sir Ronald Cohen (a venture capitalist who chaired the 2001 Social Investment Taskforce) added weight and credibility. It is worth noting that the Labour government included ministers with responsibility for the third sector, who had back-grounds in the voluntary sector or with links to the Co-operative Party.[44] In this way the policy networks around social finance were extended and strengthened, both vertically and horizontally, and it was through them that many of the ideas took shape. That said, the management of the various funding and support programmes was centralized and closely overseen. The

[43] JRF (2011) *Asset Transfer*, IVAR study.
[44] For example, OTS Ministers Phil Hope, Angela Smith, and Kevin Brennan.

Adventure Capital Fund team[45] bid successfully to run Futurebuilders, and it also managed the Community Builders Programme, the loan element of the Modernisation Fund and the Department of Health's Social Enterprise Investment Fund.

By contrast, the USA seems to have demonstrated a tendency towards more traditional patterns of hierarchical coordination and implementation of policy, albeit with consultative processes and perhaps negotiation with advocacy coalitions (especially in relation to legislation). Indeed, the USA stands out as *not* having convened and utilized a taskforce approach to policy development, prior to the G8 inspired National Advisory Board in 2013. This may be due, in part, to the relatively large size and political influence of the community finance sector in the USA, with its clear and focused legislative priorities and limited incentive to 'muddy the waters'. It is possible, too, that at least at the federal level difficulties in reaching agreement in Congress have had the practical effect of restricting what could be done by the administration to the repurposing or refocusing of existing programmes, rather than launching new initiatives.

Be that as it may, the UK and the USA have in common a reliance on the construction of temporary policy groups responding to specific issues, rather than building up more institutionalized governance systems for the field of social finance. The contrast with the more corporatist approaches in Quebec is clear. In the latter case, an economic crisis mobilized all social actors, including the private sector, to collaborate in designing an effective transformative strategy. That experience still informs many initiatives in the social economy today. But the unavoidable tension between hierarchical government and collaborative governance can occasionally erupt in the form of unilateral action. For example, in 2004 the then Liberal government reviewed the governance of the publically funded *Centres Locaux de Developpments* (CLD) and despite strong opposition, reduced the representation of civil society on their boards.[46] Government thereby transformed multi-stakeholder boards into ones dominated by elected officials. Opponents argued that a successful and innovative model of deliberative democracy was on this occasion being trumped by the centralized power of representative democracy. Keeping the militancy and the commitment to economic democracy alive has been seen as difficult as these citizen-based initiatives became institutionalized and faced all the challenges to democracy that institutionalization implies.

Another recurring feature of these policy processes are tensions and differences among the third-sector/social-economy participants—for much of the time, they were no more coherent and single-minded than government. In the UK, for example, some were enthusiastic supporters of social finance, seeing enterprise and investment as a way to reduce grant-dependency, and hence

---

[45] Since 2009 under the trading name of Social Investment Business.
[46] Bill 34, passed by the Government of Quebec in 2004, transformed the governance of CLDs. This was met with strong opposition.

gain increased autonomy and resilience. At the same time, others argued that in practice this approach meant reduced grant-giving, more scrutiny of organizational performance by funders and government and, hence, decreased independence. Of course, everyone could agree on the desirability of funds and financial institutions better tailored to the sector and its distinctive requirements. But what was the sector, and what were those requirements? For some, the new hybrid forms of organization and finance and their associated business practices were 'other' and threatened to undermine the distinctiveness and purposes of their sector. Nevertheless, traditional charities and established co-operatives tended to go along with government social finance policy (perhaps reluctantly), in order to gain access to finance for revenue and development. Comparable debates have taken place in the USA and Quebec.

Finally, it is important to stress that though these governance processes may be relatively open and inclusive, this does *not* mean that all groups will be equally embraced and their ideas absorbed into public policy mix. This is very clear in the UK where an attempt was made to connect government thinking around social finance to the debates on the future of banking and financial services—in the light not just of the 2008 crisis, but of a continuing series of scandals. Those involved included UKSIF (the sustainable investment and finance association which had been very influential in relation to community investment). UKSIF has always promoted a broader conception of social finance, one embracing the totality of ethical and socially responsible investment, not just finance for the disadvantaged or harnessing mainstream finance for social activity.[47]

This wider view was also reflected in the Carnegie UK Trust Inquiry into the Future of Civil Society in the UK and Ireland (2010) in its views on a more 'civil economy'. These went beyond brokering-in additional funds to build up a specialist, 'social sector' finance system alongside the mainstream. Rather, the idea was to bring greater financial pluralism to the mainstream, addressing the need for financial products and services to meet broader societal needs (such as long-term care or trustworthy pension provision), and greater engagement by social actors within all aspects of financial design, regulation, and provision. Despite the standing of many of those involved, the near universal and long-running concern with the problems identified, and the opportunities provided by the effective public ownership of two very large banks (and a post office system also under review), these ideas did not achieved any traction.

In summary, it is suggested here that public policy in relation to social finance seems to follow a similar broad trajectory in different jurisdictions—albeit unevenly and at different speeds of development. In the first place, it appears that policymakers have not typically started with the idea of

---

[47] <http://www.uksif.org>.

developing broad institutional structures to build a social finance marketplace in any of the ways that this and related terms are now being used. Rather, in the three countries considered here, public policies to support social finance started out as issue-driven problem-solving by governments. But as more issues were tackled using similar approaches and as these developments came to be explained and justified in terms of the broad policy narratives, the infrastructure supporting social finance grew in scale and refinement across different domains. These developments may have been proclaimed 'new'—and they do indeed often include innovative elements—but they invariably built on existing agencies and practices. Indeed, the course of development was often strongly influenced by the engagement in policy processes of those representing socially owned and/or socially responsible enterprise (in both their established and emergent forms).

At some point this emerging infrastructure with its patchwork of supportive public policies started to be recognized and labelled as 'social finance' (or some similar broad term), and considered as a distinct field with a record of achievement, a developing ecosystem of specialist practitioners, and a growing array of specialist funds and financial instruments. Then the market became more institutionalized and normalized with bespoke legal adaptations, regulatory changes, and enduring government-endorsed agencies.

It seems clear, then, that these developments were marked *both* by path-dependence (the particularities of local institutional regimes and issues matter enormously) *and* by a degree of convergence. That convergence has been limited to date, but it has been evident in the types of instruments developed and by the international transfer of policy ideas 'in good currency'. So, policy agendas focused on social finance have been developed through different institutional configurations in both liberal market economies and coordinated market economies. The G8 Social Impact Investment Task Force took this coordination across policy contexts to another level.

In all likelihood, this work will continue for many years—simply because it is not in government's gift to create a full-blown, differentiated ('mature') social finance marketplace alone. That will depend crucially on the co-evolution of investor preferences, financial instruments, social and environmental businesses, support structures and services, and so on. Indeed, some important developments—most notably, the development of web-based peer lending and crowdfunding—have been taking place quite independently of government. The current policy patchworks in the three countries considered here are also subject to continuing revision and development as various pieces of unfinished business are progressed—including the idea of a social stock exchange, and the challenge of clarifying governance and financial control issues within hybrid organizations, particularly in relation to forms of equity.

Nevertheless, this chapter's analysis suggests one answer to the question of what a mature social finance marketplace would look like: it would be one where the patchwork of measures had become quite comprehensive and familiar. However, this still begs a question around 'comprehensive in relation to what?' Or, to put it another way, to what does the *social* in social finance refer in different cultural and political contexts? Currently, there seem to be three main answers:

- Social refers to the social *sector*, and especially to socially owned enterprises within it—this is the view associated with and upheld by third sector/social economy bodies
- Social refers to the social *outcomes* of an investment—the view underpinning the impact investment movement and the concern with social innovation
- Social refers to the social (re-)*embedding* of finance—the view that the failings of financial markets and institutions are best corrected by market-shaping interventions to ensure appropriate and local/regional banking facilities and services are provided (cf. Nicholls, 2010)

Future policy developments at a national level, as well as transnational policy transfers, focused on social finance may well have to address and attempt to resolve the relationship of these three conceptualizations.

▓ REFERENCES

Alcock, P. (2012). *The Big Society: A New Policy Environment for the Third Sector?* Birmingham: Third Sector Research Centre.

Battilana, J., Leca, B., and Boxenbaum, E. (2009). 'How Actors Change Institutions: Towards a Theory of Institutional Entrepreneurship', *Academy of Management Annals*, 3(1): 65–107.

Big Society Capital (2014). *Social Investment: From Ambition to Action. Annual Review 2013*. London: Big Society Capital.

Brown, A., and Norman, W. (2011). *Lighting the Touchpaper: Growing the Market for Social Investment in England*. London: Boston Consulting Group and Young Foundation.

Cabinet Office (2014). *The Public Services (Social Value) Act 2012: One Year On*. London: Cabinet Office.

Carnegie UK Trust (2010). 'Inquiry into the Future of Civil Society into the UK and Ireland', Carnegie Trust, London.

Charity Commission (2013). 'Charities and Investment Matters: A Guide for Trustees'. (CC14). London.

CUA (Commission on Unclaimed Assets) (2007). 'The Social Investment Bank, Its Organisation and Role in Driving Development of the Third Sector', CUA, London.

Crouch, C. (2011). *The Strange Non-Death of Neo-Liberalism*. London: Polity Press.

Gregory, D. (2009). 'UK Government and Social Investment', Office for the Third Sector presentation at the Open University Business School Social Investment Seminar series.

Hall and Soskice (2001). *Varieties of Capitalism*. Oxford: Oxford University Press.

HM Government (2013). *Growing the Social Investment Market: 2013 Progress Update*. <www.gov.uk>, accessed 1 November 2014.

ICF GHK in association with BMG Research (2013), 'Growing the Social Investment Market: The Landscape and Economic Impact'. City of London.

Joseph Roundtree Foundation (2011). *Asset Transfer*. IVAR study.

Kay, J. (2003). *The Truth about Markets*. London: Allen Lane.

Kendall, J. (2009). 'The UK: Ingredients in a Hyperactive Horizontal Policy Environment', in J. Kendall (ed.) *Handbook of Third Sector Policy in Europe: Multi-level Processes and Organised Civil Society*. Cheltenham: Edward Elgar, pp. 67–94.

Lazonick, W., and Mazzucato, M. (2013). 'The Risk-reward Nexus in the Innovation-inequality Relationship: Who Takes the Risks? Who Gets the Rewards?' *Industrial and Corporate Change*, 22(4): 1093–128.

Lord Hodgson (2012). *Trusted and Independent: Giving Charity back to Charities: Review of the Charities Act 2006*. London: The Stationery Office.

Mutuals Taskforce (2012). 'Public Service Mutuals: The Next Steps'. A Mutuals Taskforce Report.

Nicholls, A. (2010). 'The Institutionalisation of Social Investment', *Journal of Social Entrepreneurship*, 1(1): 70–100.

Polanyi, K. (1945). *Origins of Our Time: The Great Transformation*. London: Gollancz.

Rubin, J. (ed.) (2007). *Financing Low Income Communities: Models, Obstacles and Future Directions*. New York: Russell Sage Foundation.

Social Investment and Finance Team (2013). 'G8 Social Impact Investment Forum: Outputs and Agreed Actions'. London: Cabinet Office.

Stiglitz, J. E., Jaramillo-Vallejo, J., and Park, Y. C. (1993). 'The Role of the State in Financial Markets', *World Bank Research Observer: Annual Conference on Development Economics Supplement*: 19–61.

Thake, S., and Lingayah, S. (2009). *Investing in Thriving Communities: The Final External Evaluation Report on the Adventure Capital Fund*. London Metropolitan University.

Weber, M. (1930). The Protestant Work Ethic and the Spirit of Capitalism. London: Alan and Unwin.

Westall, A. (2010). 'UK Government Policy and "Social Investment"', *Voluntary Sector Review*, 1(1): 119–24.

15 Building the social finance infrastructure

Rodney Schwartz, Clare Jones, and Alex Nicholls

Introduction

Over the past few years, a growing number of politicians, business leaders, media commentators, and academics have been analysing and assessing the social finance model as a source of resources for social enterprise and social business. While fiscal constraints have increasingly diminished governments' power to tackle social problems, charities have also been under financial pressure and large corporations have faced an erosion of public trust in their motives and actions—threatening long-term profits. As a consequence, many observers are hoping that the social enterprise model, and its attendant funding mechanisms, can help to solve some of society's most intractable 'wicked' problems.

A strong case has been made elsewhere for social enterprises as contributors to public good (Nicholls, 2006; Howard, 2012; Montgomery et al., 2012; Wood et al., 2012; Eggers and Macmillan, 2013). Social Enterprise UK regularly publishes reviews of the UK social enterprise sector and its importance.[1] In the 2013 survey of over 850 social enterprises, there was evidence of strong growth in the sector, with the Government reporting a £24bn contribution of social enterprise to the economy (SEUK, 2013). With mainstream players entering the social investment market, it has grown remarkably over the past five years—largely due to investment in the infrastructure (Swersky and Brown, 2012), but as much of the literature points out, it is far from institutionalized (Nicholls, 2013). Addressing infrastructure needs can prepare social finance for more rapid growth; Bannick and Goldman pointed out that:

> Industry players often have common needs that are most economically served in collective form. Infrastructure players advance a sector by addressing these collective needs, thus helping to build a supportive ecosystem for entrepreneurial innovation ... a lack of infrastructure can disrupt an otherwise burgeoning sector. (Bannick and Goldman 2012: 1)

In this context, what follows here explores the key issues in growing the social finance infrastructure to grow a mainstream market where deep, sustained

---

[1] These can be seen at <http://www.socialenterprise.org.uk/policy-campaigns/policy/research>.

Basic Requirements for a Social Economy: formation of social enterprises; available capital; enabling infrastructure

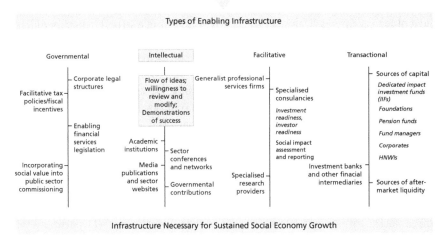

Figure 15.1. Social impact investment infrastructure

impact and scale are possible.[2] The chapter begins with an exploration of the basic requirements for a social economy, before exploring the four key types of infrastructure in which investment must be made: governmental, facilitative, intellectual, and transactional.

There are some basic requirements for a social economy—including the formation of social enterprises and available capital. Enabling infrastructure is the third of these core parts, and Figure 15.1 below demonstrates how the four types of enabling infrastructure support the development of social finance. This chapter will explore each of these in turn, analysing the areas in which each contributes to a strong and sustainable infrastructure for social finance.

Market intermediation

In social finance, as in mainstream finance, the market is structured by three interlinked elements: supply, demand and intermediation.

(Nicholls 2013: 165)

---

[2] Although much of the discussion in this chapter will be relevant to contexts throughout the world, it is largely rooted in a discussion of the situation in the UK. This is because the UK is frequently perceived to be the market leader from the standpoint of social finance innovation (Bishop and Green, 2010), where the emergent market 'fuses together two relative strengths of the UK—skill in finance and skill in civic action, organisation and delivery' (Shanmugalingam et al., 2011). For the purposes of this chapter, the process by which social enterprises secure capital is referred to as 'social finance'. In social finance, resources are harnessed to facilitate the growth and development of enterprises that generate a beneficial impact on society. Such enterprises exist predominantly to achieve social, ethical, and environmental (simplified here into 'social') benefits, and these are considered to be 'social enterprises'.

Social entrepreneurs require capital to start their organizations, to develop them past proof of concept and to bring them to scale. In the UK, successive governments have supported the growth of the sector with grants, funds, and a host of tax incentives (Cabinet Office, 2013). The single largest experiment has been the wholesale social investment bank, Big Society Capital (BSC). BSC will mobilize over £600m in funding (coming two thirds from the unclaimed assets left in high street banks and one third from large commercial banks) to grow the social sector and make it more sustainable via co-investment aimed at accelerating the social investment market. Similar experiments are underway in the USA, Canada, Australia, Germany, Japan, and at the EU level. In 2011, for example, the Australian Senate Inquiry researched how to build their impact investing market, establishing three Social Enterprise and Development Investment Funds (SEDIFs). As with BSC in the UK, the funds are designed to catalyse social impact investing in Australia. The Australian government provided $20m in grants to seed the establishment of these three social investment funds as cornerstone investments (Department of Education Employment and Workplace Relations, 2012).

UK CASE STUDY BIG SOCIETY CAPITAL (BSC)

Established by the coalition government in April 2012, this organization was originally conceived under the previous Labour government. Its overriding purpose is to create a thriving social investment marketplace in the UK and to further its global leadership of that marketplace with London as the international hub (Big Society Capital, 2012). As outlined above, BSC will be funded an initial sum from unclaimed deposits as well as by commercial banks—this amount is expected to be £600m, but we may see this sum increase considerably. In addition to its role as 'market champion', BSC makes investments in social impact investment intermediaries. Importantly, it does so as a wholesaler. Thus, rather than make direct investments into social enterprises, which would disrupt initiatives already underway, Big Society Capital supports those that already exist; its main focus is providing seed capital for impact investment funds.

In the mainstream economy, banks, investment banks, and other advisors have been established to facilitate the flow of capital into investments. These firms are the plumbing designed to make the process of capital allocation as efficient as possible (Bishop and Green, 2010). Indeed, the OECD noted the importance of infrastructure development in the UK venture capital industry to support the sector 'ultimately resulted in tremendous growth' (OECD 2004: 194), and the World Economic Forum also highlighted the importance of intermediaries themselves:

However, there are only a limited number of intermediaries in the social finance sector and many are only small, niche or specialized players. These intermediaries will need to grow in number and scale in order for the social finance market to reach maturity. Mainstream investors will need mainstream social finance intermediaries. (World Economic Forum 2013: 23)

Bishop and Green noted:

Although the mainstream financial sector can certainly do better, it is hard to fault the efforts of their [intermediary] counterparts in the social sector . . . the greatest weakness of these "good-brokers" is that they are underfunded, not least because philanthropists and indeed governments too often regard investing in infrastructure as inferior to funding programs that have a direct impact on the needy. However, the infrastructure of virtue's intermediaries may actually ensure that those direct programs deliver a far higher social return on investment. (Bishop and Green 2010: 31)

A range of research has also highlighted the importance of the intermediation function that brings social finance capital to social entrepreneurs.[3]

For intermediary firms to come into existence there must be a sufficient level of transactions taking place to ensure that any reasonable fees applied are affordable for the firms receiving the capital and that the level of fees paid is sufficient to reward the providers to offer the required level of assistance needed. These intermediaries also require an assortment of other related activities for the process to work properly—such as legal, accounting, consulting, and other relevant support services.

In the mainstream economy, all three components of this ecosystem grow at a natural pace—consistent with the underlying levels of capital flows and economic activity to which they are attached. Politicians and others—ambitious for rapid growth in social investment—have been keen for this to happen faster than a natural pace would allow.[4] In the UK in particular, where substantial budget cuts put pressure on all those providing public services, social enterprises have been looked at as somewhat of a 'Holy Grail' solution to maintaining welfare services under conditions of austerity. Some of this has proved simply unrealistic, but in the hope of accelerating market development, the UK government has poured more than £1bn into the sector, creating or fostering a range of funds with a social impact orientation. The hope was that such funds would create their own demand, as social enterprises formed in response to increased capital on the supply-side.[5] Some feel this assumption has proven overly optimistic, although there is debate on both sides as to where the balance lies. Moreover, the necessary market infrastructure has been underinvested in, and the levels of transactions are currently too low to encourage natural entry without proactive support.

Thus, it is clear that increased investment into the market infrastructure of social finance will be essential going forward (Wood, Thornley, and Grace, 2012). Well-conceived infrastructure creates substantial leverage; Emerson and Bugg-Levin suggested that:

Impact investing will take off when its pioneers and newcomers collaborate effectively, building the infrastructure that will enable the next wave of talent and capital to join the field. (Bugg-Levin and Emerson, 2011: 159)

The remainder of this chapter focuses on delineating the elements of an effective infrastructure for the social finance market into four categories: governmental, facilitative, intellectual, and transactional. These are each discussed in turn before some thoughts are offered regarding the logical ordering of these infrastructural developments and conclusions drawn.

Categories of market infrastructure

GOVERNMENTAL INFRASTRUCTURE

Governments possess a wide range of options to put in place the necessary elements of infrastructure to enable the social finance market to flourish

---

[3] For other examples, see Bishop and Green (2010); Shanmugalingam et al. (2011); Keohane (2012); Meehan and Jonker (2012); The Rockefeller Foundation (2012).

[4] See the UK government's 2013 report 'Growing the Social Investment Market' (Cabinet Office, 2013).

[5] See, for example, Ronald Cohen's interview with the GIIN:

There is huge latent demand for impact investment capital. Lack of funding is prevalent in the social sector everywhere across the world. If money isn't perceived to be available, the challenge of raising capital appears so great that skilled, successful people do not take the risk of launching themselves into a social venture. If money is perceived as being readily available, people take the risk of launching out. In this sense, increasing the supply of money will create its own demand. (GIIN, 2012)

(Wood, Thornley, and Grace, 2012). In the UK policy context, the Government defined its role as:

Increasing the supply of finance for social investment; stimulating and supporting demand for social investment; and improving the legal, tax and regulatory environment for social investment and social enterprise. (HM Government, 2012: 8)

From an analysis of policymaking over the past decade, five elements that are central to the creation of an enabling environment for the social finance can be discerned. Each is considered in turn.

Regulation

On the demand side of the social finance market, the state can innovate to create new legal forms for investee organizations that are designed to be well suited to taking social finance investment. In the USA, there has historically been a very clear delineation between 'for-profit' and 'not-for-profit' companies: for-profit companies exist to maximize value on behalf of the company's shareholders,[6] whilst charity law prescribes very carefully the extent to which not-for-profit companies are permitted to get involved in commercial activities.

Various legal forms for social enterprises in different countries can support the development of social enterprises and their capital-raising efforts. Many commentators stress the difficulty for social enterprises to raise capital with 'the lack of an appropriate legal form' (Doeringer 2010: 315), so legal structures are a key part of the infrastructure necessary for social finance to flourish.

In some cases, this will not mean a separate legal form for social enterprises but a range of other forms so entrepreneurs can choose the structure most appropriate for their aims. In New Zealand, there are a range of structures that can apply to social enterprises without one specifically assigned legal form— from limited liability companies and industrial and provident societies to co-operatives and Maori land trusts. None of these are designed specifically for social enterprises, and a recent report by the Department for Internal Affairs stressed that a new legal form was not a priority for the sector (New Zealand Department of Internal Affairs, 2013).

In Europe, legal forms are often seen as key to the development of the sector. Since the early 1990s, almost every European country has authorized its own social co-operative entity. The Italian parliament began with a social solidarity co-operative in 1991, with 7,300 of them set up in the fifteen years following. Portugal followed in 1997 with a social solidarity co-operative and

---

[6] See the famous Dodge v. Ford Motor Company case, where the Supreme Court found Henry Ford owed a duty to operate his business to profit his shareholders, rather than the community or employees—and for a counterpoint, Lynn Stout's book *The Shareholder Value Myth: How Putting Shareholders First Harms Investors, Corporations, and the Public* (Stout, 2012).

Spain in 1999 with the social initiative co-operative. Belgium attempted to set up a form specifically for social enterprises. In 1995, they set up a new corporate form—the Société à Finalité Sociale (SFS) 'a for-profit company that has additional restrictions on profit distribution' (Doeringer, 2010: 309). In reality, however, this is more like a label than a separate legal form, and due to the restrictions it offers, many social entrepreneurs prefer to avoid this form and simply set up for-profit companies. Indeed, it is generally agreed that the SFS has not been particularly successful—it is important, then, that specific legal forms for social enterprise are fit for purpose (not too restrictive, and offering benefits when compared to other non-profit or for-profit structures) if they are to support sector growth.

To foster the development in the USA of social finance, it has been necessary to begin to develop new structures that encourage this (E. T. Jackson and Associates Ltd, 2012). Social enterprises can set up as for-profit entities or non-profit corporations. Non-profit corporations have tax exempt status, but none of their net earnings can benefit shareholders or individuals, making it inappropriate for many entrepreneurs, while for-profit companies create barriers for capital raising and issues around redistribution of profits of over 10 per cent to associated charities. Recently, the benefit corporation (B-Corp) has been gaining traction; this is a private certification for for-profit entities that meet 80 out of 200 social impact measures. The "Benefit Corporation" is a corporate entity that is for-profit (currently only in 30 States) and includes positive societal impact in its legally defined goals. Additionally, the USA's hybrid legal form for social enterprises is the low profit limited liability company (L3C). The L3C is for-profit with limited liability for owners; crucially, it allows L3Cs to issue equity to raise capital and also makes it easier for them to raise 'programme-related investment' from foundations (Esposito, 2013: 682).

It is generally agreed that the UK has one of the most robust social enterprise sectors in terms of a broad range of legal structures available to social entrepreneurs looking to seek investment (Bates, Wells, and Braithwaite, 2005; Esposito, 2013). A short exploration of these different forms demonstrates how regulation can enable the creation and growth of social businesses and enterprise by offering a range of options to investors and investees. Firstly, the limited company offers a degree of flexibility for balancing the interests of stakeholders that is not possible in the USA. Even in the more mainstream company limited by shares (CLS) actions that are not of a profit-maximizing nature are permitted and the company's behaviour can be guided by its Memorandum and Articles of Association (the governing constitutional documents).

Social mission can be strengthened further within more restrictive company limited by guarantee (CLG) legal form. In the CLG, there is a requirement that members give a guarantee to cover a company's liability—in a CLG, there are no shareholders, but the company must have one or more members. The members attend general meetings and vote; they can appoint and remove directors, essentially having ultimate control over the company. However, the guarantee is nominal, normally being limited to £1. The members of a CLG become its owners and have broadly the same powers as shareholders in a CLS. The UK Labour government also introduced the community interest company (CIC) that specifically sought to enable equity shareholders and debt holders to invest in a social enterprise where assets are locked into a clearly stipulated social purpose and returns to providers of capital are capped.[7] Furthermore, the CIC was designed to provide a 'good housekeeping seal of approval' to the venture and attest to its social and ethical orientation. However, to date, CICs have paid their investors minimal returns (Regulator of Community Interest Companies, 2010; Schwartz, 2010) despite over 9,000 registrations by 2014. For investors seeking to develop co-operatives and mutually owned companies, the industrial and provident society (IPS) legal form offers a well-established regulatory form (Mason, Kirkbride, and Bryde, 2007).

It is not only companies that can take on social investment; charities can also receive funding in this way. One example of this in the UK is that of the London Early Years Foundation (LEYF). This is a charity that is over 100 years old, providing community nurseries throughout London for disadvantaged children. Wanting to source more sustainable revenues, LEYF worked with intermediary ClearlySo (with funding from the Government's Investment Contract Readiness Fund)[8] to structure a model suitable for social investment, using cross-subsidy where profitable nurseries in more affluent areas allow them to provide free or discounted places for children in more deprived communities. They have thus far raised £1.25m debt investment from two institutional impact investors—Bridges Ventures and Big Issue Invest (White, 2014).

Aside from direct debt investment, charities can also receive funding through social bonds. The UK's first institutional investment into charity bonds was into the disability organization Scope.[9] They had worked with the Investing for Good initiative to develop the first exchange-listed social bond, and raised £2m in May 2012 as the first part of a £20m social bond programme. The investment came from high-net-worth individuals, foundations, and institutional investors, including Rathbones and NESTA (The Good Analyst, 2012; Investing for Good, 2012).

Regulatory issues also affect the ability of enterprises to raise capital from trusts and foundations. While concepts of and regulation around fiduciary duty are insufficiently aligned with impact investing, capital that could be unlocked to support the mainstreaming of social finance will remain inaccessible.

---

[7] See the website of the UK CIC Association, which regulates CICs, much like the Charity Commission for the third sector: <http://www.cicassociation.org.uk>.

[8] See <http://www.beinvestmentready.org.uk> for more details.

[9] See <http://www.scope.org.uk>.

The US National Advisory Board on Impact Investing specifically high-lighted the regulatory restrictions around fiduciary duty in the USA (for pension funds as well as foundations) and restrictions on foundation invest-ments in for-profit enterprises as barriers to growing the social finance market in the USA. In the UK, meanwhile, the Social Investment Taskforce recom-mended in their 2000 report *Enterprising Communities: Wealth Beyond Wel-fare* that the Chancellor of the Exchequer produce 'legislative and regulatory changes to provide greater latitude and encouragement for charitable trusts and foundations to invest in community development finance' (quoted in Cabinet Office, 2010: 2), with the Charity Commission publishing guidance stating clearly that charities and foundations can make social investments as well as grants. The Esmée Fairbairn Foundation in the UK is one example of a foundation that has become increasingly active as an investor in this space in the past ten years.

Regulation that is supportive of social impact investing can be seen in countries like South Africa, which now requires investors 'consider any factor which may materially affect the sustainable long-term performance of the investment, including those of an environmental, social, and governance character' (US National Advisory Board on Impact Investing, 2014: 22). For now, these changes are largely more aligned with mission-related investing (MRI)[10] or The United Nations Principles for Responsible Investment (PRI)[11] than with impact investment, but this vision of fiduciary duty that encom-passes such externalities is an important precursor to the infrastructure necessary to support social finance. There are over 1,200 investors with \$34 trn in assets engaged with PRI—this includes the Norwegian Government Pension Fund (US National Advisory Board on Impact Investing 2014). With such backing for the PRI from foundations and funds that consider fiduciary duty in their investing, the stage is set for further entrants into the impact investing space; the regulatory environment, then, must encourage this if social finance is to mainstream.

Fiscal Policy

In many countries governments have put in place tax incentives to encourage investment, particularly in early-stage growth companies. Capital gains taxes are often significantly lower for social enterprises as a way to encourage such investment. In the UK, for example, capital gains tax relief is offered for certain regulated social enterprises (such as CICs or charities). It has initially

---

[10] Mission-related investing, where foundations ensure their investment portfolio makes invest-ments that are aligned with their overall aims and values—a useful report being the 2008 Rockefeller Foundation Report *Mission-Related Investing: A Policy and Implementation Guide for Foundation Trustees.*

[11] The United Nations has developed the Principles for Responsible Investment (see <http://www.unpri.org>), which offer possible options for incorporating environmental, social, and governance issues into investment practices across asset classes.

been put in place for capital gains arising from 6 April 2014 to 5 April 2019. Moreover, in many Western countries, individuals donating sums to charities will derive some fiscal benefit from doing so and this is well documented as a driver of giving (Wood and Hagerman, 2010).[12] Once in place, such fiscal incentives are very difficult to remove, as interest groups develop to secure their continuance. They are also powerful in the signalling messages they send more widely, with some arguing that improving the tax environment will itself act as a catalyst for further development of the social sector more widely (Worthstone and Wragge & Co LLP, 2013).

Social finance, owing to its relative newness, has lacked such powerful interest groups to lobby in its favour. Moreover, they have generally not secured particularly favourable tax treatment and in some countries equivalent social investments do not even generate the same fiscal advantages as conventional investments. Where some tax advantages were granted, as in the case of Community Investment Tax Relief (CITR) in the UK, so many conditions and restrictions were put in place that the amount of money flowing into this deposit scheme has been well below expectations (approximately £86m since 2003 against estimates of £200m a year, or £2bn in a decade (CDFA, 2012)). Partly to remedy this, in April 2014, the UK government introduced Social Investment Tax Relief[13] as a way of further stimulating the social finance market.

CASE STUDY SOCIAL INVESTMENT TAX RELIEF IN THE UK

Social Investment Tax Relief, officially announced in March 2014's Budget, provides incentives to investors to invest in regulated social enterprises. It complements existing UK tax relief schemes for investors such as the Enterprise Investment Scheme and the Seed Enterprise Investment Scheme. The tax relief comes as a deduction from income tax, equal to 30 per cent of the amount invested and began from 6 April 2014. The relief can be claimed if investing into a charity, a CIC, or a community benefit society (Bencom). While some critics have argued it may skew the market by prioritizing only certain types of regulated social enterprise, others have lauded it as an opportunity to bring more private capital and angel investment into the market by de-risking investments (Evill, 2014).

There are widespread arguments about how to put in place the necessary fiscal environment to accelerate social finance (Cohen, 2011). Some argue that making the sector more attractive to investors will encourage capital and accelerate its growth (Worthstone and Wragge & Co LLP, 2013). Others believe such incentives are market distortions that have very little impact on the overall levels of investment and are a subsidy to the better-off (those who usually have assets to invest). However, there is broad agreement that social finance should operate on a level playing field with mainstream investing (Heaney, 2010). A good example of this is in France where the *Projet de loi*

---

[12] These incentives range from 1% to 10% tax deductions in the Netherlands on charitable donations to the generous variable tax credit of Canada, where $200 or less will receive a 17% tax credit, and higher-value gifts attract a 29% credit (CAF, 2006).

[13] See for details <http://www.gov.uk/government/publications/social-investment-tax-relief-factsheet>.

relatif à l'économie social et solidaire proposed a new definition of social enterprise, better access for these enterprises to dedicated investments (access to Banque Publique d'Investissements funds), a secured legal environment and support to local community initiatives (Moscovici and Hamon, 2013).

One example of fiscal intervention that is often ignored comes in the form of funds established by governments to invest in social enterprises directly or into the infrastructure to support them. The existence of such funds, even if they require a private sector match, dramatically reduces the overall cost of capital in the social sector. An example of such a wholesale bank is Big Society Capital, as discussed above. In Australia, three funds have been established with a similar set of purposes with a total value of A$40.6m—A$20.6m in private investment combined with a A$20m grant from the Australian government (Cohen, 2011). The EU, both under its own auspices and within the European Investment Fund, has also explored launching funds with a similar purpose. One example is the Social Impact Accelerator (SIA) fund-of-funds—the first pan-European public–private partnership for impact investing launched in May 2013—seeking to mobilize €60m (EVPA, 2013). Similarly, one of President Obama's early actions in office was to set up the Social Innovation Fund (Trivedi, 2010). In its third iteration since 2010, the fund has made federal grants of over $177m and leveraged funding of $423m in non-federal match commitments, including from private donors (Corporation for National and Community Service, 2013). By giving grants to intermediaries of $1–$5m annually for up to five years, with intermediaries providing match funding, which they then distribute to organizations to further their reach and build rigorous evidence about what works. All these vehicles subsidize overall capital formation and are, therefore, an alternative to tax credits, grants, and other fiscal subsidies.

It is an integral part of infrastructure building that governments create facilitative fiscal environments that stimulate social impact investing, providing incentives and opportunities for institutional and individual investors to move into the market at an early stage, catalysing their capital.

Financial Services Legislation

As noted in the section above, individuals undertaking donations to charities frequently derive some fiscal advantages. To protect against abuse, it is often the case that charities are required in each country to register with a national authority that helps to ensure the charity or foundation operates in accordance with some social objective or purpose. In countries such as Italy in particular these organizations have long-standing histories and their memberships are enormous (Palmer, 1997). This is not the case for formal social enterprises, which are in general more recent entrants to the scene—although, of course, mutuals, co-operatives, and other socially oriented companies have existed in Europe for decades. One such exception is the Mondragon Cooperative

Corporation, a Spanish firm very much considered a social enterprise and founded in 1956 (Bhawuk, Mrazek, and Munusamy, 2009).

Moreover, although the pump-priming work of foundations and grant-making institutions is key in developing the market (Bannick and Goldman, 2012), social enterprises are typically not funded with grants at the point of scale, but with social impact investments. These investments are generally governed differently from charitable donations and are closer to mainstream investment. In the UK, financial investing has been regulated by the Financial Conduct Authority (FCA)[14] that aims to protect investors against fraudulent or inappropriate behaviour by financial promoters. Such regulation is understandable; however, it is relatively costly to those firms undertaking financial promotions. These costs and restrictions can prove onerous to the much smaller social finance sector (O'Donohoe, et al., 2010). Furthermore, the fact that many social investors are not seeking to maximize profits, and that many of the normal regulations assume predominantly financial objectives, means that much of the existing regulatory framework is ill suited to support social finance. A key part of the infrastructure needed for social finance to grow is not only a proactive enabling environment, but also the removal of existing barriers set up for more mainstream financial or organizational regulation that limit the potential of early-stage social ventures to grow and scale their impacts.

CASE STUDY CROWDFUNDING AND SOCIAL INVESTMENT

With the growth of crowdfunding in recent years, social entrepreneurs are finding it can be used to complement investment from individuals and institutions. Some platforms, such as Kickstarter use rewards-based crowdfunding, while others—such as Seedrs—offer investors equity in the business. Social business Breezie, which supports the digitally excluded to get online, raised £600k investment in June 2014, including £180k angel investment from Clearly Social Angels and then secured crowdfunding capital from the CrowdBnk online platform.

One of the leading UK equity-based crowdfunding platforms, CrowdCube, raised £1.6m in sixteen minutes online in July 2014 for their own capital raise; this crowdfunding was underpinned by a £3.4m investment from a venture capital firm, showing the power of the crowd when combined with institutional investment. As crowdfunding continues to grow, regulation will need to be supportive of equity-based as well as reward-based funding if social impact businesses are to garner the potential in this market.

PUBLIC SECTOR COMMISSIONING

In most developed countries, government spending represents something between one third and two thirds of economic activity. For this reason, how government behaves as a purchaser can be important. Public sector commissioning can, thus, be key in infrastructure building for the social finance.

Some evidence suggests that public sector commissioning has been historically open to abuse, and observers certainly agree that it is in the public interest for the government to try

---

[14] The previous Financial Services Authority was replaced in 2013 by the Prudential Regulation Authority (the PRA) and The Financial Conduct Authority (the FCA) <http://ukgicompliance.co.uk/fca>.

to secure good value for money in terms of purchasing products and services (Public Administration Select Committee, 2008). However, it is important to recognize that the cheapest bid may not represent the best value. Questions around what represents 'good value' have become increasingly important to those in the social enterprise sector because of the belief that socially oriented businesses generate value to governments above and beyond what is included in a bid. A growing body of supporters believe this needs to be taken into account.

In the UK there has been a governmental response to this, with legislation specifically designed to encourage public sector commissioning that is in line with the values of a social economy. The Public Services (Social Value) Act passed the UK Parliament in the first quarter of 2012 (Cabinet Office, 2013). It aimed to ensure that public sector commissioning take into account the unique social, ethical, and environmental impact of bidders. Thus, community-owned groups or social enterprises should find it easier to compete with large corporate bidders for public sector contracts because commissioners became obliged to take these factors previously considered external to the contract into account. By internalizing such externalities into the bidding process, the additional value of bids coming from social and community-owned enterprises should be clear.

In the Cabinet Office's review of the first year of the Act, they highlighted the wealth of resources created by the commissioner and provider communities to embed social value in procurement activity. One example of the outcome of the Act can been seen in the work of Trading for Good, which created a digital platform allowing small and medium businesses (SMEs) to demonstrate their social value and thus improve their access to public sector commissioning; over 3,000 SMEs are now using this service (Cabinet Office, 2014: 6).

The rules of commissioning and engagement with the private sector are another critical piece of the infrastructure necessary to foster social finance. Prior to the Social Value Act, the rules of economic activity and commercial transactions were constructed so that organizations oriented to tendering on price alone were advantaged. Governments can also move further in this direction by increasing costs to firms of negative externalities—those generated by firms where activities pass costs (such as the cleaning up of polluted rivers and lakes) on to all of society. By effectively increasing the costs of those firms generating negative externalities, governments further adjust the rules in favour of social enterprises. Such rules of engagement are another useful piece of infrastructure for the social impact investment market.

INTELLECTUAL INFRASTRUCTURE

The development and growth of the social finance market can also be facilitated by supportive intellectual infrastructure (Mitchell, Kingston, and Goodall, 2008; Freireich and Fulton, 2009). For such infrastructure to flourish there are three necessary baselines conditions that can be observed in those countries where progress has taken place:

- There must be a regular inflow of new ideas that are open to public debate
- There must be a willingness to review initiatives and be open to the possibility of having made mistakes. Not to do so runs the risk of misdirected attempts and a considerable waste of resources. For example, errors in the original conception of the CIC corporate form in the UK meant that progress was greatly slowed, with the Regulator of Community Interest Companies, recommending a host of changes to make CIC regulation more fit for purpose (Department for Business, Innovation & Skills, 2013).

The fact that the Government of the day was open to criticism meant that rules could be improved and restrictions eased so that the take-up of this legal structure was increased

- The dissemination of the social finance market's success stories is key to its development (Howard, 2012; Martin, 2013), with some recommending a sector-based, targeted public relations campaign to promote demonstrated successes (Freireich and Fulton, 2009). Having an array of widely known and understood cases of successful social businesses and enterprises will lead to a far more rapid diffusion throughout society of the possibilities contained in the social economy.

With these baselines in mind, it is worth exploring particular areas of informational or intellectual infrastructure that need to be assembled to further the advance of social finance. Key institutions engaged in building and developing this intellectual infrastructure are as follows.

Academic Institutions

In addition to the valuable research conducted by academic institutions into social finance, a central part of intellectual infrastructure that encourages the growth of the market is at the educational level (Baird, 2011; E. T. Jackson and Associates Ltd, 2012). For the most part it has been in business schools with a range of courses developing at undergraduate, graduate, and executive education levels. Student interest has also driven the creation of bespoke clubs formed around an interest in social finance. Such engagement by academic institutions has provided both the intellectual underpinning for the sector as well as helping build talent for the sector.

Sector Conferences and Networks

Sector conferences are proliferating around the world and bring together practitioners, policymakers, social entrepreneurs, with funders and financiers. They are vital in sharing best practice and spreading information about successful case studies, enabling newer entrants to benefit from the experiences of those firms active in the sector for some time (E. T. Jackson and Associates Ltd, 2012). Specifically, they also provide emotional support to those struggling within a sector that is still in the earliest stages of development—this is vital if the sector is to retain talent and experience. Increasingly, however, such conferences are more and more outward facing—in particular in the direction of the mainstream economy, the resources of which social entrepreneurs seek to tap into and from which they have a great deal to learn. In addition, the conferences are becoming increasingly international in scope. The Social Enterprise World Forum and US-based SOCAP have been leaders in this regard, with the Sankalp Forum playing a central role in building a global intellectual ecosystem, particularly in the Global South.

Networks centred on the intellectual development of the sector 'provide resources and services to grow the entire impact investment ecosystem' (World Economic Forum, 2013: 17). These can be groups such as the Global Impact Investing Network (GIIN) that aim to solidify definitions, research, and other intellectual scaffolding for the sector (O'Donohoe et al., 2010), as well as convening collaboration and sharing of best practice. Through bringing together those working globally, networks and conferences develop the intellectual infrastructure that is so important in an early-stage market.

Media Publications and Sector Websites

Every sector in development benefits from bespoke trade publications. These share best practice and offer case studies and success stories. News and information of general interest to sector participants is also disseminated. Usefully, these publications also offer information on job opportunities within the sector, assisting the human capital to flow freely and efficiently. Sector websites benefit from the immediacy and responsiveness permitted by online platforms, and as social media continues to grow, the building of social media networks centred on social finance will be a key part of the intellectual infrastructure as the sector moves towards the mainstream (Osburg and Schmidpeter, 2013).

The importance of dissemination of information about the successes of social finance is highlighted in a study of major Swedish investment institutions' willingness to get involved in the market. Jansson and Biel found that concerns over financial risk and market growth drive socially responsible investment forward (significantly more so than social and environmental concerns) (Jansson and Biel, 2014). As more case studies and successes come out of the sector, it is vital that these messages are communicated to the financial mainstream if institutional players are to truly get behind social finance.

'Grey' Research

A number of specialized providers have emerged to respond to the growing demand for research to accelerate the sector's growth most effectively. Such research is being done by sector practitioners and mainstream institutions (such as Nesta or J.P. Morgan) and is designed to inform policy and practice to build the social finance market This research aims to provide the evidence base necessary for encouraging further investment in the sector, especially when complemented by other intellectual infrastructure.

Governments can also play a role in promoting and creating the intellectual infrastructure for the sector. Governments can act as powerful conveners and sources of research and data collection and aggregation. However, such activity differs dramatically across countries. In the USA, the state has played a smaller role in the sector, whilst in France, for example, the state has played a leading role, complemented by a 'deliberative and organised social movement, which aimed at changing the institutional logics of the asset management field' (Crifo and Forget, 2012: 23).

Government support for intellectual infrastructure is not only relevant at the national level. In the UK, the creation in 2000 of the Social Investment Taskforce was significant in raising the profile of the sector, and there have been some strides made to disseminate successes and case studies (Patton, 2013). This was followed up with the Social Impact Investment Task Force set up in June 2013 as part of the UK leadership of the G8—a similar forum but excluding Russia and including Australia as an observer, and was an example of an initiative aimed at building an international policy agenda (Cabinet Office, 2013).

A key role played by government in creating intellectual infrastructure is through the sharing of aggregate data to create a transparent and clarified picture of the sector. The UK Cabinet Office released visual representations of data sets in early 2014 around the Social Incubator Fund and Social Impact Bonds (see Wood, 2010); these accessible data sets aimed to equip sector professionals, and those in the mainstream financial, third, and public sectors, with valuable information on the successes of the sector to date.

FACILITATIVE INFRASTRUCTURE

In order to grow social finance transactions there is a need for developed *facilitative infrastructure*, a key part of the 'capital curve' that has developed in the mainstream but is still developing in social finance (Bishop and Green, 2010). Facilitative infrastructure is organized to ensure that parties are ready and able to receive and undertake social finance capital. Much of this relates to the intermediary space between supply and demand—this is the 'plumbing' required in all well-functioning markets.

Generalist Professional Services Firms

In the mainstream financial sector, little gets done without the assistance of lawyers and accountants, and in social finance this is increasingly true as well. Lawyers, in particular, are essential in guiding social enterprises through an increasingly complex legal system in order to achieve the most flexible and effective financial structures and arrangements for organizing themselves to balance their social and financial objectives. These are driven also by the demands of those investors whose capital they seek and it is essential to get these structures right. In fact, in social finance this can be even more complex than in the mainstream because of the added complexity of social impact as an extra dimension.

Accountants ensure that social enterprises report in a fashion that is clear and transparent to their stakeholders—they also frequently assist in due diligence work. For the confidence of investors, the involvement of reputable accountants and lawyers in the social finance market is an important factor reducing the risk of investing in a social business or enterprise. Many UK professional services firms specialize in the social sector[15] and this has contributed to a growing depth of valuable expertise.

In addition to lawyers and accountants, demands have been growing for those firms providing other skills, both of a hard and soft nature. This is also taking place in mainstream investing, as firms look to enhance the effectiveness of their teams through skills development, upgrading management effectiveness, and other techniques. A growing set of such providers is willing to dedicate some of their services to the social sector and some providers concentrating solely on the sector are also emerging.

CASE STUDY BATES WELLS BRAITHWAITE (BWB)

BWB is the leading UK law firm representing charities and social enterprises. Although based in the heart of the City of London, it has always been viewed as a law firm with a difference—dedicated to providing leading-edge service to social sector firms as well as to mainstream clients. It has been particularly instrumental in some of the leading initiatives in the social impact investment sector. For example, is widely recognized as being the architect of the community interest company (CIC) form of legal structure utilized by thousands of UK social entrepreneurs. It is also entrepreneurial in its own right, having established joint ventures subsidiaries such as CaSE Insurance and Trustees Unlimited, both of which provide non-legal services to charities and social enterprises.

Specialized Consultancies

In addition to the firms mentioned above, there are organizations that play a vital and rather particular role in the capital intermediation process. One key area is investment readiness. Providers of investment readiness support typically seek to help social businesses and enterprises to secure capital. Such services might include work on a financial model or business plan as well as some assessment of the senior management team of the enterprise, its board of directors or trustees, and key aspects of its progress. The objective is to ensure that all the matters likely to be of interest to investors are addressed and that remedial actions are taken or begun wherever deemed necessary.

In the UK, the Cabinet Office launched an Investment and Contract Readiness Fund (ICRF) to accelerate the provision of support services for UK social

---

[15] Large players such as Boston Consulting Group and PWC conduct research and offer consultancy in the sector, with PWC creating a 'hub for social change' in South London, where they support Social Enterprise UK, the School for Social Entrepreneurs and Brigade, a social enterprise restaurant <http://firestation.pwc.co.uk/>.

entrepreneurs positioning themselves to raise at least £500k of investment or to secure contracts in excess of £1m in external investment (ICF GHK and BMG Research, 2013). The UK's Big Lottery Fund (BLF) has also set up the Big Potential Fund, directed at smaller, more early-stage ventures, delivering £10m grant funding over three years (Big Lottery Fund, 2014), while the grant-making consultancy UnLtd has been seen as a leading example of this kind of specialized consultancy for early-stage ventures (Phan, Bacq, and Nordqvist, 2014). This follows on from funding that BLF made available for a series of social enterprise incubators.

The need for accelerators and incubators for early-stage ventures is also well documented in the literature Baird, 2011; (Worthstone and Wragge & Co LLP, 2013; Eggers and Macmillan, 2013), but it can be argued that funding tied directly to investment readiness is particularly important in creating a sustainable social investing market. The OECD stressed the need for investment in such facilitative infrastructure: 'an inadequate investment infrastructure exists for both start-up social enterprises and for the replication of effective enterprises in the same city or in other markets' (OECD, 2004: 145).

CASE STUDY THE INVESTMENT AND CONTRACT READINESS FUND (ICRF)

The ICRF is an initiative of the UK's coalition government funded out of the Cabinet Office to facilitate capital-raising and contract readiness efforts of social enterprises and charities.[16] Funded initially with £10m, the programme was designed to last for three years and enable over 100 such organizations to pay for the services of key approved experts and advisors. Such funding is generally unavailable and means that social sector firms are either ill advised or unable to get the support they require to expand. The programme has been immensely popular and there are regular reports of follow-on programmes of a similar nature (Boston Consulting Group, 2014). The Social Investment Business, a hybrid charity-social enterprise organization, administered this programme.

In addition to helping social entrepreneurs become investment ready, companies are also offering support to impact-oriented investors as well, where the overall level of awareness and experience can be somewhat elementary. Firms are developing their skills in assisting investors in developing their impact investment strategies, monitoring the effectiveness of such strategies, and providing due diligence and other services to consider specific investments.

Another important focus for specialist services has been social impact assessment and reporting. Given that social impact investing is different from the mainstream in how it accommodates social impact alongside risk-adjusted financial returns, there is a growing need to measure and assess such impact, and compare and contrast it with investor expectations. Such methodologies have been developed in North America and in Europe, with obvious similarities as well as cultural differences manifesting in the metrics

---

[16]   See their website: <http://www.beinvestmentready.org.uk>.

developed.[17] Many interested parties have strived to develop common standards, although consensus has not been achieved and does not appear imminent. Nevertheless, investors, both institutional and individual, are demanding such metrics and want to have confidence in them (Social Finance, 2012). Investors' willingness to sacrifice some yield may be growing, but only if they are confident that the social impact achieved as a result of the yield sacrifice can be measured satisfactorily (Keohane, 2012). Social entrepreneurs are willing to incorporate such metrics into their reporting systems, but are often intimidated by the transaction costs of measurement or monitoring or both.

Measurement of, and reporting on, social impact are also tied to the ability of sector intermediaries to deliver their services; Keohane suggested that 'measurement and reporting standards have helped strengthen the field's infrastructure more broadly, including the work of the growing number of intermediary advisory firms' (Keohane, 2012: 98). Some commentators even suggest that at scale, the sector will need the establishment of a distinct profession of *social* auditing (Dunfee, 2003). Without robust measurement, the facilitative—and indeed transactional infrastructure—that is necessary to move the sector forward will struggle to gain traction. Investment in infrastructure that supports widely recognized measurement and reporting on social impact is an integral part of social impact investing.

CASE STUDY MEASURING IMPACT: INTENTIONALITY

Intentionality is a CIC based in the UK that supports social enterprises and programmes to measure and report on social impact. Their offer ranges from small group sessions showing entrepreneurs how to measure and report to in-depth analyses for investment-readiness work; they subcontract through the ICRF to support companies in developing their social impact reporting. They also provide all of the social impact measurement work for the Big Venture Challenge, a Big Lottery-funded programme to raise investment for early-stage social ventures.

TRANSACTIONAL INFRASTRUCTURE

It has been suggested that sector transaction costs will be high until the infrastructure that supports investors—such as deal clearing mechanisms, benchmarking data, and investment banking services—is built (O'Donohoe et al., 2010). As in the investment mainstream, the necessary vehicles, structures, and intermediaries need to be in place in order for investment to take place effectively and efficiently (Nicholls and Pharoah, 2007; Meehan and Jonker, 2012). These can be divided into three clear areas: sources of capital, financial intermediaries, and sources of after-market liquidity.

---

[17] For example, see 'Conceptions of Social Enterprises and Social Entrepreneurship in Europe and the United States: Convergences and Divergences' (Defourny and Nyssens, 2008).

Sources of Capital

All investment ultimately begins with individuals. Individuals generate the wealth that gets invested through pension funds or other product providers and managers. Even government is not the real originator of the funds it has been using to support the sector—these are provided by taxpayers. However, absent the necessary institutional pathways for funds to find social enterprises in which to invest, much less investment will take place and the growth of the market will be significantly slower than desired. The most common institutional pathways are cited below.

Dedicated Impact Investment Funds (IIFs). Some commentators highlight bespoke impact investment funds, along with intermediaries, as one of the key drivers of the growth of the social finance sector (E. T. Jackson and Associates Ltd, 2012). These funds are growing rapidly in the UK, often catalysed by governmental action. Bridges Ventures,[18] whose first fund received subsidized support (£20m first-loss investment from the Government), has now become an immensely successful player with almost £600m under management—all this remaining was raised exclusively in the private market without any state subsidy. Several other organizations have also evolved, including Big Issue Invest, the Social Investment Business, CAF Venturesome, Impetus Trust/ Private Equity Foundations and others,[19] with a preponderance of government money and some corporate support as well as some investment by High-Net-Worth Individuals (HNWIs).

This intermediary market has grown in the UK with the inauguration of a social investment wholesale bank—Big Society Capital (BSC)—that has supported several new investment funds by offering cornerstone finance. Two sizable examples of this are the NESTA Impact Investment Fund, and the joint venture fund between private bank Berenberg and LGT known as IVUK. With over £600m of capital to deploy, much of which will be dedicated to IIFs, BSC is expected to leverage over £2bn into the sector. Investment in infrastructure that supports the creation of impact investment funds is vital if social finance is to move from the margins to the mainstream (Eggers and Macmillan, 2013).

CASE STUDY NESTA IMPACT FUND

This fund was launched in 2012 and was one of the very first managed investment funds to be seeded by Big Society Capital. The fund closed with £17.6m of assets and targets key social sectors, which include: the health and well-being of an ageing population; the educational attainment and employability of children and young people; and the social and environmental sustainability of communities. With the capacity to make investments of £100,000—£1m, the fund is targeted at investments that are addressing a gap in the social investment marketplace—in

---

[18]   See <http://www.bridgesventures.com>.
[19]   See, respectively, <http://www.bigissueinvest.com>; <http://www.sibgroup.org.uk>; <http:// cafonline.org/venturesome>; <http://impetus-pef.org.uk>.

between where funding from angels stops and funding from institutions starts. The fund can invest using a variety of instruments and utilizes debt, equity, and quasi-equity instruments.

Foundations

Mostly established by a single wealthy individual or family, foundations are important players with philanthropic funding often key to catalysing market growth. Much has been written on their role in infrastructure building for the sector,[20] and it is indisputable that the pump-priming work of foundations, as well as their profile-raising work, has been integral to the success of the sector to this point; although only a small portion of the estimated £80bn of foundation endowments has been directly allocated to social investing (we estimate about £50–100m).

Foundation capital has often operated as risk—or research and development—capital with a high impact orientation and, often, a lesser need for high financial returns. The connections and networks, as well as the deep impact expertise of foundations, can also be integral in creating social finance markets. Eggers and Macmillan gave the example of Ashoka aiming to create a market for affordable housing in India by leveraging their ability to develop relationships between the mortgage companies, for-profit housing developers, and local community organizations linked to their own capital (Eggers and Macmillan, 2013). However, foundations are becoming increasingly resistant where grants are used predominantly to create private sector profit.

Foundations have also been key in creating other kinds of infrastructure—intellectual infrastructure, for example. The Rockefeller Foundation's funding created the Global Impact Investing Network (GIIN), which has 'become the pivotal platform for impact investors and their support organizations from the Global North' (E.,T. Jackson and Associates Ltd, 2012: 38). More foundations are expected to consider impact investment as part of their endowments going forward, but it is unlikely that this will become a meaningfully large pool of funds in the foreseeable future to challenge the potential of large institutions in this space.

Pension Funds

Pension funds have typically not been very active in this space, other than through fund vehicles such as Bridges Ventures (Sullivan, 2012). However, it may be that those with a strong ethical orientation (religiously affiliated, academically affiliated, and perhaps labour union funds) may, over time, allocate a growing portion of their funds to impact investing, and may, in the future, become important actors in building the sector. Indeed, in France it is already a legal requirement that pension funds offer investment into at

---

[20] See, for example, Nicholls and Pharoah (2007); Koh, Karamchandani, and Katz (2012); Bannick and Goldman (2012).

least one solidarity fund (a scheme that must invest 5–10 per cent of its capital into companies with a solidarity label, which they receive for certain features in line with the social enterprise ethos, such as employing workers from disadvantaged backgrounds) (Yermo, 2008: 7). Another leading UK initiative in this regard is Investing for Growth, while CalPERS (California Public Employees Retirement System), the largest public pension fund in the USA, has targeted social investment as part of its mainstream investment policy since 1992 (Quarter, Carmichael, and Ryan, 2008).

CASE STUDY INVESTING FOR GROWTH (I4G)

This is a landmark initiative undertaken by five leading UK local authority pension funds to utilize their substantial funds to invest not only for financial return but take into account the social impact of the investments they make. This is in accordance with the risk and return requirements of the Local Government Pension Scheme funds, to 'benefit local communities and address some of the current economic challenges' (Jones, 2014: 1). Advised by the Pensions Investment Research Consultants, this initiative is an initial commitment to invest £50m per local authority pension fund (£250m in total) into social impact investment funds that deliver a target minimum investment return of 7 per cent annually. This is significant in itself and also seems likely to catalyse billions of other pension fund assets—in particular those with an ethical orientation (such as religiously affiliated groups like the Church Commissioners), which could be deployed simultaneously for both financial gain and a positive impact on local communities.

Fund Managers

Via their socially responsible investment (SRI) activities, some fund managers are moving into the impact investment area. This is happening slowly, although the rapid growth of the SRI movement would suggest there is a great potential for engagement with impact investing, especially where lessons are learnt from engaging fund managers with the principles of SRI (Crifo and Forget, 2012). Banks such as J.P. Morgan have been leaders in seeking to raise funds with solely an impact orientation, as in their Global Health Investment fund, designed to provide financing to advance the development of drugs, vaccines, diagnostics, and other interventions against diseases that disproportionately impact low-income countries.

Corporates

Corporates have been reluctant to invest their own funds in this area to date. However, there are a few notable exceptions, such as SAB Miller with their Latin America fund, which is investing $17m over four years (Lippert, 2013), in conjunction with some of its other developing market activities. One encouraging recent exception has been the Ignite Fund,[21] launched by utility giant Centrica, that focuses on impact investments with an energy-saving or

---

[21] See <http://ignitesocialenterprise.com>.

environmental angle. Firms with heightened sensitivity to ethical issues and growing client interest have been the most active in exploring this market. There is great potential in corporate engagement to support the growth of social enterprises and the sector more widely (Waddock, 2008).

High Net Worth Individuals

Wealthy individuals have made impact investments, occasionally on their own on a direct basis and sometimes through the growing pool of family offices active in this area. There are exceptions where individuals participate through angel networks, such as the one managed ClearlySo.[22] The vast bulk of private wealthy individuals with an interest in this area invest via private banks and, to a lesser extent, IFAs, who assist them in placing a small portion of their wealth into a variety of vehicles.

Despite limited engagement by HNWIs to this point, much of the literature stresses the importance of investor-driven movements in recalibrating the financial system, arguing that they are critical to the development of socially responsible investment infrastructure (MacLeod, 2009).[23] Indeed, with intermediaries such as ClearlySo and Toniic, as well as governments cultivating networks of HNWIs,[24] the need for their support has been widely recognized.

Advisory Intermediaries

Advisory intermediaries are necessary to ease the process by which capital flows. They play a role as matchmakers, identifying suitable investors for particular social finance propositions. Furthermore, they provide corporate finance advice to enterprises, assessing capital needs and optimal funding structures. These intermediaries also play a meaningful role in assisting the enterprises to become investment ready, working with the client to build a compelling investment case. There are several classes of advisors currently operating in the social sector at this time and their number is growing.

Mainstream advisors. The big four accounting firms in the UK have all developed some advisory activities in this area. Some, like Ernst & Young, run 'Accelerate' networks, partner with providers such as UnLtd to offer advisory work, and fund social entrepreneurship awards. Others have established social enterprise advisory units as part of their existing corporate finance or advisory arms. For example, PwC has been a leading advisor to the Cabinet Office's

---

[21] See <http://ignitesocialenterprise.com>.

[22] Clearly Social Angels was the first UK angel group for social impact investing: <http://www.clearlysocialangels.com>.

[23] See also The Rockefeller Foundation (2012).

[24] In April 2014, President Obama hosted a private event at the White House for millenials who are heirs to fortunes—including the Rockefeller, Marriott, and Carlson families—to explore engaging next generation ultra-HNWIs in impact investing for global social impact (Johnson, 2014).

aforementioned ICRF programme. The large international investment banks have not become involved in this area as deal sizes are still well below their target size range.

While established intermediaries are key in offering advice and support, as the sector grows more specialized intermediaries will need to offer expertise and advice based on deep knowledge of the social impact investment space:

Established intermediaries...often play the critical role in bringing conventional investment opportunities to institutional asset owners. They will continue to do so until new, more impact-oriented intermediaries become 'institutional quality'. (Wood, Thornley, and Grace, 2012: 9)

Independent niche firms. Several advisory intermediaries have emerged in the UK specifically to work on behalf of social enterprise clients. These firms include Social Finance, Triodos (Dutch-based but active in the UK) and ClearlySo. This list also includes a growing number of smaller firms providing similar advice to social enterprises in the UK. These range from firms like Resonance, which also manages smaller investment funds, to firms with just one or a few members of staff.

CASE STUDY CLEARLYSO

Founded in September 2008, the same month Lehman Brothers collapsed, this FCA-licensed firm[25] was established to help social entrepreneurs. It does so by assisting them in raising capital for expansion. Clients consist of earlier stage social entrepreneurs seeking under £1m of investment, normally in the form of equity; more mature socially impactful organizations looking for up to £40m; and impact investment funds raising anywhere from £5m to £200m. Early-stage firms normally receive investment from business angels and ClearlySo operates the largest social business angel network in the UK, Clearly Social Angels. In addition, it markets investment opportunities to over 500 institutional investors in the UK and Europe. ClearlySo itself is an angel-backed socially oriented business and has also received investment from NESTA and Big Society Capital.

Sources of After-Market Liquidity

The limited number of sizable social enterprises in the UK, and the fact that an active social finance market has only recently begun to take shape, has meant that the demand for liquidity as a mechanism to exit an investment, or manage a portfolio of social investments has been limited. Nevertheless, this is expected to grow over the coming years as mainstream investors enter the field and seek the sort of after-market liquidity to which they are accustomed (Hill, 2011):

Exchanges and investment platforms help address the challenge that many investors face when seeking to invest in impact enterprises: identifying investable opportunities. While stock exchanges have been facilitating transactions for centuries, the first Social

---

[25] <http://www.clearlyso.com>.

Stock Exchange was officially launched in London in 2013; it showcases publically listed impact enterprises that trade on the London Stock Exchange. (World Economic Forum, 2013: 16)

There have been similar attempts to create the beginnings of socially oriented liquidity providers in other countries. Some of the better-know examples include Brazil's Environmental and Social Investment Exchange, the South African Social Investment Exchange (SASIX) (Stewart, 2012) and in Canada SVX Canada (Floyd, 2013), and the Asian Impact Investing Exchange (IIX), which is based in Singapore but uses the Mauritius stock exchange as its trading platform.[26] On a less grand—but perhaps more practical—level, Ethex was founded a few years ago in the UK as a portal for experienced private investors in ethical/social shares, to gain access to useful information about the industry and the underlying shares, and to attempt to secure liquidity for the shares they own. This venture, as with many others of a similar nature, is at the earliest stages of development—but signs are encouraging. The UK Social Stock Exchange, launched in June 2013, is another platform for investors accessing impact investment opportunities in the public markets.

Mainstream investment banks, especially the mid-sized firms, offer further sources of liquidity. For example, for years the UK broker Brewin Dolphin provided matched bargain services to shareholders in the Ethical Property Company.[27] Cannacord Capital, another mid-sized UK broker, also offers a facility for trading listed bonds in social enterprises. Finally, there has been discussion in the UK of a pool of capital that might serve a market-making function to provide liquidity to impact investors.

Commentators have agreed that the social finance market still requires significant infrastructure building and that this will include stock exchanges, a range of bespoke products and instruments, and well-developed intermediation (O'Donohoe et al., 2010; Solomon, 2011). Only through strong infrastructure and diverse product offerings will the sector truly draw in institutional and retail investment flows to transform the sector (Heaney, 2010).

Conclusion

This chapter has explored the need for a better developed supporting infrastructure to grow and develop the social finance market. This represents the main ingredient in accelerating the volume and value of social finance transactions. Rather than lump all infrastructure needs into a single pot, the types of infrastructure have been divided into categories and discussed in detail, with examples of key organizations in each category provided. Table 15.1 below is a summary, which may be useful for practitioners and policymakers in order to compare these elements and assess each from the standpoint of cost, relevance

---

[26] SASIX and IIX merged in 2014.   [27] <http://www.ethicalproperty.co.uk>.

Table 15.1. Building the infrastructure

Type of infrastructure		Cost of investing in this infrastructure	Most appropriate group to lead	Stage of market building for focus
Governmental	Corporate legal structures	Low		Early
	Facilitative tax policies	Low	Government, with social movement pressure	Medium
	Enabling financial services legislation	Low		Early
	Social value in public service commissioning	Medium		Medium
Intellectual	Academic institutions	Medium	Academic community	Early
	Sectors conferences and networks	Low	Academic community, impact networks and organizations	Early
	Media publications and sites	Low	Media, intermediaries, sector networks	Medium
	Governmental contributions	Low	Government	Medium
Facilitative	Generalist professional services firms	Medium	Professional firms	Early
	Specialized consultancies	High	Professional firms, government	Medium
	Specialized research providers	Medium	Academic community, impact network, foundations	Medium
Transactional	Sources of capital	High	Finance community, government, foundations	Early
	Investment banks and financial intermediaries	High	Finance community, government	Early
	Sources of after market liquidity	Medium	Finance community, impact network	Late

at different stages of the market, and who might take the lead in developing this element.

These governmental, facilitative, intellectual, and transactional forms of infrastructure all need investment if the social finance market is to capitalize on its success to this point and mainstream, to help create a more balanced economy that demands social, ethical, and environmental accountability. Despite these strong arguments in favour of deep infrastructure investment, there is still an infrastructure gap that must be filled:

While money is flowing reasonably well to 'scalers' where investors expect high financial and social returns, money is less readily available for industry infrastructure and for early-stage innovators—especially in markets that serve the most disadvantaged. (Bannick and Goldman, 2012: 16)

Infrastructure that enables the creation and growth of social enterprises facilitates their ability to raise investment and supports the transactions where investments are made, can set up a social economy that is sustainable and forward-looking. Infrastructure investment is also an investment in structures that encourage collaboration, interaction, and broader measures of impact and accountability, from which every early-stage sector can benefit.

REFERENCES

Baird, R. (2011). 'Seed-Stage Investment and Support: Closing the Gap to Growth in Impact Investing.' *Innovations*, 6(3): 133–43.

Bannick, M., and Goldman, P. (2012). *Priming the Pump: The Case for a Sector Based Approach to Impact Investing*. California: Omidyar Network.

Bates, Wells and Braithwaite (2005). 'Keeping It Legal: A Guide to Legal'. <http://www.bwbllp.com>, accessed 28 April 2014.

Bhawuk, D. P., Mrazek, S., and Munusamy, M. V. P. (2009). 'From Social Engineering to Community Transformation: Amul, Grameen Bank and Mondragon as Exemplar Organizations', *Peace & Policy*, 14: 36–63.

Big Lottery Fund (2014). *Big Lottery Fund Launches £10 million Fund to Get Sector Investment Ready*. <http://www.biglotteryfund.org.uk/global-content/press-releases/england/270214_eng_sib_fund-to-get-sector-investment-ready>, accessed 2 May 2014.

Big Society Capital (2012). *First Annual Report*. London: Big Society Capital.

Bishop, M., and Green, M. (2010) 'The Capital Curve for a Better World.' *Innovations: Ashoka-Lemelson Special Issue*, pp. 25–33.

Boston Consulting Group. (2014). *Review of the Investment and Contract Readiness Fund*. External Review. London: Boston Consulting Group.

Bugg-Levin, A., and Emerson, J. (2011). *Impact Investing: Transforming How We Make Money While Making a Difference*. Kindle ebook. Hoboken: John Wiley & Sons.

Cabinet Office (2010). 'Social Investment: Ten Years On'. Final report of the Social Investment Taskforce, Cabinet Office, London.

Cabinet Office (2013). 'Background Analysis on the UK Social Investment Market'. Cabinet Office, London.

Cabinet Office (2013). 'Growing the Social Investment Market: 2013 Progress Update'. London: HM Government.

Cabinet Office (2014). 'The Public Services (Social Value) Act 2012: One Year On'. HM Government, London.

CAF (2006). *International Comparisons of Charitable Giving*. London: CAF.

CDFA (2012). *Inside Community Finance: The CDFI Industry in the UK*. London: CDFA.

Cohen, R. (2011). 'Harnessing Social Entrepreneurship and Investment to Bridge the Social Divide.' EU Conference on the Social Economy, Brussels.

Corporation for National and Community Service (2013). 'Getting Results, Transforming Lives: The Social Innovation Fund 2010–2012 Investment Report.' <http://

www.nationalservice.gov/sites/default/files/documents/sif_investment_report2013_0.pdf>, accessed 28 July 2014.

Crifo, P., and Forget, V. (2012). 'Think Global, Invest Responsible: Why the Private Equity Industry Goes Green.' *Journal of Business Ethics* 116: 21–48.

Defourny, J., and Nyssens, M. (2008). 'Conceptions of Social Enterprises and Social Entrepreneurship in Europe and the United States: Convergences and Divergences.' *Journal of Social Entrepreneurship*, 1(1): 32–53.

Department for Business, Innovation & Skills (2013). 'Response to the CIC Consultation on the Dividend and Interest Caps.' 10 December. <https://www.gov.uk/government/uploads/system/uploads/attachment_data/file/264664/CIC-13-1333- community-interest-companies-response-on-the-cic-consultation.pdf>, accessed 2 May 2014.

Department of Education Employment and Workplace Relations (2012). *The Social Enterprise Development and Investment Funds: Lessons from the Implementation Process.* Canberra: Australian Government.

Doeringer, M. (2010). 'Fostering Social Enterprise: A Historical and International Analysis', *Duke Journal of Comparative and International Law*, 20: 291–329.

Dunfee, T. W. (2003). 'Social Investing: Mainstream or Backwater?' *Journal of Business Ethics*, 43(3): 247–52.

E. T. Jackson and Associates Ltd. (2012). *Accelerating Impact: Achievements, Challenges and What's Next in Building the Impact Investing Industry.* New York: Rockefeller Foundation.

Eggers, W. D., and Macmillan, P. (2013). *The Solution Revolution: How Business, Government, and Social Enterprises Are Teaming Up to Solve Society's Toughest Problems.* Cambridge, MA: Harvard Business Review Press.

Esposito, R. (2013). 'The Social Enterprise Revolution in Corporate Law: A Primer on Emerging Corporate Entities in Europe and the United States and the Case for the Benefit Corporation'. *William & Mary Business Law Review*, 4(2): 639–714.

Evill, S. (2014). 'Budget 2014: Osborne's Social Investment Tax Relief Is a Welcome Move', *Real Business*, 20 March. <http://realbusiness.co.uk/article/26101-budget-2014-osbornes-social-investment-tax-relief-is-a-welcome-move>, accessed 28 July 2014.

EVPA (2013). 'European Venture Philanthropy Association.' 15 May. <http://evpa.eu.com/blog/2013/05/eif-launches-a-social-impact-investing-fund-of-funds/>, accessed 2 May 2014.

Floyd, D. (2013). 'Social Stock Exchange: The Rise of International Competitors,' *The Guardian*, 25 October.

Freireich, J., and Fulton, K. (2009). *Investing for Social and Environmental Impact.* San Francisco, CA: Monitor Institute.

GIIN (2012). 'Investor Spotlight: Big Society Capital', Washington, DC: GIIN. <http://www.thegiin.org/cgi-bin/iowa/resources/spotlight/486.html>, accessed 15 June 2015.

Heaney, V. (2010). *Investing in Social Enterprise: The Role of Tax Incentives.* London: CSFI and Nesta.

Hill, K. (2011). *Investor Perspectives on Social Enterprise Financing.* London: ClearlySo and City of London.

HM Government (2012). *Growing the Social Investment Market: HMG Social Investment Initiatives.* London: HM Government.

Howard, E. (2012). *Challenges and Opportunities in Social Finance in the UK.* London: Social Finance.

ICF GHK and BMG Research (2013). *Growing the Social Investment Market: The Landscape and Economic Impact.* City of London.

Investing for Good (2012). *Scope Closes First Issue of Bonds under £20-million Social Investment Programme.* <http://www.investingforgood.co.uk/news/scope-closes-first-issue-of-bonds-under-pound20-million-social-investment-programme/>, accessed 28 July 2014.

Jansson, M., and Biel, A. (2014). 'Investment Institutions' Beliefs about and Attitudes toward Socially Responsible Investment (SRI): A Comparison Between SRI and Non-SRI Management', *Sustainable Development*, 22(1): 33–41.

Jones, J. (2014). 'LAPFF Schemes Commit £152m to Impact Investments', *Professional Pensions*, 14 June.

Keohane, G. L. (2013). *Social Entrepreneurship for the 21st Century: Innovation cross the Nonprofit, Private, and Public Sectors.* New York: McGraw Hill Professional.

Koh, H., Karamchandani, A., and Katz, R. (2012). *From Blueprint to Scale: The Case for Philanthropy in Impact Investing.* San Francisco, CA: Monitor Group.

Lippert, K. (2013). 'SABMiller: Supporting Retailers in Latin America.' 29 April. <http://community.businessfightspoverty.org/profiles/blogs/karl-lippert-president-sabmiller-latin-america-supporting>, accessed 2 May 2014.

MacLeod, M. R. (2009). 'Emerging Investor Networks and the Construction of Corporate Social Responsibility', *Journal of Corporate Citizenship* 34: 69–98.

Martin, M. (2013). *Status of the Social Impact Investing Market: A Primer.* London: Cabinet Office.

Mason, C., Kirkbride, J., and Bryde, D. (2007). 'From Stakeholders to Institutions: The Changing Face of Social Enterprise Governance Theory', *Management Decision*, 45(2): 284–301.

Meehan, B., and Jonker, K. (2012). 'The Rise of Social Capital Market Intermediaries', *Stanford Social Innovation Review*, 10(1): 45–53.

Mitchell, L., Kingston, J., and Goodall, E. (2008). *Financing Civil Society: A Practitioner's View of the UK Social Investment.* London: Venturesome.

Montgomery, A., Wren, P., Dacin, A., and Dacin, M. T. (2012). 'Collective Social Entrepreneurship: Collaboratively Shaping Social Good', *Journal of Business Ethics*, 111(3): 375–88.

Moscovici, P., and Hamon, B. (2013). *Projet de loi économie sociale et solidaire.* Paris: Ministre de l'économie et des finances.

New Zealand Department of Internal Affairs. (2013). *Legal Structures for Social Enterprise.* Wellington: NZ DIA.

Nicholls, A. (2006). *Social Entrepreneurship: New Models of Sustainable Social Change.* Oxford: Oxford University Press.

Nicholls, A. (2013). 'Filling the Capital Gap: Institutionalizing Social Finance', in S. Denny and F. Seddon (eds), *Social Enterprise: Accountability and Evaluation Around the World.* Oxford: Routledge, pp. 161–95.

Nicholls, A., and Pharoah, C. (2007). *The Landscape of Social Investment: A Holistic Topology of Opportunities and Challenges.* Oxford: Said Business School.

Nicholls, A., and Schwartz, R. (2013). 'The Demand Side of the Social Investment Marketplace', in L. M. Salamon (ed.), *New Frontiers of Philanthropy: A Guide to the New Tools and New Actors That Are Reshaping Global Philanthropy and Social Investing.* San Francisco: Jossey Bass, pp. 562–82.

O'Donohoe, N., Leijonhufvud, C., Saltuk, Y., Bugg-Levine, A., and Brandenburg, M. (2010). *Impact Investments: An Emerging Asset Class.* London: J.P. Morgan.

OECD. (2004). *Entrepreneurship: A Catalyst for Urban Regeneration.* Paris: OECD Publishing.

Osburg, T., and Schmidpeter, R. (2013). *Social Innovation: Solutions for a Sustainable Future.* New York: Springer.

Palmer, P. (1997). 'Auditing, Accounting and Supervision in the European Charitable Sector', *Corporate Governance: An International Review*, 5(1): 29–36.

Patton, A. (2013). 'The Social Investment Market: The Role of Public Policy in Innovation and Execution', in *Perspectives from the Social Investment Symposium 2012.* Cabinet Office, Said Business School, Oxford.

Phan, P., Bacq, S., and Nordqvist, M. (2014). *Theory and Empirical Research in Social Entrepreneurship.* Google eBook: Edward Elgar Publishing.

Public Administration Select Committee (2008). 'Public Services and the Third Sector: Oral and Written Evidence (HC 112-ii, Incorporating HC 540-i-v, Session 2006–07)'. House of Commons, London.

Quarter, J., Carmichael, I., and Ryan, S. (2008). *Pensions at Work: Socially Responsible Investment of Union-Based Pension Funds.* Toronto: University of Toronto Press.

Regulator of Community Interest Companies. (2010). *Annual Report.* London: Regulator of Community Interest Companies.

Schwartz, R. (2010). 'ClearlySo Blog.' 24 April, available at: <http://www.clearlyso.com>, accessed 15 June 2015.

SEUK (2013). *The People's Business.* London: SEUK.

Shanmugalingam, C., Graham, J., Tucker, S., and Mulgan, G. (2011). *Growing Social Ventures: The Role of Intermediaries and Investors: Who They Are, What They Do, and What They Could Become.* London: Young Foundation and NESTA.

Social Finance (2012). *Microfinance, Impact Investing, and Pension Fund Investment Policy Survey.* London: Social Finance.

Solomon, L. (2011). *Tech Billionaires: Reshaping Philanthropy in a Quest for a Better World.* New Jersey: Transaction Publishers.

Stewart, N. (2012). 'The Rise of Social Exchanges', *IR Magazine*, 23 January.

Stout, L. (2012). *The Shareholder Value Myth: How Putting Shareholders First Harms Investors, Corporations, and the Public.* San Francisco: Berrett-Koehler Publishers.

Sullivan, R. (2012). 'Impact Investing Forecast to Double.' 11 November. <http://www.ft.com/cms/s/0/9cdb0efe-29c2-11e2-9a46-00144feabdc0.html>, accessed 2 May 2014.

Swersky, A., and Brown, A. (2012) *The First Billion.* London: Boston Consulting Group.

The Good Analyst (2012). *Scope: Report No. 1.* London: The Good Analyst Ltd.

The Rockefeller Foundation (2012). *Capital Markets for Impact at Scale: Showcasing Institutional Impact and Community Investing.* New York: Rockefeller Foundation.

Trivedi, C. (2010). 'Towards a Social Ecological Framework for Social Entrepreneurship', *Journal of Entrepreneurship*, 19: 63–80.

US National Advisory Board on Impact Investing (2014). *Private Capital, Public Good: How Smart Federal Policy Can Galvanize Impact Investing—and Why It's Urgent.* Washington, DC: NAB Impact Investing.

Waddock, S. (2008). *The Difference Makers: How Social and Institutional Entrepreneurs Created the Corporate Responsibility Movement.* Sheffield: Greenleaf Publishing.

White, A. (2014). 'Big Issue Backs Deprived London Nurseries'. *The Daily Telegraph*, 24 May.

Wood, A. (2010). 'New Legal Structure to Address the Social Capital Famine', *Vermont Law Review*, 35: 45–52.

Wood, D., and Hagerman, L. (2010). 'Mission Investing and the Philanthropic Toolbox'. *Policy and Society* (Initiative for Responsible Investment, The Hauser Center for Nonprofit Organizations, John F. Kennedy School of Government), 29(3): 257–68.

Wood, D., Thornley, B., and Grace, K. (2012). *Impact at Scale: Policy Innovation for Institutional Investment with Social and Environmental Benefit*. New York: Rockefeller Foundation.

Word Economic Forum Investors Industries (2013). *From the Margins to the Mainstream: Assessment of the Impact Investment Sector and Opportunities to Engage Mainstream Investors*. Geneva: World Economic Forum, 2013.

Worthstone and Wragge & Co LLP (2013). *The Role of Tax Incentives in Encouraging Social Investment*. London: City of London and Big Society Capital.

Yermo, J. (2008). 'Governance and Investment of Public Pension Reserve Funds in Selected OECD Countries.' OECD Working Papers on Insurance and Private Pensions, No. 15, OECD Publishing, France.

Part V

Future Directions

16 Crowdfunding in social finance

Othmar M. Lehner

Introduction

In the early stages of a venture, when innovative entrepreneurs are often armed only with an idea, their good name, and their enthusiasm, financing can be very difficult and tricky. Due to the lack of a working proof of concept, these entrepreneurs can find it impossible to attract so-called 'business angels' as early investors, and banks are reluctant to lend money without the prospect of stable cash flows in the near future (Waygood, 2011).

In such cases, entrepreneurs may have to tap into the resources of 'friends and family (and fools!)' for start-up capital, or they may have to use 'bootstrapping' approaches in which advance-payments, personal loans, and other means of finance allow for a self-funded growth (Lam, 2010). However due to various constraints, these methods may not be applicable to all business models. Enterprises in need of large upfront investments or social enterprises, with blended value creation outputs, may find it difficult and, perhaps, even impossible to make use of such self-sustaining methods (Dushnitsky and Shapira, 2010).

(Social) enterprises with a high legitimacy in the eyes of society tend to attract a number of people willing to contribute various resources, such as volunteering, donating items, or even giving sums of money. This process has recently been dubbed crowdsourcing, especially when involving a multitude of contributors and communication over new social media (Howe, 2006; Kittur, 2010; Bloxham, 2011).

Tapping the crowd for significant amounts of debt and equity investment, however, remains difficult for several reasons: First, there can be important information asymmetries where there is geographical distance between investor and investee (Ketchen, Boyd, and Bergh, 2007) and, second, in many countries legislation has hindered forms of crowd-investments other than donations or simple upfront payments for expected goods.

Yet, donations are becoming increasingly scarce, as more and more social enterprises and not-for-profit organizations are competing for them. At the same time, many everyday people are seeking to invest, rather than donate, their money into social and sustainable businesses of their choice, as an alternative to other capital market offers. However, in most countries with a developed capital market, investors looking for equity or even shares of earnings have to be registered and accredited and companies offering securities have to undergo a long and expensive process, often involving external auditing, to create a share offer prospectus.

A bundle of recent developments in the technical, legal, and societal spheres, however, have created new opportunities for retail social finance. One of these has been the emergence of crowdfunding (CF). CF aims to engage large numbers of potential retail investors using social media and the Internet instead of relying on established finance intermediaries such as investment managers. Each individual member of the crowd typically contributes only a small amount but, together, these contributions add up to provide a significant *joint* investment.

Improving knowledge on CF may be especially important for social enterprises (SE), since, historically, such social mission-driven entrepreneurs have had particular problems attracting early-stage finance. Some of the reasons for these challenging circumstances have been identified in literature as being a function of the often hybrid nature of social enterprises (Dacin, Dacin, and Matear, 2010) blending social and financial value creation. Moreover, further issues include: the lack of clear metrics that can guide investors in their capital allocation; unusual legal and organizational structures in social enterprises; and deep cultural and cognitive barriers between for-profit investors and social enterprises that can hinder effective communication (Bauer-Leeb and Lundqvist, 2012). The 2008 financial crisis and the resulting credit-crunch in banks have also increased the pressure to find alternative means of funding and financing new social enterprises.

CF may offer one other option, especially suited to financing the needs of social enterprises, as crowd investors typically do not look much at collaterals or business plans, but at the ideas and core values of the firm in which they invest—often with a keen focus on its perceived legitimacy. These aspects are typically regarded very positively in social enterprise. Such crowd-based processes may well bring the additional benefit of being perceived by the public as democratic, addressing some criticisms of the market focus of social enterprises (Meyer, 2009) especially in 'Bismarckian' social welfare countries (Esping-Andersen, 2006; Lehner, 2011).

Despite its potential to support social enterprises, however, there are very few academic articles that address CF in this context—apart for a small stream focusing solely on donations (Chow, 2011). Even in the business-venturing domain as a whole, research on CF is only starting to emerge and is often merely based on anecdotal evidence. This chapter therefore sets out to examine and explore business models for CF, looks into debt- and equity-based CF, and proposes future research themes in a social enterprise context.

Financing social enterprises

For some time, finance for the social enterprise market has been constrained by the idiosyncrasies of this hybrid sector. Some arise from the entrepreneurs or founders themselves, as they often come from traditional not-for-profit organizations and have a non-business-related educational background. Their cultural backgrounds and skill sets typically do not communicate easily with traditional investors and financial intermediaries (Bauer-Leeb and Lundqvist, 2012). Their focus is often foremost on social impact rather than cash flow, liquidity, long-term financial returns, or financial planning and forecasting (Ridley-Duff, 2009). A 2003 study by the Bank of England confirmed that social entrepreneurs have had a hard time accessing traditional debt finance (Brown and Murphy, 2003). However, the success of the micro-credit market—pioneered by the Grameen Bank in Bangladesh—has helped to open up the field of social finance in the public discourse (Yunus and Weber, 2007). It has also attracted mainstream capital.

Centred upon the specifics of social enterprise investment, a specialized social finance market has emerged for social entrepreneurs (Bull and Crompton, 2006; Ridley-Duff, 2009; Fedele and Miniaci, 2010). It includes very different models of risk and reward as well different narratives and discourses compared to traditional financial markets. In addition, specialized investment and performance metrics, such as the social return on investment (SROI) model have been proposed as instruments in the capital allocation and legitimization of investments (Flockhart, 2005).

Instead of focusing on return on investment as a driver of getting finance, social entrepreneurs sometimes participate in grant-driven venture 'competitions' often organized by foundations such as Skoll or Ashoka, or, increasingly, by traditional for-profit companies as part of their CSR activities (Baron, 2007). Besides these foundations, there are several country-specific approaches to the financing situation of social entrepreneurs such as GoodBee in Austria, serving the Eastern European market, or large governmental funds, such as the Social Enterprise Investment Fund in the UK. All of these institutions have their own focus on what an eligible social enterprise is, including what kind of organizational and legal form they can take. This is in contrast to CF models where all kinds of entrepreneurs, forms, and ideas can tap into the capital of the crowd, based upon merit. The idea of CF relates closely to new models of citizen emancipation.

Many social enterprises in countries with a social-democratic or corporate-statist welfare regimes (Esping-Andersen, 2006) have typically relied at least partially on donations and public grants (Ridley-Duff, 2009; Fedele and Miniaci, 2010). However, reductions in welfare spending due to the financial crisis have made it increasingly difficult to access public money and the competition for charitable grants has also intensified. CF platforms, although mostly established in the Anglo-Saxon countries (Massolution, 2012), promise an alternative stream of finance.

Many social entrepreneurs have high levels of perceived legitimacy too and this reduces risk for investors (Ketchen et al., 2007). This helps address risk issues stemming from the inherent information asymmetry in CF models.

Crowdfunding

It is well recognized that new ventures often do not easily gain access to the necessary external finance at their early stages and alternatives are needed (Waygood, 2011). In later stages of development, business angels and venture capital funds may fill the gap for larger amounts, however the costs of funding proof-of-concept work and the first entrepreneurial steps are often only financed through the entrepreneur, her family, and friends (Dushnitsky and Shapira, 2010; Irwin and Scott, 2010; Cumming, 2012). This process is sometimes known as 'bootstrapping' (Lam, 2010), comprising working capital management and austerity.

CF may provide a much-needed alternative for raising capital in the early stages of a SE, offering access to donations, debt, and equity finance from a large audience. It should be noted, however, that CF is often considered as finite, project-based funding only (e.g. the Kickstarter platform in Table 16.1). In reality this conceptualization does not fully capture the actual scope of CF in practice. Some have suggested the term 'crowdinvesting' to differentiate between the *funding* of projects and *long-term investment* with debt or equity capital.

Scholars see the roots of CF in a movement that has been labelled as 'crowdsourcing', best understood as a process of using the crowd to obtain ideas, feedback, solutions, as well as resources in order to develop activities (Bloxham, 2011; Huppé and Hebb, 2011).

A distinct feature of the 'crowd' is seen as consisting of a large number of people, each contributing little, but with a potentially high combined impact. However, it has been suggested that the crowd is supposed to behave in chaotic and complex ways that are open to manipulation. This is in stark contrast to decision-making models centred on a small group of relatively sophisticated investors and managers. Given the large number of investors involved, CF can provide additional legitimacy to a social enterprise, as the selection process by the crowd may be perceived as democratic and participatory.

The concept of CF has been demonstrated to work well in some cases. The amounts of money obtained from the crowd for individual ventures can reach £1m, as in the case of Trampoline[1] Systems UK, a high-tech start-up. However, the CF process, from marketing to legal aspects is far from being institutionalized (Lambert and Schwienbacher, 2010). Thus, more research on cases of success and failure is needed, in order to identify the actual issues and to develop recommendations and best practice for investees and investors.

Belleflamme, Lambert, and Schwienbacher (2010) examined CF from an industrial organization perspective and linked it to pre-ordering and price discrimination for products such as music records or software. However, such

---

[1] <http://www.trampolinesystems.com>, accessed 8 June 2012.

Table 16.1. Crowdfunding platforms

Name/link	Short description	Categories/codes
Crowdfunder <http://www.crowdfunder.com>	New platform, allowing for donations, debt- and equity-based crowdfunding. Need practical demonstration of product or service. US based organizations only	Beta Stadium, debt, donations, equity, working model, US
Buzzbnk <http://www.buzzbnk.org>	Especially for social ventures. Loans and donations with small non-monetary returns	Debt, donations, pre-set funding goal as trigger
Impact Trader <http://www.impacttrader.com>	'Crowdmarket for world-changers'. Special impact points system as metric and reward, loans and later equity shares.	Debt, impact bonds, impact shares (2013+)
Kickstarter <http://www.kickstarter.com>	Finite project based, rewards mostly later products and honorary mentions. Large base of successful projects. Needs a working model. Relying on multimedia for presentation. Pre-set funding goal.	Debt, donations, pre-set funding goal—all or nothing
Kiva <http://www.kiva.org>	Small loans (25 USD+) to enable people in developing countries in starting theirs businesses, using microfinance institutions as field-partners. Kiva is a non-profit based upon additional donations. Already huge investments.	Debt, microfinance, field-partners US or UK-based businesses only, several high profile cases
Advertactivist <http://www.advertactivist.com>	Funding ad campaigns through donations. Platform takes 15% commission.	Donations, commission, campaigns
Indiegogo <http://www.indiegogo.com>	No restrictions on projects, 4–9% commission, large base of successful ventures and projects	US, debt, donations, Keep-it-all model, worldwide access, also for personal use, several high-profile cases
Ioby <http://www.ioby.org>	Environmental projects only, often local community based (i.e. urban greening). 3–5% commission	Donations, environmental projects
Microplace <http://www.microplace.com>	A PayPal company, no fees (but transaction costs), lots of fair trade and social projects, Loans with interest payments	Debt, portfolio tools, interest
CrowdCube <http://www.crowdcube.com>	A UK-based company with several successful cases of equity crowdfunding up to £600,000.	Equity financing, EIS tax relief, portfolio building, UK-based, professional investor tools
Ethex <http://www.ethex.org.uk>	A new UK-based fund, allowing the crowd to invest in equity stakes via a complex legal construction	Early-stage, ethical investment fund, equity offerings, portfolio building, UK, allowing re-selling of shares
Symbid <http://www.symbid.com>	Special legal construction with fiduciary intermediaries	Dutch-based, equity, intermediary, fiduciary
Australian Small Scale Offerings Board <http://www.assob.com.au/>	ASSOB matches entrepreneurs, job creators and business pioneers seeking growth capital with investors desirous of investing in high-growth opportunities.	Equity, Australian, professional reporting, Registered investors

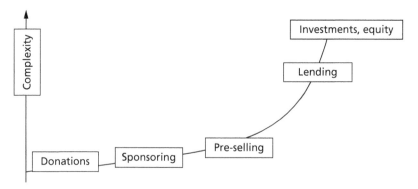

Figure 16.1. Major forms of pledging capital ranked by complexity
Source: Hemer, 2011

an analysis may not hold well in a social enterprise context as the investors' motives for investment may differ in that they are less concerned about costs but the outcome (Shaw and Carter, 2007; Delanoë, 2011).

Belleflamme et.al also provided some analysis as to why not-for-profit organizations tend to be more successful in using CF than others by examining literature on contract failure theory. This theory is based on the view that limiting the monetary motivations of owners, such as the presence of dividend caps or asset locks in some forms of social enterprise attracts donations more easily and invites other forms of participation, such as voluntary work. Limiting the potential monetary gain for owners can also be seen as a strong signal that they put a significant weight on the quality of the outcome/impact ahead of personal gain (Van Slyke, 2006; Lohrke, 2007). This links to work in information economics and signalling (Akerlof, 1970; Ketchen et al., 2007).

Pope (2011) identified the legal hurdles for equity-based CF in the USA that had been put in place by the Securities Exchange Commission (SEC). Such restrictions may also have relevance for other countries with heavily regulated capital markets. He scrutinized the difficulties for micro-start-ups to gain equity capital and their willingness to bootstrap through their own resources. As the public offering of equity is highly regulated, it brings tremendous costs for auditing, creating prospectuses, and consulting law firms and financial intermediaries. According to Pope, CF for equity in start-up ventures is being severely limited in the current legal situation. It is, therefore, logical that many forms of CF do not, so far, offer equity shares but other forms of rewards, for example early access to products, honorary recognition or some interest payments (see Figure 16.1). Hemer (2011) sees four established (and one emerging) models of CF:

- *Donations*: Investors donate money without expecting to receive tangible benefits
- *Rewards*: Investors support campaigns in order to receive some kind of reward

- *Debt*: Investors lend money and expect the future repayment. Interest payment is not mandatory in any setting
- *Equity*: Investors receive equity or equity-like shares in return for their investment.

Highly distributed equity stakes may, on the one hand, provide a clear democratic governance model for social enterprises, and, on the other, also be the missing opportunity for retail investors seeking ethical investments (Fox, 2012).

Legal and regulatory hurdles for equity CF were addressed in a ground-breaking manner by the JOBS Act in the USA. The Act lowered the restrictions on SEC Rule 506 offerings and freed seekers for small CF volumes <$100k, and to a lesser extent <$500k from several costly regulations. However, some resistance emerged (Pope, 2011; Rubinton, 2011; Heminway and Hoffman, 2012). As will be laid out more detailed later, new-institutionalism perspectives may provide insights into the power struggles behind the scenes and comparative studies are needed to address the viability of the model on an international level.

Schwienbacher and Larralde (2012) identify business models for CF, namely donations, as well as *passive* and *active* investments by the crowd. CF for donations has been a long-established means of finance for not-for-profits, non-governmental organizations, and to some extent, social enterprises (Hansmann, 1987). However, it is possible that as the number of CF initiatives and platforms rise, the resource 'crowd' for donations will become more and more scarce and competition will increase. Passive CF sees some reward for its investors, such as tailored products, honorary recognition, or other forms of revenue sharing. However, the interaction between the investee and its crowd investors is limited to the financing function. Active CF differs as its investors not only supply capital but are also involved in a dialogue with the firm: helping, for example, in designing new features, testing products, suggesting strategies for the company, and using their respective networks and individual expertise to grow the venture. This active form of CF is also very fruitful in providing a means of corporate communication and public relations. Active participation may also ultimately improve a company's perceived legitimacy.

Such a quest for legitimacy is of high value especially for social enterprises because of their position between the market, civil society, and the public sector (Nyssens, 2006). Social entrepreneurs, on the one hand, address social voids by market activities but, on the other hand, also work as social change-makers by influencing systems and policies (Cho, 2006; Drayton, 2006). Such attempts at policy change may inevitably see resistance from incumbent powers and institutions (Levander, 2010; Lim, Morse, Mitchell, and Seawright, 2010) and, therefore, needs to be strongly backed by claims to legitimacy.

CF can also have a global reach through the Internet and social media platforms. Agrawal et al. (2011) examined this in terms of the record industry, and found that CF showed a broad geographic dispersion of investors and that the potentially negative impact of distance-sensitive costs was mitigated—something in contrast to traditional finance theory, which would suggest that distrust rises with distance. This broad geographic dispersion of CF also matches well the global spread of social enterprise start-ups (Zahra et al., Zahra et al., 2008, 2009; Meyskens et al., 2010; Korsgaard, 2011). Indeed, specialized firms have created platforms on the Internet to bridge geographic distances and to act as the new intermediaries in the global CF market. Their important role will be discussed in the next section.

Modeling crowdfunding

Given the geographic distances in a global economy, tapping a large international crowd for financial support without the means of online social media would be expensive and difficult. While some well-established 'brands' such as Greenpeace may be able to operate conventional global fund-raising campaigns, this would be impossible for small start-up ventures. CF 'platforms'—as they are called by the SEC—equal software applications, developed by specialized companies, which are run on retail investors' Internet browsers to give access to global investment opportunities.

Their role, working as financial intermediaries, concerns several functions—from transporting information concerning possible investment opportunities, to collecting and representing the 'wisdom of the crowd', to address information asymmetries, and even playing 'watchdog' to prevent fraudulent misuse.

Some platforms host videos and presentations by entrepreneurs, thus providing a signalling element to allow for an easier selection by investors. Others embrace crowd evaluation tools—similar to the well-known Facebook style 'Like' buttons and comment functions. Others even work as gatekeepers as they only transfer the collected money to the ventures when a certain monetary goal (as stated in a business plan) has been reached.

The roles and functions of platforms are subject to constant development—they adjust to changing legislation, public opinion, and market trends. Microfinance entrepreneurs in developing countries have offered an important CF market (see, for example, Kiva in Table 16.1), the upfront investment by the crowd in independent records and software has also developed fast (see Kickstarter in Table 16.1), and there are increasing signs of equity investors in SEs coming on stream.

However, as many platforms are still in the early stages of development, the regulatory and legal environment in which they operate is still evolving. Moreover, there is little empirical data on the success or failure of various CF business models. When, perhaps inevitably, fraudulent CF cases emerge it is to be expected that legal and regulatory frameworks will develop to shape and restrict platforms' offerings and business models. Thus, emerging web-based platforms at the moment are acting as an intermediary between crowd-funders and individuals (Schwienbacher and Larralde, 2012), however with little regulation in an un-institutionalized sphere.

From a positive perspective, crowdsourcing platforms can be seen as enablers for innovation by facilitating new sets of practices and systems. Platform can be divided in three different types according to venture life cycles: exploration platforms, experimentation platforms, and execution plat-forms. According to Nambisan (2009), the majority of CF platforms will, over time, adapt to being execution platforms. Table 16.2 shows the capabilities of CF platforms.

CF platforms aim at facilitating transactions through their previous experi-ence and intermediary structures. The former can help circumvent legal and regulatory issues. Additionally, platforms can offer projects to new audiences with social network tools like Facebook or Twitter (Martinez-Canas, Ruiz-Palomino, and Pozo-Rubio, 2012). There are even findings that having more Facebook friends may be a predictor of later funding success (Massolution, 2012). The differing levels of specialist knowledge amongst participants in CF is mediated in various ways by specific platforms (Bannerman, 2011). Offline decisions often have to be made on relatively little data and may be, in a usually face-to-face setting, subject to cognitive biases. CF platforms are taking these concerns out of the game by embracing the so-called 'wisdom of the crowd' (Mollick, 2014).

The important role of payment providers, such as PayPal and related questions of trust, international legal regulations, transaction fees, and tax-ation have not been addressed in research and seem fuzzy in the empirical cases. Yet, the moderating power of payment platforms is clearly playing a part in bringing global crowd finance to SEs. A 2012 CF industry report, sponsored by US-based Massolutions, found 452 CF platforms (CFP) active worldwide, with a majority based in North America and Europe. Statistical data from 135 CFPs were evaluated in this study to gain insights into this new emerging

Table 16.2. Collaboration platforms

Perspective	Capabilities
Network-centric perspective	Play supporting roles, rather than controlling the collaboration process Adapt to the potentially varying goals of creators and investors Embrace non-traditional partners Leverage network resources and facilitate the flow of ideas and solutions
Modular or plug-and-play expertise	Deploy specialized expertise in diverse contexts both quickly and cost-effectively Integrate expertise with that of partners
A portfolio of success metrics	Agree on measures that reflect all stakeholder's concerns Define project goals in ways that subsume platform-specific goals

Source: Nambisan, 2009

industry, for example on income generation, geographical distribution, or types of funding offered.

The overview in Table 16.1 shows the various business models and approaches used by these platforms. It also demonstrates the importance of platforms as mediators of CF. The underlying business models are differing and constantly changing, most platforms, however, allow finite projects (such as a software or music) to be funded, with little more rewards to the investors than the actual product and some honorary stickers. Most platforms charge some form of commission from the funds. Ordanini et al. (2011) distinguished different types of CF. They took the risk–return ratio for customers (i.e. crowd members), combined with the type of pay-off expected into account to derive three different types:

- *models characterized by high levels of risk–return*; rewards are predominantly material pay–offs to consumers; activity is quite similar to what venture capitalists are doing
- *models characterized by low levels of risk–return*; have a broader set of potential rewards, allowing also for emotional rewards
- *models characterized by little or no risk*; close to charitable activities where only non-material pay-offs are expected.

Platforms typically offer various media applications, mostly videos and interactive blogs as communication strategies. Few platforms, however, have created their own viable marketing strategy and many are currently just carried along by the wider media hype around CF. Due to the close link between platforms and ventures, a possible failure of a platform might be expected to have negative impacts on the ventures listed and, perhaps, also to the overall legitimacy of CF itself. Although CF has its origins in the crowdsourcing movement, CF platforms mostly mediate project funding only and, perhaps due to the complex nature of finance, traditional crowdsourcing providers refrain from engaging in finance.

A merger or alliance of traditional crowdsourcing with CF platforms may provide them with a reliable source of income through commissions and, at the same time, offer platforms and their respective customers additional benefits. For example, the networks of the individual crowd-members can provide a rich pool of resources as part of the crowd-based strategies of new ventures. The crowdsourcing platforms OpenIdeo and Sparked are two outstanding examples of what crowdsourcing could offer, from idea generation to offering used items.

The most commonly accepted model of collecting 'pledges' from the crowd is the so-called 'all or nothing' approach. Initiators target a certain amount of money that must be raised within a pre-defined period of time. If the sum falls short of the target, then early supporters get their pledges back. Especially in a reward-based setting this 'threshold pledge system' can be seen as a means of risk reduction. Alternatively, in the 'keep it all' approach, a CF platform will immediately pay out funds to fund raisers, even if the pre-defined target is not met. This funding mode is common for projects that serve social or personal causes. Martinez-Canas et al. (2012). Massolution (2012) and Mollick (2014) found that an increase in the funding goal size is negatively associated with success within a reward- and donation-based CF setting. In addition, the increase of the pre-set duration of funding decreases the chances of success. Longer durations can be seen as a sign of a lack of confidence from the initiators.

Based on the literature and the early empirical evidence a preliminary model of CF can be developed (see Figure 16.2). Such a model can provide a framework to cluster discussion and research around the topic of CF. Its variables are based upon a careful analysis of existing platforms and key cases. However, this is only an exploratory model and further in-depth work will be needed to examine its actual utility functions and its moderator and mediator variables to allow for more precise modeling of CF functions and transactions.

Taken together, communication strategies and aspects of information economics combine with crowd members' risk tolerances and perceptions of the legitimacy of the business idea form the 'motivational effects' of a CF offer. These are further moderated by potential rewards, the offer of some control or participation and the intermediary platform's particular business model. Laws

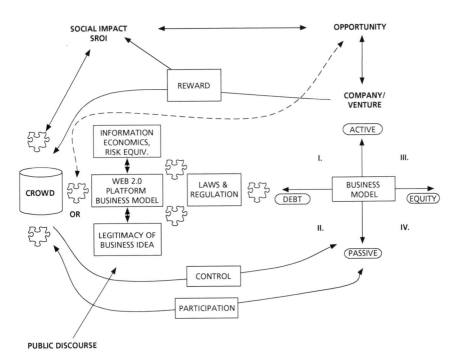

Figure 16.2. A matchmaking model
Source: Lehner, 2013

and regulation (including related costs) also form a strong mediator effect between the crowd/platform and the potential investees. This participation can take place within one of the four quadrants, spanning business models (active–passive) as well as type of capital (debt–equity).

Two elements are central to this model; first, the (social) opportunity itself as recognized and valued by the crowd and the venture likewise (Lehner and Kaniskas, 2012); second, the platform itself as it mediates the issues of information and risk and provides an institutional space to frame legitimacy (Nicholls, 2010). The (social) opportunity also frames one apparent reward in the form of a 'social return on investment' to the investee and, possibly, to the investor too in terms of psychological wellbeing.

Depending on the form of capital, the 'control' variable may have a more important role, especially when it comes to equity-based CF. Control, as a form of corporate governance, can be seen as a defining feature of social enterprise. Next, Figure 16.2 will be discussed in terms of CF business models and investor types of capital.

Debt crowdfunding: From donations to loans

From an economic perspective, choosing debt or equity CF finance may be determined by the stage and phase of a venture, its risk profile, and relevant legal regulations, as well as non-monetary goals such as corporate governance and reputational issues (Berger and Udell, 1998; Kreiser, Marino, Dickson, and Weaver, 2010).

Types of debt can be categorized by maturity from long-term bond to short-term advance payments in anticipation of future goods. Contrary to what the mainstream finance literature holds, the maturity and structure of the loans has not been seen to correlate with the required level of involvement and control in CF cases (Rubinton, 2011).

The value assessment by crowd investees of the particular outcomes of an investment (Ruebottom, 2011) appears to be a much higher motivation for active participation than monetary rewards or ownership/control. Desired outcomes could be a special software game, an independent record or a special park in the middle of New York. However, all these yields tend to display two characteristic attributes: first, a match with established normative value frames that enable opportunity recognition; second, high perceived legitimacy based upon currently constructed societal values.

As has been seen in several cases (Whitla, 2009; Kittur, 2010), active participation in addition to investment can take many forms in CF (Bloxham, 2011) from testing early prototypes to supporting viral marketing or volunteering. It even seems beneficial to the fund-raising process to invite some form of investor involvement, since participation will typically create a 'buzz' across social media that may draw in other potential investors (Belleflamme, Lambert, and Schwienbacher, 2014).

Due to legal complexities and restrictions, there have been few long-term, maturing CF bonds issued outside of traditional markets, so it is not yet clear what trends are emerging in terms of expected interest rates or the level of control and reporting expected from CF lenders (Pope, 2011; Rubinton, 2011; Schwienbacher and Larralde, 2012). Up to 2014, most cases of debt financing have been advance payments (Agrawal, Catalini, and Goldfarb, 2010; Chow, 2011; Schwienbacher and Larralde, 2012; Ward and Ramachandran, 2010) for future goods (such as music records or services).

Closely related to debt funding are donations. Donations are especially common in CF models for social enterprises. It appears that crowd investors in social enterprises do not always clearly differentiate between debt and donation since it neither case do they typically expect a conventional, risk-adjusted, financial return. On the other hand, some 'venture philanthropist' donors to social enterprises often seek a measured social return for their investments—frequently in the form of a demonstrated social outcome. Therefore, a form of reward is often involved in donations based upon the perceived likelihood of a desired outcome being achieved (social or environmental) (Chell, 2007; Nielsen and Noergaard, 2011).

In many cases, CF platforms work as fiduciary intermediaries by forwarding (or deducting in the case of credit cards) the collected money only when a pre-determined amount of capital has been raised—typically enough to start a project or venture (Ward and Ramachandran, 2010). Effective CF requires careful information management between the platform and investors, in order to facilitate future contributions and to build perceived public legitimacy. Early case evidence, however, suggests that the main focus of investor communications tends to be limited to the start-up phase of a venture: the focus of the investor relations is mainly on 'selling' a project or idea. Such an approach works well for finite projects in an early market, but will be less effective in cases of long-term debt investment (Bassen, Basse Mama, and Ramaj, 2010).

This may be especially true in the field of social enterprise, since social and sustainable investments often have a significant emotional engagement for the investor. This demands high levels of continuous communication to demonstrate credibly that desired social outcomes are being achieved. One further peculiarity of social and sustainable CF investment may be complex forms of hybrid partnerships and organizational forms that can have various legal forms (Grimsey and Lewis, 2007; Kwak, Chih, and Ibbs, 2009). For example, the New York 'Lowline' initiative[2] was structured as a combination of public contributions of land and facilities (an disused tramway station) with private CF capital. Hybrid CF investment models may also involve additional transaction costs, bureaucracy, and, perhaps, divergent logics and desired outcomes

---

[2] <http://www.kickstarter.com/projects/855802805/lowline-an-underground-park-on-nycs-lower-east-sid>, accessed 8 June 2012.

(especially in terms of profit-making) that can introduce tensions and issues over time (Biau, 2011). For example, in one case, a social enterprise created a public garden in disused public land near to New York University. Yet, the long-term survival of the project has been threatened as the NYU seeks to expand and the New York City authorities may revoke its support for the garden in order to sell the space. Next there is a discussion of equity-based CF and the diffusion of risk.

Equity: Shares and securities

Equity financing may provide the greatest challenges but also the greatest opportunities for CF-financed social enterprises. Typically, equity investments are legally linked with several rights including: rights to information and control, rights to share in the earnings or added value of the company (Berger and Udell, 1998), rights to sell shares in secondary markets and to make a profit. Compared to raising debt finance, offering shares or equity is, ultimately, a means of distributing risk to investors (Sharfman and Fernando, 2008). Investors taking on risk expect to be compensated, so equity-based CF comes at a much higher cost for ventures, often in terms of control, govern-ance, and stewardship (Meuleman, Amess, Wright, and Scholes, 2009).

Yet, the challenges of equity-based CF are multi-faceted and comprise legal and regulatory hurdles (Heminway and Hoffman, 2012; Schwienbacher and Larralde, 2012; Pope, 2011; Rubinton, 2011), as well as considerations about governance and control. Initial public offerings (IPOs) of a company's equity are usually highly regulated in most developed countries including complex and expensive registration and disclosure regulations.

In traditional for-profit finance, dispersing control is seen as a negative factor. However, its impact on corporate governance might be more positive for social enterprises, as increased shareholder participation could improve legitimacy and broaden engagement with a social or environmental issue (Ridley-Duff, 2009). Yet, there is also a risk of 'mission drift' as shareholders could pressure a social enterprise to increase profits and reduce social costs (Huarng and Yu, 2011; Vaccaro, Jansen, Van Den Bosch, and Volberda, 2012). Sometimes, such risks are mitigated by complex ownership and governance structures. Symbid (see Table 16.2) was structured so that all investments into its ventures were transferred into membership certificates with direct voting rights as part of the platform's co-operative legal form, but with only indirect voting rights into the enterprise of the investee entrepreneur and with limited transferability and dividends. There have been similar examples in the UK—such as on Crowdcube (see Table 16.2)—also addressing equity-based CF with complex contract structuring.

The JOBS Act in the USA represented a ground-breaking change in policy, as legal and regulatory hurdles were minimized to allow some forms of CF equity (Agrawal et al., 2010; Pope, 2011; Heminway and Hoffman, 2012). The Act addressed (Parrino and Romeo, 2012; Stemler, 2013):

- the registration provisions of the Securities Act governing publicly offered securities for a narrowly-defined class of offerings
- the registration provisions of the Securities Exchange Act governing the triggers that require registration of a class of securities under the Exchange Act, but only for limited purposes
- the broker-dealer registration requirements to create a SEC registered new entity, the 'funding portal', which is permitted to undertake some functions that would previously require registration as a broker.

While this US legislation may be seen as an important milestone in the further development of CF and may influence subsequent European legislation, the fragmented markets in Europe will also need to find local models that work for the various approaches to securities across the Union (De Buysere et al., 2012). The European CF Framework[3] can be seen as an early pan-European model.

Equity CF may offer a solution to reduce investees' dependency on scarce donation capital, increase enterprise legitimacy, and stakeholder-participation and may also offer a more long-term funding model than short-term CF debt finance. This may be especially true in the case of ventures with require a large upfront investment (Pope, 2011; Rubinton, 2011; Schwienbacher and Larralde, 2012).

In terms of the reward systems of shareholder value and dividends, CF investors in social enterprises are likely to follow a different rationale by being more oriented towards social impact. However the monetary aspect of dividends and the tradability of the investments will always be an important element of CF equity and the lack of secondary equity markets for social enterprise shares remains an important barrier to the further growth of this type of capital. Yet, the principal stimuli for investors—the availability of good information, projected growth, attractive value proposition, and access to control (Ketchen et al., 2007; Cumming, 2012) all apply to social enterprise investment too.

Several legal forms, tailored for social enterprises, such as the community interest company (CIC) in the UK, or L3C in the USA have built-in dividend or debt interest caps or other prohibitions (Ridley-Duff, 2008, 2009; Nicholls, 2009). These legal forms may also have an asset-lock provision that does not allow a hostile takeover to realize assets or compromise the organization's social mission. The co-operative and mutual legal form also has key equity restrictions limiting external investment or share transfer/sale.

There are also the more strategic and for-profit considerations in equity-based CF, based upon real-options logic (Tong and Reuer, 2007; Scherpereel, 2008; Levitas and Chi, 2010). Some relatively small investment at the beginning

---

[3] <http://www.crowdfundingframework.eu>, accessed 28 March 2013.

may provide access and control over the investment if it turns out to be successful later, while the downside risk is limited to the investment itself. In a social enterprise context such a real option may well provide tangible value to the investors in terms of their own legitimacy, access to ethical consumer markets, useful knowledge of hybrid market spaces and so on.

It remains to be seen, however, whether actual cost of capital calculations may lead to reappraisal of the impact of the JOBS Act in terms of its effects on the CF market. The next section of this chapter sets out an agenda for such research.

Future research

It remains clear from what has been said above that the CF market is in a state of dynamic evolution and remains very far from being fully institutionalized globally. Reflecting on some of the issues discussed in this chapter, a number of research themes can be identified for CF, particularly in a social enterprise context:

- *The crowd*: While we are talking about the crowd as a distinctive entity, little is known about the actual make up of the 'crowd'. Can its members be clustered and segmented using certain attributes? What can be said about the value propositions and utility functions specific to crowd-investors?

- *Platforms*: CF platforms are proliferating, offering various forms of crowd-sourcing and CF: from an active participation as volunteers, to monetary donations and even equity shares. There appear to be a multitude of business models under development across platforms and this would seem to imply an experimental phase. What dominant models are emerging? Are they context specific? How sustainable is the CF platform model? How do platforms and payment providers, such as PayPal team up? What is the moderating power of these providers in regards to successful CF applications and investors?

- *Applications and opportunities*: Which business models and opportunities will work especially well when tapping the crowd for funds? Early research suggest that investors are particularly attracted to creative, innovative, or socially focused enterprises (Lehner, 2013). What can be learned from cases of success or failure? What additional resources and benefits can be realized from the CF model?

- *Corporate governance*: Social enterprises typically focus on stakeholder inclusion in their corporate governance structure. However, in CF investments the number of stakeholders involved may be very large. What impact will this have on the governance structures of social enterprises? How can new interactive web-based media be used to deal with these challenges? Will the increased number of stakeholders create better or worse corporate governance structures?

- *Risk and disclosure*: In traditional investor relations a core perspective of the firm is to reduce perceived risk through transparent reporting and timely disclosure. However, CF platforms offer very limited reporting with presentations of the ventures often oriented on selling the investment. In addition, recent enabling legislation, for example the JOBS Act, have actually reduced auditing and reporting requirements, leaving crowd investors potentially more vulnerable to fraud. Will there be more fraudulent cases without proper regulation or will a 'wisdom of the crowd' element increase transparency, help share data, and, ultimately, prevent fraud?

- *The role of networks and geographies*: What is the role of cognitive and cultural closeness in the networks of CF ventures? Can the network structures of investees, investors, and/or platforms predict CF success or failure? What is the role of geographic distance? What are the implications of future developments in Internet and mobile information technologies? Which sociological theories may provide a guiding framework for CF research?

- *Discourse and legitimacy*: How does society perceive CF social enterprises in terms of legitimacy? Is CF perceived as more 'democratic' and is the dispersion of control in such models perceived as a positive thing? What is the fate of minority problems and efforts?

- *Neo-institutionalist perspectives*: From a neo-institutionalist perspective, do states or incumbent welfare institutions feel threatened by multinational CF initiatives that act upon values that are, perhaps, incompatible with some states' or religions' logics, norms, and cultures? Can CF transcend states and institutions? Are CF pioneers functioning as Schumpeterian entrepreneurs (Zahra et al., 2009), bringing about creative and disruptive (social) innovations? Who regulates and controls CF as a global phenomenon? Should it be constrained?

- *Legal and regulative perspectives in CF*: So far, platforms addressing equity-based CF have had to develop complex structuring to avoid costly rules and regulation. Have regulatory initiatives aimed at enhancing CF diluted reporting and auditing requirements in a dangerous fashion increasing information asymmetry and the opportunity for moral hazard and free-riding behaviours. In addition, further issues arise concerning the tax treatments of CF and its transaction costs. These may be particularly pertinent in the social enterprise setting with its complex and unusual legal forms (e.g. the CIC or L3C).

CF is an emergent and under-institutionalized market for social finance. But it has grown fast and seems likely to continue to do so having global implications for new ventures both social and otherwise. There remain many unanswered questions concerning its value and effects and a robust research agenda is needed to generate meaningful analysis and support future developments in practice.

Conclusion

This chapter has reviewed the limited literature on CF and has offered a market overview based on a new analytic model to structure future research and analysis. It has also attempted to contextualize CF within the social finance market in terms of its implications for providing a new source of retail investment in social enterprises.

The chapter has also suggested that there is an urgent need for a range of new research to underpin the next stage of evolution of CF. Such research needs to be interdisciplinary, borrowing its perspectives and methods from the interplay of various domains, by looking at the diverse fields of finance, economics, politics, law, international relations, communications, and entrepreneurship and business. Büscher and Urry (2009) noted the need for new strategies of inquiry in the age of mobile devices as a whole and proposed the 'mobilities' paradigm. New methodological considerations on how to conduct empirical studies that better grasp the nature of movements of people, objects, information, and ideas using social media and mobile devices will support valid research agendas for CF.

Such solid and specialized studies at the field level will ultimately help inform policymakers and practitioners too and thus contribute to building a successful CF market, a market enabling social enterprises to connect with millions of retail investors to share social agendas, start-up, scale, and overcome structural resistance.

▓ REFERENCES

Agrawal, A., Catalini, C., and Goldfarb, A. (2010). 'Entrepreneurial Finance and the Flat-World Hypothesis: Evidence from Crowd-Funding Entrepreneurs in the Arts', NET Institute Working Paper 10-08.

Agrawal, A. K., Catalini, C., and Goldfarb, A. (2011). 'The Geography of Crowdfunding', National Bureau of Economic Research, Cambridge, MA.

Akerlof, G. A. (1970). 'The Market for "Lemons": Quality Uncertainty and the Market Mechanism', *Quarterly Journal of Economics*, 84(3): 488–500.

Bannerman, S. (2011). 'Crowdfunding Culture'. Paper presented at the annual conference of the International Association for the Study of Popular Music, Canadian Chapter, Montreal.

Baron, D. P. (2007). 'Corporate Social Responsibility and Social Entrepreneurship', *Journal of Economics & Management Strategy*, 16(3): 683–717.

Bassen, A., Basse Mama, H., and Ramaj, H. (2010). 'Investor Relations: A Comprehensive Overview', *Journal für Betriebswirtschaft*, 60(1): 49–79.

Bauer-Leeb, M., and Lundqvist, E. (2012). 'Social Entrepreneurs and Business Angels: A Quest for Factors Facilitating Business Relationships'. Working Paper Danube University, Krems.

Belleflamme, P., Lambert, T., and Schwienbacher, A. (2010). 'Crowdfunding: An Industrial Organization Perspective', paper presented at the Digital Business Models: Understanding Strategies Conference, Paris 25–26 June.

Belleflamme, P., Lambert, T., and Schwienbacher, A. (2014). 'Crowdfunding: Tapping the Right Crowd', *Journal of Business Venturing*, 29(5): 585–609.

Berger, A. N., and Udell, G. F. (1998). 'The Economics of Small Business Finance: The Roles of Private Equity and Debt Markets in the Financial Growth Cycle', *Journal of Banking and Finance*, 22(6–8): 613–73.

Biau, C. (2011). 'The "Governance Gap", or Missing Links in Transnational Chains of Accountability for Extractive Industry Investment', *Journal of Sustainable Finance & Investment*, 1(3–4): 251–60.

Bloxham, E. (2011). 'Corporate Governance and Sustainability: New and Old Models of Thinking', *Journal of Sustainable Finance & Investment*, 1(1): 77–80.

Brown, H., and Murphy, E. (2003). 'The Financing of Social Enterprises: A Special Report by the Bank of England Domestic Finance Division'. Bank of England, London.

Bull, M., and Crompton, H. (2006). 'Business Practices in Social Enterprises', *Social Enterprise Journal*, 2(1): 42–60.

Büscher, M., and Urry, J. (2009). 'Mobile Methods and the Empirical', *European Journal of Social Theory*, 12(1): 99–116.

Chell, E. (2007). 'Social Enterprise and Entrepreneurship: Towards a Convergent Theory of the Entrepreneurial Process', *International Small Business Journal*, 25(1): 5–26.

Cho, A. H. (2006). 'Politics, Values and Social Entrepreneurship: A Critical Appraisal', in J. Mair, J. Robinson, and K. Hockerts (eds), *Social Entrepreneurship*. Hampshire: Palgrave Macmillan, pp. 34–56.

Chow, C. (2011). 'Establishing a Corporate Sustainability Monitoring Tool Using the Shareholder Engagement Commitment Indicator', *Journal of Sustainable Finance & Investment*, 1(3–4): 195–208.

Cumming, D. (2012). *The Oxford Handbook of Entrepreneurial Finance*. Oxford: Oxford University Press.

Dacin, P. A., Dacin, M. T., and Matear, M. (2010). 'Social Entrepreneurship: Why We Don't Need a New Theory and How We Move Forward From Here', *The Academy of Management Perspectives*, 24(3): 37–57.

De Buysere, K., Gajda, O., Kleverlaan, R., and Marom, D. (2012). 'A Framework for European Crowdfunding', European Crowdfunding Network, Brussels.

Delanoë, S. (2011). 'An Individual-level Perspective for Assessing Nascent Venturing Outcomes', *Journal of Small Business and Enterprise Development*, 18(2): 232–50.

Drayton, B. (2006). 'Everyone a Changemaker: Social Entrepreneurship's Ultimate Goal', *Innovations*, 1(1): 80–96.

Dushnitsky, G., and Shapira, Z. (2010). 'Entrepreneurial Finance Meets Organizational Reality: Comparing Investment Practices and Performance of Corporate and Independent Venture Capitalists', *Strategic Management Journal*, 31(9): 990–1017.

Esping-Andersen, G. (2006). *The Three Worlds of Welfare Capitalism*. Cambridge: Polity Press.

Fedele, A., and Miniaci, R. (2010). 'Do Social Enterprises Finance Their Investments Differently from For-profit Firms? The Case of Social Residential Services in Italy', *Journal of Social Entrepreneurship*, 1(2): 174–89.

Flockhart, A. (2005). 'Raising the Profile of Social Enterprises: The Use of Social Return on Investment (SROI) and Investment-ready Tools (IRT) to Bridge the Financial Credibility Gap', *Social Enterprise Journal*, 1(1): 29–42.

Fox, S. (2012). 'The New Do-it-yourself Paradigm: Financial and Ethical Rewards for Businesses', *Journal of Business Strategy*, 33(1): 21–6.

Grimsey, D., and Lewis, M. (2007). *Public–private Partnerships: The Worldwide Revolution in Infrastructure Provision and Project Finance*. Cheltenham: Edward Elgar Publishing.

Hansmann, H. (1987). 'Economic Theories of Nonprofit Organizations', in W. W. Powell (ed.) *The Nonprofit Sector: A Research Handbook*. New Haven, CT: Yale University Press.

Hemer, J. (2011). 'A Snapshot on Crowdfunding'. Working papers firms and region, no. R2/2011, Fraunhofer-Institut für System- und Innovationsforschung (ISI).

Heminway, J., and Hoffman, S. (2012). 'Proceed at Your Peril: CF and the Securities Act of 1933', *Tennessee Law Review*, 78: 879–973.

Howe, J. (2006). 'The Rise of Crowdsourcing', *Wired*, 14(6): 1–4.

Huarng, K.-H., and Yu, T. H.-K. (2011). 'Entrepreneurship, Process Innovation and Value Creation by a Non-profit SME', *Management Decision*, 49(2): 284–96.

Huppé, G. A., and Hebb, T. (2011). 'The Virtue of CalPERS' Emerging Equity Markets Principles', *Journal of Sustainable Finance & Investment*, 1(1): 62–76.

Irwin, D., and Scott, J. M. (2010). 'Barriers Faced by SMEs in Raising Bank Finance', *International Journal of Entrepreneurial Behaviour & Research*, 16(3): 245–59.

Ketchen, D. J., Boyd, B. K., and Bergh, D. D. (2007). 'Research Methodology in Strategic Management: Past Accomplishments and Future Challenges', *Organizational Research Methods*, 11(4): 643–58.

Kittur, A. (2010). 'Crowdsourcing, Collaboration and Creativity', *XRDS*, 17(2): 22–6.

Korsgaard, S. (2011). 'Opportunity Formation in Social Entrepreneurship', *Journal of Enterprising Communities: People and Places in the Global Economy*, 5(4): 265–85.

Kreiser, P. M., Marino, L. D., Dickson, P., and Weaver, K. M. (2010). 'Cultural Influences on Entrepreneurial Orientation: The Impact of National Culture on Risk-taking and Proactiveness in SMEs', *Entrepreneurship Theory and Practice*, 34(5): 959–83.

Kwak, Y. H., Chih, Y., and Ibbs, C. W. (2009). 'Towards a Comprehensive Understanding of Public-private Partnerships for Infrastructure Development', *California Management Review*, 51(2): 51–78.

Lam, W. (2010). 'Funding Gap, What Funding Gap? Financial Bootstrapping: Supply, Demand and Creation of Entrepreneurial Finance', *International Journal of Entrepreneurial Behaviour & Research*, 16(4): 268–95.

Lambert, T., and Schwienbacher, A. (2010). 'An Empirical Analysis of Crowdfunding', *Social Science Research Network* 1578175.

Lehner, O. M. (2011). 'The Phenomenon of Social Enterprise in Austria: A Triangulated Descriptive Study', *Journal of Social Entrepreneurship*, 2(1): 53–78.

Lehner, O. M. (2013). 'CF Social Ventures: A Model and Research Agenda', *Venture Capital*, 15(4): 289–311.

Lehner, O. M., and Kaniskas, J. (2012). 'Opportunity Recognition in Social Entrepreneurship: A Thematic Meta Analysis', *Journal of Entrepreneurship*, 21(1): 25–58.

Levander, U. (2010). 'Social Enterprise: Implications of Emerging Institutionalized Constructions', *Journal of Social Entrepreneurship*, 1(2): 213–30.

Levitas, E., and Chi, T. (2010). 'A Look at the Value Creation Effects of Patenting and Capital Investment through a Real Options Lens: The Moderating Role of Uncertainty', *Strategic Entrepreneurship Journal*, 4(3): 212–33.

Lim, D. S. K., Morse, E. A., Mitchell, R. K., and Seawright, K. K. (2010). 'Institutional Environment and Entrepreneurial Cognitions: A Comparative Business Systems Perspective', *Entrepreneurship Theory and Practice*, 34(3): 491–516.

Lohrke, F. T. (2007). 'Book Review: Ketchen, D. J., Jr., and Bergh, D. D. (eds), *Research Methodology in Strategy and Management*', *Organizational Research Methods*, 11(4): 860–4.

Martinez-Canas, R., Ruiz-Palomino, P., and Pozo-Rubio, R. (2012). 'Crowdfunding and Social Networks in the Music Industry: Implications for Entrepreneurship', *International Business & Economics Research Journal* (IBER), 11(13): 1471–6.

Massolution (2012). *Enterprise Crowdsourcing Industry Report*. Boston, MA: Massolution.

Meuleman, M., Amess, K., Wright, M., and Scholes, L. (2009). 'Agency, Strategic Entrepreneurship, and the Performance of Private Equity Backed Buyouts', *Entrepreneurship Theory and Practice*, 33(1): 213–39.

Meyer, M. (2009). 'Wie viel Wirtschaft verträgt die Zivilgesellschaft? Über Möglichkeiten und Grenzen wirtschaftlicher Rationalität in NPOs', in I. Bode, A. Evers, and A. Klein (eds), *Bürgergesellschaft als Projekt*. Wiesbaden: VS Verlag für Sozialwissenschaften, pp. 127–44.

Meyskens, M., Robb-Post, C., Stamp, J. A., Carsrud, A. L., and Reynolds, P. D. (2010). 'Social Ventures from a Resource-based Perspective: An Exploratory Study Assessing Global Ashoka Fellows', *Entrepreneurship Theory and Practice*, 34(4): 661–80.

Mollick, E. (2012). 'The Dynamics of Crowdfunding: Determinants of Success and Failure', *Journal of Business Venturing*, 29(1): 1–16.

Nambisan, S. (2009). 'Platforms for Collaboration', *Stanford Social Innovation Review*, 7(3): 44–9.

Nicholls, A. (2009). '"We Do Good Things, Don't We?"' Blended Value Accounting in Social Entrepreneurship', *Accounting, Organizations and Society*, 34(6–7): 755–69.

Nicholls, A. (2010). 'The Legitimacy of Social Entrepreneurship: Reflexive Isomorphism in a Pre-Paradigmatic Field', *Entrepreneurship Theory and Practice*, 34(4): 611–33.

Nielsen, K. P., and Noergaard, R. W. (2011). 'CSR and Mainstream Investing: A New Match? An Analysis of the Existing ESG Integration Methods in Theory and Practice and the Way Forward', *Journal of Sustainable Finance & Investment*, 1(3–4): 209–21.

Nyssens, M. (ed.) (2006). *Social Enterprise: At the Crossroads of Market, Public Policies and Civil Society*. London and New York: Routledge.

Ordanini, A., Miceli, L., Pizzetti, M., and Parasuraman, A. (2011). 'Crowd-funding: Transforming Customers into Investors through Innovative Service Platforms', *Journal of Service Management*, 22(4): 443–70.

Parrino, R. J., and Romeo, P. J. (2012). 'JOBS Act Eases Securities-law Regulation of Smaller Companies', *Journal of Investment Compliance*, 13(3): 27–35.

Pope, N. (2011). 'Crowdfunding Microstartups: It's Time for the Securities and Exchange Commission to Approve a Small Offering Exemption' *University of Pasadena Journal of Business Law*, 13: 973–87.

Ridley-Duff, R. (2008). 'Social Enterprise as a socially Rational Business', *International Journal of Entrepreneurial Behaviour and Research*, 14(5): 291–312.

Ridley-Duff, R. (2009). 'Co-operative Social Enterprises: Company Rules, Access to Finance and Management Practice', *Social Enterprise Journal*, 5(1): 50–68.

Rubinton, B. (2011). *Crowdfunding: Disintermediated Investment Banking.* <http://ssrn.com/abstract=1807204> or <http://dx.doi.org/10.2139/ssrn.1807204>, accessed 1 November 2014.

Ruebottom, T. (2011). 'Counting Social Change: Outcome Measures for Social Enterprise', *Social Enterprise Journal*, 7(2): 173–82.

Scherpereel, C. M. (2008). 'The Option-creating Institution: A Real Options Perspective on Economic Organization', *Strategic Management Journal*, 29(5): 455–70.

Schwienbacher, A., and Larralde, B. (2012). 'Crowdfunding of Small Entrepreneurial Ventures', in D. Cumming (ed.), *The Oxford Handbook of Entrepreneurial Finance.* Oxford: Oxford University Press, pp. 369–92.

Sharfman, M. P., and Fernando, C. S. (2008). 'Environmental Risk Management and the Cost of Capital', *Strategic Management Journal*, 29(6): 569–92.

Shaw, E., and Carter, S. (2007). 'Social Entrepreneurship: Theoretical Antecedents and Empirical Analysis of Entrepreneurial Processes and Outcomes', *Journal of Small Business and Enterprise Development*, 14(3): 418–34.

Stemler, A. R. (2013). 'The JOBS Act and Crowdfunding: Harnessing the Power—and Money—of the Masses', *Business Horizons*, 56(3): 271–5.

Tong, T. W., and Reuer, J. J. (2007). 'Real Options in Strategic Management', *Advances in Strategic Management*, 24: 3–28.

Vaccaro, I. G., Jansen, J. J. P., Van Den Bosch, F. A. J., and Volberda, H. W. (2012). 'Management Innovation and Leadership: The Moderating Role of Organizational Size', *Journal of Management Studies*, 49(1): 28–51.

Van Slyke, D. M. (2006). 'Agents or Stewards: Using Theory to Understand the Government–Nonprofit Social Service Contracting Relationship', *Journal of Public Administration Research and Theory*, 17(2): 157–87.

Ward, C., and Ramachandran, V. (2010). 'Crowdfunding the Next Hit: Microfunding Online Experience Goods'. Workshop on Computational Social Science and the Wisdom of Crowds at NIPS 2010.

Waygood, S. (2011). 'How Do the Capital Markets Undermine Sustainable Development? What Can Be Done to Correct This?' *Journal of Sustainable Finance & Investment*, 1(1): 81–7.

Whitla, P. (2009). 'Crowdsourcing and Its Application in Marketing Activities', *Contemporary Management Research*, 5(1): 15–28.

Yunus, M., and Weber, K. (2007). *Creating a World without Poverty: Social Business and the Future of Capitalism.* New York: Public Affairs.

Zahra, S., Gedajlovic, E., Neubaum, D., and Shulman, J. (2009). 'A Typology of Social Entrepreneurs: Motives, Search Processes and Ethical Challenges', *Journal of Business Venturing*, 24(5): 519–32.

Zahra, S., Rawhouser, H., Bhawe, N., Neubaum, D., and Hayton, J. (2008). 'Globalization of Social Entrepreneurship Opportunities'. *Strategic Entrepreneurship Journal*, 2(2): 117–31.

17 Investing for social impact

Direct foreign investment and private equity in Africa and South Asia

Peter Hinton and Sweta Penemetsa

Introduction

Development finance institutions (DFIs) and private equity (PE) have played a pioneering role in investing in sub-Saharan Africa and South Asia. Typically they have looked to achieve financial returns and to a greater or lesser degree, development or social returns. DFIs have been acting in this way for over sixty years compared with PE investors who are more recent players in these geographies. This chapter explores the evolution of the DFI sector and explores in what ways it is functioning as a source of social impact investment—acting in its own specialized way as a distinctive social finance market.

A DFI is typically a developed-country funded agency that supports the economic development of specific countries or regions through the provision of long-term capital to the private sector in the form of debt, equity, or other instruments. Major DFIs are set out in Table 17.1 below.

In contrast to DFIs typically established and funded by the public sector, PE fund managers are normally private sector-led entities. PE can be defined as equity risk financing provided for management buyouts, growth, and mature-stage private companies. It is a term that also covers venture capital (VC) where, typically, finance is provided to start-ups and early-stage companies.

This chapter aims to assess the current DFI and PE investment landscape in emerging markets. The following pages include a comparative analysis of selected DFIs and PE firms on the basis of relevant mandates, financial instruments utilized, geographic focus, and industry coverage. Notably, the analysis and commentary presented places special emphasis on the African and South Asian markets.

DFIs, by nature of their mandates and ownership structures have been providing social finance to emerging markets for many decades. Their emphasis on the importance of compliance with certain standards of environment, social, and governance aspects (often as a precondition of investing) places them firmly in the social finance space. This emphasis has often been combined with DFIs looking to measure the social impact of how their funding is used and the development impact achieved.

Table 17.1. Bilateral and multilateral DFIs

	Insitutional Name	Headquarters	Established
AFDB	African Development Bank	Tunisia	1964
ADB	Asian Development Bank	Philippines	1966
BMI	**Belgian Corporation for International Investment**	**Belgium**	**1971**
BIO	**Belgian Investment Company for Developing Countries**	**Belgium**	**2001**
CDB	Caribbean Development Bank	Barbados	1969
COFIDES	**COFIDES S.A.**	**Spain**	**1990**
CDC	**Commonwealth Development Corporation**	**United Kingdom**	**1948**
CEB	Council of Europe Development Bank	France	1956
DEG	**Deutsche Investitionsund Entwicklungsgesellschaft**	**Germany**	**1962**
DBSA	Development Bank of Southern Africa	South Africa	1983
EBRD	European Bank for Reconstruction and Development	United Kingdom	1991
EIB	European Investment Bank	Luxembourg	1957
FinnFund	**Finnish Fund for Industrial Cooperation Ltd.**	**Finalnd**	**1980**
IDC	Industrial Development Corporation of SA	South Africa	1940
IFU	**Industrialisation Fund for Developing Countries**	**Denmark**	**1967**
IADB	Inter-American Development Bank	United States	1959
IFC	**International Finance Corporation**	**United States**	**1956**
ISDB	Islamic Development Bank	Saudi Arabia	1973
FMO	**Financierings-maatschappij voor ontwikkelingslanden N.V.**	**Netherlands**	**1970**
NorFund	**Norweigan Investment Fund for Developing Countries**	**Norway**	**1997**
OeEB	**Oesterreichische Entwicklungsbank AG**	**Austria**	**2007**
OPIC	Overseas Private Investment Corporation	United States	1971
PIDG	**Private Infrastructure Development Group**	**United Kingdom**	**2002**
PROP	**Proparco**	**France**	**1977**
PTA	PTA Bank	Burundi	1985
SOFID	**Sociedade para o Financiamento do Desenvolvimento**	**Portugal**	**2007**
Swedfund	**Swedfund International AB**	**Sweden**	**1979**
SIFEM	**Swiss Investment Fund for Emerging Markets**	**Switzerland**	**2005**
SIMEST	Società Italiana per le Imprese all'Estero	Italy	1991
WADB	West African Development Bank	Togo	1973

Source: EDFI 2012 Annual Report, company websites

Note: Institutions highlighted in bold are included in the analysis that follows.

The degree to which PE funds are providing social finance is largely a function of whether they are 'finance first' (such as Actis of the UK) or 'impact first' funds (such as Goodwell of the Netherlands).

The chapter concludes by looking at key issues, with respect to social finance, that require addressing by the DFIs and PE firms, namely:

- the need for capital and the role of DFIs
- the need for a track record
- the need for financial innovation
- the need for greater risk taking
- the need for a blended view of return
- the need for locally based emerging market institutions to invest in PE.

In order to demonstrate the variety and social impact of DFI and PE investments, specific examples have been included throughout the chapter. These examples were drawn from various DFI publications.

Development finance institutions

By comparison, DFIs typically seek to promote development goals, such as poverty reduction, economic growth, and private sector development (IFC, 2011a). According to a 2011 survey conducted by the World Bank of private sector companies throughout the developing world, the major obstacles to growth were (IFC, 2011b):

- access to finance
- infrastructure
- the investment climate
- worker skills.

DFIs look to address some or all of these obstacles and have historically been established mainly by Western hemisphere governments. Consequently, DFIs ironically end up being Western government public sector controlled institutions that address private sector challenges by providing finance and knowledge to the private sector in the developing world. The justification often given is that the private sector is not prepared to invest in developing world opportunities given the perception that the risks are too high and the size of investment too small. Consequently, DFIs primarily exist to fulfil one or more of the following roles:

- provide financing to companies that have limited access to finance from other sources (particularly equity capital)
- provide project-related finance
- provide general advisory and/or technical assistance to share specialized knowledge, thereby improving investment outcomes
- act in a catalytic role by mitigating country/project risk and therefore helping to bring additional financing from other investors
- demonstrate the viability of private sector solutions in challenging markets, catalysing later investments and 'fostering safe innovation'.

The UK-based Commonwealth Development Corporation (CDC) fulfilled a number of these roles when, in 2010, CDC invested $12.6m to Seedfund 2, an investment fund that backs start-up and early-stage companies in India in the consumer, technology, retail, and education sectors that struggled to raise the required capital for their business idea. CDC's financial and advisory assistance helped Seedfund 2 raise close to $50m in capital commitments. They could then invest in RedBus which makes buying bus tickets much more efficient and organized; with a $2m investment RedBus evolved from an online start-up to a sophisticated service with over 450 employees that offer bus tickets at over 40,000 services point.

Likewise, Swiss Investment Fund for Emerging Markets (SIFEM) of Switzerland extended a $6m senior loan to AccessBank in Azerbaijan in 2007 with the purpose of using SIFEM's advanced knowledge in finance and investment to grow AccessBank's MSME (micro, small, and medium enterprises) and agriculture lending activities. Since 2007, AccessBank has maintained double-digit year-on-year growth despite the stress of the global economic downturn. In 2009 the bank had 960 employees, and used the SIFEM facility to lend 2,080 loans. In 2008 a social performance impact survey showed AccessBank's long-term clients spent 336 per cent more on education compared to new clients, versus 78 per cent more than the industry average. Likewise, expenditure on healthcare fell more for AccessBank's long-term clients (33 per cent) than for the industry (12 per cent) caused by the increased education and improved living conditions of these clients.

Similarly, in 2007, Finnish Fund for Industrial Cooperation Ltd (FinnFund) provided an investment loan and equity for OOO Volgastrap, which is the first production facility to produce high-quality steel strapping in Russia. The Finnish-owned Specta Group AG, which is a leading supplier of transport packaging and machinery for the metal and wood processing industry in Russia, is the other major investor in the project. The total value of the investment was US$20m.

For over forty years IFC has invested in Serena Hotel Groups and in 2008, they invested a further $8.1m to support a $20.8m expansion and refurbishment of the 'Serena Kigali Hotel'. A case study conducted by ODI showed that each room in the Serena Kigali creates and sustains ten jobs. Moreover, in the five years after the expansion the hotel has established linkages with many local suppliers and generated $85m of economic activity, $64m of which related to the local Rwandan economy.

Typically, DFIs help fill investment gaps in the developing world's private sector and improve the development impact of each project they invest in (IFC, 2011b). Bilateral DFIs, funded by one government, typically have specialized knowledge and expertise on certain countries, sectors, financial products, and investment partners. Some of these are based on the institution's home country's interests abroad. For example, FinnFund co-invests with Finnish companies and also finances projects that use Finnish technology or co-operate with Finnish partners.

Multilateral DFIs, funded by several governments, are typically larger, such as the International Finance Corporation (IFC), European Bank for Reconstruction and Development (EBRD), and the Asian Development Bank (ADB). Some have been in operation for over fifty years, such as the IFC (part of the World Bank) and the UK's Commonwealth Development Corporation, while others were established in the new millennium. The youngest DFIs are Oesterreichische Entwicklungsbank AG (OeEB) from Austria and Sociedade para o Financiamento do Desenvolvimento (SOFID) from Portugal.

The majority of DFIs are owned by the public sector such as:

- Commonwealth Development Corporation
- Deutsche Investitions und Entwicklungsgesellschaft (DEG)
- Norwegian Investment Fund for Developing Countries (Norfund)

- Industrial Development Corporation of SA (IDC)
- Overseas Private Investment Corporation (OPIC).

In contrast, institutions such as Proparco, Belgian Corporation for International Investment (BMI), and Financierings-maatschappij voor ontwikkelingslanden N.V. (FMO) have a mixed public and private ownership structure, while SIFEM and OeEB are privately owned—by Obvium and Oesterreichische Kontrollbank AG respectively.[1]

In most cases, private sector-oriented DFIs operate without government guarantees, sharing the investment risk on investments they make. An exception to this would be OeEB that although privately owned, has the investment risks involved in its projects covered by sovereign guarantees issued by the Government of Austria (EDFI, 2013).

Private sector investments by DFIs have grown rapidly over the past decade. In Europe there are fifteen DFIs, which serve to implement their governments' international development policies. In 2012, this group's investment portfolio accounted for over $32bn in 4,705 projects (EDFI, 2013). The sample of DFIs considered in this chapter also includes the IFC and PIDG and collectively, this sample group has invested $81bn (IFC, 2013 and PIDG, 2013). The IFC, which is the largest DFI by dollar amount invested, accounts for approximately $45bn (IFC, 2013), while SOFID at the other extreme has invested $11m (EDFI, 2013).

While a DFI's core business is to invest financial resources, most also provide technical assistance and promote environmental, social, and governance standards in the funds or companies in which they invest. An important distinction of DFIs' capital is that during times of crises when private capital recedes very quickly, DFI capital remains. This specific attribute may result in the continued importance of these types of institutions in the global investment landscape.

While most DFIs function and operate with an aim to promote both investment and development in the emerging markets, each institution's primary focus can vary based on region, sector, company size, and/or the home country's government interests and objectives. Despite the differences in their approach, DFIs strive to be innovative, influential, and impactful in the markets in which they operate. It is also common for DFIs to adapt their objectives based on the overarching macro political and economic environmental factors.[2]

---

[1] Unlike most other DFIs, the Private Infrastructure Development Group (PIDG) was established as an alliance of partners, focused on providing solutions to private sector involvement in infrastructure development. Members include Agdevco and Infraco. This institution is a donor-financed group and investors include several aid agencies (i.e. AusAID, Irish Aid) as well as DFIs (i.e. FMO, IFC).

[2] The events of the Arab Spring in 2011 have led to increased commitments throughout the Middle East and North Africa (MENA) region. More specifically, in light of the social upheaval in the region, IFC partnered with the Islamic Development Bank to launch the 'e4e' initiative, or Education for Employment, to address the disconnect between jobs, skills, and opportunity. Similarly, in 2011 the

A relatively recent development that was spearheaded by CDC in the 1990s, is that of DFIs' investment of significant sums in private equity funds rather than just financial intermediaries and companies directly which has been the historical practice. Given that most DFIs do not have an extensive office network in emerging markets investing in PE funds provides a means of reaching small- and medium-sized enterprises (SMEs) through funds that do have presence on the ground. Those with a local presence in target regions are often the best positioned to make direct SME investments due to the grassroots nature of investee enterprises.

Institutions such as IFC, Norfund, Proparco, and Belgian Investment Company for Developing Countries (BIO), provide financing either directly or through intermediary structures. In particular, BIO supports financial institutions, investment funds, enterprises, and private infrastructure projects. Norfund's strategy includes giving priority to Africa and countries that have a prominent position in Norwegian development co-operation. It has also chosen to concentrate on renewable energy, the finance sector, and agribusiness in particular.

SIFEM's primary focus is on private equity funds and financial institutions that invest in the SME sector. Occasionally SIFEM will invest in financial institutions with a microfinance lending focus or make direct equity investments. Similar to SIFEM, SMEs are one of the main target groups for DEG. However, unlike SIFEM, DEG makes capital available to them directly. Likewise, SOFID can offer financing for investments in start-ups, subsidiaries, or joint ventures.[3]

There is considerable variability in terms of the mandates for DFIs. Some are focused on specific socio-economic indicators while others are focused on facilitating access to new markets for home country companies. Not surprisingly, a few DFIs use a blended approach of the two.

The activities of IFC, CDC, OeEB, Norfund, and PIDG are generally not tied to national interests. CDC supports the building of businesses in the poorest parts of Africa and South Asia. Since May 2011, CDC has concentrated on the low- and lower-middle-income countries of sub-Saharan Africa and South Asia where 70 per cent of the world's poor live (CDC, 2012).

Other DFIs in contrast specifically operate according to national interests including, COFIDES, Spain's development institution, FinnFund, Società Italiana per le Imprese all'Estero (SIMEST), BMI, and SOFID:

EBRD began laying the foundations for the expansion of its operations to the Southern and Eastern Mediterranean region.

[3] While CDC has in the last decade primarily only invested through intermediaries, the business plan released in mid 2011 calls for new additions to investment tools used by the institution. By 2015, CDC aims to have 20% of its portfolio in direct investments and 20% in debt investments. The change in debt investments and the addition of guarantees as a financial instrument are designed to be beneficial to SMEs.

- COFIDES provides financial support for projects in developing countries in which Spanish companies are involved as investors
- FinnFund mainly invests with Finnish companies and/or these companies' business partners in international markets
- BMI and SIMEST are dedicated to supporting and promoting the activities of Belgian and Italian companies in international markets, respectively. For investments in countries outside the European Union, SIMEST can acquire up to 49 per cent of the capital (EDFI, 2013)
- SOFID supports Portuguese companies, which have investments or wish to invest in new markets, either alone or in partnerships which local investors.

In addition, IFC, SIFEM, Norfund, and Denmark's Industrialization Fund for Developing Countries (IFU) use relevant socio-economic indicators to guide their investments:

- IFC aims to commit 50 per cent of its projects in International Development Association (IDA) countries (IFC, 2011b)
- SIFEM is mandated to only invest in countries with GNI per capita below the World Bank's IBRD graduation threshold (SIFEM, c.2012). According to the latest World Bank report (c.2013) this threshold is set at $7,115
- Starting in 2011, Norfund has used a GDP per capita maximum threshold of $6,885 to determine eligibility of countries in which to invest (EDFI, 2013)
- IFU from Denmark co-finances projects in developing countries with a per capita income below $6,138. However, it is also a requirement that 50 per cent of IFU's annual investment be in countries with a per capita income below $3,228 (EDFI, 2013).

In addition to using economic indicators to determine investment eligibility, SIFEM treats Swiss Development Cooperation's and State Secretariat for Economic Affairs' partner countries with priority, with at least 60 per cent of indirect investments allocated to this group (SIFEM, c.2012). Similarly, SOFID is mandated to focus especially on beneficiary countries of the Portuguese Official Development Assistance.

Upper limits on investment amounts are also used as a guideline for certain DFIs. For example:

- IFU has a maximum investment threshold per project—DKK100m (approximately $17m) (EDFI, 2013)
- Swedfund International's focus is on equity investments of approximately SEK20m ($3m) to SEK100m ($15m) per investment (Swedfund, c.2013)
- BMI's average financing amount ranges between €500,000 ($660,000) and €2.5m ($3.3m) (EDFI, 2013). For projects in emerging markets, larger amounts are possible by co-investing with other European DFIs (EDFI, 2013)

- SIFEM invests between $5m and $7m into private equity funds (EDFI, 2013). On the microfinance side, SIFEM lends to banks and debt funds with loans of up to $7.5m (EDFI, 2013).

In addition to financial capital, most DFIs provide general and project specific technical assistance and/or advisory programs. BIO and SIMEST have the ability to provide funding for feasibility studies as well. For example, SIMEST has granted loans to Italian companies to finance market penetration programmes in non-EU countries.

While environmental, social, and governance (ESG) standards are regularly monitored and upheld by DFIs in general, some have additional requirements either prior to or after initial investment:

- BIO, for instance, requires its business partners to implement ESG standards
- FinnFund, on the other hand, has the capacity to co-invest with other DFIs in non-Finnish businesses that generate significant environmental or social benefits
- FMO supports its clients in implementing ESG best practices and can potentially offer reduced interest rates for clients who successfully implement ESG policies
- OeEB is required to support projects in developing countries that respect social and environmental standards.

Looking now at where DFIs deploy their capital, their investment portfolios can be looked at under three key dimensions: instruments, sectors, and geography.

FINANCIAL INSTRUMENTS

Most DFIs limit their participation to minority stakes (i.e. under 50 per cent) in order to partner with other DFIs or strategic investors; however, the individual thresholds vary from institution to institution. Most have a holding period of five to ten years for both equity and loans. Proparco invests for longer periods than most with average loan maturities of eight to ten years (EDFI, 2013).

In terms of equity stakes, 30 per cent seems to be a common maximum threshold for most DFIs:

- FinnFund, Swedfund,[4] and SIFEM typically do not go higher than 30 per cent (EDFI, 2013)

---

[4] Swedfund's stake can go up to a third of the total investment.

- Whilst IFU's stake is usually around 30 per cent, it can go as high as 50 per cent for some of the smaller projects in the emerging markets (EDFI, 2013). It also normally has a seat at the board of investee companies
- DEG's equity participation is usually about 5–25 per cent while Norfund ranges from 10–35 per cent of the funding (EDFI, 2013).

As Figure 17.1 illustrates, DFIs use various financial instruments for investments. The most common financial instruments are loans followed by equity and quasi-equity. Quasi-equity includes such instruments as mezzanine capital, subordinated loans, and convertible loans. Most do very little in guarantees. FinnFund only offers guarantees in exceptional cases. Securitization and structured finance vehicles are also part of Proparco's range of instruments. However, The ADB invested $750,000 in a project for secondary education sector development in Bangladesh in 2012 in the form of a multitranche financing facility (MFF). An MFF is a financing modality that supports a client's medium- to long-term investment programme where the board of directors, in this case ADB, approves a maximum amount for an MFF, and the conditions under which financing will be provided. The ADB is currently attempting to mainstream its new financial instrument.

In 2008, BIO granted a loan facility to Rwandan Mountain Tea (RMT) of $1m, which financed the rehabilitation of two existing tea units, improved the quality of the tea, and doubled the production capacity (to 4,300 ton/year). RMT is now accountable for around 18 per cent of the national production of

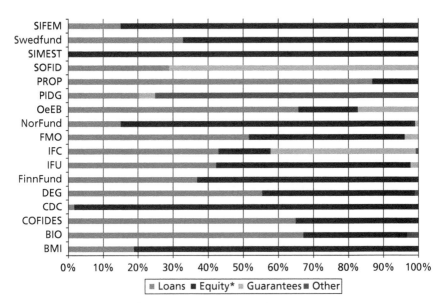

Figure 17.1. Comparative financial instruments analysis
Source: EDFI 2012 Annual Report, company reports
Note: Equity includes quasi-equity products

tea and employs about 3,600 tea pickers. BIO's project maintains 5,000 jobs in a structurally weak region and women represent more than 45 per cent of the labour force.

FMO provides a mix of funding including syndicated loans, equity, mezzanine, guarantees, and capital markets. CDC, SIMEST, BMI, Norfund, and SIFEM specialize almost entirely in equity (or quasi-equity), with each allocating more than 80 per cent to that asset class. Additionally, FinnFund and Swedfund contribute greater than 60 per cent to equity investments. In contrast, IFC and Proparco have the smallest allocation to equity instruments. Furthermore, the majority of the committed portfolio of Proparco is through loans, amounting to greater than 80 per cent. OeEB, COFIDES, and BIO also have a significant allocation to loans of greater than 60 per cent. Of all the DFIs in this analysis, SOFID has the highest allocation to guarantees, at 71 per cent of their portfolio.

SECTOR ANALYSIS

As illustrated in Figure 17.2, DFIs invest in a wide variety of sectors, from the financial sector to infrastructure and agribusiness. While some have no specific preference (i.e. CDC), a number of DFIs have a substantial focus on certain sectors.

PIDG, for instance, is entirely focused on the infrastructure sector, while SIFEM is mostly involved in the industry/manufacturing sector (over 70 per cent). Financials and infrastructure account for approximately 44 per cent of Proparco's portfolio but its sector investments have no clear pattern and like those of CDC it also invests in the environmental sector and the agricultural sector. From a strategic standpoint, SIMEST does not exclude any sectors

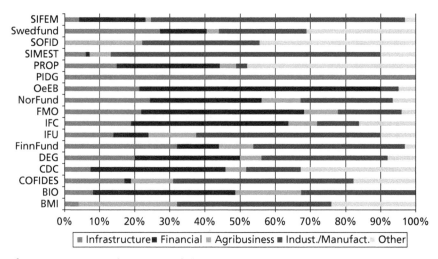

Figure 17.2. Comparative sector analysis

Source: EDFI 2012 Annual Report, company reports

since it is open to any sector in which Italian companies operate. However, looking at its portfolio, it is heavily invested in the industry/manufacturing sector, with a minor allocation to financials.

In 2010 Proparco financed the sugar cane industry in Brazil with a senior loan of $50m with partner Guarani. Guarani then improved the agricultural performances of the Brazilian production units. By financing Guarani Proparco is supporting a sector that is both an engine of Brazil's economy—the sugar cane sector—and is working to combat climate change via the development of bio fuels via ethanol that can be created from sugarcane. Ethanol projects have higher yields and have an 80 per cent to 90 per cent reduction in vehicle emissions.

In contrast, BMI has no investments in the financial sector. Finnfund chooses sectors on the basis of its perceived comparative advantage at home, which explains the relatively diversified sector investments. Renewable energy, forestry, and telecommunications are among the industries where it is eager to co-finance projects with other development financiers. While DEG finances projects in all sectors, it has a specific focus in the financial sector in order to facilitate access to long-term capital for local companies. Finally, IFC and OeEB have the majority of their investments in the financial sector.

GEOGRAPHICAL ANALYSIS

As illustrated in Figure 17.3, whilst DFIs have a specific development strategy for the emerging markets, there are various differences in the specific regions where their capital is invested. For example, CDC's portfolio is much more geared towards poorer countries than the other bilateral DFIs. Overall, Africa and Asia are well represented by most DFIs in terms of total investments. This is most likely due to the fact that DFIs follow their home country government lead in terms of the focus of their development aid across countries and typically provide financing in higher risk regions where private capital is especially scarce.

In 2008 CDC invested $46m in Himin, a company that manufactured solar-powered water heaters and is based on China's east coast. The technology is relatively simple and the product affordable for most Chinese households. Himin is part of a portfolio managed by CDH Investments (CDH), one of CDC's managers in China and a leader in the private equity industry. CDH has had a long relationship with Himin lasting over ten years. CDH is helping the company to tighten its internal controls and to strengthen its top management.

COFIDES, a DFI that operates based on national interests, seems to have a preference for South and Central America. This is indicative of the interest Spanish companies have in working with companies there. Proparco provides funding on four continents encompassing the major emerging countries and the poorest countries, particularly those in French-speaking Africa.

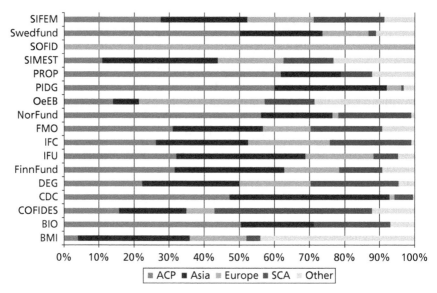

Figure 17.3. Comparative geographical analysis

Source: EDFI 2012 Annual Report, company reports

Notes: ACP = Africa, Caribbean and Pacific; SCA = South and Central America, Europe is typically Eastern Europe. The ACP position for IFC includes investments in the Middle East

PIDG also has substantial investments in Africa. While SOFID may seem to be only interested in the Africa, Caribbean, and Pacific (ACP) region, the results are skewed due to low investment numbers. It currently has only eleven investments in its portfolio. As SOFID grows its geographic allocation may very well expand.

The majority of DEG's and COFIDES' Asian investments are in China. In contrast, BIO's Asian investments are mostly in South East and South Asia, with only one portfolio project in China. FMO is another example of an institution that has significant exposure in the Asian market with over 25 per cent of projects in the region (EDFI, 2013). Furthermore, on a relative basis, CDC's 'highest country exposures are 21% in India and 15% in China' (CDC, 2012).

Private equity

Private equity expansion in emerging markets has been strongly supported by DFIs including CDC, IFC, OPIC, and FMO. By the end of 2011, IFC alone had committed $3bn to some 180 private equity funds (IFC, c.2012). Collectively, DFI participation in emerging-market private equity was critical in the early years, when most investors were reluctant to commit capital to companies in unfamiliar markets. In a study conducted by Johns Hopkins University about the growth of PE in emerging markets, one fund manager noted, 'Having the IFC in our fund as an investor is important to assuring other investors' (Leeds and Sunderland, 2003). David Wilton, the Chief Investment Officer for IFC's Private Equity and Investment Funds Department, stated in a 2010 interview, 'Ten years ago, there were only four or five emerging markets that we thought could sustain country-dedicated funds, today there are more than 20' (Meerkatt and Liechtenstein, 2010).

PE investors in the emerging markets typically offer 'patient capital', with longer investment horizons than those in the developed markets of the USA and Europe. They also aim to add value in a variety of ways during the course of their investment including management advice, corporate governance, and operational assistance. Many PE funds in transitional economies are focused on building companies rather than simply restructuring them for a quick re-sale. Furthermore, many emerging market SMEs offer significant room for improvement at operational and governance levels, allowing PE firms to add substantial value.

The primary exit strategies undertaken by private equity firms in emerging markets are industry/trade sales rather than management buyouts (MBOs) and initial public offerings (IPOs) (Arosio, 2011). Actis is one of the largest emerging-markets-focused PE fund managers and has £5.2bn in assets under management (Actis, 2013). According to a 2011 report by Responsible Research, Actis' exit strategy data indicated that the vast majority of divestments have been through a trade sale (18 out of 23) (Arosio, 2011). This is due to the fact that private equity investors in developing countries often cannot rely on IPOs. Particularly in smaller countries where firm and transaction sizes tend to be small, it is challenging to attract significant local institutional investors in an IPO and the lack of liquidity in quoted markets can be an obstacle for successful public offerings. Consequently, investors tend to rely on selling to other strategic investors via a trade sale—and in some cases achieving 'exits by selling the portfolio company to a larger regional or international enterprise' (AfDB, 2012).

According to a Harvard Business School article published in July 2012:

Several private organizations have tried to develop creative approaches to the exiting problem. Examples include the listing of the shares on an exchange in a developed country, and the acquisition of a similar firm in a developed country (which is subsequently merged with the firm in the developing nation). This is likely to be an area of continued innovation in the years to come. (Lerner, Leamon, and Vase, 2011)

AREAS OF FOCUS

According to a study by the Monitor Institute, social finance (impact investment) PE funds can be categorized according to their primary motivation for

Table 17.2. Sample list of development impact and financial first funds

Impact First	Impact and Financial	Financial First
Acumen Fund	Creation Investments	8 Miles
E+Co	Grassroots Business Fund	Actis
	IGNIA	The Abraaj Group
	LeapFrog	Bamboo Finance
	Sarona Asset Management	Elevar Equity
	Small Enterprise Assistance Funds (SEAF)	GroFin
	Summit Development Group	Helios Investment Partners
	Willow Impact Investors	Maghreb
		Phatisa - African Agriculture Fund
		Sierra Investment Fund

Note: Classification assumptions solely based on information provided on each fund's website. The Abraaj Group completed acquisition of Aureos Capital in July 2012.

investing: financial first or impact first investors (Monitor, 2009). Impact first investors are willing to give up some financial return in exchange for social impact (i.e. Acumen Fund, E+Co). Hence, these funds' investor base often consists of philanthropic investors. For instance, Acumen Fund's investors include the Rockefeller Foundation, W. K. Kellogg Foundation, Cisco Systems Foundation, Bill & Melinda Gates Foundation, and many other philanthropic and family investors.

In a similar way to DFIs investing for financial and development returns, several PE firms investing in emerging markets typically look to have a financial and development return on their investments. Table 17.2 includes a selected list of private equity and PE funds operating in emerging markets. The table illustrates the relative emphasis such funds place on development impact compared with financial returns.

In addition to those highlighted above, there exist a number of well-established social finance/impact investment funds in the developed European and US markets, serving their own geographies such as Bridges Ventures in the UK.

Finance first investors, on the other hand, seek market returns while also pursuing a positive social impact via their investments. DFIs have traditionally been the main source of capital for these funds. Sarona Asset Management 'estimates that 60–85% of the capital raised currently by private equity funds in Sarona's investable universe comes from development finance institutions' (Sarona, c.2013a). The following are some specific examples:

- GroFin, an Africa-based fund, has a number of investors that are DFIs including: CDC, IFC, FMO, Norfund, FMO, BIO, FinnFund, and SIFEM (Grofin, c.2013)
- Actis, one of the largest 'finance first' funds was established in 2004 as a result of a spin-off from a DFI, namely CDC
- Aureos Capital also had a historical relationship with CDC. It was initially established as a joint venture between CDC and Norfund and in 2008,

Aureos employees achieved 100 per cent ownership, before purchase by The Abraaj Group in July 2012[5]

- Phatisa, a pan-African Fund completed its first close in 2011 with investments from the following institutions: Agence Française de Développement, African Development Bank (AfDB), Spanish Agency for International Development Cooperation, Investment and Support Fund for Businesses in Africa, Development Bank of Southern Africa, Banque Ouest Africaine de Développement, and ECOWAS Bank for Investment and Development (Phatisa, c.2013)

- As recently as 13 February 2012, 8 Miles, a new pan-African private equity fund completed its first close of $200m with support from the IFC, AfDB, and CDC (8 Miles, 2012).

As is the case with DFIs, there seems to be no common underlying strategy for emerging-market private equity funds. Each has its own specific focus and objectives. As in any other asset class, there are generalist funds, sector-focused funds, regional funds, or some combination of the above. While funds in developing markets generally target already established firms in traditional industries, some do invest in the earlier stage businesses. One of the reasons there is limited 'technology-intensive' venture capital participation is probably due to the limited intellectual property protection in many nations (Lerner, Leamon, and Vase, 2011).

GroFin, an Africa-focused investor, for instance, supports businesses at any stage of development, from start-up through growth and/or expansion. Helios, another Africa-focused investor, prefers 'sectors with high-growth...high operating leverage, and a high degree of control over the value chain'. Furthermore, Henry Obi, Helios' Chief Operating Officer, noted that Helios' funds typically target 'returns of more than three times invested capital' (Ware, 2011).

Mahgreb Private Equity funds take on a generalist approach towards investing in SMEs in Algeria, Morocco, and Tunisia. Its strategy usually involves board representation. One fund has the specific objective of partnering with foreign companies seeking to enter the region.

IGNIA's aim is to serve as an early-stage venture capital firm that supports the 'founding and expansion of high growth social enterprises' focused on Bottom of Pyramid (BoP) markets (IGNIA, 2013). While Sarona Asset Management (Sarona) has some exposure to late-stage VC companies, it generally focuses on profitable, growth-stage companies. It also invests in countries with per capita GDP between $500 and $12,000 (Sarona, 2013b). Similar to Sarona, Grassroots Business Fund (GBF) prefers growth-stage companies but will consider early-stage businesses on a case-by-case basis. Moreover, it prefers to work with companies that directly impact in the range of 500 to 2,000

---

[5] On 24 July 2012, The Abraaj Group, a growth-markets-focused private equity firm, announced the completion of the Aureos Capital acquisition.

individuals, with potential to increase and scale at least five to ten times over the period of the investment (GBF, 2013).

One overarching trend is that there are many more funds focused on later stage growth capital than start-up ventures. In 2010, 'of the 31 funds in the Gray Ghost Ventures survey, only three were willing to invest at the start-up stage' (*Forbes*, 2010). Unless the provision of early stage capital for new enterprises increases, the future deal flow of companies wanting later stage capital will be severely limited. The pump has to be primed at the riskier but critically important early-stage life cycle of investing.

In 2012, GBF invested $1m into Jaipur Rugs Company (JRC), one of the most well-known social enterprises in India. JRC is now working on building more warehouses to optimize its supply chain and reduce costs. JRC now employs 7,000 home-based weavers using 3,000 wool spinners and creates economic opportunities for the unemployed and underemployed low-income people in rural areas of North India. The organization is training thousands of new artisans each year.

FINANCIAL INSTRUMENTS

Both finance first and impact first funds employ a similar variety of capital instruments: equity, quasi-equity, guarantees, and debt.

Bamboo Finance, Mahgreb, GBF, and Sarona all make debt and equity investments. GBF is open to utilizing guarantees as well. Additionally, Sarona has the option to utilize co-investments whenever appropriate. Most investments follow a four- to eight-year time frame.

Unlike most funds, GroFin provides medium-term debt in the majority of cases. Moreover, in addition to equity and debt instruments, Small Enterprise Assistance Funds (SEAF) provides lines of credit, working capital loans, and trade financing for certain companies in its portfolio.

Unlike developed markets, however, and due to the infancy of the sector, investors in Africa and South Asia typically work with smaller transaction sizes and longer investment horizons.

Acumen, an impact first fund, has slightly different investment guidelines. Typical commitments range from $250,000 to $3m in equity or debt with an investment horizon of up to ten years (Acumen Fund, *c.*2013).

Regardless of the financial instrument used, a study conducted by Boston Consulting Group (BCG) and IESE Business School in 2010 reported that minority deals are more successful in emerging markets. The study analysed IFC's private equity portfolio and found that minority investments 'produced returns that were three times higher than those of majority stake investments . . . minority deals were also the most common and successful type of private equity investment in emerging markets' (Meerkatt and Liechtenstein, 2010).

In 1998, E+Co provided enterprise development services and a loan to Vacvina, which sells household biogas systems for small pig farms; one unit uses pig manure to produce sufficient methane to meet the daily cooking requirements of a rural household. Later E+Co provided an additional loan making the total financing from E+Co $82,000 which helped the business to grow further, creating 200 jobs. Moreover, the systems reduce emissions by 80,000 tonnes of CO_2E per year, displace fuel wood and coal, and improve hygiene and reduce water pollution.

SECTOR ANALYSIS

The sector distribution of the selected funds' portfolios is highlighted in Table 17.3 to illustrate some of the current strategies in place. Key sectors focused on by these investors in emerging markets include agribusiness, energy, financials, education, and health care.

Each of Mahgreb's funds targets specific industries with overlap in agribusiness, telecommunications, pharmaceuticals, and financial services. Within health care, Elevar is focused on providing investments to improve rural health care specifically. Willow Impact Investors, a recently established Dubai-based fund, includes food and nutrition, the environment, and community development among its six principle sectors. They also deliver tangible positive environmental impacts and social benefits.

Some funds have a very specific mandate with regards to sector focus. For instance, Leapfrog invests in financial services businesses, mostly companies that provide insurance in Africa and Asia, such as AllLife, the only South African insurer of people living with HIV/Aids. In 2009 Leapfrog invested $6.7m in AllLife and brought financial capital, operational excellence, and a global network. Since the investment, AllLife's client base grew by 200 per cent in the first year post investment and AllLife's annual revenue more than

Table 17.3. Sector preferences

Insitutional Name	Financials	Healthcare	Education	Water	Manufacturing	Agribusiness	Housing	Environment	Energy	Other
8 Miles	✓	✓	✓		✓				✓	✓
Actis	✓					✓			✓	✓
Acumen Fund		✓	✓	✓		✓	✓		✓	
The Abraaj Group	✓	✓	✓		✓	✓			✓	✓
Bamboo Finance	✓	✓	✓	✓		✓	✓			
Creation Investments Capital Management, LLC	✓									
E+Co									✓	
Elevar Equity	✓	✓						✓		
Grassroots Business Fund						✓			✓	✓
GroFin		✓	✓		✓	✓				✓
Helios Investment Partners	✓					✓				✓
IGNIA		✓	✓			✓	✓			✓
LeapFrog	✓									
Maghreb	✓	✓			✓	✓				✓
Phatisa - African Agriculture Fund						✓				
Sarona Asset Management	✓	✓			✓	✓	✓		✓	✓
Sierra Investment Fund	✓				✓	✓				✓
Small Enterprise Assistance Funds (SEAF)		✓			✓	✓			✓	✓
Summit Development Group	✓									
Willow Impact Investors		✓	✓					✓	✓	✓

Source: company websites

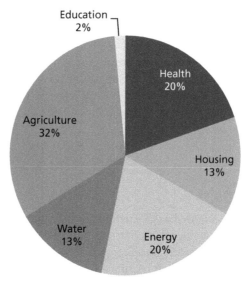

Figure 17.4. Acumen Fund's sector focus
Source: Acumen Fund

doubled. Moreover, the company sees an average 15 per cent improvement in clients' health, just from having an AllLife insurance policy. E+Co, on the other hand, only invests in projects and enterprises that benefit the energy sector.

In contrast, Acumen Fund is well diversified with investments across five different sectors: water, health, housing, energy, and agriculture. Figure 17.4 provides additional details.

Acumen Fund invested $2m equity in the Pushpagiri Vitereo Retina Institute (PVRI) in 2008, enabling PVRI to build two additional hospitals. This expanded its reach to approximately 50 per cent of Andhra Pradesh (with a population of 75 million people) and its ability to treat nearly one million patients.

Funds that generally focus on BoP markets, such as IGNIA and Sarona, focus on sectors that have a high impact on low-income populations. These include, health care, financial services, water, and sanitation investments. Generally, social finance/impact investment funds aim to make the greatest amount of positive impact with the capital that is available. Providing funding to companies that provide access to basic goods and services such as quality health care, energy, financial services, housing, education, and water may result in large-scale economic and social development for all.

In 2005, AfDB approved a $7.8m private sector investment in the Sahanivotry hydroelectric power station in Madagascar. A 15 MW hydroelectric power station was built which increased electric power output by more than 10 per cent at a competitive cost that is 50 per cent cheaper than electricity generated from diesel plants. The project created 140 jobs during the construction phase and encouraged direct and indirect supply of local goods. Moreover, the regular supply of electricity to the village boosted small and medium-size industries (like mining and hulling) and contributed to the improved living conditions in the area.

This diversity in sector objectives can be 'an advantage of impact investing that might allow for a comprehensive development impact and the scalability of the for-profit social venture model, but also could hinder the consolidation of the impact investing industry as a whole' (Simon and Barmeir, 2010).

GEOGRAPHICAL ANALYSIS

Not surprisingly, PE investors tend to focus on markets with significant economic growth opportunities but low levels of prosperity. Africa is in the midst of a profound economic transformation that is 'promoting trade, foreign direct investment, and domestic entrepreneurship' (Simon and Barmeir, 2010). The Abraaj Group has a $7.5bn portfolio (see Figure 17.5); of this total, The Abraaj Group invested $4bn in African and Asian markets (Abraaj, 2014).

Table 17.4 is a general representation of investments in various geographies by specific private equity funds.

GroFin focuses almost wholly on investing in Africa. For example, in 2009 GroFin invested $50m into fifty SMEs across East Africa with their GroFin East Africa Fund (GEAF). GEAF increased job creation by 87 per cent and turnover by 50 per cent in the fifty enterprises that had been invested in. While Maghreb primarily invests in Morocco, Algeria, and Tunisia, the firm also makes opportunistic investments in Egypt, Libya, and some European countries.

Given that Sarona's investable universe is largely dependent on per capita GDP thresholds, its universe includes approximately eighty countries (Sarona, c.2013b).

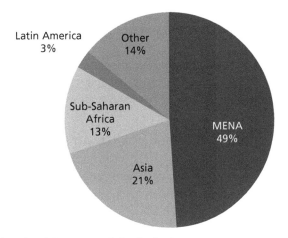

Figure 17.5. The Abraaj Group's portfolio distribution
Source: The Abraaj Group

Table 17.4. Geographical analysis

Insitutional Name	MENA	Sub-saharan Africa	Europe	Asia	Latin America	Other
8 Miles	✓	✓	✓	✓	✓	
Actis	✓	✓				
Acumen Fund		✓		✓		
The Abraaj Group	✓	✓		✓	✓	✓
Bamboo Finance		✓		✓	✓	
Creation Investments Capital Management, LLC			✓	✓		✓
E+Co	✓	✓		✓	✓	
Elevar Equity				✓	✓	
Grassroots Business Fund		✓		✓	✓	
GroFin	✓	✓				
Helios Investment Partners	✓	✓				
IGNIA						✓
LeapFrog	✓	✓		✓		
Maghreb PE	✓					
Phatisa - African Agriculture Fund	✓	✓				
Sarona Asset Management*						
Sierra Investment Fund		✓				
Small Enterprise Assistance Funds			✓	✓	✓	
Summit Development Group		✓				
Willow Impact Investors	✓	✓				

Source: company websites
Note: Sarona Asset Management's Investable universe is determined by per capita GDP range.

As of July 2012, E+Co, a clean energy-focused fund, has pursued a new strategy of supporting clean energy entrepreneurs in Africa. In response to this announced restructuring, E+Co Managing Director Chris Aidun noted, 'Forced to narrow our focus, we chose Africa, because of all of our opportunity for impactful clean energy investing.' Prior to this change, E+Co had invested in twenty countries on five continents.

Future issues

THE NEED FOR CAPITAL AND THE ROLE OF DFIS

The growing economies of the emerging markets are likely to need significant capital investments over the next decade, beyond what national governments and aid programmes can provide. Some estimates of the investment needs identified include:

- $93bn per year in Africa for infrastructure (Foster and Briceño-Garmendia, 2010)
- $83bn per year in agriculture in developing countries (FAO, 2009)
- $25–$30bn in sub-Saharan Africa for healthcare (i.e. hospitals, clinics, medical warehouses) (IFC, 2009).

Consequently, it is vital for private sector capital to work alongside governments and aid programmes to meet this demand. DFI finance currently accounts for approximately 1 per cent of capital going into private investments in developing countries and about 2 to 4 per cent in Africa (IFC, 2011b). The challenge going forward for DFIs is how they can effectively leverage their increasing presence for greater development impact. According to an IFC (2011b) report on international finance institutions (IFIs i.e. DFIs), to make a meaningful difference, they should deploy capital more strategically by doing the following (IFC, 2011b):

- focus on investment areas and approaches that have the potential of greatest development impact
- provide investment and advice not available commercially
- leverage partnerships with the private sector, DFIs, and governments in order to maximize impact.

Overall, DFIs look to add value by helping the private sector in developing economies through financing infrastructure and the private sector, thereby assisting those economies to operate better. However, for continued success, it is important to realize the importance of scalability alongside innovation. Focusing on scaling up new sectors via replication may allow for a higher level of sustainable innovation (IFC, 2011b). DFIs have improved capital flows to certain markets and have been helping countries 'create the conditions necessary to foster as much private sector involvement as possible' (Politi, 2012). Even after many of the lowest-income countries move up to 'middle-income', some policy analysts note that the primary question for DFIs would be 'how to address uneven development' (Politi, 2012). In other words, how will these institutions work with countries where certain sectors show sustainable growth while others struggle to meet critical objectives such as education and health care?

A rather interesting trend appears to be the emergence of additional development banks. Interestingly, the New Development Bank formerly referred to as the BRICS (i.e. Brazil, Russia, India, China, and South Africa) Development Bank came into being in July 2015 having been under discussions since March 2012 (Politi, 2012). This is the first multilateral bank to be created since the founding of the European Bank for Reconstruction and Development in 1991. The question that has to be asked, however, is what will such an entity do that existing DFIs are not already doing? If there are specific unmet BRICS goals, would it have been a better use of government funding to outsource specific tasks to existing DFIs or PE funds to leverage off existing capacity and networks?

Overall, DFIs will most likely maintain or grow their current operations in high impact markets.

THE NEED FOR A TRACK RECORD

According to J.P. Morgan's 2011 investor perspectives survey, investors are optimistic about the future amount of investment looking to make a development impact. However, at the present time the 'lack of a substantial track record' by fund managers in this space is a key challenge to attracting more capital:

Investor respondents signaled tempered optimism for the near term and a healthy outlook for the longer-term prospects of the impact investing industry. Over a 10-year horizon, survey participants believe that institutional and HNWI investors will allocate 5% and 10% of their portfolios to impact investments, respectively. (J.P. Morgan, 2011)

Regardless of how ambitious and optimistic some industry reports may be, this is an industry that will require at least a decade to mature before reaching a significant size and level of sustainability. Industry optimists point to the recent successes of microfinance institutions. For example, the successful 2007 IPO of Banco Compartamos in Mexico is frequently used to highlight the market potential and demand. However, it is just as important to understand that it took this organization seventeen years to attract substantial commercial interest, which eventually warranted a public offering and high financial returns. It started out as a non-profit that was funded by philanthropic capital and continued to operate under that mandate for many years. Therefore, one of the factors critical for future success is realizing how impact first capital and finance first capital can effectively complement each other. For instance, the former can finance innovation (as was the case in the Banco Compartamos), while the latter finances the scaling (Milligan and Schöning, 2011).

THE NEED FOR FINANCIAL INNOVATION

Financial creativity, greater transparency, and knowledge sharing between foundations, DFIs, and commercial investors will likely help the entire industry mature and realize both financial and social objectives.

Financial creativity is particularly helpful since 'innovation' is key in developing markets and flexible financial structures are more conducive to this than simply using traditional loans or grants. IGNIA's Rodriguez Arregui recently noted, 'loans might be appropriate at later stages of the life cycle of an organization, but not when you want them to innovate' (Milligan and Schöning, 2011). Loans can sometimes hinder innovation since management will be more focused on repaying the loan and perhaps even make poor risk-averse operational decisions.

Investments in the development sector require 'risk capital' and this normally takes the form of equity investments. However, as noted earlier, exiting equity investments in emerging markets is challenging and often limited to trade sales. Ultimately, industry practitioners will have to develop a more robust marketplace that allows for numerous exit options for investors (Milligan and Schöning, 2011). This should pave the way for more traditional investors to enter higher-risk developing markets.

The African continent has been a key area of focus for many DFIs and DFI-backed PE funds mainly because it is viewed as a market that has the potential for high developmental impact. However, at current rates of economic growth, the need for capital is far greater than the current supply. Issam Darwish, co-founder of HIS, a Nigeria-based telephone infrastructure company, recently stated that financing ventures in Africa is still 'extremely tough'. Austin Okere, chief executive of Computer Warehouse Group in Nigeria further noted that 'a lot of companies with potential die because they do not have the money to fund growth' (Wigglesworth, 2012).

Although some progress has been made with, for example, Carlyle Group, one of the largest private equity fund managers launching in 2011 its first Sub-Saharan Africa Fund of $0.7bn (Wigglesworth, 2012), mainstream institutional investors do not appear to be at a stage where they allocate significant capital to emerging (specifically frontier) markets such as Africa. In order to unlock such capital, it is imperative for DFIs and private equity funds to 'demonstrate consistent track records of successful growth' (AfDB, 2012).

What is interesting is that given the less developed nature of the capital markets system in certain emerging markets, 'private equity is being increasingly used as a proxy for the growth of the underlying economies' (AfDB, 2012). In light of strong underlying economic growth in Africa and South Asia, the demand for private equity should far exceed supply.

THE NEED FOR GREATER RISK-TAKING

It is imperative for investors to understand the importance and necessity of the following factors when working with funds and/or SMEs in the development impact arena, particularly in Africa. These types of investments typically require:

- higher risk appetite
- smaller transaction sizes
- patient and long-term commitment
- earlier-stage (i.e. VC-type) funding.

As PE developed as an industry in the USA, it was primarily led 'by investment arms of wealthy families, such as the Rockefellers and Whitneys' (*The Economist*, 2004). Investments made were usually confined to venture capital investments in small businesses. As the industry matured, a larger percentage of overall capital was allocated to expansion or buyouts of established companies.

In the emerging markets today, and particularly in Africa and South Asia, however, it appears as though practitioners are adopting a mature market approach whereas the emerging markets are just that—emerging. As in the early days of private equity the USA, more venture capital is needed for early stage SME financing than for MBOs and pre-IPO opportunities. The successful growth of the industry is highly dependent on whether sufficient capital is available at all stages of the business cycle (i.e. from idea to profitable enterprise). There seem to be many more growth capital funds providing early-stage capital. The absence of earlier-stage capital will place a break on innovative business models and in turn further expansion capital opportunities in the future unless sufficiently addressed today.

According to Michael Chu, more collaboration is needed where various participants in the development impact investing space can effectively work together. If different players can absorb risk and play meaningful roles at different stages of an enterprise's evolution the dots can be joined as illustrated in Table 17.5. Aligning sources of capital with various investment strategies may prove to be useful in helping the industry mature efficiently (Chu, 2012).

As the US private equity industry emerged in the 1980s, it was 'a place for mavericks and outsiders'. The social finance/impact investment space could benefit from this type of fund manager as it usually involves a higher tolerance for risk, which is a key characteristic of many emerging market investment opportunities.

Moreover, first-time Africa PE funds often struggle to raise capital, indicating the current risk-averse mindset of investors—including many DFIs. DFIs in particular can and should invest in the growing number of first-time African and South Asian PE funds and nurture this entrepreneurial activity.

Table 17.5. Aligning sources of capital with investment strategies

Source of Capital	Expected Financial Return	Angel Venture Capital	Seed Venture Capital	Growth Venture Capital
Venture Philanthropy (Individuals and Foundations)	Driving motivation is Sicial Impact (None)	✓	✓	✗
Public Sector / Dev. Agencies	Grants (None)	✓	✓	✗
Public Sector / Dev. Agencies	Investments (RoC to Commercial)	✗	✓	✓
Private Sector (Individuals and Institutions)	Low to Commercial	✗	✗	✓
Pure commercial Investors	Commercial	✗	✗	N.A. (Too Early)

Source: IGNIA

More leadership is needed by individual DFIs prepared to go out on a limb rather than be like sheep only investing if the rest of the DFI club invests, which is typically the case.

THE NEED FOR A BLENDED VIEW OF RETURN

While PE investors span the spectrum between impact first and finance first, it may be more useful to avoid the idea of maximizing one over the other and consider finding strategies that will result in an optimal balance of financial return and development impact for the industry as a whole. The two are not mutually exclusive and can be blended to provide a sustainable and longer-term framework for investing. The days of finance first PE funds in Africa and South Asia may very well be numbered if the importance of social finance increases and the need to demonstrate sustainable development impact is required by investors in such funds.

THE NEED FOR LOCALLY BASED EMERGING-MARKET INSTITUTIONS TO INVEST IN PE

In the same way that mainstream developed market institutions have been slow to invest in PE in Africa and South Asia, insurance companies and pension funds in Africa and South Asia have been extremely slow in investing in this asset class. David Ashiagbor of the Commonwealth Secretariat has commented that, 'if the largest African markets by assets under management were to invest 5 per cent of their portfolio in private equity, a potential \$17bn could be released to support private sector investment in Africa' (Ashiagbor, 2012). However, much education of pension funds and insurance companies is needed in addition to the reforming and liberalization of the pension sector in particular. Ashiagbor commented, 'Even in South Africa, with its sophisticated financial markets, few pension funds have experience of or knowledge of private equity' (Ashiagbor, 2012).

Insurance companies in East and West Africa have largely shied away from investing in PE—sometimes due to regulatory restrictions but mostly due to their own risk aversion and the early stage of the industry. Things are however changing as illustrated in Botswana, South Africa, and Nigeria:

- Only recently did Botswana's public pension body (BPOPF) allocate funds to PE. However, when it did so, its requirement for local ownership of PE fund management companies effectively excluded most PE funds operating in Africa
- The revised Regulation of The Pensions Fund Act in South Africa means that pension funds can invest 10 per cent in unlisted equities

- In Nigeria, 5 per cent of assets under management can be invested in private equity and alternative assets although 75 per cent need to be invested in Nigeria and funds need to have DFIs as co-investors.

The above steps in the right direction, however, need to pick up pace and further liberalization is needed. In particular, cross-border PE investing, by, for example, Kenyan institutions investing in Ugandan PE firms or Ghanaian institutions investing in Zambian funds should be encouraged and changes made to tax regimes and currency rules to encourage such intra-African cross-border investing and portfolio diversification.

Lastly, the significant participation of the DFI community in PE funds in these emerging markets underlines the need for local institutions that have significant assets under management to climb up the learning curve and put capital to work in this alternative asset class—particularly where it can have a development impact in their own countries.

Conclusions

This chapter has sought to set out the landscape of social finance in Africa and South Asia. DFIs were the early investors in this space and possess a variety of investment preferences such as geography, sector, and size. In some instances there has to be a linkage/benefit to the DFI's own country before any investment can be made. Moreover, DFIs are typically owned by governments and as such subject to foreign ministry/foreign aid policy changes. Successful investments which have had a positive social impact have certainly been made in various sectors and geographies and using a variety of financial instruments.

DFIs were largely responsible for the more recent development in the past two decades of PE funds investing in Africa and South Asia. Some funds are sector focused whilst others are generalists. Such funds lie upon a spectrum of 'impact first' funds at one end to 'financial first' funds at the other. As with the DFIs, investments have been made in different geographies and sectors utilizing a variety of financial instruments. Social impact has been achieved and this chapter has given various examples of the same.

Finally, the chapter has looked at issues facing social finance in Africa and South Asia. Specifically, it highlights the need for DFIs to take greater risk, to invest in earlier stage opportunities and support innovation. They should not be a watered down version of commercial investors, but should be pioneering and catalytic. In addition, there is still a great need for local insurance companies, pension funds, sovereign funds and other bodies to invest in PE funds. Lack of capital going into PE funds from African and South Asian sources will only constrain economic growth and the role social finance can play.

Social finance has tremendous potential particularly in emerging markets found in Africa and South Asia but long-term success of the industry will depend on how investors (DFIs, international institutions, and local institutions) rise to the challenge of deploying far more capital and far more early-stage financing to the private sector than currently is the case. If they do they can build a virtuous circle of greater investment begetting greater financial returns, begetting greater development returns, begetting greater capital being deployed.

■ REFERENCES

8 Miles. (2012). *$200m First Close achieved, supported by: IFC, African Development Bank, CDC, and Vital Capital.* <http://8miles.com/news13_feb_2012.html>, accessed 1 August 2012.

Actis (2013). *Actis in Review 2013.* <http://www.act.is/ActisPDFs/Actis_In_Review_2013.pdf>, accessed September 2013.

Acumen Fund (*c.*2013). *Patient Capital.* <http://acumen.org/investments/investment-model/>, accessed: September 2013.

Africa Development Bank Group (AfDB) (2012). *Private Equity Investment in Africa.* Tunis-Belvedere: AfDB.

Arosio, M. (2011). 'Impact Investing in Emerging Markets', *Issues for Responsible Investors, 4.* New York: Responsible Research. <http://www.sustainalytics.com/sites/default/files/impact_investing_in_emerging_markets-issues_for_responsible_investors.pdf>, accessed September 2012.

Ashiagbor, D. (2012). 'Unlocking African Institutional Capital for Private Investment in Africa', *Africa Finance Forum Blog*, 1 October. <http://aff.mfw4a.org/africa-finance-forum-blog/time/2012/10/01/blogpost/unlocking-african-institutional-capital-for-private-investment-in-africa.html>, accessed 1 October 2012.

CDC Group (CDC) (2012). *Annual Review 2012.* <http://www.cdcgroup.com/Documents/Annual%20Reviews/CDC%20Annual%20Review%202012.pdf>, accessed October 2012.

Chu, M. (2012). 'Impact Investing: Reflections from the Front Lines', presented at Latin American Forum on impact investing, 14 February. <http://www.ignia.com.mx/bop/uploads/media/Impact_Investing_Merida_14_Feb_2012.pdf>, accessed 1 September 2012.

EDFI (European Development Finance Institutions) (2013). *2012 EDFI Annual Report.* Brussels: EDFI.

Food and Agriculture Organization of the United Nations (FAO) (2009). *How to Feed the World in 2050.* <http://www.fao.org/docrep/012/ak542e/ak542e00.htm>, accessed: September 2013.

Forbes (2010). 'Impact Investing Faces Hurdles'. <http://www.forbes.com/2010/08/16/impact-investment-hurdles-business-oxford-analytica.html>, accessed August 2010.

Foster, V., and Briceño-Garmendia, C. (eds) (2010). *Africa's Infrastructure: A Time for Transformation.* Washington, DC: Agence Française de Développement and the World Bank. <http://infrastructureafrica.org/system/files/Africa's%20Infrastructure

%20A%20Time%20for%20Transformation%20FULL%20TEXT.pdf>, accessed 1 August 2012.

Grassroots Business Fund (GBF) (*c.*2013). *Impact Criteria.* <http://www.gbfund. org/investment-criteria>, accessed September 2013.

Grofin (*c.*2013). *Our Fund Investors.* <http://www.grofin.com/sme-fund-management-solutions/our-fund-investors.aspx>, accessed September 2013.

IGNIA (*c.*2013). *What We Do.* <http://www.ignia.com.mx/bop/>, accessed September 2013.

International Finance Corporation (IFC) (2009). *The Business of Health in Africa.* <http:// www.unido.org/fileadmin/user_media/Services/PSD/BEP/IFC_HealthinAfrica_Final. pdf>, accessed September 2013.

International Finance Corporation (IFC) (2011a). *Sustainable Investment in Sub-Saharan Africa.* New York: IFC <http://www.ifc.org/wps/wcm/connect/65c3300048865905b7-faf76a6515bb18/IFC_Sustainable_Investment_in_Sub-Saharan_Africa.pdf?MOD= AJPERES>, accessed: 1 September 2012.

International Finance Corporation (IFC) (2011b). *International Finance Institutions and Development Through the Private Sector.* <http://www.miga.org/documents/ IFI_report_09-13-11.pdf>, accessed September 2012.

International Finance Corporation (IFC) (2012). *Private Equity and Investment Funds.* <http://www.ifc.org/wps/wcm/connect/Industry_EXT_Content/IFC_External_Cor porate_Site/Industries/Home/Portfolio/>, accessed September 2013.

International Finance Corporation (IFC) (2013). *IFC Annual Report 2012.* <http:// www.ifc.org/wps/wcm/connect/2be4ef804cacfc298e39cff81ee631cc/AR2012_Report_ English.pdf?MOD=AJPERES>, accessed September 2013.

J.P. Morgan (2011). *Insight into the Impact Investment Market.* <http://www.thegiin. org/cgi-bin/iowa/download?row=334&field=gated_download_1>, accessed September 2012.

Leeds, R., and Sunderland, J. (2003). 'Private Equity Investing in Emerging Markets', *Journal of Applied Corporate Finance*, 15(4): 111–19

Lerner, J., Leamon, A., and Vase, A. (2011). 'Private Equity in Developing Countries', Harvard Business School Background Note 811–102. <http://www.people.hbs.edu/ jlerner/develop.html>, accessed 1 September 2012.

Meerkatt, H., and Liechtenstein, H. (2010). *New Markets, New Rules: Will Emerging Markets Reshape Private Equity?* The Boston Consulting Group, IESE Business School, November. <http://www.iese.edu/research/pdfs/ESTUDIO-127.pdf>, accessed 1 September 2012.

Milligan, K., and Schöning, M. (2011). 'Taking a Realistic Approach to Impact Invest-ing', *MIT Innovations*, Special Edition for SOCAP 2011: 161–72. <http://www. weforum.org/pdf/schwabfound/TakingARealisticApproachToImpactInvesting_ MIT_Innovations.pdf>, accessed 1 September 2012.

Monitor Institute (2009). *Investing for Social and Environmental Impact.* <http://www. monitorinstitute.com/downloads/what-we-think/impact-investing/Impact_Investing. pdf>, accessed August 2012.

Phatisa (*c.*2013). *Frequently Asked Questions about the African Agriculture Fund.* <http://www.phatisa.com/PhatisaIRRcalculatorapp/>, accessed 1 September 2013.

Politi, J. (2012). 'New World Order Sets a Double Goal', *FT Special Report*, 24 February. <http://www.ft.com/cms/c1628ce2-03a3-11e2-bad2-00144feabdc0.pdf>, accessed September 2013.

Private Infrastructure Development Group (PIDG) (2013). *2012 PIDG Annual Report.* <http://www.pidg.org/news/launch-of-the-pidg-annual-report-2012>, accessed: September 2013.

Sarona Asset Management (Sarona) (*c*.2013a). *Investment Strategy: Vision.* <http://www.saronafund.com/vision.php>, accessed September 2013.

Sarona Asset Management (Sarona) (*c*.2013b). *Investment Strategy: Strategy.* <http://www.saronafund.com/strategy.php>, accessed September 2013.

Simon, J., and Barmeir, J. (2010). *More than Money—Impact Investing for Development.* Washington, DC: Centre for Global Development. <http://www.cgdev.org/publication/more-money-impact-investing-development>, accessed 1 September 2012.

Swedfund (*c*.2013). *Our Investments.* <http://www.swedfund.se/en/our-investments/>, accessed September 2013.

Swiss Investment Fund for Emerging Markets (SIFEM) (*c*.2012). *Strategic Objectives.* <http://www.sifem.ch/med/205-strategic-objectives-of-the-federal-council.pdf>, accessed September 2013.

The Abraaj Group (Abraaj) (2014). *An Introduction to The Abraaj Group 2013/14.* <http://www.abraaj.com/news-and-insight/introduction-abraaj-group/>, accessed January 2015.

The Economist (2004). 'The New Kings of Capitalism', 25 November. <http://www.economist.com/node/3427270>, accessed September 2012.

Ware, G. (2011). *Helios Investment Partners.* London: Helios Investment Partners <http://www.heliosinvestment.com/support/uploads/1320924897Helios-Shell.pdf>, accessed August 2012.

Wigglesworth, R. (2012). 'Africa: Funding on the Frontier', *Financial Times*, 18 September. <http://www.ft.com/cms/s/0/481612d8-00be-11e2-9dfc-00144feabdc0.html#axzz2e4Cz0SIC>, accessed September 2012.World Bank (*c*.2013). *World Bank Operational Lending Category Changes.* Report. <http://en.wikipedia.org/wiki/International_Bank_for_Reconstruction_and_Development>, accessed September 2013.

18 Islamic finance as social finance

Natalie Schoon

The most powerful force in the universe is compound interest.

Albert Einstein

Introduction

An often-heard remark from a wide range of players within the Islamic finance industry is that due to the fact they operate on the basis of Islamic principles they are, by nature, founded on a stronger social footing. The principles that can be found in the *Quran* and the *Sunnah* together with a variety of secondary sources, form what is commonly known as Islamic law or *Sharia'a*. Besides guidance on faith and behaviour, *Sharia'a* also governs businesses including the way in which financial services are offered. Applying these pricipals is generally considered to be an important sign of ethical behaviour in social as well as in business undertakings. Although the modern history of Islamic finance started as recent as the early 1960s, the underlying principles have been around for a significant amount of time and generally predate Islam (Schoon 2016, 2008). This chapter explores the social aspect of Islamic finance exploring its relationship to social finance, starting with a brief overview of the history of finance to provide a context for some of the subsequent precepts of Islamic finance. Next, the most well-known prohibition in Islamic finance— the prohibition on charging interest—is reviewed. This is followed by an overview of the different product types available in this market. The next section considers other, lesser-known prohibitions specifically focused on social responsibility within Islamic finance. Conclusions draw the chapter together.

A brief history of finance

Financial services have always played an important role in the economy of societies, both via individuals acting as intermediaries and more formal financial institutions. The intermediary assumes the role of investor, mobilizing funds and applying them to facilitate trade and business. Its history is long and goes back at least as far as Babylonian times. Throughout history, we have seen periods of frantic financial as well as periods notable for the absence of any form of organized financial services.[1]

Even predating the invention of money, there was a demand for the safekeeping of valuables such a grain, cattle, and agricultural implements that, at a later stage, were supplemented as a means of exchange by precious metals such as gold. Safekeeping was often undertaken by temples since they had a continuous stream of visitors, and tended to be solidly built so would deter any would-be thief. In addition, temples were a place of worship providing yet another layer of additional protection.

Evidence exists that the priests in Babylon were engaged in lending money to merchants as early as the eighteenth century BC, and the code of Hammurabi,[2] which dates back to the same time, includes laws governing financial services in ancient Mesopotamia. The Code contained laws regulating the repayment of debt in different situations and distinguished between losses due to natural disaster and those caused by negligence. In addition, it governed the compensation to be paid for losses of articles in safekeeping and the rental amounts that could be charged for making available the use of land and different species of livestock.

The ancient Greek bankers were keen moneylenders and investors, with the representatives of the rulers and traders often undertaking financial services. Lending was typically done against a flat fee, with investments attracting a share of the profit. Trade was typically financed by using a network of traders who would, against a fee, issue credit notes that could be cashed in other parts of the empire. Credit-based banking spread in the Mediterranean world from around the fourth century BC. Around the same time, pre-eminent philosophers such as Aristotle argued that the charging of interest was unnatural. In Europe, banking activity declined with the withdrawal of the Roman Empire and the rising popularity of Christianity that placed additional restrictions on the banking system and prohibited the charging and paying of interest. Trade-based financing continued to take place, but was more likely to be undertaken by the traders than any intermediary offering financial services.

The Crusades and the expansion of European trade and commerce in the Middle Ages lead to the requirement to have funds available in different locations without having to transport coins, as well as the need to be able to borrow to facilitate trade and other business undertakings. International trade

---

[1] See further, Ferguson (2008).

[2] The Code of Hammurabi is a comprehensive set of laws, considered by many scholars to be the oldest laws established. Although it was essentially humanitarian in its intent and orientation, it contained the 'eye for an eye' theory of punishment, which is a barbarian application of the concept of making the punishment fit the crime. The Code of Hammurabi recognizes such modern concepts as corporate personality. See also King (2004).

required foreign exchange contracts, the first of which was recorded in 1156, in Genoa.[3] With the Christian prohibition on usury still in place, the use of these types of contracts expanded significantly since profits from time differences in a foreign exchange contract were not considered to be interest.

During the next two hundred years, commerce flourished and many merchants had more money than they could reinvest in their own enterprise. Instead, excess funds were invested in other areas and provided financing for individual and government consumption.[4] Initially only lending their own money, the more successful investors would also invest other merchants' capital, and over time this became their main business. Increasing urbanization and the financial requirements of the Industrial Revolution increased the need for financing and, thus, for financial institutions laying the foundations for the current financial infrastructure seen in developed economies.

Islamic financial services

During medieval times Middle Eastern tradesmen engaged in financial transactions on the basis of *Sharia'a*, which, incidentally, was guided by the same principles applied by their European counterpart at the time including justness of exchange and the prohibition of usury. They established systems without interest that were either based on trade financing or the sharing of profits and losses. These instruments catered for the financing of trade and other enterprises and were very effective during and after the era known as the Islamic Civilization that lasted from the late sixth to early eleventh century AD. As the Middle Eastern and Asian regions became important trading partners for European companies such as the Dutch East India Company, European banks started to establish branches in these countries that typically were interest-based. On a small scale, credit union and co-operative societies continued to exist, but their activities very much focused on small geographical areas.

During the period 1963 until the mid 1980s there was a slow but steady rise in demand for Islamic financial services, mainly in the Middle-Eastern and Asian regions. In the years since then, the Islamic financial industry has experienced exponential growth with an estimated size of assets under management at the end of 2011 of $1trn. Although a significant amount, this is less than mainstream banks. HSBC, for example, had assets under management well in excess of $2.5trn at the end of 2011.

---

[3] Two merchant brothers borrowed 115 Genoese pounds to reimburse the bank's agents in Constantinople by paying them 460 bezants one month after their arrival in Constantinople.

[4] Supple (1977).

Prohibition on interest through the ages

As a result of the growth of Islamic financial services, the prohibition of interest has gained renewed attention. Contrary to popular belief, however, the ban on interest is not unique to Islamic finance and has a long history going back at least as far as the Code of Hammurabi noted above. Interest has been a controversial subject and has been extensively debated over centuries by philosophers and theologians, even though in practice it was common to charge a fee for money or goods lent.

The Code of Hammurabi (c.1760 BC) included laws governing banking operations in ancient Mesopotamia and included concepts associated with such behaviour such as corporate responsibility.[5] Ancient Greeks and Ancient Romans used freely to charge interest and generally secured both the debt and the interest on the borrower, as a result of which the borrower would automatically become the slave of the creditor in the event of default.[6]

Aristotle argued that money was intended to be used in exchange, and was meant to be consumed. It could, thus, not increase and did not have an intrinsic value of its own since it was merely a human social invention with no utility in itself.[7] He specifically defined the term *usury* as 'the birth of money from money' and rejected it as the most unnatural way of making money, since money per se does not have any self-replicating properties.

By this time, the Jewish moneylender was already long established. As the result of a difference in interpretation of Deuteronomy 23:21 between Judaism and Christianity, Jews could lend at interest to non-Jews but Christians were prohibited from charging interest to anyone.

The Romans recognized the right to lend and borrow against a specified return, although fungible goods and some other basics could not attract a return, only the repayment of the lent principal.[8] Interest was only allowed if it was contractually agreed between the parties upfront, although subject to a maximum cap of 12 per cent set in 50 BC by decree of the Senate. In 533 AD, Emperor Justinian introduced a tiered interest structure in which 12 per cent was the legal maximum that could be charged for *foenus nauticum*; 8 per cent for business loans; 6 per cent for those not in business; and 4 per cent for distinguished persons and farmers.[9] Although it is unclear how the different rates were determined, it is likely that consideration had been given to the perceived risk associated with the transaction as well as the economic necessity of the loan.

With the demise of the Roman Empire from the late fourth century AD onwards and the subsequent development of the European nation states, the

---

[5] King (2004).   [6] Saleh (1986).

[7] Aristotle, 'The Politics', in Monroe (1948).

[8] *Nauticum foenus* refers to a nautical, or maritime interest rate charged to underwrite a dangerous or risky voyage: Jones (2008).

[9] Jones (2008).

individual countries over time developed their own laws. In the initial stages, the Canon laws of the Christian Church would generally be the leading body of law, but as time went on, they developed into a separate body of law. In the UK, this process took place by means of a series of royal decrees and, later, acts of parliament.

The Anglo-Saxon Laws of Edward the Confessor dealt with Jewish as well as Christian usury and evidence exists that Henry II actively prohibited Christian usury as early as 1136.[10]

The Code of Canon Law from around 1187 clearly stated that as far as the Church was concerned, the basic definition of usury was *everything* that was asked for in return for a loan beyond the value of the loan itself. In itself, the earning of money through usury was deemed to be a sin forbidden by both the Old and the New Testament. Requesting a higher price for a sale on credit was also seen as an act of usury, albeit an *implicit* one.[11] Also in the twelfth century, Innocent III argued that no interest could be charged to Crusaders, but for all others, moderate interest was acceptable and Christians should only be protected against immoderate or excessive usury. Innocent III's decree specifically referred to Jewish moneylenders, implying that the charging and paying of interest between Christians was still not permissible.[12]

The Fourth Lateran Council, which was conducted by Pope Innocent III, prohibited Jews from taking oppressive and excessive interest from Christians, but allowed them to lend money at interest as long as the rates were deemed to be reasonable. The ban on Jewish interest was, therefore, not absolute.

During the middle of the thirteenth century AD, Thomas Aquinas and his contemporaries including Ibn Rushd (Averroes) further explored Aristotle's views on the charging of interest and considered charging money for something that has been consumed to be unlawful.[13] In this respect, Aquinas also referred back to the civil law of the time. It did not reject the idea that capital could be put to productive use and anyone providing capital should be rewarded for making it available, but rather rejected the providing of a loan at interest without any economic purpose, or without the lender taking at least some form of risk.[14]

In the late thirteenth century AD, Edward I issued proclamations and statutes against usury, strongly condemning any form of it. In 1290 he expelled all Jews from England on the pretext that they were moneylenders and, thus, committing a criminal offence. Although the charging of interest was officially banned, it was hardly ever enforced under any of the Royal decrees. It was not until 1363 that the first usurers were finally taken to trial.[15]

---

[10] Seabourne (2003).   [11] Goff (1990).
[12] Stow (1981).   [13] St Thomas Aquinas *Summa Theologica* in Monroe (1948).
[14] Goff (1990).   [15] Seabourne (2003).

One of the main challenges has long been that the term usury in itself was rather loosely defined as the excess return on something that was lent. It was, therefore, unclear whether late payment penalties or selling at inflated prices for payment at a later date would fall under the prohibition or not. In addition, different rules appear to have been applied to Jews and Christians regarding the permissibility of applying an additional charge when selling on credit. Jews would be allowed to charge an additional amount over and above the sale price but Christians, on the contrary, were not. Jews could freely charge usury and were not hindered by the Government. A Charter of Henry III to the University of Oxford provided some evidence of this: it allowed the Jews of Oxford to take up to 2 pence (2d) per pound per week from the scholars of the university, as long as the interest was not compounded.[16] In the year 1363 rules were put in place to be able to act against any circumvention of the usury laws. These rules applied in London, but did not get introduced in the national legal code until 1487. The rules ware particularly aimed at the practice known as *chevisance* which consisted of entering into a combination of an artificial sales transaction, one at a higher price for future payment and the resale of the same asset at a lower price for immediate payment thus facilitating a loan against interest.[17]

During the period leading up to the introduction of the 1571 bill against usury, moneylenders were occasionally taken to court, although actions taken were fairly inconsistent. During the first part of Edward I's reign (1272–1307), any instance of usury was actively investigated and punished accordingly, and the state went as far as to evict all Jews when they continued to charge usury after the Statute of Jewry in 1275. Subsequent royal decrees tended to refer to Canon Rules, thus making the charging of usury more like a moral sin than a criminal offence. The Courts set up a special Usury Tribunal in 1363, but very few cases were pursued. It should be noted that the royal actions were, at least in part, driven by financial motivations. For example, the court of Edward I benefitted financially when actions were taken against the Jews and Italian merchant usurers, and when Edward III included an anti-usury article in 1341–3 this was, at least in part, driven by the fact that he needed funds to meet the cost of his war with France. However, whilst it might be easy to assume that anti-usury action was largely governed by a desire to enhance the financial position of the Crown, this is unlikely to have been the case. Moreover, the laws were mainly aimed at the Christian usurers and only marginally dealt with the Jews and Italian merchants, which would lead to the conclusion that the bans were mainly motivated by religious principles.[18] Around the same time, in the Ottoman Empire, all economic activity was subject to principles and rules in the *Quran* and the *Sunnah*, which prohibit all charging of interest. In practice, however, interest rates as high as 50 per cent have been recorded.

---

[16] Seabourne (2003).   [17] Seabourne (2003).   [18] Seabourne (2003).

In 1468, Henry VII introduced a law that defined usury as something that occurred when anyone lent: 'money to and for a tyme, taking for the same lone any thing more besides or above the money lente by wey of contracte of covenaunte at the tyme of the same lone, Savyng laufull penaltees for nounpa-ment of the same money lent'. Although this definition prohibited the general charging of interest, it did allow lenders to charge penalties on default.[19] In 1546, Henry VIII repealed this act and replaced it with an act on usury in which it was declared that all interest in excess of 10 per cent usurious and thus unlawful. Edward VI subsequently repealed this act, again prohibiting all charging of interest. The act appears not to have had the desired effect of eradicating lending at interest. On the contrary, there is reason to believe that instead it increased the amount of lending and in addition resulted in higher percentages charged.[20] The latter is likely to have been related to the fact that the moneylender would need to be compensated for the higher risk he was taking as a result of the prohibition.

From 1571 onwards, Elizabeth I revived the statute of Henry VIII, with the maximum legal interest rate of 10 per cent remaining in place until 1624, when it was reduced to 8 per cent.[21] The maximum interest rate was subsequently reduced further to 6 per cent soon after the Restoration, with the introduction of an act of parliament called 'An Act for restraining the taking of Excessive Usury' that simultaneously introducing a penalty of £20 and imprisonment for transgression.[22] In 1714 the legal maximum was reduced to 5 per cent where it remained until 1854 when it was finally abolished.[23]

The Statute of Usury of 1714, which limited the interest rate that could be charged in the UK to 5 per cent, is generally accepted to be the basis for all anti-usury legislation in the USA. Contrary to European countries, where usury laws were repealed between 1854 and 1867, usury laws in the USA largely remained in place. There were, however, differences across individual states in the implementation of the laws. On 31 March 1980 President Carter signed The Depository Institutions Deregulation and Monetary Control Act into law. The purpose of title two of this law—the Depository Institutions Deregulation Act—was to 'provide for an orderly phase-out and ultimate elimination of interest rate ceilings', effectively repealing the anti-usury laws at federal level.[24] Most individual states still, however, enforced a maximum interest rate, although there are significant differences of treatment in each state.

More recently, an Interest Rate Reduction Act was introduced to Congress on 19 January 2011 that was designed to amend Section 107 of the Truth in Lending Act to introduce a maximum interest rate of 15 per cent.[25] In the

---

[19] Jones (1989).   [20] Smith (1776).   [21] Smith (1776).
[22] Charles II (1660) 'An Act for restraining the takeing of Excessive Usury'.
[23] Horack (1941).   [24] Federal Reserve Bank of Boston (1980).
[25] Congressional Bills 112th Congress, 1st Session. H.R. 336 Introduced in House.

current version of the Act no such restriction is in place.[26] The recurring theme throughout the ages is that interest on money is disadvantageous since it creates inequality between rich and poor, does not reflect the profitability of the investment, and can result in inefficient allocation of available resources in the economy which may in turn lead to instability of the system.

Islamic financial products

The previous section demonstrated that prohibitions on interest are not a new phenomenon. Even though it was recognized that a cost was associated with providing capital, the charging of interest in return for a loan was deemed to be disadvantageous for individuals as well as the economy in many cultures. However, whilst the prohibition on usury has typically been relaxed in many states from all interest to only excessive interest, it is still in place in Islam where restrictions cover all interest and are absolute and unqualified. A return on investment or a profit on trade, however, is permissible as long as there is an underlying asset or enterprise with which the capital is associated. In order to be able to redistribute capital, the following transaction types are in place in Islamic finance (see Table 18.1).

By far the most popular structure in Islamic finance is the *commodity murabaha* or its variety the *tawarruq* transaction. In this transaction an unrelated commodity is purchased and sold at a higher price against deferred payment. There are a number of reasons for the popularity of these transactions including the fact that they are easy to understand and do not have any adverse tax implications.

Pricing of the transactions is typically benchmarked to local or international interest rates since, in the end, it is recognized that the ability to use capital has a cost associated with it, and interest is still the benchmark that allows for the pricing of the cost of capital, risk, opportunity costs, and future growth.

Other principles underlying Islamic finance

In addition to the prohibition on interest there are a number of other prohibitions within Islamic finance that are often not considered to the same extent. The other major prohibitions are *gharar* (unnecessary uncertainty or risk) and *maysir* (gambling). Equally important, however, are

---

[26] FDIC Law, Regulation and Related Acts, 15 U.S.C. 1606.

Table 18.1. Islamic finance products

Name	Description	Usage
Murabaha	Trade-based transaction in which the seller of the asset charges the original purchase price plus a pre-defined mark-up to be paid on an agreed date	Secured personal loans Trade finance Working capital Credit cards
Commodity murabaha	Trade-based transaction in which a commodity (typically an LME base metal) is bought and sold to provide one party with a deferred payment obligation	Unsecured personal loans Interbank placements Real estate finance
Ijara	Lease transaction that can either be structured as a finance or an operating lease	Equipment leasing Mortgage
Salam	Production and pre-harvest financing transaction in which the full amount of the good purchased is paid in advance against delivery at a later date	Short-term production finance Pre-harvest finance Short-term liquidity
Istisna	Project finance in which the construction of a non-existing asset is financed. Payments can be made up front but are more likely to be scheduled in accordance with progress	Project finance
Sarf	Currency exchange contract in which an amount in one currency is exchanged for an equal amount in another currency for immediate delivery	Spot foreign exchange
Qard hassanah	The loan of an amount of money which needs to be repaid in full. The loan does not attract any charges	Deposit taking for current accounts
Wakala	Agency agreement in which one person appoints another to execute a service	Deposit taking for savings accounts Asset management
Wadia/amanah	Deposit-type agreements similar in nature to the use of a safety deposit box. The client may give permission to the bank to use the funds in their day-to-day operations	Deposit taking for current accounts
Musharaka	Partnership transaction in which all parties provide capital as well as skills and expertise. Profits are shared in accordance with the contract and the profit ratio will reflect the level of input of the partners. Losses are distributed in proportion to capital provided	Direct investments Venture capital Project finance
Mudaraba	Partnership transaction in which one party provides capital and another provides skills and expertise. Profits are shared in accordance with the contract and the profit ratio will reflect the level of input of the partners. Losses are distributed in proportion to capital provided, and hence all losses are for the partner providing the capital unless the business manager has been negligent	Direct investments Venture capital

limitations on the assets in which investment can be made and other principles that need to be adhered in business to such as honesty and fairness.

UNNECESSARY UNCERTAINTY AND GAMBLING

Within the framework of *Sharia'a*, two further major prohibitions are identified in addition to the prohibition on *riba*: *gharar* (unnecessary uncertainty) and *maysir* (gambling). Their existence does not, however, mean all risk is prohibited as is detailed further next.

Gharar

Gharar is generally translated as *uncertainty*, although there are differences of opinion between various schools of thought on what *gharar* actually includes. The literal meaning of *gharar* is 'unknowingly to expose oneself or one's property to jeopardy' and is interpreted in each of the following ways:[27]

- *Gharar* applies exclusively to cases of doubtfulness or uncertainty as in the case of not knowing whether something will take place or not, which for instance applies to uncertainty over the asset for sale and can be extended to uncertainty of specifications or ownership
- *Gharar* only applies to the unknown, but not to cases of doubtfulness. This view is adopted when the purchaser does not know what she has bought or the seller does not know what she has sold
- *Gharar* applies to a combination of the above that covers both the unknown and the doubtful: *gharar* occurs where the consequences of a contract are not known. This approach is favoured by most jurists.

Generally speaking, uncertainty regarding the asset, its price, delivery or payment date all cause *gharar*. In essence then, *gharar* refers to acts and conditions in exchange contracts, the full implications of which are not clearly known to all parties. Ibn Rushd argued that *gharar* in sales transactions causes the buyer to suffer damage and is caused by a lack of knowledge regarding the asset or its price,[28] or general ignorance. Ignorance applies equally to all parties. *Gharar* does not apply to business risks such as an investment in a company. In addition, minor levels of uncertainty are allowed such as, for example, linking a price to the market price on an agreed date or linking the payment date to a harvest period that, although not exactly certain, can be estimated to fall within a reasonable date range.

Maysir

Maysir occurs when there is a possibility of total loss for one party, and has an element of *gharar*, since it involves a level of uncertainty. But not all *gharar* is *maysir*. *Maysir* is associated with games of chance or gambling. Similar to the exceptions for *gharar*, anything related to the broad uncertainties of life and business activities involving an element of chance and risk-taking are not subject to *maysir*.

PERMISSIBLE RISK-TAKING

One of the distinguishing features of Islamic finance is the sharing of risk between entrepreneurs and financiers, and, hence, not all types of risk-taking are prohibited. The following risk types are generally permitted:

---

[27] Iqbal and Molineux (2005).   [28] Saleh (1986).

- *Entrepreneurial risk incurred in the normal course of business*: Enterprises make profits and occasionally incur losses. Generally profits tend to outstrip any losses since otherwise no society would have any entrepreneurs at all. Willingness to take an entrepreneurial risk is not deemed to be a moral evil and Islam encourages investment. It is fulfilling a need that a society cannot do without, and the risk and associated uncertainty are permissible
- *Possibility of natural disasters and calamities occurring*: These risks are completely out of the control of an individual or business and are, therefore, acceptable risks to take. Protection against these risks, also known as *force majeure*, by means of mutual insurance is permissible
- *Risks that arise from uncertainties related to activities voluntarily undertaken which are not part of everyday life and arise from types of 'games' people devise*: The risks involved are unnecessary for the individual (the risk does not have to be taken) and unnecessary for society (taking the risk does not add any economic value to the wealth of the society). These risks are akin to gambling that is prohibited.

Social responsibility

Sharia'a places a particular strong emphasis on social responsibility, which is not only evidenced by the major prohibitions as outlined in the previous sections, but also upon a set of commercial ethics. Within *Sharia'a* these are based on five main principles:

- *Stewardship of humanity on earth*: Private ownership is permitted, but any ownership is deemed to be temporary since man is entrusted to look after it on behalf of Allah. Ownership is, thus, not an end in itself, but a means to provide a decent life for the owner, his family, and society
- *Integrity*: All acts including business dealings should be governed by integrity
- *Sincerity*: All stakeholders need to be treated in a sincere and fair way
- *Piety*: Everyone has to be devout in private and in public and the values, norms, and rules of *Sharia'a* will always need to be adhered to
- *Righteousness and perfection at work*: All duties should be undertaken to the best of one's capability.

During the early years of Islam, the city of Medina was largely a market economy, and many of the behavioural norms and values associated with these ethical principles relate to commerce. Generally speaking, due to the lack of emphasis on fairness, justness, and transparency in most free market contexts, it can be said that Islam combines the concepts of free market with a more socially embedded approach to economics. The norms and values that must be observed are strongly linked to what is sometimes known as *social responsibility* and include, but are not restricted to, not lying about products sold, honouring promises, and not attempting to deceive or defraud. The essence of this is structured in the following ten rules:

- *Avoid riba*
- *Avoid gharar*
- *Trade honestly and fairly*: Any trade manipulation including, for example, the use of black markets, taking advantage of a information asymmetry, manipulating weights and measures, and concealing defects, is prohibited. All trades need to be executed fairly
- *Full disclosure*: Although it is prohibited to conceal defects, it is not forbidden to sell a defective good. The seller may stipulate that he is not liable for any defects as long as he discloses all defects of which he is aware
- *Avoid misrepresentation*: Traders should not make false declarations about the goods or services they sell
- *Do not interfere in a transaction that is (being) concluded*: Although bargaining and sale by auction are permitted, it is not allowed to interfere in a transaction that is being concluded by, for example, offering the same good at a lower price, or offering a higher price for a good subject to a private sale
- *Avoid forbidden (haram) items*: In addition to the assets that are generally deemed illegal such as drugs, there are a number of other assets that a Muslim cannot invest in. Although the exact list varies slightly depending on the individual, generally speaking anything that is harmful should not be invested in. The consensus among scholars is that the following assets are deemed to be *haram*:
  - conventional banking and insurance charging interest
  - weapons and defence
  - alcohol including distilling and marketing, but excluding medicinal alcohol
  - tobacco
  - pork
  - adult entertainment
  - gambling
- *No hoarding*: Although there is no prohibition on wealth creation, both hoarding assets and an excessive love of wealth are strongly condemned
- *Open markets*: All goods, assets, and services should be sold in the open market and all parties must be aware of the state of the market before the transaction is concluded. Neither the buyer nor the seller should take advantage of another's ignorance of market prices and conditions
- *Do not take advantage of a seller's helplessness*: When a person is falling on hard times, it is not acceptable to take advantage of this by purchasing her assets at a heavily discounted price. Instead, other assistance should be provided.

In combination, these rules ensure the incorporation of social values in Islamic business. Similar principles can be found in the mainstream socially responsible investing (SRI) market, and are also enshrined in some financial regulations. The Treating Customers Fairly (TCF) initiative in the UK, for example, attempted to achieve some of the same goals when it came to transparency and fairness. The main difference is that TCF was biased in favour of customers where as the Islamic principles in commerce apply to all parties. In light of the global financial crisis on 2008, the final rule above is of particular interest. Many investors with funds at their disposal have purchased what is known as *distressed property*. The term refers to heavily discounted assets, typically real estate, for which the price is depressed due to the fact that the seller is experiencing financial difficulties. Within the framework of *Sharia'a*, the buyer should, instead of using the seller's situation to drive the price down, look for other options that can be explored to assist the seller.

From a markets perspective, these rules are also interesting. The fact that goods need to be sold in fully transparent and open markets should promote healthy competition and limit the potential for monopolies. In general it is fair to say that the principles embedded in Islam promote trade and commerce, but at the same time ensure fairness and transparency.

Islamic finance in practice

For a number of reasons such as the requirement to conform to existing regulations, the relatively short history of modern Islamic finance, the small size of the institutions, and the desire to be part of the larger financial industry, many financial structures in Islamic finance have been developed to mimic conventional finance. Unsurprisingly this has resulted in some scepticism about the spiritual integrity of these transactions, particularly since the underlying economic reality of the debt transactions is often the same as those of conventional lending.

Many of the players in the Islamic financial industry attempt to show that they can play a role in the international financial industry and keep on placing money with other financial institutions using *commodity murabaha*. The *commodity murabaha* transaction is, by far, the most popular instrument in Islamic finance: this is largely due to the ease with which it can be compared to conventional loans and deposits. Investing in, and lending to, local enterprises is often dismissed as too risky since the companies are small and not well diversified. Although this has an element of truth in it, the amounts to be invested are typically lower thus allowing for diversification of investments by the financial institution. In addition, the closer relationships that can be developed have a risk-mitigating element.

One of the most risky ventures to provide financing for is the agricultural sector. Prone to natural disasters and other uncontrollable elements such as changing weather conditions, most financial institutions will only hesitantly finance agriculture and associated businesses. Agriculture finance is typically associated with high interest rates and collateral requirements to cover the risk.

From an Islamic financial institution's point of view, the easiest way to finance agriculture is the same way as most other transactions are financed: namely, the *commodity murabaha* transaction, in which an unrelated commodity is purchased and sold to the client on a deferred payment basis. In this case the financial institution purchases a commodity, sells it to the client with a mark-up and against deferred payment, after which the client requests the institution to sell it as their agent against immediate payment. Although relatively risk free, since the client will have the obligation to pay for the asset, it involves an asset neither the client nor the financial institution has any particular use for.

A better way of dealing with this would be to identify an asset the client requires such as, for example, agricultural inputs. These consist of seeds, fertilizer, tools, pesticides, and other related assets. The asset can be purchased by the financial institution and sold to the farmers for a price plus mark-up to be paid one month after the harvest period. However, from the financial institution's perspective, there are a number of challenges with this approach:

- *Exposure to the asset*: For a brief period of time, the financial institution may be exposed to fluctuations in the asset price. This is typically resolved with fixed-price purchase contracts and agreed sale prices
- *Price determination*: Due to the requirement to sell goods in an open market, the wholesale to retail price can be used as an approximation for the mark-up, but varies per type of good. In Afghanistan, for example, for some types of agricultural inputs such as fertilizer, the mark-up between the wholesale and retail price is around 2.5 per cent: for others, such as tools, the mark-up can be up to 20 per cent. Rather than being able to charge one flat fee over the whole amount, a complex composite structure may be required
- *Payment date*: For agricultural finance repayment dates would typically match crop and harvest cycles. Although harvest dates are predictable within a range, they are not usually known exactly. Payment dates can, for example, be determined as one month after completion of harvest.

One of the additional challenges with agriculture is the fact that it is prone to natural disasters and changes in weather conditions that are out of the control of the farmer. In countries such as Afghanistan where insurance is not readily available, this risk needs to be addressed in a different way. Risk diversification in this sense can be achieved by lending via co-operatives or farm service centres that serve a number of farmers—ranging from 10 to 1,000—that are typically spread over a larger area and, in some cases, multiple provinces. The geographical range will reduce the risk that all farmers are subject to losses from natural disasters and can limit the overall loss risk. Another opportunity here would be to charge an additional mark-up or profit share that is contributed to an Islamic trust (or *Waqf*) that will only pay out in the event of a proven loss from a natural disaster.

Agriculture finance is high risk at best, and even more so in a country like Afghanistan where, besides varying weather conditions and earthquakes, other elements are at play. However, developing the agricultural sector is not only of importance to the individual farmer, but for the community as a whole. It will help in increasing the quality and quantity of produce that, in turn, enhances the competitiveness of local farmers in global markets. In a country that depends for a significant amount of its food supplies on neighbouring countries with many associated problems (i.e. border closures and transportation costs), being able to buy locally can provide a tremendous benefit to the local society as a whole. From an Islamic point of view, the development of the local society is at least as important as the prohibition on interest.

The perception of high risk is an important reason why many banks, both conventional and Islamic, shy away from agricultural finance. However, there are also less tangible issues. Financing local farmers does not hold the same appeal when it comes to showing that the Islamic financial industry is a full player within the overall financial industry. Financing local farmers is not glamorous, and does not show global reach. But it does benefit the local economy, allow for diversification and innovation, and has a potential to reduce risks when businesses depending on good quality agricultural produce are starting to develop.

Conclusion

The prohibition on interest is generally cited as the issue that sets apart Islamic from conventional finance. This argument, however, has two flaws. Firstly, the prohibition on interest is, as can be seen from history, not unique to Islamic finance. In addition, the prohibition on interest has long featured in the laws of Europe. In the case of the USA, there are still laws against the charging of usury at the level of individual states. The view on interest in Europe and the USA has changed over time and now only covers excessive interest.

Other principles governing Islamic finance are often overlooked but are equally important. The second main tenet of the *Sharia'a* view of commerce is the prohibition on *gharar* or unnecessary uncertainty. This does not mean that calculated risks are forbidden, but that unnecessary risks should not be taken. *Gharar* occurs when there is excessive uncertainty regarding the asset, price, or delivery and payment date. As Ibn Rushd argued, *gharar* in sales transactions causes the buyer to suffer damage. It does, however, not apply to business risk.

From a social responsibility perspective, *Sharia'a* includes many strong guidelines such as the requirement that all transactions have to be transparent for all parties, that parties should not deceive each other, and that all trans-actions need to take place in the open market thus stimulating competition and reducing monopolies. In turn, these principles ensure that none of the trading parties is disadvantaged compared to another. Wealth creation is encouraged, however, as long as the principles that need to be adhered to such as honesty and fairness are taken into consideration.

In addition to the major prohibitions, the commercial ethics within *Sharia'a* are based on five main principles: stewardship of humanity on earth, integrity, sincerity, piety, and righteousness and perfection at work. In combination with an emphasis on trade, these principles ensure that restrictions are placed on the free-market mechanism to ensure fairness, justness and transparency. This socially embedded version of the free market has links with mainstream socially responsible investing, co-operative and mutual finance and commu-nity development finance.

In practice, Islamic financial institutions typically apply the instruments that are easiest to reconcile with their local regulations. In addition, there appears to be a growing desire to be seen as a part of the mainstream financial industry. Many Islamic financial structures have been developed to mimic conventional financial instruments and this has raised scepticism about the spiritual basis of the industry. Investing in small- and medium-sized local enterprises has often been dismissed as too risky and is also not attractive from the perspective of the Islamic finance industry's determin-ation to be seen as a global player. There are, however, a number of advantages to investing in local enterprises, most of which are particularly suited to the *Sharia'a* principles. Closer relationships are forged between the financial institution and the client thus leading to greater trust, social capital, and openness in transactions. The case of agricultural finance is a special one, particularly when applied in countries like Afghanistan where strengthening the agricultural sector will not only be of benefit for the farmers but also for their entire society. As such, providing agricultural finance, even in high-risk environments, could further meet the broader social responsibility requirements embedded in *Sharia'a*. After all, from an Islamic point of view, the development of a local society and stewardship of humanity on earth is at least as important as the prohibition on interest. The higher risk that is always present in agriculture financing cannot always be avoided, particularly when considering the risk of natural disas-ters and unpredictable weather. However, it does benefit the local econ-omy, allows for diversification and innovation, and has a potential to reduce risks when businesses depending on good quality agricultural prod-uce are starting to develop.

When considering the full array of prohibitions and principles, it becomes clear that the socially responsible elements of *Sharia'a* are all inclusive. Applied to finance, they provide a framework similar to what is called ethical or socially responsible investment and is closely matched to merchant banking when it first originated.

■ REFERENCES

Aquinas, St Thomas (1948). 'Summa Theologica', in A. E. Monroe (1948), *Early Economic Thought: Selections from Economic Literature Prior to Adam Smith*. Cambridge, MA: Harvard University Press, pp. 51–78.

Aristotle (1948). 'The Politics', in A. E. Monroe (1948), *Early Economic Thought: Selections from Economic Literature Prior to Adam Smith*. Cambridge, MA: Harvard University Press, pp. 1–30.

Charles II (1660) 'An Act for restraining the takeing of Excessive Usury', *Statutes of the Realm*: v: *1628–80* (1819), Public Records Office, London, pp. 236–7.

Congressional Bills 112th Congress, 1st Session. (2011). H.R. 336 Introduced in House. <http://www.gpo.gov/fdsys/pkg/BILLS-112hr336ih/html/BILLS-112hr336ih.htm>, accessed 15 June 2015.

FDIC Law (2011). Regulation and Related Acts, 15 U.S.C. 1606 <http://www.fdic.gov/regulations/laws/rules/6500-200.html#fdic6500107>, accessed 1 November 2014.

Federal Reserve Bank of Boston (1980). 'Depository Institutions Deregulation and Monetary Control Act of 1980: Summary Booklet'. <http://www.bos.frb.org/about/pubs/deposito.pdf>, accessed 22 May 2011.

Ferguson, N. (2008). *The Ascent of Money: A Financial History of the World*. London: Allen Lane.

Goff, J. Le (1990). *Your Money or Your Life—Economy and Religion in the Middle Ages*. New York: Zone Books

Horack, B. S. (1941). 'A Survey of the General Usury Laws', *Journal of Law & Contemporary Problems*, 8(1): 36–53.

Ibn Rushd (2000). *The Distinguished Jurist's Primer*. Lebanon: Garnet Publishing Ltd.

Iqbal, M., and Molineux P. (2005). *Thirty Years of Islamic Banking: History, Performance and Prospects*. London: Palgrave Macmillan.

Jones, N. (1989). *God and the Money Lenders: Usury and the Law in Early Modern England*. Oxford: Basil Blackwell Ltd.

Jones, N. (2008). 'Usury', *EH.Net Encyclopedia*, ed. R. Whaples, 10 February 2008. <http://eh.net/encyclopedia>, accessed 15 June 2015.

King, L. W. (2004). *The Code of Hammurabi*. Whitefish, MO: Kessinger Publishing.

Saleh, N. A. (1986). *Unlawful Gain and Legitimate Profit in Islamic Law: Riba, Gharar and Islamic Banking*. Cambridge: Cambridge University Press.

Schoon, N. (2008), 'Islamic Finance: An Overview', *European Business and Law Review*, 9: 621–35.

Schoon, N. (2016). *Islamic Banking and Finance*. London: John Wiley & Sons.

Seabourne, G. (2003). *Royal Regulation of Loans and Sales in Medieval England: Monkish Superstition and Civil Tyranny*. Woodbridge: The Boydell Press.

Smith, A. (1776). *An Inquiry into the Nature and Causes of the Wealth of Nations*. Complete and Unabridged Version (2000). New York: The Modern Library.

Stow, K. R. (1981). 'Papal and Royal Attitudes toward Jewish Lending in the Thirteenth Century', *AJS Review*, 6: 161–84.

Supple, B. (1997). 'The Nature of Enterprise', in E. Rich and C. Wilson (eds), *The Economic Organization of Early Modern Europe*. Cambridge: Cambridge University Press.

19 Environmental impact investing

Co-managing the ecological and economic household

Jacob Harold, Joshua Spitzer, Jed Emerson, and Marieke Spence

Introduction

It is no coincidence that the words 'economics' and 'ecology' begin with the same three letters drawn from the Greek word *eco*, meaning *household*. In the modern context *eco* refers to the discipline of how scarce resources can be best allocated and refers back to the original meaning of effective *household* management.

This chapter explores this intersection of households, the economics of environmental management, and the environmental consequences of economic investment.[1] The analysis is organized into four main components: the first section begins by exploring principal themes in environmental economics. It continues by investigating the link between environmental impact investing and financial return. Finally, the section suggests a framework for understanding the different forums in which environmentally oriented investment occurs. The second section posits ten propositions on how environmental concerns influence and are influenced by financial investment. The third section focuses on one particularly tangible domain—real estate—and includes three case studies to illustrate existing strategies for incorporating environmental value into real estate investment. The fourth and final section offers conclusions and recommendations for further research.[2]

---

[1] For the purposes of this chapter's discussion, 'impact investing' refers to distinct strategies that account for environmental, financial, and other dimensions of value creation. 'Blended value' is what those strategies create and measure. Blended value may be understood as an understanding of value creation, which integrates economic, environmental, and social components into a value proposition, either at a capital or corporate level.

[2] This chapter draws heavily from two papers by the authors, both published in 2007 by the Skoll Centre for Social Entrepreneurship at the Oxford Said School of Business: 'Blended Value Investing: Integrating Environmental Risks and Opportunities into Securities Valuation' and 'Blended Value Investing: Innovations in Real Estate.'

The intersection of environmental economics and finance

ENVIRONMENTAL ECONOMICS

The natural environment makes the human economy possible. Supplies of critical 'goods' such as timber, grain, meat, and medicinal plants rely on a delicate balance of natural factors such as weather patterns, the nitrogen cycle, and predator–prey networks. Similarly, large parts of the human economy are protected and enhanced by the stability of 'services' provided by natural systems that filter water, prevent flooding, and support the production of natural goods. Hurricane Katrina highlighted the critical role of the Greater Mississippi Delta's wetlands in protecting—or failing to protect—human settlements from tropical storms.

The problem is a classic 'tragedy of the commons' (Ostrom, 1990): individuals might benefit fully from developing a wetland, but they only pay a small part of the broader social cost of losing that wetland's filtration and protection functions—costs they may not even understand or know to consider when capturing financial value from an activity.

Creating strategies to avoid future tragedies of the commons may offer a variety of benefits to society as a whole, but such strategies also face significant political and operational challenges. Some argue for regulations that prevent individuals from exacting such social costs; others claim that clear property rights will solve the problem; still others look to cultural change. Such potential solutions can be difficult to design, launch, and execute. Nevertheless, a set of examples has emerged in which individual or institutional investment can trump the tragedy of the commons and generate both financial and environmental benefits. A discourse often identified with 'ecosystem services' or 'natural capital' explores the protection of ecosystems by pricing the services they provide society.[3] When people define the services offered by the natural world and then compare them to human-made alternatives, it can be cheaper in many cases to protect natural capital rather than allow it to be degraded and replaced by inferior substitutes. Several examples discussed throughout this paper fit under the ecosystem services rubric. Nevertheless, this paper does not explore the ecosystem services and natural capital discourses specifically. Instead, readers would be advised to consult the extensive literature that explores those concepts in great depth.

---

[3] Gregory Unruh, professor of global business at the Thunderbird School of Global Management and director of the Lincoln Center for Ethics in Global Management at the University of Arizona, has said of measuring ecosystem services: 'What's the right way to calculate that value? You know that a forest or wetland provides the service of purifying the water you use, but putting a price on that is very difficult. Because it's so difficult, most companies just don't try. You can't be precisely correct, so you decide to be precisely wrong; you put the price at zero.' Cited from Bredenberg (2012).

EFFICIENT MARKETS

An understanding of efficient markets and risk-adjusted time-value of money helps establish a context for environmental impact investing. To begin, it is commonly understood that some assets are valuable for what they will be able to do continuously into the future. For example, a piece of land may be valuable because it can produce wheat or grapes into the foreseeable future. It is worth more than simply the value of one year's crop because a purchaser would believe the land will produce the bounty of future harvests. On the other hand, it is worth less than the value of a hundred years' of harvests because there is risk that drought or plague could reduce future crops. Also, most investors prefer to receive money now instead of in the future.

The productivity of a given piece of land may be improved but over time will reach a ceiling according to available technology and fundamental physics. In contrast, investors in other more liquid assets face fewer constraints. Traditional corporate valuation practice would assert that a company's profits may grow indefinitely but are nevertheless subject to economic and non-market constraints. Thus, the current value of an asset is not only a reflection of current productivity and perception of risk it is also a reflection of hope for the future. In simple terms, a stock is worth the sum of the future profits of its constituent company. Financial valuation is therefore an exercise involving both quantitative and qualitative—even emotional—judgements.

In 1970 economist Milton Friedman made his famous claim that the social responsibility of corporate managers is to make money for investors.[4] Friedman argued that managers pursuing any other goals—beyond following the law and basic morality—were betraying their fiduciary duty. Since then, many authors have corroborated that idea; others have attempted to modulate Friedman's unqualified stance; and still others have directly challenged Friedman's approach both on economic and ethical bases.

The 2008 financial crisis and continuing economic turmoil have deepened public scepticism of large financial institutions, corporate managers, and the opaque instruments they often use. Meanwhile, the news has been full of environmental disasters such as the BP oil spill in the Gulf of Mexico, radiation concerns in Japan following the 2011 earthquake, and more frequent extreme weather occurrences—most recently Hurricane Sandy.[5,6] These failures, both financial and environmental, have strengthened critics of Friedman's strict interpretation of social responsibility and have increased pressure to better strike the 'economy–ecology' balance. Against this backdrop, investment strategies that deliver both social or environmental and

---

[4] Friedman (1970).   [5] Borenstein (2011).
[6] Tom Karl, director of NOAA's National Climatic Data Center, notes that troubling weather extremes in 2011 were 'abnormal... but part of an ongoing trend we've seen since 1980'. Worldwide insured losses from disasters in the first three months of 2011 were more than any entire year on record with the exception of 2005, when Hurricane Katrina struck (Borenstein, 2011).

financial returns, and more accurately price environmental factors including risk, are increasingly appealing.

Environmental impact investing

Investor engagement with social and environmental issues is a global phenomenon, but the best data is available for the largest market, the USA. At the start of 2010 assets oriented toward social and environmental investment strategies totalled $3.07trn in the USA, a rise of more than 380 per cent from $639bn in 1995. Altogether, this pool of capital accounts for 12.2 per cent of all assets under management in the USA.[7] Represented another way, nearly one out of every eight dollars under professional management in the USA today is tied to some type of SRI strategy. Much of this capital flows through financial mechanisms tied to a broadly defined social good, but increasing amounts are specific to a particular issue, often environmental protection. As one example of many, in 2011 Wells Fargo provided a record $2.8bn in environmental loans and investments, ranging from LEED-certified commercial and community developments, to solar and wind projects and beyond.[8]

Individual investors' appetite for investment products that focus on environmental returns appears to be growing. A recent survey by Allianz Global Investors found that 71 per cent of respondents believe environmental technology is the next great American industry. Even more striking is a 70 per cent increase in the number of investors claiming to have capitalized on environmental trends between 2007 and 2010. In the same survey, more than half planned to invest in clean tech over the next year, while 63 per cent classified the environment as the most desirable investment opportunity out of 11 categories listed including sectors such as financial services, commodities, and traditional energy companies.[9] Another study cites environmentally themed investment products and impact or programme-related investing as two major drivers of rapid SRI growth in the USA.[10]

Regardless of this enthusiasm, it is not yet clear how environmentally oriented investment strategies will influence financial returns over the long term. Ample evidence (cited throughout this chapter) suggests that some investments do offer both a financial return and substantive environmental returns. Less clear, however, is whether such investment strategies as a

---

[7] Social Investment Forum Foundation (2010).   [8] Wells Fargo (2012).
[9] Baden (2010).   [10] SIFF Report, p. 11.

category can *consistently* achieve financial returns that are the same as or better than traditional strategies.

A key, correlating question has to do with the goals of an individual investor. As with all investors, impact investors vary in their risk profiles—but they also vary in the social and environmental returns they seek. Their investment strategies range from simple negative screens (e.g. no investment in tobacco companies) to highly proactive investments in transformative technologies for which there may not yet be a fluid, highly functioning market (e.g. investments in carbon sequestration technologies). Thus, even when an investor aims to create blended value, there is no single, monolithic blended value investing strategy or asset allocation framework, no 'Green Monte Carlo Scenario' to help guide the investment process.

The empirical evidence

The evidence on the relationship between social and financial returns is complex and contradictory, no surprise given the richness and complexity of the topic. There is certainly significant evidence that impact investing can generate returns comparable to or better than investment strategies aiming only for risk-adjusted market rate financial returns. Between 2007 and 2010, for example, a period when major market indices like the S&P 500 declined, assets tied to sustainable and socially responsible investing increased more than 13 per cent.[11] Furthermore, a study of 160 socially responsible funds by the Social Investment Forum found that 65 per cent outperformed their benchmarks in 2009.[12]

Likewise, a recent study testing the impact of environmental, social, and governance (ESG) issues on portfolio performance found promising results: introduction of the ESG criteria into stock selection actually increased probability of outperformance over the longer term.[13] Importantly, the five-year period under analysis, 2006 to 2010, encompassed strong market growth, a market crash, and an emerging rebound. One recent literature review boldly states that there is now clear, empirical evidence for a positive correlation between corporate social and financial performance, and that studies claiming otherwise are relying on outdated evidence.[14]

On the other hand, while several researchers have found positive correlations, others claim no connection or a negative relationship between

---

[11] SIFF Report, p. 8.   [12] Keane (2010).
[13] RCM, 'Sustainability: Opportunity or Opportunity Cost?' July 2011, pp. 1–12. The study notes, 'investors could have added 1.6 percent a year over just less than five years to their investment returns by allocating to portfolios that invest in companies with above-average ESG ratings.'
[14] Van Beurden and Gossling (2008).

proactive environmental action and financial value creation. For example, a 2008 study by State Street Global Advisors found that companies with poor ESG ratings delivered better financial returns than their peer group, with the largest polluters outperforming by a wide margin.[15] A different investment consultant noted frustration that for each study claiming ESG factors made a difference to financial returns, there was one that implied otherwise.[16]

Socially responsible and ESG investments comprise a more inclusive category than the subject of this chapter. Most studies have not definitively proven that the *environmental practices* of a given firm have clear effects on its securities' prices, or that blended value investment in the real estate marketplace consistently offers attractive financial returns.

Turning to studies with a narrower breadth can provide more definitive, actionable conclusions. For example, one landmark study completed in 2010 and evaluating 582 firms over an eleven-year period, found a robust link between better environmental performance and lower cost of debt. The report concludes that results 'are consistent with the view that the regulatory implications of climate change have sensitized lenders to the downside risk of poor environmental practices'.[17] A second study looking at responsible property development from 1999 to 2008 found that the properties in question had net operating incomes, market values, price appreciation, and total returns that were either higher or the same as conventional properties, with lower costs of capital.[18] A common theme in all studies however is the dearth of evidence and the need for more rigorous research to underpin investment decisions.

For investors, these inconclusive results may in fact be very good news. They suggest that while more attention is being paid to environmental considerations as they pertain to real assets, by and large these factors remain inconsistently reflected in asset prices, indicating opportunities for astute, alpha-seeking investors, those who seek to identify investments that will outperform their market segments thanks to factors inherent in the specific investment vehicles themselves, to achieve outsize returns by deploying their specific insight into environmental opportunities and risks. Accordingly, the early twenty-first century may be a particularly good time to be an impact investor in the environment and real estate space:

- Investors have access to an ever-increasing amount of information.
- Regulators are learning how to use market mechanisms to reach environmental goals.

[15] Kennedy, Whiteoak, and Ye (2008).   [16] Carter (2012).
[17] Bauer and Hann (2010).   [18] Pivo and Fischer (2010).

- An increasing number of consumers seek environmentally responsible products
- Environmental considerations are beginning to (albeit, inconsistently) manifest in pricing.

As the evidence cited above indicates, the tools and perspectives of impact investing may help an investor identify, and profit from, the financial manifestation of previously un-priced environmental value. The prospect of concurrent profit and environmental return sounds alluring, but the challenges are significant, and incautious assumptions and generalities do a disservice to potential investors. Desire to protect natural resources or investing savvy are not enough. Making smart environmental impact investments requires an expanded toolkit, including (but not limited to) facility with the language, products, and marketplace of traditional finance; insight into unique opportunities that deliver the right mix of environmental and financial risk and reward; understanding of the frequently regulated markets where these transactions take place; and access to reliable metrics to measure complex, blended value outcomes.

A framework for environmental investment

How should environmental impact investments and transactions be organized? Shedding some light on this question is the evolution of capital investment, which transpires in three different forums: first in specific *deals*, then in professionally managed *funds*, and ultimately in increasingly organized *marketplaces*.

DEALS

Many innovative investments are first initiated on a project-by-project basis, wherein investors finance a particular venture in what could be called 'niche deals'. While individually financed projects permit creativity and innovation in capital structuring, the process is time-consuming and difficult to scale. Nevertheless, such complex deals are the first critical step toward understanding the dynamics of innovative financing strategies.

Environmental Impact Application

Examples abound of niche deals in this space. Some of this can be attributed to the unique nature of blended value projects, where investors may prioritize financial gains, environmental gains, or any balance in between. Contracts may also be complicated; for example, conservation easements tend to be highly customized. The diversity of deals reflects, quite appropriately, the diversity of the natural world they seek to protect.

FUNDS

After managers and investors learn from multiple projects, they may develop pools of capital, allowing professional fund managers to invest in deals as they see fit with greater efficiency and risk mitigation. This aggregation affords diversification across multiple deals, thereby decreasing risk, maximizing value creation, and enabling rapid deployment of capital. Managers may then begin standardizing investment vehicles and management structures. Such consistency often brings lower costs and less waste, which in turn results in more investors moving more capital through a greater number of deals.

Environmental Impact Application

The number of real estate-focused funds seeking environmental impact is growing rapidly. Institutional investors are also crowding into this arena. Norwegian pension fund NBIM recently announced plans to invest $16bn, fully 5 per cent of the fund's overall value, to ESG-screened real estate. Alternative investment funds dedicated to responsible property investment are also proliferating, with 95 identified within the USA in 2011, holding $44.3bn in assets.

MARKETPLACES

Standardized investment vehicles and increased capital flows set the stage for increasingly organized marketplaces, where transactions become easier and cheaper to effect. Standardized investment vehicles engender standardized measures of performance, transaction sizes, and market intermediaries.

Environmental Impact Application

Organized marketplaces for blended value products of all types are only just emerging. Ratings systems, social stock exchanges, trading platforms, and advisory firms oriented toward impact investing are in their infancy. Until more consensus on these criteria can be reached, the path toward an impact investment marketplace, let alone common platforms focused on environmental returns, promises to be halting and non-linear at best.

As this field matures, environmental or real estate-focused investments may, in particular, continue to conform to the capital markets framework; nevertheless, it may necessitate new, innovative transactional frameworks and investment tools (e.g. Social Impact Bonds). Some experts have cautioned against over-reliance on traditional investment structures, noting that blended value investments may 'require greater patience than a closed-life private equity fund can offer'.

Ten propositions on environmental impact investing

As investors work to understand how environmental considerations will be priced into asset market valuations, they should consider several market characteristics and how markets manage new information. This section outlines ten propositions about how markets receive and absorb environmental data. These ten propositions are not mature 'empirical truth', but instead are informed hypotheses drawn from emerging evidence in a rapidly changing world.

ENVIRONMENTAL FACTORS DIRECTLY AND INDIRECTLY INFLUENCE FINANCIAL VALUE

Environmental risks can influence valuation through short-term impacts to companies' financial results, but they may also destabilize companies' strategies over a longer time horizon. Short-term risks may include, for example, boycotts, spikes in commodity prices, and inadvertent pollution releases. Strategic risks include unfavourable regulatory changes, reputational damage, tort liability, and the long-term introduction of unanticipated risk. Similarly, opportunities arise. Toyota's Prius and Ben & Jerry's ice cream are famous examples of the economic benefits that rise from a favourable consumer demand-side reaction to products that are more environmentally benign.

Many environmental considerations directly influence and can be measured in real estate investments. Impact assessments and environmental due diligence are hallmarks of any real estate transaction, and as such these environmental considerations often have direct and fairly clear (if ad hoc) influences of financial valuation. Nevertheless, the same forces that may affect a company's strategy can bear out on environmental real estate investment strategies.

Imagine an investment in a large-scale property development within or adjacent to a Superfund site, classified as an uncontrolled or abandoned place where hazardous waste is located, possibly affecting local ecosystems or people. The investment strategy will likely include consideration of location, potential liability for clean-up costs, land use restrictions, the cost of environmental insurance, and myriad other factors. Yet it is clear not all factors qualify as negatives: the purchase price, for example, may be deeply discounted, and properly managed and structured such a deal could promise attractive returns.

Another example demonstrates the influence of environmental risk on both valuation and strategy: less than two months after the fateful explosion on BP's Deepwater Horizon rig, shares of the company had plunged 40 per cent, its market capitalization shrank by approximately $20bn, and UK pension funds lost £12bn.[19] Residential home values on the Gulf coast plummeted, while insurance premiums for offshore drilling rigs and their operators increased dramatically.

Some issues will affect an entire industry, and others will alter the valuation of individual players. For example, controversy over tobacco control would have an impact on valuations for all tobacco companies, but climate change will carry different implications for individual energy companies better able to adopt clean fuel technologies than for competitors dependent on traditional fossil fuels.

PRICE ADJUSTMENT LAGS BEHIND THE EMERGENCE OF NEW INFORMATION ABOUT AN ENVIRONMENTAL ISSUE

Broadly speaking, markets efficiently aggregate the opinions of many different investors. Given the complexity of environmental systems and a still-incomplete understanding of how certain environmental factors will interact with any asset's economics, intelligent market participants can have different opinions about how environmental information will affect specific companies. Initially, the magnitude of a new risk or opportunity will make its way into the market in fits and starts. For example, as studies about the science of climate change are published, the market will not immediately process the economic implications for companies in different industries. Similarly, complex or contradictory research may emerge that brings additional uncertainty to public understanding of an issue.

As long as there are sceptics regarding impact investing, securities' market prices will lag the expected valuation ascribed by blended value investing disciples. Impact investing could be a strategy that wins (on strictly financial terms) in some markets and loses in others. In a sense, impact investors are simply 'value investors', seeking to identify investments that are being under-priced by the broader marketplace, who have insight into new dimensions of financial value creation and destruction. This assertion, that one can be an environmental impact investor in the real estate forum, can have critical impacts on management strategies.

As the economics of an industry become more closely aligned with a social or environmental concern, either through consumer or regulatory pressure, the market may begin to develop a more precise evaluation of a risk or

---

[19] Gardner (2010).

opportunity. For example, in 2010 the US Securities and Exchange Commission (SEC) formally recognized the potential materiality of water risks stemming from climate change; the move forced many companies to report previously undisclosed water risk exposure. Since that regulatory change, Coca-Cola has disclosed that quality and scarcity of water may negatively affect production costs and capacity, and energy giant Exelon Corporation has stated that the availability of water to cool its electricity generating assets could affect operations.[20] Such disclosures remain largely voluntary however, and market reaction to the new information is not always easy to predict. As a recent study by Ceres notes, 'in growing numbers, investors are clamouring for more robust information that is standardised, comparable and easily accessible to inform their investment decisions'.[21]

Of course, as information filters into the marketplace in piecemeal fashion, there is a danger (or opportunity) that the market will overreact. Here again, the BP oil spill is instructive. Shortly after the explosion, market participants overreacted and share prices fell more than was warranted; environmentally agnostic investors were able to buy low and sell high (or hold the stock).[22] For the would-be environmental impact investor, the example is a warning not to jump to judgement and a reminder that pricing environmental risk is trickier than it might at first appear (see Figure 19.1).

Understanding the extra-financial aspects of these investments (scientific, political, and regulatory) may help impact investors take advantage of price movement, up or down. Several factors help explain imperfect market reactions to new environmental risks or opportunities. Each presents a chance for investors to capture value with thoughtful research and prediction. The lag may be explained in part by how certainly the newly revealed information will have a financial impact on a particular company. Another slowing factor is the extraordinary liquidity of certain markets. Thus, investors may believe the risk of climate change will in fact lower the value of relatively dirty industries; nevertheless, knowing they can eventually sell quickly, the investors hold their securities until the market begins pricing in that environmental risk.

The valuation impact of environmental information can also vary across political geography. For example, some investors cite the Kyoto effect by

---

[20] Branca (2012). A report released by Ceres in June 2012, 'Clearing the Waters,' surveyed 82 publicly traded companies in eight water-dependent sectors: beverage, chemicals, electric power, food, house-building, mining, oil and gas, and semiconductors.

[21] Branca (2012).

[22] The rebound in BP's stock price may be traced to the following factors: 1) high demand for the asset; 2) a liability cap in place that would have made BP liable for only $75m in clean-up costs; and 3) restoration of public image when BP agreed to cover the full cost of the oil spill and make payments to businesses and people affected. Once overselling of BP stock stopped, the stock price took a turn for the better and continued to climb during the rest of the year. Anyone who invested in May of 2010 and cashed out in May 2011 would have made a profit of around 50% ('Current Events Can Be an Investor's Best Friend', *InfoBarrel*, <http://www.infobarrel.com/Current_Events–Potentially_an_Investors_Best_Friend#ixzz1yqgfBvxx)>, accessed 10 July 2012.

HYPOTHETICAL MODEL OF THE INCLUSION OF FINANCIALLY–
RELEVANT SOCIAL INFORMATION IN A VALUATION

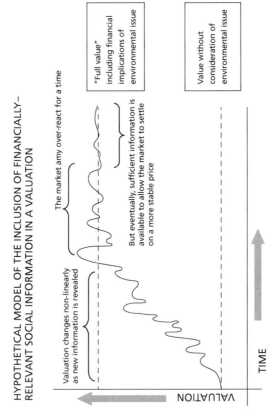

This chart shows how the market begins to price the impact of an emerging social or enviormental issue into the valuations of securities affects by the issue. This chart could, for example, represent the price of renewable energy equities over the time period (1980–2005) when emerging information about climate change science began to diffuse into the markets.

The challenge for an individual investor is to determine where the market is at a given point in this reevaluation process – whiche woule determine abuy/sell/hold strageegy.

The market amy over-react for a time

Valuation changes non-linearly as new information is revealed

But eventually, sufficient information is available to allow the market to settle on a more stable price

"Full value" including financial implications of environmental issue

Value without consideration of environmental issue

TIME

VALUATION

Figure 19.1. Temporal issues in environmental investment valuations

which energy companies face different valuations depending on whether or not their home country has ratified the Kyoto Protocol. Further integration of the global economy will depress these kinds of variations, but they are not likely to disappear.

There are several categories of regulatory innovation that could effect valuations. These can be broken down into two types: innovations that change the intrinsic value of an investment and innovations that change investor behaviour. Examples of the first include regulations that force companies to internalize externalities (such as carbon taxes) and tort law that implies corporate liability for environmental damage. Examples of the second include changes that reduce market turnover or increase investment horizons and accounting changes that force inclusion of environmental risks in financial statements.

EXTERNAL STAKEHOLDERS CAN INDIRECTLY INFLUENCE VALUATIONS AND VALUE

With the retreat of government oversight from corporations in many parts of the world, civil society organizations have moved to fill the vacuum. In essence, there has been a partial privatization of regulation, in which non-governmental organizations have taken responsibility for holding corporations accountable to public concerns. The divestment of companies operating in Sudan following genocide there and previously, South Africa during apartheid is perhaps the most prominent example of investors' non-market concerns changing corporate strategies.

Similarly, efforts in the late 1990s to pressure apparel manufacturers to improve labour conditions led to increasingly sophisticated activism as organizations examined the structures of global supply chains and connected companies' positive public images (e.g. Nike and The Gap) with an uglier private reality (sweatshops) down the supply chain. In these examples, activists have invoked non-market action (boycotts, protests, etc.) in order to initiate market actions (changes in business practices). In recent years, investors have invoked a similar kind of activism, using capital market actions (buying and selling securities, and engaging in shareholder activism) to influence companies' non-market actions (such as reducing pollution). For example, Boston-based group Ceres helped form the Investor Network on Climate Risk, which supports 100 institutional investors with assets totaling $10trn, identify financial opportunities and risks in climate change. The group also addresses policy and governance issues that impede investor progress toward more sustainable capital markets.[23]

Civil society strategies have, over time, increased in sophistication and effectiveness. For example, consider the efforts to decrease logging pressure

---

[23] Ceres homepage, <http://www.ceres.org/incr>, accessed 6 July 2012.

on old-growth forests led by ForestEthics and Rainforest Action Network. As pressure on leading paper-producer Boise Cascade faltered, these organizations began targeting Boise's customers, most prominently in successfully encouraging Kinko's to cancel its contract with the paper company.

These sophisticated efforts go beyond mere public relations; they target the core business propositions of multinational corporations, especially those selling products with low switching costs. Facing such external accountability, many companies have made cosmetic changes in practice while others (including Boise Cascade) have substantively altered their operations. There is relatively little evidence that these kinds of consumer campaigns have a direct bottom-line impact on poor performers, but concerns about reputational damage make these civil society actors very effective.

Civil society organizations are generally not attempting to alter the valuation of their targets—which could, in fact, be considered racketeering by financial regulators—but instead they aim simply to change practices. However, the existence of these now-powerful external actors is a likely implicit factor in market valuations.

ENVIRONMENTAL INFORMATION RELEVANT TO PRICE IS OFTEN COMPLEX AND/OR UNAVAILABLE—BUT, IT IS BECOMING INCREASINGLY ACCESSIBLE TO INVESTORS

Financial markets thrive on information. Valuations can be based on complex economic models or whispered rumours, but in each case they are based on information. Emerging issues are often complex, and both industry-wide and company-specific implications can be unclear. Investors seeking relevant information may be forced to make their way through obscure or even contradictory scientific and economic research to understand an issue. It can also be very difficult to gauge the timing and degree of regulatory and civil society response to an emerging issue.

Increasingly, multinational corporations are publishing sustainability reports that provide data allowing benchmarking of specific aspects of environmental performance. Historically thin, unreliable, and inconsistent, they have since improved significantly, allowing investors to differentiate among companies in a given industry. Publicly available data are also burgeoning, with the number of sustainability indices increasing from twenty-one in 2000 to 108 as of October 2010.[24] Such indices include FTSE4Good in Europe, Bovespa in Brazil, and the Dow Jones Sustainability Index in the US.

Importantly, financial services institutions increasingly provide analysis to aid investors in understanding the valuation impacts of environmental issues.

[24] Williams (2010).

Analytic shops such as KLD Research & Analytics and Ethical Investment Research Service (EIRIS) provide comprehensive reports and issue-specific information. Perhaps more importantly, mainstream investment banks have begun issuing reports and recommendations on environmental issues.

Impact investors who see themselves as value investors are likely to believe this proposition holds true. As environmental information becomes more available to investors, the markets will begin to 'catch up' to the previously un-priced extra-financial value. That perspective also suggests the next hypothesis.

IMPACT INVESTING OPPORTUNITIES ARE CHANGING AS THE CORE ECONOMICS OF BUSINESS BECOME MORE ALIGNED WITH ENVIRONMENTAL VALUES

The fundamental economics of capitalism are not always well aligned with environmental value creation. The tragedy of the commons demonstrates how members of a community may draw from a resource in ways that are individually beneficial but collectively unsustainable. The structures of modern corporations geographically, politically, and legally separate investors from the consequences of their investment. The globalization of capital can exacerbate this problem.

Many of the efforts cited in this chapter are part of broader efforts to *internalize* externalities into the economics of individual businesses and investors. Increased transparency and public pressure may close the gap between market price and the 'intrinsic' values that include the costs and opportunities of environmental problems. Similarly, market-based regulations such as the Kyoto Protocol directly align the economics of businesses with the environmental goals (or, at times, lack thereof) of policymakers.

Government regulation of real estate assets with an aim toward environmental benefit is no exception. Consider the evolution of the 'green' building certifications and initiatives. Regulation encourages responsible property development through expedited permitting and density bonuses, as well financial incentives such as tax credits and abatements, in particular through the US Green Building Council's LEED certification program. The value of stocks related to green building construction grew by 10.1 per cent in 2009, far outpacing both the S&P 500 and the NASDAQ.[25] Falling technology prices and a surge in consumer demand for energy efficiency is buoying this growth. One leading industry publication notes that while government regulation may be forcing the issue for now, market forces will become an equal—if not leading—driver for environmentally responsible development.[26]

---

[25] McQuilkin (2010).
[26] PricewaterhouseCoopers and Urban Land Institute (2011).

EMERGING MARKETS MAY OFFER THE MOST APPEALING OPPORTUNITIES FOR ENVIRONMENTAL IMPACT INVESTORS—BUT THEY PRESENT SIGNIFICANT ADDITIONAL CHALLENGES

In recent years, major emerging market economies have grown more rapidly than developed world economies. This has held true even during the global recession: China had a 9.5 per cent annual growth rate in 2011, and India grew at 6.5 per cent over the same year. In comparison US growth has hovered around 2 per cent and a full-blown banking and debt crisis in Europe has pushed growth down to the 1 per cent mark. Thus, many of the most appealing financial opportunities in coming years may well be found in the Global South.

These markets tend to have less-developed financial and environmental regulatory structures. Some have strong environmental laws that are simply left unenforced (Russia and India, for example). Others see a large part of their gross domestic products generated through informal, often illegal, channels (pirated CDs, illegal drugs, and government corruption, for example). Their consumer markets are as yet less responsive to environmental concerns. Nevertheless, the central financial institutions of these countries are increasingly providing investors with access to environmental information (e.g. the Bovespa market in Brazil) and pressuring managers to reform environmental practices (e.g. substantive activities by the Confederation of Indian Industry and other industrial groups in India).

The Global South also faces a number of looming environmental challenges—many of which have political and economic implications. Continuing, large-scale unrest in the Chinese countryside can in large part be traced to the economic impacts of environmental degradation.

In short, many of the same dynamics that make markets in the Global North ripe for blended value investors are at play in the Global South. Investors face significant challenges, given relatively underdeveloped financial infrastructure, high transaction cost, and weaker available information. It can be more difficult to untangle valuations in the Global South than in the developed world, but exactly that sort of uncertainty provides opportunities for impact investors.

ENVIRONMENTAL IMPACT INVESTING RELIES ON LONGER TIME HORIZONS THAN 'TRADITIONAL' INVESTING; THAT DIFFERENCE IN TIME HORIZON WILL BE AN ONGOING TENSION—AND SOURCE OF VALUE

A key issue cutting across these difficulties is the investor's time horizon. A short-term investor or manager can often consider environmental value as an externality. For example, two investors may both believe that all of an American oil company's operations will eventually abide by restrictions on greenhouse gas emissions, though the USA will be slow to implement such constraints domestically. The investor with the shorter time horizon may not consider the financial consequences of the company's emissions, as they will have sold the stock long before its valuation reflects the cost of managing carbon emissions. The longer-term investor will include the costs and opportunities of carbon constraints and will integrate them into their valuation of the company.

As one investment analyst put it, 'The disconnect many see between the short-term time horizons of traditional financial analysis and the long-term nature of the business impacts of ESG investing is one of the challenges to overcome on the road toward a more sustainable economy'.[27]

New impact investing terms and funding mechanisms are beginning to address the time horizon differential. For example, Acumen Fund has coined the term 'patient capital' to refer to debt or equity investment in early-stage social or environmental enterprises with anticipated payback or exit in roughly seven to ten years.[28] While Acumen's timeframe may seem long to traditional investors, environmental impact investments, particularly those oriented toward real estate, may require many multiples of that to realize returns. Some experts advocate for pushing the investment outlook for ESG factors to twenty years, noting that while today's investors are preoccupied with energy scarcity, increasing scarcity of water and arable land will prove to be the big market changers.[29]

As suggested elsewhere in this chapter, the various time horizons of market participants complicate the manifestation of environmental value in a company's stock price. Any changes in the market or non-market environments that push investors to have longer time horizons and/or companies to internalize externalities will remove some of that complexity.

STANDARDIZATION OF INFORMATION ARCHITECTURE CAN AND WILL HELP ACCELERATE THE GROWTH OF THE ENVIRONMENTAL INVESTING MARKET

Markets are fueled by high-quality information to inform participants' decisions. Impact investors can speed the development of more efficient markets by sharing information on the investments they have already made. In fact this, task remains critical in the evolution of most types of impact investment. Of the microfinance and community economic development investments, this

---

[27] O'Sullivan (2012).   [28] See <http://www.acumen.org>.
[29] Carter (2012).

chapter's authors wrote in a previous study: 'Open communication about investment methodologies, pricing, failures, and equity holders' profits will be essential to pricing these blended value investments correctly. Keeping the data private introduces the chance that other funds will erroneously price risk. When substantial capital enters (or fails to enter) a market based on mispriced risk, that market is prone to dramatic failure.'[30] Markets cannot accurately price the risk associated with their securities unless they openly explore failures as well as successes. The emerging blended value capital markets simply cannot afford for participants to be secretive about their data, ashamed of their failures, or fragmented in their terminology.

The categorizations established to provide structure to a market can have immense implications on the future of that market. For example, land-use expert Christopher Leinberger observed of the American commercial real estate market, 'there are 19 standard real estate product types that can readily obtain financing ... [and] these are the only products most banks and publicly traded real estate investment trusts (REITs) can build, finance, trade, and own.' He claims the categories homogenized real estate development, promoted suburban sprawl, and inhibited progressive mixed-use development: 'We built the wrong product in the wrong location, and nobody wants it any more. That's the reason for the housing crisis, and therefore the mortgage crisis, and therefore the Great Recession.'[31] More optimistically, Leinberger says the slowdown may incentivize developers to create more environmentally responsible real estate products. As such products proliferate and prove financially sound, they may invite a new era of industry categorization and typology—helping financiers expedite analysis and comparison, more accurately understand and predict financial performance, and open the door to more capital.

Additionally, real estate markets include a variety of information clearing houses, most notably the Multiple Listing Service (or MLS). Information forums like the MLS are not financial exchanges, but rather provide information about property for sale and historical sale prices. The blended value real estate industry could move towards such clearing-houses, which would require market participants to share information about transactions.

Forums like the Katoomba Group's Ecosystem Marketplace, which publishes thought-leading studies and other relevant ecosystem services market information, suggest the future of information sharing. The recent development of general impact investment reporting and ratings systems is also highly relevant, pointing toward continued evolution toward an organized marketplace for such investments. The Global Impact Investing Network (GIIN) in collaboration with the Rockefeller Foundation, Acumen Fund, and B Lab has created IRIS, or Impact Reporting and Investment Standards, to provide a

---

[30] Spitzer and Emerson (2006).   [31] Badger (2011).

framework and underlying set of definitions for impact-related terms, thereby facilitating comparisons of impact data across investments.[32] Investors can access IRIS metrics through different aggregators; for example Pulse is a portfolio data management system solely concerned with reporting social and environmental performance. Pulse runs for free on the popular Salesforce.com platform, increasing its prospects for usability and widespread adoption. Concurrent development by B Lab of the Global Impact Investment Ratings System, styled after Morningstar or Capital IQ financial analytics, and integrating IRIS analysis, further suggests an emerging maturation of the field.[33]

ENVIRONMENTAL IMPACT INVESTING REQUIRES THE INTEGRATED CONSIDERATION OF MULTIPLE FACTORS

In several ways, building blended value real estate funds is analogous to developing a high-technology product that can have many features. Often it is not the most feature-laden, capable device or product that succeeds in the marketplace. Instead, the most successful products offer exactly the right features for the customers who purchase them (even when the customers have not articulated exactly which features they want and need). Blended value investments themselves are like feature-rich products: they offer complicated ranges of risk–reward profiles, different types of social and environmental value creation and various geographic emphases. Furthermore, most of those dimensions are interrelated in complex ways. Building viable blended value investment vehicles requires financial structuring expertise and experience in managing the social value creation mechanisms, but the task also requires a keen eye for product–market fit and product marketing.

THERE IS A FUNDAMENTALLY PERSONAL, EMOTIONAL, AND HUMAN ASPECT TO ENVIRONMENTAL IMPACT INVESTING

Many limited partners in blended value funds are themselves principal investors (venture capitalists, private equity fund general partners, or hedge fund managers) who have an interest in conserving land, enjoy outdoor recreation, or who own ranches. Ultimately, impact investment funds may generate more interest in their funds by offering limited partners a unique set of privileges, including recreational access to the fund's properties, the opportunity to co-invest in the fund's deals, and a right of first refusal to make market-rate purchases of properties upon resale.

---

[32] IRIS website, <http://iris.thegiin.org/about-iris>.
[33] GIIRS website, <http://www.giirs.org>.

Three case studies in environmental impact investing: A focus on real estate

CASE STUDY TIMBERLAND INVESTMENT MANAGEMENT:
LYME TIMBER COMPANY

The Lyme Timber Company, LP is a private timberland investment management organization (TIMO) that focuses on the acquisition and sustainable management of lands with unique conservation values. Since its founding in 1976, the company has followed a disciplined and value oriented approach to investing in forestland and rural real estate.

The Lyme team has extensive experience managing and operating land throughout the Northeast, Appalachian region, and Lake States of the USA. The company's current portfolio includes 475,000 acres of forestland located in New York, Wisconsin, Pennsylvania, Maine, Massachusetts, Tennessee, Virginia, Delaware, and Louisiana. Company lands are primarily certified under the Forest Stewardship Council (FSC) certification programme. Over 30 million board feet of FSC certified logs are harvested from Lyme lands annually.

The Lyme Timber Company began investing in timberland and rural real estate in 1976. During its first 25 years, Lyme made a series of $1m to $10m investments in forestland properties throughout the eastern USA. In 2002, Lyme organized the Lyme Northern Forest Fund with $64.5m in capital commitments from eighty-eight limited partners. At the close of its investment phase in 2005, this fund had invested in five properties totaling 260,000 acres of timberland. The following year, Lyme organized The Lyme Forest Fund with $190.6m of committed capital from 171 limited partners. At the close of its investment period in March 2009, this second fund had invested in seven properties totalling 433,000 acres. In 2010, Lyme organized The Lyme Forest Fund III that closed on February 15, 2011 with $160.4m in capital commitments from 180 limited partners. Deal sizes range from $4m to $80m, with a nominal return from 11 to 25 per cent.

An investment from Lyme's third fund illustrates exactly how it achieves environmental goals, alongside a very competitive return for investors. In late 2004, Lyme purchased 85,000 acres of woodland in northern New York for $18.5m, with almost half of the financing secured through a New Markets Tax Credit at a low interest rate. The Nature Conservancy paid $600,000 for the option to purchase a conservation easement on the property. Four years later, Lyme sold a $10m conservation easement to the State of New York, ensuring public access to 38,400 acres, maintenance of private hunting club leases, and restriction of all further development. In 2009 the company sold the remaining property, subject to a conservation easement, for $20m. Taking into account all operating income and losses, the sale of the easements and the sale of the property, the investment generated an IRR of approximately 22 per cent.

Lyme's success can be derived in part from a management team well versed in negotiation and sale of working forest conservation easements that restrict development on lands, but allow income generation from sustainable timber harvesting and recreational leasing. The Lyme team also has expertise structuring advantageous debt arrangements (e.g. New Markets Tax Credit financings), restructuring forestry and timber operations, and developing new opportunities such as wetland mitigation banks.

CASE STUDY CONSERVATION REAL ESTATE: BEARTOOTH CAPITAL

As a conservation-focused investor in ranch lands, Beartooth Capital is distinctive in the field of responsible property fund managers. The firm was founded in 2005 with the aim of restoring and conserving important natural lands in western America while pursuing competitive financial returns for investors.

Based in Bozeman, Montana, Beartooth acquires ranches that are undervalued, often due to environmental degradation. The firm then works to turn those properties around by partnering with conservation groups and government agencies to restore their ecological health and resolve any existing issues, such as zoning or property access. Because ecosystem restoration and protection frequently increase natural beauty, wildlife diversity, and agricultural productivity, Beartooth can add substantial environmental value to its properties through conservation. In addition, the relationships Beartooth has built with conservation groups now provide a source of deal flow and funding for the firm.

Beartooth Capital's first fund focused on relatively smaller ranches, where the partners could deploy a similar suite of improvements across all properties. The principals found their value proposition appealed most strongly to investors whose personal values (and in many cases whose philanthropic efforts) aligned with Beartooth's conservation mission. Co-founder Carl Palmer reported that while investors cared deeply about the preservation of open spaces and valued the fund's conservation goals, most investors were interested first in the economic fundamentals of the strategy. To get commitments of capital, Beartooth had to demonstrate that it was investing in an inefficient market where the partners could generate outsize returns through their domain expertise and unique strategies.

In cases where all or part of a property has been identified as high-priority for conservation, Beartooth not only restores the property, but also works with its partners to place a conservation easement on that area, protecting the land from irresponsible development in perpetuity. The firm makes little to no use of debt, eliminating potential loss from leverage. Sale of easements and funding for restoration provide early revenue and offset expenses; investors receive all proceeds until they achieve an 8 per cent preferred return, aligning management and investor interests. Beartooth distributes revenues to investors as they occur during the ten-year term of its fund, rather than re-investing proceeds in additional deals.[34]

As of this writing, 11,141 acres, 50 per cent of Beartooth Capital's total acres under management, are now permanently protected. On two of its ranches, Beartooth has achieved the dual goals of conservation and community benefits by selling property to conservation groups or local governments. In 2010, Beartooth sold 1,640 acres in the South Park basin in Colorado to the county to create the Cline Ranch State Wildlife Area. The new park is managed by Colorado Parks and Wildlife and is open to the public. The environmental returns of Beartooth Capital's work manifest themselves on its restored ranch lands in a variety of ways. After purchasing the Big Springs Creek ranch in central Idaho in 2008, Beartooth worked with The Nature Conservancy, Idaho Fish and Game, and other conservation partners to remove several irrigation diversions and barriers that had disrupted the creek's natural flow. In the first year after restoration, the number of spawning sites for wild Chinook salmon jumped from two to sixty-nine, with similar results the second year. Importantly, a conservation easement ensures the Creek will remain a vibrant riparian ecosystem for threatened wild salmon and steelhead populations.

Palmer had some words of wisdom for investors who aim to recreate Beartooth's blended value returns. 'The key to success for the field and for individual firms at this stage is focusing on getting it right at a small scale to start—accomplishing bona fide conservation while exceeding investors' return targets—and doing so in a highly transparent way...This industry has the potential to advance conservation efforts at a scale that is otherwise not possible. Those of us working in the field feel a weight of responsibility to live up to that potential, along with the very real responsibility we have to our investors.'

CASE STUDY WETLANDS MITIGATION ECOSYSTEM: ECOSYSTEM INVESTMENT PARTNERS

Based in Baltimore, Maryland, Ecosystem Investment Partners (EIP) pursues competitive financial returns through a business model based on monetizing environmental assets, also known as payments for ecosystem services (PES). When property developers (either private or public) incur

---

[34] Financing Fishers Conservation (2011).

unavoidable negative impacts on wetlands, they are required by the government to offset the impact by restoring equivalent acreage elsewhere. Developers can either do this themselves (termed 'self-mitigation') or they may contract with a third party such as EIP.[35] The third party identifies and purchases suitable properties, which are then certified by the federal government as 'mitigation banks.' Once lands are restored, the government gives the firm credits, which can be sold at a profit to developers who must purchase them to comply with the law. The most established and active PES markets are wetland, stream, and endangered species mitigation banking. The market is significant and growing; every year over $3.8bn is spent to mitigate the impact to these federally protected natural resources, and there are now over 1,000 mitigation and conservation banks covering over 1 million acres in the US.[36]

Founded in 2006, EIP is now recognized as a leader in advancing a private capital investment model to address land conservation. The firm's mission is twofold: to deliver risk-adjusted market returns to investors, and to provide a positive and enduring impact on land conservation efforts in the USA. EIP targets rural real estate that meets three criteria. First, it must be an ecologically significant property with degraded or threatened aquatic or habitat features that can be restored; second, it must be an area with active property development that generates demand for mitigation credits; and third, it must be subject to strict enforcement of environmental laws that require mitigation. Once restoration is complete, which can take several years, EIP receives and subsequently sells credits. The firm may also employ other cash-flow strategies such as sustainable timber management, sustainable agriculture, or leases for recreational land use. Ultimately, it may sell the land, protected by easements, to conservation buyers.

One sample investment from EIP's first fund showcases these various cash-flow strategies. In June 2007, EIP acquired 1,030 acres within the boundary of the Great Dismal Swamp National Wildlife Refuge in southeastern Virginia. Much of the acreage had been ditched and drained, then converted to agriculture, and US Fish and Wildlife Services (FWS) had tried for more than a decade to acquire the property but lacked the financial resources to do so. Working with the FWS, The Nature Conservancy, the Commonwealth of Virginia, and the US Army Corps of Engineers, EIP used mitigation banking on 963 acres of the land to pay for conservation and restoration as well as generate an attractive return for EIP's investors. EIP also conveyed a permanent conservation easement over the mitigation area to The Nature Conservancy. Another primary component of the deal's value is endangered species mitigation, through the establishment of a protected habitat for the endangered canebrake rattlesnake. Secondary cash-flow strategies include the temporary leasing of farm fields to a reputable farming operator, and leasing of property to an adjoining landowner for recreational use.

EIP's land acquisitions average between $5m and $20m per transaction, and target properties range from 1,000 to 10,000 acres. In June of 2012 the firm announced the final close of its (oversubscribed) second fund, EIP II, with $180.7m in equity capital commitments from a traditional mixture of private equity LPs, including public pensions, endowments, and High-Net-Worth Individuals. EIP II aims to purchase 10–15 properties to be used primarily as mitigation banks, with an expected return in the mid-teens.[37]

Of course, mitigation banks—and other PES markets—are not without risks. Nick Dilks, EIP Managing Director, noted 'you've got to really know these sites. That's part of the value we add . . . you've got to be very careful in selecting just the right properties.' Co-founder Fred Danforth pointed out that mitigation markets are driven by regulation and, as such, may scare off traditional investors. But he also expressed optimism that as these markets mature, they will show sufficient deal flow and a track record of producing repeatable returns.[38]

---

[35] Under a new 2008 federal law, purchasing credits from an approved bank is now the preferred method for providing compensatory mitigation.

[36] EIP website, www.ecosystempartners.com.

[37] Witkowsky (2012).

[38] Witkowsky (2012) and from EIP website <http://www.ecosystempartners.com>.

Conclusion

The investment examples presented in this study focus on how to capture a portion of the financial value created by environmental improvement. This paper's examples demonstrate that astute investors can generate real financial returns through conservation, remediation, and related strategies that create environmental value. However, simply because an investment *can* generate blended value, does not make it the most *efficient* at achieving environmental return, raising the larger question of whether linking conservation to profit is the best way to create environmental value.

Overly simplified, this impact-measurement situation can be posed in three complementary theses:

- *Thesis A:* One can generate competitive financial returns by practising conservation and responsible property development
- *Thesis B:* One can have a significant positive environmental impact through financial investing
- *Thesis C:* Conservation impacts can be most significant when achieved through non-market strategies.

The first two theses better articulate the sentiments behind the increasingly tired phrase 'doing well while doing good'. Thesis A indicates people may pursue financial goals in ways that also enhance the natural world. Thesis B, a more complicated proposition, asserts financial investments may be especially expedient ways of enhancing the environment. Thesis C speaks to strategies this inquiry has not explored in depth. Nevertheless, many such strategies, including top-down regulations, organized protests and boycotts, and civil disobedience, have been vitally important to the creation and preservation of environmental value.

Investors aiming to align a financial investment strategy with a programmatic one may be content to invest under Thesis A. Investors deciding between making a grant or engaging in a blended value conservation investment may seek to understand the extent to which Thesis B applies to their situation. While this paper explores the second thesis in part, it remains a question with which the field still struggles. Both of the first two theses appear to reject Thesis C, but the authors would assert that the three are compatible if examined with more subtlety. The degree to which each is true depends significantly on the specific context: In certain cases, Thesis B is likely to be strongly true, while in other cases it will be patently false. The authors believe that deeper, more nuanced exploration of these theses will be critical to wise investment.

Assessments of Thesis B are few, and rarer still are tests of Thesis B comparing a blended value investment strategy to a more traditional grant-making or government-mandated solution. Such a test might ask if one generates more environmental impact by seeking the donation of land to conservation organizations or by advancing a conservation-development investment model, such as that pursued by Beartooth Capital. The lack of such studies reaches to the heart of the impact measurement issue. One must first agree on the appropriate measure of value by which to compare the grant-making and blended value investment opportunities. Assuming one could determine an impact metric, one must implement it. Then, one needs to develop an experimental design that would compare the impact generated by the two different strategies.

Even without a scientifically valid test of Thesis B, one can assert that in the following circumstances Thesis B is likely to be true:

When top-down control is difficult: In the case of the American Clean Air markets (which regulate acid-rain and smog-forming pollutants through cap-and-trade market mechanisms), Thesis B would seem to be true. In theory, aggressive command and control regulations could have lowered SO_2 and NO_X pollutants below those achieved with the EPA's pollution credit-trading programme. Nevertheless, attempts to do so would have met with stiff political opposition, legal challenges, and a number of other obstacles to implementation. Thus, the pollution markets probably had a higher than expected environmental value than did the command and control policy. This condition holds because the non-impact solution (in this case regulation) would be expensive and difficult to enforce, while the blended value strategy decentralizes decision-making and motivates companies to comply.

Where impact investing brings new capital to bear on environmental problems: A simplified example may help to illustrate this point. A grant may create 100 units of environmental value, while an investment strategy might, with the same amount of capital, create only 50 units of environmental value. However, if the blended value strategy attracts three times the amount of capital, it would generate more overall environmental value than the standard method. An impact investment strategy whose returns have a weak correlation with other real estate investment vehicles may draw capital that would otherwise have been invested in environmentally agnostic or even destructive enterprises.

Where capital can be recycled efficiently: When capital can create environmental value, be returned to the investor, and then be redeployed to create more of the same value, such a strategy can be more environmentally valuable than an alternative 'one-time charity' strategy that does not recycle capital. This condition only holds when the environmental value is created by the input of financial capital and is not erased by its withdrawal. One impact investment that does not leverage the recycling of capital would be a below-market-rate loan used to make a conservation purchase and which must be repaid by grant funds.

When regulatory change creates fungibility or other appropriate conditions: In some circumstances, changes in the non-market environment—the advent of tradable property rights or the forum for market-based exchanges—can encourage impact investment strategies that may outperform traditional strategies. When regulators initiated the fungibility of certain wetlands, thereby permitting compensatory mitigation, they changed the overall environmental game such that mitigation banking may become more effective than alternative approaches to protecting wetlands.

Where new models can permanently alter incentive systems or cultural assumptions: The greatest potential for Thesis B is not necessarily in those investments explicitly called 'blended value'. Instead, enough examples may shift cultural assumptions to the point that it is no longer acceptable to think about a deal without considering environmental value—and the incentive systems that guide behaviour change to reward multiple kinds of value. Such 'mainstreaming' change is the hardest to measure and the riskiest to bet on, but it might ultimately create the most value.

With these examples in mind, researchers and investors would still be wise to consider impact investing as an innovation that remains imperfectly understood and, at this time, inefficiently deployed.

Both in the USA and around the world, environmental impact investing is in a relatively early stage of market adoption. The pioneers in this field, who have accumulated knowledge about structuring and managing investments, are only just developing a sense of where and how their models will eventually be deployed and which may become dominant. But as a booming population exerts its inexorable pressure on the natural world and companies are increasingly forced to internalize environmental externalities, it would not be surprising to see creative investment strategies begin to outperform current mainstream approaches. Not long ago the concept of wetland mitigation banking was all but unfathomable; today, over $3.8bn is spent annually to mitigate the impact to federally protected natural resources in the USA, with over 1 million acres protected. No matter what the exact evolution looks like, a long-term perspective and an appreciation for partnerships public and private will be essential to success.

Of course, some conservationists may look at blended value strategies and conclude they underperform traditional approaches to creating environmental value. Some investors may conclude that returns are unreliable, or risk is too high. Meanwhile, entrepreneurs like those at Lyme, Beartooth, Ecosystem Investment Partners, and others will continue to grow, test assumptions, and ultimately expand the utility and efficacy of the impact investing field. Each year brings new innovations around what kinds of environmental value may be created through these methods. In certain areas—and with increasing momentum—these impact entrepreneurs will demonstrate in which scenarios Thesis B holds true. Ultimately, there may be no limits to the ways that creative financial engineering and innovative environmental strategies can enhance ecological value and deploy capital more effectively.

Integrating environmental opportunities and risks into asset valuation generates a host of challenges. Many have been suggested in the previous pages: disentangling the various components of price, measuring environmental value, predicting changes in the external context, and more. Even given its simple premise, the operational complexity of this topic is difficult to overemphasize.

Some say that every environmental discussion is a discussion about balancing the concerns of the grandparent and the grandchild. Perhaps, the future of environmental impact investment offers an opportunity to align financial inheritance with ecological inheritance.

▨ REFERENCES

Baden, B. (2010). 'Investors Say Environment Is Key for Economic Turnaround', *US News and World Report*, 3 March.

Badger, E. (2011). 'The 19 Building Types that Caused the Recession', *The Atlantic Monthly*, 25 October. <http://www.theatlanticcities.com/jobs-and-economy/2011/10/buildings-that-caused-recession/345/>, accessed 9 July 2012.

Bauer, R., and Hann, D. (2010). 'Corporate Environmental Management and Credit Risk,' 23 December. <http://ssrn.com/abstract=1660470> or <http://dx.doi.org/10.2139/ssrn.1660470>, accessed 10 July 2012.

Borenstein, S. (2011). 'US Natural Disasters: 2011 An Extreme and Exhausting Year', The Associated Press, 3 September.

Branca, A. (2012). 'Water Disclosure Rising, But So Is the Risk—Ceres', *Environmental Finance*, June.

Carter, D. (2012). 'Towers Watson Shifting ESG Focus even more Long Term', *Pensions & Investments Online*, 23 January. <http://www.pionline.com/article/20120123/PRINTSUB/301199999>, accessed 8 July 2012.

Friedman, M. (1970). 'The Social Responsibility of Business Is to Increase Its Profits', *The New York Times Magazine*, 13 September.

Gardner, D. (2010). 'BP Market Plunge Wipes Billions off UK Pension Funds as Shares in Oil Giant Suffer Fresh Falls', *MailOnline*, 2 June. <http://www.dailymail.co.uk/news/worldnews/article-1282870/BP-shares-plunge-15-oil-giant-admits-oil-spill-August.html>, accessed 9 July 2012.

Keane, R. (2010). 'Socially Responsible Funds Outperformed Investing Benchmarks in 2009', *AdvisorOne*, 27 January. <http://www.advisorone.com/2010/01/27/socially-responsible-funds-outperformed-investing>, accessed 10 July 2012.

Kennedy, T., Whiteoak, J., and Ye, T. (2008). 'A Comprehensive Analysis of the Relationship between ESG and Investment Returns', *State Street Global Advisors*, 17 November: 1–3.

McQuilkin, A. (2010). 'Consumer Demand Drives Green Construction Growth', *Green Real Estate Investing News*, 13 September. <http://greenrealestateinvestingnews.com/green-real-estate-investing/consumer-demand-drives-green-construction-growth.html>, accessed 8 July 2012.

Ostrom, E. (1990). *Governing the Commons*. Cambridge: Cambridge University Press.

O'Sullivan, G. (2012). 'ESG Investing on the Rise', *State Street*, 18 January. <http://www.statestreet.com>, accessed 1 July 2012.

Pivo, G., and Fischer, J. D. (2010). 'Income, Value and Returns in Socially Responsible Office Properties', *The Journal of Real Estate Research*, 32(3) July/September: 243.

PriceWaterhouseCoopers and Urban Land Institute (2011). 'Emerging Trends in Real Estate', p. 43.

Social Investment Forum Foundation (SIFF) (2010). '2010 Report on Socially Responsible Investing Trends in the United States', December, p. 8.

Spitzer, J., and Emerson, J. (2006). 'Blended Value Investing: Capital Opportunities for Social and Environmental Impact', World Economic Forum, March.

Van Beurden, P., and Gossling, T. (2008). 'The Worth of Values: A Literature Review on the Relation Between Corporate Social and Financial Performance', *Journal of Business Ethics*, 82(2): 1.

Wells Fargo (2012). *Wells Fargo Environmental Finance Report*, April: 3.

Williams, R. (2010). 'Are Sustainability Ratings Sustainable?' *Future Energy*, 25 October. <http://www.futureenergyinvesting.com>, accessed 5 July 2012.

Witkowsky, C. (2012). 'Ecosystem Investment Partners Raises Conservation Fund', *Private Equity International*, 25 June.

Postscript

Is there a co-operative alternative to capitalism?

Dan Gregory

Is it really 'easier to imagine the end of the world than the end of capitalism[1]'? Perhaps, with the kind of perverse logic in which the 'popularizer' of this remark, Slavoj Žižek, himself indulges, the truth of this statement was diluted just as it was uttered: for in admitting even the faintest possibility of an alternative, this rendered it at least imaginable.[2]

Subsequently, and rather suddenly it seems, this possibility of an alternative to capitalism has become easier to imagine. Putting aside, at least temporarily, the views of those who have long advocated other models for organizing our productive forces, a range of evidence suggests that after many decades of 'actual existing capitalism', this model is presently failing to deliver, even on its own terms.

First, as it is failing to deliver for many of the nation states in which capitalism has been longest established on its core promises of growth, employment, returns to capital, material security, and stability. For many, growth has turned from an expectation into a memory; unemployment is at record levels in many European economies; capital lacks sufficiently convincing investment propositions that even the negative returns offered by German Federal bonds are oversubscribed; and financial collapse was only recently averted.

Second, the negative externalities that the market mechanism generates are now frighteningly large—and seemingly growing. Inequality continues to rise in the UK and further afield, the riots of 2011 bear witness to bubbling social tensions, environmental uncertainty, child poverty, and mental health problems are not going away, and if anything, are increasingly worrying. Over 40 per cent[3] of the economy now falls under the command and control of the public sector, funded mainly through taxation, in a seemingly hopeless attempt to mitigate the social and environmental fallout of market failure.

So while public interventions can crowd out private enterprise and may be obstructing the market's ability to deliver jobs and growth, there are few, if any

---

[1] Z. Slavoj (2010) *Living in the End Times.*

[2] An edited version of this chapter was previously published in *People over Capital: The Co-operative Alternative to Capitalism* (2013) edited by Rob Harrison.

[3] HM Treasury (2012) 'Budget'.

credible voices suggesting that if the state just got out the way, the market alone would somehow begin to correct its own environmental and socially destructive tendencies. We are damned if we do and damned if we don't. We can't leave it to the market alone to deliver social and economic well-being but neither have we found an effective way to step in and pick up the pieces through public interventions. At best, then, our capitalist system is operating at 60 per cent efficiency.

In this light, it is revealing that the net value of both the public and private sectors is actually negative![4] Businesses and the government both owe more than they own. Even with the vast and unprecedented financial underpinning by the state of recent years, the private sector alone is now officially worth less than nothing. We seem to have descended into a destructive duel between the public and private, fighting to stand on each other's shoulders and all the time, sinking together lower into the mud. We have stumbled into a kind of accidental state capitalism, which combines, on one hand, a monstrous version of Keynes interventionist state, clumsily interfering for longer and to a greater degree than he would have ever envisaged. On the other, a pathetic mutation of Hayek's invisible hand, which despite its pervasive reach into the public and social spheres, is now failing to deliver the goods. At this rate, Keynes' quip that 'in the long-term we're all dead' looks optimistic.

Finally, returning to those who object to the capitalist system of production per se, the moral objections against it appear to be gaining ever wider support, as public disgust with bankers and bonuses becomes the norm, and as the commodification of social relationships and a reliance on a consumerist model is brought into question.

An investigation that seeks out an alternative to capitalism must inevitably begin in the private sector. What exactly seems to be the problem?

First, private enterprise does not appear to be delivering the returns which capitalism expects, for example, with returns for venture capital funds since the dotcom bubble close to zero.[5] Private sector growth is low or negative in many Western economies despite historically absurdly low interest rates. Many are starting to believe that the growth we assumed was normal over the past few decades was built on an unsustainable bubble of housing, debt, and the trickery of financialization.

Second, the free market is not very free. The competitive drive of the private sector which should move the invisible hand and prompt the effective allocation of scarce resources does not appear to be functioning in a very competitive way. Putting aside the demonstrable difference between individuals' rational behaviour in economic text books and in practice, the increasing workload of the Competition Commission[6] and the dominance by a handful of businesses of our food retail, banking, and energy sectors demonstrates the

---

[4] Office for National Statistics (2012).   [5] NESTA (2011) 'Atlantic Drift'.
[6] Competition Commission (2012) 'Annual Report and Accounts'.

increasing concentration of ownership in the private sector, the presence of oligopolies, barriers to entry, and the stifling of new enterprise and diversity.

Third, private businesses' increasingly narrow and short-term focus on a single, financial bottom line logically results in a corresponding rise in externalities. The increasing demands on central and local government, whether bailing out banks or providing welfare, are a testament to the extent to which these externalities are frequently negative.

Fourth, finally and perhaps most frightening, is that despite the signals, we don't really know if the private sector is failing or not, as our economic dashboard has become disconnected from our vehicle. We have coasted blindly into a bewildering landscape of economic postmodernism where value is always on the surface, is always negotiated, often through secondary and tertiary markets where the multiplication of intermediaries have ruptured the connections between signifier and signified. It is often near impossible for a layman to decode quarterly financial statements; interest rates do not reflect actual lending rates; much of our national infrastructure is not included in the national accounts; trillions of pounds' worth of contingent liabilities are hidden; and copy produced by PR executives for press notices often bear little relation to the underlying economic conditions.

This schism between reality and rhetoric endangers our well-being as we have, neither collectively nor individually, any real certainty about what is really happening in the productive economy. It is as if Wile E. Coyote is wearing virtual reality headgear, oblivious to whether he is on safe ground, hovering over the abyss or already plunging downwards. As far as we know, we may be close to the point of doing irrevocable damage to the economy and the planet while the numbers on the screen flash a reassuring green or, indeed, a more ominous red. Who knows what's really behind them?

So is it possible that a co-operative model could offer us remedies to each of these maladies? Is it possible that 'where the invisible hand fails, the handshake may succeed'?[7]

First, co-operatives and social enterprise that eschew conventional capitalist forms of ownership, perversely, have been financially outperforming red-blooded businesses within their own capitalist game. In the UK, the co-operative sector grew by more than 25 per cent between 2008 and 2011;[8] RBS report that social enterprises are 'flouting the fiscal gloom to grow faster than the rest of the UK economy';[9] social enterprises are outstripping SMEs for growth, business confidence, and innovation;[10] and Spanish co-operatives have seen an increase in employment of by an average of 7.2 per cent in the last quarter of 2011, despite wider unemployment at record

[7] S. Bowles and H. Gintis (2011) *A Cooperative Species: Human Reciprocity and Its Evolution*.
[8] *Guardian* (2011). 'The Cooperative Sector Has Grown more than 25 Per Cent'.
[9] Social Enterprise Live (2011) 'Vibrant Sector Defies Downturn with Powerful Growth'.
[10] Social Enterprise UK (2011) *Fightback Britain*.

levels. Furthermore, co-operatives have higher resilience in economic crises, based on research by Roelants and Bajo.[11]

Second, co-operatives can offer two solutions to the anti-competitive conundrum. On the one hand, as their ownership structure is inherently inclined to subdivision into smaller units, since subsidiarity and democracy are at the heart of the co-operative model. On the other, many co-operatives and social enterprises provide a defence against takeovers and conglomeration through an 'asset lock', democratic ownership, or disallowing dividends. As a consequence, co-operatives can sidestep the anti-competitive problem by turning such behaviour into a virtue! Co-operation and collusion are of course two sides of the same coin. Observing from a distance the assumption in the Competition Act, in EU law, and inside the Competition Commission that being anti-competitive is a bad thing reveals policymakers', economists', and regulators' blinkers. Co-operatives are bound by their principles to co-operate for public benefit rather than collude for private interest. This enables us to imagine a world other than the inhuman one into which we have stumbled where co-operation—let's spell that out, 'working together'—is an illegitimate and illegal activity.

Third, co-operatives and social enterprises are set up with a responsibility to worry more about the externalities of their trading activity. Their wider obligations beyond the purely financial offer the promise of a less crass and rampant capitalism and instead, a more humanized economy in which businesses price in environmental and social costs. As suggested by the financial performance of co-operatives, this can actually represent a business advantage, rather than a hit on the financial bottom line, as co-operatives capture loyalty and attract trust, for example. Even if this were not true, and internalizing social and environmental costs did mean sacrificing a few percentage points on return to capital, there is much wriggle room between single digit returns and –40 per cent.

Fourth, the co-operative model provides an exit route from the pointless (or worse dangerous) dead end of postmodern economics, not by retreating to traditional models but through turning to each other. Under co-operative ownership, financiers and owners *are also* the consumers or producers. As one and the same, or as peers, they are therefore connected in a more meaningful way than, say, the relationship between a supermarket shopper in the East Midlands and a trader's spreadsheet in Boston. The existence of these more direct and authentic connections can avert the dangers of distance and dislocation by re-establishing more concrete relationships between the constituent components of the economy. Furthermore, under the co-operative model, as the motivations of producers, owners, and consumers are held more in common, the incentives to manipulate 'signifiers' to misrepresent the underlying economic 'signified' are fewer, reintroducing a more meaningful

---

[11] C. Bajo and B. Roelants (2011) *Capital and the Debt Trap: Learning from Cooperatives in the Global Crisis.*

and transparent relationship between economic indicators and the real economy.

What might this mean in practice if we decided to pursue a transition towards a more co-operative market economy? It could mean, for example:

- The creation of more phone, water, energy, and other utility companies along co-operative lines in order to reconnect the incentives between customers and financiers
- The further spread of community-owned shops and pubs to show the large retails chains how real engagement with customers can deliver diversity and remarkably successful financial performance (only 3 per cent of community shops to open have ever closed)[12]
- The appointment of more laymen, charity representatives, customers, and other stakeholder on the boards of banks in order to bring to banks a dose of realism and humanity to the governance of our financial institutions
- The takeover of football clubs by supporters' trusts in order to bring ownership to the people who have the greatest vested interest in clubs' success
- Consumer co-operatives running rail franchises, creating better incentives for owners as customers
- The transformation of the Port of Dover into the so-called 'People's Port' through a community trust model
- Customers moving their money to 'challenger banks' and/or a mutual, co-operative, or credit union to create a more sensible financial system more focused on both the longer-term and the real economy.

But the failures of actual existing capitalism rest as much with the public sector as with the private. Markets are rarely truly free: the state sets the rules, offers subsidies, provides revenue, investment, taxes, and tax breaks which create the playing field and can distort markets. If the state had been able to find a way effectively to harness and steer the private sector, without weighing sufficiently heavily on its back fatally to compromise its horsepower, and used a proportion of the winnings to tidy up the mess left behind, then capitalism would be clearing the fences. Yet successive governments in the UK and across Western capitalist economies have fallen at every hurdle. But could co-operative principles help the public sector play a more constructive role within the capitalist model?

There are three conventional levers at the disposal of policymakers to correct market failure in pursuit of any given policy objective: spending, taxation, and regulation (not to mention 'nudging'—although both the extent to which the population of the UK is willing to be nudged by politically divisive figures, and their ability to nudge sufficiently accurately and with the necessary nuance is yet to be proven).

---

[12] Plunkett Foundation (2011) 'Community-owned Village Shops: A Better Form of Business'.

Both taxation and regulatory interventions could be more intelligently constructed in order to create a more co-operative relationship between the state and the private sector, working with business to incentivize the reduction of negative externalities in order to achieve policy goals in return for fiscal or regulatory rewards. By going beyond the conventional black and white policy choice of taxing or regulating simply either (a) more or (b) less—and instead using shades of grey to bring an increasing tax or regulatory burden only on those businesses which fail to pursue desired behaviours—the state can bring about the development of a private sector which is both less burdened by taxation and regulation while at the same time making a greater contribution to social and environmental, as well as economic prosperity.

Again, what would this mean in practice? We can already see how this works in the environmental sphere through, for example, the state coming down more heavily on those businesses that emit a greater level of CO_2. For this model to be improved upon and extended to the social sphere is not so far-fetched: the Government has recently floated the possibility of relaxing health and safety regulation for those businesses with a strong track record of compliance. If this model could be extended to employment of long-term out-of-work, training and development, R&D, working with local communities, and so on, then this could represent an evolution toward a more liberal and proportionate state which links rights and responsibilities and rewards good corporate behaviour rather than clumsily burdening all businesses with blanket state interference.

For example, tax breaks for investors—such as the Venture Capital Trust (VCT) and Enterprise Investment Scheme (EIS)—could be tweaked to provide greater reliefs for enterprising activities that alleviate poverty, create jobs for NEETs, or support environmental objectives. Relief would be reduced for trade in tobacco, fast food, and other less socially useful sectors and overall, the net corporate tax burden would not change in the short-term while subsequently decreasing in the longer-term as corporate behaviour started to shift.

On the spending side, public services have conventionally been delivered either in-house by public servants within the bosom of the state or put out to competition to be delivered by the most convincing bidder, often from the private sector. Yet there are significant flaws with both models.

Evidence against the statist model can be found where teachers, nurses, and other public servants have entered their profession with a commitment to making a difference and have subsequently been ground down by bureaucracy, paperwork, endless policy reversals, and organizational upheaval. Or for others, where their passion has been dampened as they have become accustomed to job security, pensions, and habit. Furthermore, public budget holders have few incentives to reduce costs and consequently indulge in a ludicrous and shameful annual rush to get money 'out of the door' by the end of the financial year in order to justify and protect their budgets from one year to the next.

The alternative of 'privatization', 'marketization' or 'commercialization' is no less scandalous. First, through the way in which departmental and local silos institutionalize waste. EU law, for example, explicitly states that a commissioning authority is not allowed to take into account wider policy objectives in contracts where they are 'not relevant'. In practice, this means it is understood to be practically illegal for a commissioner of hospital equipment, for instance, to specify that the manufacture of this equipment should engage people far from the labour market. Second, dissatisfaction with the commissioning process in sectors as diverse as the voluntary sector and the architectural profession—evidenced from their respective specialist press[13]— demonstrates another failure of public markets. This is not unjustified whinging—often hundreds of architectural practices apply resources bidding for one single contract. In the East of England, one charity estimated that it took them hundreds of hours of staff time to bid for a contract to deliver children's services, which they subsequently failed to secure. By multiplying that time wasted by the number of bidders, and then again across hundreds of local authorities, and again across dozens of service areas, we can start to get a sense of the immense scale of waste. Even worse, subsequently, contractual negotiations, legal fees, the establishment and maintenance of targets, monitoring, inspection, and reporting regimes absorb billions of pounds. Finally, perverse incentives are contractually enshrined as providers of services are under compulsion to compete with each other and are even disallowed from working across geographical and institutional boundaries in support of citizens.

So is there a co-operative alternative? The rhetoric, if not the reality, of the cross-party enthusiasm for such a model suggests there is, with Labour's Co-operative Councils initiative and the Conservatives' Mutuals Programme. In practice, neither initiative has made any significant advances into the bipolar territory ruled over by cultural, technical, and legal assumptions of only in-house and outsourced options. For human resources staff in foundation trusts, for procurement professionals in local authorities, and for strategic policy-makers in central government, the conventional levers with which they are familiar remain command and control versus compete and contest. It is rare to find any guidance on how to co-operate and collaborate in the rule book, the HR handbook, and the commissioning textbook.

Yet there are several examples where a co-operative alternative has been pursued. *Mutual Ventures'* Andrew Laird and Jessie Cunnett describe how local authorities can take 'a more proactive "market-making" approach and engage with local organisations to bring potential providers together . . . by and large, these organisations would rather come together in collaboration rather than be forced into winner-takes-all competition with each other'. Similarly, under the previous government's Right to Request policy, hundreds of PCT (Primary Care Turst) staff and community health service contracts worth almost a billion pounds annually were 'spun-out' into new employee-owned

---

[13] See a number of third sector magazines (<http://www.thirdsector.co.uk>) and BD articles (<http://www.bdonline.co.uk>).

mutual and social enterprises with an uncontested initial contract. We could imagine more service users co-operatively owning organizations that deliver public services, each with a legal obligation to pursue the common interest, public service beneficiaries, or the local community.

So there is an alternative. But what makes this a promising one is the potential for enterprising public service providers unleashed from some of the restrictions of the public sector, yet driven by community purpose, asset locked, and with greater levels of staff and community engagement. This opens up the possibility to manage the application of public money through appropriate governance at the highest level—which aligns incentives between taxpayer, providers, and service users—rather than the minutiae of contractual legalese, not least reducing complexity and transaction cost.

Taken together, steps like this would represent an evolution towards a more co-operative state, in the way it exploited the fiscal, regulatory, and spending levers at its disposal. This would, in turn, prompt the development of a more co-operative private sector, itself working more in the common interest. This could be a 'shortcut' to the more roundabout route of the private sector pursuing a more blinkered financial perspective, with a necessarily higher level of fiscal transfers, and the maintenance of a costly, complex, and contested state apparatus.

So a co-operative model may offer an alternative to some of the failures of the public and private sectors. But, as Raymond Williams pointed out as early as 1962, 'We have been reduced to making contrasts between the speculator and the bureaucrat, and wondering which is the blacker devil. The real barrier, perhaps, is that we see these as the only alternatives.'[14]

So what about the sector that defines itself through its social, and supposedly more co-operative ethos: civil society, the social sector, or the voluntary and community sector? Whatever we call it and however we define it, and despite its positive net worth in comparison to its public and private cousins, the social sector too suffers from a number of flaws and failures.

First and foremost, the social sector relies to a massive degree on the other two sectors. Organizations that exist beyond the control of the state for a social purpose rather than private profit are hugely reliant on the benevolence of public grants or contracts and private handouts. While they are defined in theory by their independence of governance, their practical existence is characterized by financial and indeed other forms of dependence.

In contrast to communist regimes, liberal democracies pride themselves on the role of a strong civil society existing independently of the ruling state ideology. Civil society under communism, to the extent it would exist at all, would be regulated, funded, and governed in a way that was dominated by the state apparatus. Civil society groups would be (a) restricted from political activities; (b) significantly reliant on state funding; and (c) not truly independent,

---

[14] R. Williams (1962).

with the state directly influencing decision-making and governance. Yet, worryingly, we can also recognize each of these patterns in the relationship between civil society and the state in the UK today.

When it comes to regulation, Charitable Law regulates many civil society organizations. Most think tanks are charities. Yet a charity cannot exist for a political purpose, which includes 'securing or opposing a change in the law, policy or decisions' and 'an organisation will not be charitable if its purposes are political'. Yet organizations are incentivized by the state to adopt charitable status and thus fall under these rules through—as Dame Suzi Leather puts it— 'generous tax breaks and other advantages'.

On the funding side, the state is a dominant source of income for the social sector: the 2012 NCVO Almanac tells us that between a third and a half of the voluntary sector's income comes from statutory sources.[15] Much of the rest comes from private sources, from individual donations, businesses, and customers, but relatively little from within the sector itself.

In terms of governance, the 2011 Panel on Independence of the Voluntary Sector reported that the 'state appears to exercise undue influence over the governance of charities...in some cases there is a sole trustee who is a local government employee...pressure can be put on them to include a local authority representative on their Boards'.[16]

So for civil society in the UK today, political activities are restricted, government funding is critical and the state can restrict the independent governance of the sector. As the Independence Panel concluded, there are 'real and present risks' to independence and 'indirect and sometimes direct pressure towards self-censorship, muting the voice of some in the sector'.

A second major failure of civil society is that in accepting, albeit often reluctantly, the pervasiveness of the market mentality, the sector is increasingly tending towards the methods and mindset of competition, yet with no corresponding benefit to society. The transaction costs of competing for funds are enormous. Funds administered by NatWest, for example, as well as the Government's Social Action Fund and Communitybuilders have seen hundreds of organizations competing for resources with only a tiny percentage (as little as less than 1 per cent) ultimately attracting funding. It is hard to see who is benefitting from such competition and how beneficiaries could not fail to see some rewards if charities co-operated to a greater extent.

So a case can be made that imagines a more co-operative economy, in the sense that each distinct sector adopts a more co-operative approach—with co-operative businesses taking a higher market share and organizations in the public and third sector mutualizing or embodying more co-operative principles. Yet this is only a co-operative alternative to capitalism in a limited

---

J. Clarke, D. Kane, K. Wilding, and P. Bass (2012). *UK Civil Society Almanac 2012.*

Panel on the Independence of the Voluntary Sector (2012) *Protecting Independence: The Voluntary Sector in 2012.* (<http://www.independencepanel.org.uk/wp-content/uploads/2012/01/Protecting-Independence-final.pdf>, accessed 27 September 2012).

sense—simply more co-operative actors playing the capitalist game. As far as it goes, this is perhaps not so hard to imagine.

But from a more fundamental perspective, which may be as difficult to conceive as Žižek suggests, such changes could be a stepping-stone to the transformation of the relationships not only *within* but *between* the sectors, and the creation of a system of production that could be defined as an alternative to capitalism—or co-operativism.

This co-operative alternative to 'actual existing capitalism' would recalibrate a co-operative dynamic between sectors rather than the current competitive and antagonistic tension. This means players within the system realizing through enlightened self-interest that they will each benefit from working more effectively together to create a more successful, balanced, and mutually supporting democratic mixed economy.

The ONS[17] figures tell us that the public and private sectors are less than worthless, while the voluntary sector and private households maintain a net value of many trillions of pounds. Simplistically, this could be interpreted that we, both as individuals and in association, are collectively carrying the public and private institutions. Alternatively, it could be argued that private business and government have overreached themselves for our sake—trying to deliver us the financial returns we have come to expect as investors, and the public services we have come to expect as citizens.

Either way, or perhaps a more accurate interpretation lies elsewhere, these figures illustrate how the interrelation between sectors is important for the on-going viability and sustainability of the UK's economy and society. Yet this dynamic between sectors is bafflingly ignored by economists and demands greater consideration, especially as our two sectoral giants are currently practically bankrupt, if not technically insolvent. There are very few serious attempts to understand how the two spheres of labour and capital interrelate within our economy.

We do have theories of market socialism, such as the Lange model of Pareto efficiency,[18] studies of common resource management, led by Elinor Ostrom,[19] and Yochai Benkler's recent inquiry into how 'co-operation triumphs over greed'.[20] Indeed Benkler does go some way into exploring the relationship between different sectors of the economy, highlighting the extremes of Hobbes' Leviathan and Adam Smith's The Invisible Hand.

But what do we really understand about the interrelationship between private individuals and businesses (competing to create financial wealth) with public bodies (which command or control resources to create public

---

[17] Office for National Statistics (2012). 'UK Worth £6.8'.
[18] O. Lange (1936) *On the Economic Theory of Socialism*.
[19] E. Ostrom (1990) *Governing the Commons: The Evolution of Institutions for Collective Action*.
[20] Y. Benkler (2011) *The Penguin and the Leviathan: The Triumph of Co-Operation over Self-Interest*.

goods and services) and with the groups, charities, trusts, and associations (which co-operate to make the UK a more socially or environmentally rich place to live)? In other words, what are the positive and negative economic dynamics between (crudely drawn) liberté, egalité, and fraternité?

Can the state provide the infrastructure that helps businesses? Can businesses reinvigorate communities? Does the private sector generate tax revenues? Can social action save government money? Do markets rely on trust and social capital? And more destructively, do businesses generate negative externalities that bring costs to the Exchequer? Does the public sector crowd out social action? Can the welfare system stifle enterprise?

Of course the answer is yes to all the above, to various degrees and dependent on the circumstances. A co-operative alternative to capitalism then, would see the pursuit of actions, policies, and entrepreneurial approaches which lead to more positive supporting, catalysing, and enabling dynamics and less stifling, undermining, and crowding out. The UK economy can be highly inefficient when these three different sectors work selfishly and destructively in opposition. With the state asked every year to pick up a bigger tab to solve the externalities and failures of the market, the private sector feeding the public sector's addiction to tax revenues, and the social sphere ever more reliant on handouts to shoulder the burden of mopping up failure elsewhere. Instead, a more harmonious and symbiotic alignment of the different spheres of capital and labour could lead to more sustainable public finances, more responsible business, and to a more effective social sector.

This is related to some Labour ideas focused on 'pre-distribution' with the intention of reducing the need for fiscal transfers later. It is also linked to the Conservative's 'Big Society', with the argument that if the state gets out of the way, then social action can flourish. But this is only half the side (and the gloomy side at that) of a triangle. Equally 'pre-distribution' only considers the dynamic between the private sector and the state.

This is not a theory, then, which proposes market socialism from a negative position—as an alternative to the expropriation of surplus value by capitalists—but rather a positive construction of a political economy which is more efficient *as well as* more social.

Admittedly, there is currently little evidence that such a system would indeed be more efficient but perhaps encouragingly, not because attempts have been tried and failed (and as a starting point, it seems we only need to improve upon a model running at 60 per cent efficiency).

Where there is some relevant evidence, perhaps, is in the natural world, where a range of research suggests that co-operation can be evolutionarily advantageous. The biologist Lynn Margulis, for example, has received much praise even from the supposed high prince of selfish, Richard Dawkins (who himself is now keen to point out the occasions in nature when nice guys finish first) for examining how co-operation has been key to our evolution, for example, arguing that 'life did not take over the globe by combat, but by networking'.[21] In *Evolutions Arrow*, John Stewart argued that 'evolution can exploit the advantages of co-operation by finding ways to make cooperation pay for the individuals who cooperate'.[22]

Work by Robert Trivers on 'reciprocal altruism'[23] suggested that helping another at your own cost in the short term may be beneficial in the long term and therefore evolve into a more permanent co-operative strategy. Axelrod's *Evolution of Co-operation*[24] follows his work on the 'Prisoners Dilemma' that concluded that the most successful players were those who co-operated on the first move and then reciprocated what the other prisoner did on the previous move. Similarly, Martin Nowak's *Super Co-operators*[25] argues that 'co-operation, not competition, is the key to life' and that many of our great innovatory evolutions, from the molecular level to language and the city, have been driven through co-operation. Bowles and Gintis' *Cooperative Species*[26] also explores how co-operation has been crucial to human survival and progress.

In contrast to the bibliography of inter-sectoral economics (!), the list goes on. But while we still await the emergence of a convincing new economics, these lessons from nature, together with recent evidence of the success of co-operatives on the ground, may be in themselves enough to suggest that the exploration of an economic system that more accurately reflects humanity, its motivations and behaviours may be worthy of more serious consideration.

So is there a co-operative alternative to capitalism? Perhaps not, if what we mean by capitalism is a mixed market economy. But the answer is almost certainly yes, if we are in the market for an alternative to 'actual existing capitalism'. The recent history of the private, public, and social sectors—and also the story deep inside us—could prompt a dawning realization by participants in the economy that a more co-operative approach could potentially deliver a more efficient, human, and harmonious market economy in a world with ever scarcer resources. A co-operative economy can be in both our common and our self-interest. As Robert Owen says 'the union and co-operation of *all* for the benefit of *each*'.[27] Imagine.

■ REFERENCES

Axelrod, R. (1984). *The Evolution of Cooperation*. New York: Basic Books.

Bajo, C., and Roelants, B. (2011). *Capital and the Debt Trap: Learning from Cooperatives in the Global Crisis*. New York: Palgrave Macmillan.

---

[21] L. Margulis D. and Sagan (1996) *What is Life?*
[22] J. Stewart (2000) *Evolution's Arrow: The Direction of Evolution and the Future of Humanity*.
[23] R. Trivers (1971) 'The Evolution of Reciprocal Altruism'
[24] R. Axelrod (1984) *The Evolution of Cooperation*.
[25] M. Nowak (2011) *Super Cooperators*.
[26] Bowles and Gintis (2011).
[27] R. Owen (1826) *The Social System: Constitution, Laws, and Regulations of a Community*.

Benkler, Y. (2011). *The Penguin and the Leviathan: The Triumph of Co-Operation over Self-Interest*. New York: Crown Business.

Bowles, S. and Gintis, H. (2011). *A Co-operative Species: Human Reciprocity and Its Evolution*. Princeton, NJ: Princeton University Press.

Clarke, J., Kane, D., Wilding, K., and Bass, P. (2012). *UK Civil Society Almanac 2012*. London: NCVO.

Competition Commission (2012). *Annual Report and Accounts*. London: The Stationery Office.

Guardian (2011). 'Co-operative Sector Has Grown more than 25 Per Cent', 26 June. <http://www.guardian.co.uk/business/2011/jun/26/co-operative-sector-has-grown-more-than-25-per-cent>, accessed 27 September 2012.

Harrison, R. (ed.) (2013). *People over Capital: The Co-operative Alternative to Capitalism*. Oxford: New Internationalist and Ethical Consumer.

Lange, O. (1936). 'On the Economic Theory of Socialism, i', *The Review of Economic Studies* 4(1): 53–71.

Margulis, L., and Sagan, D. (1996). *What Is Life?* London: Weidenfeld & Nicholson.

NESTA (2011). *Atlantic Drift*. <http://www.nesta.org.uk/library/documents/AtlanticDrift9.pdf>, accessed 27 September 2012.

Nowak, M. (2011). *Super Cooperators*. New York: Free Press.

Office for National Statistics (2012). 'UK Worth £6.8 Trillion'. Press release. <http://www.ons.gov.uk/ons/rel/mro/news-release/uk-worth–6-8-trillion/nbsnr0812.html>, accessed 27 September 2012.

Ostrom, E. (1990). Governing the Commons: The Evolution of Institutions for Collective Action. Cambridge: Cambridge University Press.

Owen, R. (1826). The Social System: Constitution, Laws, and Regulations of a Community.

Plunkett Foundation (2011). 'Community-owned Village Shops: A Better Form of Business'. <http://www.plunkett.co.uk/templates/asset-relay.cfm?frmAssetFileID=1062>, accessed 27 September 2012.

Social Enterprise Live (2011). 'Vibrant Sector Defies Downturn with Powerful Growth', 11 July. <http://www.socialenterpriselive.com/section/se100/management/20110711/vibrant-sector-defies-downturn-powerful-growth>, accessed 27 September 2012.

Social Enterprise UK (2011). *Fightback Britain*. <http://www.socialenterprise.org.uk/uploads/editor/files/Publications/Fightback_Britain.pdf>, accessed 27 September 2012.

Stewart. J. (2000). Evolution's Arrow: The Direction of Evolution and the Future of Humanity. Canberra: The Chapman Press.

Trivers, R. (1971). 'The Evolution of Reciprocal Altruism', *Quarterly Review of Biology*, 46(1): 35–57.

Williams, R. (1962). *Communications*. Harmondsworth: Penguin.

Zizek, S. (2010). *Living in the End Times*. London: Verso.

INDEX

AADD (All About Developmental Disabilities) 100, 103
Aavishkaar India Impact Fund 22
Abraaj Group 561
  portfolio distribution 561 Fig. 17.5
Absolute Return for Kids 118
academic institutions 501
accelerators 54, 443–4, 505
AccessBank, Azerbaijan 545–6
ACCION, USA 473
Actis 555, 556
Acumen Fund 208, 219, 228, 231, 556, 558, 605
  best alternative charity option (BACO) 267, 323
  sector focus 560, 560 Fig. 17.4
Adams, D. 394, 404, 446
Adapt (Harford) 121, 122
ADM Capital Foundation, Hong Kong 200
advanced market commitments 56
Adventure Capital Fund (ACF), UK 53, 465, 466, 483
Advocacy Partners, UK 194
affordability and redistribution, not-for-profit role 71–2
affordable housing 208, 210, 402, 434, 437, 439
  India 508
Afghanistan, agricultural finance 585, 586, 587
Africa:
  agricultural development 128
  capital needs 565
  cellular phones 117
  co-operatives and mutuals 144
  direct foreign investment and private equity 543–71
  economic transformation 561
  healthcare 219 Box 8.2, 220 Case 8.1
  lack of investment-ready projects 237
  poverty 217
Africa Media Development Initiative 117
African Agricultural Capital Fund 229
African Development Bank (AfDB) 557, 560
'Age of Reason' 129
Age UK 61
ageing population 114, 370, 387, 446
Agrawal, A. K. 527–8
Aidun, Chris 562
Alcoholics Anonymous 61
Allen, Graham 343

Allen & Overy law firm 343
Alliance for Useful Evidence, UK 59
Allianz Global Investors 592
Allied Dunbar Charitable Trust, UK 192
AllLife 559–60
Alternative Public Offerings (APOs) 12–13
American Clean Air markets 612
American Diabetes Organization 69
Amity Foundation, China 202–3
Annenberg Challenge 121
Annie E. Casey Foundation 227
anti-drinking advertisements 299–300
apparel manufacture 601
Aquinas, Thomas 576
architectural practices 622
Aristotle 573, 575, 576
Armendáriz, B. 168, 171
Arregui, Rodriguez 564
Ashiagbor, David 567
Ashoka 192, 342, 508, 523
Asia:
  direct foreign investment and private equity 543–71
  engaged-giving circles 201–2
  and the globalization of philanthropy and social entrepreneurship 198–9
  'Green Revolution' 128
  microfinance 164
  new generation of entrepreneurial philanthropists 199–201
  poverty, West Asia 217
  social finance instruments 12–13
  venture philanthropy 197–203
  wealth creation 197–8
Asian Development Bank (ADB) 546, 551
Asian Impact Investment Exchange (IIX) 512
Asian Venture Philanthropy Association (VPA) 199
Aspen Network of Development Entrepreneurs (ANDE) 233
asset allocation 19–21
asset locks 12, 19, 75, 89, 526, 619, 623
  community interest companies (CICs) 23, 85, 89, 102, 465, 535
Attanasio, O. 167–8
Aureaos Capital 556–7
Australia:
  community development investment 425
  government as convenor 408

Australia: (*cont.*)
  government funds for social
    enterprises 497–8
  High-Net-Worth Individuals 197
  open data initiatives 305
  SEDIF initiative 433, 434
  Social Impact Bonds (SIBS) 323, 358, 359
    Tab. 12.1, 449
  tax incentives 437, 438
  venture philanthropy 202
Australian Senate Inquiry (2011) 490
Australian Social Enterprise Development and
  Investment Funds 213–14, 433
Axelrod, R. 627
Ayadi, R. 148

B Lab, USA 21, 85, 90, 101, 231, 270, 606, 607
Baan, Paul and Joan 196
Babylon 573
Bajo, C. 619
Bamboo Finance 558
Banca Etica, Italy 46
Banca Prossima, Italy 46
Banco Compartamos, Mexico, IPO 172–3,
  213, 238, 564
BancoSol, Bolivia 162, 166–7
Banerjee, A. 177
Bangladesh 158, 161, 551; *see also* Grameen
  Bank
bank bailouts, UK 145
bank crises, increasing incidence 145
Bank of England 146, 523
  Financial Stability Report (2010) 145
  as Lender of Last Resort 146
Bank Rakyat Indonesia (BRI) 162, 172
banking, ancient 573
banks:
  co-operatives and mutuals 141–2
  effects of competition from co-operatives
    and mutuals 136
  microfinance 165
  'too big to fail' 146
Bannick, M. 404, 414, 444, 485, 513
Banque Publique d'Investissement,
  France 10–11
Barby, C. 291
Barclays Wealth survey (2010) 198
Baron, D. P. 76, 77, 80
Barrow Cadbury Trust, UK 192
Bates-Wells Braithwaite (BWP) case study 504
Bauchet, J. 177
Beartooth Capital 608–9, 612
behavioural science 255, 267
Belgian Corporation for Investment
  (BMI) 547, 548, 549, 552, 553

Belgian Investment Company for Developing
  Countries (BIO) 548, 550, 551–2,
  554, 556
Belgium:
  Société à Finalité Sociale (SFS) 493
  solidarity economy 384
Bell, Daniel 51
Bellagio meetings (2007, 2008) 208
Belleflamme, P. 524–6
Ben & Jerry's 23, 100, 101, 597
Benefit Corporations (BCs, B-Corps),
  USA 5, 21, 23, 52, 85, 85–6, 89, 101, 426,
  440, 473, 494
benefits theory 27–8, 97, 103–6, 109–10
  and capital financing 106–9
Benkler, Yokhai 625
Berger, Ken 124
Bertha Centre for Social Innovation, South
  Africa 444
Bethnal Green Ventures, UK 54, 55
Better World Books 101
Big Issue 51, 62
Big Issue Invest, UK 54, 55, 495
Big Lottery Fund, UK 57, 59, 505
  Commissioning Better Outcomes 58
Big Potential Fund, UK 505
Big Society Capital (BSC), UK 8, 15, 52, 55,
  58, 59, 125, 214, 241, 272, 324, 344, 435,
  468, 469, 497, 507
  case study 490
  Outcomes Matrix 272–3, 304, 430
Bill & Melinda Gates Foundation 119, 120,
  213, 227, 556
  Advance Market Commitments 122
Bishop, M. 113, 491
Black Rock 23
Blair, Tony 192
Blakeborough, Adele 193–4
'blended value' 3, 116, 208, 256, 283, 284,
  311, 384, 567, 593, 594, 595, 598,
  604, 611, 613
  measuring 241, 267–8, 279, 612
  real estate industry 594, 596–7, 606, 607
  and upfront spending 307
Bloomberg, Michael 15, 114
Bloomberg Philanthropies, USA 25, 57
Blumberg, G. 290–1, 298, 299
BNP Paribas 15
Body Shop 51
Boise Cascade 602
Bolivia 161
  commercialization of microfinance 173,
  179–80
BonVenture, Germany 54
'bootstrapping' 524, 526

Boston Consulting Group (BCG) 558
Bottom of the Pyramid (BoP) markets 47, 48,
    217, 224, 242, 557, 560
Bowles, S. 627
BP Deep Water Horizon oil spill 598, 599
Brainer, Paul 191
Brakman Reiser, D. 81, 82–3, 84, 91
Branson, Richard 127
Brazil:
    Clean Development Mechanism 437
    sugar cane industry 553
Breakthough, UK 193–4
Breezie 499
Brewin Dolphin, UK 512
BRICS development bank proposal 563
Bridges Ventures, UK 2, 54, 55, 58, 208,
    240, 287, 289, 323, 324, 464, 495,
    507, 508, 556
    Social Enterprise Fund 229, 466
    Social Impact Bond Fund 471
    Sustainable Growth Fund, UK 433, 434
Bridgespan 123–4
Brilliant, Larry 125–6
Brin, Sergey 125
British Broadcasting Company (BBC) 117
Brookes, Martin 124, 343
Buffet, Warren 108, 113, 116, 120, 123, 198
Buffini, Damon 193–4
Bugg-Levin, A. 491
building societies, *see* mutual building
    societies
Büscher, M. 538
business succession 150–1
Buzzbnk 324, 525 Tab. 16.1

Cafédirect 54
    pricing case study 325–9
Caja Laboral, Basque country 46
California Fresh Works 213
CalPERS, USA 509
Calvert Foundation 223
    Community Investment Note 26
Cameron, David 62, 114
'Campbell's law' 260
Canada:
    credit unions 140
    international development initiatives 22
    policy context and agenda 31, 361
    Social Impact Bonds (SIBs) 323, 358
Canadian Task Force on Social
    Finance 388, 435
Cannacord Capital, UK 512
capacity building 19, 53, 73, 200, 205, 237,
    297, 441, 465
    UK 55, 465–7, 469–70
    USA 475

Capgemini RBC World Wealth Report
    (2012) 197–8
capital asset pricing model (CAPM) 283, 318–19
Capital Regionel et Coopératif (CRCD),
    Quebec 481
capital sources, institutional pathways 507–10
'capital stacking' 240, 243
capitalism:
    cooperative alternative 616–27
    holistic approach 384
    inefficiency 616–21
    and inequality 616
    moral objection to 617
    'narrow' conception 403
    new, improved 116
    reality/rhetoric schism 618
    reorientation 113
    'under siege' 383
    and unemployment 616
    varieties of 461
carbon reduction markets 56
Caritas, Germany 61
Carlyle Group 565
Carnegie, Andrew 117, 119
Carnegie UK Trust Inquiry (2010) 484
'carpet-bagging' 139
Carter, Jimmy 578
Case i3 initiative, Duke University 444
catalytic capital 25, 431–5
    layered capital structures 432 Fig. 13.7
CDC Group 22
CDH Investments 553
Center for Effective Philanthropy (CEP) 124
Central Surrey Health 52
Centre for European Policy Studies (CEPS) 144–5
Centre for Social Impact Bonds, UK Cabinet
    Office 471
Centres Locaux de Developpments,
    Quebec 483
Ceres, Boston 599, 601
Chantier de l'économie sociale, Quebec 480
charitable donations and legacies 16, 99, 100,
    103; *see also* philanthropy
charitable foundations, *see* foundations
charities:
    and collective goods 69
    contract funding 7
    formalization of sector 8
    mission-related investment 8
    non-distribution constraint 3
    registration requirement 498
    revenue streams, USA 98–9
    social investment funding 494–5
Charity Bank, UK 46, 54, 467
Charity Commission, UK 55, 423, 464,
    470, 495

charity law:
and civil society organisations 620
UK reform 52
Charity Navigator 124
Chen, James 201
Chen, Annie 201
Chen Foundation 201
ChevronTexaco 212
Children's Investment Fund Foundation 118
China 126, 159, 200, 201
direct foreign investment 553, 554
economic growth 198, 604
Foundation Center 203
High-Net-Worth Individuals 197, 198
philanthropy 199
venture philanthropy 202–3
Christianity:
Code of Canon Law 576, 577
prohibition on interest/usury 573, 574,
575, 576, 577
Chu, Michael 172, 566
Čihák, M. 149
Cisco Systems Foundation 556
Citibank 'EQ2' structure 210
Citigroup 175
City Leader's Group, UK 56, 343, 344
City Year 105
civil society 2–3, 6
China 202–3
corporation oversight 601–12
funding 6
and philanthrocapitalism 116–17
and the state 623–4
Clarke, C. 234
Clarke, Kenneth 345
Clean Development Mechanism, Brazil 234
clean/green energy 8, 34, 126, 220–1, 393,
402, 434, 437, 560–1, 562, 598
ClearlySo 17, 495, 510
case study 511
climate change 227, 264, 307, 319, 445, 553,
594, 598, 599, 601
Clinic Africa, Uganda 220 Case 8.1
Clinton Global Initiative 28, 123
Clontarf Football Academy, Australia 300
CNN 119
Coalition Government, UK 114, 142, 146,
344–5, 468–72, 490
Big Society agenda 114, 468–9, 477, 626
welfare privatization 469
Coca-Cola 599
Code of Hammurabi 573, 575
COFIDES 548, 549, 553, 554
Cohen, Ed 190
Cohen, Ronald 36, 244, 394, 442, 462, 482
Co-Investissment Coop, Quebec 481

collaborative economics 445
collective goods ('public goods') 66–7, 90
contract failure 67
corporate social responsibility and joint
production of private and 75, 76
excludable 67
for-profit provision 73
non-excludable 66, 74
not-for-profit provision 69
scholarships as 105
society-wide, benefits theory 104, 105, 107,
109, 110
specific target groups, benefits theory 104,
105, 106, 108–9, 110
collective impact 204
College Summit, USA 88
co-mingling funds 222, 223, 409, 431–2
Commission on Ownership Report (2012),
UK 148
Commission on Unclaimed Assets,
UK 341, 468
Commonwealth Development Corporation
(CDC), UK 208, 545, 546, 548, 460, 552,
553, 554, 556, 557
Community Action Network (CAN), UK 51,
52, 192, 193
community associations 159–60
Community Builders Programme,
UK 466, 483
Community Development Corporations
(CDCs) 49
Community Development Finance
Association, UK 464
community development finance institutions
(CFDIs) 16, 17, 140, 209, 234, 463,
464, 473
Community Development Financial
Institutions (CDFI) Act (1994),
USA 473
community economic development
corporations (CEDCs), Quebec 479
community enterprises 441–52
Community Innovation UK 467
Community Interest Companies (CICs),
UK 23, 52, 83, 85, 88, 89, 102, 127, 465,
494, 501, 535
Community Investment Tax Relief (CITR),
UK 234, 341, 437, 464, 496–7
Community Reinvestment Act (CRA, 1977),
USA 48–9, 208, 234, 425, 437,
472, 474
community sector:
innovation at the intersection with public
sector and market 445–51
UK policy for investment
(1999–2002) 425, 463–4, 495

Communitybuilders 624
companies limited by guarantee (GLG)
    form 494
companies limited by shares (CLC) form 494
Competition Act EU 619
Competition Commission, EU 617, 619
Confédération des syndicats nationaux (CSN) 480
conferences 501–2
Conservative Party, UK 344
consultancies, specialised 504–6
Consultive Group to Assist the Poor
    (CGaP) 162–3
consumer co-operatives 134
contingent liability bonds 263
contingent revenue bonds 56, 342–3
Contract and Investment Readiness Fund,
    UK 441
contract failure 67, 526
    in commercial markets 69–70, 72, 74,
        81, 90
    in hybrid organizations 89
Cooper Hohn, Jamie 194
cooperative alternative to capitalism 616–27
    alternative public services delivery 622–3
    authentic connections 619
    cooperative market economy 620
    cooperative relations between state and
        private sector 620
    as model 618–19
co-operatives and mutuals 8, 13, 28, 35,
        101–2, 133–55, 284–5, 498, 574
    access to finance 135–6, 137–8, 144,
        149–50, 151
    access to investment capital 153
    benefits to the financial sector 136, 151
    and business succession 150–1
    and corporate diversity 137, 144–7
    creating permanent 149
    finance raised and provided 133
    global developments 140–2
    governance 138
    historical context 139–40, 152
    inherent benefits 151
    legislative and regulatory regime 148
    low risk appetite 148
    main arguments in favour 147
    market for mutual finance 148–51
    motivation for founding or choosing
        structure 135
    'mutual' term 135
    ownership and 'cashing in' 138–9
    ownership structures 133–5, 619
    profit distribution 138
    public service mutuals 469
    and public services delivery 136–7
    and public services reform 142–4

Quebec 478
research needs 153
sector assets 10
seven principles 134
types of 133–4
see also credit co-operatives; social
    co-operatives
Co-operatives Group 61
coordinated market economies (Quebec) 461,
    463, 478–82
corporate diversity 137, 144–7, 148–9, 151
corporate investment funds 509–10
corporate philanthropy 100
    extent 79
    limitations on 79
Corporate Quid Pro Quo x 103
corporate social responsibility (CSR) 73,
        75–7, 100, 113, 212, 477
    and cost reduction 75–6
    Disclosure Rule, Malaysia 234
    effect on personal donations 79
    and enhanced revenue 75
    and increased investment 76–7
    informational asymmetry 81
    limitations on 79–81
    and the market for control 77–8
    and reduced regulation 77
    reporting 255
    unsustainability issues 80
corporate sponsorship, benefits theory 104,
        105–6, 107, 109, 110
corporate takeovers 78
cost-benefit analysis 6, 267–8, 303, 318, 436
    welfare outcomes 255
Council of the European Union 409
Council on Social Action, UK 342
Cox, P. 139
'craft knowledge' 50
Credit Coopératif, France 18, 46
credit co-operatives 159–60
credit unions 55, 133, 165, 466, 574
    Mexico 143
    origins and growth 140
    Quebec 478
Crépon, B. 177
Cross Cutting Review (2002), UK
    Treasury 464
cross-sector partnerships, UK 463–4
CrowdBnk 499
CrowdCube 525 Tab. 16.1, 499, 534
crowdfunding 13, 26, 32, 63, 113, 324, 426,
        485, 521–42
    active investments 527
    all or nothing approach 530
    case study 499
    collaborative platforms 529 Tab. 16.2

crowdfunding (*cont.*)
  'crowd' concept 524, 536
  debt 527, 532–4
  donations 526, 533
  equity 526, 527, 534–6
  financing social enterprises 522–3
  future research 536–8
  global reach 527–8
  major forms of pledging capital 526 Fig.
    16.1
  mission drift 534
  modelling 528–32, 531 Fig. 16.2
  passive investments 527
  platforms 525 Tab. 16.1, 528–9, 533, 536
  regulation 426
  reward 526, 533
  threshold pledge system 530
crowdsourcing 524, 530
Crusades 573
Cuevas, C. E. 142
Cull, R. 166
Cunnett, Jessie 622
Curtin, Edmond 343

d.o.b. Foundation, Netherlands 54
DAC (Development Assistance
    Committee) 114
  Busan Declaration (2011) 114
  Paris Declaration on Aid Effectiveness
    (2005) 114
Dalberg Associates 215
Darwish, Issam 565
Dasra Giving Circles 202
Davies, W. 150
Dawkins, Richard 626
'deadweight calculations' 264
Deardon-Phillips, Craig 194
debt funding 11–12, 221, 222 Fig. 8.2
  crowdfunding 527, 532–4
  development finance institutions 551–62
  private equity in emerging markets 558
demand side (capital users) 18–19
  direct investments and financial
    structures 228–30, 229 Tab. 8.6
  policy initiatives to develop 440–53, 474–5
  see also benefits theory
Demos 462
DenokInn Social Innovation Park, Bilbao 54
Department for International Development
    (DFID) 430
  Impact Programme 22, 235
Depository Institutions Deregulation and
    Monetary Control Act (1980),
    USA 578
Deshpande, Gururaj 'Desh' 199
Deutsche Bank 9, 214, 286

Eye Fund investment structure 229, 230
  Fig. 8.4
Deutsche Investitions und
    Entwicklungsgesellschaft (DEG) 546,
    548, 551, 553, 554
developing countries 22, 126, 158, 174–5, 234,
    242, 343, 471
  aligning sources of capital with investment
    strategies 566 Tab. 17.5
  co-operatives and mutuals, welfare
    role 143–4
  crowdfunding market 528
  demand-side actors 229 Tab. 8.6
  economic growth and high poverty levels 233
  environmental investment 218–19
  impact investing market 235, 236
  lack of market regulation 397
  microsavings 171
  obstacles to growth 545
  population growth 210
  social innovation strategies 401–2
  unmet needs 12, 387–8
  see also emerging markets
development aid 210
  limits on 385
  plateauing of 242
development finance institutions (DFIs) 32,
    543, 545–54, 568–9
  bilateral and multiple 544 Tab. 17.1, 546
  financial instruments 550–2, 551 Fig. 17.1
  future issues 562–668
  geographical analysis 553–4, 554 Fig. 17.3
  need for capital and the role of 562–3
  sector analysis 552 Fig. 17.2, 552–3
development guarantees 439
Development Impact Bonds (DIBS) 21–2,
    219, 448, 450
Devoto, F. 177
Diggers movement 8
direct public offerings 13
Divine Chocolate 52
Dodd-Frank Act (2010), USA 147
Doeringer, M. F. 88
Dormant Bank and Building Society Accounts
    Act (2008), UK 468
Draper Richards Foundation, San Francisco
    Bay 191
Drexler, M. 432
Drucker, Henry 192
Duflo, E. 177
Dupas, P. 178
Dutch Est India Company 574

E. T. Jackson and Associates 213, 223
  market infrastructure framework 224–5,
    225 Tab. 8.4

E+Co 559, 560, 562
early-stage investment funds 54
Ebrahim, A. 255
Eccles, Toby 344, 366
Echoing Green 190
  Fellowships 88
eco 589
'economic chivalry' 36
Economist, The 113
Ecosystem Investment Partners 609–10
'ecosystem services'/'natural capital' 590
Edelgive 200
Edelweiss Group, India 199–200
Edward the Confessor 576
Edward I 576, 577
Edward III 577
Edward VI 578
Edwards, Michael 116, 117, 118
Egerton-Warburton, Chris 343
Eggers, W. D. 508
8 Miles 557
Einstein, Albert 572
EKO Asset Management Partners 25
Elders, The 128
Elevar 559
Eli Lilly and Company 65
Elizabeth I 578
emerging markets 26, 208–9
  environmental impact investing 604
  expected rates of return 223
  foreign direct investment and private
    equity 8–9, 439, 32, 543–71
  limited track record 238, 243
  as impact investing destination 216–17,
    242
  impact investing policies 234
  lack of regulation 398
  sectors of interest 216–18
  see also developing countries
Emerson, J. 116, 208, 234, 290, 292, 451, 491
employee buyouts 151
employee co-operatives 134
Employee Retirement Income Security Act
    (ERISA, 1979), USA 424
Endeavour 237
engaged-giving circles 201–2
EngagedX 241, 271–2, 428
'enlightened self-interest' 116
Enterprise Investment Scheme (ENS) 621
'entrepreneurial social finance' 185
Environmental and Social Investment
    Exchange, Brazil 512
Environmental Defense Fund (EDF) 126
environmental degradation 210, 218–20,
    242, 604
environmental disasters 591

environmental impact investing 3, 25–6,
    32–3, 218–21, 589–615
  availability of environmental
    information 602–3
  business economics/environmental values
    alignment 603
  deals 595–6
  efficient markets 591–2
  emerging markets 604
  empirical evidence of social/financial
    relationship 593–4
  environmental economics 590
  environmental factors and financial
    value 597–8
  external stakeholder influence 601–12
  framework for 595–9
  funds 596
  integrated consideration of multiple
    factors 607
  market places 596–7
  personal, emotional and human aspect 607
  price adjustment delays 598–603, 600
    Fig . 9.1
  real estate case studies 608–10
  standardization of information 605–7
  three complementary theses 611–14
  time horizons 604–5
environmental, social and governance (ESG)
    integration 9, 20, 21, 34, 79
  additional standards, direct finance
    institutions 550
  and financial performance 593–4
  time horizons 605
Equitas Micro Finance 240
Equity Bank, Kenya 172
equity capital 12–13, 88, 172, 221, 222 Tab. 8.2
  crowdfunding 526, 527, 534–6
  development finance institutions 550–1,
    552
  for-profit access 80, 83
  reverse vesting 331
  see also private equity
equity-tranche 84, 87, 89
Ernst & Young 510
Esmee Fairburn Foundation 54, 175, 346, 495
  Venturesome investments 289
ESOP (Employee Stock Ownership Plan),
    USA 13
ESRC 59
Ethex, UK 269, 525 Tab. 16.1
ethical consumption 269
  rise of 35–6
ethical for-profits 70
Ethical Investment Research Service
    (EIRIS) 603
Ethical Property Company, UK 54, 324, 512

Europe:
  economic growth 617
  evolution of venture philanthropy 191–7
  legal forms of social enterprise 493
  private equity, hedge fund and family office
    venture philanthropy funds 195 Tab 7.2
European Bank for Reconstruction and
  Development (EBRD) 546
European Commission Single Market Act
  (2008) 234
European Investment Fund 9, 286, 497–8
European Social Impact Accelerator 435
European Social Investment Taskforce 234
European Union:
  carbon trading market 56
  'Standard for Social Impact' 21
European Venture Philanthropy Association
  (EVPA) 185, 193, 196, 199
  annual conference 233
evidence-based approaches 55, 59,
  118–19, 441
  and social probability risk reduction 298–9
Exelon Corporation 599
exits 238, 427–8
  private equity firms in emerging
    markets 555, 564
Eybam, Rosalind 118–19

Facebook 528, 529
F. B. Heron Foundation 227
facilitative infrastructure 489 Fig. 15.1, 503–6,
  513 Tab. 15.1
  generalist professional services
    firms 503–4
  specialized consultancies 504–6
Fair Finance, UK 14–15
Fair Trade movement 5, 35–6, 75, 135
family businesses 150, 151, 198, 199, 200
family philanthropy 200–1
Faula Kenya 168–7
Fiducie du Chantier de l'économie sociale,
  Quebec 480
field shaping:
  UK 475–6
  USA 476
'finance first' investments 2, 4, 14, 54, 226,
  402, 544, 564
  both/and 'impact first' 226–7, 242–3, 307
  development funds 556 Tab. 17.2, 556–7
Financial Conduct Authority (FCA), UK 498
Financial Institution Reform and Recovery
  Act (FIRREA, 1989), USA 472, 474
financial instruments 11–15
  development finance institutions 550–2,
    551 Fig. 17.1
  impact investing 221–3, 221 Tab. 8.2

  private equity in developing
    countries 558–9
financial sector:
  benefits of corporate diversity 136, 144–7
  destructive innovations 50–1
  post-boom confidence 46
  post-boom guilt 46
  surge, post-1970 46
financial services:
  history 572–4
  Islamic 574
  legislation 498–9
Financierings-maatschappij voor
  ontwikkelingsanden N. V. (FMO) 547,
    550, 548, 554, 556
FinnFund 546, 548, 549, 550, 551, 553, 556
First Book 103
First Fundamental Theorem of Welfare
  Economics 73–4, 87
fiscal policy 495–7
Fischer, C. E. 142
FISEA fund 22
Flexible Purpose Corporations, USA 83, 86,
  473
Fondaction, Quebec 480
Fondazione CRT, Italy 54
Fonds de développement de Montréal (FDEM),
  Quebec 479
Fonds de solidarité des travailleurs (FTQ),
  Quebec 478–9
Fonds locaux de solidarité, (FLS), Quebec 479
food and agriculture sector 217, 218
  and Islamic finance 584–6, 587
  sugar cane industry, Brazil 553
Ford Foundation, USA 472
foreign direct investment (FDI) 8–9, 32, 439
ForestEthics 602
for-profit organizations 64
  access to capital 91
  advantage 73–5
  case examples 81–3
  case for social investment in 72–83, 90, 91
  and civic value creation 117
  and contract failure 69–70, 90
  efficiency 86–7, 91
  efficiency claims exaggerated 87
  excludable collective goods 69
  historical mistrust 139
  legal structures, USA 493–4
  limitations on social enterprise 78–81
  and the market for control 77–8
  price discrimination 72–3
  provision of merit goods 71
  rights of owners 65
  social mission lock-in 23
  see also hybrid organizations

for-profit/not-for-profit delineation,
    USA 492–3
Fortune at the Bottom of the Pyramid, The
    (Prahalad) 171–2
Foundation for International Community
    Assistance (FINCA) 167
foundations/charitable foundations:
  China 203
  as donors not investors 204
  impact first/finance first investments 227
  late 1980s practices, USA 188–9
  programme-related/mission-related
    investing 9–10
  sector assets 9
  sixteenth century 117
  social impact value of grants vs. social
    investments 323
  and transactional infrastructure 508
Fourth Lateran Council 576
France 497
  co-operatives and mutuals 102, 141,
    142, 160
  international development initiatives 22
  90/10 Solidarity Investment Funds 426
  pension funds and solidarity funds 508–9
  policy design principles 411
  policy support for social finance 10–11
  social and solidarity economy 7, 384
  social and solidarity economy legal
    framework 391, 440
  Solidarity Investment Funds 424
  state role in creating intellectual
    infrastructure 503
free market ideology 145, 222, 257, 587
  inefficiency 616–17
free rider behaviour 24, 105, 108, 110
Freireich, J. 431
French Development Agency 439
Fresh Works, California 217
Friedman, Milton 77, 116, 127, 591
Fulton, K. 431
fund managers 509
fund of funds 201, 435
Futurebuilders, UK 53, 341, 434–5,
    465–6, 483

G8:
  funding 'gap' 387
  Social Impact Investing Forum 10, 21, 62,
    235, 390, 408, 427, 471, 593
  Summit, London (2013) 10, 21, 62, 212
G20 114
Gagliardi, F. 148
Gan, J. 291
Gates, Bill 108, 113, 114, 116, 118, 120, 123,
    127–8, 198

Gates Foundation, *see* Bill &; Melinda Gates
    Foundation
Georgia Justice Project (GJP) 99–100
Germany 391, 449, 490
  co-operatives and mutuals 140, 141,
    142, 106
  international development initiatives 22
  small business banks 46
  welfare system 7, 398
Ghana 178
Ghana Social Investment Fund 433, 434
Ghana Venture Capital Trust Fund 435
Giné, X. 167
Gintis, H. 627
GiveWell.org 124
'Giving Pledge', USA 113, 116, 123, 198–9
Glennerster, R. 177
Global Development Innovation Ventures
    (GDIV) 22, 433
Global Environment Fund (GEF) 220
global financial crisis (2007–8) 47, 113, 114,
    118, 126, 136, 144, 207, 233, 242, 313,
    383, 522, 591
  aftermath 212–13
  and distressed property investment 584
  factors behind 146
  and focus on market regulation 397
  legacy problem 145
  and risk calculation weaknesses 283
  and trend towards demutualization 152
  US response 147
Global Fund for Women 116
Global Impact Economy Forum, USA 408
Global Impact Investing Network
    (GIIN) 125, 221, 231, 232–3, 243, 253,
    270, 392, 428, 430, 432, 502, 508, 602; *see
    also* Impact Reporting and Investment
    Standards (IRIS)
Global Impact Investing Ratings System
    (GIIRS) 21, 215, 231–2, 241, 243, 255,
    270–1, 274, 304
  areas evaluated 271
  rating example 232 Fig. 8.6
Global Learning Exchange 412, 471
Global Living Labs 54
Global Reporting Initiative (GRI) 21, 261
Golden Lane Housing 54
Goldman, P. 404, 414, 444, 485, 513
Goldman Sachs 9, 15, 114, 124, 126
  '10,000 Women' programme 126
Good Deals conference, UK 233, 467
GoodBee, Australia 523
Goodwill, North Georgia 99
Google Inc. 82–3
Google.org (DotOrg) 82–3, 125–6
Gospel of Wealth (Carnegie) 119

government, *see* public policy; state
government funding, *see* public (government)
    funding
governmental infrastructure 489 Fig. 15.1,
    492–500, 513 Tab. 15.1
    financial services legislation 497–8
    fiscal policy 495–7
    public sector commissioning 498–9
    regulation 492–5
'grace capital' 288
Grameen Bank, Bangladesh 62, 156, 158, 159,
    161–2, 167, 168, 169, 523
Grand Challenges Canada 22
grants 11, 221, 222 Tab. 8.2
    and risk mitigation 287
    traditional vs. venture philanthropy 185
Grassroots Business Fund (GBF) 219, 557–8
Greek, ancient:
    bankers 573
    interest charging 575
Greece, modern 391, 440
    development contributions drop 210
    social co-operatives 102
Green, M. 491
Green Building Councils LEED certification,
    USA 603
green energy, *see* clean/green energy
greenhouse gas emissions 605
Greenko Group, India 220
Greenspan, Alan 145
'green-washing' 81, 91
Greenwich Leisure 52
Gregory, D. 481–2
GroFin 212, 556, 557, 558, 561
    East Africa Fund (GEAF) 561
Growing the Social Investment Market: 2012
    Progress Update, UK 234–5
Guarani, Brazil 553
guarantees 438–9
    development finance institutions 551
Guidestar 124

Hackney Community Transport, UK 325
Haldane, Andrew 146
Ham, C. 143
Hansmann, H. 67, 74
happiness/well-being measures 255
Harvard Business School's Social Enterprise
    Initiative 442–3
Harvard Kennedy School Social Impact Bond
    Technical Assistance Lab 390, 450
Hauser Centre for Non-Profit Studies,
    Harvard University 444
Hauser Institute for Civil Society Initiative for
    Responsible Investment 235
Havens, J. J. 198

healthcare 217, 218
    Africa 219 Box 8.2, 220 case 8.1
    costs of reaching Millennium Development
        Goals 387–8
    developing countries 171, 559
Heateo SA, Estonia 197
hedge fund managers, and venture
    philanthropy 194
Helios 557
Hellenic Social Investment Fund,
    Greece 54
Hemer, J. 526–7
Henry II 576
Henry VII 578
Hess, M. 394, 404, 446
Hesse, H. 149
high commitment work systems 143
High-Net-Worth-Individuals (HNWIs) 210,
    224, 227, 510
    Asia Pacific 197–8
    developing countries 233
    UK 507
Hill, K. 306
Himin, China 553
Himmelstein, J. L. 79
Hirsch, Jerry 122
HMP Peterborough, *see* Peterborough
    (Prison) pilot Social Impact Bond
Hobbes, Thomas 625
Hodgson Review (2012) 470
Hohn, Chris 194
Home Depot 105
Hong Kong 198, 200, 201
    government funds for social enterprise
        development 214
Hope Consulting 215
Hornsby, A. 290–1, 298, 299
Horton, R. 65
housing 60–1, 218; *see also* affordable housing
HSBC 574
100 per cent Impact Network 20, 226, 233
Hurricane Sandy 591
Hurricane Katrina 590
Husk Power, India 228
Hutchison, David 34
hybrid funding 2, 221, 222 Fig. 82, 286
hybrid organizations 18, 27, 35, 64, 66, 83–6,
    90–1, 102–3, 106, 108
    access to capital 88
    contract failure 89
    efficiency 86–7
    evaluating 86–90
    possible benefits of social investment 91
    sustainability 89–90
    see also Community Interest Companies (CICs)
hybridization 98

IA-50, The 211
Ibn Rushd (Averrroes) 576, 581, 586
If Pigs Had Wings (Siever) 203–4
IFMR Capital 240
IGNIA, Latin America 223, 557, 560, 564
Ignite fund, USA 509
Impact Assets (USA) 17, 26
IMPACT-Australia 408, 409
impact DNA 23
'impact first' development funds 4, 14,
    32, 402, 544, 555–6, 556 Tab. 17.2,
    564, 568
    both/and 'finance first' 226–7, 242–3, 307
impact investing 29, 207–46
    achieving impact 224, 225 Tab. 8.3
    aligning capital 238–9
    assessment of social risk, philanthropy
        compared 297
    capacity building 237
    challenging deal economics 237–8, 238 Fig.
        8.7, 243
    context and trends 209–13
    definition 207
    demand-side actors: direct investments and
        financial structures 228–30, 229
        Tab. 8.6
    investing examples 211 Tab. 8.1
    financial instruments 221–3, 221 Tab. 8.2
    future challenges 235–41
    geographic focus 216–17, 217 Fig. 8.2
    growth and potential 1–2, 9, 125
    impact investors (asset owners and
        managers) 224, 226–8, 228 Tab. 8.5
    impact measurement challenges 241
    industry networks 232–3
    innovation financing 239–40, 243
    intermediation capacity 240–1, 243–4
    key characteristics 215–24
    limited supply of investment-ready
        deals 236–7, 243
    limited track records 238
    market infrastructure 224–33
    marketplace-building phase 213–15, 222
    metrics and standards initiatives 215
    origins of the term 208
    performance measurement and standard
        setting 230–2
    phases of market evolution 214 Fig. 8.1
    pioneers 208
    practitioner literature 5
    public policy 233–5
    Quebec 481
    return expectations 222–4
    sectors of interest 217–18, 218 Fig. 8.3
    as separate 'asset class' 19–20
    service providers 224–5

size of the industry 1, 209
   see also development finance institutions;
      environmental impact investing; private
      equity
Impact Investing 2.0 24–5
Impact Investing Capital, Singapore 324
Impact Investing Initiative (Rockefeller
    Foundation and J. P. Morgan) 175
Impact Investing Policy Collaborative
    (IIPC) 34, 212, 235, 390, 412, 472
    policy design principles 410–11
    see also London Principles
Impact Investment Funds, UK 507
impact measurement, *see* social impact
    measurement
Impact Reporting and Investment Standards
    (IRIS) 21, 215, 231–2, 241, 243, 270, 274,
    304, 606–7
ImpactAssets 210–11
Impetus Trust, UK 43, 55, 194
Imprint Capital (US) 17
incubators 54, 443–4, 505
India:
    Andhra Pradesh crisis 173–4, 253
    commercialization of microfinance 173–4,
        179–80
    direct foreign investment 545
    economic growth 198, 604
    engaged-giving circles 202
    philanthropy 199
    right to form co-operative societies 144
    securitization of micro-loans 240
    venture philanthropy 199–200
India Inclusive Innovation Fund 401–2
India Integrated Rural Development
    Programme (IRDP) 160–1
Indian National Innovation Council 401–2
Indian Philanthropy Forum 202
Indonesia 161, 162, 219
    High Net Worth Individuals 198
Industrial Development Corporation of SA
    (IDC) 547
Industrial Revolution 139, 574
Industrialization Fund for Developing
    Countries (IFU), Denmark 549, 551
inequality:
    and capitalism 616
    public concern 114–15, 128
    some necessary for social prosperity 120
information asymmetries 400, 521, 523
infrastructure building 413–30, 414 Fig. 13.5,
    415 Fig. 13.6, 488–517
    facilitative 489 Fig. 15.1, 503–6, 513
      Tab. 15.1
    governmental 395–6, 489 Fig. 15.1,
      492–500, 513 Tab. 15.1

infrastructure building (*cont.*)
  intellectual 489 Fig. 15.1, 500–3, 513
    Tab. 15.1
  market intermediation 489–92
  PFI funding 99
  transactional 489 Fig. 15.1, 506–12,
    513 Tab. 15.1
  types 489 Fig. 15.1, 513 Tab. 15.1
initial public offerings (IPOs) 213, 534
  microfinance institutions 172–3, 174
Innocent III 576
Innovation Exchange for the third sector,
  UK 469
innovation funds 54
Insitut de Développement de l'Economie
  Sociale (IDES, France) 17–18
'Inspiring Impact' project, UK 21
institutional investors 215, 240, 241
  social impact value pricing 323–4
insurance companies:
  co-operatives and mutuals 142
  private equity investments in Africa and
    South Asia 567–8
  see also microinsurance
intellectual infrastructure 489 Fig. 15.1,
  500–3, 513 Tab. 15.1
  academic institutions 501
  'grey' research 502–3
  media publication and sector websites 502
  sector conferences and networks 501–2
Intentionality, UK case study 506
interest, prohibition 575–9
  Christianity 573, 574, 575, 576, 577
  definition of usury 575
  Islam 574, 577, 579, 586
Interest Rate Reduction Act (2011),
  USA 578–9
intermediaries 17–18, 47, 214, 33
  advisory 510–11
  development 443–4
  lack of capacity 240–1, 243–4
  philanthrocapitalism 122–5
  policy supporting 489–92
  International Center for Research on
    Women 117
International Co-operative Alliance
  (ICA) 134, 137, 141, 144, 150, 153
international development 21–2
  evidence-based approaches 118–19
  public-private partnerships 114
  see also development aid; development
    finance institutions; development
    guarantees
International Finance Corporation (IFC) 208,
  228, 237, 546, 547, 548, 549, 553, 554,
  555, 556, 557, 558, 563

International Finance Facility for
  Immunization (IFFI) 211, 343
International Labour Organization (ILO) 137
International Symposium on Social Impact
  Bonds, (2012), London 235, 471
International Year of Co-operatives
  (2012) 141
'Invest to Save', UK Treasury 469
investees, range 5
Investing for Good, UK 272, 495
Investing for Growth, UK case study 509
Investissment Québec 481
Investment and Contract readiness Fund
  (ICRF), UK 237, 470
  case study 505
investment readiness 53, 236–7, 243, 441,
  504–5
Investor Network on Climate Risk 602
Investor's Circle 210
IRS 88
Islamic finance 32, 572–88
  and the agricultural sector 584–6, 587
  brief history of finance 572–4
  Commodity Murabaha 579, 580 Tab. 18.1,
    584, 585
  financial products 579, 580 Tab. 18.1
  financial services 574
  financial structures 587
  finance *Gharar* (uncertainty)
    prohibition 579, 581, 586
  Maysir (gambling) prohibition 579, 581
  permissible risk-taking 581–2
  in practice 584–6
  principles underlying 579–82
  prohibition on interest through the
    ages 575–9
  prohibition on interest 574, 577, 579, 586
  social responsibility 582–4, 586–7
  Tawarruq 579
isolated impact 204
Israel 49, 221
  Social Impact Bonds (SIBs) 358, 390–1, 448
Italy 78, 97, 141, 210, 426, 498
  Church-related bank tradition 46
  international development initiatives 22
  policy support for social finance 10
  social co-operatives 102, 143, 493
  Social Impact Bonds (SIBs) 390–1, 448
IVUK 507

J.P. Morgan 125, 209, 214, 232, 286, 392, 502
  Global Health Investment fund 509
  impact investing initiative 175
  impact investing studies and
    reports 217–18, 223, 224, 236, 237, 238,
    239, 563–4

J.P. Morgan/Global Impact Investment
    Network Survey 221, 391
Jackson Cole, Cecil 192
Jaipur Rugs Company, India 558
Janeway, W. H. 403
Japan 141, 142, 159, 202, 591
    High-Net-Worth Individuals 197
    policy support for social finance 10
Jet Li One Foundation, China 203
Jobs Act, USA 527, 534–5, 536
John Lewis Partnership, UK 61, 135, 469
Johnson, Bob 212
Joseph Rowntree Charitable Trust, UK 192
Judaism/Jews:
    moneylending 575, 576, 577
    Statute of Jewry (1275) 577
Just Another Emperor? (Edwards) 116
Justinian, Emperor 575

Ka-Boom! 105
Kania, J. 204
Karlan, D. 167, 177
Katoomba Group's Ecosystem
    Marketplace 606
Katz, R. A. 80
Kelley, T. A. 83
Kellogg Foundation 227
Kendall, J. 463
Kenya 160, 168, 178, 428
Keohane, G. L. 506
Ketley's Building Society 140
Kholberg, Kravis, Roberts (KKR) 126
Kickstarter 499, 525 Tab. 16.1, 524
Kinnan, C. 177
Kitzmueller, M. 73
Kiva 61, 113, 324, 426, 525 Tab. 16.1
KLD Research & Analytics 603
Kohlberg, Kravis, Roberts and Co 23, 190
Kramer, M. R. 126, 204, 451
Kyoto effect 599–601
Kyoto Protocol 56, 603

Laing, N. 290
Laird, Andrew 622
Lambert, T. 524–6
Lange model of Pareto efficiency 625
Larralde, B. 527
Last Chance Thrift Store, Atlanta,
    Georgia 100, 103
Lazonick, W. 477–8
Leadbeater, C. 192
Leader, Nick 348
leadership:
    government 408, 431, 452
    multilingual 25, 244, 447
Leapfrog Investment 389, 559

Leather, Suzi 624
Legacy Venture 201
Lehman Brothers crash 113, 118
Leinberger, Christopher 606
Lenovo Venture Philanthropy Project,
    China 203
Lewis, John Spedan 150
LGT Venture Philanthropy 228
liberal market economies 461
    synthesis 474–8
    UK 463–72
    USA 472–4
Limited Liability Companies (LLCs) 83
liquidity 427–8, 511–12
Living Labs 54
Llewellyn, D. T. 145
loans linked to contracts 55
Local Initiatives Support Corporations
    (LISC) 49
Lodestar Foundation collaboration prize 122
London Early Years Foundation (LEYF) 495
London Principles (IIPC) 235, 236 Box 8.2,
    390, 411–12, 436
London Review of Books 115
London Social Stock Exchange 125, 279, 324,
    427, 475, 511–12
Low Income Housing Tax Credit, USA 437
Low-Profit Limited Liability Companies
    (L3Cs), USA 83, 84, 91, 101, 234, 473,
    475, 494, 535
    access to capital 88
    contract failure 89
    sustainability 89
Lyme Timber Company 608

MacCormac, S. 80
Mackey, J. 76, 80
Macmillan, P. 508
Mahgrab Private Equity 557, 558, 559
malaria 219
    eradication 127–8, 129
    investment risk options example 294
Malthus, Thomas 129
Manchester-Bidwell Corporation 103
Mao Zedong 203
marginal impact contract failure 67, 69, 81,
    89, 90
Margulis, Lynn 626
market:
    dynamics 397–406, 398 Fig. 13.1
    environmental impact investing 596–7
    innovation at the intersection with public
        sector and community sector 445–51
    intermediation 489–92
market socialism theories 625–6
Marshall, A. 36

Martinez-Canas, R. 531
Massolution 531
materiality 261–2, 263
Maude, Francis 620
Maude Mutuals Programme 622
Mazzucatto, M. 405, 477–8
McBain, John 212
McKinsey Consulting 123
Media Development Investment Fund,
    Prague 196–7
media publications 502
mental accounting 91
merit goods 67–8
    not-for-profit provision 71
Mesopotamia 573, 575
mezzanine capital 215, 221, 222 Tab. 8.2, 551
Michie, J. 150
microcredit 12, 48, 62, 523
    microfinance distinguished 158
    Quebec 479
    sixteenth century 117
Microcredit Summit Campaign
    (MSC) 162, 164
microfinance 5, 29, 156–84, 397
    Andhra Pradesh crisis 173–4, 253
    breadth of product-service offering 170
        Fig. 6.4, 170–1
    commercialization 157, 171–4, 179–80
    critical features 157, 166–71
    criticism 213
    definition 157
    developed vs. emerging markets 217–18
    dynamic incentives 169–70
    evolution 216 Box 8.1
    geographic coverage 163–4, 164 Fig. 6.2
    group vs. individual lending 166–8
    growth 162–3, 163 Fig. 6.1
    historical context 158–61, 179
    historical private equity transactions 172
        Tab. 6.2
    impact 157, 174–9
    impact assessment 176–7, 180
    implications for social finance 179–80
    India's Integrated Rural Development
        Programme 160–1
    institution size 164, 165 Tab. 6.1
    institution type 164–6, 165 Fig. 6.3
    landscape 163–6
    microcredit distinguished 158
    mission drift 171, 253
    modern movement 161–3, 179
    M-Pesa and group lending 168–9
    'microfinance plus' 171
    poverty alleviation 158, 161
    public repayment 168
    randomized controlled trials results 177–9

repayment frequency 169
Rockefeller Foundation and J. P. Morgan
    Impact Investing Initiative 175
securitization 240
and social inclusion 158
terminology 157–8
Microfinance Act, Kenya 234
Microfinance Information Exchange (MIX) 164
microinsurance 157, 171
    evaluation 178
microsavings 157, 171, 178
Miliband, Ed 626
Millennium Development Goals 141, 387–8
Minority Business Development Agency
    (MBDA), USA 472, 475
missing middle 18, 215
mission drift 12, 19, 22–3, 534
    crowdfunding 534
    microfinance 171, 253
mission 'first and last' 23, 25, 244
mission-related investment, see programme-
    related/mission-related investment
Mo Ibrahim Prize for African Leadership 119
Mollick, E. 531
Mondragon Cooperative Corporation,
    Spain 498
Mongolia 167–8
Monitor Group 123
Monitor Institute 175, 209, 213, 221, 392, 414,
    502, 555
Morduch, J. 168, 170, 171
More Love Foundation, China 203
Morino, Mario 191
Mouvement Desjardins, Quebec 478
Mozambique Malaria Performace Bond
    (MMPB) 219
M-Pesa 117, 168–9
Mulgan, Geoff 116, 253, 343
multilingual leadership 25, 244, 447
Multiple Listing Services (MLS) 606
multi-systemic therapy 298–9
multitranche financing facility (MMF) 551
mutual building societies:
    demutualization, UK 139
    historical context 139–40
mutual savings 48
Mutual Support Programme (MSP),
    UK 469–70
mutual, see co-operatives and mutuals

Nambisan, S. 529
Narada Foundation, China 203
National Community Development Initiative,
    USA 52
National Endowment for Science Technology
    and the Arts, UK 444

National Rental Affordability Scheme, Australia 437
Nature Conservancy's Conservation Note 25
NBIM, Norway 596
NCVO Almanac (2012) 624
neo-classical economic 384, 396, 403
neo-liberal agenda 340
NESsT, Budapest 197
NESTA 52, 55, 59, 462, 467, 495
 Impact Fund case study 507
 Social Investment Fund 466
 standards of evidence proposal 60
net present social value (NPSV) 307
Netherlands Green Funds 426, 437
Netmums 61
networks 502
New Horizon Landscaping Company 99–100
New Labour government, UK 56, 114, 192, 342, 344, 461–2, 463–7, 482, 490, 494
 The Compact 461–2
 Co-operative Councils initiative 622
 policy rationales 476
New Markets Tax Credits, USA 437
New Philanthropy Capital (NPC), UK 124
New Philanthropy Circle, UK 343
New Profit, Boston 191
'new public management' 340
New Schools Venture Fund, San Francisco Bay 191
New South Wales Benevolent Society 301
New York City Acquisition Fund 229, 434
New York 'Lowline' initiative 533–4
New Zealand 141, 142, 424, 426
 social enterprise structures 493
 Social Impact Bonds (SIBs) 394
Newman, Paul 81–2
Newman's Own Foundation 81–2, 100
Newpin social benefit bond, Australia 449–50
NGOs 25, 54, 61, 144, 389
 influence on valuation and value 601–2
 microfinance 165, 166, 173
NHS (UK) 476
 Regional Innovation Funds, UK 54
 social enterprise commissions 52
Nicholls, A. 3–4, 489
Nixon, Richard M. 472
Noaber Foundation, Netherlands 196
Nobel Peace Prize 156
Noble, A. 432
Norwegian Investment Fund for Developing Countries (Norfund) 546, 548, 549, 551, 552, 556
not-for-profit (non-profit) organizations 27, 64, 96, 98–100
 access to capital 74, 90
 benefits theory 97, 104

case for social investment in 68–72
and contract failure 70
inefficiency claims exaggerated 87
legal structures, USA 493
provision of collective goods 69
provision of merit goods 71
role in affordability and redistribution 71–2
rights of owners 65–6
sustainability 90
unrealized potential 442
see also hybrid organizations
not-for-profit/for-profit delineation, USA 492–3
Nowak, Martin 627
nudging 620

Oasis Fund 228
Obama, Barack 498
Obi, Henry 557
Occupy Movement (2011) 115
Ocean 25
O'Donohoe, N. 12, 20, 207
Oesterreichische Entwicklungsbank AG (OeEB), Austria 546, 547, 548, 550, 553
Office for Civil Society (OCS) 468–9
Office of Social Innovation and Civic Participation, USA 473
Office of the Third Sector (OTS), UK Cabinet Office 466, 467
Official Development Assistance (ODA) 210
OhmyNews, South Korea 62
Okere, Austin 565
Omidyar, Pierre 121, 212
Omidyar Network 121, 122
One/Make Poverty History 119
OOO Volgastrap, Russia 546
OpenIdeo 530
Ordanini, A. 530
Organisation for Economic Cooperation and Development (OECD) 114, 393, 410, 436, 444, 471, 490, 505
Ostrom, Elinor 625
Ottoman Empire 577
Outcomes Matrix 272–3, 304, 430
Overseas Private Investment Corporation (OPIC) 22, 547, 554
Owen, Robert 51, 627
Ownership Commission, UK 137

Pacific Community Ventures 208
 InSight team 235
Page, A. 80
Page, Larry 125
Palmer, Carl 609

Parienté, W. 177
participatory management practices, and
    employee ownership 143
'patient capital' 605
pay-for-success (payment-by-results)
    models 27, 55–60, 62
  Social Impact Bonds (SIBs) 338, 448
  US exploration 450
  welfare services 341
Peak Timbers, Swaziland 220
Pearson, Roberta 82
peer-to-peer finance 62
pension fund managers 305
pension funds 239, 508–9
  and climate change 227
  investment regulations 424
  private equity investments in Africa and
    South Asia 567
People Tree 52
Permira, UK 193–4
Peterborough (Prison) pilot Social Impact
    Bond 31, 58, 229–30, 303, 323, 338, 341–
    58, 449, 471
  and the Big Lottery Fund 344–5, 346, 347
  changes (2014) 365–7
  collaboration 357
  connections workers-prisoner
    engagement 349–50
  contractual flexibility 352
  development and first pilot 342–5
  frontline services 350–1
  interim results 367–8
  key aspects 354
  key innovations 356–8
  long-term contracts 356
  measurement and payment 347–9, 348
    Fig. 12.4
  Meganexus data system 351
  and the Ministry of Justice (MOJ) 323,
    341–2, 344, 345, 346, 347, 348, 351, 365,
    367
  One Service 345–6, 347, 348, 357, 358,
    365, 367
  One Service in action 349–53
  One Service learning process 353–6
  and Ormiston Children and Families
    Trust 342, 346, 351, 355, 357
  outcome-based funding model
    risks 352–3
  and Peterborough and Fenland Mind 342,
    346, 350, 355
  Rand Europe evaluation 346, 348–9,
    366, 371
  randomized controlled trials 303
  service innovation 358
  single-outcome contracts 357

  and Social Finance 323, 342, 343–4, 345,
    346, 365
  Social Finance commentary 369–70
  and Social Impact Partnership SPV 345,
    346, 347
  and SOVA 342, 346, 350
  and St Giles Trust 342, 346, 350, 353, 355,
    356, 358, 458
  structure 345–7, 346 Fig. 12.3
  voluntary engagement 351–2
  and YMCA 342, 346, 352
Pharaoh, C. 3–4
Phatisa 557
philanthrocapitalism 6, 28, 29, 113–29, 193
  big companies and social
    innovation 125–7
  and civil society 116–17
  critiques 115–21
  diversity 119
  governmental interest 114
  historical context 117
  intermediaries 122–5
  obsession with measurement 118–19
  philanthropic capital, important
    role 221–2
  privatizing the good 119–21
  and profit/social value contradiction 115–17
  and public concern at inequality 114–15
  regulation 120–1, 127
  risk and failure 121–2
  squeeze on wealth risk 128
  war and conflict risk 128
Philanthrocapitalism (Bishop and
    Green) 113, 114, 121, 123, 125, 126, 127
philanthropy 2, 55, 103
  assessment of social risk, impact investing
    compared 297
  benefits theory 104, 105, 106,
    108–9, 110
  boundary with investment 288
  emergence 117
  globalization of 198–9
  'golden ages' 117, 128–9
  and risk mitigation 287–8
  transactive approach 189
  see also charitable donations and legacies
Philippines 167
PhiTrust, France 54
Phoenix Fund, UK 53, 464
Plutocrats (Freeland) 119–20
Policy, see public policy
Poor Economics (Duflo and Banerjee) 118
Pope, N. 526
population growth 129, 210
Porter, M. 123, 126, 451
Portugal 440

social economy legislation 386
Social Innovation Fund 433
social solidarity co-operatives 102, 493
postmodern economics 618, 619
Power, M. 269
pre-distribution 626
price discrimination 72
pricing, *see* social impact value pricing
prisoner's dilemma' 627
private cost of capital model (PCOC) 297–8,
320–2
private equity (PE) 32, 46
convergence with social
entrepreneurship 193–4
'exit events' 188
misleading portrayal 50
and venture philanthropy 196
private equity in emerging markets 543, 544,
548, 554–62
areas of focus 555–8
financial instruments 558–9
future issues 562–8
geographical analysis 561–2,
562 Tab. 17.4
and microfinance 172, 172 Tab. 6.2, 173
need for locally-based investment
institutions to invest in 567–8
sector analysis 559 Tab. 17.3, 559–61
Private Equity Foundation 54
private finance initiatives 56, 306, 340
Private Infrastructure Development Group
(PIDG) 547, 548, 552, 554
privatization:
of regulation 601
Social Impact Bonds (SIBs) as 362
of welfare 144, 469, 477
Pro Mujer, Latin America 171
producer co-operatives 133–4
professional services firms, generalist 503–4
profit-with-purpose businesses 23–4
programme-related/mission-related
investment (PRI/MRI) 8, 9–10, 11, 55,
88, 101, 103, 106, 110, 227, 287, 323–4,
403, 423, 472, 495–6, 592
Charity Commission guidance 55, 423
L3Cs 101, 494
and risk mitigation 287
UK development 464
US development 473
projection-valuation-pricing (PVP)
model 30, 312–14, 313 Fig. 11.1, 332
performance projections 310 Tab. 11.1,
314–17
pricing 322–9
term sheets 330–2
valuation 317–20

Projet de loi relative à l'économie social et
solidaire, France 497
Promotion of Co-operatives
Recommendation (ILO,2002) 137
proof of concept funding 53–4
Proparco 22, 547, 548, 550, 551, 553
Prudential Insurance, USA 210
public finance initiatives (PFIs) 57, 99
public (government) funding 6, 55, 99, 103,
109, 274, 362–3, 384, 445
Australia 497–8
benefits theory 104, 105, 107, 109, 110
drop in development aid 210
relationship with philanthrocapitalism 120
supporting social enterprise 213–14
public offerings 54
public policy 10–11, 62, 110–11, 212, 243,
361, 383–452, 460–87
case for action 387–97
catalysing demand and
intermediaries 439–44
catalytic capital 431–5
and catalytic investment 431–51
and co-operatives 621–2
coordinated market economies 478–82
contexts and agendas 31
customization for local conditions 412
enabling and endorsing 409–10
and financing social
enterprises 110–11
government as convenor 408–9
government as market participant 395
government as market steward 395–6,
401, 411
government role 392–7
guarantees 438–9
and impact investing 233–5
and infrastructure 413–30, 414 Fig. 13.5,
415 Fig. 13.6
and initiative design 410–12
innovation at the public sector/community
sector/market intersection 445–51
liberal market economies 463–78
liquidity and exits 427–8
and market dynamics 397–406, 401
Fig. 13.2
market lens 399–402
measurement and metrics 428–9
policy map 413, 416–22 Tab. 13.1
'policy symbiosis' 24–5, 406–7
policy toolbox 31, 407
Fig. 13.4, 407–8
tax incentives 436–8
translating into practice 406–13
value innovation lens 403–6, 405 Fig. 13.3
see also regulation; UK policy; US policy

public-private partnerships 56, 340, 396
　distinction challenged 383–4
　next generation 451
public sector, innovation at the intersection
　　with community sector and
　　market 445–51
Public Service (Social Value) Act (2013),
　　UK 470
public service commissioning 499–500
　contracts bidding system, UK 622–3
　flaws and failures 623–5
　free-market mentality 624–5
　levers of policymakers 620
　more open markets, Europe 62
　public/private blurring, UK 401
　reform 142–4
Public Services (Social Value) Act, (2012),
　　UK 234–5, 500
public service delivery 114, 295, 301, 360, 398,
　　429, 464, 621–2
　co-operatives and mutuals 136–7, 142–4,
　　153
　cooperative alternative to 622–3
　market models 340–1, 402
　opening to independent. non-state
　　organizations 52
　structural and operation changes 340–1
　see also Social Impact Bonds (SIBs)
Pulse 607
PwC 510

quasi-equity 13, 551
Quebec:
　corporatist approaches 483
　policy developments 462, 478–82
　social economy action plan 395–6
　social economy legislation 390
Quirk Review (2007), UK 467
Quran 572, 577

Rabobank, Netherlands 142
Rai, A. 169
Raiffeisen, Friedrich Wilhelm 140
Rain Forest Action Network 602
Ramaswamy, Venkat 200
Ramdas, Kavita 116
randomized controlled trials
　　(RCTs) 118, 124, 157, 177–9, 255, 267,
　　276–7, 303
Rangan, V. K. 255
Rare 25
Rathbones 495
real estate:
　case studies 608–10
　distressed property 584
　environmental regulation 603

incorporating environmental value 33,
　　589, 594, 596, 597, 598, 606, 607,
　　608–10, 612
'reciprocal altruism' 627
Red Cross 61
RedBus, India 51
Reed-Tsochas, R. 168
Reformation 128
regulation 423–6, 492–6
　environmental, and valuation 601
　financial 397
　investment 495–6
　legal forms 492–5
　philanthrocapitalism 120–1, 127
　privatization of 601
Regulation 28, South Africa 234
'reinventing government' movement 340, 387
Renaissance 117
Renewable Energy for Affordable Living
　　(REAL) Housing project, Israel 221
Réseau québecois du credit communautaire
　　(RQCC), Quebec 479
Réseaud'investissement social du Québec
　　(RISQ) 480
Restoration 578
retail investment 26
　regulation 426
　social impact value pricing 324
Retail Solutions Inc. 201
revenue-based financing 13
revenue redemption structures 13
Rikers Island SIB, USA 230, 231 Fig. 8.5
Rise of the Social Entrepreneur, The
　　(Demos) 52
risk and return 2, 3, 14, 30, 33, 282–310, 313
　capital asset pricing model (CAPM) 283
　philanthropy/investment boundary 288
　post-financial crisis changes 212
　probability risk 282–3
　mitigations models 287–8
　uncertainty risk 283
　variance risk 283
risk and return, financial 284–93
　correlation patterns 289 Fig. 10.3, 289–90
　correlation patterns in mainstream
　　finance 288, 289 Fig. 10.2
　in mainstream finance 282–4
　measurement 303
　spectrum 286–8, 287 Fig. 10.1
risk and return, social 293–306
　contextual, negatively correlated 302
　correlations 298–306, 302 Tab. 10.2
　data availability 18–19, 294, 295 Fig. 10.5
　as distinct variable 289–90, 293–4
　distinctive features 284, 293–8
　investor perspectives 297–8

measuring and modelling 302–6
organizational, uncorrelated 301
population 299 Fig. 10.8, 299–300, 300 Fig. 10.9
probability 294, 295 Fig. 10.4, 297 Tab. 10.1
probability correlations 298–300, 302 Tab. 10.2
reputational correlation 301
responsiveness, negatively correlated 302
uncertainty 296 Fig. 10.7, 296–7, 297 Tab. 10.1, 436
uncertainty correlations 302, 302 Tab. 10.2
variance risk 295, 296 Fig. 10.6, 297 Tab. 10.1
variance risk correlations 300–2, 302 Tab. 10.2
Risk Capital Fund, UK 53
Road From Ruin (Green and Bishop) 116
Roberts, George R. 190–1
Roberts Enterprise Development Fund (REDF) (formerly Homeless Economic Development Fund) 190, 204
Roberts Foundation 190–1
Robin Hood Foundation 118, 190
Robinson, David 343
Robinson, J. 178
Roca, Massachusetts 301
Rochdale Pioneers 8, 139
Roche, Chris 118–19
Rockefeller Foundation 57, 175, 208, 209, 227, 231, 232, 508, 556, 606
Impact Investing Initiative 390
Roddick, Anita 51
Rodgers, T. J. 80
Roelants, B. 619
Rome, ancient 575
Roscas 159
Rose-Ackerman, S. 71
RS Group, Hong Kong 201
Rwandan Mountain Tea (RMT) 551–2

SAB Miller, USA 509
Sabin, N. 168
Sahanivotry hydroelectric power station, Madagascar 560–1
Sahlman, W. A. 394
Said Business School 235
Saisudhir Infrastructure Ltd., India 220
Sankalp Forum 502
Sankalp Social Enterprise Awards, India 233
Sarona Asset Management 556, 557, 558, 560, 561
SBA Impact Investment Fund, USA 473, 477
Scarman Trust 462
Schervish, P. G. 198

School for Social Entrepreneurs 51, 52
Schwab Foundation 387, 401
Framework for Government Action 404–5, 405 Fig. 13.3
Schwienbacher, A. 524–6, 527
Scope, UK 495
Scottish Social Investment Fund 54, 433
Securities and Exchange Commission (SEC), USA 526, 599
securitization 240
development finance institutions 551
seed capital 400, 431, 432
Seedfund 2, India 545
Sen, A. 36
Serena Kigali Hotel, Rwanda 546
Shah, Rashesh 200
Shah, Vidya 200
Shanmugalingam, C. 17
shared value approaches 126–7, 384, 389, 403
shareholder control 77
Sharia'a 572, 574, 582, 584, 587
Shell Foundation 212, 228
Shimshack, J. 73
Shoemaker, Paul 191
Sierra Leone 168
Siever, Bruce 203–4
SIFEM, Switzerland 545–6, 549, 550, 552, 556
SIFIs 468, 470
Silicon Valley Social Venture Fund (SV2) 202
Silwal, A. 169
SIMEST 550, 551–2
Singapore 198
SITRA, Finland 54
Sjostrom, T. 169
Skoll, Jeff 116, 125, 128
Skoll Centre for Social Entrepreneurship, Oxford University, UK 444
Skoll Foundation, USA 476, 523
Skoll World Forum, (2014) Oxford 24, 233, 244
Slivinski, A. 87
small and medium-sized enterprises (SMEs) 211, 431, 480, 500, 587
in developing countries 228, 555, 557, 548, 561
Small Enterprise Assistance Funds (SEAF) 558
Small and Micro Enterprise Programme 169
Small Business Administration programme, USA 472
Smith, Adam 73, 285, 625
SoCap (Social Capital Markets Conference, San Francisco) 24, 502
'social accounting' 303, 305
Social Action Fund 620
social auditing 506

social banks 46, 54
Social Benefit Bonds, Australia 8, 15
Social Bond Act (proposed), USA 425
social bonds 495
Social Business Trust, UK 54, 194
Social Capital Markets Conference (SOCAP),
    USA 233
social co-operatives 102, 143, 493
Social Economy Act (2013), Quebec 395–6,
    409–10
Social Enterprise Access to Investment
    (SEATI) programme, UK 467
Social Enterprise Coalition, UK 465, 475
Social Enterprise Investment Fund (SEIF),
    UK 434–5, 466, 483, 523
Social Enterprise Unity, UK 464
Social Enterprise World Forum 502
social enterprises:
    benefits theory 27, 103–10, 107 Fig. 3.1
    complexity 96
    financing 96–112, 522–3
    growth in 618
    Horton's definition 65
    limited pubic understanding 96
    range and diversity 97, 98–103
    see also for-profit organizations; hybrid
        organizations; non-for-profit
    organizations
social entrepreneurship:
    agnosticism about sources of support 97,
        109
    convergence with private equity 193–4
    as emerging trend in Asian
        philanthropy 200
    globalization of 198–9
    rise of 192–3, 196, 259
    and venture philanthropy 190–1, 196
Social Entrepreneurship Sandbox, India 199
Social Exclusion Unit, UK 52, 463
social finance 1–41, 45–63, 64–95
    absorption scenario 34–5
    accountability 256–7, 261
    building momentum 390–1
    challenges to further
        institutionalization 33–4
    co-evolution with evidence 59–60
    confusion over terms 49–50
    as critique of extant financial system 4
    debates and issues 19–26
    definitional issues 61, 64–5
    different types 47–9
    drivers 7–11
    enabling conditions 52–3
    evolving a UK ecosystem 51–5
    financial risk and return 284–93
    growth 392, 485

    growth potential 1–2
    hype 45
    implication of microfinance 179–80
    institutional transformation scenario 35–6
    instruments 11–15, 14 Tab. 0.1
    instruments spectrum 4, 5 Fig. 0.2
    issues and challenges 60–2
    lifecycle 53 Fig. 1.1
    market structure 15–19
    meaning of 'social' 2–3, 486
    'missing middle' 18–19, 215
    new market 1
    parallel institutionalization scenario 35
    paucity of academic literature 5–6
    pay-for-success models 55–60
    power issues 63
    returns issues 60–1
    roots and precursors 8
    scale issues 61–2
    spectrum 4–5, 5 Fig. 0.1
    term compared to social investment 2
    under-institutionalization 332
    value creation/value appropriation
        bifurcation 285, 316
    weak evidence base 27, 49, 60
    what should it invest in? 27, 64, 66–8
    what works? 49–51
    why now? 45–7
    with whom should it invest? 27, 64, 68–90
Social Finance, UK 56, 211, 241, 511
    definition of SIBS 338–9
    launching 342
    and Peterborough (Prison) pilot Social
        Impact Bond 323, 342, 343–4, 345, 346,
        365
social impact:
    achieving 224
    definition 256
Social Impact Accelerator (SIA) fund-of-
    funds 498
Social Impact Analysts' Association
    (SIAA) 124
Social Impact Bond Act, USA 450
Social Impact Bonds (SIBs) 31, 56–60, 62, 86,
    110, 211, 219, 229–30, 241, 243, 263–4,
    272, 333, 335, 336–9, 410, 429–30, 447–
    50, 471, 503
    access to capital 88
    benchmark methods and data sets 305
    benefits 360–1
    challenges 57–8, 361–3
    definitions 338–9, 369
    development timeline 378 A.12.10
    government-service provider-investor
        collaboration 336
    historical context 340–1

legacy 363–4
negotiating and drafting contractual arrangements 377 A.12.9
New South Wales Benevolent Society 301
outcome-based contracts 338, 448
pricing structure 322–3
social impact metrics 336
stakeholder interest alignment 337
stakeholder perspectives 369–73, 374 Tab. 12.2
structure 339 Fig. 12.1, 447, 448 Fig. 13.8
tests of appropriateness 376 A.12.8
theoretical value-form-money calculation by government 373–4 A.12.5
UK 8, 358, 359 Tab. 1.2, 375 A.12.6, 450, 461
US 8, 9, 15, 114, 408, 473
worldwide adaptation and development 323, 358, 359 Tab. 12.1, 375 A. 12.7, 391, 448
see also Peterborough (Prison) pilot Social Impact Bond
Social Impact Investment Taskforce (G8 plus Australia) 6, 10, 34, 235, 335, 390, 392, 400, 430, 452, 453, 471, 485
high level recommendations (2014) 36–7
Measurement Working Group 429
Mission Alignment Working Group 23–4, 426
National Advisory Boards 412, 423–4, 471
report (2014) 396
social finance market analysis 15
Working Group on Impact Measurement 410
social impact measurement 21, 30, 56, 61, 215, 230–2, 253–81, 304
assurance, compliance and audit 269
attribution of outcomes 264
balanced scorecard approaches 268
benchmarking 264
beneficiary participation 315
bespoke social finance metrics 269–73
certification and audits 269, 276
challenges 241, 243, 259
contingency framework 255, 276–7
contingency model 256, 273–8, 276 Fig. 9.1
cost-benefit models 267–8, 303
critical issues framework 255, 256, 258–65
critical theory methods 265, 267–8
data set development 304–6
developmental evaluation 277
distinctiveness of social finance 256–8
estimating the counterfactual 264
government role 428–30
how to measure? 264–5
interpretive methods 265, 268–9
logic models 258, 266–7
methodological approaches 265–73, 266 Tab. 9.2
microfinance 174–9, 180
participatory approaches 268–9, 276
and philanthrocapitalism 118–19, 124–5
positivist methods 265, 266–7
'process' and 'product' 224
Social Impact Bonds (SIBS) 336
specialist services 505–6
stakeholder participation and engagement 261, 262, 263, 265, 267, 268
standardization issues 254–5, 304, 315
'strategy approaches' 268
and symbolic power 278–9
what to measure? 260–2
when to measure? 263–4
who measures? 262–3, 262 Tab. 9.1
why measure? 260
see also EngagedX; Global Impact Investing Network (GIIN); Impact Reporting and Investment Standards (IRIS); Outcomes Matrix; randomized controlled trials (RCTs); Social Return on Investment (SROI)
social impact performance projections 314–17
attribution adjustments 315–16
causality 315–16
conversion 314–15
deadweight adjustments 315–16
gatekeepers of capital 317 Fig. 11.2, 317
integration 316
social impact valuation 30, 317–20
capital asset pricing model (CAPM) 318–19
discount rates 318–19, 319 Tab. 11.2
private cost of capital model (PCOC) 320–2
venture capital discount rates 320 Tab. 11.3, 320
social impact value pricing 30, 322–9
Cafédirect case study 325–9
foundations 323
governments 322–3
institutional investors 323–4
retail investors 324
tranching 324–4
Social Impact VCT, UK 437
Social Incubator Fund, UK Cabinet Office 434, 441, 470, 503
social incubators *see* incubators
social innovation:
financing 27–8, 49, 96–112
importance of policy action 403–5, 405 Fig. 13.3
UK policy for (2010–2015) 10, 400–1, 468–72

Social Innovation @ MaRS, Toronto 54
Social Innovation Fund, USA 498
social investment *see* social finance
Social Investment Business, UK 54
Social Investment Consultancy survey
  (2010) 79
Social Investment Forum Foundation
  (SIFF) 79, 593
social investment funds 54
Social Investment Taskforce, UK 3, 52, 62,
  388, 389–90, 391, 463, 464, 495, 503
Social Investment Tax Relief (2014), UK 62,
  235, 335, 467
  case study 497
social marketing 71
social mission lock-in 22–3
Social Outcomes Fund, UK 58, 361
social portfolio theory 307
social purpose businesses 96, 100–1
Social Responsible Investing (SRI) 8, 9, 509,
  584, 592
Social Return on Investment (SROI) 21, 241,
  255, 261, 267–8, 269, 271, 277–8, 285,
  303, 304, 475, 523
  deadweight and attribution
    adjustments 315–16
  principles 262–3
Social Stock Exchange, London *see* London
  Social Stock Exchange
social stock exchanges 49, 427–8, 467
Social Value Act (2012), UK 304, 341, 409
social venture capital funds 2
Social Venture Fund, Germany 197
Social Venture Partners International
  (SVPI) 202
Social Venture Partners-Seattle 191
Social Ventures Australia 18
social weight adjusted cost of capital
  (WACC) 307
Sociedada para o Financiamento do
  Desenvolvimento (SOFID),
  Portugal 546, 547, 548, 549, 554
Società Italiana per le Impres all'Estro
  (SIMEST) 548, 549
Société à Finalité Sociale (SFS),
  Belgium 493
Societé d'Investissement France Active
  (France) 17
Societe Generale 14–15
Sodexo private management company 356
solar power 220–1
solidarity economy, Europe 384
'solution revolution' 384
Soros, George 115, 116, 119
South Africa 12, 234, 390, 475, 559, 567, 601
  investment regulation 424, 495

South African Social Investment Exchange
  (SASIX) 512
Spain 141, 142, 391, 440
  cooperatives 493, 618–19
  development contributions drop 210
  regional and co-operative banks 46
Sparkassen network, Germany 142
Sparked 530
Speaking Up, UK 194
specialist social finance organizations 17–18
Startup America Partnership 473
start-up capital 10, 11, 106, 107, 239,
  466, 558
state:
  changes in shape and function 8, 340 Fig.
    12.2, 340–1
  and civil society 623–4
  provision of merit goods 71
  role in creating intellectual
    infrastructure 502
  role in encouraging innovation 31, 396–7,
    399, 403–6, 409
  role in social finance market 391–2, 393,
    396–7
  see also individual states; public
    (government) funding; public policy;
    public service commissioning; public
    service delivery
state capitalism 617
state-owned banks 46
state-owned development banks 158, 159, 160
Statute of Usury (1914) 578
Steinberg, R. 70
Stewart, John 627
Stiglitz, J. E. 461
Strom, S. 90
structured finance 14–15
Sunnah 572, 577
supply side (capital providers) 15–17, 47,
  285–6
  segmentation 16
  policy measures, UK/US 474
sustainability indices 602
Sustainable Accounting Standards Board
  (SASB) 21
SVX Canada 512
Swayam Krishi Sangam (SKS), India 172,
  174, 213
Swedfund International 549, 550
Swiss Investment Fund for Emerging Markets
  (SIFEM) 547, 548
Symbid 534

Tax Act (1969), USA 472
tax incentives 52–3, 62, 235, 436–8, 474, 496–7
  start-up capital 111

taxation:
  and inequality 120
  and philanthrocapitalism 128
Teachers Insurance and Annuity Association–
    College Retirement Equities
    Fund (TIAA-CREF) 214, 227
Technology Strategy Board, UK 54
term sheets 330–2
  drag-along rights 332
  financial information 331
  material change 332
  milestones 330
  option pools 331
  pre-money valuation 330
  protective provisions 331–2
  vesting 330–2
Thailand, High-Net-Worth Individuals 198
Thaler, R. 91
The Children's Investment Fund (TCIF),
    UK 194
Thiel, Peter 122
Thornley, B. 400
Threadneedle, UK 240
'three-dimensional capital' 3
Tiernay, Tom 123
Timberland 105
Tokyo cap and trade mechanism 437
Toniic 233, 510
Total Foundation Asset Management 20
Total Impact Advisors, USA 241
total portfolio approach 4, 20–1, 201, 226
Toyota Prius 597
tracker funds vs. managed funds 50
Trading for Good 500
'tragedy of the commons' 590, 603
Trampoline Systems, UK 524
tranching 324–5, 330
transactional infrastructure 489 Fig. 15.1,
    506–12, 513 Tab. 15.1
  advisory intermediaries 510–11
  corporates 509–10
  foundations 508
  fund managers 509
  High-Net-Worth Individuals 510
  pension funds 508–9
  sources of after-market liquidity 511–12
  sources of capital 507–10
Transforming Local Infrastructure
    Programme, UK 470
Transforming Rehabilitation (TR),
    UK 365, 366
Transition Fund, UK 469
Treating Customs Fairly (TCF), UK 584
TriLinc Global 26
Triodos Bank, Netherlands and Belgium 46,
    54, 511

Trivers , Robert 627
Turner, Ted 119
Twitter 529

UBS 214
UBS-INSEAD study (2011) 200
UKSIF 484
Unilever 100
  'Vision 2020' strategy 126–7
United Kingdom (UK):
  affordable housing guarantees 439
  commitment to Social Impact Bonds 58
  community development finance 425
  community interest company
    structures 440
  demand-focused initiatives 434, 441
  ecosystem for social finance 27
  eighteenth century philanthropy 128–9
  elevating social finance discourse to global
    platforms 390
  endowment assets available for social
    finance 16
  evolving a social investment
    ecosystem 51–5
  G8 presidency (2013) 10, 408, 471, 503
  government 'market stewardship' role 395
  hybrid organizations 83, 85
  impact investing support 213, 234–5
  international development initiatives 22
  investment-readiness support 237
  investment regulation 423, 495
  legal structures 494–5
  Open Data Strategy 305
  potential growth in social finance
    market 286
  public sector commissioning 500
  riots (2011) 616
  shift from grants to contract funding 7
  social co-operatives 143
  social enterprise funds 434–5
  social enterprises as 'Holy Grail' 491
  Social Impact Bonds (SIBS) 8, 358, 359
    Tab. 12.1, 371 A.12.6, 450, 461
  social services costing data
    availability 430
  tax incentives 437, 438, 496–7
  venture capital 49, 50
  venture philanthropy 192–4
United Kingdom (UK) policy 243, 341,
    361, 490
  for community investment
    (1999–2002) 463–4, 461–2, 463–4
  for social innovation (2010–2015) 10,
    400–1, 468–72
  government role 492
  instruments 474–6

United Kingdom (UK) policy (*cont.*)
rationales 476–8
for social enterprise investment
(2002–2010) 10, 51–2, 464–7, 482–4
United Kingdom (UK) Cabinet Office 403,
408, 410, 466, 500
accessible data sets 503
catalytic capital study 432
Centre for Social Impact Bonds 450, 471
co-mingling report 222, 224, 229, 409
and 'Inspiring Impact' 21
Investment and Contract Readiness Fund
(ICRF) 505
Mutual Support Programme (MSP) 469–70
Social Exclusion Unit 463
Social Impact Bond definition 339
Social Outcomes Fund 58, 361
United Nations (UN) 387
Environment Programme Finance
Initiative 25
Food and Agriculture Organization
(FAO) 218
International Year of Microcredit
(2005) 156
Principles for Responsible Investment
(PRI) 9, 496
support for co-operatives 140–1
Ted Turner's support 119
United States of America (USA)
challenge.gov platform 445
community development finance 425
engaged-giving circles 202
environmental impact investing 592
financial sector boom 46
for-profit/not-for-profit delineation 492–3,
493–4
government role as convenor 408
hybrid organizations 83–4, 85–6
impact investment dominated by private
debt and equity 12
income mixes among not-for-profits 98–9
international development initiatives 22
investment regulation 423, 424, 425, 495
legal structures 493–4
open data initiatives 305
origins and development of venture
philanthropy 188–91
public funds for pay-for-success
projects 214
Social Impact Bonds (SIBS) 323, 358, 359
Tab. 12.1, 408, 450
usury laws 578–9, 386
venture capital 49
United States (US) policy 11, 31, 361, 462,
472–4, 483
instruments 474–6

rationales 476, 477
US National Advisory Board on Impact
Investing 396, 495
US Overseas Private Investment
Corporation 433, 439
US Small Business Administration initiative
(2012) 439
USAID 22, 232, 430, 476
US-SIF 209
Unitus Capital, India 241
UnLtd, UK 53, 464, 505, 510
Urgent Global Threats Fund 125–6
Urry, J. 538
usury, *see* interest, prohibition

Vaccine Bond 263
Vacvina 559
value creation/value appropriation
separation 4, 257–8
venture capital (VC) 49, 424, 473, 543, 557,
565–6
misleading portrayal 50
UK infrastructure development 490
venture capital discount rates 319, 320 Tab.
11.3, 320
Venture Capital Trust (VCT) 621
venture philanthropy 11, 29, 35, 46, 63, 121,
185–206, 284, 286, 477
Asia 197–203
core elements 204–5
criticisms 203–4
deal flow 186
early-stage finance 227–8
evolution in Europe 191–7, 195 Tab. 7.2
exit ('graduation') 188
funds 54
investment appraisal 186
matrix of investment and organizational
policies 187 Tab. 7.1
operational principles 185–6
origins and development in US 188–91
portfolio management 186
regional networks 34
Venture Philanthropy Partners 191
Venturesome, UK 54, 289, 3978
report (2009) 19
Vibrant Oceans Initiative 25
Victorian era 8, 117
'village banking' models 167
Vinnova, Sweden 54
VoiceAbility, UK 194
volunteers 105–6

Waitrose, UK 135
Wall Street 189–90
Wall Street Crash (1929) 191

Wal-Mart 127
Wanless, Peter 345
water risk exposure 599
WCLV radio station 100, 101
websites 502
weighted average cost of capital
    (WACC) 307, 320–1
Weisbrod, B. 69
Welch, Jack 145
'welfare dependency' 129
welfare economics 255, 267, 303
Wells Fargo 592
'what works centres' 59
Wheeler, Peter 343
White House Office for Social Innovation and
    Civic Participation, USA 408
Whole Foods 80
wholesale and intermediary funding 55
'wicked problems' 2, 128, 242,
    477–8, 485
Wikipedia 87
Williams, Raymond 623
Willow Impact Investors 559
Wilton, David 555
Wise Group, Glasgow 61–2

W. K. Kellogg Foundation 556
Wood, Arthur 342–3
World Bank 217, 387, 549
    Green Bonds 213
    survey (2011) 545
World Bank Group Multilateral Investment
    Guarantee Agency 439
World Economic Forum 50, 390, 415, 424,
    427, 431, 435, 438, 490–1
    Global Agenda Council on the Future of
    Government 385
    Davos meetings 123
World in Need, UK 192

X-Prize 122

YouChange, China 203
Young, D. R. 104
Young, Michael 51
Young Foundation 54, 55, 343, 462
Yunus, Muhammad 80, 156, 158, 159, 161–2,
    169, 172–3, 180
Zadek, S. 451
Zinman, J. 177
Žižek, Slavoj 114, 115, 616, 625